First Corinthians

An exegetical-pastoral commentary

Gary S. Shogren

Revised edition, 2020

First Corinthians

An exegetical-pastoral commentary

Gary S. Shogren

Revised edition, 2020

© 2020 Publicaciones Kerigma
First Cotinthians: An exegetical-pastoral commentary

© 2020 Publicaciones Kerigma
Salem Oregón, Estados Unidos
http://www.publicacioneskerigma.org

Todos los derechos son reservados. Por consiguiente: Se prohíbe la reproducción total o parcial de esta obra por cualquier medio de comunicación sea este digital, audio, video escrito, salvo para citaciones en trabajos de carácter académico según los márgenes de la ley o bajo el permiso escrito de Publicaciones Kerigma.

Diseño de Portada: Publicaciones Kerigma

2020 Publicaciones Kerigma
Salem, Oregón
All rights reserved

Pedidos: 971 304-1735

www.publicacioneskerigma.org

ISBN: 978-1-948578-76-9

Impreso en los Estados Unidos
Printed in the United States

For our children
Steve, Tim, Ben, Victoria

Contenido

Abbreviations 9
Preface 11
Bibliography 13

INTRODUCTION 27
I. Historical Background 27
II. Why did Paul write 1 Corinthians? 42
III. The Formal Structure of 1 Corinthians 51

COMMENTARY 57
I. INTRODUCTION (PRESCRIPTO) 1:1-4 57
II. THANKSGIVING (PROEMIUM) AS EXORDIUM 1:4-9 61
III. BODY 1:10-16:4 69
    A. The Main Issue that Paul wishes to raise in the letter: unity working through love 1:10-4:16 (*Probatio*) 71
    B. Other Issues that concern the church in the world, based on oral report 5:1-6:20 146
    C. Issues that the Corinthians have raised in their letter – 1 Cor 7-15 184
IV. CONCLUSION (POSCRIPTO) 16:5-24 393
    A. Itinerary 16:5-12 393
    B. Final exhortation 16:13-14 395
    C. Commendations 16:15-18 395
    D. Secondary greetings 16:19-20 395
    E. Autograph 16:21 396
    F. Benediction (and malediction) and Final Greetings 16:22-24 397

About the Author 403

Abbreviations

AB	Anchor Bible
ACCS	Ancient Christian Commentary on Scripture
AnBib	Analecta Biblica
ANF	*Ante-Nicene Fathers*
BA	*Biblical Archaeologist*
BECNT	Baker Exegetical Commentary on the New Testament
BETL	Bibliotheca ephemeridum theologicarum lovaniensium
BNTC	Black's New Testament Commentaries
BTB	*Biblical Theology Bulletin*
CBC	Cambridge Bible Commentary
CGTC	Cambridge Greek Testament Commentary
CSEL	Corpus scriptorum ecclesiasticorum latinorum
EKKNT	Evangelisch-katholischer Kommentar zum Neuen Testament
EvQ	*Evangelical Quarterly*
HNT	Handbuch zum Neuen Testament
HTS	Harvard Theological Studies
HUT	Hermeneutische Untersuchungen zur Theologie
ICC	International Critical Commentary
JBL	*Journal of Biblical Literature*
JETS	*Journal of the Evangelical Theological Society*
JSNT	*JSNT Journal for the Study of the New Testament*
JSNTSup	Journal for the Study of the New Testament: Supplement Series
JTS	*Journal of Theological Studies*
KNT	Kommentar zum Neuen Testament
LCL	Loeb Classical Library
LEC	Library of Early Christianity
LNTS	Library of New Testament Studies
Neot	*Neotestamentica*
NIBC	New International Biblical Commentary
NICNT	New International Commentary on the New Testament
NIDNTT	*New International Dictionary of New Testament Theology*
NIGNT	New International Greek Testament Commentary
NovT	*Novum Testamentum*
NPNF	Nicene and Post-Nicene Fathers

Abbreviatons

NTD	Das Neue Testament Deutsch
NTS	*New Testament Studies*
RNT	Regensburger Neues Testament
SNTSMS	Society for New Testament Studies Monograph Series
TDNT	*Theological dictionary of the New Testament*
THKNT	Theologischer Handkommentar zum Neuen Testament
TJ	*Trinity Journal*
THKNT	Theologischer Handkommentar zum Neuen Testament
TLG	*Thesaurus linguae graecae*
TNTC	Tyndale New Testament Commentaries
TynBul	*Tyndale Bulletin*
WC	Westminster Commentaries
WTJ	*Westminster Theological Journal*
ZNW	*Zeitschrift für die neutestamentliche Wissenschaft und die Kunde der älteren Kirche*

Preface

This is the English version of a commentary published by CLIE, Barcelona, Spain; it is also available in both languages as part of Logos Bible Software; this version reproduces the 2012 Logos edition, with some editorial improvements.

Because I have my foot in two worlds, some applications of the text will be informed by the Latin American church, others by the North American. We make reference to the best of ancient wisdom as well as modern scholarship – some of which is out of reach, due to my geographical distance from a research library – in order to expose the reader to the varying currents of interpretation. In order not to distract from the epistle itself, I have kept the footnotes to a minimum. Comments on the Greek will appear only when needed for understanding, and readers who wish to do so can find further technical help in other works.

I have been especially impressed by two or three commentaries that combine technical help with a strong emphasis on the practice of the Word. It will be clear in this commentary where my sympathies lie: with those who insist that the interpreter the Word not be content only with details of exegesis, textual criticism, historical background, or rhetoric. Hence, "as Christians, we read the Bible with personal faith – not only to understand it but to embrace its message and theological worldview as true for the world in which we live." (So Craig Keener, *Spirit hermeneutics: reading Scriptures in the light of Pentecost*, Eerdmans, 24; in Spanish, *Hermenéutica del Espíritu*, Kerigma), Thus, our ultimate aim must be the understanding that leads to love for God and obedience to him. For that reason, much of this volume deals with putting the Word into practice, and how a preacher might proclaim 1 Corinthians to God's people.

In fact, 1 Corinthians is astonishingly relevant for God's church in the 21st century, both in Latin America and in the English-speaking church. I pray that the Spirit will direct the reader to rediscover "what God has prepared for those who love him" and to put the truth into daily practice.

My thanks to my family, my co-workers at Seminario ESEPA, Costa Rica and my Tico brothers and sisters in Christ.

Bibliography

A note about sources

This commentary is based on a study of the Greek text (the 28th edition of Nestlé-Aland), but a knowledge of Greek is not necessary to use it. We will follow the text of the New International Version (1984). It is my opinion that the NIV 2011 is generally an improvement on the 1984 edition; please visit my blog to read an article on how the NIV 2011 handles 1 Cor 1-7.[1] Nevertheless, since I wrote this commentary before the appearance of the NIV 2011, we will mention it only in a few passages.

Beyond our own exegesis of the Greek text, we will interact with the best in English, Spanish, German and French comments on the epistle, as well as with Greek and Latin material from the early church.

New sources…

As a general rule, we should rely on newer commentaries, since they are more likely to have fresh information and to correct the factual errors of older works. Other insights from recent years include the ongoing excavations at the site of Corinth, which have led to fresh sociological insights into the epistle. In addition there is a renewed attention to the use of rhetoric in the composition of 1 Corinthians. Also of growing interest is the meaning of Paul's teaching in 1 Cor 6:9, and whether he meant to exclude homosexuals from the kingdom to come. Finally, there is a growing consensus is that Paul did not encounter Gnosticism in Corinth. Many scholars have affirmed the useful theory that Stoicism, that all-pervasive philosophy of the "wise" rulers of the empire, was infecting the church at Corinth. We will pay attention to all these themes, as well as other hot issues of today, such as the spiritual gifts, the role of women in the church, the work of missions, the ministry of apostles, the church and finances, and above all, the nature of Christian leadership.

The best commentary I have used is the four-volume set in German by Wolfgang Schrage, *Der erste Brief an die Korinther*, in the EKKNT series. Anthony Thiselton's work in the NIGNT series is in a virtual tie for first place. David Garland's commentary in BECNT and Joseph Fitzmyer's volume in the Anchor Bible are also useful, and Ben Witherington offers many of his characteristic insights in *Conflict and community in Corinth*. The best commentary in Spanish, and one of the best in English, is the volume by Gordon Fee.

…and old sources:

---

[1] See my analysis of the use of gender in the NIV 2011 in https://openoureyeslord.com/2020/05/26/the-new-international-version-1984-and-2011/

The Law said that "Rise in the presence of the aged, show respect for the elderly" (Lev 19:32). In this case it is the ancients of the early church to whom we should direct our attention. Perhaps more than in the case of any other New Testament document, 1 Corinthians is best studied by the light of patristic literature. First we should mention the Greek-language commentators: fragments of homilies by Origen, and the 44 sermons by John Chrysostom; these two provide expositions of a *koiné* text, proclaimed in *koiné* Greek, to an audience whose daily language was that of the 1st-century apostles. Other Greek commentators are Didymus the Blind, Theodore of Mopsuestia, Gennadius of Constantinople, Severianus and most notably, Theodoret of Cyrus. An excellent Latin commentary, falsely attributed to Ambrose of Milan, was written in the 4th century; its unknown author is called Ambrosiaster.

The earlier fathers did not write full commentaries on 1 Corinthians, but their works are filled with useful information. *1 Clement* deals principally with divisions and party spirit in Corinth at the end of the 1st century. The Epistles of Ignatius and the *Didache* say much about church order. The Christians of the 2nd century, Polycarp, Justin Martyr, Irenaeus, Clement of Alexandria, Origen, Tertullian inhabited the world of Paul and the Corinthian believers, in which the cross was ever "a stumbling block to Jews and foolishness to Gentiles" (1 Cor 1:23). On one side, the fledgling church was dwarfed by the hundreds of thousands of Jews scattered in the Diaspora. Israel was putting its own house in order after the destruction of the Temple, and they were stubbornly unconvinced that the Christian movement had any insight into the Scriptures. From the world of the pagans, Christianity was mocked as a religion for fools and slaves, a faith for people who knew no better than to worship a crucified man. These church fathers lived in a world where the charismatic gifts, veils for women, philosophical wisdom, persecution from the empire, Gnosticism and doubts over the resurrection of the body were not simply words from a history book, but everyday issues. I provide relevant quotations from the fathers and other ancient sources, on the assumption that much of this material is not readily available to the typical reader.

We follow the abbreviations of *The SBL Handbook of Style* (2nd edition).

Ancient Commentaries and other Ancient Resources

Ambrosiaster. *Commentaries on Romans and 1-2 Corinthians*. Edited by Gerald L. Bray. Downers Grove, IL: IVP, 2009.

_____. *In epistulas ad Corinthios*. Edited by Heinrich Joseph Vogels. CSEL 81.2. Wien: Hölder-Pichler-Tempsky, 1968.

Ante-Nicene Fathers. Edited by A. Roberts and J. Donaldson. 10 vols. Edinburgh: T. & T. Clark, 1867-73.

Bray, Gerald, ed. *1-2 Corinthians*. 2nd ed. ACCS 7. Downers Grove, IL: IVP, 2006.

Charlesworth, James H., ed. *The Old Testament pseudepigrapha*. 2 vols. New Haven, CT: Yale, 1983.

Didymus the Blind. *Fragmenta in epistulam i Corinthios*. In *Pauluskommentar aus der griechischen Kirche aus Katenenhanschriften gesammelt*. Edited by K. Staab. Münster: Aschendorff, 1933.

Bibliography

Epictetus. *Enchiridion*. Translated by Elizabeth Carter. Online: http://classics.mit.edu/Epictetus/epicench.html.

Eusebius. *History of the church*. Edited by Paul L. Maier. Grand Rapids, MI: Kregel, 1999.

Flavius Josephus. *The works of Flavius Josephus*. Translated by William Whiston. New updated edition. Peabody, MA: Hendrickson, 1987.

Gaius. *Institutes of Roman law*. Edited by Edward Poste. 4th ed. Oxford: Clarendon, 1904.

García Martínez, Florentino and Eibert J. C. Tigchelaar, eds. *The Dead Sea Scrolls*. 2 vols. New York: Brill, 1998-99.

Gennadius of Constantinople. *Fragmenta in epistulam i Corinthios*. In *Pauluskommentar aus der griechischen Kirche aus Katenenhanschriften gesammelt*. Edited by K. Staab. Münster: Aschendorff, 1933.

Gregory the Great. *Pastoral care*. Online: http://www.newadvent.org/fathers/3601.htm.

John Chrysostom. *In Acta apostolorum*. In *Patrologiae Cursus Completus, Series Graeca*. Edited by J. P. Migne. 161 vols. Paris: Imprimerie Catholique, 1857-1866. Volume 60:13-384.

_____. *In epistulam i ad Corinthios*. In *Patrologiae Cursus Completus, Series Graeca*. Edited by J. P. Migne. 161 vols. Paris: Imprimerie Catholique, 1857-1866. Volume 61:381-610; also NPNF[1] 12.

_____. *In principium Actorum apostolorum*. In *Patrologiae Cursus Completus, Series Graeca*. Edited by J. P. Migne. 161 vols. Paris: Imprimerie Catholique, 1857-1866. Volume 51:65-112.

_____. *Oportet haereses esse*. In *Patrologiae Cursus Completus, Series Graeca*. Edited by J. P. Migne. 161 vols. Paris: Imprimerie Catholique, 1857-1866. Volume 51:251-60.

Kock, T., ed. *Comicorum Atticuorum fragmenta*. Leipzig: Teubner, 1880.

Kovacs, Judith L., ed. *1 Corinthians interpreted by early Christian commentators*. Church's Bible. Grand Rapids, MI: Eerdmans, 2005.

Lightfoot, J. B., J. R. Harmer and M. W. Holmes, eds. *The Apostolic Fathers: Greek texts and English translations of their writings*. 2nd ed. Grand Rapids, MI: Baker, 1999.

Martial. *Epigrams*. Edited by A. Ker. LCL. 2 vols. Cambridge, MA: Harvard University Press, 1919.

Neusner, Jacob, ed. *The Misnah*. 2nd rev. ed. New Haven, CT: Yale, 1988.

Roberts, A., J. Donaldson, P. Schaff and H. Wace, editors. *Nicene and Post-Nicene Fathers*. 28 vols. Edinburgh: T. & T. Clark, 1886-1900.

Oecumenius. *Fragmenta in epistulam i ad Corithios*. In *Pauluskommentar aus der griechischen Kirche aus Katenenhanschriften gesammelt*. Edited by K. Staab. Münster: Aschendorff, 1933.

Origen. *Fragmenta ex commentariis in epistulam i ad Corinthios*. Edited by C. Jenkins,

"Documents: Origen on I Corinthians," *JTS* 9 & 10 (1908).

Plutarch. *Moralia*. Edited by F. C. Babbitt, 2nd ed. Cambridge, MA: Harvard University Press, 1959.

_____, *Vitae Parallelae*. Edited by K. Ziegler. 4th ed. Leipzig: Teubner, 1969.

Pseudo-Phocylides. *Sententiae*. In *Theogonis*. Edited by D. Young. Leipzig, Teubner, 1971: 95-112.

Quintilian. *Training of an orator*. Edited by H. E. Butler. LCL. Cambridge, MA: Harvard University Press, 1920.

Severianus. *Fragmenta in epistulam i Corinthios*. In *Pauluskommentar aus der griechischen Kirche aus Katenenhanschriften gesammelt*. Edited by K. Staab. Münster: Aschendorff, 1933.

Tacitus. *Complete works of Tacitus*. Edited by Moses Hadas. Translated by Alfred John Church and William Jackson Brodribb. New York: Random House, 1942.

Theodoret of Cyrus. *Commentary on the letters of St. Paul*. Edited by Robert C. Hill. 2 vols. Brookline, MA: Holy Cross Orthdox Press, 2001.

_____, *Interpretatio in xiv epistulas sancti Pauli*. In *Patrologiae Cursus Completus, Series Graeca*. Edited by J. P. Migne. 161 vols. Paris: Imprimerie Catholique, 1857-1866. Volume 82:36-877.

Theodoret of Mopsuestia. *Fragmenta in epistulam i Corinthios*. In *Pauluskommentar aus der griechischen Kirche aus Katenenhanschriften gesammelt*. Edited by K. Staab. Münster: Aschendorff, 1933.

Reformed and Modern Commentaries

Allo, E.-B. *Première épitre aux Corinthiens*. 2nd ed. Paris: Gabalda, 1956.

Bachmann, Philipp. *Der erste Brief des Paulus an die Korinther*. 2nd ed. KNT 7, Leipzig: Deichert, 1910.

Baker, William, *1 Corinthians*; Ralph P. Martin, *2 Corinthians*. Cornerstone Biblical Commentary. Carol Stream, IL: Tyndale House, 2009.

Barrett, C. K. *The first epistle to the Corinthians*. BNTC. London: Black, 1968.

Blomberg, Craig. *The NIV application commentary series: 1 Corinthians*. Grand Rapids, MI: Zondervan, 1994.

Calvin, John. *Commentary on the epistles of Paul the apostle to the Corinthians*. Translated by John Pringle. 2 vols. Edinburgh: Calvin Translation Society, 1848.

Conzelmann, Hans. *1 Corinthians*. Translated by James W. Leitch. Hermeneia. Philadelphia: Fortress, 1975.

Dods, Marcus. *The first epistle to the Corinthians*. Expositor's Bible. London: Hodder & Stoughton, 1906.

Fascher, E. and Christian Wolff. *Der erste Brief des Paulus an die Korinther*. 2 vols. 2nd ed. THKNT: 7. Berlin and Leipzig: Evangelische Verlagsanstalt, 1975, 1982.

Fee, Gordon. *The first epistle to the Corinthians*. NICNT. Grand Rapids, MI: Eerdmans,

Bibliography

1987.

Fitzmyer, Joseph A. *First Corinthians*. AB 32. New Haven, CT: Yale University Press, 2008.

Foulkes, Irene. *Problemas pastorales en Corinto*. San José, Costa Rica: DEI-SBL, 1996.

Garland, David E. *1 Corinthians*. BECNT. Grand Rapids, MI: Baker, 2003.

Godet, Frederic Louis. *Commentary on First Corinthians*. Grand Rapids, MI: Kregel, 1977 [orig. 1889].

Goudge, H. L. *The first epistle to the Corinthians*. 4th ed. WC. London: Methuen & Co., 1915.

Grosheide, F. W. *The first epistle to the Corinthians*. NICNT. Grand Rapids, MI: Eerdmans, 1953.

Hays, Richard B. *First Corinthians*. Interpretation. Louisville, KY: John Knox, 1997.

Héring, Jean. *The first epistle of Saint Paul to the Corinthians*. Translated by A. W. Heathcote and P. J. Allcock. London: Epworth, 1962.

Hodge, Charles. *The first epistle to the Corinthians*. New York: Robert Carter, 1857.

Horton, Stanley M. *I & II Corinthians*. Springfield, MO: Gospel Publishing House, 1999.

Kistemaker, Simon J. *1 Corinthians*. Grand Rapids, MI: Baker, 1998.

Kuss, Otto. *Die Briefe an die Römer, Korinther und Galater*. RNT 6.1. Pustet: Regensburg, 1940.

Lietzmann, Hans and W. G. Kümmel. *An die Korinther I/II*. 4th ed. HNT 9. Tübingen: Mohr, 1949.

Morris, Leon. *The first epistle of Paul to the Corinthians*. TNTC. Grand Rapids, MI: Eerdmans, 1958.

Murphy-O'Connor, Jerome. *1 Corinthians*. Doubleday Bible Commentary. New York: Doubleday, 1998.

Nicoll, W. Robertson, ed. *The first epistle of Paul to the Corinthians*. In *The Expositor's Greek Testament*. 4 vols. New York: George H. Doran, 1897-1910.

Olshausen, Hermann. *First and Second Corinthians*. Edinburgh: T. & T. Clark, 1855.

Orr, William F. and James Arthur Walther. *I Corinthians*. AB 32. New York: Doubleday, 1976.

Parry, R. St. John. *The first epistle of Paul the apostle to the Corinthians*. CGTC. Cambridge: Cambridge University Press, 1937.

Robertson, Archibald and Alfred Plummer. *First epistle of St. Paul to the Corinthians*. 2nd ed. ICC. Edinburgh: T. & T. Clark, 1914.

Schrage, W. *Der erste Brief an die Korinther*. 4 vols. EKKNT 7.1-4. Neukirchen-Vluyn: Neukirchener, 1991-2001.

Soards, Marion. *1 Corinthians*. NIBC 7. Peabody, MA: Hendrickson, 1999.

Talbert, Charles. *Reading Corinthians: a literary and theological commentary on 1 and 2 Corinthians*. New York: Crossroads, 1987.

Thiselton, Anthony C. *The first epistle to the Corinthians*. NIGNT. Grand Rapids, MI:

Eerdmans, 2000.

Thrall, Margaret E. *I and II Corinthians*. CBC. Cambridge: Cambridge University Press, 1965.

Walter, Eugen. *The first epistle to the Corinthians*. New York: Crossroad, 1981.

Weiss, J. *Der erste Korintherbrief.* 2nd ed. Göttingen: Vandenhoeck & Ruprecht, 1910.

Wendland, Heinz Dietrich. *Die Briefe an die Korinther*. 8ª ed. NTD 7. Göttingen: Vandenhoeck & Ruprecht, 1962.

Wesley, *Notes on 1 Corinthians*. Online: http://wesley.nnu.edu/john_wesley/notes/1Corinthians.htm.

Witherington, Ben, III. *Conflict and community in Corinth: a socio-rhetorical commentary on 1 and 2 Corinthians*. Grand Rapids, MI: Eerdmans, 1995.

Monographs and Reference Works

Arnold, Clinton E. *Ephesians: power and magic: the concept of power in Ephesians in light of its historical setting*. Grand Rapids, MI: Baker, 1992.

Aune, David E. *The New Testament in its literary environment*. LEC 8. Louisville, KY: Westminster John Knox, 1987.

_____. *Prophecy in early Christianity and the ancient Mediterranean world*. Grand Rapids, MI: Eerdmans, 1983.

Barrett, C. K. *The Acts of the Apostles*. 2 vols. ICC. Edinburgh: T. & T. Clark, 1994.

_____. *Christianity at Corinth: essays on Paul*. Philadelphia: Westminster, 1982.

Barth, Karl. *The resurrection of the dead*. Translated by H. J. Stenning. New York: Fleming H. Revell, 1933.

Barth, Markus. *Ephesians 4-6*. AB 34A. New York: Doubleday, 1974.

Bauckham, Richard J. *Jude and the relatives of Jesus in the early church*. Edinburgh: T. & T. Clark, 2000.

Baumert, Norbert. *Woman and man in Paul: overcoming a misunderstanding*. Collegeville, MN: Liturgical, 1996.

Beale, G. K. and D. A. Carson. *Commentary on the New Testament use of the Old Testament*. Grand Rapids, MI: Baker, 2007.

Beker, J. Christiaan. *Paul the apostle: the triumph of God in life and thought*. Philadelphia: Fortress, 1980.

Berkhof, L. *Systematic theology*. Grand Rapids, MI: Eerdmans, 1941.

Bornkamm, Günther. *Paul*. Translated by D. M. G. Stalker. London: Hodder and Stoughton, 1971.

Boswell, John. *Christianity, social tolerance, and homosexuality: gay people in Western Europe from the beginning of the Christian Era to the fourteenth century*. Chicago: University Press, 2005.

Bousset, Wilhelm. *Kyrios Christos: a history of the belief in Christ from the beginnings of Christianity to Irenaeus*. Translated by John E. Steely. Nashville: Abingdon, 1970.

Bibliography

Bultmann, Rudolf. *The theology of the New Testament*. Translated by K. Grobel. 2 vols. New York: Charles Scribner's Sons, 1951, 1955.

Burgess, S. M. and G. B. McGee, eds. *Dictionary of Pentecostal and Charismatic movements*. Grand Rapids, MI: Zondervan, 1988.

Calvin, John. *Institutes of the Christian religion*. Ed. John T. McNeill. Translated by Ford Lewis Battles. Two volumes in one. Louisville, KY: Westminster John Knox, 1960.

Carson, D. A. *The cross and Christian ministry: an exposition of passages from 1 Corinthians*. Grand Rapids, MI: Baker, 1993.

_____, ed. *From Sabbath to Lord's Day: a biblical, historical and theological investigation*. Grand Rapids, MI: Zondervan, 1982.

_____. *Showing the Spirit: a theological exposition of 1 Corinthians 12-14*. Grand Rapids, MI: Baker, 1987.

Catechism of the Catholic Church. New York: Doubleday, 1992. Online: http://www.vatican.va/archive/ccc/index.htm.

Cerfaux, L. *Christ in the theology of St. Paul*. Translated by G. Webb and A. Walker. New York: Herder and Herder, 1959.

Clarke, Andrew D. *Secular and Christian leadership in Corinth: a socio-historical and exegetical study of 1 Corinthians 1-6*. Paternoster Biblical Monographs. Leiden: Brill, 1993.

Coenen, L., E. Beyreuther and H. Bietenhard, eds. *New international dictionary of New Testament theology*. Edited by Colin Brown. 4 vols. Grand Rapids, MI: Zondervan, 1986.

Cullmann, Oscar. *Christ and time: the primitive Christian conception of time and history*. London: SCM Press, 1962.

_____. *Christology of the New Testament*. Rev. ed. Philadelphia: Westminster, 1963.

_____. *The early church*. Edited by A. J. B. Higgins. London: SCM, 1956.

Dalman, Gustav. *The words of Jesus*. Translated by D. M. McKay. Edinburgh: T. & T. Clark, 1902.

Deidun, T. J. *New Covenant morality in Paul*. AnBib 89. Rome: Pontifical, 1981.

Deissmann, G. Adolf. *Light from the Ancient East*. Translated by L. R. M. Strachan. London: Hodder & Stoughton, 1910.

Deming, Will. *Paul on marriage and celibacy: the Hellenistic background of 1 Corinthians 7*. 2nd ed. Grand Rapids, MI: Eerdmans, 2004.

Dodd, C. H. *According to the Scriptures*. London: Nisbet, 1952.

Doty, W. G. *Letters in primitive Christianity*. Philadelphia: Fortress, 1973.

Dunn, James D. G. *Baptism in the Holy Spirit*. London: SCM, 1970.

_____. *Jesus and the Spirit: a study of the religious and charismatic experience of Jesus and the first Christians as reflected in the New Testament*. Grand Rapids, MI: Eerdmans, 1997.

_____. *The theology of Paul the apostle*. Grand Rapids, MI: Eerdmans, 1998.

Ensberg-Pedersen, Troels. *Paul and the Stoics*. Louisville, KY: Westminster John Knox, 2000.

Evans, Craig A. and Stanley Porter, eds. *Dictionary of New Testament background*. Downers Grove, IL, IVP, 2000.

Fee, Gordon D. *God's empowering presence: the Holy Spirit in the letters of Paul*. Peabody, MA: Hendrickson, 1994.

_____. *Pauline christology: an exegetical-theological study*. Peabody, MA: Hendrickson, 2007.

Finney, Mark T. *Honour and conflict in the ancient world: 1 Corinthians in its Greco-Roman setting*. LNTS: 460. London: T & T Clark, 2012.

Fitzmyer, Joseph. *According to Paul: studies in the theology of the apostle*. Mahwah, NJ: Paulist, 1992.

Forbes, Christopher. *Prophecy and inspired speech in early Christianity and its Hellenistic environment*. Peabody, MA: Hendrickson, 1997.

Freedman, David Noel, ed. *Anchor Bible dictionary*. 6 vols. Garden City, NY: Doubleday, 1992.

Furnish, Victor Paul. *The moral teaching of Paul: selected issues*. 3rd ed. Nashville, TN: Abingdon, 2009.

_____. *The theology of the first letter to the Corinthians*. Cambridge Cambridge University Press, 1999.

Gardner, P. D. *The gifts of God and the authentication of a Christian: an exegetical study of 1 Corinthians 8-11*. Lanham, MD: University Press of America, 1994.

Garcilazo, Albert V. *The Corinthian dissenters and the Stoics*. Studies in Biblical Literature 106. New York: Peter Lang, 2007.

Gómez, V., Jorge I. *El crecimiento y la deserción en la iglesia evangélica costarricense*. San Francisco de Dos Ríos, Costa Rica: IINDEF, 1996.

González Ruíz, José María. *El evangelio de Pablo*. Madrid: Marova, 1977.

Grant, Robert M. *Paul in the Roman world: the conflict at Corinth*. Louisville, KY: Westminster John Knox, 2001.

Green, Michael. *I believe in the Holy Spirit*. Rev. ed. Grand Rapids, MI: Eerdmans, 2004.

Grudem, Wayne A. *The gift of prophecy in the New Testament and today*. Rev. ed. Wheaton, IL: Crossway, 2000.

Harris, Murray J. *Raised immortal: resurrection and immortality in the New Testament*. Grand Rapids, MI: Eerdmans, 1983.

Harrison, E. F., ed. *Baker's dictionary of theology*. Grand Rapids, MI: Baker, 1982.

Hawthorne, Gerald F., Ralph P. Martin and Daniel G. Reid, eds. *Dictionary of Paul and his letters*. Downers Grove, IL: IVP, 1993.

Hay, David M., ed. *Pauline theology, Volume II: 1 & 2 Corinthians*. Minneapolis, MN: Fortress, 1993.

Hendriksen, William. *The Bible on the life hereafter*. Grand Rapids, MI: Baker, 1987.

Bibliography

Hengel, Martin. *Cruxifixion in the ancient world and the folly of the message of the cross*. London: SCM, 1977.

Hooker, Morna D. *Not ashamed of the gospel: New Testament interpretations of the death of Christ*. Grand Rapids, MI: Eerdmans, 1994.

Horton, Stanley M., ed. *Systematic theology*. Rev. ed. Springfield, MO: Gospel Publishing House, 1994.

_____. *What the Bible says about the Holy Spirit*. Rev. ed. Springfield, MO: Gospel Publishing House, 1976.

Hurd, John Coolidge, Jr. *The origin of 1 Corinthians*. 2nd ed. Macon, GA: Mercer, 1983.

Hurley, James B. *Man and woman in biblical perspective*. Grand Rapids, MI: Zondervan, 1981.

Inwood, Brad, ed. *The Cambridge companion to the Stoics*. Cambridge: Cambridge University Press, 2003.

Jewett, Robert. *Paul's anthropological terms*. Leiden: Brill, 1971.

Käsemann, Ernst. *New Testament questions of today*. Philadelphia: Fortress, 1969.

Keener, Craig. *Paul, women & wives: marriage and women's ministry in the letters of Paul*. Peabody, MA: Hendrickson, 1992.

Kittel, G. and G. Friedrich, eds. *Theological dictionary of the New Testament*. 10 vols. Grand Rapids, MI: Eerdmans, 1964-1976.

Ladd, George E. *A theology of the New Testament*. Rev. ed. Grand Rapids, MI: Eerdmans, 1992.

_____. *I believe in the resurrection of Jesus*. Grand Rapids, MI: Eerdmans, 1987.

Lanci, John R. *A new temple for Corinth: rhetorical y archaeological approaches to Pauline imagery*. Studies in Biblical Literature 1. New York: Peter Lang, 1997.

Lewis, C. S. *The Screwtape letters*. New York: HarperCollins, 2001.

Lincoln, Andrew. *Paradise now and not yet: studies in the role of the heavenly dimension in Paul's thought with special reference to his eschatology*. SNTSMS 43. Cambridge: Cambridge University Press, 1981.

Marshall, I. Howard. *Last Supper and Lord's Supper*. Grand Rapids, MI: Eerdmans, 1981.

_____. *New Testament theology: many witnesses, one gospel*. Downers Grove, IL: IVP, 2004.

Martin, Dale B. *The Corinthian body*. New Haven, CT: Yale University Press, 1995.

_____. *Sex and the single savior: gender and sexuality in Biblical interpretation*. Louisville, KY: Westminster John Knox, 2006.

Martin, Ralph P. *The Spirit and the congregation: studies in 1 Corinthians 12-15*. Grand Rapids, MI: Eerdmans, 1984.

Meeks, Wayne A. *The first urban Christians: the social world of the apostle Paul*. 2nd ed. New Haven, CT: Yale University Press, 2003.

_____. *The moral world of the first Christians*. Philadelphia: Westminster, 1986.

Mitchell, Margaret M. *Paul and the rhetoric of reconciliation: an exegetical investigation of the language and composition of 1 Corinthians*. HUT: 28. Tübingen: Mohr, 1991.

Morris, Leon. *I believe in revelation*. Grand Rapids, MI: Eerdmans, 1983.

Murphy-O'Connor, Jerome. *St. Paul's Corinth: texts and archaeology*. Collegeville, MN: Liturgical, 1983.

Newton, Derek. *Deity and diet: the dilemma of sacrificial food at Corinth*. JSNTSup 169. Sheffield: Sheffield University Press, 1998.

Pagels, Elaine Hiesey. *The Gnostic Paul: Gnostic exegesis of the Pauline letters*. Philadelphia: Fortress, 1975.

Pentecost, J. Dwight. *Things to come: a study in biblical eschatology*. Grand Rapids, MI: Zondervan, 1965.

Plummer, Robert L. *Paul's understanding of the church's mission: did the apostle Paul expect the early Christian communities to evangelize?* Paternoster Biblical Monographs. Milton Keynes, UK: Paternoster, 2006.

Porter, Stanley E. *Handbook of classical rhetoric in the Hellenistic Period, 330 B.C.-A.D. 400*. Leiden: Brill, 1997.

Ridderbos, Herman. *Paul: an outline of his theology*. Translated by John R. de Witt. Grand Rapids, MI: Eerdmans, 1975.

Savage, Timothy. *Power through weakness: Paul's understanding of the Christian ministry in 2 Corinthians*. SNTSMS 86. Cambridge: Cambridge University Press, 1995.

Schmithals, Walter. *Gnosticism in Corinth: an investigation of the letters to the Corinthians*. Translated by J. E. Steely. Nashville, TN: Abingdon, 1971.

Schnabel, Eckhard J. *Paul the missionary: realities, strategies and methods*. Downers Grove, IL: IVP, 2008.

Schnackenburg, Rudolf. *God's rule and kingdom*. Translated by John Murray. New York: Herder and Herder, 1963.

Schowalter, Daniel and Steven J. Friesen, eds. *Urban religion in Roman Corinth: interdisciplinary approaches*. HTS 53. Cambridge, MA: Harvard University Press, 2005.

Schrage, Wolfgang. *The ethics of the New Testament*. Minneapolis, MN: Fortress, 1990.

Schweitzer, Albert. *The mysticism of Paul the apostle*. Translated by W. Montgomery. Baltimore, MD: The Johns Hopkins University Press, 1998 [orig. 1930].

Scroggs, Robin. *The New Testament and homosexuality*. Philadelphia: Fortress, 1983.

Shogren, Gary S. *The Pauline proclamation of the Kingdom of God and the Kingdom of Christ within its New Testament context*. PhD diss., University of Aberdeen, 1986.

South, J. T. *Disciplinary practices in Pauline texts*. New York: Mellon, 1992.

Stauffer, Ethelbert. *New Testament theology*. Translated by John Marsh. New York: MacMillan, 1955.

Stendahl, Krister. *Paul among Jews and gentiles*. Philadelphia: Fortress, 1976.

Stott, John. *The cross of Christ*. Downers Grove, IL: IVP, 1986.

Strack, H. L. and P. Billerbeck, eds. *Kommentar zum Neuen Testament aus Talmud und Midrasch*. 4 vols. München: C. H. Beck'sche Verlagsbuchhandlung Oskar Beck, 1922-28.

Theissen, Gerd. *Social setting of Pauline Christianity: essays on Corinth*. Translated by J. H. Schutz. Philadelphia: Fortress, 1982.

Thomas, Robert L. *Understanding spiritual gifts: a verse-by-verse study guide of 1 Corinthians 12-14*. Rev. ed. Grand Rapids, MI: Kregel, 1998.

Welborn, L. L. *Politics and rhetoric in the Corinthian epistles*. Macon, GA: Mercer, 1997.

Wiens, Arnoldo. *Los cristianos y la corrupción: desafíos de la corrupción a la fe cristiana en América Latina*. Barcelona: CLIE, 1998.

Wikenhauser, Alfred and Josef Schmid. *New Testament introduction*. New York: Herder and Herder, 1963.

Wimbush, V. L. *Paul the worldly ascetic: response to the world and self-understanding according to 1 Cor. 7*. Macon, GA: Mercer, 1987.

Winter, Bruce W. *After Paul left Corinth: the influence of secular ethics and social change*. Grand Rapids, MI: Eerdmans, 2001.

_____. *Roman wives, Roman widows: the appearance of new women and the Pauline communities*. Grand Rapids, MI: Eerdmans, 2003.

Wire, Antoinette Clark, *The Corinthian women prophets: a reconstruction through Paul's rhetoric*, Fortress, Minneapolis, MN, 1990.

Witherington, Ben, III. *Women in the earliest churches*. SNTSMS 58. Cambridge: Cambridge University Press, 1988.

Wood, D. R. W. and I. H. Marshall, eds. *New Bible dictionary*. 3rd ed. Downers Grove, IL: IVP, 1996.

Yamauchi, Edwin. *Pre-Christian Gnosticism: a survey of the proposed evidences*. Rev. ed. Grand Rapids, MI: Baker, 1983.

Articles

Brookins, Tim. "The wise Corinthians: their Stoic education and outlook." *JTS* 62.1 (2011): 51-76.

Deming, Will. "The unity of 1 Corinthians 5-6." *JBL* 115.2 (1996): 289-312.

Derrett, J. D. M. "'Handing over to Satan': an explanation of 1 Cor. 5:1-7." *Revue Internationale des Droits de l'Antiquité* 26 (1979): 11-30.

Dodd, C. H. "*Ennomos Christou*." Pages 96-110 in *Studia Paulina*. Edited by J. N. Sevenester and W. C. van Unnik. Haarlem: Bohn, 1953.

Finney, Mark T. "Honor, rhetoric and factionalism in the ancient world: 1 Corinthians 1-4 in its social context." *BTB* 40.1 (2010): 27-36.

Gebhard, Elizabeth R. "The Isthmian games and the sanctuary of Poseidon in the early empire." Pages 78-94 in *The Corinthia in the Roman period*. Edited by Timothy E. Gregory. *Journal of Roman Archaeology* Sup Series 8. Ann Arbor, MI, 1993.

Gill, David W. J. "The importance of Roman portraiture for head-coverings in 1 Corinthians 11:2-16." *TynBul* 41.2 (1990): 245-60.

_____. "The meat market at Corinth (1 Corinthians 10:25)." *TynBul* 43.2 (1992): 389-93.

Hammer, Paul L. "A comparison of *klēronomia* in Paul and Ephesians." *JBL* 79 (1960): 267-72.

Haufe, Günter. "Reich Gottes bei Paulus und in der Jesustradition." *NTS* 31 (1985): 467-72.

Hooker, Morna. "Authority on her head: an examination of 1 Cor 11:10." *NTS* 10 (1964): 410-16.

_____. "Hard sayings: 1 Corinthians 3:2." *Theology* 69 (1966): 19-22.

Instone-Brewer, David. "1 Corinthians 7 in the light of the Graeco-Roman marriage and divorce papyri." *TynBul* 52.1 (2001): 101-15.

_____. "1 Corinthians 7 in the light of the Jewish Greek and Aramaic marriage and divorce papyri." *TynBul* 52.2 (2001): 225-43.

Jeremias, J. "'Flesh and blood cannot inherit the kingdom of God' (1 Cor. xv. 50)." *NTS* 2 (1955-56), 151-59.

Jongkind, Dirk. "Corinth in the first century AD: the search for another class." *TynBul* 52.1 (2001): 139-48.

Liefeld, Walter L. "Women, submission and ministry in 1 Corinthians." Pages 134-60 in *Women, authority & the Bible*. Edited by Alvera Mickelsen. Downers Grove, IL: IVP, 1986.

Manson, T. W. "The Corinthian correspondence (I)." Pages 190-209 in *Studies in the gospels and epistles*. Edited by M. Black. Manchester: Manchester University Press, 1962.

Martin, Dale B. "*Arsenokoites* and *malakos*: meanings and consequences." Pages 117-36 in *Biblical ethics and homosexuality: listening to Scripture*. Edited by Robert L. Brawley. Louisville, KY: Westminster John Knox, 1996.

Meeks, W. A. "'And rose up to play': midrash and paraenesis in 1 Corinthians 10:1-22." *JSNT* 16 (1982): 64-78.

Mitchell, Margaret M. "Concerning PERI DE in 1 Corinthians." *NovT* 31.3 (1989): 229-56.

Oster, Richard. "Use, misuse and neglect of archaeological evidence in some modern works on 1 Corinthians." *ZNW* 83 (1992): 52-73.

Pablo VI. "*Humanae Vitae.*" Online: http://www.vatican.va/holy_father/paul_vi/encyclicals/documents/hf_p-vi_enc_25071968_humanae-vitae_en.html.

Peterman, G. W. "Marriage and sexual fidelity in the papyri, Plutarch and Paul." *TynBul* 50.2 (1999): 163-72.

Poythress, Vern S. "Linguistic and sociological analyses of modern tongues-speaking: their contributions and limitations." *WTJ* 42.2 (1980): 367-88.

Bibliography

Ross, J. M. "Floating words: their significance for textual criticism." *NTS* 38 (1992): 153-56.

Shogren, Gary S. "Christian prophecy and canon in the second century: a response to B. B. Warfield." *JETS* 40.4 (December 1997): 609-26.

_____. "How did they suppose the 'the perfect' would come? 1 Cor. 13:8-12 in patristic exegesis." *Journal of Pentecostal Theology* (Sheffield) 15 (1999): 97-119.

_____. "Is the kingdom of God about eating and drinking or isn't it? (Romans 14:17)." *NovT* 42.3 (2000): 238-56.

_____. "Una ofrenda para los pobres." *Apuntes Pastorales* 23.4 (2006): 18-24.

_____. "The 'ultracharismatics' of Corinth and the Pentecostals of Latin America as the religion of the disaffected." *TynBul* 56.2 (2005): 91-110.

_____. "'The wicked will not inherit the kingdom of God': a Pauline warning and the hermeneutics of Liberation Theology and of Brian McLaren." *TJ* 31.1 (2010): 95-113.

_____. "The 'wretched man' of Romans 7:14-25 as *Reductio ad absurdum*." *EvQ* 72.2 (April, 2000): 119-34.

Thiselton, Anthony C. "Realized eschatology at Corinth." *NTS* 24 (1977-78): 510-26.

_____. "The significance of recent research on 1 Corinthians for hermeneutical appropriation of this epistle today." *Neot* 40.2 (2006): 320-52.

Thompson, Cynthia. "Hairstyles, head-coverings, and St. Paul: portraits from Roman Corinth." *BA* 51.2 (1988): 99-115.

Witherington, Ben, III. "Not so idle thoughts about *eidolothuton*." *TynBul* 44.2 (1993): 237-54.

Wuellner, Wilhelm. "Paul as pastor: the function of rhetorical questions in First Corinthians." Pages 49-77 in *L'apôtre Paul: personnalité, style et conception du ministère*. Edited by A. Vanhoye. BETL 73. Leuven: Leuven University Press, 1986.

Zaas, Peter S. "Catalogues and context: 1 Corinthians 5 and 6." *NTS* 34 (1988): 622-29.

Introduction

1 Corinthians is Paul's definitive statement on how the Spirit leads God's people to be humble, loving and unified as they grow together in the true wisdom. It is through the cross that God has revealed himself, demolishing any mere human inquiry after knowledge; it is through that same cross that God transforms the unredeemable.

I. Historical Background

The epistle was sent to a church stationed deep within paganism. In Corinth as in no other place to that date, the God of Jesus Christ was pitted against the god of this world. The church sprang up in a soil that was saturated with idolatry, philosophical posturing and social stratification, all driven by a service economy that provided opportunities for the clever and made many rich off the sweat of slaves and the poor. Here Christianity could show in stark relief how it might transform the arrogant, the oppressed, the hopeless, the corrupted and the dissipated.

A. The Second Missionary Journey

Corinth was the main focus on Paul's second journey (Acts 15:40-18:23), which he launched immediately after the apostles settled the question of gentile salvation. After passing through Galatia to reinforce his churches there (16:1-5), he moved westward as if he were going to settle in Ephesus (16:6). But the Spirit prompted him and his team across the Aegean to Macedonia (16:7-10), to continue downward in a counter-clockwise arc. Planting churches in Philippi, Thessalonica and Berea, he sailed down the European side of the Aegean, past Mount Olympus to Athens and Corinth.

In the famous Macedonian call, Paul saw "a man of Macedonia standing and begging him, 'Come over to Macedonia and help us'" (Acts 16:9). He might have been forgiven if he expected the Macedonians to thank him for taking the gospel to new areas. Instead, the second journey had all the marks of a grand disaster, a monotonous cycle of Paul preaching the gospel, Paul encountering opposition, Paul being beaten or driven out, Paul moving southward. What had started as a formidable mission team of himself, Silas, Timothy, Luke, and perhaps others, began to decrease as he left one member or another along the way in order to conserve their small victories, working in the tiny congregations that clung to Christ. Paul finally arrived, quite alone, to evangelize Athens in Achaea – the town of Socrates, Plato, Aristotle and Zeno the Stoic. He spoke as a guest preacher in the synagogue. He also engaged passersby and the professionally curious in the town marketplace, and even spoke to the city fathers on the Areopagus.

One persistent interpretation of the Athens campaign is that it was a failure, attributable to Paul's own blunder.[2] The case is built on two suppositions: the first is that because they laughed at his message on the Areopagus, then his time in Athens was unsuccessful. The second assumption is that 1 Cor 2:1-2 records Paul's return to an older strategy – "When I came to you, brothers, I did not come with eloquence or superior wisdom as I proclaimed to you the testimony about God. For I resolved to know nothing while I was with you except Jesus Christ and him crucified" (See commentary on this text). From these inferences is born the theory that Paul had tried to impress the philosophers of Athens by downplaying the crucifixion of Jesus, but that his cleverness only emptied the gospel of its transforming power. Thus, badly chastened by his blunder, he went back to preaching the cross on his very next stop, Corinth.

In fact, Paul's treatment in Athens certainly compared favorably with, for example, the beating he received in Philippi. He was, predictably, laughed at on the Areopagus for teaching the resurrection, a ridiculous doctrine that he hadn't bothered to remove from his gospel. His note in 1 Cor 2 was prompted by the Corinthians' pseudo-sophistication rather than a change of method on his part. No, Paul's message to the Corinthians was what he had been preaching all along in all places, even in Athens.

B. *Driving to Modern Corinth*

Paul probably walked the 60 km from Athens to Corinth over the course of three days, stopping for the night at Eleusis and Megara.[3] Today Highway 8A runs along that same route. Where the isthmus is at its narrowest, the sudden cluster of tourist restaurants and bus stops heralds the approach to the Corinthian Canal. The canal was in planning stages several times in Greek and Roman history – notably by Julius Caesar, then by Nero, who himself dug the first basket of earth in AD 67 and sent 6000 Jewish prisoners of war to toil, before the project was finally abandoned.[4] The modern canal was dug at the close of the 19th century. To appreciate this manmade marvel, it is best to park and walk out onto the pedestrian bridge with the other sightseers. This is no Panama Canal with its locks and twists and turns, but a deep 6 km long gash cut straight across the limestone as if by a giant laser. At the bottom lies a blue ribbon of water that stretches in either direction to the horizon and the sea.

Nevertheless, even before the canal was built, Corinthians were able to move ships east-west, using a clever feat of engineering. Along the north, mainland side there is evidence still of a narrow paved track that looks as if it could have been cut by miniature earthmoving equipment; in reality it is the remains of the *diolkos* or ancient railway. Already centuries old when Paul visited Corinth, this stone path was like a railroad track on which platforms laden with cargo or even small ships were wheeled the short distance overland. It saved 300 kilometers off the east-west sea route, a shortcut that let sailors avoid the treacherous area south of the Peloponnesian coast at Maleae. Ships could dock at Corinth's port towns, Cencrea on the Aegean side or Lechaeum just 2.5 km to the northwest, and there wait their turn while the cart returned along the single-track. The

---

[2] As states, for example, Eugen Walter, *The first epistle to the Corinthians* (New York: Crossroad, 1971), 41; also Otto Kuss, *Die Briefe an die Römer, Korinther und Galater*, RNT 6.1 (Regensburg: Pustet, 1940).
[3] C. K. Barrett, *The Acts of the Apostles* (ICC; Edinburgh: T. & T. Clark, 1994), 2:860.
[4] Suetonius, *Life of Julius Caesar* 44; *Life of Nero* 19; Josephus, *Wars*, 3.10 §540.

system was still being used as late as the 9th century AD.[5]

The ruins of Corinth lie to the southwest, and have been the site of a great deal of excavation and study in the last three decades. From ancient times its fortress on the Acrocorinth has overlooked this narrow nexus of sea and land routes. The Corinthian region in its store of legends could boast of Herakles (Hercules) and Jason; Theseus had performed his feats of daring; evil queen Medea had ruled the city; king Sisyphus had started the major Isthmian games nearby; and they said that on the Acrocorinth itself was captured the winged horse Pegasus.

Set apart from the modern town of Korinthos, ancient Corinth was actually two cities: (1) Greek Corinth, which was utterly destroyed by the Romans two centuries before the gospel arrived; (2) Roman Corinth, the city that Paul visited.

The original Greek Corinth was nicknamed "wealthy Corinth" as early as Homer's *Iliad* (2:570). Into it flowed taxes, *diolkos* fees, port duties, as well as travelers, sailors, soldiers, government officials, worshippers of the local gods, visitors for the Isthmian athletic games, all with money to spend or schemes to get rich. They came to Corinth to corrupt and be corrupted, to fornicate, that is, "get corinthianized" as Aristophanes jokingly termed it.[6] Probably its morals were no lower or higher than in other Greek cities; but being a wealthy port, its opportunities for trouble were more numerous.

Because of its rebellions, the Romans completely wiped out Greek Corinth in 146 B. C., the same year they leveled another perennial nuisance, Carthage. The Corinthians were shipped off as slaves and the ruins left to the poor and to the neighboring cities. An observer wrote: "Where is thy celebrated beauty, Doric Corinth?...Not even a trace is left of you, most unhappy of towns, but war has seized on and devoured everything."[7]

In 44 B. C. Julius Caesar took the decision to rebuild Corinth as a Roman colony. *Colonia Laus Iulia Corinthiensis* ("Colony of Corinth in Honour of Julius") was built on top of the old city center but was laid out according to the Roman plan, as a rectangular grid. Latin was the language of the ruling classes, and this accounts for the presence of Latin names on city inscriptions. In AD 44 the region was given over to the Senate and the management of the senatorial proconsuls – among whom was a man named Gallio. Quickly Roman Corinth's location and natural resources made it thrive anew, becoming a regional banking center.[8] They even reinstituted the famous Isthmian Games, a sports festival that Paul may have watched in AD 49 and 51, and which may have provided his race imagery in 1 Cor 9:24-27.

Today the ruins of the two Corinths lie within a few acres, fenced in to form a sort of outdoor museum. Only the stray cats call the ancient city home. When the tour buses

---

[5] Jerome Murphy-O'Connor, *St. Paul's Corinth: texts and archaeology* (Collegeville, MN: Liturgical, 1983), 87-89; Robert Grant, *Paul in the Roman world: the conflict at Corinth* (Louisville, KY: Westminster John Knox, 2001), 17. See the video "Corinth Canal and Diolkos" https://youtu.be/T9kOK3QMu6Y and even better, "Diolkos for 1500 Years" https://www.youtube.com/watch?v=3GtE0kfWDuU

[6] T. Kock, ed., *Comicorum Atticuorum fragmenta*, vol. 1 (Leipzig: Teubner, 1880), frag. 354 line 1.

[7] Murphy-O'Connor, *St. Paul's Corinth*, 40. There is new evidence that some Greeks continued to live at the site of Old Corinth during the century before its reestablishment. See Nancy Bookidis, "Religion in Corinth: 146 B. C. E. to 100 C. E.," in Daniel Schowalter and Steven J. Friesen, eds., *Urban religion in Roman Corinth: interdisciplinary approaches* (HTS 53; Cambridge, MA: Harvard University Press, 2005), 141-64.

[8] Murphy-O'Connor, *St. Paul's Corinth*, 110. There has recently been research on the private dwellings of Roman Corinth, leading us to believe that the population ranged from the very rich to the very poor, with a strong middle-class as well. See Dirk Jongkind, "Corinth in the first century AD: the search for another class," *TynBul* 52.1 (2001): 139-48.

fill up and drive away, the ruin lies silent and a pleasant breeze blows across the flattened homes, shops, streets, and civic buildings of the dead city. In the spring poppies grow in the town square, and tall weeds threaten to hide the scattered blocks of stone.

C. Corinth as Paul encountered it

It was not so serene when Paul first stopped there. Roman Corinth was a large, bustling city of many thousands.[9] A broad paved road led straight from the city gate to the port at Lechaeum. The city center was not huge; one could walk from one end of the city proper to the other in a half hour, or from the city gate down to the Lechaeum harbor in the same time. The streets were jammed with shoppers, slaves carrying burdens, vendors, tourists, business travelers, worshipers and priests, prostitutes, soldiers, the rich cruising the city with their retinues, the dazed and the poor, and wide-eyed sailors and dockworkers on holiday.[10] In the very center stood a Roman-style forum, an open square over 100 meters long that contained the government buildings and civic monuments, including a large temple dedicated to the "divine Caesar." Around the center stood the markets (or *agora*). But the most impressive buildings were monuments to the gods. On the western edge of the city center on small rise stood the massive stately temple which had survived the destruction of ancient Corinth. It may have been a temple to Apollo, god of the sun, poetry, and science. An observer at that temple could look to the SE for a magnificent view of the Acrocorinth, a mountain, flattened at the top. On it stood the citadel and also the small temple of Aphrodite, goddess of love and protectress of the city.[11] From the mountain, if one had a telescope and looked northeast several kilometers in the direction of the *diolkos*, ships could be seen apparently sailing up and over dry land.

In Corinth was a building that in later years would bear the sign that now stands in the Corinth museum: "Synagogue of the Hebrews." It was the spiritual home for a sizeable Jewish population in this palpably pagan town. 1st-century AD Philo names Corinth as a Jewish center[12] and in the 130's AD the Jewish refugee Trypho made Corinth his home.[13] The synagogues in the Diaspora watched out for their own people, seating men according to their trades so as to foster business connections. Paul had no trouble finding the appropriate section for a tentmaker, or more likely, a general worker

---

[9] There is no certain population estimate. Bruce W. Winter, *After Paul left Corinth: the influence of secular ethics and social change* (Grand Rapids, MI: Eerdmans, 2001), 294, says there may have been 80 thousand in and around Corinth. John R. Lanci, *A new temple for Corinth: rhetorical y archaeological approaches to Pauline imagery,* Studies in Biblical Literature (New York: Peter Lang, 1997), Chapter 2, provides a vivid description of life in Roman Corinth.

[10] See the fine article by Anthony C. Thiselton, "The significance of recent research on 1 Corinthians for hermeneutical appropriation of this epistle today," *Neot* 40.2 (2006): 320-52, for a description of Corinth as a "service economy."

[11] Were there sacred prostitutes dedicated to Aphrodite in Roman Corinth? For a long time this was the assumption, but current scholarship all but eliminates the possibility: see for example, John R. Lanci, "The stones don't speak and the texts don't lie: sacred sex at Corinth," in *Urban religion in Roman Corinth,* 205-20; also Murphy-O'Connor, *St. Paul's Corinth,* 55-57. People who have not done proper research keep circulating Strabo's claim that there were a thousand prostitutes dedicated to Aphrodite. Nevertheless, Strabo was referring to the earlier city, Greek Corinth, not Roman Corinth; even then he was probably grossly exaggerating or was simply ill-informed. Roman Corinth had prostitutes, as did any city, and if their numbers were high it was because Corinth was a thriving port.

[12] Philo, *Legation to Gaius* 281.

[13] Justin Martyr, *Dialogue with Trypho* 1.

in leather, and happily ran into a man and then his wife, a couple who would become lifelong friends and coworkers. Aquila and Priscilla (Acts 18:2-3) had just been expelled from Rome and apparently were already Christians.

Nevertheless, Paul was the first to visit Corinth on a deliberate evangelistic mission (2 Cor 10:14). Corinth was just the sort of city where he liked to work: it was no isolated village, it was bursting with people, and it daily sent and received hundreds of potential Christians and lay missionaries to every part of the empire, by boat or by foot. Corinth was never an "easy" field (Jesus himself had to encourage Paul to stay, Acts 18:9-10). But there Paul's gospel met and conquered territory where the devil seemed at his strongest.

D. *Paul's Sojourn at Corinth*

Paul had a relatively lengthy stay in Corinth, 18 months to two years, as much time as he spent at the rest of the stops on this second journey combined. It was not as if Paul had skimped on Athens or the Macedonian churches. Nevertheless, in some cases it was impossible for him to stay longer, and at least in Corinth he enjoyed a respite before the situation turned ugly and his old companion persecution returned. The other churches, deprived of Paul, made do with Silas, Timothy and Luke for their spiritual formation. The so-called "we" sections of Acts imply that the author Luke was not present in Achaia on this journey nor on the next, apparently remaining to work in Asia or Macedonia in the north. But Silas and Timothy traveled back and forth from Paul, leaving with his instructions and at least two epistles (1 and 2 Thessalonians); Paul himself could not return to these volatile cities (1 Thess 2:17-18). Was Paul trying to create in Corinth a missionary base for the region, as would do during his 2-3 years in Ephesus on his next journey? If this was his aim, it seems to have been a failure: in the 50's the Corinthian church was a net drain on Paul. Even later from Ephesus he had to expend a great deal of energy to keep his Corinthian disciples on track. The Corinthian missionary work may have suffered from the dissensions and from their tendency to magnify individual charismatic experiences. Meanwhile, the hastily planted works at Philippi (Phil 1:27, 4:3) and Thessalonica (1 Thess 1:8) thrived as missionary centers.[14]

It was not the purpose of Acts or of Paul's letters to chronicle every single event of the early church or even of Paul's experiences. Acts does not even mention that Paul wrote any epistles, let alone the two he seems to have written from Corinth to the Thessalonians and later on one to Rome. Nor does it mention the "painful visit" (2 Cor 2:1, 12:14, 13:1) or the discord in the church that prompted 1 Corinthians.[15] There are many missing data about the movements of the individual members of the Pauline team.

Yet the record is more than adequate to create a general picture. First, Paul worked for a period of time, while living with Aquila and Priscilla, plying his leather trade to support himself (Acts 18:3; see 1 Cor 9:3-19). Leathercraft in ancient times was not the mechanized production that it is today. Paul and Aquila would have worked with hand

---

[14] Despite the claims of some, it was certainly Paul's intention that his churches be actively evangelistic in their regions. See the wonderful study by Robert L. Plummer, *Paul's understanding of the church's mission: did the apostle Paul expect the early Christian communities to evangelize?* (Paternoster Biblical Monographs; Milton Keynes, UK: Paternoster, 2006), especially 81-96.

[15] See the comparison of Acts and the epistles by John Coolidge Hurd, Jr., *The origin of 1 Corinthians* (2nd ed., Macon, GA: Mercer, 1983), 23-25.

tools in a tiny shop (a *taberna*) that opened off the *agora*, that is, the public marketplace. The street would have been busy all day with potential converts, and people could sit and talk about the gospel as Paul worked. Although the hours were long, Paul did not have to answer to a foreman. In addition, he could visit the synagogue every Sabbath and execute his ancestral prerogative to expound the Torah to the congregation; failing that, at least he could open a dialogue with the attendees (Acts 18:4).

When Silas and Timothy arrived from Macedonia, Paul was able to take up evangelism full-time (if that is indeed the sense of Acts 18:5). Perhaps it was this fresh burst of energy that led to his break with the synagogue, when finally they opposed him with force (18:6). Paul left they synagogue and made his headquarters in the house of Titus Justus – a gentile Christian with a Latin name – winning over synagogue president Crispus and other Corinthians to the gospel (18:7-8, probably the same Crispus of 1 Cor 1:14). Paul experienced a vision in which Christ directed him to prolong his visit in Corinth (18:9-10) and so stayed at least a year and a half (18:11). It seems likely that the bulk of this time lay after Paul left the synagogue.

Later came the explosion: the Jews took Paul to the tribunal court of the senatorial proconsul, Annaeus Julius Gallio. This seems to have taken place shortly after Gallio took office, late in 51 or early in 52.[16] Paul appeared before the *bema* or judgment seat, perhaps the same raised platform that today stands in the middle of the Corinthian ruins. Their exact aim is unstated in Acts: perhaps it was no better formed that than they wanted to get Paul "in trouble" with Rome.

The Jews' plan failed utterly. The first duty of Gallio as a Roman judge was to decide whether he should even consent to listen to a suit. If it was his common sense that kept him from intervening in the doctrinal dispute of a minority sect (18:14-16), it was his apathy that sealed his decision; Acts 18:17 gives a perfect snapshot of his callousness. As a result, the Jews could not induce Gallio to punish Paul for being a bad Jew, or to offer any ruling at all. Gallio in effect chose not to see Christianity as a religion distinguishable from Judaism, which in the 1st century enjoyed legal recognition from Rome (that it, Judaism was *religio licita*). After the case was thrown out of court, "they" (the Jews? Gentile bystanders? the original is not clear) beat another synagogue rule, Sosthenes, in front of the court. This may be the same man as Paul's associate in 1 Cor 1:1, although Sosthenes was a common name and it is not clear that the man in Acts was a Christian, or would become one. Perhaps the beating made no real sense to anyone: the Jews were frustrated, and so they took out their anger on the first person that came to hand.

Paul at any rate was not forced to leave the city. He made his own choice to depart, but only, literally, after "a number of days" (18:18). This stands in contrast with the hasty exits from Philippi (16:39-40), Thessalonica (17:10) and Berea (17:14; see also 13:49-51; 14:6, 20).

Finally, Paul laid the base for his third missionary journey while he was still wrapping up the second, by passing through Ephesus and leaving Aquila and Priscilla there. When he returned to Ephesus in 54 he had a ready base with his friends, and a new center of operations, across the Aegean Sea from Corinth.

---

[16] See the full discussion on dates by Murphy-O'Connor, *St. Paul's Corinth*, 151-59.

Introduction

Application: God's Will and Paul's Missionary Plans, or, How did Paul know where he was supposed to go?

Let us suppose that a Christian believes that God is calling him or her to the mission field. One of the most pressing questions always is: *I know I'm going; but where should I go? How can I be sure when the whole needy world lies before me?* One's tendency might be to select out one passage of Scripture, such as the vision of the Macedonian man in Acts 16:9-10, and regard that as some sort of formula. In fact the New Testament shows us a range of ways in which a missionary should make missionary decisions. Because Acts and the Pauline epistles record a number of data about his major missionary journeys, Paul is the best case study.

The question: *How did Paul, as a Spirit-filled missionary, know where to go? When he was at a crossroads, how did he know to turn to the right or to the left? How did he know it was time to leave and when it was time to stay longer?*

> **The New Testament (in Acts and in Paul's epistles) describes 49 distinguishable turning points in Paul's missionary work.**

Human motivations are complex, especially when made by Christians led by God, and Paul had multiple motivations at some of these 49 junctures. For example, one move is recorded in both Acts 9:23-25 and 2 Cor 11:32-33. Both texts mention a death threat as one motivation. But it is also implicit that Paul wished to meet with the apostles in Jerusalem.

Beyond this complexity, it is certain that while the text of Scripture describes Paul's movements with accuracy, it does not give his entire set of reasons for each move. Hence, Paul elected to stay in Ephesus because "a great door for effective work has opened to me" (1 Cor 16:8-9), but the text leaves open the possibility that he had further motives. Beyond that, there are plenty of passages where the text tells us nothing about motivation (e.g., the trip to Corinth in 1 Cor 16:5-7) or where the text may imply a reason but the reader is not certain. And let us not forget that Paul made many moves that were simply not recorded at all, including his acts during his "silent years."

Yet, having affirmed all this, we can nevertheless find much useful data, and these available data are likely to represent the broad range of experiences in Paul's life.

Two motivations show up nine times each:

travel in response to direct divine revelation;
travel in response to dangerous local circumstances.

Direct revelation:[17] Paul received revelations by prophecy, vision, audible voice, and angelic visitation. The messages could be positive (*go here!*) or negative (*don't go there! don't be afraid! don't leave here now!*). It is not known how the Spirit blocked Paul's entry into Asia and Bithynia, but that leading was clear to Paul and his team (see Acts 16:6-8). Another unexplained supernatural impediment came through "Satan's

---

[17] I would include: Acts 9:29-30/22:17-21; Acts 11:30; Gal 2:1-5; Acts 13:3-4; Acts 16:6-7; Acts 16:8-10; Acts 18:9-10; Acts 20:22-24/21:4/21:10-14; Acts 27:21-26.

hindrance" (1 Thess 2:17-18).[18]

Of course, the Damascus Road vision was the foundation of Paul's entire ministry. This call, which rivaled any experience of the Hebrew prophets, not only made Paul a missionary, but summoned him to evangelize the gentiles in far-flung areas. Everything Paul did subsequently, he did in order to carry out that vocation. He also understood his work in light of the Scriptures, particularly Isaiah (cf. the allusions in Acts 26:18, the quotations in Rom 15:8-12).

What is noteworthy by its absence is any reference to inner leading or inaudible voices. When Paul made statements like *the Lord told me to go to Macedonia*, he meant that he had heard audible words or seen visible revelations.

Dangerous circumstances:[19] These included death threats, plots and expulsion. The Lord had already instructed his disciples that they should depart from cities where they were persecuted, rather than await their own destruction (Matt 10:23); Paul sometimes took advantage of this right. To this category we may add that Paul preached to the Galatians due to an illness (Gal 4:13-14). Acts leaves the reader with the impression that the greatest opposition to Paul came during his initial visit to a place. However, that may simply be Acts' style of reporting pioneer work in greater detail, perhaps leaving out accounts of whatever persecution broke out during subsequent visits (see for example 1 Cor 15:32, where Paul's tangling with "wild beasts" goes unmentioned in Acts).

We hear Christians seeking for God's "open door," presuming that God will leave open one – and only one – opportunity, and will close every single other possibility? Did Paul make his decisions that way? To be sure, he spoke of open doors and closed doors. Yet there is never any indication that he perceived only one sole open door at a time. Therefore, let us not ask God to close doors if we are not also willing to pray and study hard in order to determine the most biblical course of action.

Missionary Strategy:[20] Strategic planning for ministry is a topic in itself. There are a dozen or so texts where Paul seems to have moved from one place to another simply "because it was there" and because it fit in with his initial call; see especially the movements in his third journey. It should not be surprising, then, to find Paul taking one step after another without reference to fresh "Macedonian visions." We see him working strategically, and managing these complex comings and goings of himself, his letters, and his deputies. For example, Paul wrote 1 Corinthians from Ephesus, then went to Troas for a rendezvous with Titus, who was heading there from Corinth, apparently by way of Macedonia. Titus didn't show up, so Paul became concerned and went ahead to Macedonia. There Titus finally met him and conveyed the relatively good news about

---

[18] One sticky issue is what to make of the interaction between the Spirit's guidance and Paul's plans in Acts 20-21. First of all, Paul believed that Christ had directed his collection for Jerusalem. He also said he was "compelled" to go, which probably means that he believed it was God's direction. Second, he was told several times that he would face hardship or death, and that he should not go to Jerusalem. Paul responded by brushing aside the prophetic notices with the rejoinder that he was willing to risk his life (Acts 21:13) Perhaps we should understand the prophetic words not as direct orders, but as warnings that Paul was free to set aside if he was willing to accept the risk.

[19] Here I would include: Acts 9:23-25/2 Cor 11:32-33; Acts 9:29-30/22:17-21; Acts 13:50-51; Acts 14:5-6; Acts 14:20; Acts 16:35-17:1; Acts 17:10; Acts 17:13; Acts 20:3.

[20] At the least I would include Acts 14:21-23; Acts 14:24-28; Acts 15:36; Acts 18:18; Acts 18:23; 2 Cor 10:15-16; Rom 15:17-22. The list could easily be augmented.

the Corinthian church. In response, Paul wrote 2 Corinthians. All this took place in just a few months, and reveals the existence of deliberate strategic movement. The schedule was flexible, too: his original design had been to go first to Corinth and later to Macedonia.

How do we reconcile the three main motivations: *revelation, circumstances, strategy*? It looks as if Paul's did not depend on these occasional appearances of angels and prophecies. It was his assignment from the Damascus Road that drove him, and these further revelations or circumstances were nudges, given to fine-tune his route one way or the other.

Aloud or in writing, Paul was comfortable with using language such as "I plan, wish, desire, hope, I have decided, it is my ambition, my prayer." His changes of plans led some Corinthians to suspect him of equivocation (2 Cor 1:15-2:4, our comments on 1 Cor 16:5-7), but Paul responded with careful reasons for the altered timetable. He strikes us as a man who was constantly thinking ahead, moving in optimum fashion and always with prayer.

We are inundated today with claims of *God told me this, God sent me there, I felt God's leading.* People boast a level of contact with God that neither apostle or prophet of old ever claimed. If Paul believed the Lord was also leading him with some sort of inner prompting or feeling, would he not have given God credit in 2 Cor 1 and said "I made my plans, but God told me to visit you *later on* rather than *immediately*"? In fact no single verse gives us that impression: (1) Paul never mentioned inner leading, notably in those places where we might expect to have heard about it; (2) Paul changed his mind often enough that he was clearly not following an infallibly-communicated heavenly plan.

Romans provides us with the best example of prayerful and spiritual strategizing. Here is what we know about the apostle's plans for the late AD 50's:

- Rom 1:10-11 – He has prayed that God would allow him to visit in Rome, so that he could teach there.
- Rom 1:13 – He has laid plans to travel to Rome before, but been prevented so far. We do not know what the hindrance was, but part of it was that he has wanted to finish the work in the East (15:22-23).
- Rom 15:24-25 – Paul plans to visit Jerusalem, then Rome, then Spain.

In these texts we see Paul praying and setting an itinerary. His plans were carefully measured against his divine calling to plant churches in new areas. However, the text offers us little help in answering why Paul chose Spain as his ultimate goal. We can make a good guess: Paul was moving westward anyway, Rome was already evangelized, and Spain lay to its west. Spain was in the empire; it was "virgin territory," fitting with Paul's method. But why Spain rather than, say, Gaul? Why not the German barbarians? Indeed, why not Africa or Mesopotamia? We simply cannot say. It is clear that Paul never wrote that he had felt in his heart that God told him to go to Spain.

But what happened to the Spain mission? Paul could not carry out his schedule, at least not in the way he had conceived it. He would not get to Rome for another three years. If he ever got to Spain (and it is doubtful) it was at least another eight years after writing Romans.

The best way we can approach these texts is not with the agenda, *How did Paul know it was God's will for him to go to some location, such as Spain?* Rather, the real question is, *Did he usually know that it was God's will for him to go to some location?* We conclude that Paul normally did not possess that knowledge, and would be certain only when he got there. In the meantime, Paul could say, "I pray that now at last by God's will the way may be opened for me to come to you" (Rom 1:10).

If Paul had stood before the Antioch Missions Committee how would he have answered the question, *Brother, do you believe in your heart, beyond a shadow of a doubt that God wants you in Spain?* Paul would have had to answer that he did *not* know that, and that he would have that assurance if and when he arrived on Spanish shores. Yet at another point in his career, he could have stated that he *was* certain that God indeed wanted him to sail from Asia to Macedonia or that he *was* certain that God wanted him to stay longer in Corinth despite the opposition.

Let us summarize what we have seen from Paul's life:

(1) Paul was driven fundamentally by Christ's commission on the Damascus Road, an incontrovertible divine message. Paul understood that he was to focus on planting Gentile churches in unreached areas.
(2) Paul never mentioned "inner" promptings when he talked about how he decided where to go.
(3) Paul mentioned "open doors" and on the other hand was prohibited from some areas, but he never hints that that is his main source of direction or that God normally gave him only one "open door" at a time.
(4) Paul sometimes received new revelations from God, but he moved ahead with his work with or without them. When they came, these direct revelations gave help in the details, but not with the basic direction.
(5) Paul was almost constantly on the move, and he laid plans that he understood to be in line with the Bible, his commission, and a wisely-conceived strategy. When asked, he could articulate the reasons for his itinerary.
(6) Paul sometimes changed his plans for strategic reasons, or had his mind changed for him by revelation or circumstances.
(7) Paul followed the directive of Jesus (Matt 10:23) to leave dangerous areas unless otherwise directed by God. However, while he took seriously the warnings to avoid Jerusalem, he seems to have known that he was permitted to accept the risk and go anyway.

There is no reason for missionary candidates to limit themselves to one or two of these principles.

E. The Corinthian Church in the early 50's

There are scraps of information regarding events at Corinth between Paul's departure from the city (AD 51-52) and his return (AD 56-57; see Acts 20:2).

The church in the house of Gaius. Gaius is probably the man whom Paul baptized (1 Cor 1:14). This house church, mentioned in Rom 16:23, was one of several in Corinth. Likely, all the house churches at Corinth met together only for special events. How many Christians were there in Corinth when Paul wrote 1 Corinthians? Estimates are made by calculating the probable number of house churches with the probable maximum space in each house, and by noting the 14 Corinthians who are named in Paul's letters.[21] The typical estimate is 100 or fewer adult believers, with one estimate as low as 40.[22] Others suggest 100 or more.[23] Given the variety of parties in the church, and given that the 14 named Christians were probably among the few who were well-off, an estimate between 60-100 is reasonable. There was also a church in one of Corinth's ports, Cencrea (Rom 16:1-2).

Ministry of Apollos. He moved the church further along, "watering" what Paul had planted (1 Cor 3:6). Apollos became a Christian only after meeting Aquila and Priscilla in Ephesus (Acts 18:24-26). He departed quickly to work in Achaia, and thus he ended up in Corinth to build on Paul's foundation (18:27-19:1).

Ministry of Cephas. Some Corinthians claimed, "I follow Cephas." Does that imply that Cephas had visited that city? The scholars are divided, but the evidence points to at least a brief visit. Cephas is the Aramaic form of "Peter" (John 1:42), and we take Cephas to be none other than the apostle Simon Peter (see under 1:12, below). Cephas had an itinerant work in Antioch (Gal 2:11), and probably in Galatia, in Corinth, and in northern Asia Minor, the destination of 1 Peter. In addition he would up in "Babylon" (1 Pet 5:13), a coded reference to Rome; according to tradition he was martyred in that imperial capital.[24] The Corinthians knew that he traveled with his wife (1 Cor 9:5). Cephas is mentioned in the traditional list of resurrection appearances (1 Cor 15:5). This is all to say that Peter/Cephas was a person known to the church in Achaia, someone whose name or his habits could be mentioned without having to give further details. There is some external evidence for Peter's visit: Dionysius, the 2nd-century bishop of Corinth, wrote that "For both [Peter and Paul] sowed in our Corinth and instructed us together."[25] While it seems unlikely that they worked at the same time – wouldn't Paul have mentioned that fact in 1 Cor 3? – Dionysius is probably remembering a real visit of Peter to the city.

Titus. There is no doubt that Titus played a large role at Corinth during the third journey. Paul had "urged" Titus and another brother to visit Corinth (2 Cor 12:18), a visit that had already taken place sometime earlier. It was his meeting with Paul that gave the occasion for 2 Corinthians (2 Cor 7:6).

Application: Paul as Pastor

Paul was a traveling apostle, not a local pastor. Nevertheless, he had to deal with the members of this flock in a pastoral way, teaching, encouraging and rebuking them; see 1 Thess 2:1-12 in particular.

I must admit honestly, that if I had been Paul, I would have been heavily tempted to abandon the Corinthian church, and that long before he wrote his epistle in AD 56. The fact that Paul did not do so is a testimony to what God was doing at Corinth.

---

[21] W. Schrage, *Der erste Brief an die Korinther* (EKKNT 7.1-4; 4 vols.; Neukirchen-Vluyn: Neukirchener, 1991-2001), 1:31.
[22] Murphy-O'Connor, *St. Paul's Corinth*, 156-57.
[23] See, for example, Mark T. Finney, *Honour and conflict in the ancient world: 1 Corinthians in its Greco-Roman setting*, LNTS: 460 (London: T & T Clark, 2012), 64-66.
[24] Eusebius, *The Church History* 2.25.
[25] Quoted by Eusebius, *The Church History* 2.25.

As mentioned above, there were perhaps 60-100 Christians in Corinth, distributed among 3-4 congregations, which met in private homes. It took two years to plant that church; it had then received five years of further apostolic care from Paul, then Apollos, probably Cephas/Peter, not to mention Timothy, Titus and other team members. It carried on regular written correspondence with Paul. It was a church for which Paul anxiously prayed every day (2 Cor 11:28).

Yet compared with the other churches, Corinth gave back poor returns for Paul's investment. He does not commend them as he does Philippi or Thessalonica for their evangelistic work, and 2 Cor 10:16 may imply that Corinth had not gotten far into evangelizing their own region, Achaia; meanwhile both Achaia and Macedonia had heard about the gospel work in Thessalonica (1 Thess 1:7-8). The Corinthians consumed more resources and energy than they produced; they ate up the apostle's time and energy when he should have been focusing on the "open doors" in other places (1 Cor 16:8-9). Some deprecated Paul's work, even though they owed him their souls. They laughed behind his back that he was crude and simplistic, a loser. Some devalued his gospel by ranking it second to popular philosophy. They rejected entire apostolic doctrines, such as the resurrection of the dead. They were arrogant and boastful, and cruel to their own poor. They justified themselves for rejecting marriage on one hand or for visiting prostitutes on the other. They took each other to court and hurled insults at each other.

If Paul were a pastor like us, wouldn't he have left the church, walked across the city and planted a new work of Christ from scratch? Wouldn't common sense tell him that if he stopped wasting his time with these few dozen people, he could start another work and surpass that number in a very short time? Why not pour his time into a New Corinthian Church?

He could not do so because Christ would not allow it. For these bothersome individuals were not simply marks in a ledger that should be written off as a bad investment. Rather they were God's chosen people. And despite the inexcusable things they did and said, Paul perceived that the Spirit was working in them and would continue to do so (1 Cor 1:4-9).

What modern pastor can endure months of this treatment, let alone years? We are in a rush to reap results that we can measure and boast of before other shepherds. We forget that God is not in a hurry. What foolishness it would be to storm off from God's flock when he may be preparing to do a fresh work among them in a few short years.

When a pastor becomes furious at his sheep for their slowness or stubbornness; when he berates them for their stupidity; when he threatens to leave them; when he beats them in anger rather than chastise them in love; then this pastor has left behind the ministry of Christ and wandered into a ministry of the flesh. Anger cannot accomplish a work for God; impatience, boasting, rudeness and sarcasm are never tools of God's Spirit.

Excellent advice from two pastors from long ago:

In this commentary we will be exploring the wisdom of the early church fathers in order to understand and apply 1 Corinthians. Our first example comes from the hand of Ignatius, around the year AD 117.[26] He wrote to Polycarp of Smyrna in order to warn

---

[26] Ignatius, *Polycarp* 2.1. I do not accept Ignatius's doctrine of the monarchical bishop, that is, the idea that each church must have one supreme leader. This is not a teaching of the New Testament, which everywhere assumes that the church has multiple elders or bishops (also translatable as overseers); see for example the

him about spending time only with eager disciples of the congregation: "If you love [only] good disciples, it is no credit to you; rather with gentleness bring the more troublesome ones into submission."

The best book that I know on the topic of pastoral care was written by a Roman pope in the 6th century AD. *Pastoral care* by Gregory the Great is simple and biblical and worth a hundred others combined.[27]

F. Third Journey – The Sojourn at Ephesus and the Return to Corinth

The third journey was Paul's Asian campaign. Beginning about AD 54, he spent about three years in Ephesus, training disciples who would go on to plant the gospel in towns such as Laodicea, Colossae, Hierapolis, and eventually the churches of Rev 2-3. Ephesus was the pinnacle of Paul's life work. But always staring at him from due west, some 300km across the "wine-dark sea," was the church at Corinth. So like an adolescent: argumentative, sullen, factious, arrogant, yet full of potential and never far from Paul's heart.

With a fair degree of confidence we can reconstruct Paul's subsequent dealings with Corinth:[28]

- Paul arrived in Ephesus from Antioch, worked with Aquila and Priscilla and stayed for three years.
- He sent the "Previous Letter" – This note at the least contained Paul's instruction "not to associate with sexually immoral people," a point that raised questions about the Christian in the world (1 Cor 5:9). Hurd believes that he can reconstruct other points of this letter, although this is speculative.[29]
- A letter arrived for Paul from Corinth: it is clear from 1 Cor 7:1, "Now for the matters you wrote about," that the Corinthians had sent a written communication

---

elders of the church of Ephesus in Acts 20:17; also the overseers of Philippi in Phil 1:1. A "senior pastor" or sole pastor who regards himself as "God's man" for the flock will find no justification for this office in the New Testament; it is based on the idea of priesthood from the Old Covenant. Still, the wisdom of both Ignatius and of Gregory the Great which we quote here is not dependent on their notion of a monarchical bishop, but has everything to do with high-quality pastoral ministry.

[27] Gregory the Great, *Pastoral care* 3.8 (the whole text is available online, http://www.newadvent.org/fathers/3601.htm) – "For we then best correct the forward, when what they believe themselves to have done well we shew to have been ill done; that whence glory is believed to have been gained, thence wholesome confusion may ensue. But sometimes, when they are not at all aware of being guilty of the vice of forwardness, they more speedily come to correction if they are confounded by the infamy of some other person's more manifest guilt, sought out from a side quarter; that from that which they cannot defend, they may be made conscious of wrongly holding to what they do defend. Whence, when Paul saw the Corinthians to be forwardly puffed up one against another, so that one said he was of Paul, another of Apollos, another of Cephas, and another of Christ (1 Cor. 1:12; 3:4), he brought forward the crime of incest, which had not only been perpetrated among them, but also remained uncorrected, saying, *It is reported commonly that there is fornication among you, and such fornication as is not even among the Gentiles, that one should have his father's wife. And ye are puffed up, and have not rather mourned, that he that hath done this deed might be taken away from among you* (1 Cor. 5:1, 2). As if to say plainly, Why say ye in your forwardness that ye are of this one or of the other, while shewing in the dissoluteness of your negligence, that ye are of none of them?"

[28] See especially Hurd, *Origin*.

[29] Hurd, *Origin*, cap. 6, "The contents of Paul's previous letter."

- to Paul, most likely carried by the leaders mentioned in 16:15-18.
- Oral information from Corinth. At the same time as the letter from Corinth, Paul received other information from two sources: the official Corinthian delegation (16:15-18) but also unofficially from Chloe's people (1:11). It is doubtful that the official letter contained a report of the schisms that divided the church, and this creates a conundrum: the Corinthians had written about certain doctrinal and lifestyle issues, but did not inform Paul about the divisions in the church. Their questions, though valid, seemed to Paul to be secondary, and they served to obscure the deeper problems of the church. In his return letter (our 1 Corinthians), Paul would answer all of their queries, but he would work through each of them from the standpoint of the cross and its implications: unity, peace, mercy, and above all charity. He would also make the issue of church divisions his highest priority in 1 Cor 1-4.
- Paul sends Timothy on a journey with instructions to visit Corinth (1 Cor 4:17); we do not know when he arrived, only that he eventually did so (Acts 20:4).
- Paul sends 1 Corinthians (c. AD 56). This may have been carried by Titus; otherwise Titus arrived in Corinth between Paul's two letters. Paul mentions that rather than paying a call to Achaia first – as the Corinthians had apparently been led to expect (2 Cor 1:15-16) – he would pass through Macedonia. He planned for Titus to travel north, perhaps getting as far as Troas for a rendezvous with Paul.
- The "Painful Visit." Between 1 and 2 Corinthians, Paul dropped in on the Corinthians for a short visit, not mentioned in Acts, but recalled in 2 Cor 2:1. This would be the second visit implied by the "I am ready to visit you for the third time" in 2 Cor 12:14.
- Paul sent the so-called "sorrowful letter." It is very difficult to determine whether the letter mentioned in 2 Cor 2:9 and 7:8-9 was 1 Corinthians itself, another letter in between 1 and 2 Corinthians, or some other written message. We take the position that it is a lost epistle that he wrote before or, more likely, after his Painful Visit.
- Paul traveled to Troas and then to Macedonia (Acts 20:2). He met up with Titus, after a delay in Troas while he vainly awaited word about the Corinthians. Although Paul heard some disappointing news from Titus, he was pleased to hear that the Corinthians still loved him.
- Paul sent 2 Corinthians (AD 56 or 57). He wrote in order to warn about certain Judaizing "super-apostles" that were already operating in the Corinthian church. He also had to save the Corinthians from the embarrassment of not being prepared to give to the Jerusalem fund, concerning which he wrote 2 Cor 8-9. For partition theories regarding 2 Corinthians, consult the standard reference works; the present commentary assumes the unity of both Corinthian epistles.
- Paul arrived in Corinth (c. AD 57). The meager reference in Acts 20:2 is that he went to Greece (that is, Achaia) and stayed there three months. Timothy and Erastus[30] had gone ahead of him to Macedonia (Acts 19:22) and Timothy at least was with Paul again in Corinth (Rom 16:21). Here Paul wrote his epistle to the Romans, mentioning that he was staying with Gaius (Rom 16:23) and that the

---

[30] Of Erastus we know nothing, unless he was the Corinthian Erastus mentioned in Rom 16:23.

letter was being carried by Phoebe, a Christian leader from the Cencrea church (Rom 16:1-2). Tertius the scribe, Quartus and Erastus the "director of public works" (*aedile*) were probably Corinthian Christians (Rom 16:22-23). Once again the Jews plotted against him (Acts 20:3), prompting him to change his travel plans and to return by road to Macedonia rather than head straight for Jerusalem. Timothy was with the group that left with Paul (Acts 20:4). Luke was already in Macedonia and rejoined Paul on this return loop (Acts 20:6).

G. Later history of the church at Corinth

After the writing of Romans, the church at Corinth disappears from the pages of the New Testament. We possess several pieces of information from the late 1st and 2nd Christian centuries that shed further light on 1 Corinthians:

Earthquake! The city was nearly destroyed by earthquake in AD 77, but the Christian congregations and the Jewish colony survived.

Epistle of 1 Clement. Although formally anonymous, this earliest of the post-apostolic literature was ascribed to Clement of Rome, presbyter and correspondence secretary of the Roman church. It was probably written just after the persecution of Domitian (thus c. AD 96) and is thus contemporary with the Revelation. The letter implies that a handful of malcontents had led a revolt against the presbyters. The presbyters are spoken of in the plural, implying that neither in Rome nor in Corinth at this point was there a single or "monarchical" bishop, as there already was in many Eastern churches.[31] It is a common error to conclude that the church had been in continual internecine warfare between the 50s and the 90s. Just the reverse is true: four decades had elapsed between these two outbreaks of schism, and Clement makes the point that this new conflict was recent (*1 Clem* 3) and that for a long time Corinth had been renowned for its unity and love (*1 Clem* 1-2). The epistle makes full use of 1 Corinthians, indicating that both Rome and Corinth possessed a copy of that letter. Like Paul, Clement spends some time developing the doctrine of the resurrection. *1 Clement* was still being read publicly in the Corinthian church in the days of Dionysius (see below) and was immensely popular in the post-apostolic church.

Bishop Dionysius. Eusebius recounts the pastoral work of Dionysius, the Corinthian bishop from around the year AD 170. This bishop was a letter-writer, and Eusebius knew eight of his collected epistles:

> As Bishop of Corinth, Dionysius gave inspired service not only to those under him, but also those distant, especially through the general epistles he wrote for the churches.[32]

Later history. Corinth was plundered by marauding tribes in the 3rd and 4th centuries,

---

[31] For the earliest description of the monarchical bishop, see the *Epistles of Ignatius*, penned some two decades after *1 Clement*; for example, Ignatius, *Ephesians* 2.2 – "it is proper, therefore, in every way to glorify Jesus Christ, who has glorified you, so that you, joined together in a united obedience and subject to the bishop and the presbytery, may be sanctified in every respect."

[32] Eusebius, *The Church History* 4.23.

but survived and continued for many years as a commercial and trading center. In the late Middle Ages it declined and shrank, finally falling with all Achaia to the Muslim Turks in 1458.

II. Why did Paul write 1 Corinthians?

Paul did not write letters simply to stay in touch. As with all his epistles, 1 Corinthians was part of the written material that arose in his missionary work.[33] Paul was an itinerant worker, and during his absences he wrote in order to give his churches direction. This written teaching was usually not new information, but a call to be faithful to the truth they already possessed.

We possess more information about the circumstances of 1 Corinthians than we do about any other Pauline epistle. The immediate causes for this letter are (1) the disturbing news that Paul had heard from "Chloe's people"; (2) the delegation of Stephanus, Fortunatus y Achaicus, who brought (3) a letter from the Corinthians to Paul, asking him about issues for which they wanted fresh clarification. Their seven questions may be deduced from Paul's responses, which take up the second half of 1 Corinthians and are often introduced by "concerning..." or "and now..."[34] We provisionally define them as:

- Isn't marriage just the institutionalization of carnal desire (7:1)? There may have been several questions concerning this theme.
- Shouldn't a well-informed Christian have the right to eat meat that has been sacrificed to idols (8:1)?
- How serious were you, when you said women had to wear veils in the meeting (11:5)?
- Is it true that speaking in tongues is the surest sign of spiritual status (12:1)?
- Do we really need to accept that crass superstition of the resurrection of the body, or doesn't the idea of an eternal spiritual existence do complete justice to the Christian tradition (15:12)?
- What should we do about this Jerusalem offering (16:1)?
- Why hasn't Apollos come to visit us (16:12)?

Beyond this Paul had heard things about the church, especially from Chloe's people (1:11).

From these questions and from the text of the letter, we may provisionally synthesize the theological currents and practices within this small church:

---

[33] I say letter, singular, since I see the unity of 1 Corinthians as beyond reasonable doubt, that is, that it was written as one composition and is not a pastiche of Pauline fragments. See Hurd, *Origin*, 43-46 or the standard introductions for the various theories.

[34] Hurd, *Origin*, cap 5, "The Corinthians' letter to Paul." One should consult the thorough study by Margaret M. Mitchell, "Concerning PERI DE in 1 Corinthians," *NovT* 31.3 (1989): 229-56. She argues that *peri de* ("now concerning") does not necessarily imply an answer to an asked question. She is technically correct with regard to the phrase as generally used, but with respect to *this* epistle it does seem as if *peri de* introduces answers to questions.

Introduction

1. A combination of attitudes and opinions that include: (a) Partisanship, (a) Elitism based on the boast of a supposed philosophical sophistication, (c) A false epistemology (philosphy of knowledge), (d) Triumphalism, that is the attitude that the true Christian need not struggle

It is a notoriously difficult task to listen to one side of a conversation (in this case, an epistle) and try to infer what was going on in the church. Paul's main exhortation in 1:10 has to deal with partisanship; but when he goes ahead and develops why divisions are wrong, his argument is based entirely on the Corinthians' misunderstanding of the gospel and its ministry. Some Corinthians had lately developed a craving for philosophical wisdom. Their error was partly due to a false epistemology, that branch of philosophy that asks the question: *How do we know what we know?* They believed that rational speculation could let them make sense of the universe, and on this quest they were downplaying the simple message of the cross that Paul had preached (see *Commentary* for detailed discussion). "Amongst so many freshly awakened and eager but undisciplined minds, the Greek intellectualism took on a crude and shallow form; it betrayed a childish conceit and fondness for rhetoric and philosophical jargon (i. 17, ii. 1-5, etc.), and allied itself with the factiousness that was the inveterate curse of Greece."[35]

As it invariably does, this approach led to bitter arguments over which philosophical method was superior, who best understood the nature of truth, and who should be regarded as the elite, able to judge the motives and actions of others. Very few of the Corinthians were affluent enough to have been born into this intellectual culture (1:26). In fact the few who were wealthy enough to host house-churches or to make a sea voyage to Ephesus seem to have been on good terms with Paul; they were not the culprits in this situation (16:15-18). Yet some converts had an education and thus an interest in things intellectual. They accepted the assumptions of the popular schools of thought: that the powerful, those from well-placed families, the rich, the well-educated, the comfortable were best qualified to make up the wise elite; that the poor, the unconnected, the disenfranchised, the ignorant, and the suffering were least likely to reach any level of sophistication, and should allow themselves to be led by their betters.[36]

2. A spiritual, disembodied eternal destiny

Some Corinthians doubted that the human body would be resurrected at the return of Christ. They did not deny the resurrection of Jesus, for that would mean that they were not Christians at all. Apparently they saw Jesus as a unique case rather than the first fruit of what God would do for the church. They probably held to a doctrine of the immortality of the soul, which would exist in a disembodied state.

Some scholars argue that the Corinthians' attitude in 1 Cor 4:8 – "you have become kings!" – was based in some local misinterpretation of Christian eschatology. According

---

[35] W. Robertson Nicoll, ed., *The first epistle of Paul to the Corinthians*, in *The Expositor's Greek New Testament*, 4 vols. (Cambridge: Cambridge University Press, 1897-1910), 2:731.

[36] In the main, commentators assume that the Corinthians had a shallow understanding of popular philosophy and could use slogans and sayings without having a profound knowledge. A possible alternative, furnished by Tim Brookins, "The wise Corinthians: their Stoic education and outlook," *JTS* 62.1 (2011): 51-76, is that the "wise" Corinthians had taken a formal education at the Corinthian gymnasium, perhaps under the tutelage of Lucian the Stoic.

to this viewpoint, Paul had taught them that the kingdom of God would come in the future, and that only then would they fully enjoy the new creation and the resurrection (see 1 Thess 2:12; 2 Thess 1:5; Rom 8:18-25). Meanwhile, life in this age, rich though it be with the blessings of God, would involve suffering and weakness. This apostolic program is called *theologia crucis*, the theology of the cross. Later, the Corinthians, under some influence or another, supposedly came to believe an "*over*-realized eschatology," that is, that God had already "realized" or done for them things that were supposed to come only in the age to come. Some have suggested that the Corinthians held to something like the teaching in 2 Tim 2:18 – "who have wandered away from the truth. They say that the resurrection has already taken place, and they destroy the faith of some." Of the false teaching in 2 Timothy we have little knowledge.

An alternative to this viewpoint is that Paul had taught them that they were already raised with Christ (as in Rom 6:11 – "In the same way, count yourselves dead to sin but alive to God in Christ Jesus"). The Corinthians for their part embellished Paul's doctrine into the distorted idea that there is no future resurrection and that Christians fully reign already in a spiritual kingdom.

Gordon Fee and others have argued that an over-realized eschatology could explain many features of the letter: not only the denial of the future resurrection (1 Cor 15) but also their tendency toward charismatic ecstasy and their "liberty" to eat meat sacrificed to idols.[37]

Yet the viewpoint has a number of serious weaknesses. First, there is a problem of methodology. Scholars as a whole prefer unified solutions to all of the theological and practical issues that are found in an epistle. For example, some have tried to identify Gnosticism as the "root cause" of all of Corinth's problems (see below). Nevertheless, the whole notion that a church must have one root error, from which grow all other problems, is a questionable one. This is where a pastor might have a better sense of how to interpret an epistle than a scholar would: every pastor knows that even in a small church, there can exist a whole range of problems side-by-side, matters which are not necessarily related one to the other. In Corinth some members brought lawsuits, others went to prostitutes, others denied the resurrection, others didn't want to touch meat sacrificed to idols. It is quite possible that none of these issues were interconnected.

Second is the historical problem: nowhere in the history of the early church is there evidence for a group that combined over-realized eschatology with charismatic excess. The theologian must invent such a religion for Corinth, tying together various data into one synthesis.

Third, nowhere does Paul deal head-on with any denial of future eschatology in Corinth. Even in 1 Cor 15, the Corinthians did not reject the future coming of Christ and the kingdom; what they rejected was the resurrection of the body.

Fourth, the epistle everywhere assumes that the Corinthians had a strong future eschatology as taught them for a year and half by Paul. The apostle touches upon the coming of Christ from the beginning, for example in 1:7 – "as you eagerly wait for our

---

[37] See Gordon Fee, *The first epistle to the Corinthians* (Eerdmans, Grand Rapids, MI, 1987); Victor Paul Furnish, *The theology of the first letter to the Corinthians* (Cambridge: Cambridge University Press, 1999), 9-12; Anthony C. Thiselton, "Realized eschatology at Corinth," *NTS* 24 (1978): 510-26; Anthony C. Thiselton, *The first epistle to the Corinthians* (NIGNT; Grand Rapids, MI: Eerdmans, 2000), 357-59; Schrage, *An die Korinther*, 1:338-40; Heinz Dietrich Wendland, *Die Briefe an die Korinther* (NTD 7; 8ª ed.; Göttingen: Vandenhoeck & Ruprecht, 1962), 35-36; J. Christiaan Beker, *Paul the apostle: the triumph of God in life and thought* (Philadelphia: Fortress, 1980), 164-66; many others.

Lord Jesus Christ to be revealed." He does not offer the slightest hint that anyone denied or minimized the return of Christ.

The theory that a radically "realized" eschatology was the root Corinthian error should be laid aside due to lack of proof.

3. Exaggerated detachment from the world

Some Corinthians had misinterpreted a statement of Paul to mean that they should remain aloof from the people of the world (5:9-13). Some were being judgmental of outsiders, but, ironically, some were lax toward sin within the church of God. In 7:1, Paul is perhaps quoting one of their own slogans – literally "it is good for a man not to touch a woman" – which may indicate their rejection of sex and marriage as contaminants to the spirit or at least a distraction from a higher calling.

4. Lawsuits

Some Christians were taking much advantage of the world system, settling their differences by bringing suit against each other in the court system (6:1). This was probably a sin of the wealthier power elite of the church, since bringing suit was beyond the reach and legal rights of the poor.

5. Libertinism and toleration of incest

One member of the church had taken his father's wife (his stepmother) as his mistress (5:1ff.). We do not know the man's justification for his behavior, nor why some were "proud" in condoning the sin.

6. Eating meat sacrificed to idols

This issue had two levels – (1) whether it is intrinsically a sin or an invitation to demonic invasion to eat such food, even if by accident (as in 10:25, 27); (2) whether a Christian can participate in a banquet or ceremony which is openly dedicated to a pagan god (8:10; 10:14-22). Some members saw through the illusion of pagan idols to the fakes that they were: *if there are no "gods" but our God, then what harm can there be in eating their offerings? In fact, isn't that freedom a sign of our greater wisdom of we wise Christians? And isn't the fear of the less-sophisticated a sign of their weakness?*

7. Issues concerning women

Some Corinthians did not believe that women should wear head coverings in the assembly; Paul does not mention why. 14:33b-35 may hint at some sort of disorder caused by women in the meetings.

8. Class divisions

There have been some recent studies that argue that divisions of wealth and status were the main issue threatening the church.[38] It is better to say that the social hierarchy, while not the root cause for the church's problems, provided a context for their manifestation. The Lord's Supper, supposedly the sign of Christian love and unity, had come to symbolize of the chasm between the comfortable and the poor and powerless (11:20-21).

9. Fixation on speaking in tongues in Christian meetings

In 1:4-7 Paul remarks that one of the outstanding positive features of the church is its rich experience of the spiritual gifts or *charismata*. He will go on to show in 1 Cor 12 and 14 that these good gifts were being used to divide the church rather than build it up in love. The main (but not the only) attraction was the gift of tongues; the Corinthians were using it in meetings to give themselves individual satisfaction and status, rather than a blessing to the group. This led to disruptive meetings.

What may we make of these nine phenomena, and is there any way to tie them all together? Do these stars form any recognizable constellation or are they merely random points of light? One is always tempted to try to explain as many points as possible by one grand theory. Thus some have argued that #3 (detachment from the world) and #7 (sexual egalitarianism?) were caused by #2 (a spiritual eternal destiny), which would see sexuality and marriage as transitory and thus not relevant for those who had already tasted the coming age. Or perhaps the Corinthians were super-charismatic, that is, so possessed by the Spirit of God (as they imagined) that conventional prohibitions against idolatrous food (#6) or incest (#5) were laid aside. Or perhaps some systematized heresy, for example, Gnosticism, was the underlying problem.[39] After all, why else would Paul keep mentioning the key word, *gnōsis* ("knowledge"; see 1:5, 8:1, 7, 10, 11, 12:8, 13:2, 8, 14:6) if he were not trying to reinterpret what is true knowledge? Since it is known that Gnostics denied the bodily resurrection (#2), and were by definition elitist (#1) and tended to be ascetics (#3) and tended to blur gender roles (#7, although the notion that Gnosticism was egalitarian owes more to modern scholarship than to historical data), surely, say some, Gnosticism was the "Corinthian heresy."

The problem with this type of approach is the impossibility of bringing all nine data together in one explanation without the additional need to invent more assumptions. This is especially the case with the Gnostic interpretation of this and other Pauline letters. All the information we have of Gnosticism comes from the 2nd century AD or much later, and it has not been demonstrated that it existed as a movement in Paul's day.[40] In fact, the Gnostics came to use 1 Corinthians as "proof" of their own system: after all, didn't

---

[38] Gerd Theissen, "Social integration and sacramental activity: an analysis of 1 Cor 11:17-34," in *The social setting of Pauline Christianity: essays on Corinth* (Philadelphia: Fortress, 1982), 145-74.

[39] See the major commentaries; especially, Walter Schmithals, *Gnosticism in Corinth: an investigation of the letters to the Corinthians*, tr. J. E. Steely (Nashville, TN: Abingdon, 1971). Schmithals was the main proponent of the Gnostic hypothesis, but he is widely thought to have exaggerated the evidence. In the last few decades all but a few have rejected Gnosticism as the matrix for the Corinthians' problems. Nor is the category of "pre-Gnostic" any more satisfactory: what are designated as pre-Gnostic ideas – for example, the denial of the resurrection – were actually generally-held beliefs in Paul's day, which had no historical connection with the later Gnostic movement.

[40] The definitive statement is still by Edwin Yamauchi, *Pre-Christian Gnosticism: a survey of the proposed evidences* (rev. ed.; Grand Rapids: Baker, 1983).

Paul teach the existence of three classes of human beings, the worldly, the soulish (Christians), and the spiritual (Gnostics, who could receive the higher truths)? The very ease with which Gnostics incorporated the epistle seems to mean that Paul would have had to have missed the point of their system, and that his refutation was a botched job.

Some of these nine points (such as #3 and #5) are mutually contradictory, hinting that if there was false theology in Corinth, then we are dealing with more than one system of belief. Thus another approach is to try to describe the four parties that we know existed (see our notes on 1:12). By deduction and imagination some argue that the Apollos group was the more philosophical, while the Cephas group was Judaizing. The fatal problem is the total lack of proof. The fact that different scholars can deduce radically different interpretations of the same group is telling: was the Cephas group conservative, since he was one of the Twelve? Or was it in favor of gentile Christians, given Peter's pioneer work among gentiles (Acts 10-11)? In fact, it is impossible for us to determine which of the factions might have denied the bodily resurrection or which scrupled at eating meat sacrificed to idols. As we will argue later on, their attraction to Apollos, Cephas and Paul were based on their taste in each person's status and ministry style. By acclaiming, for example, Cephas as their hero, some Corinthians were attaching themselves to an influential figure, whose status was then reflected in their own, less glamorous, lives.[41]

We will have better success if we look to the historical *milieu* to see whether we can explain the Corinthians' teachings without recourse to multiplied assumptions. Paul himself implies that it is their craving for the status, gained by human wisdom, that was the root cause for the factions. In 1:22 he describes his own experience as an evangelist: "Jews demand miraculous signs and Greeks look for wisdom." How does this help to unlock the errors at Corinth? There were some Jewish believers in the church, but as with all the Pauline congregations, Greek gentiles were in the majority. It is telling then that Paul spends all of his time in this epistle, not dealing with unbelieving Jews or Judaizing Christians (as in Galatians), but with philosophical wisdom, that is, the stereotypically Greek error. He is dealing not with Christians who are tempted to receive circumcision, but those who are tempted to interpret the universe through rationalistically rather than through divine revelation.

Philosophical opinions in Achaia varied, but we can deduce how their common points might have affected the fledgling Christians at Corinth:

- every current philosophical system shared an epistemological assumption, stressing the importance of reason over tradition or revelation
- every system believed that its own approach was the wisest and most commendable, and each system was perpetually in conflict with the others
- every system, intentionally or not, fostered elitism, reserving its highest honors for those who were intellectually equipped to devote themselves to the quest for wisdom
- every system offered advice concerning the relationship of the individual to society; the Epicureans valued the private life and the Stoic, public involvement
- most systems valued logic, rhetoric and an attractive presentation of their truths, one goal being the enlistment of wealthy patrons and students; the Cynics street

---

[41] See especially Mark T. Finney, "Honor, rhetoric and factionalism in the ancient world: 1 Corinthians 1-4 in its social context," *BTB* 40.1 (2010): 27-36.

preachers were an exception, but they were widely regarded as buffoonish
- every philosophy had a strongly developed opinion on whether the traditional Greek gods existed, what was the nature of God/gods and what was our duty to God/gods
- every system (whether Stoic, Peripatetic, Epicurean, popular paganism of the poets, and especially Platonism) ridiculed the idea of bodily resurrection (see Acts 17:18, 32)

The philosophical school that best reflects the issues of 1 Cor 1-10, 15 is Stoicism, which in fact is known to have strongly influenced Roman Corinth at the time of Paul. "Stoicism was not only the most popular among Hellenistic philosophies in the 1st century, but it was particularly popular among the wealthy."[42] One of the living voices of Stoicism in Paul's day was Seneca, brother of the very Gallio who was serving as proconsul of Corinth. A certain "Lucian the Stoic" was actively teaching in Corinth around the time of the Corinthian epistles.[43] All of this to say that, we do not have to rely upon the anachronism of a 1st-century version of Gnosticism, since it can be firmly demonstrated that Corinthians would have been in regular contact with Stoic ideas, namely:

- A rationalistic approach to knowledge and to morality
- Abstinence from polluting influences (see 1 Cor 7:1)
- A passion for self-examination as an instrument of the moral life (see 1 Cor 4:3-4)[44]
- Relative indifference to marriage and childrearing (cf. 1 Cor 7)[45]
- A keen interest in living according to "nature" (*phusis*; cf. the use of the word in 1 Cor 11:14-15)[46]
- Belief in the "spirit of this world" (1 Cor 2:12)[47]
- A denial of the resurrection (see 1 Cor 15:12)
- A belief that the soul survives death, but is not conscious, and will be absorbed into the universe
- An expectation that the universe will be periodically purified by fire (cf. 1 Cor

---

[42] Tim Brookins, "The wise Corinthians," 47. See too Albert V. Garcilazo, *The Corinthian dissenters and the Stoics* (Studies in Biblical Literature 106; New York: Peter Lang, 2007). According to Garcilazo, the elite of Roman Corinth were under the strong influence of Seneca and other leaders of Roman society. He points to the Stoic emphasis on wisdom, freedom and self-sufficiency as the key to understanding the epistles. Will Deming, *Paul on marriage and celibacy: the Hellenistic background of 1 Corinthians 7* (2nd ed.; Grand Rapids, MI: Eerdmans, 2004), gives some solid background of Stoic slogans and thinking in the letter. Unfortunately, his theory suffers from the multiplication of assumptions, since he argues that there were also Jewish sapiential and apocalyptic elements in Corinth, syncretized within a basically Christian framework. One must remember that the church of Corinth was composed of perhaps a hundred people, very few of whom would have had any appreciation for philosophical thinking.

[43] Brookins, "The wise Corinthians," 59.

[44] Richard B. Hays, *First Corinthians* (Interpretation; Louisville, KY: John Knox, 1997), 66.

[45] So Clement of Alexandria, *Stromata* 2.23 – "According to the opinion of the Stoics, marriage and the rearing of children are a thing indifferent."

[46] Brad Inwood, ed., *The Cambridge companion to the Stoics* (Cambridge: Cambridge University Press, 2003), 239-46.

[47] Thiselton, *First Corinthians*, 262-63.

3:13-15)[48]
- A slogan: "All things are belong to the wise man" (cf. 1 Cor 3:21b)[49]
- A teaching that "a temple...ought not to be regarded as holy" (cf. 1 Cor 3:16-17, 6:19-20)[50]
- Most strikingly, the Stoics regarded the wise man (the philosopher) as in control of his world: "The Stoics teach what is in conformity with this, assigning kinghood, priesthood, prophecy, legislation, riches, true beauty, noble birth, freedom, to the wise man alone."[51] This is a very close parallel to 1 Cor 4:8, where Paul parodies some Corinthians for being "sated, rich, kings already."

The Corinthians had not converted to Stoicism, nor was there a coherent fusion of the Christian and Stoic horizons. Rather, some Christians picked up on Stoic and other ideas because they presented themselves as the deeper source of wisdom for the elite or upwardly-mobile person. A philosophy strong in Stoicism would provide answers to #1 and 2 above, and perhaps play a role in #4, 6 and 8. It does not provide any sort of explanation for #5, libertinism.

To bring them back to the true gospel and to the unity it engenders, Paul will argue that God has revealed himself in the cross of Christ. And while some scholars argue that the problem throughout the letter is super-spirituality, we argue that life in the Spirit, or a "charismatic" gospel, is precisely what Paul presents as the solution to many of the Corinthian problems.

In antiquity the craving for wisdom tended in daily practice to produce self-promoting preachers who used their skills for their own gain. For every wise and sincere Epictetus or Marcus Aurelius, there were dozens of slick manipulators – people who were often lampooned by their contemporaries, and whose speeches and writings history has decided not to preserve for us. Still, even the best and most sincere philosopher could not come close to hearing God speak. It was the Christian gospel, revealed to humankind a scant 25 years before this epistle, that presented the will of God, and that certain Corinthians were labeling as too elementary. It was this spirit of condescension, not some heretical system, which constituted the heart of Corinthian error. It was Paul, not the Corinthians, who saw that their problem was at heart theological – that people who acted as they did were babies, not grownups; were foolish, not wise; were thinking like the world, not thinking through the perspective of the cross. "In order to overcome these sources of discord Paul gives in his letter a lengthy discourse on concord or reconciliation using deliberative rhetoric. *He is convinced that even social problems have theological roots and ethical implications.*"[52]

---

[48] So Clement of Alexandria, *Stromata* 5.1; Inwood, *The Stoics*, 129, 133-38.

[49] Hays, *First Corinthians*, 60; Grant, *Paul in the Roman World*, 29; the Stoic philosopher Seneca, *De Beneficiis*, 7.3 – "if you think of all the creatures of the earth, all the riches which the bounty of nature lavishes, it shows a great spirit to be able to say, as though you were a god, 'All these are mine.'" He went on in 7.4 to say, "omnia sapienti sunt," that is, "all things belong to the wise man."

[50] Zeno, *Republic*, quoted by Clement of Alexandria, *Stromata* 5.11 – "'that we ought to make neither temples nor images; for that no work is worthy of the gods.' And he was not afraid to write in these very words: 'There will be no need to build temples. For a temple is not worth much, and ought not to be regarded as holy. For nothing is worth much, and holy, which is the work of builders and mechanics.'" See also Inwood, *The Stoics*, 177.

[51] Clement of Alexandria, *Stromata* 2.4.

[52] Ben Witherington III, *Conflict and community in Corinth: a socio-rhetorical commentary on 1 and 2 Corinthians* (Grand Rapids, MI: Eerdmans, 1995), 75, emphasis added.

Up until this point, one major issue in Corinth goes unexplained: what of speaking in tongues (or "glossolalia"), the issue that provides the context for 1 Cor 12-14, including the famous "Love Chapter"? Paul does not specifically connect the yearning for wisdom in the early chapters with the mania for revelatory gifts later in the letter. Greek philosophy cannot explain it, and attempts to make the Corinthian philosophers "enthusiasts" or "super charismatics" are bound to fail. After all, Paul specifically tells the so-called wise to return back to the apocalyptic supernatural revelation of the Holy Spirit, which will have to do with the gospel of the cross (2:6-16).

The modern Pentecostal movement suggests a solution. It is an accepted truism that charismatic experience tends to be highest among the poor and dispossessed, and lowest among the wealthy. It has even been observed that a sign of upward mobility in the church is the leaving of extreme charismatic experience in favor of education and social power: society's powerful cannot afford to be seen in an ecstatic state.[53]

Corinth is a microcosm of this same phenomenon. There were no denominations to cater to taste or social stratum. Rather in one small network of churches we see the very rich next to the very poor next to the social climbers. As in the city as a whole, competition was intense, and those with any possibility to get ahead tried to do so. Among these are people who dabbled in philosophy, perhaps the local version of Stoicism. Groups formed around Paul and the others to reflect personal taste, but also for the purpose of social jockeying for power and prestige. These issues make up the bulk of Paul's criticisms in this epistle.

Meanwhile, at the very bottom, economically and educationally, were those who have no hope to compete with their social "betters." These were the slaves, the day laborers, the illiterate, the unconnected of the church. When the rest of the church was playing its social game, what did these people do? How did they define themselves and their relationship to heaven?

We suggest that the mania for charismatic gifts was a backlash against rationalism and the elitism that it fostered. Paul affirms without reservation the value of the spiritual gifts, or *charismata*. Nevertheless, disenfranchised Christians were approaching tongues as an escape from social competition: *Very well, boast about your books (which I cannot read), your philosophy (which I cannot understand), your rich friends (who mock me). I'll just stand over here and have direct, supernatural communication with God! And we'll let God decide who is the better Christian!* In this context, the spiritual gifts of serving or administration or even prophesying could not hope to compete with the aura that attached to glossolalia. For in that activity, carried on in an uproar during the church's meetings, the charismatic could finally outshine the rich and the powerful.

To sum up: 1 Corinthians was written mainly to counteract the rationalism of the elitists, which is foolishness from the standpoint of God's revelation. It was written secondarily to correct the ultracharismatics, although not with the harsh rebuke or the sarcasm that Paul used with the other group. He affirms their gifts, but reminds them that their first duty is to love, not to use their gifts to build themselves up. Rather, let them find satisfaction in being of service to the church, since even the poor and ignorant,

---

[53] I explore this theory in detail in Gary S. Shogren, "The 'Ultracharismatics' of Corinth and the Pentecostals of Latin America as the religion of the disaffected," *TynBul* 56.2 (2005): 91-110. Dale B. Martin, *The Corinthian body* (Yale University Press, New Haven, CT, 1995), 102-03, takes the opposite viewpoint: he argues, based upon little evidence, that higher class people of antiquity would be the most naturally attracted to ecstatic charismatic experience. Martin then seems to contradict himself on pp. 239-42.

empowered by the Spirit, are useful parts of the body of Christ.

III. The Formal Structure of 1 Corinthians

There has been in recent decades a fresh appreciation for the Graeco-Roman epistolary form.[54] How do these new studies illuminate Paul's letter?

1. Paul follows many of the conventions of the 1st-century letter and of classical rhetoric. While this has been exaggerated by some scholars, it remains true that Paul writes as an educated man of the Roman empire.
2. Paul's letters have their closest parallels in the epistles that philosophers sent to their disciples, to instruct and exhort them to be true to their beliefs.
3. Paul's letters are lengthy by contrast with the day-to-day business or personal letters which we possess from his time.
4. Paul's writing style is notable for being more vivid, passionate, and caring than that of the average writer. Since his habit was to dictate his letters to a scribe (see Rom 16:22), they have the flow of a talk rather than a stale document. It is likely that some of the paragraphs that we possess in epistolary form had earlier been given orally on different occasions.
5. Paul follows the custom of taking the pen in his own hand at the end of the letter to sign his name or to give some final words of greeting or exhortation (1 Cor 16:21; Gal 6:11; 2 Thess 3:17).

Apart from the epistolary opening and closing, the body of 1 Corinthians is composed of three major sections.[55] The first part is 1 Cor 1:10-4:21, which in formal terms looks as if it could have functioned as a complete letter. Here, Paul deals with the main issue at stake in Corinth, which he heard about through Chloe's people. It is introduced and summarized in 1:10:

> I appeal to you, brothers, in the name of our Lord Jesus Christ, that all of you agree with one another so that there may be no divisions among you and that you may be perfectly united in mind and thought.

This statement serves as the theme of the first section (see comments on 1:10), but it is also the idea that to which Paul will return throughout the other two sections. In the first section Paul uses some conventions of classical rhetoric to prove his point (see how we label these in the outline, below). These Latin terms may be defined:
- What point do I want to tell you (*propositio*)?
- Why will I be talking about this (*ratio*)?
- What proof can I offer that my point is correct (*confirmatio*)?
- How should you live now that you see my point (*peroratio* or *exhortatio*)?

---

[54] See especially P. T. O'Brien, "Letters, Letter form," in *Dictionary of Paul and his letters*; also Wikenhauser, *Introduction*, 346-50; W. G. Doty, *Letters in Primitive Christianity* (Philadelphia: Fortress, 1973); the partially-outdated insights by G. Adolf Deissmann, *Light from the Ancient East*, tr. L. R. M. Strachan (London: Hodder & Stoughton, 1910), 143-246.

[55] Contra Witherington, *Conflict and community*, 75-76, who sees 1:18-16:12 as one long *probatio*.

The second section is 1 Cor 5-6. It deals with three other points that Paul has heard about, perhaps from Chloe's people.

The third section is 1 Cor 7:1-16:4. It is made up of Paul's responses to their questions. Perhaps he responds to them in the order in which they were asked.[56] Nevertheless the logic seems to flow along Paul's own agenda, and it is likely that he has ordered his answers to suit his purposes.[57] When Paul responds to their questions, he keeps returning to what he knows to be their lack of love, unity and humility. This section includes a chapter about Paul's voluntary sacrifices for the gospel in 1 Cor 9 as well as the famous love chapter 1 Cor 13, general exhortations which correspond to what the ancients called *egressio*.[58]

Paul does not complain outright, but the Corinthians had not been entirely honest with him. They told him the truth about themselves, but not the whole truth. They had written a letter and even sent him a delegation, but their "confession" was itself part of a conspiracy of silence to cover up the deeper problems of the church.[59] So, the Corinthians wanted to know whether widows should remarry, or what unmarried girls or people married to unbelievers should do – all valid questions. But how is it that they failed to mention that one of their members was openly living in incest? They ask him about whether women really needed to cover their heads in the meetings. *Very well*, said the apostle, *and I will give you the best answer that I can*. But surely Paul must have wondered how the church could have written him about this fine point, but failed to mention that those same meetings were bitterly divided.

Thus, Paul will answer their letter, but sprinkled throughout the letter are *I hear that…* or *Chloe's people told me…*, and every one is an implicit rebuke: *…and why did I hear about this second-hand, when there exists regular communication between us? Why have you embarrassed me – let along discredit the gospel – by carrying on like this while asking me these relatively minor questions?*

The very structure of the letter is marked by this tension between what Paul has been told officially and what he has heard indirectly. He gives in 1 Cor 7-16 some of the longest sustained teachings in any of his letters, showing that he took their concerns with all pastoral seriousness. But he does not allow their questions to lead him away from what he now knows about the church. He had already devoted 1 Cor 1-6 to answering the unasked questions. He sets the agenda for the entire letter, widows, veils, tongues, resurrection and all, with his appeal in 1:10, that the Corinthians be of one mind, that there be no divisions but that they church be knitted together in love. This is who 1 Cor 13 should not be regarded as extraneous; rather he is communicating that, *of course, I will tell you how the gift of tongues should function in the church: but what you really*

---

[56] Hans Conzelmann, *1 Corinthians*, tr. James W. Leitch (Hermeneia; Philadelphia: Fortress, 1975), 6.

[57] Mitchell, "PERI DE," 257: "The composition, structure and arrangement of 1 Corinthians is determined by Paul's rhetorical purpose, and not by the Corinthians' letter."

[58] See Witherington, *Conflict and community*, 191. See the rhetorical expert Quintilian, *Training of an orator* 4.3.10, who taught that in the *egressio* the author would digress into a theme that was pertinent to the case at hand, while also providing his hearers with an emotional break from the strong tone: "We shall therefore employ such utterances as emollients to soften the harder elements of our statement, in order that the ears of the jury may be more ready to take in what we have to say in the sequel and to grant us the justice which we ask. For it is hard to persuade a man to do anything against the grain."

[59] It is telling that he heard of the main problem, divisions, from Chloe's people, not from Stephanus, Fortunatus and Achaicus (16:17). It must remain speculative what role they played in the misrepresentation.

need to see is that love surpasses tongues or knowledge or prophecy, and that if you really understood agapē, *you would know already how to use your gift to the building up of your fellow Christian.*

Our commentary will follow this outline, and we will explain technical terms in context:

Outline of 1 Corinthians
I. Introduction (*Prescripto*) 1:1-4
    A. Sender (*Superscriptio*) 1
    B. Recipient (*Adscriptio*) 2
    C. Greeting (*Salutatio*) 3
II. Thanksgiving (*Proemium*) as *Exordium* 1:4-9
III. Body 1:10-16:4
    A. The Main Issue that Paul wishes to raise in this letter: unity working through love – 1 Cor 1:10-4:16 (*Probatio*)
        1. Purpose for Writing (*Propositio*) 1:10
        2. Reason for Writing (*Ratio*) 1:11-17
        3. Confirmation (*Confirmatio*) 1:18-4:21
            a. Proof from the gospel: the gospel does not foster divisions based on pride in one's wisdom 1:18-25
            b. Proof from the Corinthian reality: they were not high or wise to begin with and thus have nothing of which to boast now 1:26-31
            c. Proof from the apostolic example: they should remember how Paul first brought them the gospel in humility 2:1-5
            d. More proof from the gospel: God's true wisdom is revealed through the cross/the Spirit 2:6-16
            e. More proof from the Corinthian reality: they are acting like the world's people 3:1-4
            f. More proof from the apostolic example: all true Christian workers labor for God's glory, not their own 3:5-17
        4. Exhortation (*Peroratio*) 3:18-4:16
            a. Seek true wisdom from God, not through human wisdom 3:18-23
            b. Have the right attitude toward the apostles 4:1-5
            c. Follow the apostles in their humility and suffering rather than in triumphalism 4:6-16
        5. Itinerary y Conclusion: Paul will judge the arrogant Corinthians when he comes, so they should prepare themselves 4:17-21

    B. Other Related Issues that Paul raises, based on oral report – 1 Cor 5-6
        1. Incest and Moral Separation 5:1-13
            a. Specifically, this case of incest must be judged by the church itself 5:1-8
            b. Generally, Christians should expel worldly elements from the church 5:9-13
        2. Lawsuits 6:1-11

a. Situation – Christians are suing each other in court 6:1
b. Solution – the church should handle matters between Christians; failing that, it is better to drop the matter 6:2-8
c. Rationale – Christians who sue are living like those who will be damned 6:9-11
3. Libertinism 6:12-20

C. Issues that the Corinthians have raised in their letter – 1 Cor 7-15
1. Concerning marriage: "Isn't marriage just the institutionalization of carnal desire?" 7:1-40
   a. General principle: People may be gifted for marriage or for celibacy; in general, Christians should marry, and married Christians must not abstain from sexual relations 7:1-7
   b. Specific directions to the "unmarried" and to widows 7:8-9
   c. Specific directions to men or women who are married to believers 7:10-11
   d. Specific directions to "the rest," that is, those married to unbelievers 7:12-16
   e. General exhortation: right now, stay where you are; but don't use your circumstances as an excuse for laxity 7:17-24
   f. Specific directions to virgins 7:25-28
   g. General exhortation, continued: why you should stay where you are 7:29-35
   h. Specific directions to those engaged to virgins 7:26-38
   i. Recapitulation, with a word to widowed women 7:39-40
2. Concerning food offered to idols: "Shouldn't a well-informed Christian have the right to eat meat that has been sacrificed to idols?" 8:1-11:1
   a. The basis for deciding the question 8:1-6
   b. Eating sacrificial meat harms other Christians 8:7-13
      PARENTHESIS: PAUL'S GENERALIZING PARANAESIS (*ENGRESSIO*): CHRISTIAN LOVE MEANS THAT WE SET ASIDE OUR OWN LIBERTY IF IT IS FOR THE GOOD OF THE OTHER 9:1-27
   c. Israel's history shows us the danger of dabbling in idolatry 10:1-14
   d. Eating sacrificial meat is a sign of divided allegiance and thus offends God 10:15-22
   e. Specific instructions for some marginal related issues 10:23-11:1
3. Concerning meetings (they perhaps had written): "How serious were you, when you said that women had to wear veils in the meeting?" 11:2-16
4. Paul – And by the way, about your meetings: don't you know that the Lord's Supper should show the church at its most unified in love? 11:17-34
5. Concerning the spiritual gifts: "Is it true that speaking in tongues is the surest sign of spiritual status?" 12:1-14:39
   a. The key truth is the unity of the body as fostered by the one Spirit 12:1-31

Introduction

        PARENTHESIS: PAUL'S GENERALIZING PARANAESIS (*ENGRESSIO*): THEIR ROOT PROBLEM IS A LACK OF *AGAPĒ*. WITH LOVE, ALL THESE PROBLEMS ABOUT CHARISMATIC GIFTS WOULD RESOLVE THEMSELVES 13:1-13

    b. From the perspective of love, it is obvious that prophecy is a better blessing to others than is the gift of tongues 14:1-40

  6. Concerning the Christian's future: "Do we really need to accept that crass superstition of the resurrection of the body, or doesn't the idea of an eternal spiritual existence do complete justice to the Christian tradition?" 15:1-58

    a. The saving gospel is a gospel of the bodily resurrection of Jesus 15:1-11

    b. Denying the resurrection of the body means denying the resurrection of Jesus, and thus the saving gospel 15:12-19

    c. The resurrection of Jesus must imply the resurrection of his people 15:20-28

    d. The acceptance or denial of the resurrection of the body affects one's lifestyle in this age 15:29-34

    e. The objections to the resurrection stem from a lack of faith and a poor understanding of God's power as creator 15:35-49

    f. Besides, the resurrection of the body is revealed truth 15:50-58

  7. Concerning the collection for the believers: "What should we do about this Jerusalem offering?" 16:1-4

IV. Conclusion (*Poscripto*) 16:5-24
    A. Itinerary 16:5-12
    B. Final Exhortation final 16:13-14
    C. Commendations 16:15-18
    D. Secondary greetings 16:19-20
    E. Autograph 16:21
    F. Benediction (and malediction) and Final Greetings 16:22-24

Commentary

I. INTRODUCTION (PRESCRIPTO) 1:1-4

At least until the advent of email and text messaging, we were taught to follow a fixed form when writing a letter. The convention is so fixed that word processors offer templates for both letter and envelope, which the writer only need fill in. After the address and date we begin the communication with "Dear + Name." At the end of the letter, the sender both prints his name and signs it, and the letter is folded and put it in an envelope in a certain way.

In the Greco-Roman world, short letters were written on one sheet; longer ones on a scroll. Typically they began with the so-called *prescripto* formula:

Sender to Recipient(s), Greeting! ("greeting" = the Greek word *chairein*)

This would be followed by a short, formal prayer to the gods for the health and happiness of the recipient. Here is an example of a letter opening, sent from a soldier in the Roman fleet to his father during the 2nd century AD:

> Apion to Epimachus, his father and lord, very many greetings. Before all else I pray for your health and that you may always be well and prosperous, together with my sister and her daughter and my brother. I thank the [god the] Lord Serapis that when I was in danger at sea he straightway saved me. On arriving at Misenum, I received from Caesar three gold pieces for travelling expenses. And it is well with me.[60]

1 Corinthians is an example of Paul's adaptation of this contemporary form, but with a strongly Christian imprint.

1:1 (Sender / Superscriptio)

The *superscriptio* named the sender right at the beginning, to allow the reader to identify him immediately without having to unroll the scroll to the end.

Paul followed the normal form of *prescripto*, but he tended to expand the various parts. Here he tells something about himself; he then describes the church at Corinth in a way that leads us into the message of the letter. Paul is writing to them with the authority of an apostle; he has been called to this work by Christ Jesus, and **by the will of God**. Paul has the authority to instruct and correct them as their "father" in the gospel (4:14-16).

---

[60] Select Papyri #111, ed. A. S. Hunt and C. C. Edgar, from The Loeb Classical Library.

It was very rare to mention a co-sender in Greco-Roman letters, but Paul frequently did so. It is most likely that these names are to remind the readers of other members of Paul's team, not that they were literally co-authors. **Sosthenes** is named a **brother**, not an apostle, apparently someone they knew without further description. It is possible that this man is the same synagogue leader who was beaten in Corinth (Acts 18:17), but as his is a common name it is impossible to prove that they are the same.[61] There is no further reference to Sosthenes in this letter or in 2 Corinthians.

1:2 (Recipients / Adscriptio)

The *adscriptio* foreshadows the warning to careless workers in the church, which is God's temple and holy (3:17b). First, he reminds them that God has called them, set them apart to be **sanctified** and his **holy people**. This is not some wish of the apostle that they would behave better than they have, but a declaration of fact. "Sanctify" does not always mean to be made holy, as we use the term today. Rather it means that God has chosen to dwell among this group and set them aside to be holy. Paul gives greater details about this work of "initial" sanctification in Rom 6:1-23.[62]

Second, by the phrase **church of God**, he locates the church within the world-wide plan of God.[63] One of the Corinthians' faults is that they thought themselves a group apart, above the rules that applied to other churches: "the Corinthian concern for 'autonomy' led them to devalue the trans-local character of Christian identity."[64] But Corinth was not unique; God has called them along with individuals and congregations **everywhere**. The churches at Ephesus, Athens, Philippi, Antioch and Jerusalem also **call on the name** of Christ. These are not some generalized religious words to make them feel good about being Christians. Rather, Paul needs to lay the groundwork for what he will say through the letter, that all his churches received one and the same teaching (see 4:17; 7:17b; 11:16; 14:33b).[65] The Corinthians cannot claim the Christian experience for their very own, nor can any one group in the church claim to be specially "of Christ" (1:12). The repeated references to Christ, Christ Jesus, Jesus Christ, our Lord Jesus Christ, or [God's] Son, Jesus Christ our Lord in 1:1-9 show Paul to be Christ-centered (that is to so, christocentric). If their apostle is christocentric, then it is also the duty of Corinth – whether one is speaking of the entire church, a house group, a partisan group or the individual – to be focused entirely on the one Savior.

---

[61] Calvin is sure it was the same man, see John Calvin, *Commentary on the epistles of Paul the apostle to the Corinthians*, tr. John Pringle (Edinburgh: Calvin Translation Society), 1:50; C. K. Barrett, *The first epistle to the Corinthians* (BNTC; London: Black, 1968), 31, says it is "more than possible" that they are the same man; Fee, *First Corinthians*, 31, says they are probably the same man. Eusebius, *The Church History* 1.12.1 says that Sosthenes, Barnabas and the Cephas of Galatians 2:11 were among Jesus' 70 disciples mentioned in Luke 10:1. We have no way of knowing Eusebius's source, although Paul's reference to 500 Palestinian disciples who had witnesses the resurrection (15:6) provides a tantalizing possibility.

[62] See George E. Ladd, *A theology of the New Testament* (Eerdmans, Grand Rapids, 1992), ch. 37.

[63] See E.-B. Allo, *Première épitre aux Corinthiens* (2nd ed.; Paris: Gabalda, 1956), 2; also the use of the same phrase "churches of God" when speaking of the Jerusalem congregations in 1 Thess 2:14.

[64] Thiselton, "The significance of recent research on 1 Corinthians," 330. He goes on (334) to argue that Corinth fell into the same trap as post-modern Christians, assuming that truth is whatever the community decides it to be, rather than what the cross of Christ shows it to be. See also David E. Garland, *1 Corinthians* (BECNT; Grand Rapids, MI: Baker, 2003), 28-29.

[65] Contra Joseph A. Fitzmyer, *First Corinthians* (AB 32; New Haven, CT: Yale University Press, 2008), 50, who thinks this may be simply a liturgical formula; he doubts whether Paul intended anyone outside Corinth to read the epistles.

Introduction 1:1-4

Paul has established a pattern with the verb "call": he is **called** to be an apostle; the Corinthians are **called** to be holy; Christians are those who **call on** the name of the Lord.

Application: "Terminal uniqueness" 1:2

The United States is often criticized for its "exceptionalism," the belief that it is unique in history and unique among nations, that the normal laws and lessons of history do not apply to it. It can be summarized as the philosophy which says: *Yes, this is normally true, except in our case, because we are different from everyone else.*

The church of Corinth too believed in its own exceptionalism. They felt that they had grown past the point where they needed to follow the rules that every other church upheld: *We're not being disobedient*, they might have claimed, *it's that we're different! We have a different set of circumstances.* Exceptionalism affects most Christians and congregations at some time.

It is a lesson in irony to look at congregation after congregation, all more or less the same, and to hear many argue that the rules should not apply to them:

- "No, normally a pastor should not badger his congregation about obeying him absolutely, but our situation is so different that it is allowable."
- "Yes, normally churches should test prophecies, but this prophet is so anointed that it would be a lack of faith to raise questions."
- "No, normally a church's accountant should not falsify the books, but our church is in a situation that is so special that it is permissible this time."
- "Our church has been uniquely called by God to bring the Word to all other churches;" or "Our pastor has been called as an apostle to lead all other churches in our nation;" or "Our nation has been called to be the unique launch pad to bring the gospel to all nations."

I have an abiding interest in church history, as my many quotations from the church fathers demonstrate. When I took a course on the early church in university, many of my fellow students wondered why they should be wasting their time studying what happened in AD 325 or 1447, when there were so many exciting things happening today that needed our attention. Later on, as a pastor, I saw the reason why: history keeps repeating itself. It is said that there are no new heresies, that most of the false teachings we encounter today had already turned up in the first five centuries of the church. Thus when Jehovah's Witnesses appear at your door to tell you that "Jesus is a god, but not God eternal," they are teaching the fourth-century heresy of Arianism.

But how many times do we hear things like this:

- "God is working today (whether it be in 1995 or 2002 or 2015 or 2032) in a fresh way; this has never happened before, and so we have to put aside all past

experience and start anew."
- "Yes, Christians should read their Bible; but we cannot put new wine into old wineskins, so we should ignore those who tell us what we're doing is not biblical. How could they possibly know how God is working today? *The letter kills, the Spirit gives life!*"
- "The devil has bothered this nation since before Columbus; but just this year we have prayed this certain prayer, and so from now on the devil and his demons cannot have a foothold anywhere in this territory!"
- "Yes, Paul told the Christians not to speak aloud in tongues in a meeting unless there was an interpreter; but we live in the time of the "latter rain," and we cannot contain the Spirit as we did in the past!"
- And above all: "We cannot put God in a box!"

In fact, these very people are the great offenders when it comes to placing limits on what God can do; they imply that "he specially or uniquely reveals himself to me and my group, this month and year, in this town." They sin by ignoring that God works outside of our little experiences and has worked for thousands of years around the world.

Alcoholics Anonymous, by a striking coincidence, points out that many addicts feel that their situation is unique: *People shouldn't drink heavily, but my situation is different! People should be able to handle their problems without taking drugs, but I'm not built that way! My situation is so unusual that I should have the right to use a chemical to relax! We creative people are high-strung and we need extra drink or drugs to relax.* This attitude is called "terminal uniqueness." It is labeled "terminal," because this belief has fatal results. The person will die or lose his mind while still shouting, *But I'm not like all the others!*

All around the world and all through history there have been huge churches and influential movements that have caught the same virus. And the result, every time, is that Christians with terminal uniqueness are on the path to their own destruction. All Christians should rather obey what God has commanded for all churches in all times, and also listen to other believers who are trying to follow God's leading.

1:3 (Salutation / Salutatio)

The *salutatio* of a letter simply means the greeting. In their letters, the Greeks used the infinitive *chairein* ("Greetings!" as in Acts 15:23, 23:26; James 1:1; also 2 John 10-11). The Jews, meanwhile, used *shalom* (peace! greetings! farewell!) in their epistles. Paul seems to have christianized these two greetings to the dual form **grace and peace** from **God our Father and our Lord Jesus Christ**, substituting for *chairein* the similar-sounding *charis* ("grace"). This is the form used in Paul's letters (but see the exception "grace, *mercy* and peace" in 1 and 2 Timothy).

II. THANKSGIVING (PROEMIUM) AS EXORDIUM 1:4-9

For centuries, readers have wondered how Paul could be so positive and affirming about their spiritual gifts and the riches of the Spirit in these opening verses, when later on he will be sarcastic about their being "rich" (4:8), and rebuke their abuse of the gifts as childish (14:20)?

We are helped today by a century of investigation into the nature of ancient letters, which shows that 1:4-9 is a Pauline adaptation of a common form. Greco-Romans letters typically followed the *prescripto* (in this case, 1 Cor 1:1-3) with a *proemium* or an *exordium*.

Proemium – a thanksgiving to the gods, mentioning the author's gratitude for the recipient's health, for their friendship, or for some recent divine help. In the letter we cited earlier, the *proemium* is "I thank the [god the] Lord Serapis that when I was in danger at sea he straightway saved me, etc." The closest parallels to 1 Corinthians 1 are the thanksgivings in 1 Thess 1:2-10 and Phil 1:3-11; all three texts end on a note of hope for Christ's return. Among Paul's letters, only Galatians lacks a thanksgiving, probably because he was too disturbed by their impending apostasy to say anything positive about them.

Exordium – a short section, which might appear after the *prescripto*, and before the author got down to the business of saying why he was writing. It was an expression of friendship and respect that served to re-establish the relationship between sender and recipient. In social terms, it would be like offering your guest a cup of coffee and talking for a while about family and shared interests; then, when you are both comfortable, you might say, *Carl, the main reason I wanted to talk to you was...* Perhaps Carl will be better disposed to hear something difficult, given that you have already reaffirmed your friendship. In a letter the writer was not able with smiles, gestures and general conversation to communicate that he was the friend of the recipient. For that reason, he ran the risk of moving too quickly to a difficult theme and possibly alienating his friend. So he would write something positive and friendly in the beginning as a reminder of his continuing love, and only then go on to the hard issues.[66]

In 1 Corinthians, as in most of Paul's letters, he uses a *proemium* thanksgiving, making it function as an *exordium*.[67] That is to say, in 1:4-9 he tells them, **I always thank God for you**, the Corinthians, using that to remind them of his love and interest in their welfare. Since Paul's letters were meant to be read aloud, publicly, from beginning to end (see 1 Thess 5:27; Col 4:16), the recipients would hear first section first and could not skip ahead to the rest of the letter. When Paul reveals his main theme in 1:10, it comes as a surprise – it's possible that no-one save "Chloe's household" (1:11) had any idea that Paul even knew about their divisions.

Was Paul, as many street preachers and letter-writers of his day, merely trying to flatter his audience? Was he saying things he did not mean in order to manipulate their feelings and thus leave them vulnerable to coercion? Our answer to this must be, no. Paul will condemn throughout this letter the sin of empty rhetoric. He is truly is grateful for the work of God among them, even if they have misused some of his gifts.

---

[66] David E. Aune, *The New Testament in its literary environment* (LEC 8; Louisville, KY: Westminster John Knox, 1988), 186.
[67] Witherington, *Conflict and community*, 87.

Application: Telling all the truth 1:4-7

A caricature is a sketch of a person which exaggerates some aspect of his appearance, sometimes to be humorous and sometimes to demean. When a Christian distorts the truth about another Christian it is the grave sin of giving false testimony (Exod 20:16).

Paul is about to condemn the Corinthians for harboring an incestuous church member (1 Cor 5) and for negating the meaning of the Lord's Supper (1 Cor 11), among many other faults. He will speak frankly and at time angrily. But that does not prevent him from sincerely noting the Corinthians' spiritual successes in the *exordium*.

The myth has arisen that preaching that is true and faithful is by nature harsh:

> "This congregation has not tithed; there is no way that it has any commitment to the Lord!"
> "There has never been a church as gossipy as this one!"
> "You are not clapping loudly enough; clearly you don't love the Lord."
> "When I go to pastors' meetings, I'm ashamed to speak of the things that go on among us!"

Yet Paul, who we believe to have spoken apostolic truth, did not dwell on the negative side overmuch, even in a situation as nasty as the Corinthians.'

What does it mean to speak the truth? It means to describe the other's state in relation to the gospel, neither excusing wrong nor ignoring the good. To tell the truth does not mean simply to say accurate things. It also means to avoid exaggeration or distortion.

In the *exordium*, Paul does not depict Corinth from a mere human perspective. He carefully links what he sees with the ongoing work of God. The Corinthians are not by nature clever in word and knowledge; in fact, it is their union with Christ that makes them so. They are not simply steadfast; they are being held steadfast by God until the coming of Christ. This too is part of the truth, as seen by one who knows God's mysteries.

1:4

Here Paul reports on how he prays, using **always** to show that it is his habit.[68] Primarily he thanks God for the richness of spiritual gifts and experience of the Corinthians. He is thankful because of the **grace** God has given them in Christ. **Grace** (*charis*) is closely related to the word *charisma* (a gracious **spiritual gift**, as in 1:7; see Rom 12:6; 1 Cor 12:4, 9, 28, 30, 31; 1 Tim 4:14; 2 Tim 1:6; 1 Pet 4:10) and can sometimes stand in for that term. These gifts are not some clever skill of which someone could boast; rather they are supernatural abilities to be used for God's purpose, the building up of the church (12:7).

1:5-6

Paul will later speak ironically of their attitude of being rich (4:8), but here he speaks

---

[68] Conzelmann, *1 Corinthians*, 26 shows that the word "always" (*pantote*) was typically used in Greek *proemia*. It is used in prayer language in other Pauline letters: Rom 1:10; Eph 5:20; Phil 1:4; Col 1:3, 4:12; 1 Thess 1:2; 2 Thess 1:3, 11, 2:13; Phlm 4.

sincerely: they are in fact endowed with God's riches. This giftedness is shown in two areas: **in all your speaking and in all your knowledge**. As 1 Pet 4:11 does with "words" and "service," Paul is sketching out two types of endowment. Gifts of **speaking** might include, among other activities: teaching, speaking in tongues, interpretation of tongues, prophecy, word of wisdom and word of knowledge.

What Paul means by **knowledge** is harder to determine, since Paul will later criticize their tendency to run roughshod over other believers with their supposed superior knowledge (8:1; cf. 13:8). Also, Paul will not support their supposed philosophical sophistication, which has led to divisiveness in the church (beginning in 1:19-20).[69] The empty words and boastful knowledge of some are devoid of the power of the Holy Spirit that blesses the work of God's kingdom (4:20). At this point in the *exordium* he looks beyond those false forms of knowledge to the true knowledge of God.

In these blessings and others has the work of God through the preaching of Christ has been visibly and truly **confirmed in you**. At this point, Paul is just beginning to distinguish true knowing from rationalistic speculation. He is grateful that God has broken through the barrier through the Spirit, the Spirit who reveals the gospel and also speaks in the assembly.

1:7

Paul thanks God that they lack no **spiritual gift** (again, *charisma*) during this age.[70] As a counterpoint, he will later remind them that tongues and prophecy are limited to this age; thus Christians should focus on the eternal virtue of love rather than any spiritual gift (13:8-10). Still, up until Christ's return, the Corinthians should delight in the full supply of spiritual gifts that God has given them.

This is the first reference in the epistle to Christ's coming, when he will be **revealed**. From that same word we get the title of the last book of the New Testament, and Paul uses it technically of Jesus' return only here and in 2 Thess 1:7 ("when the Lord Jesus is revealed from heaven in blazing fire with his powerful angels"; but see also 1 Peter 1:7, 13, 4:13). The return of Christ is a revelation of God's heavenly truth; it is a vindication for the Christian who may look a fool for believing in the cross-gospel; it also is a judgment as God reveals his hidden evaluation of people's thoughts and actions (see 1 Cor 3:13). In other contexts the term has different senses: of a revelation made by the Holy Spirit to the congregation (14:6, 26) or the revelation that God has made of the gospel of Christ (2:10).

Paul says that during this age the Corinthians **eagerly wait for** the revelation of the Lord. This raises a key question about the Corinthians' theology. As we saw in the Introduction, one theory about Corinth is that it had become so other-worldly that it had abandoned or diminished its expectation of the Second Coming; or that it had accepted Gnostic ideas and rejected traditional eschatology. According to that interpretation,

---

[69] Witherington, *Conflict and community*, 88, sees "in all your speaking and in all your knowledge" a foreshadowing of the rejection of worldly knowledge in 1 Cor 1:18-4:21, but this interpretation cannot stand: he was not giving thanks to God for that pseudo-intellectual speech and knowledge. Rather Paul is thinking ahead to the spiritual gifts in cap. 12-14, which are true workings of God, even if the Corinthians have abused them.

[70] See the parallel in Ignatius, *Smyrnaeans* preface – "to the church of God the Father and of the beloved Jesus Christ at Smyrna in Asia, mercifully endowed with every spiritual gift, filled with faith and love, not lacking in any spiritual gift, most worthy of God, bearing holy things."

Paul's comment is a subtle correction rather than a declaration of fact, in other words he means to say *you should eagerly await him.*[71]

In fact, Paul says just the opposite. His teaching style is that he typically demonstrates some difficult or contentious point by appealing to a truth upon which he and his readers agree. Eschatology plays a very key role in this letter, but not because he is trying to convince the Corinthians to renew their belief in Jesus' return. Time and again he appeals to the future in order to argue for the need of some present behavior. The return of Christ is not as something he proves, but is itself a proof or illustration of some other point, thus: *You who believe in Jesus' coming should realize that what I'm saying is true.*

And so it is in this epistle that he uses the eschatology of B to prove A:

A: Paul tries to convince them:	B: Since the Corinthians agree with him that:
We should take care how we build	The fire will reveal our works
We should not judge now	Christ will bring everything to light
We should excommunicate now	The sinner's spirit might be saved
We should not sue other Christians	We shall judge the world/the angels
We should continue in what state we're in	The time is short
We should judge ourselves now at the Lord's table	God will judge the world
We should not boast about tongues or knowledge	We shall know all even as we are known
We will be resurrected	Christ has to reign until the last enemy is destroyed, (and that enemy is death)

The Corinthian church had plenty of eschatological hope in their lives. They had not spiritualized away the second coming, as the 2nd century Gnostics were to do. Their fault, rather, was in not seeing how the end of the age should affect their behavior (and in one case – the resurrection of the body – their doctrine). Their triumphalism, their arrogance, their uncontrolled charismatic experiences and their libertinism can all be better explained without recourse to some hypothesis of over-realized eschatology or enthusiastic denial of the end.

1:8

Thus Paul uses the end of the age, specifically **the day of our Lord Jesus Christ**, to demonstrate that they should now pursue holiness. This phrase is a Pauline reworking of the traditional "day of Yahweh" (or simply "the day") in the Old Testament (see Isa 13:6, 9; Joel 2:1, 11, 31, 3:14; Amos 5:18; Zeph 1:7). It was the day both of salvation

---

[71] See especially Gordon D. Fee, *God's empowering presence: the Holy Spirit in the letters of Paul* (Peabody, MA: Hendrickson, 1994), 55-58; 89.

and of judgment, and the concept is taken over in the New Testament and made a component of the Christian gospel.[72]

How the apostles regarded Jesus comes into sharp relief when one examines how they applied to Old Testament to him. They consistently attributed the acts of Jehovah to the Lord Jesus (see John 5:27; note the use of Isa 6:10 in John 12:40-41; Joel 2:32 in Rom 10:13), using, for example, the Day of the Lord Jesus Christ as a variation of the Day of Jehovah. This means that the biblical authors understood the acts of Jesus to be no less than the acts of Yahweh himself. When Paul speaks in 1 Cor 8:6 of "one Lord (*kurios*), Jesus Christ, through whom all things came and through whom we live," he applies to the Lord Jesus the language of Deut 6:4 – "The LORD [Yahweh in the Hebrew, *kurios* in the Greek Septuagint] our God, the LORD is one." This is why Paul rarely has to state that "Jesus is God." He is writing to people who knew the Bible, and every time he quotes or alludes to Yahweh language from the Old Testament and finds its fulfillment in Jesus, he affirms that Jesus is God eternal, the creator.[73]

A disciple does not just say and know the correct things, but exhibits **blameless** behavior. Here we are in the realm of prayer: Paul expresses thanks to God that in the final resort the firmness of their faith depends on Christ. This is partly diplomatic on his part, but also an act of faith. The Corinthians are hardly to the human eye without reproach; in fact, he is about to issue them some stern words. But he believes that they are in Christ's hands, and that despite appearances he will continue to work in that church. The nearest parallel is in Phil 1:6: despite the divisions in the church of Philippi, "being confident of this, that he who began a good work in you will carry it on to completion until the day of Christ Jesus."

Application: "Strong to the end" 1:8

Evangelicals are divided over the doctrine of sanctification, which answers the question "how does a person become holy before God."

First we will deal with two false extremes:

- No Christian sins
- Christians sin in this lifetime and always will, and it matters relatively little

---

[72] The New Testament uses "that day" (Matt 7:22, 2 Thess 2:3, 2 Tim 1:18, 4:8), "the day" (2 Thess 1:10, 1 Cor 3:13, Heb 10:25), "the day of wrath" (Rom 2:5, see 2:16), "the Day of the Lord Jesus" (1 Cor 5:5 some manuscripts; 2 Cor 1:14), "the day of Jesus Christ" (Phil 1:6), "the day of Christ" (Phil 1:10, 2:16), "the day of the Lord" (Acts 2:20, 1 Cor 5:5, 1 Thess 5:2, 2 Thess 2:2, 2 Pet 3:10), "the day of God" (2 Pet 3:12, Rev 16:14). It is a mistake to try and carve out a different meaning for each term, as if the Day of Christ, the Day of Christ Jesus, and the Day of Jesus Christ all refer to different concepts. Traditionally, Dispensationalists have tended to make unwarranted distinctions between semantically varied expressions. The Scofield Reference Bible (1917 edition), for example, assures the reader that "the 'day of Christ' relates wholly to the reward and blessing of saints at his coming, as 'day of the Lord' is connected with judgment." But what then of the Day of the Lord Jesus, or the Day of God; are all of these to be distinguished one from the other? Part of the problem has to do with a mistaken definition of the Day of the Lord, which in fact could speak both of blessing and damnation. What's more, the sole reference to "the day of the Lord" in the Corinthian letters (1 Cor 5:5) has to do with Christ's dealings with the church, not the world.

[73] The best study on this theme is by Gordon D. Fee, *Pauline christology: an exegetical-theological study* (Peabody, MA: Hendrickson, 2007).

The first extreme denies 1 John 1:8, 10, 2:1, which are after all addressed to Christians. It also contradicts Paul's epistles, which are always addressed solely to Christians and which consistently warn Christians about falling into sin (see especially Gal 5:16-17). Some Christians argue that while the body or the flesh sins, the spirit does not, so that "I" am not really sinning. This is playing with words and dividing the Christian person in a way which the Bible does not allow; plus it flatly contradicts 1 John 1:8, where "we" believers sin.

The other error appears in heresies that allow Christians to do whatever they feel like doing, teaching that their consciences need not feel bothered. Or it may show up in the attitude, *Oh well, we all sin; we can always confess it and be made right with God, so there is no need to panic.* These Christians forget the offense that every sin directs against God.

Even among evangelicals with mainstream views there exist real differences. Often it has to do with the "eschatological" element of sanctification, that is: assuming the Bible teaching about the resurrection and transformation of believers when Christ returns, what role do we assign that final victory and what possibility do we see for the Christian in this life? Thus we have the teachings:

- The Christian may not achieve perfection in this life but must await the resurrection
- The Christian may achieve perfection in this life, although much depends on one's definition of "perfection"

Most Dispensationalist and Reformed Christians gravitate toward the first response, while some Wesleyan and some Pentecostal Christians (but not the Assemblies of God, for example) believe that the second better reflects the biblical teaching. They argue that a believer may experience a work of grace (or second blessing, or the baptism of the Spirit) that leaves him purified of willful sin and able to serve God perfectly. Such an experience is received through faith, and those who do not have it are responsible to seek it.

The tension here, as in so many doctrines, is between the present and the future sanctification: what may the believer seek and hope for in the "now," and what is it that that remains "not yet." What does 1 Corinthians reveal of this?

Past: Christians have been sanctified as part of their conversion. They are all properly said to be "sanctified in Christ Jesus and called to be holy" (1:2); also, "you were washed, you were sanctified, you were justified in the name of the Lord Jesus Christ and by the Spirit of our God" (6:11). Most evangelicals are in the habit of speaking of sanctification as progressive or future, but biblical references frequently place it at the point of conversion (see also 1:30; Acts 26:18; 2 Thess 2:13; 1 Pet 1:2).

Present: Christ continually gives Christians strength during this life (1:8) and continues to sanctify them (1 Thess 4:3; 5:23). Yet Christians, who in the past were already sanctified, do not live in consistent obedience. We might even leave aside the gross cases of the incestuous man or those who went to prostitutes: even then, most or all of the Corinthians seem to have sinned in arrogance, childishness and factiousness. Some do faulty work in the church or even sin grossly, and yet will still be saved (1 Cor

3:15; 5:5; 11:32). In this age we are all of us relatively childish, ignorant and blinded (13:9-11). Yet before God they had no excuse to be sinful (2 Cor 7:1), nor could they claim that they could not act any differently; if that were so, why would Paul bother telling them to change?

Future: Paul wants them to be perfect at the return of Christ (1:8; see 1 Thess 5:23); his orientation is future and eschatological. He equates perfection in maturity and knowledge only with the second coming of Christ (13:9-11), as does 1 John 3:2 – "when he appears, we shall be like him, for we shall see him as he is."

How can we apply this to the modern church, which has such variety in its doctrine of sanctification? 1 Cor 1:8 shows the way, along with passages such as Rom 6:1-11 and Gal 5:18-19. The Christian life is not meant to be a constant defeat by sin – as some claim, appealing to Rom 7:14-25 – still the struggle is going to be constant and life-long.[74] In Latin America we are often guilty of promising instant victory over sin: that once a person raises his hand for an invitation; walks to the front to be prayed for; receives the laying on of hands; makes what feels like a complete commitment to Christ; speaks in tongues; or some other experience, that the battle with sin will either be at a complete end or rendered sufficiently over that the believer will not be seriously buffeted by it.

These are grave dangers in these approaches. In Costa Rica, for example, it has been demonstrated through field research that the promise of instant victory tends to produce short-lived disciples:

> ...when the [ex-evangelical] interviewees were asked about the possibility of whether a convert can sin, 22.9% indicated that it is not possible. Another 5.8% did not wish to give an opinion. Therefore, at least ¼ of those interviewed spoke about the possibility of living in "perfection", without sinning...they added that, as an outcome of salvation the Christian cannot be tempted again (11.1%), fall into temptation (10.0%), or experience anguish (11.2%). It is clear then, that 21.2% of the interviewees rejected the possibility of falling into temptation or of even being tempted...It is noteworthy that the churches with less desertion have a lower percentage of members who view the transformation [of the emotions, the feelings and the mind] as an immediate experience.[75]

Of course, many of the teachers of these people would retort that they had never promised any such thing, or that these people had misinterpreted what was said! But remember the great responsibility that teachers have, to make themselves absolutely clear and to eliminate misinterpretations. If so many people *think* they heard this, then they were not adequately informed, period. I have heard teaching that, given its most reasonable interpretation, promised such "complete victory." Is it possible that some church leaders are giving the impression that their special new brand of sanctification has higher octane than in other, less-anointed ministries? If so, they are boosting their

---

[74] But see Shogren, "The 'Wretched Man' of Romans 7:14-25 as *Reductio ad absurdum*," *EvQ* 72.2 (April, 2000): 119-34, in which I argue that the passage is not about the Christian's struggle.

[75] Our own translation from Jorge I. Gómez V., *El crecimiento y la deserción en la iglesia evangélica costarricense* (San Francisco de Dos Ríos, CR: IINDEF, 1996), 103.

own status and reputation at the cost of souls for whom Christ died. This is a grave sin against Christ (8:12).

1:9

Paul's hope rests on his faith that God is **faithful** who called them to **fellowship** with his Son Jesus Christ, our Lord. Paul will use the same term, *koinōnia*, to speak of our "communion" or sharing in Christ's body and blood in the Lord's Supper (10:16). But the communion in 1:9 is not sacramental; rather it refers to the church's entire union and relationship with Christ, the "being-in-Christ" that is the essence and definition of salvation. The term is particularly important in 1 John 1:3, 6, 7 as a metaphor of salvation.

Here closes Paul's *exordium*. Reminding them of his prayers and thanksgiving, he has renewed the warm bond between apostle and church, by telling them:

- He regularly thanks God for them
- He believes that God has richly blessed them
- Their experience of the spiritual gifts of speaking and knowing is genuine and lacking in nothing
- The gospel obviously has worked well in Corinth
- They are looking forward to Christ's return
- It is God's work to maintain them firm and blameless in the faith until his return
- God has called them to have fellowship with Christ

In the next section and indeed throughout the letter he will supplement but not overturn this opinion. They have several grievous faults that can exist alongside of these positive traits:

- They are arrogant in their supposed riches and unwilling to suffer for the gospel
- They are self-centered in the way they use the spiritual gifts and give little heed to the rest of the local congregation and the world-wide body of Christ
- Through their pride they are in danger of ruining the temple of God, his church
- They have committed several egregious moral errors
- Their expectation of Christ's return lacks a key element, the resurrection of the body
- And, first and foremost on Paul's agenda: they have committed sacrilege by in effect tearing Christ into many pieces

To this issue we now turn.

III. Body 1:10-16:4

1 Cor 1-4 is a connected series of arguments, a development of Paul's appeal for unity in 1:10 and followed by proofs for that appeal. In these chapters Paul demonstrates that unity is not simply making up one's mind to get along with others. Rather it is the supernatural outflow of the true gospel, and unity will come only when the Corinthians have an accurate appraisal of Christ's work. Let us paraphrase his argument, using the rhetorical terms mentioned above:

Propositio (or, What point do I want to tell you? 1:10): I'm entreating you Corinthians to live in unity, free from typical human divisions, and that you mend your divisions by thinking and living in the same direction.

Ratio (or, Why will I be talking about this? 1:11-17): I'm bringing up this unity issue right from the first, even though it is not one of the questions you asked me. This is because I've heard how you're really behaving, that you are breaking into factions and warring with each other. You can't tear Christ apart, you know! We're not founding rival schools of thought, but rather one people of Christ.

Confirmatio (or, What proof can I offer that my point is correct? 1:18-3:16): If you would only think through the meaning of the gospel instead of playing around with Greek "wisdom," and if you lived according to the gospel, you wouldn't be having these schisms. Why? [Some of Paul's rebukes are implicit rather than explicit, but they would have been plain enough to the people in Corinth; we will put in brackets the subtext of Paul's statements]

    a. Proof from the gospel: the gospel does not foster divisions due to pride in one's wisdom (A, 1:18-25). Only saved people can understand the Christian message. The Old Testament predicted (Isa 29:14, for example) that when God finally acted in history, he would overturn the world's wisdom. All you have to do is remember that our Jesus saves us through being crucified to realize that that has now come to pass – no philosopher is going to think a Roman cross is a clever idea. So if Greek philosophy can't begin to grasp the one fundamental fact of God's gospel, why do you act as though philosophy will take you deeper into the truth? [Implicit subtext: and why are you alienating your fellow believer in the cross with something as marginal as philosophical boasting?]

    b. Proof from the Corinthian reality: they were not high or wise to begin with and thus have nothing of which to boast now (B, 1:26-31). I was there when you Corinthians initially received the gospel, and we both know that you make poor candidates for being the wise elite. The fact that God picked individuals of your low caliber to be his people shows that he is not operating according to the standards of Greek philosophy. [None of you is deserving, so live in unity as the benefactors of God's gracious choice]

    c. Proof from the apostolic example: they should remember how Paul first brought them the gospel in humility (C, 2:1-5). The Holy Spirit did miracles and changed your lives through my preaching – and as you'll recall, I was nervous and notoriously unclever. Obviously, God gave his approval to my cross-gospel and not to your philosophy. [If you really believe in the gospel, show some humility around each other.]

    d. More proof from the gospel: God's true wisdom is revealed through the cross/the Spirit (A'; 2:6-16). We humans don't arrive at the truth of God through reason and speculation; God has to show us ultimate truth through revelation, because only God knows what is on God's mind. God just recently revealed his truth to us, and it was revealed in the cross. The so-called wise elite, both Roman and Jewish, were the very ones who rejected and crucified Jesus, so what can they possibly know? The way to God's truth is through the Holy Spirit's revelation, not through our reason. [Implicit rebuke: And what does the Holy Spirit tell us? He teaches us to be unified as God's chosen people, so, listen to him.]

    e. More proof from the Corinthian reality: they are acting like the world's people (B'; 3:1-4). When I came to you, you were really shallow and ignorant of the truth [so don't start telling me how philosophically sophisticated you've become in five short years!]. I gave you the gospel in the simplest form I could. You're still babies; you think you want profound truths, but even now I can't teach you the gospel in a deeper way. You're acting like human beings devoid of the Spirit! [Implicit warning: the route you've chosen leads you only worse into childishness. Grow up by focusing on the mature truth, the gospel, and stop picking at each other like little children.]

    f. More proof from the apostolic example: all true Christian workers labor for God's glory, not their own (C'; 3:5-17). Apollos and I and any other reputable Christian worker toil for God; God is the Master that we follow, not some clever human leader. Even the most important among us are farm hands and slaves in God's house; we live with a sense of God's impending evaluation of our work. God will judge us by whether we built up or tore down God's people, who are his holy "temple." [And you Corinthians had better watch out too, because you're tearing God's temple into pieces!]

Peroratio* or *exhortatio (or, How should you live now that you see my point? 3:18-4:16): Paul is not simply tacking on some devotional thoughts. A *peroratio* by its very nature states that *the truths we've expounded are not simply words; they must be lived out, or else I've argued my case is in vain*. Paul urges that they be centered in the cross-gospel, and as they do so, they must act out one particular truth of that message: mutual love which expresses itself in church unity. Paul's exhortation takes three directions:

    a. Seek true wisdom from God, not through human wisdom (3:18-22)
    b. Have the right attitude toward the apostles (4:1-5)
    c. Follow the apostles in their humility and suffering rather than in triumphalism (4:6-16)

Itinerary and Conclusion (4:17-21): Paul will judge the arrogant Corinthians when he comes, so they should prepare themselves.

A. The Main Issue that Paul wishes to raise in the letter: unity working through love 1:10-4:16 (*Probatio*)

1. Purpose for writing (*Propositio*) 1:10

1:10

Someone who attempts to deduce the questions that the Corinthians had written to Paul (see 1 Cor 7:1) would see that their letter could have been a few short pages. Not so for 1 Corinthians: it arrived written on a forebodingly heavy scroll that unrolled to about six meters. Reading it aloud non-stop would have taken at least an hour and a half. What could have possessed Paul to write such a long letter? His reason comes quickly in his initial appeal, whose importance one can scarcely overemphasize. The main point is framed as an "exhortation formula" (**I appeal to you**...; see 1 Thess 4:1). He asks them a favor, not as from a friend, but **in the name of our Lord Jesus Christ**. Of course this is a serious matter, since Paul invokes the divine name he would use to cast out a demon (Acts 16:18) or to expel a wicked member from a congregation (1 Cor 5:4; 2 Thess 3:6).[76]

The NIV 1984, which we follow, has Paul addressing the **brothers** here and elsewhere in the epistle. The 2011 revision has "brothers and sisters," which I would argue is a more accurate and literal translation of the Greek.[77] Like the NIV 2011, the NRSV translates 1 Cor 1:10 with "brothers and sisters" at 1 Cor 1:10 and in other epistles, but nevertheless adds a footnote saying "G[ree]k *brothers*." The editors thereby imply that while they have given "brothers and sisters" as an acceptable *paraphrase*, the Greek *literally* has "brothers." This note is misleading, since *adelphoi*, depending on the context, may equally refer to a group of only males, "brothers," or to "brothers and sisters" or "siblings." Odder still is the ESV. In the body of the text it renders *adelphoi* as "brothers" (never "brothers and sisters"). Then at the first use of the term in each letter, one encounters a footnote, as for 1 Cor 1:10: "Or *brothers and sisters*. The plural Greek word *adelphoi* (translated 'brothers') refers to siblings in a family. In New Testament usage, depending on the context, *adelphoi* may refer either to men or to both men and women who are siblings (brothers and sisters) in God's family, the church." In other words, the ESV editors concede that rendering *adelphoi* as "brothers *and sisters*" in this context would be the more accurate and literal rendering – they give no explanation as to why they didn't choose the better translation.[78]

He implores them in several clauses to come together in harmony and to mend the torn fabric of the city's house-churches. **That all of you agree with one another**, found in the NIV and other versions, is an acceptable paraphrase of what is literally "that you all say the same thing" (his usual formula, "*think* the same thing," appears in Rom 12:16, 15:5; 2 Cor 13:11; Phil 2:2, 4; 4:2). But this is not merely to mouth the same words or to "act as if" they lived in unity. "Say the same thing" was a political expression from

---

[76] See Bray, 9.

[77] See my blog https://openoureyeslord.com/2020/05/26/the-new-international-version-1984-and-2011/ for my essay on the NIV 2011 of 1 Cor 1-7.

[78] Even the traditionalist Colorado Springs Guidelines would not take issue with our "brothers and sisters," since it states that "the plural *adelphoi* can be translated 'brothers and sisters' where the context makes clear that the author is referring to both men and women. See "Colorado Springs Guidelines": http://www.bible-researcher.com/csguidelines.html.

that era, and Paul was asking the Corinthians to act as though they were all on the same side, part of the same team.[79]

Now that he has expressed it positively, Paul puts the same truth negatively, that is, **that there may be no divisions among you**. Within five years of its founding, there were schisms in this small network of house-churches, fractures which were visible during the celebration of the Lord's Supper (11:18) and in the exercise of the spiritual gifts (12:25). The word for **divisions** is the Greek *schismata*, which word later came to refer specifically to religious splits. Here the meaning is more generally any sort of divisiveness.[80] Beyond individual disunion, the Corinthians did not appreciate that all of the missionary workers were members of Christ's one team.

Finally, he appeals **that you may be perfectly united in mind and thought**. "United" in other contexts is literal, meaning to mend tears in a fabric; there as in the metaphorical use in 1:10, the goal is not simply trying to hold everything together, but restoring the oneness that had been lost. They are all to think the same thing and have the same purpose. Clearly Paul values unity, but what specifically is he talking about? What would it look like for a group of believers to be united in thought and purpose? It is telling that Paul does not instruct them to forsake some false doctrines and come back to the unity of a creed. Nor does he tell followers of Cephas or Apollos to conform to the mentality of the Paul group, whatever that might have been. Rather, the unity of the many should arise from each individual being centered in the simple gospel of the cross.[81] In that way they will act as they should, as God's one field, his sole construction project in Corinth (3:9), united together in one baptism of the Spirit (12:13) even as they exercise different functions on the body (12:7-12).

Application: Unity 1:10

Much of this epistle springs from the exhortation, "that there may be no divisions among

---

[79] See Margaret M. Mitchell, *Rhetoric of reconciliation, Paul and the rhetoric of reconciliation: an exegetical investigation of the language and composition of 1 Corinthians* (HUT 28; Tübingen: Mohr, 1991), 69-70; also Thiselton, *First Corinthians*, 115-18.

[80] See the 2nd-century parallels in *Barnabas* 19.12 – "You shall not cause division, but shall make peace between those who quarrel by bringing them together"; Ignatius, *Philadelphians* 7.2 – "To be sure, there were those who suspected that I said these things because I knew in advance about the division caused by certain people." *1 Clement* speaks of the "schisms" of Corinth decades later (*1 Clem* 46.9, 49.5), but again these seem to have nothing to do with doctrine and everything to do with ambition (see *1 Clem* 47) – "Truly [Paul] wrote to you in the Spirit about himself and Cephas and Apollos, because even then you had split into factions. Yet that splitting into factions brought less sin upon you, for you were partisans of highly reputed apostles and of a man approved by them. In contrast now think about those who have perverted you and diminished the respect due your renowned love for the brotherhood. It is disgraceful, dear friends, yes, utterly disgraceful and unworthy of your conduct in Christ, that it should be reported that the well-established and ancient church of the Corinthians, because of one or two persons, is rebelling against its presbyters."

[81] Ambrosiaster on 1:10 (Bray, 9) – "He wants them to be perfectly united in the teaching which he had given to them." While unity is clearly the main message of 1 Cor 1-4 and in other passages, Margaret Mitchell stretches the point too far when she states that unity is the theme of the entire epistle: Mitchell, *Rhetoric of reconciliation*, 1 – "...1 Corinthians is throughout an argument for ecclesial unity, as centered in the *prosthesis*, or thesis statement of the argument, in 1:10..." One must be prepared to allow for other matters, such as the pollution of individual Christians by consorting with prostitutes, confusion about widowhood or the philosophical doubts that were raised about the resurrection, to be themes in their own right and not simply sub-topics of "unity."

you and that you may be perfectly united in mind and thought."[82] Unity is not simply the more pleasant option; it matters to God that his children cannot get along with fighting and that their divisions do massive damage to the work of the gospel.

There are also false forms of unity, and their danger is so great that we must identify them first before laying out a positive model –

False unity:

Unity as being shut up. One quick way to make a church look unified is to shut up or repel anyone who seems different. This is not Christian, and it is not what Paul did. After all, he did tell the followers of Apollos and Cephas to be quiet; he told all Corinthians, including the Paul group, to love Christ and each other.

Unity based on fear, deception, social pressure, anger, shouting. It is possible to use the tools of "the sinful nature" in Gal 5:16-21 to forge some sort of false unanimity. But woe to us if we do that in the name of Christ.

"Let's have 'one way of thinking'...that is, *my* way of thinking." Some leaders say, *we will think my way and only my way and thus find unity*. But our model for unity is Christ, not one of Christ's lowly human servants who thinks to set himself up as a model. Even Paul said, "follow my example, as I follow the example of Christ (11:1)."

"We should find our unity in the Bible – but I control access to the Bible." It is tragic to see Jehovah's Witnesses come to the door and tell how hard they study the Bible. But the truth of their lives is very different. The Witnesses are never allowed alone with the Bible. Any time that they open the book, they have an approved teacher or a guide that comes directly from headquarters. (For that reason, by the way, when I speak to a Witness, I ask them to try this: "I promise I'll read your magazine carefully, if you promise me that for a month you read the Bible and only the Bible." I'm sad to say that few people agree to my offer). May it never be that we evangelicals try to enforce unity by restricting access to God's word or by implying that it cannot be read without our authoritative interpretation.

Unity as uniformity. I've known churches where everyone had the same kind of Bible in the same version; where the women uniformly wore skirts that covered their knees; where men always wore a white shirt and dark tie; where people talked, smiled, laughed and frowned identically; where everyone said "Amen" in perfect unison; where they sang the same songs in perfect harmony. The appearance they give is impressive: it looks as if an entire army in perfect order is marching off on some great mission. But looking alike and talking alike does not make people unified.

Unity enforced by tribalism. Some leaders try to unify their local tribe by encouraging

---

[82] These are words that could have been written specifically for Latin America, since we seem destined to divide into factions. For example, one may cite a study taken here among Costa Ricans, who are known for their friendly dispositions: about 28.6% of evangelicals list "arguments, divisions and gossip" as a reason the church does not grow. Similarly, 26.2% suggest "harmony and love in the church" as the solution for preventing desertion. Gómez, *El crecimiento y la deserción*, 121-23.

hatred of the other Christians and groups (of course, no Christian ever uses the word "hatred"!). It is a psychological trick of world leaders throughout history to impose unity within their nation by making another nation the adversary. This happened on all sides during the Cold War, and it happens in Christianity as well.

True unity: Let us infer from 1 Corinthians what true unity will look like –

It is about Christ. Christians who live in real unity do so because they love Christ, and because Christ has designed them to love his other people. Unity is not dedication to another human being or to a set of principles; it is a unity of family. John 17:20-21 is Christ's prayer that "that all of them may be one," revealing what was important to Jesus on the eve of his crucifixion.

It is about the cross. This epistle shows us that it is the humiliation of the cross that unites us, not our personalities. Without the cross and the forgiveness it brings us there is no unity.

It arises from within. George Orwell's *1984* is a chilling book, and deserves to be read in every generation. The hero, Winston Smith, believes that he can rebel against Big Brother in his thoughts, even if he must obey in all outward appearances. The horrifying conclusion is that the state is so powerful that it intrudes into his very thinking. This is a satanic parallel to what happens in the new birth, which prompts us to love other children of God and gives us the power to do so.

It is rooted in spirituality. Unity has to do with the fruits of Spirit, not about cultural, racial or class homogeneity. Christians who affirm and practice love, patience, generosity and other fruits will be the ones who know what to do when conflict arises. Without love, uniformity and a cool head are just a gray "sameness" and have nothing to do with God's work in us. But with true growth, we are like each other because as individuals we are growing to be more and more like Christ.

It is a unity of mission, and our first mission is to glorify God in love. A short while ago I witnessed a young Christian man give a "rap" performance. I don't normally associate rap music with bringing glory to God. Yet as I listened, I could hear an unambiguous message of love and purity and service in the gospel. How could any believer not be pleased to hear that message, even if it arrives in an unusual form? Real unity looks to unity of mission, not uniformity of packaging.

It values each brother and sister. A leader gets up to describe his vision for the church. He announces, *From now on this church is going in this direction, and those who don't like it are free...that is, free to leave and not come back!* True unity is not satisfied when 99% of the sheep are safe in the fold; it does not sacrifice sheep on the altar of a personal vision.

It values majors as majors, minors as minors. Some issues are more important than others; the paramount issues are love for God and love for others (see Matt 22:34-40; Rom 13:9). Augustine made this truth plain with his slogan: "In essentials unity, in non-essentials liberty, in all things charity." There are many issues in the church that are not directly based on biblical teaching. Rather they are this year's theological fashions or questions of taste in church organization or worship style. True unity insists that we will stay together on central Bible teachings, and allow variety on things that are transient.

It possesses courage and frankness. True unity does not live in terror of disagreement, nor does it give up in disgust when disagreement occurs. I say this again: a person who is truly loving and living in unity with the church will at times say hard things, not because it is pleasant to do so, but because it is loving. Unity means that in a sinful world, even godly people will have occasional frictions, even sharp arguments (see Acts 15:36-40; Gal 2:11-21). Unity leaves room for loving disagreement over details and disagreement over major issues. Unity does not seek calm for its own sake, but because that peace is the best way to represent God's truth.

Additional reading: I cannot recommend too strongly, Dietrich Bonhoeffer's *Life Together*, especially his emphasis on the gospel as the only true basis for unity.

2. Reason for writing (*Ratio*) 1:11-17

1:11-17 corresponds to the classic rhetorical device known as *ratio*, which answers the question, for what reason has Paul written in 1:10, "that all of you agree with one another so that there may be no divisions among you."

1:11-12

He is writing because of the information given him by people who know the real situation in the church at Corinth. **Chloe's household** is a broader group than "Chloe's family" or "relatives." She was perhaps the head of an extended family or business, as was Lydia (Acts 16:14-15). We know not who she or her people were, or whether they lived in Corinth, Ephesus or elsewhere. These people may have been slaves or freedmen in her household, that is, people of low social status. At any rate, they somehow came to know the true state of the church in Corinth, and Paul credited their report to the extent of naming his source: Paul has accurate and damning information about Corinth, and his reference to "Chloe's household" means the Corinthians now know it too. He goes on to describe the church's party spirit, but he does not immediately tell them to stop. It is not until 3:21 that he directly commands them: "So then, no more boasting about men!" [better "about people"]. Until then it enough to describe their error and leave the rebuke implicit.

Application: Should Christian leaders act on gossip? 1:11

We turn to a delicate aspect of pastoral ministry. If a leader discovers someone in sin, he or she has a natural opening to approach the offender and try to fulfill what Paul says in Gal 6:1 – "Brothers, if someone is caught in a sin, you who are spiritual should restore him gently..." But what happens in practice is not so clear-cut. Let us imagine that a member of the congregation is abusing alcohol. It is not he who tells his pastor, nor his wife nor his children; the pastor himself never discovers him under the influence. But the pastor hears from his own wife information that must have come fourth- or fifth-hand: *John is drinking and becoming violent with his family. He may lose his job. His behavior is harming the testimony of the gospel.*

The pastor now has information that may or may not be accurate. He believes that he should act on it. Yet the medium of communication is tainted: he knows what he knows because one or more people have gossiped. This puts him in a very awkward position:

1. He could ignore what he has heard and preach a sermon against the sin of gossip, but then if John is really having troubles he won't be getting any help. Alternately, he could preach about alcohol abuse. This too is awkward and may be of little use.

2. He could question the friends or family of John, although that may fuel the gossip more and it will probably get back to John.

3. He could ask John directly if what he has heard is true. The difficulty is that it may make John bitter against his gossipy brethren, no matter if the thing is true or not; alcoholics, after all, tend to shift the blame for their behavior onto others.

4. He could tell his wife to tell the person who told her, and so on, that instead of talking about John among themselves, they should be seeking to help John. But what if John's wife told one of her friends in desperation – that female friend should not confront John, should she? Besides which, if anyone has ever tried to send a message back up a chain of gossip, it takes only one individual to realize, *And why should I be the one to do the confronting, it's none of my business.*

Paul's situation is that he heard from Chloe's people that the church had divided into schisms. It is likely that Chloe's people told him other negative things, perhaps about people overeating and drinking before the Lord's Supper. That is, Chloe's people told Paul about the sins of a third party. They may or may not have tried to solve the situation themselves before they told him. They may not have had much opportunity to heal the divisions themselves, since Chloe's people (if, as is likely, they were Corinthians too) were perhaps in a position of less social status than the schismatics. Thus, they were complaining to a higher authority figure (Paul) about local people who were richer and more powerful than they. In so doing they were risking retribution: the powerful do not have a sense of humor or fair play when their inferiors squeal on them.

What does Paul do?

1. He seems sure that the information is accurate or close enough to accurate to warrant a rebuke without further questions. This does not mean that he jumped to conclusions. He had several sources and verified his information as best he could from a distance. Paul was not the type who would rush off an angry email without first checking his facts.

2. He spoke to the Corinthians about the Corinthians; he did not speak to the Philippians or the Galatians about the Corinthians.

3. He himself intervened and did not ask Chloe's people to return and rebuke the schismatics on their own. Nevertheless, at this point we must take into account that as an apostle, Paul held authority over his churches to a degree that is rare today.

4. He analyzed the problem. That is, he did not just tell them that schisms are wrong and to stop it immediately. He rooted everything he said in the broader picture of the gospel. Of course, we must beware of trying to analyze people's problems at a distance. But in this case, Paul was confident that he has enough information to tell them what is

the root of their divisions.

5. He gave them space to repent. Paul prayed and expected that a Christian, upon knowing the truth, would repent and change his ways (see especially 4:6). Paul is a pastor of hope, not of disgust and despair. And his hope was rewarded: the later epistle *1 Clement* shows that the Corinthians did give up their schisms and return to love, at least for a period of some decades (see Introduction), which is probably a good record for any church.

It turned out well that Chloe's people spoke up. This is not to give Christians the license to gossip about others – a sin that Paul condemns elsewhere (2 Cor 12:20). In this case it was appropriate that Paul made use of second-hand information. As apostle, he had a right to know what was happening and Paul was going to employ it for the church's own good.

The Corinthians seemed to have created a "conspiracy of silence," sometimes known as the "elephant in the room," an issue which everybody sees but no-one dares to mention. Paul broke the silence with information obtained from people who refused to keep quiet no longer: Chloe's people.

This social dymanic sheds light on the hypothetical case of our drinking man, John. The first action that sin takes is to camouflage itself. Rare indeed is a person confronted about a chronic sin that immediately admits his fault and goes on to repent. Especially those with addictions will have invented a complex net of excuses, justifications, deceptions, hiding places, and downright lies. In that case, the loving thing to do is to refuse to accept the person's lies, and to consistently and calmly speak the obvious truth of his condition. This is not to say that we have a perfect solution to the rumors of John's drinking. But what is clear is that a Christian pastor will pursue the issue for the good of John, will not for his part engage in gossip, will value the truth above all, and will speak that truth – to John, to those around him – in love.

What of the action of Chloe's people, who reported on the sin of other people? Did they, like children, "run and tell mother" about what his sibling has done? Was that wrong? The words of Jesus in Matt 18:15-17 are pertinent here, showing that the uncovering of sin should begin at the most intimate level and only then grow by stages that will include more "witnesses." Most Christians around the world would rather die than go and speak to an individual about his sin. We want to believe that this is the pastor's job, or that if we gossip to the right people, then somehow good might come of it. But no matter what our cultural leanings, the Bible is the truth that God expects us to follow. People should not clap and shout and claim to be full of the Spirit's power if they find themselves powerless to do what is loving toward an erring brother or sister.

And what happens when such means are exhausted, and "he refuses to listen to them" (Matt 18:17)? Let us not deceive ourselves: to love means to speak the truth out loud. When Christians speak out about sin, it is embarrassing, shameful, dangerous. Take the case of a quiet person of little status in the church. What will happen when he or she speaks out against the obvious financial corruption of its leaders? Group psychological being what it is, he or she may discover that the congregation will turn its wrath on *him* for saying something unpleasant. He will discover that the real crime is not theft, but being "disrespectful to God's anointed," or "saying awkward things."

Of course, those who speak out better be certain that they have their facts right and their goal is to help, in love, and not to gain status or to harm others. We can only hope that Chloe's people had a holy attitude when they spoke to Paul about their church's secrets. If they did not, we can be confident that Paul had strong words for them as well.

For their part, Christian leaders are very often guilty of passing along information when they should not, or on the other hand keeping it to themselves when they should speak up. And woe to the pastor who gossips about one member of his flock to another member or to other pastors, especially when he refuses to take the difficult steps that Christian ministry requires of us.

I follow __ is typical of the language of social groups or political parties.[83] According to one interpretation, based on 4:6, the Corinthians were not really following Paul and the others. As the theory goes, the apostle is speaking of unnamed leaders in Corinth, hence his meaning would be: *One of you says, I follow Paul, another, I'm for Apollos – but we all know it's not Paul and Apollos, don't we; but let's not mention names.* Hence the 4th-century John Chrysostom: "But he signifies that if these were not to be leaned on, much less others."[84]

It is much more likely that the Corinthians had indeed broken into parties based on these three leaders. Besides Paul and Apollos, the apostle refers to Cephas (see Introduction). This is the Aramaic word for a "rock" and corresponds to the Greek *Petros*, the nickname of the apostle Simon Peter. Cephas is almost certainly Peter here and in Gal 1:18; 2:11, 14; Paul seems to identify Cephas as Peter in Gal 2:9, the only time Paul uses the Greek name. That Cephas is Peter was the view of *1 Clement*, written a mere 40 years later, when he speaks of this passage mentions that the Corinthians had been "partisans of highly reputed apostles [i. e., Cephas, Paul] and of a man approved by them [i. e., Apollos]" (*1 Clem* 47.4). In addition, Cephas is named as one of the principal eyewitnesses of the resurrection in 1 Cor 15:5, a role that is fitting for Peter rather than some other Cephas.

Paul had not given permission to any group to use his name as their team slogan. He apparently assumes that all the names are being used without their owners' consent.[85] If Cephas/Peter were guilty of faction, then Paul would not have hesitate to rebuke him as he had him some ten years earlier in Antioch (Gal 2:11). Paul also takes special care to show that Apollos is, not a part of his missionary team, but a friend of it (1 Cor 3:6; 16:12); Apollos too has not created his own club.

The slogan **I belong to Christ** is a puzzle. Although some have argued that the clause was not part of the original text, but the textual evidence in its favor is unanimous.[86]

---

[83] Cf. L. L. Welborn, *Politics and rhetoric in the Corinthian epistles*, Mercer, Macon, GA, 1997), who shows that "I am of..." is political language typical of the Greco-Roman environment. Welborn cites a parallel in Quintilian, *Training of an orator* 2.11.1-2: "Alius percontanti Theodoreus an Apollodoreus esset?" [Another person, asked if he was 'of Theodore' or 'of Apolodorus'] responded "egone?...parmularius" [Me? I am of the gladiators! [lit. Thracians, who were known for being gladiators].

[84] Chrysostom, *i ad Corinthios* 3.4.

[85] As Fee, *First Corinthians*.

[86] See Thiselton, *First Corinthians*, 129-33. Some argue (1) that the text originally read "I of Crispus." Others say that the exclamation "But I am of Christ" was (2) written by Paul as a statement of his own feeling, or (3) added in by an early scribe who was copying the text; with respect to this hypothesis, Schrage, *An die Korinther*, 1:147, points out that *1 Clem* 47:1-3 mentions Paul, Cephas and Apollos, but not a Christ group, indicating that perhaps Clement did not have "I am of Christ" in his copy of the epistle. The interpretation (2) is awkward, and (1) and (3) are conjectural, there existing no manuscripts to support "Crispus" or the absence of the phrase. It is better to interpret the text as we have it in every single extant manuscript – "still another, I follow Christ."

Others argue that no group named itself after Christ, but that Paul invented it as irony.[87] The simplest explanation is that there indeed existed a group in Corinth who claimed to be followers of Christ. But if so, what was its nature? Paul tells us nothing about any of the groups, and it is hardest to nail down what this fourth group believed. Some, like F. C. Baur (see below), argue that the group is Judaizing; after all they use the Jewish term *Christos* (or Messiah). This is hardly telling, since every Greek-speaking Christian used *Christos* every day. A more fruitful approach is to show not what the group believed but at their attitude. *My* faction – not Paul's! not Cephas'! – follows Christ and has the right to his name. Others have suggested with somewhat more plausibility that this faction rejected all human leadership, following no human apostle.[88] In that case, Paul's description of the apostolic ministry later in this section was meant to show that, in fact, it is important to listen to Christ's human messengers. At any rate, these "Christ-followers" share guilt with the other factions, because they were making Christ the head of their faction alone.[89]

Scholars have been divided for centuries over whether there was fundamental doctrinal schism in Corinth; much erudition has gone into reconstructing those differences from the text.[90] Most famously, F. C. Baur's *Tendenzkritik* (popularly called the "Tübingen Theory") suggests that the Cephas party represented a form of Judaizing Christianity, while the Pauline party held to a Spirit gospel that included freedom from the Mosaic Law.[91] Baur thought that he could make two groups out of the four names: Cephas/Christ vs. Paul/Apollos. But if this were the case, then why would Paul will go to some length in 3:5-23 to prove that he and Apollos are undivided? And why does Paul write a long letter without offering the slightest criticism of Judaizing Christianity or of Cephas?

One searches in vain for doctrinal differences between one group and another. The only purely "theological" issue in the letter is the denial of the resurrection of the body (15:12), a deviation for which neither Cephas nor Apollos nor Paul nor Christ could be credited. Nor does Paul ever state that any one party is doctrinally correct and another party mistaken. The list of questions that Paul will answer beginning in 1 Cor 7 seems to have come from the whole church, and in his responses Paul does not explicitly affirm or counter any group. He never summons the church to join his own namesake faction, but rather to imitate him as he imitates Christ (11:1) and to enjoy God's blessings through Christ and through all apostles (3:21-23). The most plausible candidate for a special doctrine of a "Paul group" would be their freedom to eat meat sacrifice to idols.

---

[87] See especially Schrage, *An die Korinther*, 1:148; also Theodoret of Cyrus (Bray, 10); the discussion by Fitzmyer, *First Corinthians*, 145.
[88] See Wikenhauser, *Introduction*, 388.
[89] Allo, *Corinthiens*, 9-10. Chrysostom, *i ad Corinthios* 3.5, states that Paul adds "I am of Christ" to condemn all three groups, since all were saying something like "I am of Cephas, and my group alone really follows Christ," etc.
[90] See the attempts at defining precisely the proclivities of each of the four groups: Kuss, *Die Briefe an die Römer, Korinther und Galater*; Archibald Robertson and Alfred Plummer, *First epistle of St. Paul to the Corinthians* (ICC; 2nd ed.; Edinburgh: T. & T. Clark, 1914), 11-12; T. W. Manson, "The Corinthian correspondence (I)," en *Studies in the gospels and epistles*, ed. M. Black (Manchester: Manchester University Press, 1962), 190-209; C. K. Barrett, *Christianity at Corinth: essays on Paul* (Philadelphia: Westminster, 1982), 1-27.
[91] See especially the skepticism toward defining the four groups by F. W. Grosheide, *The first epistle to the Corinthians* (NICNT; Grand Rapids, MI: Eerdmans, 1953), 35-37. Also Wikenhauser, *Introduction*, 387-89.

But however much Paul agrees with the theoretical basis for a strong conscience, he spends the bulk of his time in 1 Cor 8-10 (esp. 8:9-12) rebuking the careless words and actions of those who might have imagined that they were siding with him.

In the end, it is not some doctrinal peculiarity that perturbs Paul,[92] but the fact that Christians who partake of the one Spirit (12:13) could foment any factions: "…Paul's rhetorical strategy is to combat the *phenomenon* of factionalism itself, not each individual faction directly."[93] At least in 1 Cor 1-4, factionalism as such is the cardinal Corinthian error; its root is their superficial and unreflective understanding of the cross.

One of the explanations for the Apollos faction has to do with a description of him found in Acts 18:24-28. He was from Alexandria in Egypt; he was "an eloquent man, well-versed in the scriptures"; he spoke in the synagogue "with burning enthusiasm;" he was a skilled public debater. Some have wondered whether his Alexandrian background points to a Hellenistic Jewish theology which Paul found objectionable. Witherington argues that Apollos's skills as a rhetorician accidentally caused the competition between him and the other apostles.[94] But in truth, neither the Acts account nor Paul voices any objection to Apollos, his theology or his methods. To the contrary, he holds up Apollos as an example of a Christian worker, worthy in his commitment to the gospel and his humble service to the Lord (3:5-9) and is entirely willing that Apollos revisit Corinth (16:12). In the end Paul gives no hint as to why one might imagine Apollos or Cephas or Paul to be the more appealing.

Application: Divisions, Part I: Why they are offensive to God 1:12

The church is named after God (1 Cor 1:1) and Christ (Rom 16:16); yet it may take attitudes that bring shame to their namesake. One of these is the sin of dividing into groups based on church heroes. The underlying psychology of hero-worship is that people of lesser fame try to gain status by attaching themselves to the more famous. Think of the screaming mobs who would give anything to be associated with their favorite singing star. Young girls even sleep with the famous, not because they are hungry for sex, but for the high rank it gives them in the eyes of their friends.

Christians typically do not jump up and down and scream at their favorite preachers. Yet, they do tend to link themselves with the powerful of the church. Thus, for example, Roger often mentions the name of TV preacher and blogger "Dr. Martin" in his Bible study. While others share their opinions, Roderigo prefers to quote another, and almost exclusively, for the glory that accrues to him. The implicit idea is: *Dr. Martin is a brilliant Bible scholar, and because "I am of Martin," I reveal myself to be deep and discerning.* The same goes for those who limit themselves to those few whom they claim to be the only true Spirit-filled teachers or prophets. This group-identification takes its most extreme form in the cults, where only "our leaders" have the Spirit, and those outside are foolish and superficial, that is, if they are authentic preachers at all!

I had written the paragraph above, but now I have to qualify it: just now a friend tells

---

[92] As shows Grosheide, *First Corinthians*, 41; Thiselton, *First Corinthians*, 115-20; Fee, *First Corinthians*, 59.
[93] Mitchell, *Rhetoric of reconciliation*, 67-68, emphasis added.
[94] Witherington, *Conflict and community*, 130; see also Wikenhauser, *Introduction*, 387-88.

me of when an internationally famous preacher (it was Benny Hinn) came to our city and spoke in a football stadium. The people physically struggled, physically fought with each other, to get into the stadium. They stood in long lines, just to be able to touch this man. Preachers are the new rock stars.

The members of the little congregations in Corinth split and split again. And Corinth was hardly unique: without the intervention of the Spirit, your church too will be divisive, even if its fault lines are invisible. It happens so easily – at the end of your service on Sunday, take a minute and analyze the patterns of conversation and movement of the people. People will clump together with people who are like themselves: those of the same language, culture, race, but especially social and economic level. The university-educated will stick together, as will the manual laborers and the truly poor. We look for someone like ourselves to identify with. This is a tendency of everyone, rich or poor; however, it is the rich who have a special responsibility to reach out to others, since they more easily cross the same social barriers that the poor so keenly feel.

Perhaps it is just as well that we do not know along which lines the church of Corinth divided, or what made an Apollos more appealing to certain persons than a Cephas. Rather Paul deals with the spiritual problem: that those who tear apart the church tear apart Christ, for the church is his body.

This sin expresses itself in larger structures, too. The existence of denominations may be due in part to positive causes – some denominations emphasize the evangelistic mission, for example – but in part to carnal ones. Do you belong to a church that emphasizes God's grace? Wonderful! But, how can you feel boastful because you understand just how helpless you are without God's gracious intervention? Is your church a center of miracles and the power of God? What a lovely gift from heaven! This means that you have the Spirit's power to live in love, humility and helpfulness with people of other groups! Is your pastor famous for his preaching and for his university degrees? Excellent! But what glory does that bring you, for choosing to listen to God's Word? Or what glory does that bring to the pastor, for that matter, for communicating truth that he never could have invented on his own?

What do you think when you meet another Christian, a person who by definition has experienced God's forgiveness in Christ? Do you immediately analyze them by race, sex, age, education, nationality? Do you impose on them a grid of Pentecostal or no, Calvinist or Arminian, member of a megachurch or not, follower of Apostle So-and-So or not? Does their value for you depend on whether they know and use the same Christian slogans that you know? God help us if this is our attitude. For us the matter of first importance is whether this person knows Christ; and if he knows Christ, then he is family; and if he is family, he has the right to my love.

Application: Divisions, Part II: Was Darwin right? 1:12

Primate studies have to do with the many species of non-human primates, such as apes, chimpanzees and gorillas. It has been discovered that male primates compete to produce as many offspring as possible, following their instincts to preserve their seed. Among gorillas, for example, the alpha male is an adult who controls access to the females. A great deal of our scientific knowledge of primates is devoted to understanding the complex "dominance hierarchy" in which they live. Individuals move up or down the hierarchy through competition. Like humans, primates might practice deception and slyness. They will gang up to attack other animals or other groups of primates, usually standing erect on two feet or banging on their chest to show aggression and strength.

Of course, people never act like this. Yet there are human parallels to beating one's chest, baring one's teeth, stealing the mate of another, fighting for better food and higher status. Human beings make themselves practice faultless courtesy but at the same time angle for more power, money and sex. They plot each other's downfall. They measure themselves against each other and may have detailed knowledge of what model car or what sort of watch are signals of higher levels on the hierarchy. The next time you see two Christians in a power struggle, the next time you hear the equivalent of "I am of Apollos," you may find yourself thinking of gorillas baring their teeth and beating their chests to become the alpha male of the troop.

Was Darwin right? Are today's Christians simply evolved apes, replacing grunts and physical blows with gossip, power plays and competition?

Not at all. The problem with our competition is not ape-like tendencies. After all, apes are animals and they cannot be expected to act as beings made in God's image. We human beings are in his image, and with the new birth in Christ able to serve God in the power of the Spirit. We are not apes when we fight among ourselves to establish a hierarchy. Rather we are human beings who need to forsake our normal human patterns and grow more Christ-like.

1:13

Has Christ been divided? is, according to some manuscripts, "Christ isn't divided, is he?"; both readings result in a similar meaning. Here Paul refrains from giving a step-by-step logical proof for why this is wrong and turns immediately to a set of rhetorical questions, all of which are highly disturbing in what they suggest – that a factious spirit is tantamount to tearing Christ himself apart, as bad as hailing Paul as its crucified savior, as bad as baptizing people in a man's name. To dividing Christ is not in the sense of sharing in the one body in the bread of communion (1 Cor 11), but of tearing off a piece of Christ to make "our church." Chrysostom paraphrases: "You have cut in pieces Christ, and distributed his body."[95]

Was Paul crucified for you? Here Paul offers what is called *Reductio ad absurdum*, that is, taking the Corinthians' attitude to its absurd logical consequence. If his statement is shocking, it is because that is his intent, to try to snap the Corinthians back to reality: how can some of you name yourself for Paul, when that could imply that he was your savior?

Or were you baptized in the name of Paul? Another absurd idea: why claim Paul as your redeemer? In the New Testament, one is baptized in the name of the triune God or of Jesus.[96] To "baptize in the name of Paul" would be blasphemy.

---

[95] So Chrysostom, *i ad Corinthios* 3.5.
[96] There is a single biblical reference to being baptized in the name of the Father, Son and Holy Spirit (Matt 28:19). Typically, baptism is in the name of the Lord Jesus (Acts 8:16, 19:5; see 19:3; *Didache* 9.5 – "baptized into the name of the Lord"; also Hermas, *Visions* 3.7.3). Some argue today that Matt 28:19 was a later addition to the text of Matthew and that only baptism in the name of Jesus is valid. Among those are

1:14-16

Continuing his strong language of ridicule, Paul will go so far as to thank the Lord that he didn't baptize many in Corinth. From his freedom to name **Crispus** and **Gaius** Paul must be confident that these men did not abuse the privilege of being closely linked to him. He refers to **household of Stephanus**; as with Chloe, the group would not necessarily be limited to Stephanus's blood relatives, but might include his servants and freedmen (see as a parallel, Acts 16:31, "you will be saved, you and your household"). He names this group as the "first converts of Achaia" and states that "they have devoted themselves to the service of the saints" with work and toil (16:15-16). Stephanus was present with Paul as he wrote this letter (16:17). Paul names these people in an off-handed way: perhaps these too, perhaps there are others, **I don't remember**, but what does it matter so long as one is baptized into Christ? The people Paul mentions must have been a small fraction of the church; otherwise his argument would make no sense. Acts 18:8 states that "many of the Corinthians who heard him believed and were baptized." It is not clear how or why Paul could have spent as much as two years in a city and made dozens of converts but personally baptized so few. Paul assumes (1 Cor 12:13; Rom 6:3; Col 2:12) that baptism is the common experience of all Christians; someone else performed the rite at Corinth.

We know Crispus, Gaius and Stephanus from other texts. Crispus (a Latin name) was the leader of the Corinthian synagogue before Paul's break with it (Acts 18:8). Gaius (Latin) is likely the Gaius who hosted Paul and a Corinthian house-church according to Rom 16:23; there is a different Gaius, from Macedonia, mentioned in Acts 19:29. The fact that Paul commends Stephanus (a Greek name; 16:15-18) hints that he was not involved in the schism.

1:17

Paul's extreme rhetoric continues, for he goes onto declare that **Christ did not send me to baptize**.[97] The verb Paul uses, "send" (*apostellō*), is the verb that lies behind "apostle" (*apostolos*), that is, "a sent one, an envoy" (see 1:1 and elsewhere). But did not Christ commission all of his disciples to baptize their converts (Matt 28:19)? We do well to compare this hyperbole with his statement in 1 Cor 9:9-10a: "For it is written in the Law of Moses [in Deut 25:4]: 'Do not muzzle an ox while it is treading out the grain.' Is it about oxen that God is concerned? Surely he says this for us, doesn't he?" A reader who is excessively literally-minded might conclude that God has no concern for the humane treatment of oxen, despite the fact that Deut 25:4 is precisely about that theme. But there, as here, Paul uses the language of "either/or" in order to drive deeply home which is the lesser truth and which the greater:

Paul: God doesn't care anything for oxen!
(Well, of course he *does*, but that's not what's important at this moment)

---

people who are anti-trinitarian, those who charge the later church with corrupting the New Testament text in order to promote a new doctrine. Yet no manuscript omits Matt 28:19, and there are other verses (for example, 2 Cor 13:14) which are equally strong in their affirmation of three divine persons.

[97]In the 2nd century there was a heretical group called the Cainites. They refused to baptize, based on this verse in 1 Corinthians. According to Tertullian, *On baptism* 1 – "a viper of the Cainite heresy, lately conversant in this quarter, has carried away a great number with her most venomous doctrine, making it her first aim to destroy baptism."

Paul: Christ did not send me to baptize!

(Well, of course he *did*, but the important thing is preaching the gospel, not making sure that people are baptized by Paul)[98]

So then, Paul baptized a few of the initial converts, but left the baptizing mainly to others; now, in hindsight, Paul is glad he did not baptize many in Corinth. This leaves the main question, therefore: why does Paul seem to degrade baptism here? Why does he bring it up at all if it wasn't really an issue to begin with? Some have suggested that the Corinthians had become sacramentalists, and that they attached some sort of magical protection to the baptism of the living (10:1-3) or to baptism on behalf of the dead (15:29).[99] Although we cannot absolutely rule out that hypothesis, it is not the natural reading of 1 Cor 1. Paul does not state that the Corinthians imagined that there was powerful magic if an apostle baptized a person. What he is saying is that there is no ground for bragging about what great person you're connected with. Paul is speaking hypothetically: *Considering how you're dividing into factions just by mere hero-worship, it's a good thing that baptism was never a factor; imagine how awful it would be if things had gone that far!*

Paul emphasizes that Christ sent him to **preach the gospel**. This is not some casual reference to Paul's calling as an evangelist, nor is **the cross of Christ** a merely pious reference. Rather, the apostle is giving us a hint at what he will develop in the *confirmatio*: to the extent that one truly understands the gospel of the cross of Christ, and applies it in one's relationships with fellow Christians, then to that extent boasting, party spirit and divisiveness will be rendered impossible.

The second half of 1:17 marks the transition from the *ratio* to the *confirmatio*, where Paul will show the rationale for his call for unity. He spoke without **words of human wisdom**. In contrast to the false wisdom of the Corinthian parties, Paul had communicated with the Corinthians with direct, unpolished speech. They should have a vivid memory that the apostle delivers the gospel so as to make its message clear, not to give himself the reputation of cleverness or skillful oratory.

Now we must ask the question of whether Paul was a mediocre public speaker. Some Corinthians seemed to think he was a better letter-writer than he was a preacher; Paul quotes their complaint back to them in 2 Cor 10:10 – "His letters are weighty and forceful, but in person he is unimpressive and his speaking amounts to nothing" (the Spanish NVI has "as an orator, he's a disaster"). On the other hand, the Pauline sermons which are recorded in Acts are rhetorically striking. One of them is preserved today at the entrance to the Areopagus in Athens; the tourist passes by a bronze plaque with the full Greek text of Paul's speech there from Acts 17:22-31. One cannot help but be impressed with Paul's skills as he begins with a local phenomenon ("you Athenians are very religious; you even have the altar to the Unknown God"), moving to a rejection of any god who needs to be served in a temple, and then to a proclamation of the true God and Creator and the resurrection of Jesus. Some mistakenly claim that Paul made a serious error when he preached that message (see Introduction). Yet here as in all of his

---

[98] Of course, Paul did baptize – he has just named some, and Acts specifically says that he baptized people: Lydia and her family (Acts 16:15), the Philippian jailor and his family (Acts 16:33), and certain Corinthians (Acts 18:8). He probably baptized the Athenian converts, there being no one else to administer the rite (Acts 17:34).

[99] Fee, *First Corinthians*, 61.

speeches we have the same positive impression: they are faithful to the gospel yet appropriately contextualized; they are simple, direct, yet graceful. His epistles reveal him to be of man of some education. They have a style all their own, nicely balancing logical development with heartfelt passion. The New Testament contains examples both of a very simple writing style (1 John) and impressive rhetorical skill (Hebrews, 1 Peter). One gets the impression that the authors all had different levels of capability, but that everyone communicated to the very best of his ability as directed by the Spirit.

It is against this context that we must examine the claim that he evangelized Corinth without "words of human wisdom" or "eloquence or superior wisdom" (2:1). Paul means that while the gospel reveals God's power to save, an evangelist could drain the gospel of its power because of the style in which he announced it.[100] It is possible to mismanage the gospel's power by exalting the messenger. The medium becomes the message, the attraction. People come to love the gospel, not because it is God's love for them in Christ, but because so-and-so presents it so beautifully.

Throughout the ages, God's people have preferred one style of preaching over another. In the 1st century, as Paul states, pagan Corinthians wanted to hear clever messages, full of reason and persuasive arguments. In fact, plenty of the popular teachers of the day were full of hot air, using words to gain a living; others offered content of greater value. Nevertheless, tastes have changed. Today's Christian is more impressed if the preacher uses a microphone, strides back and forth across the platform, repeats certain phrases and formulas in a thumping rhythm. People "feel" the Spirit's presence; or are they merely having a reaction to what they are seeing and hearing, not to the work of God? Here too, great care must be taken to ask: *Is what I'm hearing the clear, biblical gospel message of the cross, or is someone trying to impress me by adopting a fashionable style?*

3. Confirmation (*Confirmatio*) 1:18-3:17

What proof does Paul bring forth to show that his point is correct, that in fact the true gospel of the cross will lead to harmony and a united voice? He has much to say, and that "confirmation" will take us through 3:17. In this section he appeals to the cross gospel itself (twice), to what the Corinthians are like (twice), and then to Paul's own style of ministry (twice). These paragraphs are not random thoughts about the Christian message; rather they are specifically designed to reinforce the appeal to unity in 1:10, unity that is threatened by the proud Corinthians who are seeking after philosophical wisdom.

The NIV renders the Greek *gar* with **for**, which might also be rendered "I'll explain" – Paul shows *why* the cross gospel is the basis for unity between Christians.

a. Proof from the gospel: it does not foster divisions based on pride in one's wisdom 1:18-25

---

[100] Thiselton, *First Corinthians*, 145-47, is particularly good here when he asks, what is the connection between the use of clever speech and the danger of robbing the cross of its power.

1:18

The careless reader might overlook the nature of the transition between 1:10 and 1:18. Paul started out by appealing to the Corinthians to be unified; disunity is what we might label the "problem" which the apostle will now resolve. But when he moves on to offer a "solution" to the problem, the apostle's argument takes an unexpected turn. We might have thought, Paul is going to talk about the importance of getting along, or maybe give a devotional on the commandment to love one's neighbor. Perhaps he will invite them to attend a seminar on how to settle their differences in a constructive fashion. Instead, Paul takes them to **the message of the cross**.[101] He knows that the Corinthians' problem was not mere divisiveness; rather, they fundamentally misunderstood and misapplied the basic gospel message, which is centered on a crucified savior.[102] If you really come to grips with the cross, he teaches, then you will realize that the gospel doesn't divide people by levels of cleverness or education or wealth, but unites all of us together in following a shamefully crucified savior.

The message of the cross is a good rendering: some have interpreted "message" (*logos*) in this verse as the "preaching" of the cross, that is, the actual delivery of an evangelistic message. But it is not Paul's oral presentation that is **foolishness**: it is rather the very content of the message (see the parallel "the foolishness of what was preached" in 1:21).[103] Its fatal public relations flaw is that it features the crucifixion of a man, a supremely shameful event.

Here is where some sociological insight will help the reader. We modern people (especially those of us who are formed by Western ideals) tend to think of shame as coming from within the person, from some inner failure. We tell our children, what does it matter what the others think of you, so long as you know yourself to be in the right? The opposite was the case in Paul's day, as in the East today, and to a great extent in Latin America. Shame was a public issue: if you were put to public shame, then you were disgraced. "A person born into the 1st-century Mediterranean world, whether Gentile or Jewish, was trained from childhood to seek honor and to avoid disgrace. Honor is essentially the affirmation of one's worth by one's peers and society, awarded on the basis of the individual's ability to embody the virtues and attributes that his or her society values."[104]

The cross has been so transformed for us that it is hard to think of it without thinking of our savior. To capture the original rational for crucifixion, we might try to imagine a man being lifted off his feet and stapled to the wall of a public building in order to die there. The cross was an extreme form for execution; it was the most shameful, dehumanizing method, and supposed to be the supreme deterrent against violent crime.

---

[101] Hay, *Pauline theology*, 2:95-97; also Furnish, *Corinthians*, 18.
[102] As says Conzelmann, *1 Corinthians*, 40-41.
[103] See Calvin, *First Corinthians*, 1:78 – "This statement, therefore, must be understood in this way: 'However the preaching of the cross, as having nothing of human wisdom to recommend it to esteem, is *reckoned foolishness* by *them that perish*; in *our* view, notwithstanding, the wisdom of God clearly shines forth in it'"; also Charles Hodge. "The cross not only establishes what we are to preach, but how we are to preach," as says D. A. Carson, *The cross and Christian ministry: an exposition of passages from 1 Corinthians* (Grand Rapids, MI: Baker, 1993), 9.
[104] P. 518, D. A. deSilva, "Honor and shame," *DNTB*: 518-22. This insight is helpful in the interpretation of Heb 12:2. The text does not say, as we with our culture might put it, "Jesus would not let himself feel shame, because he knew he was in the right." Rather it means that Jesus, though publically shamed, refused to give any value to that shame: "he endured the cross, scorning its shame."

It was used on slaves, rebels and the trash of society and it signified the public debasement and destruction of what was once considered a human being.

Here Paul divides the world in two: people who perceive the divine power that flows through the cross are on their way to salvation. Meanwhile those who reject the message are on the road to perdition.[105] Paul anticipates the coming of divine judgment that is promised in the Isaiah quote in 1:19: **destroy** and **frustrate** are both renderings of the same verb *apollumi*.

Herein lies an implicit rebuke to the parties of Corinth. Human philosophers cannot reconcile a crucified savior with what it imagines about the nature of the universe.[106] If some Corinthians wished to add more philosophical depth to the Christian message, they ran the risk of smothering the cross with layers of false human wisdom. They fell into the temptation of wanting to be like those outside the church, those who are offended or ashamed at the idea of a cross-religion. They would be imitating those who are on the road to God's judgment.

Application: The power of the cross 1:18

You go downtown to the park, where there are always people begging for money; selling something; preaching some idea or another. You circulate around to see what new doctrines are in the air. In this corner there is a new guy, talking to a small group: *The heart of my message is ___* he begins, uttering a filthy word. You do a double-take, and listen more closely. Again he says: *The power for living, being right with God, and eternal life is___,* and he mouths the same word. You shout out, *Hey friend, there are small children running around here and there are ladies present – can't you talk about something more pleasant than...<u>that word</u>?*

But that is exactly how it would have seemed in a 1st century Greek city, running into a man who calls himself Paul the apostle. His dirty word? *Stauros*, that is, "the cross." He was preaching a message of the cross, and "cross" itself was a word so obscene that polite people did not use it. The fundamental conundrum of his mission lay in how to preach a concept that was almost unmentionable.

Within us lies the desire to seek a nicer religion than this. We naturally prefer a faith that gives us useful guidance and lofty ethics and the promise of something better in the life to come. Instead Jesus offers us the gospel of "pick up your ___ and follow me."

Yet it is the cross that gives Christians their hope for forgiveness and eternal life. How interesting it is that as early as the 2nd century, the cross had become the most common symbol of Christianity. People began to "cross themselves," a custom that goes back to the very early days of the church. Why the change in attitude? Because Christians found that the cross delivered on what it promised: it is what led directly to a radical change of direction in their lives.

We might ask of Paul the difficult life questions:

Paul, are you really saying that the fact that a man was crucified by the Roman provincial government in c. AD 30 makes a difference, really?

You mention people who are excluded from the future kingdom (6:9-10), for example, drunkards. Do you really think that the father who has an insatiable craving for

---

[105] See Barrett, *First Corinthians*, 50.
[106] Here I am indebted to Tertullian, *Adversus Marcionem* 5.5.

drink, and who will hide bottles, and lose job after job, and will lie up and down that he hasn't touched the stuff – do you really perceive that the cross has anything to tell him?

And what about slanderers? Someone will point to this old woman who has engaged in malicious gossip every day for the last 60 years, whose entire life is arranged around that pleasure – does the fact that a man was tortured to death by being hung on crossed beams of wood supposed to have some effect on her?

And what of swindlers – what about the young man whose whole life up to this point has been one long con game – popping open security gates, purse-snatching, car-theft, drug-dealing? Are you saying that one regrettable death in Palestine has anything for him?

Someone will ask: Paul, are you saying that of all the events in this world's history, the one big event that actually changes people's assumptions and behavior and emotional reactions and motivations...that it could possibly be the execution of Jesus in a remote place and time? Are you saying that *this* is God's big intervention, his plan to reconcile people to him? Is this the key, Paul?

And what would he say? *Yes, and yes, and yes, a thousand times yes!*

Let that be our answer, too.

1:19

Paul brings forward as proof an oft-cited chapter of Isaiah. Isa 29:18 is used in the Synoptics gospels (Matt 11:5; Luke 7:22). In Rom 11:8 Paul looks back to Isa 29:10, and observes that the "a spirit of stupor" has overtaken Israel in this age (see also Isa 29:16 in Rom 9:20). But here Paul cites Isa 29:14b:

> The wisdom of the wise will perish,
> the intelligence of the intelligent will vanish.

The context of Isaiah is that people who are far from God will base their religion in "rules taught by men" (Isa 29:13). Those supposedly wise and discerning masters will learn just how blind they have been once God enters in human history to judge their sins. These "wise" yet blind imaginings are not due only to their limited human perspective; rather they arise from a moral lack. They are the doctrines which result when people use their God-given brains to find some way to avoid his righteous gaze.

Now is the time, Paul says, this is the moment when God has stepped in to human history with the ultimate in revelation. And just as Isaiah predicted, people who imagine themselves as wise are blinded by the light.

1:20

Paul has not finished with Isaiah; here he paraphrases Isa. 33:18 LXX and, like the prophet, uses rhetorical questions to throw down the gauntlet to those who imagine themselves clever: *Come forward and refute what God has said he would do!* He lists three groups:

Wise man (*sophos*), or more literally, "wise person" – the term reflects the human wisdom (*sophia*) that is disparaged throughout this section

Scholar – (*grammateus*), literally "the scribe," a person who is by implication well-read. The Jewish scribes copied the sacred scrolls by hand and made themselves expert in the text of God's word. Some believe that Paul refers specifically to shallow preachers of Greek wisdom, the *sophists* (wise) and Jewish *scribes* (scholar)[107] but the two terms are in fact applicable to either group. Besides, Paul's choice of wording is probably dictated by Isaiah LXX.

Philosopher of this age (*suzētētēs*) – This phrase is not taken from Isa 33. *suzētētēs* is related to other words that have to do with philosophical debate. Fee says that the word is "quite rare," but that is not precisely correct.[108] In fact, in all of the extant Greek literature through the 5th century AD, the form appears only here and in several patristic quotations of this same verse from 1 Corinthians.[109] Because of that, we are justified in saying that Paul either invented the word, or else used a word so rare that it was intentionally ridiculous – as if he had given a challenge to wise men, scholars, and "debatationists" or perhaps "philosophicalists." Who else but a silly person would try to out-guess Jehovah?

God has turned all their genius into absurdity: Paul uses a strong negation (*oichi*) to phrase the last question: **Has not God made foolish the wisdom of the world?** Or perhaps, "It's absolutely true, isn't it, that God has made foolish the wisdom of the world?" The cross is God's way of showing that there are only two options: either God is true and everyone else is mistaken, or the reasonings of people, without the gospel and without the Spirit, are the truth; there is no in-between. As Paul would later show in Rom 12:2a, "Do not conform any longer to the pattern of this world, but be transformed by the renewing of your mind." This does not only mean that the believer should avoid immoral thoughts. It implies that the world offers a way of thought that stands against the cross of Christ. The responsibility of the believer is to daily analyze the world from the perspective of God, and then to act according to that perspective. Just as there are sins of the body, sins of the emotions, social sins, so it is possible to sin with the intellect.

Application: Are you worldly? 1:20

Paul speaks against worldliness in this letter, and also in the famous Rom 12:1-2. Traditionally we have identified worldliness as a set of behaviors that non-evangelicals do, but which we should avoid:
    Cigarettes
    Alcohol
    Listening to or dancing to secular music
    Young men wearing an earring
    Tattoos
    All kinds of details about women's dress

---

[107] J. Jeremias, "*grammateus*," *TDNT* 1:742.
[108] Fee, *First Corinthians*, 71. Fitzmyer, *First Corinthians*, 156, following Lautenschlager, says that it was a known philosophical term, but this is not correct: the philosophers used *cognates* of *suzētētēs* to refer to the philosophical quest, but from earlier than Paul there is no reference to the noun *suzētētēs* as such.
[109] See e. g. Ignatius, *Ephesians* 18.1.

> Movies, plays or other entertainments
> Missing a worship service

Of course, the gospel does have great implications for how we dress or behave ourselves. Some of our lists even have warrant in the Bible. Yet our definitions of worldliness miss the deeper implications of the gospel and so emphasize the relatively minor. For example, a Christian's reputation is lowered because he wears an earring, but not for acting unloving or impatient. Christ, who emphasized that some issues are weightier than others, starting with justice, mercy and faithfulness (Matt 23:23). Let us make sure that our lists include all things which are forbidden in the Bible, for example corruption; paying our employees less than we should; refusing to forgive; shutting our ears to other Christians and making ourselves the unique fount of truth.

D. A. Carson makes an excellent point, that "worldliness" is not merely sexual sin or the world's pleasures. One can be carnally *religious* too: "Far from being sold out to the world, the flesh and the devil, they pursue spiritual experience, if sometimes unwisely."[110] This would become particularly important in 1 Cor 12-14, where some Corinthians were bragging about their superior experience of the Spirit, especially in speaking in tongues.

1:21

Verse 21 is as difficult and repetitious in the Greek as it is in English. We may unpack the verse thus:

> *The world in all its supposed wisdom could not come to know God.*
> *Therefore God in his true wisdom decided that he would save people thus:*
> > *he would save whoever put his trust in him;*
> > *he would save them through what was in the eyes of nonbelievers a*
> *scandalously foolish message.*

The latter phrase, **the foolishness of what was preached** (*kērguma*) has been interpreted in two directions, and the decision over its meaning will affect how we apply the text. On the one hand Paul may have meant that "we preach in a crazy fashion." In that case, he is anticipating 2:1 (also 2:4-5), "I did not come with eloquence or superior wisdom as I proclaimed to you the testimony about God." On the other hand, Paul might have meant "we preach a message that looks crazy." This second explanation is preferable: the noun *kērguma* typically refers to the content of the message itself rather than to the style of delivering it. It is the very "foolishness" of the "message of the cross" (1:18), the preaching of "Christ crucified" (1:23), the gospel itself that is in the eyes of the world's wise men, a display of **foolishness**. Only a simpleton would imagine that God's power could be unleashed in a cross. Such foolishness is so extreme that it can be called moronic, a message that even at first glance is obviously absurd.

---

[110] Carson, *The cross and Christian ministry*, 74.

1:22

Now Paul will summarize why the gospel has no credibility or appeal, and he describes the audience as he has seen it in the eastern Mediterranean world. The Jews – whether in their homeland or as a minority in Diaspora – lived in a sea of Greek-speaking pagans. And both groups had an extreme inherent prejudice toward the gospel:

Jews demand miraculous signs. To be sure, God did confirm the gospel through healings and other miracles (Acts 3:16, 4:16, 21-22). Paul performed miracles in Corinth (see 2 Cor 12:12, probably implied in 1 Cor 4:20), but most Jews still remained unconvinced. The "ask for" of some translations (NLT, NASB) does not quite capture of the meaning of *aiteō*, which is better rendered "they demand." In his experience in Judea and elsewhere in the eastern empire, Paul saw the same phenomenon that the Lord Jesus did among the Jews in Mark 8:12 – "Why does this generation ask for a miraculous sign?" As C. K. Barrett notes, Israel historically had been guilty of pressing God for a demonstration of his power (as in Num 14:22, where Yahweh states that Israel "tested me ten times"). This sin of "putting the Lord to a test" is a deceptive one. *Look at my audacious faith!* someone claims, when actually what he has is its evil twin, the impudence of demanding that God perform a trick for him. That sin "implies a refusal to take God on trust; [God] must present his credentials in the form of visible and identifiable acts in which his claim upon men, and his ability to meet their need, are validated."[111] It was this very sin that Jesus rejected in his temptation to leap from the pinnacle of the temple (Matt 4:5-7).

The Jews, Paul sighs, want to be amused by magic, not amazed by the true gospel. If Paul's language seems to be an abrupt dismissal of the entire Jewish nation, it must be recalled that in the 1st century they did indeed want God to demonstrate by a powerful miracle – the destruction of Rome, usually – as proof that God favored Israel above all other nations. Paul for his part preached that God would accept Jew and gentile alike, if they believed in the gospel of the cross. Those Jews who kept holding out for more evidence were already in rebellion and falling behind those gentiles who had faith.

On the other hand, **the Greeks look for wisdom**. If the Jews objected to the message, so did the pagan majority. Not only did the gospel entail a thought-world remote from Greek culture, but it could not begin to promise a system to tell people how to live their life in the world. Where was the wise counsel of a Socrates, a Plato, an Epicurus, nuggets of wisdom that could be applied by anyone? Where was the practicable counsel of the Stoic Seneca? The Christian gospel gave no universally-valid ethic, lifestyle or wisdom; what it gave was an offer to submit to a crucified Lord.

---

[111] Barrett, *First Corinthians*, 54.

Application: The Jews seek signs, the gentiles wisdom. What do we seek today? 1:22

Why did the Jews seek signs, and the gentiles wisdom? Because they wanted to possess an integrated world view that would help them make sense of the universe and to feel safe within it. Whether in the Jewish or Greek or any of the thousand other versions, this craving for security is part of who we are as human beings. We are uncomfortable at leaving the universe in God's hands, and wish to become gods ourselves (Gen 3:5).

The Jews seek signs, the gentiles wisdom, and we seek...?

1. We take an opinion poll. We feel secure knowing that 28% of the people feel this way, 47% the other way, and the rest are unsure. We convince ourselves that we have found "reality."

2. We formulate an ideology. We find security by acquiring a full system that promises to answer all questions and provide "scientific" truth about the universe. It doesn't matter whether the system is by Freud, Marx, Weber, or some theologian. The outcome is that it makes us feel like someone has all the answers and that we are wise for affirming that set of truths.

3. We seek a conspiracy theory. Adolf Hitler wrote *Mein Kampf* to "prove" that all of the problems of post-war Germany were the result of the plotting by European Jews. He gave many weak-minded people the sense that there was a simple explanation for every problem, if one knew where to look for it.

4. We seek a fortune-teller. Whether it is an economic futurist or the traditional Gypsy, people want to know the future so that they can control the present.

5. We crave popularity in order to feel secure. We surround ourselves with people who agree with our every word.

No Christian should seek out these pale substitutes for God's truth, or let them detract from the centrality of Christ's cross, which tells us to give up this yearning for control and to submit to God.

Application: When demanding signs of God is a sin 1:22

Both Jesus and Paul charged the Jews with "demanding signs," that is, miracles that would prove the gospel message. Paul uses the Greek word *sēmeion*, one word among several that are used for "miracle," a term highly favored by the gospel of John. In the gospels there lies a tension between two poles: on the one hand, it is right to believe in Jesus and to have faith to ask for a miracle; plus faith may in turn be bolstered by seeing a miracle (John 2:23). On the other hand, seeing a miracle does not necessarily convert someone to faith and may actually provoke envy and vengeance (Mark 3:6; John *in loc.*). On more than one occasion (Matt 12:38 and Luke 11:29; Matt 16:1 and Mark 8:11) the Jewish leaders insisted: *Show us a sign that proves without a doubt that you are God's Son!* Jesus refused to grant their demand, for they were testing God: coercing God to do a miracle in their presence, not to glorify God but to satisfy themselves. There are plenty of examples of this in the Old Testament, where in the wilderness alone Israel tested Jehovah ten times (Num 14:22). That is, they demanded that God do what they wanted: "Men test God by behaviour which constitutes in effect a defiant challenge to him to prove the truth of his words and the goodness and justice of his ways…to goad God betrays extreme irreverence, and God himself forbids it."[112] In the same way Satan demanded that Jesus prove himself by turning stones into bread (Matt 4:3-4). Jesus refused to "test God" when the devil told him to throw himself off the temple (4:5-7); he replied, "It is also written: 'Do not put the Lord your God to the test,'" quoting Deut 6:16.

In the decades after the resurrection, apparently, the Jews were still seeking some heavenly proof that Jesus was their Messiah. Like their forefathers, their attitude was, *We refuse to believe until God jumps through some hoop which we have chosen.* This is not faith; in fact, it is a textbook symptom of unbelief. Ironically, Paul *did* do signs and miracles to prove his gospel message (see throughout Acts; also 1 Thess 1:5; Rom 15:19; see Heb 2:4), but for some this was not enough: they wanted to test God on their own terms.

How might we fall into this sin?

Demand of God a miracle. I maintain a running list of miracles for which I'm asking, in faith. True faith by definition is humble dependence. Yet how terrible to hear people dress up "testing God" as if it were true faith: *You have the right to a miracle; God told you that he would heal you and he cannot break his word; so you just march up to the throne and tell God what you want, when you want it, and don't take No for an answer! God will not diminish his glory by refusing you!* We think we have God trapped in a corner and that he cannot fail to give us what we require of him. True faith, on the other hand, says that God will not fail us because of who he is, and not because we have gained the upper hand with him.

Tell God, "Do this or I won't obey." We must be very cautious about the whole practice of putting out a fleece to test God's will, as Gideon did in Judges 6. Read the chapter with care and you will see that Gideon's experience was an example of God's patience and grace with his weakness, not a formula that we should imitate. After all, Gideon knew from the start by divine revelation what was God's will (Judges 6:14); yet he delayed to obey until God confirmed it again (by the angel waiting until Gideon brought food) and then a second time (the sign of a fleece) and a third time (another fleece) and a fourth time (7:13-15). Gideon did not ask for a single "sign of the fleece," but four signs, indicating that he did not fully trust God. For our part, how dare we read God's commands and then tell God that he simply must give us some extra sign before we will obey him? What of the Christian woman who is living with a man outside of marriage. She knows that this is a sin; yet she prays, *If you want me to move out of this apartment, then you must make my phone ring in the next 30 seconds;* or *I must see a white cat on the way to work today;* or *I will win the lottery this week.* And then, even if such things do come to pass, she might even shrug them off as coincidences and look for another sign. If they don't come to pass, she takes that as a *No*, or begins to wonder if God is listening at all.

Those who say, "If God is doing miracles among you Christians, then show me one right here and now!" Suppose someone approaches you and doubts that God is doing

---

[112] *New Bible Dictionary*, ed. D. R. W. Wood and I. H. Marshall (Downers Grove, IL: IVP, 1996), "Temptation," 1162.

miracles in your midst; or doubts that people are speaking in tongues or prophesying today: *If you have the gift of tongues, then go and speak to this Indian about Christ in his own language; then I'll believe you!* or *Heal this child instantaneously if you really have the Holy Spirit!* Do not misunderstand me: true miracles are shown by their evidence, not by our boasts about miracles. I believe that it is possible to disprove mere *claims* of miracles. Nevertheless, we might fall into the sin of demanding that miracles follow our own criteria instead of what God is pleased to do.

God is our creator and redeemer and has every right to command us. He is not obligated to show us his credentials on demand. When he is kind to us and shows us a special sign of his love or guidance, we should be grateful, not triumphant that we figured out how to beat his system.

1:23
Here is the heart of the matter: Paul is not authorized to give either Jews or gentiles what they want to hear. He is called to preach the gospel, and that gospel comes in only one flavor: **we preach Christ crucified**. To the Jew it was a **stumbling block**, something that causes revulsion and offense, not only intellectually but on a gut level.[113] "Stumbling block" is used in the Bible as something that gets in the way between a person and God; the fault always belongs to the human party. The cross, offered by God as the means of reconciliation, itself is the object of disgust for those who reject God. A study of Jewish messianic hopes in the 1st century reveals precisely what we might expect: nobody seems to have expected a suffering Messiah. If in hindsight the church pointed to Psalm 2 or Isa 53 as predictions of the cross, neither mainstream Judaism nor any of its sectarian groups exegeted those texts in that way. The very phrase **Christ crucified** was an oxymoron, a contradiction in terms; Judaism looked forward to a "Christ Majestic" or a "Christ Victorious." A parallel to Paul's point can be found in Jesus' trial before Pilate (John 19:21-22) – "'Do not write *The King of the Jews*, but that this man claimed to be king of the Jews.' Pilate answered, 'What I have written, I have written.'" The insult that Pilate delivered to Israel seems to have been deliberate, since he had earlier proclaimed "Here is your king" (John 19:14, see also v. 15). Every time a Christian evangelist opened his mouth, a Jewish listener's blood would have boiled in patriotic and religious resentment.

To the gentiles (or, more broadly, the non-Jewish) a message of the cross was **foolishness** on many levels. The Romans worshipped strength and beauty, and both were antithetical to the cross. Roman citizens were not crucified; rather, they put people to death by crucifixion. The Greeks wanted to find the perfectly deduced system of thought to explain the universe, and would see the cross as part of the "problem of pain," not part of its solution. The deities of the Greek philosophers were by definition beyond suffering or any change by outside force. This meant that for centuries, Christians were taunted about their fixation on their crucified Lord. For example, Cornelius Fronto wrote anti-Christian propaganda in the 2nd century and said (I paraphrase): "Their ceremonies are all about a man put to death for his crime on the fatal wood of the cross. Just to state this out loud is to assign to these abandoned miserable people the sanctuaries which are

---
[113] See the useful analysis by J. Guhrt, "*skandalon*," *NIDNTT* 2:707-10.

appropriate to them and the kind of worship they deserve."[114] Only a wretch could fall for such a wretched idea!

1:24

We come now to those who embrace the gospel, **those whom God has called, both Jews and Greeks**. We have heard of God's calling already in 1:2, "called to be holy." It is all the same if a believer has Jewish or gentile roots. In later times Christians would come to be called the "third race" a nation that is not Jewish or gentile but is culled from all nations. The author who wrote the letter *To Diognetus* put it most poetically:

> For Christians are not distinguished from the rest of humanity by country, language, or custom. For nowhere do they live in cities of their own, nor do they speak some unusual dialect, nor do they practice an eccentric life-style. This teaching of theirs has not been discovered by the thought and reflection of ingenious men, nor do they promote any human doctrine, as some do. But while they live in both Greek and barbarian cities, as each one's lot was cast, and follow the local customs in dress and food and other aspects of life, at the same time they demonstrate the remarkable and admittedly unusual character of their own citizenship. They live in their own countries, but only as aliens; they participate in everything as citizens, and endure everything as foreigners. Every foreign country is their fatherland, and every fatherland is foreign.[115]

The call of God has two distinct meanings in the New Testament. It may refer to a general invitation to respond to the gospel. Paul here, as he usually does, employs the more specific sense, the act of God in summoning individuals to faith, a special call that indeed results in belief. "The sun, after all, is light to those who see, but darkness to those who are blind."[116] All Christians and only Christians have been called in this sense (1:2; Rom 8:28-30, etc.). That the call is effective in 1:24-29 is seen from the fact that all "called people" now understand the wisdom of the gospel, an understanding that is absent in the minds of those who have not heard the gospel, or of those who have heard it (general call) and not believed. This gospel does not only appear to be correct – for to a fool, any idiocy might seem sensible – but it is powerful in changing lives.[117] The cross reveals the work of God in a way that Judaism nor Hellenism cannot.

Here Paul draws his listeners to the reality they well know. Before they came to faith in Christ, the gospel may have struck them too as "foolishness" or a "stumbling block." But now they are numbered among the "called" (1:2). For that reason, they can hear this supposed "foolishness" with different ears. And if God has truly called them, then they must abandon this notion of finding other "wisdom" by means of Greek philosophy. And if God has called them, he has called them to one name, and they are baptized in one

---

[114] See Martin Hengel, *Cruxifixion in the ancient world and the folly of the message of the cross* (London: SCM, 1977); also John Stott, *The cross of Christ* (Downers Grove, IL: IVP, 1986). The so-called "Palatine graffito" shows one attitude toward Christ in second-century Rome. The text reads "Alexamenos worships his god," and it portrays a man on a cross with a donkey's head.

[115] *Diognetus* 5.

[116] Theodoret of Cyrus, *Commentary on the letters of St. Paul*, ed. Robert Charles Hill (2 vols.; Brookline, MA: Holy Cross Orthodox Press, 2001), 1:164.

[117] Theodore of Mopsuestia (Bray, 16), "The power and wisdom of God is not the divinity of Christ as such but the preaching of the cross."

name, that of the crucified one.

1:25
Paul now turns to irony: the **foolishness of God** is an oxymoron, a contradiction in terms. God the all-wise cannot admit of any foolishness; *but if he did, that would still be wiser than the wisest of human wisdom*. Yet another oxymoron appears in the phrase the **weakness of God**. See how Paul overturns the values of those Corinthians who admired Greek wisdom: you "wise" people will never even come close to God at his most foolish or most weak – as if we could speak that way of God. But that which to humans seems to be the most weak and foolish fact (the cross) is the superlative wisdom, since the almighty and all-wise God has chosen to act in that way.[118]

b. Proof from the Corinthian reality: they were not high or wise to begin with and so obviously have nothing of which to boast 1:26-31

1:26
Paul picks up the personal reference that he began with the "called" in 1:2. Here he speaks in embarrassing specifics of his Corinthian friends and invites them: **Brothers, think of what you were when you were called.** His point is that if God really had regard for human categories of wisdom and strength, he certainly would have selected a better bunch of people for the church of Corinth.

Paul's argument rests on his belief that God has chosen individuals and has called them to faith – apart from this presupposition his argument falls apart (see Rom 1:5-6; 8:30), for then a Corinthian could claim that his decision to believe the gospel was evidence of his superior discernment. But in fact, the makeup of the Corinthian church shows that the least discerning, the crudest, the poorest educated, the people from the most obscure families tended to end up as believers.

I was there, Paul reminds them, *and I know all about you!* Here, as in 6:9-11, he reminds them of their own sordid past, not to shame them, but to show how great is the power of the gospel. He uses the rhetorical device "litotes" (negating a negative for effect): that is, he says **not many of you were wise** instead of the positive *many were foolish*, perhaps to soften any thought of insult. The Greek does not supply a verb, and so it is not obvious if Paul means they "are not wise" presently or, as is more likely, "were not wise" in the past, that is, when they came to faith (NIV, ESV, NRSV). The church reflected all strata of society from slave to wealthy, but in Corinth generally and in the church specifically, the majority was relatively poor and uneducated and there were relatively few from the society's elite. The church membership roll was an illustration that the "wise," those with casual knowledge of philosophy or actual education in it, tended not to receive the gospel. Nor were most Christians powerful or well-born: meanwhile, the various philosophies of the day usually wanted to attract powerful people from good families.

The gospel of Christ is not elitist. In fact, Jesus himself delighted in receiving the marginalized of Palestinian society: sinners, lepers, Samaritans, the poor, day-workers,

---
[118] Cf. especially Fee, *First Corinthians*, 77.

tax collectors, fanatics, women, children, the crippled. The fact that the gospel appealed to the poor did not commend it in the eyes of the world, which valued family ties, training, wealth, and civic influence. In fact, one of the most important opponents of Christianity in the 2nd century, Celsus of Ephesus said:[119]

> ...the following are the rules laid down by them. *Let no one come to us who has been instructed, or who is wise or prudent (for such qualifications are deemed evil by us); but if there be any ignorant, or unintelligent, or uninstructed, or foolish persons, let them come with confidence.* By which words, acknowledging that such individuals are worthy of their God, they manifestly show that they desire and are able to gain over only the silly, and the mean [poor], and the stupid, with women and children.

An invitation such as "Give me your tired, your poor, your huddled masses" might warm the heart of an American, but in antiquity, such a gospel was a joke. Yet, even taken on its own merit Celsum's charge was unjust – his contemporaries included many able Christian thinkers, including Justin Martyr and the other apologists. In his majestic work to refute Celsum, Origen replied that "the object of Christianity is that we should become wise," citing the examples of Solomon, Daniel and others.[120] But, he adds, Christian wisdom is based on God's revelation, not on the false wisdom of the world.[121]

1:27-28

God exalts one person, and puts another to shame, and he called these Corinthians to faith in Christ, in part, to **shame the wise** and **the strong**. As we saw in 1:18, honor and shame were of supreme importance in the 1st century. This may have been especially true in Corinth, with its upwardly-mobile businessmen and go-ahead spirit. There was nothing of greater importance than positive, open recognition; there was nothing worse than the public humiliation of poverty, scandal or family troubles. For a Roman, public embarrassment was a common reason for suicide.

The theme of "shame" is a common one in Jesus' parables: the prodigal brought shame to his father, making the father's immediate forgiveness that much more conspicuous (Luke 15:11-32). Those who threw the son out of the vineyard openly shamed the owner (Matt 21:33-44), and those who rejected the invitation to the king's feast publically shamed him (Matt 22:1-14). Jesus' gospel was a message to the dishonored known sinners (Luke 15:1-2), often to the disgust of those with wealth, family power, or the public recognition of their "righteousness."

That the membership of the Corinthian church tends to be **lowly, despised** and **things that are not** is no mere question of demographics or sociology: it was by his own sovereign choice that God summoned such riffraff to be his church. If the divine plan in the messianic age is to exalt the lowly (see especially the Magnificat of Mary, Luke 1:46-55), then it should be no surprise that God's chosen ones should function both as a sign of his mercy and also a rebuke to the well-favored, that is, **things that** [supposedly] **are**

---

[119] Quoted by Origen in his *Contra Celsum* 3.44.
[120] Origen, *Contra Celsum*, 3.45.
[121] For information about divine revelation in Greek philosophy, see Inwood, *The Stoics*, 160-62, 173, 184 – the Stoics, who rejected superstitions, nevertheless believed that God could reveal the future through divination, oracles and astrology.

in this world of false values.

For the Corinthians, it could not have been pleasant to hear, *One of the reasons you are a Christian, and you, and you, is because when unbelievers see you they will think how silly the whole Christian business is; and when God finally comes to judge the hearts of all, you losers will put the winners to shame.*

1:29

God is not capricious, elevating one person and lowering another, simply to amuse himself. He has a purpose: **so that no one may boast before [God]**. Paul might be speaking generally here, that no-one has any just cause to boast, even though in reality they still go on doing so. Nevertheless, it is likely that his meaning is eschatological, as it seems to be in the parallel passage, Rom 3:19 – "so that every mouth may be silenced and the whole world held accountable to God"; "every mouth," that is, Jews and gentiles both. The word **boast** peharps anticipates the Jeremiah quotation coming up in 1:31; still it is typical Pauline vocabulary. The world boasts in its riches and wisdom – no matter, Paul will boast in his weakness (2 Cor 11:16ff.)! If God humiliates the well-placed, his goal is to reduce all to the level of need and dependence upon him. If no-one can boast, Paul implies, then no Christian has the grounds for boasting either – most of them were chosen specifically for their ignorance, ineffectiveness and absurdity in the world's eyes.

1:30

It is **because of him** (literally, "from him," that is, from God) and his elective choice that the Corinthians are today **in Christ Jesus**. When he says that Christ **has become for us wisdom from God**, Paul does not speak like a post-modernist, allowing that one person might have his truth and another person hers. It is because Christ figures in God's plan that he has **become wisdom**, and **for us** (literally, "our") simply means that "we" have recognized it. That God's wisdom is not merely intellectual, but also relational, as shown by these words:

> **justification** (or righteousness) – a just God declares people right before him
> **sanctification** (or holiness) – holistic transformation into different people, changed by God's power, and not by philosophical reflection
> **redemption** – the experience of being delivered from bondage to sin, the world, the devil

There is a clear parallel here with 6:11, which also declares the transforming power of the gospel in triad form: "you were washed, you were sanctified, you were justified."

1:31

Paul returns to his thought found in 1:29 and finally quotes directly the Jeremiah text that has been influencing his thinking and language in this section – **"Let him who boasts boast in the Lord"** (see the same quotation in 2 Cor 10:17). It is not precisely taken from the Hebrew nor from the Septuagint; rather, Paul telescopes into a compact phrase the thoughts of Jer 9:23-24a, where the Lord rebukes the wise, the strong, the rich:

> This is what the LORD says:

> "Let not the wise man boast of his wisdom,
>> or the strong man boast of his strength,
>> or the rich man boast of his riches,
> but let him who boasts boast about this,
>> that he understands and knows me,
>> that I am the LORD..."[122]

Again, this is not a call to boast that we have a special connection with God that exalts us above other believers. Boasting in the Lord means precisely what it says: that we stop trying to exalt ourselves and instead go around talking about how wonderful is the Lord. By word and deed we must show in clear terms how much we needed God's mercy toward us. It also means that we will not boast about mere human leaders (1 Cor 3:21).

Application: How do we boast? 1:31

Boasting about ourselves, even about our spirituality, is a sin. Our boasting or glorying should be about the Lord. When we imply to others that we are superior in our wisdom or knowledge or experience we are at the same time bragging in the very presence of God and detracting from his glory. This attitude is the very opposite of becoming like a little child (Matt 18:3-4). It is the opposite of being justified by faith, which comes to a person who "shuts his mouth" by the knowledge of his sin and need (Rom 3:19).

We deceive ourselves if we imagine that being religious is the opposite of human boasting. In the plotlines of the four gospels, much of the human boasting the reader encounters is religious in nature. Luke 18:9-14 shows that a relatively righteous man may accurately describe his actions before the Lord yet still be guilty of boasting. Could he not have justified his speech by saying, *After all, I am boasting in the Lord, not myself; did I not plainly say, "God, I thank you that I am not like other men"?*

In our perverseness we try to dress up boasting about ourselves as if it were the praise of God. This leads to offering the Lord a polluted sacrifice, even while we are unconscious of the enormity of our crime. Two people can say the exact same words and yet one is glorifying God and the other glorifying self:

> God raised up this ministry! I started out as a pastor of a flock of 20 in a storage room, and we began to reach the people. Obviously we are in the center of God's will to be blessed this way.
> I didn't go to university nor do I have advanced university degrees. Yet now thanks to God's grace I sit on the platform with Ph D's and talk with them as an equal.
> I just stick to the Word of God, even though the others do not.

Beware, all those who use God's name to give themselves honor and glory!

---

[122] See the citation of this passage in *1 Clem* 13, although Clement is probably alluding to 1 Corinthians.

c. Proof from the apostolic example: they should remember how Paul first brought them the gospel in humility 2:1-5

Here the apostle will give the first of several examples of his own character and actions. The student of Paul will affirm that he often appealed to his own experience.

2:1

In the ancient world a teacher was expected to personify the principles for which he stood, and Paul frequently uses himself as a model for his disciples. In Corinth particularly, the Christians should imitate Paul's example, even as he follows Christ (4:16; 11:1). Here he looks back 5-6 years to when **I proclaimed to you the testimony** [better "the mystery"] **about God**, a reference to his first appearance in Corinth.[123] It repeats the sense of 1:17, which describes the calling of Paul "preach the gospel—not with words of human wisdom." His point is, that if you were converted without the benefit of **eloquence or superior wisdom**, then these must not be necessary to unleash the gospel's power; if that is true, therefore, your pursuit of such worldly "wisdom" has nothing to do with Christ.

Why did Paul take such pains *not* to impress the Corinthians with powerful rhetoric? It was because his goal was that their faith rest in God's power, not in Paul's power to convince. After all, someone might come along afterward (and in fact, they did, in Corinth, Galatia, Colossae, Ephesus) who would seem at the moment to be more convincing then Paul – then where would their faith be?

2:2

One reading of the verb "resolved" in **I resolved to know nothing** (see Introduction) is that Paul had tried to preach a clever message in Athens and that he ended in failure. Thus chastened, he made a decision just before he entered Corinth that he would go back to the simple gospel of the cross. In fact, a better rendering would be "I did not resolve to know anything."[124] That is, Paul is not describing a decision he made, but rather a decision he would never take: he did not opt to adorn the gospel to make it prettier for his audience. Rather he did as he always did: he focused on Christ. This too was the experience of the Galatian believers, "Before your very eyes Jesus Christ was clearly portrayed as crucified" (Gal 3:1).

At the core, his message was **Jesus Christ and him crucified**. Paul does not mean to exclude, of course, other aspects of the Christian message, and from 1 Corinthians it is obvious that he taught them a well-rounded message about Christ (his last supper, death, burial, resurrection, second coming) and the Holy Spirit and his gifts.[125] Yet his words were never far from the cross, and any portion of the apostolic message was understandable only by reference to crucifixion.

---

[123] Some of the older manuscripts do not have *marturion* ("testimony," as in the NIV, ESV, NASB), but rather *mustērion* ("mystery," thus NA[28], NRSV, NLT). The reading *marturion* ("testimony") is probably a scribal error.

[124] Thiselton, *First Corinthians*, 211; Nicoll, *First Corinthians*, 2:775.

[125] Contra Augustine, *On the Trinity* 1.12 – "For the apostle also says, 'I determined not to know anything among you, save Jesus Christ, and Him crucified;' because he was speaking to those who were not able to receive higher things concerning the Godhead [deity] of Christ."

Commentary 1:10-4:16

Application: The gospel of the cross 2:2

What does it mean today to preach the gospel of the cross, the revealed mystery of God? The obvious response is: *Well, we describe the death of Jesus – and of course his resurrection – and invite people to come to him.* While true, that answer has deeper implications.

Paul here returns to the nature of the gospel: the entire message of the cross was designed to go against the received wisdom of humanity. Paul is in accord with the prophetic wisdom of Daniel: "there is a God in heaven who reveals mysteries" (Dan 2:28, read in its context). The cross-message was a divine "mystery" (2:1) that God revealed, to the great surprise of all. On an epistemological level, then, Paul is pulling them away from a rationalistic method (*what does my reason say to be true?*) to a prophetic one: *what has God revealed to be true by the cross and by the Spirit at the end of history?* In practical terms this means than when people are guided by the Holy Spirit, they will be taken back to the cross of Christ. And in turn this wisdom of God will bring unify Christians together as no human insight will.

The gospel we preach must be rooted in the manifestation of God in human history, especially in the events of Jesus' incarnation, suffering and death, burial, resurrection, ascension, and the gift of the Spirit on Pentecost. Before Christ, things were one way; when Christ came, things changed; when Christ returns a second time, things will change yet again. This is sometimes called redemptive history or a redemptive-historical approach to theology.

We cannot limit false gospels to those which eliminate the cross of Christ entirely. After all, every Mormons believe in the death of Christ. No, a false gospel is any gospel that makes the cross less than what God says it is.

The alternative is all too common today. Someone will preach a series or write a book, saying: *We have discovered certain truths, principles, ideas, mechanisms or formulas. These things were true thousands of years ago and will always be.* One of the best examples of this phenomenon is the best-selling book *The Secret* by Rhonda Byrne, who promises that "In this book, you'll learn how to use *The Secret* in every aspect of your life – money, health, relationships, happiness, and in every interaction you have in the world. You'll begin to understand the hidden, untapped power that's within you, and this revelation can bring joy to every aspect of your life." Imagine! You don't need a crucified and resurrected Savior, you don't need the Spirit – you were born with all you need already "within you." And so all you need is to buy this book from the supermarket and you will be as wise as Solomon and as creative as Leonardo da Vinci!

We need to meditate on the victory of Jesus in his cross, resurrection and ascension and unambiguously state that truth to the church and to the world. These are concepts that are offensive to unbelievers, as Paul already knew. He reminded the Corinthians not to try to sound cleverer than they were, with all their talk of principles, ideas and philosophies. What matters is the death of Jesus for us sinners: it is true and it is God's Truth.

2:3

An audience will, often unconsciously, "read" a speaker for clues to his message: how he dresses, his style of speaking, his posture, whether he seems confident or unsure of himself. This is why politicians spend so much time with coaches, who tell them how to stand, speak, use gestures, what tie to wear and so forth. In the Greco-Roman world, rhetorical style was of huge importance and a major theme in the educational system: the boys were taught not only what to say but how to present themselves well, with strong arguments and with confidence. Failures were scorned. One example is a certain Maximus; when he refused to use logical "demonstrations" to prove his point, his listeners brushed him off.[126] A speaker who appeared nervous or humble was disdained, since it implied that he did not have confidence in his own message.

Paul failed on two counts. He paid little attention to style, and did not offer elaborate logical proofs to try to convince his audience of his truth. The fact that he spoke **in weakness and fear, and with much trembling** would have given people the impression that he had nothing valid to teach them.

Of what was Paul afraid to the point that he was trembling with fear? He uses similar language in Phil 2:12 and Eph 6:5, where he refers to our attitude toward God; but that is not the case here. Here in 1 Cor 2 it seems to be general nervousness: he was aware of the weakness of his presentation if judged by human standards.

Paul's humble attitude was not attractive to the Corinthians. They wanted a strong man who would come to town and tell them what to do. They laughed that Paul was meek when he was with them, but "'bold' when away" (2 Cor 10:1); "in person he is unimpressive and his speaking amounts to nothing" (2 Cor 10:10). For their part, the Corinthians "put up with anyone who enslaves you or exploits you or takes advantage of you or pushes himself forward or slaps you in the face" (2 Cor 11:20). Why? Because those men showed strength and confidence in their message. "The Corinthians want assertiveness and demagoguery...[Paul] gives them only words of weakness and humility."[127]

2:4-5

Just as David refused Saul's armor, Paul would not gird himself with **wise and persuasive words** to prove the truth of the gospel; from his culture's perspective, his case was weak. On the other hand, Paul argues, his truth was entirely convincing: Paul's message, not the others', was accompanied **with a demonstration of the Spirit's power**. Some take this demonstration as their conversion: the fact that they were convinced by such a poor presentation shows that the message was backed up by the Spirit, who was working in their hearts.[128] While that is certainly true, it is best to understand this verse as a parallel to 2 Cor 12:12, that in Corinth Paul showed "the things that mark an apostle – signs, wonders and miracles."[129] By contrast the teachers

---

[126] Thiselton, *First Corinthians*, 220, quoting Eunapius, *Lives of the Sophists* 466-69, 475.
[127] Timothy Savage, *Power through weakness: Paul's understanding of the Christian ministry in 2 Corinthians* (SNTSMS 86; Cambridge: Cambridge University Press, 1995), 73.
[128] So Thiselton; Grosheide; Kistemaker. Fee, *First Corinthians*, 95, takes it as *both* conversion *and* their experience of the Spirit and tongues.
[129] Theodoret of Cyrus, *Commentary*, 1:165 – "Miracle working testified to the proclamation of the Spirit." Cf. Hays, *First Corinthians*, 36; Stanley M. Horton, *I & II Corinthians* (Springfield, MO: Gospel Publishing House, 1999), 33. The early fathers used this same sort of logic to show that God favored the church, not the Jews or the pagans: Justin Martyr, *Dialogue* 82, 88; Irenaeus, *Against heresies* 2.32.4 and 5.6.1, who was quoted approvingly by Eusebius, *The Church History* 5.7. See pp. 614-15 of Gary S. Shogren, "Christian prophecy and canon in the second century: A response to B. B. Warfield," *JETS* 40.4 (Dec 1997): 609-26.

described in 1 Cor 4:19-20 were superficially convincing, but they did not have the power of God's kingdom in their work. Paul, by the way, is assuming for the moment that only true preachers will be able to do miracles; for now he leaves aside the problem of "lying miracles, signs and wonders" (which I take to be actual Satanic miracles in the end times) from 2 Thess 2:9-10.

His point is that God doesn't perform miracles randomly; he gives them to authenticate the message of which he approves, and only that message. Since Paul's gospel came with miracles and other clear evidences of the Spirit's power, then it must be what God is affirming to be truth. The parallel passage in Gal 3:5 works the same way:

> Gal 3: It was my gospel that came with miracles, not the gospel of the legalist; therefore, my gospel is true and the legalistic one is not
> 1 Cor 2: It was my gospel that came with miracles, not the polished message of the rhetorician; therefore, my gospel is true, and not the message of philosophers

Application: Spirit power in the Christian life 2:4

The Holy Spirit enables the Christian to live for Christ in power, in holiness and in Christian virtues (Acts 1:8; 2:1-4; Rom 8:5-6, 1 Cor 12; 2 Cor 3:3, 18; Gal 5:22-23; many other passages). But how does this function?

There was once a popular set of TV commercials that featured the Energizer Bunny, which run on batteries. One was running on "our brand" of batteries, the other on brand X. Both toys chug along, until the brand X batteries run down, and "our brand" is vindicated as the powerful one.

Is that how the Holy Spirit is? Is he simply a better battery that makes us live holy lives or perform powerful things? When we feel drained does that mean that our Spirit-battery has worn down?

No, the power of the Spirit is not like that at all. First, the Holy Spirit is not simply a power or a force like electricity. This is one of the false doctrines of the Jehovah's Witnesses. The Bible for its part teaches the Spirit is a person and he is God. One of the best proofs of that is found in 1 Cor 12:11 – "he gives them to each one, just as he determines." That is, the Spirit is not a force, but one who makes decisions about who receives what spiritual gift.

Second, Christians do not simply "run down" when they lose touch with the Spirit. In fact, they may continue to go through many of the same motions as before: go to church, maybe pray and read the Bible – so that it may not be obvious to other Christians that something (Someone!) is missing. God knows, however, how weak and ineffective is our life and work.

So the Spirit is not in us just to make us do activities, but to do things effectively, in God's way, that is, in a way that brings God glory. For that we need to ask some important questions:

1. Why does the Holy Spirit give us power?
2. How do we get this power?
3. What is it like to be empowered by the Holy Spirit?

I. Why does the Holy Spirit give us power?

This issue seems simple, but in fact people complicate it. We may become so caught up in the Spirit's power that we forget that it is power *in order to do something*. We are like the person who brags about the voltage that pours into his home, yet has no intention of using it for any useful purpose.

In basic terms, God empowers us for one main reason: so that we may do his work in a powerful way.

In the Old Testament some of the earliest references to the Spirit's power have to do with Sampson and his extraordinary physical strength (Judges 13:25; 14:5-6, 19, 15:14-15). But God did not give him this strength just for his own amusement. No, his job, bizarre as it seemed, was to create random havoc among the Philistines.

But now we live in New Testament days, and God's power comes upon us for other goals than maiming the bad guys. Luke 24:49 is an excellent place to start, and in this context the power of the Spirit is power to proclaim the gospel – "repentance and forgiveness of sins will be preached in his name to all nations, beginning at Jerusalem" (Luke 24:48). The author of Luke-Acts continues the narrative from Luke 24, and we find the same evangelistic mission in Acts 1:6-10. Here the power is power to carry the gospel to other nations. The first manifestation of the Spirit happens in Acts 2:1-4. The Spirit fills them with power; but power to do what? To speak in tongues, to be sure, but for what purpose? So that all present would "hear them declaring the wonders of God in our own tongues!" (Acts 2:11). And why did the Spirit have them glorify God in foreign languages? In part to open the door to evangelize the Jews that had gathered around the disciples (Acts 2:14-42). And those listeners did not just hear the message expressed well; the Spirit was working inside them as they listened (Acts 2:37; this is a fine parallel to 1 Thess 1:4-6).

Remember that it is possible to convince people of something by mere human persuasion. For example, politicians convince us to vote for them and not their opponent; companies convince us that their laundry soap will give us cleaner clothes; shysters convince us to give them our credit card number. But remember, we're speaking here about doing God's thing in God's way. No-one can make another person truly repent and turn to God merely with persuasive words, even if they're quoting Bible verses; it is a miracle.

II. How do we get the Spirit's power?

In Eph 5:18 we are told to "be filled with the Spirit," a command that we tap into his life and power. We are speaking of the life of faith here, not of some special magic formula whereby we do Steps 1-17 and the Spirit will arrive.[130] Asking God for the gift of the Spirit or for his filling are simple acts of faith: "how much more will your Father in heaven give the Holy Spirit to those who ask him?" (Luke 11:13). The heart of faith is an acknowledgment of our own inability apart from him, and it is connected to a life of service and love for God.

---

[130] Luke 24:49 is sometimes taken to mean that we should hold special meetings. In fact, Jesus' command here was a very specific order that the disciples wait until the Spirit came, and the Spirit wasn't going to come before the feast of Pentecost, at least 10 days after Jesus uttered these words. See Stanley M. Horton, *What the Bible says about the Holy Spirit* (rev. ed., Springfield, MO: Gospel Publishing House, 1976).

III. What does it look like to be empowered by the Spirit?

We mentioned a problem at the beginning of this section: that of Christians might go through the motions of the spiritual life, but using their own power. So how do I distinguish between my own power and the power of the Spirit?

1. The life of the Spirit is God-centered, not me-centered. The Spirit does not empower us so that we may live for ourselves. Rather he leads us to live for God, even at a cost to our own ego.

2. The life of the Spirit is the life of Christ and vice versa. If we are not interested in living for Christ, then by definition we do not want to have the Spirit's power. People who are Spirit-filled love Christ, and people who are really serving Christ know the power of the Spirit. A friend once told me that in his church, the pastor boasted of seeing flames shoot from his hands; I was not present and do not know what really happened. I do know that there is no need to boast about it. If it is of the Spirit, then the Spirit of Christ is the hero, and if it is genuine it is still trivial compared with being in love with Christ.

3. The life of the Spirit frequently is a life of suffering. Oh, how this runs contrary to our common sense, but it is true, as 2 Cor 11:23-33 and many other passages prove. Paul could speak of miracles and visions, but when he wanted to demonstrate that God really was using him in power he listed his trials and tribulations. He even experienced a "thorn in the flesh," about which we know almost nothing except that it made him suffer. Yet this suffering was proof – not disproof – that God was mightily using him (2 Cor 12:7-10). He could boast in the weakness (2 Cor 11:30) that was his even while he carried God's power in himself.

In spite of all your weakness, tiredness and frustration, God's Spirit does things through you, and he is glorified despite your own human limits.

---

d. More proof from the gospel: God's true wisdom is revealed through the cross/the Spirit 2:6-16

Paul cannot simply point to his own experience to prove his point. He invites the Corinthians once again to consider how the message of the gospel was designed to go against the received wisdom of humanity. Some commentators regard 2:6-16 as a digression, where Paul supposedly wanders into a new theme, one that doesn't readily help his case.[131] In fact, Paul is merely developing a connected truth, that the gospel is a gospel of the Holy Spirit. Some Corinthians were trying to find truth through human reason; Paul pulls them away from that and directs them to the cross and to the Spirit.[132] In practical terms, when people experience the work of the Holy Spirit, he will draw them toward the cross of Christ, and also into unity one with the other.

---

[131] Without any manuscript evidence, some scholars view 1 Cor 2:6ff. as an interpolation; see the review by Thiselton, *First Corinthians*, 36-41.

[132] The systematic theologians tend to use the categories of general and special revelation, placing all special revelation into the category of biblical inspiration. See especially L. Berkhof, *Systematic theology* (Grand Rapids, MI: Eerdmans, 1941), 36-40; also Leon Morris, *I believe in revelation* (Grand Rapids, MI: Eerdmans, 1983), ch. 2. Because they do not want people to claim that the Spirit is giving new authoritative revelation, theologians might play down the role of the Spirit in guiding the Christian from day to day, the very theme that Paul is teaching in this chapter.

2:6

Paul now says that in fact the apostles **speak a message of wisdom**, leading some to imagine that he has contradicted what he has just said about its uselessness of the human mind to seek God's truth. But the point here is that there is a true wisdom, one which is completely different from the fake wisdom of the world. Once we see things God's way, the gospel message *is* wise, because it reveals the plan of creator God for us. The truth is available **among the mature**. "Mature" is a translation of *teleios*, which may have the meaning "perfect" in other contexts. Nevertheless Paul is not speaking of perfect human beings here, but those who have reached a higher level of understanding. They are contrasted with "the one without the Spirit" in 2:14, and in 3:1, the "immature," that is "mere infants in Christ" whom Paul is compelled to instruct in baby-talk. Paul is being deliberately ironic those who feel themselves mature because of their acquaintance with Greek reasoning, **the wisdom of this age**. They are in reality pseudo-*teleioi*, priding themselves on being wiser, deeper, better instructed, better developed intellectually than their fellow Christians. Their wisdom is passing away and will come **to nothing** at the final judgment.

The apostle uses a conceptual framework which is sometimes associated with the prophets and also with the apocalyptic Judaism of the intertestamental period. In his universe, God leaves the elite in the darkness created by their own sin and limitations. But he always intended to reveal his wisdom in a point of time in history, and Paul adds that this happens in the coming of his Son. This approach to divine revelation is distinctively biblical and runs contrary to the philosophical approach of the Greeks, which did not permit such an "in-breaking" of God.

The gospel also contradicts the thought-world of the Gnostics, a movement which the church battled from the mid-2nd century AD.

> The Gnostics claimed special esoteric or secret knowledge. It could be possessed only by that section of humanity which was "pneumatic," o spiritual...There was a second class of men, those who were only "psychic" and could not get beyond faith...A third class represented the overwhelming mass of human kind. They were merely "hylic" (i. e., subject to matter)..."[133]

But Paul was not dealing with Gnosticism as early as the 1st century. Indeed, the later Gnostics made 1 Cor 2:6 one of their key texts: they imagined that the apostles had left an oral tradition that only the "perfect" (or *teleioi*, that is, the Gnostics) could receive and understand.[134] They fancied that Paul is here hinting at some deeper teaching that he could not give to the Corinthians because they were inferior beings.[135] To be sure, they could be taught the message of the cross, but the "perfect" could go on to learn that the cross message is a second-tier doctrine, to be set aside by the illuminated. But Paul's point is just the opposite: there is one gospel, the one about the cross. An apostle of

---

[133] "Gnosticism," in *Baker's dictionary of theology*, ed. E. F. Harrison (Grand Rapids, MI: Baker, 1982), 237.
[134] See Irenaeus, *Against heresies* 1.8.1 – "Such, then, is their system, which neither the prophets announced, nor the Lord taught, nor the apostles delivered, but of which they boast that beyond all others they have a perfect knowledge."
[135] One commentator whose interpretation is similar to the Gnostic one is Jean Héring, *The first epistle of Saint Paul to the Corinthians*, tr. A. W. Heathcote and P. J. Allcock (London: Epworth, 1962), 15, who states that this "mysterious, divine wisdom" was some sort of theosophical instruction for the elite.

Christ teaches only one message, even if he has to teach it simply for some and more profoundly for others.[136]

2:7

Now, Paul says, **we speak of God's secret wisdom**; the secret or "mystery" is the wisdom previously hidden in God but now revealed in Christ (see the parallels in Rom 16:25-26, Col 1:26, Eph 3:5; we have stated that "mystery" is the better reading of 2:1, "I proclaimed to you the testimony of God"). And he has revealed it in the historical event of the crucifixion of Jesus, which took place some two decades previous to the first Corinth campaign. It is **destined for our glory before time began**. The mystery is not some set of practical ideas for daily living; it is the "announcement about God's apocalyptic intervention in the world, for the sake of the world."[137] Since Christ's death during the Passover, everything about the universe has changed.

2:8

None of the rulers of this age understood the plan of God (cp. John 1:10-11). They went so far as to take an active part in crucifying the **Lord of glory**, who was hidden in human form. They did this not to aid the plan of God, but because of their hatred and ignorance.

Throughout the centuries people have asked, who specifically are the **rulers** of 2:6 and 2:8?[138] One reading is that Paul is referring to the invisible demonic principalities and powers that ultimately sought to destroy Jesus, including the devil, who pushed Judas to betray him (John 3:2).[139]

Although that opinion is plausible, the other viewpoint fits better in this context: Paul is referring to the human rulers who arranged the crucifixion, that is, the Jewish priests, Herod Antipas and Pilate, representing the empire.[140] Paul's other use of this word in the plural definitely refers to human rulers (Rom 13:3; also Acts 3:17, 13:27). This would make the statement parallel to Acts 4:25-29, where the apostles pray and quote Psalm 2:1-2 – "Why do the nations rage and the peoples plot in vain? The kings of the earth take their stand and the rulers gather together against the Lord and against his Anointed One." They go on to pray that "Herod and Pontius Pilate met together with the gentiles and the people of Israel in this city to conspire against your holy servant Jesus, whom you anointed. They did what your power and will had decided beforehand should happen." There are other indications that Paul is thinking of human rulers. First, he is not now contrasting the gospel with "doctrines of demons," as he does in 1 Tim 4:1. Rather, the tension lies between the gospel and *human* wisdom, the sort that a Pilate or

---

[136] So note Marion Soards, *1 Corinthians* (NIBC 7; Peabody, MA: Hendrickson, 1999), 58; Robertson and Plummer, *First Corinthians*, 36.
[137] Hays, *First Corinthians*, 28, also 43. Also G. Finkenrath, "Mystery," *NIDNTT* 2:94-98.
[138] See the excellent review of the issue by Thiselton, *First Corinthians*, 233-39.
[139] For the "angelic/demonic" view see Origen, *De principiis* 3.3.2; Augustine; Thomas Aquinas; Walter; Allo; Héring; Schrage.
[140] So Theodoret of Cyrus, *Commentary*, 1:166; also Tertullian, *Adversus Marcionem* 5.6; Hays, *First Corinthians*, 43-44; Frederic Louis Godet, *Commentary on First Corinthians* (Grand Rapids, MI: Kregel, 1977 [orig. 1889]), 136 (especially the Jewish leaders); Nicoll. Ambrosiaster (Bray, 22) makes it the human rulers, but including the demons that lay behind them; so too Margaret E. Thrall, *I and II Corinthians* (CBC; Cambridge: Cambridge University Press, 1965), 25-26; Garland, *1 Corinthians*, 94; and importantly, Oscar Cullmann, *Christ and time* (London: SCM Press, 1962). Ignatius, *Trallians* 11 (long rescension) alludes to the verse and states that false teachers too "killed the Lord of glory."

a Caiaphas might claim to have. Second, the reference to "no eye, no ear no mind" in the Isaiah quotation in 2:9 fits better with a reference to human beings. Paul's point then is that human power structures are passing away; so why look to them for insight into God's truth? They would not have crucified Jesus had they known God's plan, and thus they cannot provide wisdom to the Corinthian church.

2:9

The Scriptures back up what Paul is saying:

> *No eye has seen,*
>   *no ear has heard,*
> **no mind has conceived**
>   **what God has prepared for those who love him.**

The first two phrases (in italics) are taken from Isa 64:4:

> Since ancient times
> *no one has heard, no ear has perceived, no eye has seen* any God besides you, who acts on behalf of those who wait for him.

However, the last part, beginning with "no mind," is not from Isaiah. It is perhaps Paul's extension of Isaiah's language, or maybe a Jewish tradition based on Isaiah which Paul found ready-made.[141] This citation backs up what Paul has said in 2:7, that God has planned to reveal his truth from ages past.[142]

2:9 is commonly taken out of context to mean that the Christian cannot possibly conceive what blessings God has in store for us *in heaven for when we die*.[143] That is not the point here. Paul is speaking the truth that can be known in the here and now, since the crucifixion. No human being could ever guess or observe or reason out the blessings of the gospel of Christ, but we Christians already understand them (see 2:10).

2:10

Already **God has revealed it to us by his Spirit**, that is, the Spirit reveals to us the meaning of the cross of Jesus.

When our Bibles are speaking about the Holy Spirit, it capitalizes the word Spirit. When it is not speaking of the Spirit but of "a spirit," it does not capitalize the word. Modern editors do this in order to help the reader understand the specific reference. But in the 1st century, written Greek did not differentiate between lower and uppercase

---

[141] Origen, *Commentary on Matthew* 27.3-10, 5.29, claimed to have seen the whole reference in a certain *Apocalypse of Elijah*, but his testimony raises difficulties; see Fitzmyer, *First Corinthians*, 177-78; Thiselton, *First Corinthians*, 251-52.

[142] *1 Clem* 34.8 cites the saying as Scripture. Presumably he knows the text by means of 1 Cor 2 and not independently, explaining the different ending – "what great things he has prepared for those who *patiently wait for him."*

[143] So *1 Clem* 34.8; Isaac de Nineveh (Bray, 23), who died around 700 AD. *Martyrdom of Polycarp* 2.3 quotes 2:9 and states that the soon-to-be martyrs understood the hidden things, "which were shown to them by the Lord, for they were no longer men but already angels." Elaine Hiesey Pagels, *The Gnostic Paul: Gnostic exegesis of the Pauline letters* (Philadelphia: Fortress, 1975), 58, thinks that the Gnostics used 1 Cor 2:9a at their initiation ceremony.

letters: the word *pneuma* could mean Spirit or spirit; it all depended on the context. Quite often the context is clear. Nevertheless, there is some confusion about Paul's use of *pneuma* in this chapter, and the difference is not a minor one.

Pneuma may have various meanings. First is the parallel to modern language: we use the word "spirit" to speak of an attitude, such as the spirit of the spirit of generosity. This is its sense in 1 Cor 4:21, but it does not serve in 1 Cor 2.

The Bible also uses "spirit" to refer to the immaterial part of a human being, as in 1 Cor 2:11, 7:34, 2 Cor 7:1, 1 Thess 5:23. If the human spirit is in fact his meaning in 2:10, then Paul would be teaching mysticism, that through our inner self we experience immediate contact with God. In the 2nd century, the Gnostics would misinterpret 1 Corinthians in a similar way. In today's language, once might claim to know God "in my heart," as if there were some part of us that had immediate contact with God. However, that would be to contradict what Paul has just said, that this wisdom was revealed at a specific point in human history, in the cross, and that it is something that the human mind could not conceive without God's specific work in that person through the Holy Spirit.

The interpretation that makes best sense is found in the NIV, that the *pneuma* in 2:10 is "*the* Spirit," that is "the Spirit of God" (2:11b), and thus capitalized in English. We have received God's Spirit (2:12), we have been taught by him (2:13), received his gifts (2:14), and been given "the mind of Christ" (2:16). Moreover, when Paul speaks of "spiritual" people (2:13, 15), he is not speaking of some class of people who are in closer touch with their inner selves. For example, in internet forums where people are searching for love, one encounters "Single, intelligent, focused, *spiritual*, seeks a young and energetic woman." "Spiritual" in this context has little or nothing to do with Christian faith, and perhaps the man is simply trying to portray himself as deep and sensitive in order to impress women.[144]

In Paul's epistles "spiritual" – whether spiritual gifts, spiritual people, spiritual understanding – denotes "having to do with the (Holy) Spirit." The unspiritual or soulish person is "the one who does not have the Spirit." As Irenaeus said, "the apostle terms [those who have spiritual gifts] 'spiritual,' they being spiritual because they partake of the Spirit, and not because their flesh has been stripped off and taken away, [nor] because they have become purely spiritual."[145] Thus in our minds we might capitalize the adjective as "Spiritual." The outpouring of the Spirit at Pentecost was a part of God's plan in history (Joel 2:28). It is this same Spirit who speaks within the Christian (Rom 8:16, 26-27) and who brings the spiritual gifts in (1 Cor 12:4) or a direct spoken revelation from God (1 Cor 14:23-25).

The Spirit knows all of God's truth: **the Spirit searches all things, even the deep things of God**, he knows "the thoughts of God" (2:11). No human system and no revelation can go beyond the knowledge that the Spirit possesses, and what he knows and shares with us is God's message of the cross. It is a message that the Spirit is pleased to back up with miraculous signs (2:4). The true person of the Spirit will be distinctly cross-centered, and such people are not divisive like the Corinthians, but humble and loving (see James 3:17-18 – "But the wisdom that comes from heaven is first of all pure; then peace-loving, considerate, submissive, full of mercy and good fruit, impartial and

---

[144] The NIV 2011 edition is superior to the older editions with regard to the use of *pneuma* in 1 Corinthians, see my blog: https://openoureyeslord.com/2020/05/26/the-new-international-version-1984-and-2011/
[145] Irenaeus, *Against heresies* 5.6.1.

sincere. Peacemakers who sow in peace raise a harvest of righteousness").

2:11

Just as a human being knows what is going on inside his or her own mind, at least to a limited extent, so the eternal Spirit of God is the one who best knows **the thoughts of God**. This truth was taught in the Old Testament:

> He reveals deep and hidden things,
> He knows what lies in darkness (Dan 2:22a).
>
> Can you fathom the mysteries of God?
> Can you probe the limits of the Almighty? (Job 11:7)

2:12

Christians have not received **the spirit of the world**. Paul is not referring to the Satanic powers specifically (as he does in Eph 2:2) but to the world of human experience; similarly he speaks of "human wisdom" in 2:13. We might paraphrase him as *we have received the Spirit of God, not the "spirit" of worldly philosophy.*[146]

2:13

Again, Paul teaches **not in words taught us by human wisdom but in words taught by the Spirit**. Literally the phrase is "not in teaching of a human but teaching of a spirit," or better, "the Spirit." Some manuscripts add the word "holy" to "Spirit;" some scribe altered the text so that it said what he thought Paul meant.

The latter part of 2:13 is capable of several meanings, and poses some difficulty to the interpreter: *pneumatikois pneumatika sunkrinontes*. We might begin with the third word, which might be translated as "comparing," but which is probably better taken as the NIV has it, "expressing."[147]

The first two words are both forms of *pneumatikos*, a word Paul uses 15 times in this letter (for example, 2:13, 2:15, 3:1). The adjective *pneumatikos* is related to the noun *pneuma*, "spirit/Spirit." We have already observed that when Paul speaks of *pneuma*, typically he is referring to the Holy Spirit. It makes good sense to apply that meaning to the adjective: Paul is "expressing spiritual truths (*pneumatika*)." It is synonymous with "the things that come from the Spirit of God" in 2:14.

The other usage (*pneumatikois*) is capable of two meaning: (1) "in spiritual words" (so the NIV)[148] or (2) "to those who are spiritual" (so the ESV).[149] Either one makes senses in this passage; (2) is preferable, since in 2:14 Paul draws a contrast with people who do not have the Spirit. We will take Paul thus: *"we speak, not in teaching that comes from a human, but teaching that comes from the Spirit; thus we are explaining those Spirit-truths to those who have the Spirit."*

---

[146] Theodoret of Cyrus, *Commentaries*, 1:167 - "...We did not receive a created spirit, nor were we in receipt of the revelation of divine things through an angel – rather, the Spirit that proceeds from the Father taught us the hidden mysteries."

[147] See Fitzmyer, *First Corinthians*, 181-82.

[148] Conzelmann, *1 Corinthians*, 67, agrees with this interpretation. The NIV 2011 is superior with its "with Spirit-taught words."

[149] So the analysis by Thistelton, *First Corinthians*, 264. It would be better, "to those who have the Spirit."

2:14

By contrast, the things that the Spirit teaches will make no sense to **the man without the Spirit**. Paul uses another pair of terms here: the *pneumatikos*, the person with the Spirit, is contrasted with the *psuchikoi*, "people of the *psuche* or soul." The NIV rendering is a paraphrase, although one that catches the idea of the context, as does "the natural man." **They are spiritually discerned**; and again, "spiritually" does not mean the person must be in touch with his own human spirit, but listening to the gospel that the Holy Spirit reinforces.

No wonder then that the philosopher and the wealthy and the well-born think the Christian gospel is nonsense! They may be well-trained in the world's intellect, but without the Spirit of God they have no hope of understanding the deepest wisdom of God. They are constitutionally incapable of seeing what "no eye has seen." And if this is true, then, by implication, the Corinthians ought to stop acting as if philosophy is going to take them beyond the "simple" gospel into deeper truths.

2:15

This verse too is difficult. Some argue that **the spiritual man** [better, the person who has the Spirit] **makes judgments about all things, but he himself is not subject to any man's judgment** is a slogan of the proud Corinthians, that they were saying (or acting as if) that they could be critical of other Christians but would not tolerate criticism in turn. This hypothesis runs into difficulties: first, one should always exercise caution in saying that such-and-such is not Paul's teaching, that he is merely quoting his opponents. Second, if Paul is quoting his opponents in order to correct them, one would expect the context to make that clear, that is, he should go on to correct them by what follows (as he does, for example, in 1 Cor 6:12, when he emends the slogan "everything is permissible for me"). Third, Paul seems to uphold and affirm this statement in 2:15a with the Isaiah quotation in 2:16; his statement here seems to be an application of Isaiah to this situation. We take the statement then to be Paul's own.

For centuries people have used 1 Cor 2:15 to justify their own actions and to condemn their opponents: *Since I have a generous portion of the Spirit, I must be in the right and can judge others; and if my opponents disagree, then they must not have the Spirit of God.*[150] That cannot be Paul's meaning here, since he is going to great pains to tell the Corinthians that a lofty and judgmental attitude is of the world. He is not describing a superior type of Christian who is allowed to judge everyone but who can live without fear of reproach. In fact, Paul will show in 1 Cor 5:1-5 that a certain offender in the Corinthian church must be judged for his actions. No, in 2:15 Paul is contrasting once again the world's wisdom with God's.

We are helped by a study of the verb in question: *anakrinō* may mean "to judge," but it may also mean "discern, examine." The wise person is supposed to be able to discern what is true. In the world of philosophy, one uses reason; in the church, one knows the truth through the Spirit, who teaches us the truth of the gospel. Therefore we paraphrase the statement thus: *The person who has the Spirit and thus understands the wisdom of the cross can discern and judge all other supposed "wisdoms"; but his wisdom cannot be properly judged by anyone in the world system, because it is from*

---

[150] This is how the Gnostics read 2:14-16, see Pagels, *Gnostic Paul*, 59.

God and not from the world (see 1 Cor 4:3).

2:16
Paul again quotes Isaiah LXX (see 1 Cor 1:19, 2:9), condensing Isa 40:13-14:

> Who has known the mind of the Lord,
> > and who has been his counselor to instruct him?
> Or whom did he consult,
> > and he instructed him?

The prophet poses rhetorical questions in order to show that human wisdom cannot possibly fathom the wisdom of the Creator. **"For who has known the mind of the Lord…?"** Long ago, Isaiah said that the mind of God is unknowable.[151] But wait, says Paul, who takes the point a step further and gives an answer to the rhetorical questions. **But we have the mind of Christ**. This is not to say that Christians know all there is to know about God, but we do know the central truth of the gospel. The world does not know God, but we have the "mind of the Lord" (2:16b), as some ancient manuscripts have it; or better, we have **the mind of Christ**.

Paul gives a strong affirmation of the Trinity as he closes this chapter: Jehovah's mind as such is unknowable to mortals, but those who have the mind of Christ have the mind of Jehovah; those who have the Spirit have the mind of God; those who have the Spirit understand the cross of Christ, and the Spirit backs up the preaching of the cross with miraculous signs, and all "so that your faith might not rest on men's wisdom, but on God's power" (2:5). And with all this they will have the "mind of Christ": not simply a set of facts, but the mind of Christ that will make the Corinthian house-churches supernaturally "may be perfectly united in mind and thought" (1:10).

Application: Would Paul have disdained theological education? 2:16

As a Jewish rabbi, Saul would have passed through rigorous training. He was fluent in Hebrew, as well as Aramaic, Greek and – given that he planned to evangelize Spain – probably Latin. He constantly quoted the Scriptures, which he would have memorized in Hebrew and in the Septuagint, the Greek version which he quoted in his epistles. He was trained to preach and teach. His epistles reflect a solid education in rhetoric and composition. He was at home in the pulpit of any synagogue in the world and could speak lucidly to any Greek philosopher.

When Paul came to know Christ, he did not throw away his formation. His statement, "whatever was to my profit I now consider loss for the sake of Christ" (Phil 3:7) does not mean that he turned his back on his Bible training, but rather any hope of gaining God's favor apart from Christ. When Paul said that "Has not God made foolish the wisdom of the world?" (1 Cor 1:20) he meant that we could never come to know and love God through human reason apart from the cross. He was not speaking of godly

---

[151] See Paul's use of Isa 40:13 along with Job 41:11 in Rom 11:33-36, where the inscrutability of God's ways are the cause for praise.

knowledge, but the mindset of pagan philosophers.

It is unfathomable, this approach in some sectors of the church, that a leader should not receive training, but should simply rely on the Spirit to tell him what to say. We have only to look at Paul, who relied on the Spirit, but at the same time provided plenty of fuel for the Spirit's fire by studying the Scriptures. How dare we ask that he supply us words to say, when we have deigned only to dabble in his written Word?

To be sure, I have met Christians who have little education and training, and many of them are wonderfully used by the Lord – but that despite a handicap. On the other hand, I have never met anyone who would be a better Christian or pastor if only he knew *less* about the Bible, sound doctrine, or practical tools for ministry. Solid training is the friend, not the enemy, of the Spirit's work.

e. More proof from the Corinthian reality: they are acting like the world's people 3:1-4

3:1

Paul's two recollections of his visit to Corinth (here and in 1:26-31) are less than flattering. Here he also describes how he perceives their current spiritual state: when I came to you originally to evangelize,[152] you were **world, mere infants**, and, he implies, you still are.

His logic runs like this: *With regard to the gospel, you were of the world when I met you; then you because babies in the true wisdom of God. I could not even give you the deeper explanation of the gospel, you were so childish. Now some of you imagine that you're all grown up with your worldly learning, but you're not adult and wise at all; you're still very immature in the gospel, let alone in your silly use of philosophy.*

3:2

Milk and **solid food** are common symbols for childish or mature needs. Just as an infant cannot chew or derive nourishment from a steak, and will only spit it up again, so the Corinthians still lack the ability to eat grown-up food. This must have been galling for the Corinthians who prided themselves on their wisdom.

However, this does not mean that milk is the gospel of the cross and the meat something other than that same gospel. This is the same misinterpretation that the 2nd century Gnostics would give this verse: *the Corinthians were mere normal Christians (people of the soul), and could never hope to hear or understand the higher teaching that the Gnostics (people of the spirit) alone could handle.* This is a complete misunderstanding of the point. Paul proclaimed only one gospel. What he is speaking about is a deeper, more mature presentation of the very same gospel of the cross, apart from which he had no message for Corinth (2:2). "…his wisdom can, by the very nature of the Gospel, only be a deeper understanding of the message which he has already proclaimed, a realization in the Corinthians' lives of the proclamation of Christ crucified…"[153] The error of the "wise" Corinthians was in thinking that the simple gospel

---

[152] He uses the same verb, *laleō*, that he used for communicating the gospel in 2:6, 7, 13.
[153] Morna D. Hooker, "Hard sayings: 1 Corinthians 3:2," *Theology* 69 (1966): 22. Also Fee, *First Corinthians*.

was fine for the immature and simple, but for the elite something more substantial – deep philosophy! hot debate! – was preferable. Their so-called intellectual depth, since it is not based on the gospel of the cross, is a token that they are still infants spiritually. This involves an implicit rebuke: *After these years, if you had kept growing in the right direction, you would have grown beyond spiritual infancy.*[154]

3:3-4

Paul concludes that, based on what he has heard, the Corinthians are still **worldly**; in the Greek it is *sarkikos*, literally "fleshly." While that adjective sometimes is used to refer to material beings, that is far from Paul's point here. The New Testament also uses "flesh" (the noun form, *sarx*) to speak of people who are unregenerate (Rom 8:9) or Christians who follow their own human desires and not the Spirit of God (Gal 5:16-21).[155] One should understand "flesh" as "merely human," and in fact Paul uses that language twice in these verses. He knows that some are living according to the old ways, once again pointing to their **jealousy and quarreling**: if they form factions, then they are living as people in the world live, who do not have the Spirit. **Jealousy** (*zēlos*) can have a positive sense, as in 2 Cor 7:7, 11, 9:2, 11:2, but this same negative sense of unholy competitiveness is found here and in 2 Cor 12:20. Also in that passage appears the word **quarreling** (*eris*), and both words appear in Gal 5:20 as works of the flesh.

If we have any doubt about what the apostle is referring to, he mentions the factions of Paul and Apollos (see 1:12). Those who are acting in accord with merely human standards are "carnal." Of course the Christians are human beings, but they are acting like every other human being in the world and not as people who have received God's redemption in Christ.[156] Let the Greeks act if they understood philosophy, and pick fights with those who disagreed with them. But when the Corinthian Christians do so, they are not being good Christians; they are not even noble people of the world.

Application: May I be a carnal Christian? 3:1-4

A church member is cold or lukewarm to the things of Christ; he is backsliding into the old patterns and sins; he reads his Bible and prays only at church, when he is there at all; he feels guilty when he takes the Lord's Supper, but not badly enough to repent. His patterns of thought and behavior are more like those of the unbeliever. Although he may deceive people at church, his relatives and close friends may sense that something is amiss.

In both North and South America this is a major problem. People drift in and out of the church; or they drift back into traditionalism; or they wander into the world with little to mark them as Christians.

Such a person must turn to God in repentance, preferably with the guidance of another believer. Never should he delay for a better time. Nor should he focus on introspection, punishing of himself, making pledges based on his own strength. After

---

[154] The same idea is found in Heb 5:12-14, where the author wishes that he could give them something beyond simple milk. The same metaphor, without the connotation that drinking milk is a childish behavior, is found in 1 Pet 2:2.

[155] See in particular Ladd, *Theology*, 509-17.

[156] See Thiselton, *First Corinthians*, 294, "like any merely human person."

all, our guilt feelings do nothing to help us unless they push us back toward the cross. Rather he should focus on the perfect work of Christ and draw near to him in love. In short, the way for the mature believer, the sinning believer, or the unbeliever is always the same: seek the cross of Christ.

At this point we should mention that, contrary to intuition, it is often the spiritual Christians who are most conscious of their own sin. The closer they draw to Christ, the grosser their own failings seem. But the spiritual Christian is at the same time the one most conscious of the cross, and of the cross, which is deeper than all sin. On the other hand, nothing characterizes the unspiritual Christian more than carelessness and superficiality.

There is another shelter to which a Christian flees, but it turns out to be a trap set by an enemy. He may be told by well-meaning preachers not to panic. After all, isn't it true that apart from the mature believer and the unbeliever, there is a third type of person: the carnal Christian? This is also sometimes defined as the person who has received Christ as Savior but not as Lord. Depending on where he goes to church, he may be told: *Don't worry, it's impossible to lose your salvation once you have raised your hand in a meeting; so your sinful works won't have eternal ramifications for your salvation.* This reminds me of a funeral that I once attended. The man was irreligious and a notorious sinner in our town. Yet the priest announced that he would be saved because as a baby his parents had baptized him as a baby. *How ridiculous!* we evangelicals retort, but our doctrine may look just as foolish from a biblical perspective.

The carnal people of 3:1-4 are professing believers who "acting according to merely human criteria." Corinth is a church of extreme cases: the incestuous man in 5:1, the fornicators in 6:15 or the elitists in 1:12; 11:20-21, etc. It may be no coincidence that Paul wrote Rom 6 from the church at Corinth, where he reminds them that 6:1-2, 12:

> What shall we say, then? Shall we go on sinning so that grace may increase? By no means! We died to sin; how can we live in it any longer?...Therefore do not let sin reign in your mortal body so that you obey its evil desires.

In Rom 8:1-11 Paul speaks only of two groups of people: those who live according to the flesh and who will perish, and those who live according to the Spirit. A person who is supposedly a Christian but who lives in the flesh is, to all human senses, an unbeliever. To be saved means to be on the road to holiness: "knowing God's commands is what counts" (1 Cor 7:19), and so of course is the doing of them.

The category "carnal Christian" is not a safe haven for someone who wants to live like the world but still receive salvation in the end. Nor does the Bible give any justification to people who want Christ as Savior but not as Lord. Rather – and I say this as one who believes in the doctrine of eternal security – these verses are stern warnings that the person must repent, and urgently.

In the case of the incestuous man, the Corinthians were to take an extraordinary step: "hand this man over to Satan" (1 Cor 5:5). That is, they were to put him out of the church, to treat the man as a non-believer. His "fruit" (see Matt 7:20), the visible elements of his behavior, show that he does not belong with the people of God. That is, Jesus taught us that a person who looks like he is unsaved is, most likely, unsaved, no matter what he says with his mouth. In the case of the sinner in 1 Cor 5, Paul hopes that it will turn out that "his spirit saved on the day of the Lord." It may be that the church's discipline will drive false hope from his heart.

But what of the people in 1 Cor 3:15, "he will suffer loss; he himself will be saved, but only as one escaping through the flames"? Can a person take hope in that sort of promise? Perhaps; or perhaps 3:17 is the relevant verse: "If anyone destroys God's temple, God will destroy him." The important truth here is that only a fool will run the risk of God's judgment, and that a person who is not concerned with offending God should examine himself to see whether he is really a follower of Christ.

Recommended reading:
Dietrich Bonhoeffer, *The Cost of Discipleship*; J. I. Packer, *Knowing God*.

f. More proof from the apostolic example: All true Christian workers labor for God's glory, not their own 3:5-17

The last proof of the *confirmatio* is again taken from the apostle's own example: just as Paul came with fear and trembling, just as he labored hard to simplify the gospel message for his audience, so he and Apollos modeled how a Christian leader should behave. And by implication, this was how all disciples of Christ should comport themselves. The implication is that the Corinthians should have seen their example during their formative years and been imitating the apostles right now.

Why does Paul leave out Cephas until 3:22? It is because Paul and Apollos were closely associated because of their work in Corinth and then again in Ephesus (1 Cor 16:12). The Corinthians cannot have doubted the unity and teamwork that these two have shown. If Cephas had at some time visited the Corinthian church (as seems likely, see Introduction), then his work was not so visibly connected with Paul's, and so did not provide as clear an example.

Paul will describe the work of God (his people, the church) by two metaphors: (1) a planted field (3:6-9), and (2) a building under construction (3:9b-15); this generic "building" later develops into God's "temple," his dwelling place (3:16-17). The booming city of Corinth witnessed all kinds of building and renovation projects in Paul's day. It was also surrounded by farms. He is probably thinking of one of the sprawling agricultural enterprises that covered the Mediterranean world, agricultural businesses which employed hundreds or thousands of workers.[157]

3:5

Once again Paul wonders aloud, why anyone would form a party based on himself or on Apollos. **What, after all, is Apollos? And what is Paul?** He asks, not "who is?" but "what is?"[158], what kind of a *thing* are these prominent leaders? Are they wise philosophers or colorful demagogues to command such a following? No, they are merely servants, workers on the construction site or on the farm during planting or watering season. They do what the master orders and nothing else. Whatever the boastful philosopher-elitists of Corinth thought of themselves, "servant" was not a label they

---

[157] So Soards, *1 Corinthians*, 69.
[158] This was corrected in some early manuscripts to "who is?" It is noteworthy (see Witherington, *Conflict and community*, 184) that agricultural slaves were considered of lower status than domestics, and possessed fewer legal rights.

would have chosen for themselves.

Paul goes on to draw some lessons from the cultivated field:

Apollos and I (and others) are servants of a Master
The planter and the waterer are working as a team
The planter and the waterer are nothing, but God who makes things grow
Faithful servants will receive a reward
(Once again) The servants work together as one

3:6

God's work is like a "field" (3:9). **I planted the seed**, that is, he evangelized the city for the first time and won the original converts – and yes, baptized a handful of them. Paul's divine mandate was that he not cultivate where someone had already planted (Rom 15:20) nor, apparently, baptize, but to break the ground for the first time. For his part, **Apollos watered it**. This does not mean, as some have suggested, that Apollos "sprinkled" them with the water of baptism.[159] Rather, the metaphor is that he took the Corinthians further in their walk with Christ, according to Acts 18:27-19:1, after Paul had left the city. But, as in a real farm, it is not the planter or the waterer, but God, **who makes things grow**.

3:7

In the end, neither the planter or the waterer **is anything**, but only God: Paul repeats himself by saying it is God **who makes things grow**. This is not to say that the apostles are superfluous; in fact, Paul will go on to state that they are necessary and that the Corinthians should give them heed. Nevertheless, God is the main actor in this business of new birth and growth. The lesson is thus: *What is Paul? Paul is nothing! Focus on God!*

3:8

On a farm, the work of the waterer is nothing if a man hasn't first planted – he can pour water on the soil if he likes, but all he will produce is a muddy mess. Likewise, the planter needs the waterer in the many regions of the world where human irrigation is necessary.

There are two ways to interpret the next clause. Literally the Greek *hen eisin* is that "are the same" (so ESV, NASB), but in what sense? Perhaps Paul means that they are equal in value; the problem with this interpretation is that Christian workers are *not* obviously on the same level or of equal worth: they will receive compensation according to their value (3:8b, 12-14), and some do work that is of no value at all (3:15). Rather, Paul's major theme throughout this passage is "that you may be perfectly united in mind and thought." That is how we understand him here: "the one who plants and the one who sow want only one thing;" not personal fame or reward, but to glorify God by serving him in his field. The NIV is correct when it says that the various workers **have one purpose**.

Paul next mentions compensation, that **each will be rewarded according to his own labor**. This may seem out of place here, but Paul anticipates the warning inherent in his

---

[159] So Ambrosiaster (Bray, 30).

building metaphor, beginning in 3:9b. Paul is not simply saying that the good worker will feel a sense of satisfaction in this life, but that in God's kingdom every action has an eschatological value; our work has future consequences.[160] Every worker must constantly keep one eye on God's future judgment, because that day will be a day of revelation.

3:9

We (Paul and Apollos and, by extension, others) are **God's fellow workers**, "those who work together with God and are engaged in a common endeavor with God himself, who is the principal worker."[161]

The Corinthians, by analogy, **are God's field, God's building**. "God's" is emphatic in the Greek – not Paul's work, not Apollos's, but *God's*. The apostle now closes the metaphor of a cultivated field and opens the metaphor of a building/temple. His language bears a strong resemblance to Jer 1:10 which has both farm and construction language as metaphors for Jeremiah's prophetic preaching:

> See, today I appoint you over nations and kingdoms
> > to uproot and to tear down,
> > to destroy and overthrow,
> > to build and to plant.

3:10

Paul draws a number of analogies from the second metaphor:

> The building belongs to God, not to any man
> Paul is a wise master builder in the construction at Corinth
> Paul laid the right foundation, the only possible one – Christ crucified
> Other people add on to the foundation
> Having a good foundation does not ensure a good superstructure, so everyone must build well
> > The building will eventually be tested by fire, so everyone must build to last
> > Faithful builders will be rewarded by God; careless builders will come to shame
> > > The building not only belongs to God – it is the dwelling of God, his Temple, and should be labored on with special care

Paul will now describe his special role in Corinth. On the one hand he is one of the "servants" (3:5). But Paul is not only a manual laborer; he is also the **expert builder** (in Greek, the *architektōn*, a word found only here in the New Testament). The meaning of this Greek word might seem obvious; nevertheless, one of the rules of word study is that that a word in the Greek does not necessarily mean the same thing as its near equivalent in English. For example, *dunamis* does not mean "dynamite," but rather "power, authority." In this case, *architektōn* is not identical to our word *architect*, which has to do mainly with designing a building. The post of *architektōn* was to oversee the design

---

[160] We agree with Thiselton, *First Corinthians*, 394-05. He lists four possibilities for the meaning of "will be rewarded" and settles for the idea of eschatological reward at the final judgment.
[161] Fitzmyer, *First Corinthians*, 195-96. The alternative is to paraphrase, as the NLT – "we are both God's workers." See the comments by Thiselton; also Fee.

and the construction of the entire project:

> For as the master builder [*architektōn*] of a new house must be concerned with the whole construction, while the one who undertakes its painting and decoration has to consider only what is suitable for its adornment, such in my judgment is the case with us (2 Macc 2:29 NRSV).

As the church's general designer-engineer, **I laid a foundation**, that is, established it in the gospel of Christ Jesus (3:11). Paul did not found a church upon the changing tastes of philosophy, as some Corinthians would have preferred. Since he is a wise master builder, then it must be assumed that he knows what the most appropriate foundation is, and that he wishes to see others build a superstructure that is suited to such a fine foundation. **And someone else is building on it** does not refer to a specific person;[162] it can refer to all who work in Corinth, or to be sure, anyone who wishes to serve God throughout the ages.

Here appears Paul's first imperative of the letter (apart from the Jeremiah quote in 1:31). **But each one should be careful how he builds.** Apollos was the next prominent builder to add to that foundation, but there are others, including Cephas, the current leaders of the church and also the supposedly wise thinkers among them.

3:11

Why does Paul mention that no-one can lay another foundation, in what seems a parenthetical statement? C. K. Barrett suggests that the Cephas party was already leaning toward papist ideas: since Christ had said to Peter that he would build his church on the rock (Matt 16:18), Cephas/Peter or some of his followers wanted to make Peter the foundation of the Corinthian church.[163] Paul would then be saying: *Peter is not the foundation of the church, it's **Jesus Christ**; this is what I, Christ's apostle, told you from the start.* This reading of course supposes that we can figure out what each of the four groups of 1:12 believed and desired, an assumption that is highly speculative to begin with. It also means that Paul is condemning the Cephas group in favor of the Paul and Apollos groups on the basis of their ecclesiology, an unlikely theory, given that Paul's point is to condemn all forms of partisanship, and to that end he draws their attention to **Jesus Christ**.

3:12

When we see what materials individual builders use – **gold, silver, costly stones, wood, hay or straw** – we can deduce a great deal about their attitude toward Christ, the church, and themselves. These are materials with which every Corinthian would be familiar, depending on the nature of the building. "Precious stone" evokes the idea of marble blocks. Gold and silver are used for costly adornment and for facing rather than for the structure, in order to show the costly investment in the project. On the other end, there are cheap, combustible materials: wood (for roofs or for cheaper framed houses), and hay and stubble, which they used to make the thatched roofs that were so common in private dwellings.

---

[162] In the 21st century there is a certain teacher who claims that he himself fulfills Paul's "prediction," the "other who would come and be a new apostle." Such an eccentric idea scarcely requires refutation.

[163] Barrett, *First Corinthians*, 87-88.

The materials are listed in descending order, from gold all the way down to thatch. The man who builds with costly materials is thinking of the future and for the lasting glory of God. One is reminded of David's preparation for the Jerusalem Temple and how he told his son Solomon:

> I have taken great pains to provide for the temple of the LORD a hundred thousand talents of gold, a million talents of silver, quantities of bronze and iron too great to be weighed, and wood and stone. And you may add to them. You have many workmen: stonecutters, masons and carpenters, as well as men skilled in every kind of work in gold and silver, bronze and iron – craftsmen beyond number. Now begin the work, and the LORD be with you. (1 Chron 22:14-16)

Meanwhile, the one who builds with thatch is thinking in the short term: *If the wind blows the thatch roof off my house this winter, I'll just put on another one in the spring*. But in the church, one does not have to be "wise, influential, of noble birth" (1:26) in order to build with costly marble and with precious metals. All Christians have the power to preach one and the same precious gospel, and it is a matter of choice rather than cost that makes one person pick thatch when there is plenty of gold available.[164]

3:13

All of this construction is metaphorical; it has to do with building up the people of God. That's why the main anxiety is a not a surprise visit from the municipal building inspector; in God's plan **his work will be shown for what it is, because the Day will bring it to light**. The crisis that Paul evokes is **fire**. The ancients lived in dread of fire, especially those who lived in poorer neighborhoods where cheap building materials were highly flammable. There were few of the modern protocols, such as building codes, emergency exits, smoke alarms or even functioning fire companies. One spark could burn down a block – or a while city. This would happen on a grand scale in a scant seven years or so, when in AD 64 Rome itself burned for six days, wiping out huge portions of the capital.

But, Paul says, a fire is not simply a possibility – it is a certainty. The "building" will burn because God himself will light the fire, to test **the quality of each man's work**. Paul uses traditional language of divine judgment: **fire**,[165] **revealed**,[166] and **reward**.[167] This combination of terms and the sense of a coming fiery disaster indicate that he is speaking of God's final judgment, a reality that hangs over every decision and action.

Is one faction or another his target here? Does he think the work of one party will burn while his group will survive? We think not. Rather his point is summed up in the opening exhortation of 3:10b: "each one should be careful how he builds it." Paul and

---

[164] Alternatively, Pelagius (Bray, 33) makes the six materials six kinds of *hearer*; others think of different types of *teaching*, for example, Godet, *First Corinthians*, 182-84.

[165] Among many other verses see Isa 66:16, Amos 1:4-2:5, Matt 3:10-12, 2 Thess 1:8, Heb 10:27, 2 Pet 3:7, Rev 18:8. Fire may be God's judgment during this age as well, as in Gen 19:24. See also Christ's "eyes like a flame of fire" in Rev 2:18.

[166] The idea of making manifest or revealing is taken from the adjective "revealed" (*phaneros*; cf. Matt 12:16, 1 Cor 3:13) and verb *apokaluptō* (cf. Luke 17:30). Both may be used of God's unveiling of that which was hidden, whether in this age or in the return of Christ.

[167] The term *misthos* is neutral in itself, that is, it may denote a reward for good or punishment for doing evil. Cf. the eschatological use of the word in Matt 5:12, 10:41-42, 20:8, 2 Pet 2:13, Rev 22:12.

Apollos and presumably Cephas have given the church a good start; so beware how you others build.

On another occasion he says that the teacher of "a different gospel" (Gal 1:6) is worthy of damnation: "Let him be eternally condemned!" In Philippians, those who preach a circumcision gospel are "dogs" (Phil 3:2ff.), using the Jewish term for people outside the covenant. But in 1 Cor 3, Paul is not describing a heretic. The closer parallel is found not in Phil 3, but in Phil 1: self-serving preachers of the true gospel are distasteful, but in the end they are preaching the true gospel (Phil 1:12-18). In Phil 1:15 as in 1 Cor 3, what constitutes poor construction is not false doctrine – that would be to reject the Christ foundation. The sin of the evangelists in Phil 1:15 is "envy and rivalry," language that is strikingly similar to 1 Cor 1:11, 3:3, where work offered by someone who is boastful, partisan, childish, self-seeking, neglectful of God's revelation in favor of philosophy.[168] Paul will not pronounce the *anathema* on them as he does with the Judaizers of Gal 1:8-9.

3:14-15a

A builder can paint wood with gold-colored paint, but it is still inferior material. A fire is coming, and in the aftermath it will be possible to analyze what burned and why. The final judgment of God may leave many bewildered – what they thought was pretty and shiny may burn like so much straw, and what some thought to be plain material (such as Paul's sermons) may turn to be well constructed. The decisive point is whether the work **survives** or is transient and perishes.

As is the manner of the Scriptural authors, Paul does not teach about the end times in order to entertain his audience. His purpose is to warn or encourage people in the present age with a prediction of **reward** or **loss**. 2 Cor 5:10 has the same approach: "that each one may receive what is due him for the things done while in the body, whether good or bad." The building is on fire, but the construction of good quality will stay standing. The builder will receive his pay, not because he is clever or persuasive or physically impressive, but because his work is sound. The Corinthians should not concern themselves about what that future reward will be, but rather, think about what they are doing right now.

But the negative side is true too: when the fire comes and the building burns, some builder will be caught inside his own firetrap! He runs outside, but his work is consumed, and he receives no reward. Probably the image is of a building under construction, as the people of God always is. It burns down due to poor building materials, the builder is liable. His loss is not only the loss of reward for putting up the building, but also the loss of time and material that he's already invested in the work. It would have been better that he never started the project, it's a **loss**.

3:15b

Paul concludes that such a careless builder **will be saved, but only as one escaping through the flames**. This statement has intrigued Christians since the beginning, and has been a doctrinal battleground. First of all, this has been taken as the main New Testament proof for the doctrine of purgatory, that upon death the faithful will pass through a time of cleansing and will finally come to eternal salvation. The Roman

---

[168] See Cox, quoted in Thiselton, *First Corinthians*, 312.

Catholic expression of this idea is as follows:

> All who die in God's grace and friendship, but still imperfectly purified, are indeed assured of their eternal salvation; but after death they undergo purification, so as to achieve the holiness necessary to enter the joy of heaven.[169]

There are a number of problems with the doctrine.[170] (1) The most important is that the doctrine of a purgatory is not mentioned here and must be imported; (2) theologically, purgatory is the logical outworking of a particular Catholic doctrine, whereby the believer must regularly partake of grace through the sacraments in order to receive justification for sin; sins which are not confessed during this life must be atoned for (as in 2 Macc 12:45) in the next life, a doctrine that is absent from the Hebrew and Christian Scriptures and that draws attention away from the power of the cross to cleanse all sin; (3) the fire in 1 Cor 3 is not hellfire nor purgatory, but a *metaphor* for the destruction of a building; the worker escapes **as one escaping through the flames**;[171] (4) the metaphor that Paul uses is applied to broadly to support the doctrine, which states that almost all Christians must pass through purgatory; (5) the chronological order is wrong: Paul says that God will test the house by fire in what is probably the eschatological judgment, *after which* the good builder is rewarded and the negligent one suffers loss. In the Catholic doctrine, the "builder" dies, goes immediately into the fire of purgatory, is released and goes to heaven; only later in the end he faces Judgment Day.

Yet it is at the same time a consistent Pauline teaching, that all who are justified by faith, will also be judged by their works. The same thought is present in 2 Cor 5:9-10, where Paul speaks of Christ's tribunal, the "*bēma*," before which all must appear (see also Rom 14:10). Much is made of the fact that *bēma* may be used of the judges' panel in athletic events.[172] In fact, it usually referred to a tribunal in the court system: that is its meaning in 2 Cor 5:10. Paul had the misfortune to appear before the Corinth tribunal during his sojourn, to stand before Gallio (Acts 18:12, 16, 17 uses *bēma*; the term is likewise used to refer to the tribunal of Pilate in Matt 27:19, John 19:13; governor Festus en Acts 25:6, 17; the emperor in Acts 25:10-11). In the same way, each Christian will stand before Christ's tribunal, perhaps to see the great evangelical work that he has constructed be consumed, as it were, in flames.

---

[169] *Catechism of the Catholic Church* §1030. Besides this passage, the Roman church adduces as proof the apocryphal verse 2 Macc 12:45b NRSV – "Therefore he made atonement for the dead, so that they might be delivered from their sin;" also Matt 12:32 – if there are sins that won't be pardoned "in the age to come," it is reasoned, then by implication there must be sins that *may* be pardoned in the afterlife. So Gregory the Great, *Dialogues* 4.41 (Bray, 34) – "We should remember that in the world to come no one will be purged of even his slightest faults unless he has deserved such a cleansing through good works performed in this life"; Augustine, *Enchiridion* 68-69 quotes our passage and observes that tribulations during this life serve to purify the believer. He goes on to state: "And it is not impossible that something of the same kind may take place even after this life. It is a matter that may be inquired into, and either ascertained or left doubtful, whether some believers shall pass through a kind of purgatorial fire, and in proportion as they have loved with more or less devotion the goods that perish, be less or more quickly delivered from it." The doctrine of purgatory is not limited to the Roman church, but is also found among the Orthodox and Anglicans.

[170] See Fee, *First Corinthians*, 144. See the review of early patristic interpretations by Thiselton, *First Corinthians*, 331-32.

[171] So Hermann Olshausen, *First and Second Corinthians* (Edinburgh: T. & T. Clark, 1855), 69.

[172] J. Dwight Pentecost, *Things to come: a study in biblical eschatology* (Grand Rapids, MI: Zondervan, 1965), 219-25.

And what of that unfortunate person? **He himself will be saved**.[173] "Salvation" is most often used by Paul to speak of the *eschatological* salvation: we believe in Christ in this life, therefore we will be saved in the end. Eph 2:8 is one of the few exceptions. Most of the references in 1 Corinthians (see our commentary on 1:18) are ambiguous as to time, while 5:5 is clearly eschatological: *his spirit will be saved on the day of the Lord*.

The question then arises, whether the man has almost lost his salvation, or indeed whether such a thing is possible. Technically the question is not one of loss of salvation, because this man gains eschatological salvation *after* his narrow escape. It is all future tense: the person will suffer loss, but will be "saved" after all. Has he just barely escaped the fire of hell, entering heaven with the smell of the smoke still on his clothing? This is not the idea at all. He does not get threatened with hellfire; **through the flames** is not in the sense of "near to" the flames. He enters heaven after he passes through the testing fire of God's judgment. Once again, 1 Cor 5:5 provides some theological context: if the church were to judge the incestuous man in this age, and bodily cast him out from the church, then there is the hope that on the day of judgment his spirit will be saved.

The apostle's warning to the elitist Corinthians, then, is: *I'm not doubting that you are Christians, but all your hard work in the church is headed for destruction! Your clever teachings, your grandiose philosophical vocabulary, your ability to impress the mob, all of them are so much flammable material. So, change your ways now, so that your labor may abide in the end; don't let your life work go up in smoke!*

Application: Building Right 3:10-17

You may have heard sermons which go like this: *What kind of a Christian are you? Are you building gold in your life, or straw? Do you see that Christian over there with a glass of brandy? He's just lowered his rating from gold to silver or worse.*

This section, however, is not about lifestyle issues for the Christian, but how one goes about doing Christian ministry. Paul offers himself and Apollos as examples to show why the church is not about picking one's heroes, as they were doing in 1:11-12. In that game for status, the Corinthians didn't just affirm which preacher they liked; they also denigrated the others.

For some, like the Corinthians, a successful ministry is what makes me, as God's "servant," look successful. *What makes me sound clever? What allows me to impress people with my depths of learning and wit? How may I mention that the successful and the rich seek my counsel, that I get invited to important places, that I have lunch with prominent people?*

Of course, we justify our values by imagining that we are seeking status in order to spread the gospel to more places. Paul on the other hand compares the gospel ministry to low forms of manual labor, for example, farm work. A ministry built of self will burn up in the end; a ministry that is Christ-centered will endure.

How I wish there were a simple test from the pharmacy that could tell us whether we are glorifying Christ or merely seeking prestige for ourselves. Instead, we must look for symptoms of self-seeking and be open to others as they tell us where they see our faults, such as:

---

[173] Fee, *First Corinthians*, 144, notes the close parallel in Amos 4:11.

1. I am concerned more for appearances than for reality. We have seen that Paul made tents so that he could offer the gospel free of charge. The Corinthians actually had the nerve to use that against him, since manual labor was looked down on. Today's "builders" might be tempted to use literal fine materials in their huge church buildings in big cities, instead of building with the true gold of humility and service.

2. I use the fame or reputation of another to give myself glory. I make it a point to tell others what important people I know; I display photos of myself with them.

3. I pay more attention to people who can do things for me, and less attention to those who can't. Both in North and Latin America we are taught to take advantage of whatever situation which we find ourselves. Our culture pushes us to seek out people with connections, with money, with power. Likewise, the poor and the powerless are less attractive are life's "losers."

4. I do unethical things and then tell myself that (1) after all it's the work of the Lord, and therefore it's allowed, or (2) the Lord is obligated to save me from the consequence if I am doing work in his name.

5. I measure success by whether or not I am lifted up. Of course, no-one would express it so baldly. We prefer terms such as "lift up this work," "confirm this ministry," "uphold the movement of God in our midst," etc. Yet when a rival is lifted up, we are disappointed, even if the name of God has been magnified.

How then should we measure success?

- not how many people see and hear me; but whether people see Christ in me
- not whether I can prove that my ministry is more vital than others; but whether I live in harmony with others and without divisiveness (1 Cor 1:10)
- not that am I recognized as the best, let us say, evangelist; but when I share the gospel, do people say, *Isn't Jesus wonderful!*
- not whether famous and important people seek me out; but whether those who do seek me come away thinking about Jesus

One consequence of the World Trade Center tragedy in 2001 was that experts in construction and design could later study how well the towers had been originally built in the 1960s. They could calculate in real terms that the towers collapsed after they suffered this much impact and so much heat; that therefore they were built poorly or well. An actual disaster is, sadly, a much better test than a computer simulation. For us, the final judgment is the reality that hangs over every decision and action and motive. On that day we will find out how much of our work was flammable junk and how much of lasting value. Many an evangelical empire will have its final end in that holocaust.

3:16

Paul now extends the building metaphor to a new level by reminding them that they are not throwing together just any building, but a temple, *the* Temple of God! In fact, the costly materials that he mentions in 3:12 take on a new sense: these are like the materials that were described over and over again in the description of Solomon's temple (1 Kings 6, 1 Chron 28-29). He uses the rhetorical device (**Don't you know that...?**) known as a "disclosure formula"[174] to remind them of what they should already know: that the people of God is the dwelling place of the Spirit of God himself.

What is the sense of **you yourselves are God's temple**? Some have interpreted this statement in light of 1 Cor 6:19, that is, so that 3:16 would mean that the Spirit lives in every individual Christian:

3:16 – Don't you know that you yourselves are God's temple and that God's Spirit lives in you?
6:19 – Do you not know that your body is a temple of the Holy Spirit, who is in you, whom you have received from God?

In both verses the plural "you" is used, but there is a different sense in each context. In 6:19 "you" means something like "the body of each one of you." However in 3:16 it is more natural to picture one single building, one temple. It is not the human body that is the temple, but "you believers" collectively: *you all together constitute the temple of God; the Spirit of God dwells in you as a group.*[175] It is the language of the Old Testament temple that is now applied to the Christian church, the sum total of the gathered congregation. This collective use of temple is found again in 2 Cor 6:16, where being God's temple means that God lives and walks among them rather than within each person. Paul will speak of the one temple as God's people in Eph 2:21 – "In him the whole building is joined together and rises to become a holy temple in the Lord." The metaphor is developed even further in 1 Pet 2:4-8 – "you also, like living stones, are being built into a spiritual house;" the "spiritual house" (better "the Dwelling Place for the Spirit") is the temple, the place where are offered "spiritual sacrifices." 2 Corinthians, 1 Peter, Ephesians and 1 Cor 3 all work from the same assumption: that it is the Christian people of God who are the true temple, constitute the real priesthood and offer the sacrifices that please God. Only in 1 Cor 6:19 does Paul apply the metaphor to the individual believer.

The Corinthians were entirely familiar with pagan temples, and probably had seen them under construction. The center of town, the "forum," was surrounded by temples, in particular the large new building dedicated to the worship of Caesar. Nevertheless, Paul's image works best in terms of comparing the church to the Jerusalem temple; after all, it is God's house, filled with the Spirit of God, not some pagan idol.[176]

In both 1 Cor 3:16-17 and 1 Cor 6:19, the word for **temple** is *naos*. Properly speaking this refers to the inner "sanctuary" (the smaller inner structure that housed the Holy Place and the Most Holy Place, see Matt 27:51, Luke 1:9), rather than the much larger complex of the Second Temple.[177] Paul invokes the image of the divine "Shekinah," the glowing

---

[174] See the rhetorical question in some form like "don't you know...?" in 5:6, 6:2, 6:3, 6:9, 6:15, 6:16, 9:24; also the positive statements "I want you to realize that" in 11:3, "I tell you that" in 12:3 and "I want to remind you" in 15:1.

[175] So Simon J. Kistemaker, *1 Corinthians* (Grand Rapids, MI: Baker, 1998), 116; William F. Orr and James Arthur Walther, *1 Corinthians* (AB 32; New York: Doubleday, 1976), 174; Walter; Ladd. Contra Calvin, *First Corinthians*, 1:142, who translates this as "you are the temples [plural] of God;" he later changes his mind and states that the temple is "collective" here.

[176] Lanci, *A new temple for Corinth*, makes the unlikely suggestion that Paul is thinking of the Greco-Roman temples which dominated the city of Corinth, not the Jerusalem temple. He also theorizes that Paul was the first ever to use the temple metaphor to denote a special people.

[177] The whole complex would conventionally be called the *hieron* and the inner sanctuary the *naos*. Although this distinction does not hold up in every context, the distinction is observed in descriptions of the Jewish

cloud that visibly marked God's presence in the tabernacle: "Then the cloud covered the Tent of Meeting, and the glory of the LORD filled the tabernacle" (Exod 40:34) and later in the Temple of Solomon (1 Kings 8:10; 11; 2 Chron 7:1; see also Ezek 43:1-5). This glory of the Lord was not some gaseous cloud, but the presence of God himself. Paul will later connect this glory with the Christians' possession of the Holy Spirit in 2 Cor 3:18 – "And we, who with unveiled faces all reflect the Lord's glory, are being transformed into his likeness with ever-increasing glory, which comes from the Lord, who is the Spirit."

Is this temple a symbol of a *local* church or of the church universal (as it is in Matt 16:18, Eph 5:25, and perhaps in the temple imagery in Eph 2 and 1 Pet 2)? In this context the local church fits better.[178] First, a parallel in 5:4-5 is telling: when Corinthian Christians assemble together in one place, the power of the Lord Jesus is among them; their expulsion of a sinful member has its roots in the teaching of Matt 18:18-20. Second, the symbolism in this chapter all seems to point to a church in a particular city: Paul laid the foundation for *this* church, but not for every church; Apollos worked on *this* temple, but not on others. Other Christian workers in Corinth had better take care with building on that foundation.

3:17

Paul gives a final stern warning to the careless and self-centered workers in God's sacred temple: **if anyone destroys God's temple, God will destroy** him or her. The word he uses is *phtheirō*, which can mean "destroy" (as in most versions), although "ruin" is better for this context: God will ruin the person by consuming all which he thought was valuable (3:13-15) but not will not "destroy" him in the everlasting flames.[179] *If you ruin the temple, God will ruin you; honor it and God will honor you.*

A well-known anecdote from Paul's day came from the 4th century B. C.: the magnificent temple of Artemis in Ephesus was burned down by a fanatic named Erostratus, who committed the deed merely to make his own name immortal. Although the building was made principally of stone, he was able to set fire to the wooden beams of the roof. How much grosser the deed of one who harms the sanctuary of the living and true God?

How might someone ruin God's temple? In the Old Covenant, the apostasy of the nation often led to the neglect of the physical structure (see 2 Kings 12:4-16, 22:3-7) or to the desecration of the temple with idols (see Ezek 8:1-18). Along that line, Barrett claims that the destruction of the temple in our verse refers to the corrosive effect of false teaching, for example, a Judaizing gospel.[180] Yet one seeks in vain for evidence of doctrinal error in this chapter. Rather, Paul is thinking of the "wise by the standards of this age" (3:18), who harms the church through personal ambition or worldly wisdom, despite the fact that he has built upon the true gospel foundation (3:10). In this case it is not the destruction of the church by its enemies that concerns Paul but rather the harm done by its "friends." If the whole thing goes down in flames, Paul implies, it is your

---

temple in the Septuagint (see Fee, *First Corinthians*, 146). In any case, it is the inner sanctuary that is the dwelling place of the divine glory, and that is the point of Paul's metaphor.

[178] See William Baker, *1 Corinthians* (Cornerstone Biblical Commentary; Carol Stream, IL, Tyndale House, 2009), 58.

[179] Paul will use the same verb *phtheirō* to claim that he has not ruined anyone in his apostolic ministry in 2 Cor 7:2. See also Fitzmyer, *First Corinthians*, 203.

[180] Barrett, *First Corinthians*, 91.

fault, not mine; for my part, I laid the right foundation.

Paul's language in this verse is similar to the *lex talionis* of the Torah:

Eye for eye, tooth for tooth, hand for hand, foot for foot, etc. (Exod 21:24-25)

Even closer parallels are found in Jesus's eschatological pronouncements:

With the measure you use, it will be measured to you – and even more (Mark 4:24)

If anyone is ashamed of me and my words in this adulterous and sinful generation, the Son of Man will be ashamed of him when he comes in his Father's glory with the holy angels (Mark 8:38).

And it is parallel to Paul's own language in Galatians:

Do not be deceived: God cannot be mocked. A man reaps what he sows. The one who sows to please his sinful nature, from that nature will reap destruction; the one who sows to please the Spirit, from the Spirit will reap eternal life (Gal 6:7-8).

Paul bases his pronouncement on the fact that **God's temple is sacred, and you** [all together] **are that temple.** The latter phrase is terse in the original Greek, but the paraphrase of the NIV gets the sense right (that is, Paul did not say, "you are the temple, and *you* are holy").[181] Was Paul thinking back through the centuries to the sinful, beaten and partly rebuilt city that God's man still referred to as "Jerusalem, the holy city" (Neh 11:1)? In the same way, the childish and fault-filled church of Corinth is composed of "those sanctified in Christ Jesus and called to be holy" (1 Cor 1:2); it is holy because God has chosen it to be the very dwelling of the Spirit.

Application: We are a temple, not a pile of blocks 3:17

God calls individuals to receive salvation. What is more, he invites them to join his people and to be part of his "temple."

It is a great tendency in the Western church, and a growing one in Latin America, that we define the Christian experience as "God and I." *I come to God, I'm accountable to God, God blesses and guides me.* If other Christians don't suit our taste, we leave them to find another group, or perhaps we drop out of the church altogether.

This is exactly what Satan wishes us to do, according to C. S. Lewis. He imagines that the devil pushes the new Christian to scorn the church; for that reason, Lewis tells the story of a new "tempter," who is given this instruction:

When he gets to his pew and looks round him he sees just that selection of his neighbours whom he has hitherto avoided. You want to lean pretty heavily on those neighbours. Make his mind flit to and fro between an expression like "the

---

[181] See Barrett, *First Corinthians*, 92. The Vulgate has the right idea with "templum enim Dei sanctum est quod estis vos," that is, "For the temple of God is holy, which you are."

body of Christ" and the actual faces in the next pew. It matters very little, of course, what kind of people that next pew really contains.[182]

But here and in many other verses we're told that God does not just relate to me; he also relates to the "us" of whom I am a member. What a strong lesson against radical individualism! God cares for his church, and if you toy with it, no matter how beloved or Spirit-filled you feel yourself to be as an individual, God will come to you in judgment.

4. Exhortation (*Peroratio*) 3:18-4:16

In ancient rhetoric, a speaker would prove his case, and then move to a *peroratio* or *paraenesis* in order to sum up his teaching and press the hearer to do it. A *peroratio* is a call to action. Up to this point, Paul has pointed out the true way to the Corinthians but has not in so many words told them what they should be doing. Now he speaks more directly about their high-mindedness and divisiveness, and the very grammar of the letter now changes. The apostle has been spare in his use of the imperative verb (e.g., 3:10); now he begins to give a string of commands (see 3:18, 3:21, 4:1, 4:5, 4:16).

a. Seek true wisdom from God, not through human wisdom 3:18-23

3:18
Do not deceive yourselves could also be rendered, "let no-one deceive you." This is conventional language of rhetoric, but there is a real possibility that some Corinthians are in fact deceived (cf. the comments on 4:3-4). They had swallowed this idea that being wise **by the standards of this age** is an asset in God's kingdom. The truth is that it is such an impediment to true wisdom, and the Christian should resist its charms. Paul uses the same word for "deceive" (*exapataō*) for Satan's temptation of Eve (2 Cor 11:3; 1 Tim 2:14). Here, as in Eden, one is enticed to believe a distorted view of God's universe. The "wise" Corinthian should **become a "fool"** of the world's wisdom **so that he may become wise** in God's eyes.

3:19-20
God's program always has been to trip up the so-called wise man. Do the wise look down on the cross? What does it matter, since **the wisdom of this world is foolishness in God's sight**. With **as it is written** once again Scripture shows the way, specifically Job 5:13 and Psalm 94:11:

The book of Job provides a perfect scriptural example of God's wisdom *versus* human: **"He catches the wise in their craftiness."**[183]

"The Lord knows that the thoughts of the wise are futile" is from Psalm 94:11 (93:11 LXX), except that Paul substitutes **of the wise** for "of men" in order to give it

---

[182] C. S. Lewis, *The Screwtape letters* (New York: HarperCollins, 2001), 6.
[183] The quotation from Job 5:13 is closer to the Hebrew than it is to the Septuagint (LXX), which has "catches the wise in their intelligence."

sharper application for the elitists of Corinth.[184] Paul and the Septuagint use a philosophical catchword for **thoughts** (*dialogismos*). These "reasonings" include the popular philosophical methods of oral debate, argument, discussion. The God who knows all knows how superficial and useless are the deep ponderings of human beings.

3:21a

It may not be clear to us modern readers, without the first-hand knowledge that the Corinthians possessed, where exactly Paul has been going with all this. If so, then with **So then, no more boasting about men!** he finally shows us the link between the party spirit of 1:11-12 and the long discussion on the gospel, divine wisdom, revelation and humility. The *confirmatio* (1:18-3:17) as it now turns out, was not a wandering discussion about human wisdom; rather, all that has been said after 1:18 has been to talk the Corinthians out of boasting in men in favor of boasting in God (1:29, 31) and having a humble respect for the gospel.[185] Inherent is a sharp rebuke: *For all of the reasons which I just gave you, do not be deceived!*

3:21b-23

In this world, the human instinct is to choose a leader, follow him right or wrong, deprecate followers of other groups – or maneuver other groups for one's own ends – and gain victory over other people. The Christian, on the other hand, has both the right and the responsibility to enjoy the ministry of all God's servants. In God's kingdom **all things are yours, whether Paul or Apollos or Cephas**. But Paul goes beyond these human servants to a truly cosmic vision: the Christian is the heir of all, of everything that may be name, in this age and the age to come (see also 6:9-10; Rom 8:38-39; Eph 1:21).

"All things are yours" is very similar in wording to certain Stoic slogans, such as the Latin *omnia sapientis sunt* or "all things belong to the wise man" (see Introduction). The Stoic's highest good was independence and self-sufficiency, and a man can gain them if he has wisdom. It may very well be that Paul is taking over a Stoic saying and giving it an ironic twist. In Paul's mouth, "all things are yours" has an entirely different ring to it: the Christian's end is to glorify God and to enjoy the full range of his gifts while surrendering any thought of autonomy in favor of a life of service.

You have Christ, but even more important **you are of Christ**. The language Paul uses here is the same he has used in 1 Cor 1:12 and 3:4, literally "I am of Paul," etc. We might broadly paraphrase Paul's meaning here in a way that I think captures his meaning: *All things are yours. That is, everyone of you may claim that "I am of Paul/follow Paul" and at the same time "I am of Apollos" and of course "I am of Cephas," because really your fundamental identity is "I am of Christ," and Christ says in effect, "you are mine and I am of God."*

This means that Paul uses the plural of "you" for a purpose. A Christian cannot claim to have Christ without at the same time affirming that all Christians have Christ. He will later develop this same though in 1 Cor 12:3 – "no one can say 'Jesus is Lord,' except by the Holy Spirit." That is to say that if your fellow Christian confesses Jesus as Lord, he or she has the Spirit; if you experience the Spirit's work, you are under divine obligation to affirm his work in others.

---

[184] A very few witnesses correct the text back to "of men" or better "of human beings" (*anthrōpōn*).
[185] So Thiselton. So also the rendering of NRSV: "Let no one boast in human *leaders*."

The phrase **and Christ is of God** has caused some to stumble, as if it said that Christ is less than divine (see too our discussion of 11:3 and 15:28). But nothing of that sort need be found here. Rather, Christ is "the Lord's Christ," a messianic title (see Luke 2:26), likewise "the Christ of God" (Luke 23:35). Paul means to say that to be in Christ is to be in God and to have access to him, as in the highly trinitarian statement of Eph 2:18 – "For through [Christ] we both have access to the Father by one Spirit." To be in God means to be given what only God knows, what no human eye could perceive (1 Cor 2:9, 16), and this must be only through Christ and through the Spirit. It is the unity of God's work in the world, and thus the unity of God's people, that Paul has in view in 3:23.

It may be that Paul is offering a rejoinder to the Christ party ("I follow Christ," 1:12), also in 3:5 and 4:1. First, God himself has chosen to use these human instruments in his work, and they should be accorded the Corinthians' full attention. Second, Paul sweeps away all claims that one group or another – especially if that group is a faction – is uniquely the people who have Christ.

Application: Accept all teachers of sound doctrine 3:21-23

One day you bring me a large, beautiful box of chocolates. There are all kinds, too, every type imaginable: some with nuts or cookies or caramel; some with raisins or cherries or other fruits; some with dark or light or white chocolate or a mixture. It's the wide variety that makes it so impressive – and probably expensive – a gift.

But what do I do? I bite into one at a time, and not finding what I like I look for another. Not only that, but I'm rude enough to spit the candy into the trash can while you watch, and make a face of disgust. I don't even bother tasting the white ones before throwing them away. *I only like the ones with dark chocolate*, I say, glaring as if I blame you for not giving me just those. Chocolate dribbles down from my mouth as I spit out one after another of the expensive candies. I make loud satisfied noises when I gobble up the kind that I like.

I have a suspicion that we do the same thing with God's gifts. He sends our way a wide variety of his servants. He sends a pastor who is not a deep preacher but whose specialty is visiting the sick and helping the needy. He sends other people who write all sorts of good books. He sends us teachers, all of them different. I am not speaking here, of course, of false teachers or deceivers, but of the various true servants of God.

The God who gave Paul to the church of Corinth also gave Apollos and Cephas and others (1 Cor 3:22); to reject one of God's faithful servants was to reject the gift of God. This was the sin of Diotrophes in 3 John 9-10: he discriminated against sound teachers who were not part of his power circle, apparently because it pleased him to exercise his authority and increase his own status. How foolish for the Corinthians to focus on an Apollos and to depreciate the two apostles that God has sent them. The Paulinists too should be sitting at the feet of Cephas and Apollos and thus enjoying the full richness of God's gifts. Those who delight in the seed planter should affirm the waterer too, or rather, honor the Master who has sent both planter and waterer.

Of course, in our experience not everyone is a Paul, a Peter or an Apollos. There are plenty of unpleasant teachers and poor writers and neglectful pastors. But let us make very sure that we show appreciation for all the things God gifts us by intentionally enjoying each of them as much as is possible.

This is not just true for a single congregation; it is applicable from church to church and from denomination to denomination. If we are Baptists, let us also learn as much as we can from our brothers in the Assemblies of God. If we are Pentecostal, let us also avail ourselves of those famous Presbyterian theologians. If we are independent congregations, let us appreciate denominations, and vice versa. Let's not be so proud that we cannot admit that others might have God's Spirit too. "So then, no more boasting about men! All things are yours, whether Paul or Apollos or Cephas..." (3:21-22). Let us open our hearts to all of God's gifts to us, not just the ones that meet our refined personal standards.

b. Have the right attitude toward the apostles 4:1-5

4:1

The Greek text steers us to a new application of what has been said; *houtōs* in the NIV is **so then**; some versions leave it untranslated. Paul's point is that, in light of what he has said in the previous section, he Corinthians must have the right estimation of God's apostles, his "envoys." This is a theme that will dominate 2 Corinthians, although in that letter the arrival of new false teachers adds a new element.

And so the next exhortation is that they **regard us** ("us," not just Paul) as **servants** whom Christ has sent into his field to work.[186] They are servants, but because they have Christ as their master, they should be listened to. The apostles are also **entrusted**, they are literally "stewards" (*oikonomoi*) of the **mysteries of God**.[187] Paul uses language that is very similar to that of contemporary mystery religions, where certain officers would guard the secret knowledge from outsiders. Yet the mysteries of which Paul is thinking are not esoteric knowledge that an officer would impart to a novice. It is information that God himself must reveal, else it remains unknowable.[188] These are the same mysteries that we have seen in 2:7ff., most importantly, that God reveals himself in a crucified Messiah. The revelation of Christ is a public gospel, not a secret one.[189] The apostles were not doling out obscure tidbits to the few initiated. As Jesus himself had said, "What you have said in the dark will be heard in the daylight, and what you have whispered in the ear in the inner rooms will be proclaimed from the roofs" (Luke 12:3).

---

[186] "Servants" here is from *hupēretēs*, rather than the synonymous *diakonoi* used in 3:5. Much has been made of the supposed deeper meaning of *hupēretēs*, which centuries before had *sometimes* been used of "under-rowers," that is, the lowest of the three banks of rowers on a trireme. In Paul's day this imagery of there rowers was long forgotten. The translation "servants" of the NIV (and ESV, NLT, NASB, etc.) is entirely suitable. Josephus used the term for temple workers (*Wars* 2.15 §321). Relevant for 1 Cor 4:1, Josephus chides the Israelites for despising the leadership of Moses, "servant [*hupēretēs*] of God" (*Antiquities* 3.1 §16). See also Ignatius, *Polycarp* 6.1 – "Train together with one another: struggle together, run together, suffer together, rest together, get up together, as God's managers, assistants, and *servants*."

[187] Although Origen (Bray, 37) says that steward and servant are two very different roles.

[188] See G. Finkenrath, "*mustērion*," *NIDNTT* 3:501-06.

[189] Of course, this goes directly contrary to what the later Gnostics would try to do, insisting that there was one level of truth for the *psuchikoi* (normal Christians) and another higher one for the *pneumatikoi* (the Gnostics). For example, note the tone of the preface to the *Gospel of Thomas*: "These are the secret sayings that the living Jesus spoke and Didymos Judas Thomas recorded."

4:2

The key virtue for **those who have been given a trust** is not to be clever or appealing or original, but rather to **prove faithful**. This word "faithful" (*pistos*) is a favorite Pauline adjective for his co-workers (4:17, 7:25). Presumably, a faithful servant will not only convey the data of the gospel with accuracy, but will also model the gospel by rejecting personal glory in favor of Christ. He or she will dole the mysteries freely to all comers, avoid partisanship and self-aggrandizement – that is, he will build with gold, silver and precious stones (3:12).

4:3

Lest people should imagine Paul to be unworthy, he implies that he believes himself to be faithful. But first he argues that his worth is not to be decided or judged (*anakrinō*, as in 2:14-15 and 9:3) **by you or by any human court**. Of course, Paul did sometimes find himself before tribunals. The Roman governor Gallio (Acts 18:12-17) listened impatiently to charges against Paul and then threw out the case as some religious quarrel that had nothing to do with Roman law. Gallio was "of the world," and could not judge between the truths of Paul and those of his opponents. Nor could Paul's worth be judged by a vote by "you" (plural), the Corinthians.

In fact, come to think of it, isn't Paul himself a "human court" in some sense? For that reason **I do not even judge myself**. It is likely that Paul is devaluing a common practice of Stoicism, the movement that was so popular in Corinth. Part of the Stoic ethos was to practice self-examination. Look into your heart and mind, said the Stoic, as a daily practice, and the wise man can be confident that he will be able to truly discern his motives and actions and continue in them or correct them.[190] Paul for his part has examined his conscience (4:4). Nevertheless, he knows how self-deceived people may be; he stands in the tradition of Prov 21:2 –

> All a man's ways seem right to him,
> But the LORD weights the heart.

4:4

Paul's conscience is clear, so that is not at issue here.[191] Nevertheless, a clean conscience is not a trustworthy guide, and **that does not make me innocent**. For Paul, **It is the Lord who judges me**. The judgment of a human being is in God's hands, and in the final judgment God will reveal what he alone fully knows. This is the same theme that the apostle has begun in 3:10b-15, "his work will be shown for what it is, because the Day will bring it to light."

4:5

It's all very well to leave judgment in God's hands, but what of 5:3-5, where the church should judge one of its own members now? And what of 6:1-6, where Paul argues that, because Christians will judge angels in the end, therefore they should be able to pass

---

[190] So Hays, *First Corinthians*, 66.
[191] Krister Stendahl makes much of this verse, especially in the light of Phil 3:6 and Rom 7:14, concluding (rightly) that Paul was not ridden with guilt, either as a Jew or Christian, and that he was blessed with a "robust conscience." See Krister Stendahl, "The apostle Paul and the introspective conscience of the West," in *Paul among Jews and gentiles* (Philadelphia: Fortress, 1976).

judgment on one another in this age? In both cases, the fact of God's coming tribunal is the basis (even more, the imperative) for judging other Christians in this age. But has Paul set up a double standard when he says that in his own case the should **judge nothing before the appointed time**? May all Christians be tried by the church, but only Paul's verdict left pending until Doomsday?

As Thiselton points out, Paul is hardly urging a "suspension of all judgment."[192] The tension between *judging now* and *leaving judgment with God* is due to the circumstances in Corinth; Paul knows that he is dealing with worldly people. We do not know how he would have reacted had Apollos and Cephas taken him aside to rebuke him for sin or some doctrinal fault. No, his point here is as follows: *I'm not going to submit my work to any merely human court for its opinion; you Corinthians too tend to think like "mere men" and would only judge an apostle by standards of the world. I (who am spiritual) have examined myself and found nothing; more than that, even I do not rely on my own conscience, which could be deceiving me – God is the higher judge.*

Paul backs up this point with traditional language of divine judgment, influenced by Jewish Scriptures; most important is Jer 17:10 –

> I the LORD search the heart
>   and examine the mind,
> to reward a man according to his conduct,
>   according to what his deeds deserve.

The key here is that **at that time each will receive his praise from God** (as in Matt 25:21). It is the same way for the "rewarded" farm worker of in 3:8 and the "reward" for faithful builders in 3:14.

Application: "Examine yourself" 4:3-5

To an extant Paul knows his own heart (4:4). Yet he cannot "judge himself" in an ultimate way but leaves final judgment to God. As we have seen, he says this because he does not want the Corinthians to judge him. But the apostle was also giving a blow to the conventional wisdom of his culture. It would be normal for the Stoics to spend time at the end of each day, examining their own consciences to see what offence they might have given. They believed themselves to be wise men with the ability to detect error, correct it and avoid it. Paul shows that no-one truly is able to be objective with himself, and that true knowledge comes through divine revelation (1 Cor 2:13). Even Christians may mislead themselves (1 Cor 3:13, 18). For example, a man in Corinth continued in incest and apparently did not feel badly enough to change his lifestyle; in addition, the church allowed his behavior and actually "boasted" (1 Cor 5:1-2).

Paul's point in 1 Cor 4 is that only God can sort out the competing motivations, attitudes, actions, words and thoughts of a human individual, and in the end only he can decide whose work deserves to endure and whose deserves to be conserved in the fire.

In Latin America there is an exaggerated level of optimism about one's ability to know his corazón. *I know it looks like I'm doing wrong...but in my heart, my corazón, in my person of persons, I know that I am pure!* This dangerous idea is far removed from

---

[192] Thiselton, *First Corinthians*, 342.

the truth of the Bible. Paul himself knew of no offense in his heart, but conceded that he could be badly mistaken, and that only God knows these things. Even Paul has to wait until the Day of Judgment to be completely certain of his motivations. This is because sin has an affect not only on the mind, the will, the actions, the emotions, but also "the motives of men's hearts" (1 Cor 4:5).

Many of our Christian leaders have sealed themselves away from others; although they are public figures, they live in isolation. When they are challenged, they interpret that as a challenge against God himself. Their defence is that they will allow only God to judge them; and their hearts are clear. What a perilous route; how many more examples do we need of pastors, supposedly anointed of the Holy Spirit, who deceive themselves and fall into deeper and deeper layers of sin, ignoring all the warnings from their fellow human beings?

How do we avoid this trap? One may suggest the following:

1. Never imagine that the Holy Spirit speaks uniquely to you or even especially to you. The Holy Spirit teaches us in our hearts, but also in and through his church. If another Christian has a word for you, you are obligated to discern it and be helped by it.

2. Don't put your confidence in your own heart. The human heart can be deceptive, even when the Spirit indwells it. God never promised that you individually would have perfect or even decently reliable self-knowledge. This is a thing that not even Paul claimed to possess. You have no way of knowing for certain whether your heart is deceiving you. When Jesus said, "My sheep listen to my voice; I know them, and they follow me" (John 10:27), he was not speaking of a silent inner voice or feeling, but of the fact that his people hear his message and follow him with their lives.

3. Be extremely careful in using the claim *The Lord told me...* Very often, people mean that they have had words run through their mind, thoughts or feelings which they have then interpreted to be a message from God. But how do you, with your busy human mind, which processes thousands and thousands of thoughts per day, know for certain what is from God, what is from Satan, what is from your own imagination? If you say *The Lord told me something and my heart told me it was truly from him*, you are merely adding two weak links together: your mind and your heart.

4. Have around you people who will tell you the truth. You might meet regularly with them so that they may ask you hard questions about your motives and your actions. Many leaders surround themselves with team members who either agree with him or, well, get fired. This means that their salaries and their status depend upon their full agreement with the leader. How then can they be free to state the whole truth? It is much better to also have one or two who are not dependent on you or in competition with you, who will speak to you as a fellow Christian with nothing to gain or lose. John Wesley made much of this discipline. He organized small weekly groups in which the members would "speak each of us in order, freely and plainly, the true state of our souls, with the faults we have committed in thought or deed and the temptations we have felt since our last meeting. The attention grew more personal: "To desire some person among us to speak his own state first, and then to ask the rest, in order, as many and as searching questions as may be, concerning their state, sins, and temptations."[193]

---

[193] See John Wesley, "Rules of the Band Societies," online http://www.godrules.net/library/wesley/274wesley_h8.htm

John Wesley was a firm believer in the Spirit's presence in the believer, but also in the need for other believers to challenge what we say we have in our conscience.

c. Follow the apostles in their humility and suffering rather than in triumphalism 4:6-16

At this point Paul interjects with **brothers**, to switch to more confrontational style. He will show the contrast between the apostles and the triumphalistic Corinthians, by which we mean believers who think they can glide through life as if they were royalty.

4:6

He uses *metaschēmatizō*, which is captured adequately by the NIV with **I have applied these things to myself and Apollos for your benefit.** Still, Paul's intention is not immediately clear. One interpretation, made famous by Chrysostom, is that Paul and Apollos – not to mention Cephas – were not the heroes around which parties had formed; rather, their names were merely substitutes for the real partisan leaders, whom Paul did not want to mention by name so as not to shame them.[194] According to this reading, the groups in 1:12 are followers of unnamed Corinthians. The better interpretation is that **to myself and Apollos** means that he and Apollos really did have their followings. Thus he means: *I have shown you an illustration of how Apollos and I worked in unity in the church in chapter 3*.[195] The Corinthians must **learn** from these two men how one serves God in truth.

The next problem is his purpose, **learn from us the meaning of the saying, "Do not go beyond what is written."** Go beyond what is written where, exactly? Thiselton describes seven possibilities.[196] The best interpretation is that it refers to what is written in the Old Testament, specifically the many references from Jeremiah, Job, Psalms and in particular Isaiah that Paul has used in the previous chapters (see our comments on 1:19, 31; 2:9, 16; 3:19, 20).[197] The Bible itself gives the Corinthians guidelines about fallible human wisdom *versus* God's truth.

With **take pride**, Paul uses one of his favorite words in 1 Corinthians, *phusioō*, which can also mean "puffed up" (see the other occurrences of the Greek verb in 4:18, 19, 5:2, 8:1, 13:4; cf. Col 2:18[198]). Here there sin is proud partisanship, to **take pride in**

---

[194] Chrysostom, *i ad Corinthios* 12.1 – "So long as there was need of expressions as harsh as these, he refrained from drawing up the curtain, and went on arguing as if he were himself the person to whom they were addressed; in order that the dignity of the persons censured tending to counteract the censurers, no room might be left for flying out in wrath at the charges. But when the time came for a gentler process, then he strips it off, and removes the mask, and shows the persons concealed by the appellation of Paul and Apollos. And on this account he said, 'These things, brethren, I have transferred in a figure unto myself and Apollos.'"

[195] So Barrett; see the full discussion by Thiselton, *First Corinthians*, 348-51.

[196] Thiselton, *First Corinthians*, 351-56. Conzelmann, *1 Corinthians*, 85, thinks the reference is "unintelligible."

[197] So Fee, *First Corinthians*, 167-68; Hays, *First Corinthians*, 69; Schrage; Barrett, *First Corinthians*, 106-07.

[198] See the use of "puffed up" (*phusioō*) in the letters of Ignatius, for example: *Smyraeans* 6.1 – "'The one who accepts this, let him accept it.' Do not let a high position make anyone proud, for faith and love are everything; nothing is preferable to them"; *Trallians* 7.1 – "Therefore be on your guard against such [heretics]. And you will be, provided that you are not puffed up with pride and that you cling inseparably to

one man over against another, that is, being for some leader and thus against the others, whether these leaders are in Corinth or from without.

4:7

Now Paul will speak, using the strong language of Greco-Roman diatribe, which is "distinguished by its dialogical orientation, in which questions and answers are given by the speaker and his interlocutor (whether hypothetical or real)."[199] Paul asks the three questions of 1 Cor 4:7, not to get answers, but to challenge them to think about their incorrect behavior: *Why are you so special? Why do you think the rules apply to all others, but not to yourselves?*

The second rhetorical question is one of the best statements about Christian humility in the Scriptures: **What do you have that you did not receive?** God gave them salvation; the Spirit; the spiritual gifts; even their teachers, whether they are apostles or others. The Corinthians in turn had brought nothing of value to salvation (6:9-10). So then, how can they have cultivated this fine degree of discrimination between one spiritual gift and another (1 Cor 12), between one field worker and another?

4:8

Paul is now at his most ironic. The first three sentences may be translated as statements (most versions) or as rhetorical questions; the meaning is not changed thereby. The Corinthians feel themselves full and rich and kingly, and so look down on Paul and the others, a theme that will resurface in 2 Corinthians. But why were they thinking this way, and what means Paul's answer?

We must take issue with a popular interpretation, according to which their problem was not simply attitudinal, but theological. They thought, says the hypothesis of "over-realized eschatology," that they didn't have to wait for Jesus' return, that they had already entered the eschatological realm and in a real sense **have become kings**.[200] We have concluded already that this is based on a misreading of the epistle, which everywhere assumes that the Corinthians had a strong future eschatology (see Introduction), despite the tendency of a few to reject the eschatological resurrection.

On the contrary, the Corinthians were triumphalistic and divisive through the influence of local philosophy.[201] In fact, Stoics had for centuries used the specific terms "rich," "satiated" and "king" to describe the philosophical man, the one has learned to be independent and self-sufficient through being wise. For example: "I alone am rich; I alone am king in the world."[202] Some Corinthians rejoiced in their own wisdom and the supposed power it gave them – the power to be individualistic and thus unloving – and despised Paul who spoke poorly, who suffered much, and who kept emphasizing the crucifixion. For that reason, the best parallel to 4:8 is Rev 3:17 ("You say, 'I am rich; I

Jesus Christ and to the bishop and to the commandments of the apostles."

[199] Stanley E. Porter, *Handbook of classical rhetoric in the Hellenistic Period, 330 B.C.-A.D. 400* (Leiden: Brill, 1997), 575. Rom 2-3 contain a long passage of "diatribe."

[200] Conzelmann, *1 Corinthians*, 87-88; Fee, *First Corinthians*, 172-73; Wendland, *An die Korinther*, 34-35; Thiselton, *First Corinthians*, 357. Contra Garland, *1 Corinthians*, 137-39.

[201] So Nicoll, *First Corinthians*, 2:800-01; Hays, *First Corinthians*, 70.

[202] Thiselton, *First Corinthians*, 357; Schrage, *An die Korinther*, 1:338; Fee, *First Corinthians*, 174-75; J. Weiss, *Der erste Korintherbrief* (2nd ed.; Göttingen: Vandenhoeck & Ruprecht, 1910), 107. Many commentators mention the philosophical parallels to 4:8, but do not draw out the implications, that the main problem is that Corinth had been infected, not with heresy, but with popular notions of self-sufficiency.

have acquired wealth and do not need a thing.' But you do not realize that you are wretched, pitiful, poor, blind and naked"). Like the Corinthians, the Laodiceans were arrogant, not because of some fault in their eschatology, but because of the common reasons of pride and complacency.

What means Paul's response? He reminds them of what the future holds: *Oh that you were kings, because by that time we'd be kings too and could lay down this apostolic suffering!* This will take place when each "will receive his reward" (3:14). At the resurrection, Paul says in another place, the believer will "reign" with Christ (2 Tim 2:11-12).

4:9

Paul makes himself and the other apostles models, taking up the plural again: **God has put us apostles on display at the end of the procession**. They are on special display for their suffering. Paul speaks of being a **spectacle**; the Greek word *theatron* may refer to a show in the arena or better, a parade of triumph (see the same word in 2 Cor 2:14-16). A triumph to honor a victorious Roman general was made up of marching soldiers, but also booty and prisoners that the general had brought back to Rome to show off; most epic movies about Roman times include one of these impressive spectacles! At the end of the parade would come the foreign insurgents, marching in chains or locked in cages, brought all that distance only to be executed. That's what the apostolic lifestyle is like, says Paul. We come last, condemned to die, a spectacle to be displayed to the **universe**, to be mocked **to angels as well as to men**. Paul leaves unspoken the implication that, most cruelly, the apostles are also mocked by arrogant Christians.

4:10

Paul offers three pairs of contrasts, glancing backward at previous themes as he ties this all up: fools/wise, weak/strong, honored/dishonored. Here he goes beyond the careful reasonings of chapters 1-3 and becomes in the *peroratio* ironical and even sarcastic: *you claim to be wise, strong and honored, but as I've told you before, we all know that you are not.*

4:11-13

Paul goes on to give a list of his sufferings, a type of argument that comes to full flower in 2 Cor 11:16-12:10. As an itinerant missionary, Paul knew well the perils of travel: hunger, thirst, heat, cold, exhaustion and physical danger. We should note that the translation "we are naked" (KJV) is not the best English equivalent; the verb *gumniteuō* means to go without adequate clothing, especially during inclement weather (see the use of the cognate noun *gumnotēs* in 2 Cor 11:27): hence "we are inadequately dressed" or in the NIV paraphrases it, **we are in rags**. According to 4:12a he works with his own hands. In Jewish circles this was considered honorable for a rabbi, but in philosophical circles it was a sign of low social station; if an instructor could not raise money through his teaching, he was considered an embarrassing failure (see comments on 9:6).[203]

In 4:12b-13a the abuse is both physical and verbal. This time Paul contrasts the way the apostles are treated and their response in turn, in a style reminiscent of the Sermon on the Mount, where Jesus taught:

---

[203] See also Martin, *The Corinthian body*, 51.

> Blessed are those who are persecuted because of righteousness,
>   for theirs is the kingdom of heaven.
> Blessed are you when people insult you, persecute you
>   and falsely say all kinds of evil against you because of me. (Matt 5:10-11)

4:13b has a statement that is a difficult to translate, although the general sense is clear enough. Paul refers to the apostles as **the scum of the earth** (*perikatharma*) and **refuse of the world** (*peripsēma*). He probably means the two words as synonyms. Since the removal of **scum** is a symbol of atonement in Prov 21:18 LXX ("and a lawless one is the refuse of a righteous one"), some have thought that *perikatharma* contains the idea of an expiatory sacrifice,[204] meaning that there might be a parallel in Col 1:24. Nevertheless, the fact that Paul goes on to use *peripsēma* as a synonym, a word with no hint of sacrifice, seems to indicate that these are mere terms for trash in general; the word is not to be pressed further.[205]

Application: Suffering for Christ 4:9-13

No-one likes to suffer. If one has a religion, at the very least one wants it to alleviate human anxiety. Yet in the apostolic faith, to follow Jesus may involve more pain and suffering in this life than if we had stayed where we were. If Paul had remained a rabbi, he would never have received the beatings that were his constant lot in life.

There is a critical point to be made in 4:16 – "Therefore I urge you to imitate me." That is, the Corinthians should follow Paul and the other apostles even to the point of suffering for the name of Christ. This means that the apostles are not special cases. They do not suffer because they are apostles; they suffer because all Christians suffer (see 1 Thess 2:14), and the apostles happen to be prime examples of how all Christians are to live.

For some Christians there is a fundamental contradiction here. They wish to say that suffering is due to a lack of faith. All sickness and pain may be vanquished by a *rhēma*, the spoken word of faith.[206] But what does 1 Cor 4:8 say? On the one hand are the Corinthians, who are speaking with complete positiveness of their wealth and power. According to the *rhēma* doctrine, the boastful Corinthians were doing precisely the right thing: Paul should have heartily commended them for their ability to speak riches and victory into existence. But what do we read? Paul rebukes them for their arrogance. He also speaks aloud and openly of his own suffering and illness. Do we really wish to say that Paul was not deep enough to understand the principle of faith? That it was his fault that he suffered poverty, because that is what he spoke into existence? Not at all: in the

---

[204] Hans Lietzmann and W. G. Kümmel, *An die Korinther I/II*, HNT 9 (4th ed.; Tübingen: Mohr, 1949), 21.
[205] As affirm Fee, *First Corinthians*, 180; Thiselton, *First Corinthians*, 364-65. Ignatius uses *peripsēma* of himself in *Ephesians* 18.1 – "My spirit is a humble sacrifice for the cross," and perhaps with a sacrificial idea in 8.1.
[206] Likewise, there are some who detect the prosperity doctrine in 2 Cor 2:14 – "thanks be to God, who always leads us in triumphal procession in Christ." But the context, like that of 1 Cor 4, has to do with the *sufferings* of the apostles, that were so extreme that it seemed like they were in a death march to their own execution. That is, "triumph" is defined not as prosperity, but faithful suffering that leads to the spread of the gospel.

end it is the apostle who is correct and exemplary, willing to accept poverty and suffering for his Lord.

This prayer nicely captures Paul's teaching:

> O God, who by the passion of thy blessed Son didst make an instrument of shameful death to be unto us the means of life: Grant us so to glory in the cross of Christ, that we may gladly suffer shame and loss for the sake of thy Son our Savior Jesus Christ; who liveth and reigneth with thee and the Holy Spirit, one God, for ever and ever. Amen.[207]

4:14

Paul assures them that **I am not writing this to shame you, but to warn you**. Because his language has been strong, he ends his rebuke with a loving embrace and a reminder to the Corinthians that they are **as my dear children**. He uses *teknon*, which does not have the connotation of being small children, as does the "infants" (*nēpios*) of 3:1. His words have not been a rejection or an attempt to make them look foolish, but the sort of admonishment a good father gives to his children.

4:15

Paul continues the father-children imagery with a reminder that he had an unusual role in their Christian experience: **I became your father** (or "I begot you") in the gospel when he came to initially preach Christ (see 1 Cor 3:6ff.).[208] In this Paul breaks a bit with his earlier remarks that all teachers are equal: compared with Paul the other servants take second place, at least in Corinth. In 3:10, Paul is one builder among many, but he alone has the role of the "expert builder" who does more than lay the foundation: in effect, he is indirectly responsible for whatever subsequently happens in the church. Compared with him the others are **guardians**, people of great value, but not their father. Very key to Paul's authority is that he begot them **through the gospel** – that is, not through a show of wisdom, not through philosophy, but through the gospel of the cross (2:2).

4:16

Paul states **I urge you to imitate me**, as their father. A few inferior manuscripts add the phrase "as I imitate Christ;" it was inadvertently placed here by a scribe who was thinking of 1 Cor 11:1. The educational method of *mimēsis* (learning by imitation of an example) was fundamental for Paul, as it was in the Greco-Roman and Jewish worlds of his day. In the Western university system, the highest goal is to create independent learners who will go beyond their instructors and even contradict them. In the ancient system the goal was to turn out disciples or imitators, whether of a rabbi or a philosophical sage.[209]

And so he concludes the *peroratio* with fatherly encouragement: *Be like me, your father, and live free of "wisdom" and contentions just as I, Paul, did when I walked*

---

[207] The prayer for Tuesday of Holy Week from the Book of Common Prayer, see online http://justus.anglican.org/resources/bio/243.html.
[208] Calvin, *First Corinthians*, 1:167-72, emphasizes the sacrifices and involvement of a father.
[209] See Conzelmann, *1 Corinthians*, 92.

among you.

5. Itinerario y Conclusion: Paul will judge the arrogant Corinthians when he comes, so they should prepare themselves 4:17-21

It was typical of epistles to follow the *peroratio* with an *itinerario*, that is, a description of the writer's travel plans. Although this is not the end of 1 Corinthians, Paul closes this section with some concrete plans, showing how he hopes to right the wrongs of their relationship.

4:17

I am sending to you Timothy, who is **faithful**, just as Paul is in 4:2. The aorist tense (literally, "I sent Timothy to you") could be a so-called "epistolary aorist," with the meaning "I'm sending Timothy to you, bringing this letter;" or it could refer to a past action, that "Timothy has already left, but hadn't reached you by the time you Corinthians wrote to me."[210] The fact that Timothy is not mentioned in 1 Cor 1:1 implies he had left before Paul penned 1 Corinthians; also, in 16:10 he writes "if Timothy comes." The order seems to be that Timothy left Paul to visit several churches (Acts 19:22 mentions Macedonia), including, eventually, Corinth; Paul then wrote 1 Corinthians, to inform them that his assistant was on his way.

The role of Timothy is part and parcel with the method of teaching by imitation (otherwise known as *mimēsis*) of 4:16. Timothy will remind them of what Paul would have done, not only with his words but with his own exemplary behavior. At some later point, but before 2 Corinthians, Paul sent Titus to Corinth for similar reasons, and Titus was an excellent role model too: "I urged Titus to go to you and I sent our brother with him. Titus did not exploit you, did he? Did we not act in the same spirit and follow the same course?" (2 Cor 12:18).[211] Paul points out here that the Corinthians do not have to follow a stricter set of rules than do the other churches; they hear what **agrees with what I teach everywhere in every** church (see our comments on 1 Cor 1:2).

4:18

The Corinthians are frequently puffed up (from *phusioō*), and at this point some **have become arrogant**, smirking that Paul the "loser" would not dare come back to Corinth. Although some (most?) Corinthians still honored Paul, it was easier in his absence to negate his influence. Timothy's upcoming visit (4:17) will help rectify that, as presumably will whoever was sent with 1 Corinthians.

4:19

Nevertheless, **I will come to you very soon, if the Lord is willing**. Paul had the apostolic trait of tenacity, refusing to quit the field even at the cost of considerable

---

[210] So the majority of commentators, for example, Conzelmann, *1 Corinthians*, 92, 297; Barrett, *First Corinthians*, 116.
[211] He met up with Titus again in Macedonia (2 Cor 2:12-13, 7:5-16).

personal shame (cf. Galatians, Colossians, and especially 2 Corinthians). The Corinthians probably won't be following Paul's style of ministry, as described in 1 Cor 2:4 – "My message and my preaching were not with wise and persuasive words, but with a demonstration of the Spirit's power." In contrast, he suspects that his opponents in the city are all high talk, mere words and worldly attractiveness. The GNB is helpful here: "Then I will find out if the ones who are doing all this bragging really have any power." As in 2:4 there are two ways of interpreting what Paul means by **power**: one interpretation is, *Does their speech lead to the God-given divine results of conversion and growth?*[212] The better interpretation, as in 2:4, is that Paul is referring to apostolic miracles, *Is their ministry just empty words, or does God do miracles to back up what they say?*[213] These are the signs that he performed in Corinth: "The things that mark an apostle – signs, wonders and miracles – were done among you with great perseverance" (2 Cor 12:12). He implies in 2 Cor 12:11 that the "super-apostles" cannot do miracles. The same test and the same logic work here, if we may paraphrase his point:

We are agreed that I performed miraculous signs among you;
  therefore, God has confirmed my message.
I imagine that those "wise men" among you are doing no miracles;
  therefore, is this not one more proof they are *not* doing the work of God?

Once more, it is the true gospel (divinely revealed, cross-centered, of the Spirit) pitted against the false wisdom (rationalistic, philosophically sophisticated, and verbose).

4:20

After all, **the kingdom of God is not a matter of talk** (that is, fancy rhetoric) **but of power** that comes from the Spirit. This statement about the kingdom is surprising, coming as it does without warning. The use of **kingdom** here may have been suggested by the Corinthians, who "have become kings" (4:8).

The kingdom of God is the truth that God would break into human history and rule over his creation anew. He would use his divine power to impose justice and to root out and judge all evil. In the 19th century there was a strong tendency to picture the kingdom as an inner sense of God's kingliness.[214] But this interpretation turns the coming of God in power into an individualized experience. It is better to understand God's kingdom as the unleashing of God's power that began in the coming of Christ and will be fully realized at Christ's coming.

In all of Paul's letters, there are perhaps 14 references to God's kingdom (*basileia*), the bulk of which (1 Thess 2:12, 2 Thess 1:5, Gal 5:21, 1 Cor 6:9-10, 15:50, Eph 5:5; see also Acts 14:22) derive from the tradition of "inheriting the kingdom" and refer to the eschatological coming of God as king (see also 1 Cor 15:24).

Here the apostle uses a different formula, as he does in Rom 14:17 – "For the kingdom of God is not a matter of eating and drinking, but of righteousness, peace and

---

[212] So Schrage, *An die Korinther*, 1:362.
[213] So Chrysostom, *i ad Corinthios* 14.3 who interprets it as "that our teaching is divine and really announces the Kingdom of Heaven we give the greater proof, namely, our signs which we work by the power of the Spirit." Hays, *First Corinthians*, 75, likens 4:19 with Elijah's contest with the priests of Baal in 1 Reyes 18; only the true prophet could invoke fire from heaven.
[214] Godet, *First Corinthians*, 236: "the Kingdom of God in the spiritual sense in which it already exists in the souls of the believers."

joy in the Holy Spirit." In Romans, he speaks of the power of God which manifests itself in the Spirit's work since Pentecost, in advance of the future kingdom; in 1 Cor 4:20, the Spirit does miracles, right now in this age.

The most natural interpretation of the present tense "is" in Rom 14:17 (the present tense is implicit in 1 Cor 4:20) is that the kingdom is in some manner present. The end has not arrived, but the death, resurrection and ascension of Christ mean that he has given his people the Holy Spirit in anticipation of the future age.

Some scholars deny that Paul taught the presence of the kingdom.[215] But he, like Jesus (see Matt 12:28), used *basileia* and other kingdom language to refer both to a future realm and also to God's present acts as King. That is why the "gospel of the kingdom of God" is a message that includes both the present and eschatological acts of the King (see Acts 19:8, 20:25, 28:23, 31; Col 4:11; also Acts 1:3, 8:12).

In 1 Cor 4:20 and Rom 14:17, Paul appeals to the kingdom in order to gauge what truly matters and what does not in the eyes of God.[216] He uses an approach that is found in the Septuagint:

> 1 Mac 3:19 – In is not on the size of the army
> that victory in battle depends,
> but strength comes from Heaven.

In two other passages, Paul uses the same logic:

> 1 Cor 7:19 – Circumcision is nothing, and uncircumcision is nothing;
> but obeying the commandments of God is everything.

> Gal 6:15 – For neither circumcision nor uncircumcision is anything;
> but a new creation is everything!

Given Paul's use of **the kingdom of God** as a present reality in 4:20, it would be surprising if the Corinthians had an over-realized view of the kingdom of God, that is, that their theology lessened or eliminated the futurity of the kingdom in favor of a purely present kingdom. In that case, Paul would be playing right into their hands, giving the false teachers further ammunition. It is better to take this reference in the context of 1 Cor 2:6-13 – only in the divine revelation of the cross can we hope to understand the mind of God (2:11-12). And, if God as King has truly broken through into history to subvert human wisdom, then it is no wonder if we encounter a battle of the words of the old age *versus* the power that comes through the cross message.

Application: What happens when we replace the kingdom of God with mere chatter? 4:20

The kingdom of God is not about talk, but about power. In Corinth this meant that some

---

[215] E. g., Kümmel, 173, who dissents with Lietzmann's "present kingdom" viewpoint, found in Lietzmann and Kümmel, *An die Korinther*, 22.
[216] See Gary S. Shogren, "Is the Kingdom of God about eating and drinking or isn't it? (Romans 14:17)," *NovT* 42.3 (2000): 238-256. Also Ladd, *Theology*, 451.

were using fine language and educated-sounding expressions to build themselves up. For his part, Paul cared little for status and concentrated instead on the cross-gospel and in showing forth God's power in apostolic miracles and signs.

Let us start with some obvious parallels and then move to the less obvious:

1. Status-seeking through language which signals our formal education

Paul lived in an age unlike our electronic culture, in which poor grammar and lack of polish are thought to come from "naturalness of speech." He lived in an age that valued eloquence, the ability to supply an apt quotation, a rich vocabulary and impressive logic. Schoolboys learned rhetoric, and public speeches were common events. Orators competed for prizes.

Was Paul denigrating an education in rhetoric in order to compensate for his own poor skills? Almost certainly not. In fact, his educational credentials were remarkable, and his letters show a deep understanding of the Scriptures and the philosophical currents of his day. But he does argue in 1:17 and here in 4:20 that eloquence can detract from the simple gospel and even be a liability to the kingdom of God.

Take as an example the professor who is asked a question for which he has no answer; his defense against shame might be to use big words and concepts to confuse the student! How unlike our Master, whose teachings were given in clear, concise terms, with common words, with helpful repetition, so that even the dullest disciple could follow him.

On the other hand, I have consistently observed that it is not the truly wise and knowledgeable who speak to overwhelm and impress. Rather, the boastful ones are more often the pretenders, those whose education and intellect is mediocre but who therefore work harder to impress their hearers that they are the mental equal of any. Surprisingly, in the church the clearest minds and the deepest thinkers I have met are brothers and sisters of humility. One reason is that the more one studies – as in a good PhD program – the more one realizes how ignorant he or she is about a hundred different topics. In a Christian, advanced study should produce humility, reasonableness, charity and openness to learning more. In the hands of the Spirit a good intellect will be the friend, not the enemy, of Christian humility.

In Paul's day, some slaves were given a good education in order to make them more valuable to their masters. It was not at all uncommon to run into professors or doctors or philosophers who were owned by someone else. So it is with Christ: a good education, even it came at great cost to you, is a gift as much as having a handsome face or a good family name or the gift of tongues. Our learning is only for the purpose of making us better slaves.

2. Status-seeking through language calculated to remind others of our social class

In many cultures one's class may be identified by speech patterns. A person of a higher status has a better vocabulary, can quote famous books or thinkers, has a smoother accent, and "sounds" wealthy. Great Britain, for example, traditionally had a class system, and people were divided by accent.

In this context, Paul might have said something like this: for the Christ, what matters is what kind of servant he is, and that depends on how powerfully the Spirit uses him. *I, Paul, speak well, but what does it matter?* If someone speaks like a rustic, but can do miracles of healing, and brings people to the Lord, and manifests the Spirit's fruits, then that is where the kingdom of God is operating. And if a person speaks like a university graduate and uses his pronouns properly in every case and speaks lovely English, what does it matter if that is all that he has to offer?

There is an equal and opposite sin. Some Christians affect a low-class accent for the opposite reason: *Once it is granted that the Spirit blesses through the poor, and if I speak with poor grammar and "country" expressions, then people will naturally assume that I am more authentically spiritual.* It is the game of anti-status – more popular in the USA than in Europe or South America – to try to convince people how humble and poor and ignorant was your background, in order to impress them with what you have become. This too is boasting and sin, and it grieves the Spirit.

3. Status-seeking through mere words about the Spirit

We come then to a form of status-seeking that is rampant in our continent. Paul might have put it like this:

> It is not talking about the Spirit's power
> but the real manifestation of it
>   that reveals the kingdom of God.

Boasting of the Spirit's power in itself is not wrong – Paul did the same thing in 1 Cor 4:19-20, after all – but it may be deceptive. Let us think of words *versus* deeds: a woman in a wheelchair is healed not when the preacher shouts; not when he paces back and forth and uses his special formula for healing; not when she declares that she has faith to be healed; not when the congregation calls out encouragement; not when she testifies about the anointing of the preacher; not when the preacher tells other churches about the remarkable things the Lord is doing; not when others whisper that this ministry is specially blessed. These are words – good words, perhaps, but only words. In themselves they are not "the kingdom of God." The power of the kingdom of God is to be found in *the healing itself.* When this lady shows measurable improvement – not just momentarily feeling better – and the doctor affirms that she has been changed, then the kingdom of God has been made manifest. (By the way, this is why the Christian should be bold about going to a doctor to confirm a healing. The results of God's healings are visible and evident to an outsider). Paul might have said, *I would rather heal one person in the power of the Holy Spirit than expend 10,000 words telling you how mightily God blesses my ministry.* For a pastor, it's better to invest time in quietly visiting the sick (James 5:14-16) and laying hands on five people and see some of them healed than to spend those same hours talking about healing. If this temptation exists in local congregations, how much greater it is when the preacher is on television. There he stands, with reams of prayer requests stacked before him, each page, he tells you, telling of a miracle that came from his anointed ministry. Remember the next time you watch an hour of talking about miracles on television, that the kingdom of God has little to do with words, but much to do with powerful deeds.

Likewise, the devil is not driven out of a person when we boast about him being driven out, or shout, or testify, or write books or give conferences; rather, he is driven out, well, when he is driven out.

4. Status-seeking through special jargon

It is not a uniquely modern problem, but I suspect that it has grown in the last generation: that is, people who seek status and control by using the latest theological, sociological or managerial models and terminology to describe the Lord's work. Each one with its special conferences and books and videos. But let us remember that the kingdom of God is not revealed by using the language or categories of some group or another. The kingdom of God shows itself through powerful manifestations of evangelism or discipleship.

4:21

He ends once more with paternal language. Do they want Father Paul to arrive to administer a spanking or do they want him to be peaceable? It's up to the Corinthians.

His travel plans were to stir up further controversy. The Corinthians had apparently understood that Paul was going directly to Achaia from Ephesus. In fact, he went north to Troas, to Macedonia, and only then south to Achaia and Corinth. This led to charges that he was vacillating (2 Cor 1:12-2:4).

We know from 2 Corinthians something of what happened next. 2 Cor 2:1 refers to a "painful visit" and a follow-up letter, now lost (see Introduction). This visit seems to have been designed to be brief, and not part of his regular travel plans. He caused them pain (2 Cor 2:2), implying that he had to bring out the **stick**; this caused hard feelings but eventually led the disciples to repentance.

And so Paul concludes this letter-within-a-letter (1 Cor 1-4) with an open question. The Corinthians now have all they need to follow the gospel: a true epistemology (theory of knowledge), reminders of what they already had heard, sound theology, relevant Bible verses and apostolic examples to show them what God expected of them. **What would you prefer?** Which way, concludes Paul, shall we go?

B. Other Issues that concern the church in the world, based on oral report 5:1-6:20

Up to this point in the epistle, Paul has dealt with partisanship and its roots. In so doing he has laid the groundwork for understanding the universe, philosophy, the gospel, Christian life and ministry, and the holy temple that is the church. Before he responds to their letter, beginning in 7:1, he will deal with some remaining more pieces of hearsay: that the church has been tolerating incest, and that some Corinthian had defrauded another brother, and in turn that brother had sued him in public court. Although for Paul these are shocking lapses by individual people, it is to the church that he offers his rebuke. The apostle speaks in terms of black and white, unlike the careful explanations that he offers in 1 Cor 7-15.[217] Once again, it is fruitless to ask whether it was "those of Paul" or "those of Cephas" who committed or condoned these sins.[218]

There are themes that tie this section with the previous one, connections that make unnecessary those hypotheses which divide them into two separate sources. The boasting of the Corinthians comes up again (5:2); the holiness of the church (3:16) is related to the dwelling of the Spirit in the individual (6:19); the right of the spiritual to judge all things (2:15) underlies the church's responsibility to judge its own members for sin (5:12-13) and to adjudicate disputes between members (6:4-5).

In 1 Cor 5 he begins with the specific case – the church's inaction in the face of gross sin – and then moves to a broader principle, at the same time correcting a misimpression from a previous letter. In 1 Cor 6, he deals with lawsuits, and then broadens the theme in 6:12-20 to include what may have been slogans among the Corinthians: *Everything is permissible for me!* and *Food for the stomach and the stomach for food, and God will destroy them both!*

1. Incest and Moral Separation – 5:1-13

a. Specifically, this case of incest must be judged by the church itself 5:1-8

5:1
The wicked deed has been **reported** publically, and Paul apparently heard a report about it second-hand. His strong tone is due to the fact that the Corinthians had "thrown the fault into the shade"[219] and not been forthright with him. Paul does not reveal the source of the scandalous tidbit, whether it had come from "Chloe's people" (as in 1:11) or from elsewhere. In this outraged tone he speaks of a case of **sexual immorality** (*porneia*). This noun appears five times in 1 Corinthians. *Porneia* is a generic term that may refer to any type of sinful sexual act. The Jews characterized gentiles always as fornicators-idolaters, but here was a crime so stunning **that is not found even among pagans**. Of

---
[217] Thiselton, *First Corinthians*, 381-82.
[218] Lietzmann and Kümmel, *An die Korinther*, 25, suggest that in 1 Cor 5-6, 8-10 the Corinthians had misunderstandings stemming from the Jerusalem Decree (Acts 15:20, repeated in 15:29), which had instructed gentile Christians not only "abstain from wht has been sacrificed to idols" but also "fornication."
[219] To quote Chrysostom, *i ad Corinthios* 15.1.

course the Jews found it even more abhorrent: it was one of the capital crimes of the Mosaic Law (see Lev 18:8 – "You shall not uncover the nakedness of your father's wife; it is the nakedness of your father").[220]

What was the exact sin? One of the men of the church is living in incest. The NIV's "a man is *living with* his father's wife" is entirely inadequate; literally he "has" (*echō*) her, the verb used in a technical sense of "having sexual relations," with or without marriage. "Father's wife" (*gunē patros*) is an Old Testament and rabbinic term for one's stepmother, not biological mother.[221] Thus a member of the church was having an affair with his father's wife, perhaps after the death of the father or perhaps while the father was still alive and married to the woman. If the man were still alive, Roman law stated that the husband would have to divorce his wife, and she might be exiled or even executed. This means that the church might have been tolerating criminal activity.[222]

Their relationship could not have been a legal marriage, as it was not permitted to marry one's stepmother under Roman law.[223] "Has her" does imply that it was a continuing relationship. At any rate, the Corinthian church knew all about it, and so did others: the news had reached Paul in faraway Asia Minor.

If this perverted arrangement seems beyond credibility, it must be remembered that in Roman society a man might marry several times, and his latter wives could be as young as or younger than the older sons, who themselves might be living with the extended family. Thus a temptation arose when the *pater familias* had died or become enfeebled; a young man and woman could find their proximity under the same roof a cause for temptation.

How could a Christian have justified a man sleeping with his stepmother? We can rule out the influence of Stoicism in this case, since they generally stood firm against

---

[220] For the Mosaic teaching, see also Gen 35:22. From the Second Temple period: Josephus, *Antiquities* 3.12.1 §274 – "[Moses] also abhorred men's lying with their mothers, as one of the greatest crimes; and the like for lying with the father's wife, and with aunts, and sisters, and sons' wives, as all instances of abominable wickedness." See also Philo, *Special Laws* 3.20-21, who condemns sex with one's biological mother or step-mother: "But our law guards so carefully against such actions as these that it does not permit even a step-son, when his father is dead, to marry his step-mother, on account of the respect which he owes to his father, and because the titles mother and step-mother are kindred names, even though the affections of the souls may not be identical; for the man who is thought to abstain from her who has been the wife of another man, because she is called his step-mother, will much more abstain from his own natural mother." The Mishnah states in *Sanhedrin* 7.4 – "These are [the felons] who are put to death by stoning: He who has sexual relations with (1) his mother, (2) with the wife of his father, (3) with his daughter-in-law, etc…R. Judah says, 'He is liable only on account of her being his mother alone.' He who has sexual relations with his father's wife is liable on her account because of her being his father's wife and because of her being a married woman, whether this is in the lifetime of his father or after the death of his father, whether she is only betrothed or already married [to the father]."
[221] Thus: "has his father's wife" (ESV; see also NIV, NASB, KJV); "stepmother" (CEV; see also GNB, NJB). Origen refers to her as a "stepmother." Lietzmann and Kümmel, *An die Korinther*, 23, take this meaning, and add that the man's father was perhaps dead.
[222] Fitzmyer, *First Corinthians*, 231-32.
[223] Contra the GW version – "a man is actually married to his father's wife." Also contra Origen (Bray, 45), who says that they had been legally married, but that Paul uses *porneia* since it is fornication if the marriage is unlawful. Giving the Roman perspective, Gaius, *Institutes* 1 §63, said – "[A man] may not marry one who has been his wife's mother or his son's wife or his wife's daughter or his father's wife. I say, one who has been so allied, because during the continuance of the marriage that produced the alliance there would be another impediment to the union, for a man cannot have two wives nor a woman two husbands." See Lietzmann and Kümmel, *An die Korinther*, 23; also Conzelmann, *1 Corinthians*, 96.

sex outside of marriage.[224] Some link this sin with the supposed "over-realized eschatology" or "enthusiasm" of the church: if the Corinthians had entered the kingdom and begun to reign (4:8), then they lived in a realm beyond the normal conventions of marriage. In that case it might be possible to punctuate 5:3-4 to make the sin a consciously religious act, that he committed this sin "in the name of our Lord Jesus Christ."[225] While this view is workable in theory, it lacks the support of history: when Gnostic heretics arose in the 2nd century, they were typically ascetics who disdained the sins of the flesh, including sexual ones. A different "theological" explanation is that the pair had a "spiritual marriage," that is, they lived together as a couple but did not have sexual relations.[226] This too would become a practice in the church in the 2nd century (see comments on 7:36-38). But if this were the case, Paul is ignoring the facts; he treats the relationship as if this were literal incest.

In fact, there is no firm evidence for any theological current in the 1st-century church by which a Christian could justify incest. The transgression was likely of the same nature of most sexual sins which human beings fall into, that is, a work of the flesh.

5:2

This may be a question ("And are you proud?", see GNB) or an exclamation (as NIV and most versions), **And you are proud!** The Corinthians not only tolerated the sin, but were still, literally, "puffed up" (*phusioō*, see comments on 4:6). There are several ways of explaining their attitude: first, that some Corinthians were proud of the tolerance that they showed for their members, loving and accepting them no matter the crime.[227] More likely is the view of the majority of commentators, who argue that this should be translated as, *You continue to be proud people, despite the fact that this sort of thing is happening in your midst.*[228]

Taking a sociological perspective, some have suggested that the church fully recognized the relationship as sinful, but was unable or unwilling to deal with it because of the status of the offender: as a man of wealth or power he was safe from censure. This is similar to an older viewpoint, popular among the church fathers, that they were proud of the man because he was one of their eloquent teachers.[229] This approach, though more likely than the "theological" explanations, lacks positive proof. We have no data to suggest that the Corinthians were particularly solicitous toward this one man as against

---

[224] See F. Hauck y S. Schulz, "*pornē*," TDNT 6:583-84.

[225] Thus the NRSV has as an alternate reading: "on the man who has done such a thing in the name of the Lord Jesus." See the discussion in Fee, *First Corinthians*, 206-08, who allows this as one possibility; likewise Craig Blomberg, *The NIV Application Commentary Series: 1 Corinthians* (Grand Rapids, MI: Zondervan 1994), 104. Hurd, *Origin*, 277, says in this regard: "It is hard to overestimate the enthusiasm which appears to have existed in this early Christian community." This comment is based on a particular interpretation of Corinth's problems; the rest of Hurd's thoughts on the passage (277-78) are, at best, eccentric.

[226] Hurd, *Origin*, 278.

[227] So Baker, *1 Corinthians*, 79-80 – the church was "openly condoning this illicit sexual relationship as though it were an excellent advertising campaign for freedom in Christ to draw their neighbors to the Christian faith." See too Fee, *First Corinthians*, 201-02.

[228] See the analysis by Thiselton, *First Corinthians*, 388-90.

[229] This is similar to Chrysostom, *i ad Corinthios*, Introduction, who speculates that the offender was one of the partisan leaders, "a leader of the multitude, and gave occasion to his followers to be conceited." Thus his eloquence was the cause of the pride (5:2) that would protect him from reproof, see *i ad Corinthios* 15.2. See too Thiselton, *First Corinthians*, 389.

some other individual. It is better to regard their error as a unwillingness to offer discipline, perhaps because it was too difficult, perhaps because it would upset the triumphalistic atmosphere of the church: the Corinthians had little talent for being glum.

Rather (*ouchi mallon*, only here and in 1 Cor 6:7, 2 Cor 3:8 in Paul's letters) they should **have been filled with grief and have put out of your fellowship** this man (or perhaps, "mourn because his actions have led to their expelling him"[230]). "Put out (a literal translation of *airō*) from among you" is somewhat vague in the Greek, but the idea is clear and the GNB is correct to use "expel" (see also NJB, "turned out"). Origen several times uses another verb, *ekballō* (the technical term for excommunication: "expel, cast out"), in his commentary on 5:2. The church must take decisive action. The synagogue of Paul's day practiced expulsion and other disciplinary actions, such as corporal punishment; "Five times I received from the Jews the forty lashes minus one," said Paul (2 Cor 11:24). It is therefore not necessary to trace Paul's teaching, as some suggest, specifically to Qumran,[231] whose rules are similar to the normal practice of Judaism. Paul gives no rules, not even as general as those laid out in Matt 18:15-17. It is probable that the Corinthians already knew what to do and how to do it; the missing element was the will to take action.[232]

5:3

As for Paul, he would have no trouble taking decisive action. He begins:

> **Even though I am not physically present,**
> **I am with you in spirit.**

The phrase **in Spirit/spirit** raises some questions. It is followed up by **as if I were present.** The NIV and most translations have *as if he were present, but in fact he is not.* We moderns would typically gloss over this with "he was present in his thoughts," a plausible view in light of the parallel in Col 2:5 – "though I am absent from you in body, I am present with you in spirit."[233] As a more likely alternative, one can have recourse to the fact that in Paul *pneuma* means Holy Spirit unless there is some hint of another meaning.[234] In the Spirit, then, Paul can be present to a degree beyond natural human ability, as evidenced by 1 Cor 5:4, "I am with you with the power of the Lord Jesus in

---

[230] See Thiselton, *First Corinthians*, 388.
[231] Cf. Barrett, *First Corinthian*, 122-23; also Richard A. Horsley, "Paul's assembly in Corinth: an alternative society," in *Urban religion in Roman Corinth*, 371-95. For an example of the Qumran practice, see 1QS col v.24-vi.1 – "One should reproach one another in truth, in meekness and in compassionate love for one's fellow-man. *Blank*. No-one should speak to his brother in anger or muttering, or with a hard [neck or with passionate] spirit of wickedness, and he should not detest him [in the fore]sk[in] of his heart, but instead reproach him that day so as not to incur a sin because of him."
[232] It is hardly surprising that commentators through the centuries find in the text an affirmation of their own ecclesiastical polity. A century and a half later, Origen would comment: "Let us take the sin before the *bishop*, so that such a one might lawfully be expelled from the church" [my own translation]. Calvin, *First Corinthians*, 1:182-83, says that this means that the matter should be taken to the *presbytery*, and their verdict affirmed by the congregation.
[233] See Barrett, *First Corinthians*, 123. This was the typical interpretation from the 19th century up through 1950, according to Thiselton, *First Corinthians*, 390-91.
[234] So Fee, *First Corinthians*, 204-06. Origen points to Paul's reference to the Spirit's words in 1 Tim 4:1ff. and 2 Tim 3:1ff., and concludes that since Paul obviously possessed the gift of prophecy, he could deal with the situation supernaturally even though absent.

the Spirit." Although we may be unclear as to how the Holy Spirit allows Paul to be "present" when he is physically hundreds of kilometers away, this seems to be supernatural communion rather than human empathy.[235]

How strange it seems that from a distance and with no further evidence **I have already passed judgment on** this case. Paul must have been convinced by the report that the charge was true, that the church knew that it was true, and that there could be no extenuating circumstance. This case goes beyond the mediating steps of Matt 18:15-17, or indeed of Paul's own teaching in Gal 6:1-2: the man should be judged and expelled right now, without delay.

5:4

As we implied above, there are various options for punctuating this sentence.[236] That of the NIV is best, **when you are assembled in the name of our Lord Jesus.** Again, Paul is present "through the Spirit" and thus giving his apostolic authority to the discipline. The supernatural element is key: although this is a congregational action, it is done in the name of Jesus (see 1:10) and with his power.

5:5

Paul gives directions concerning **this man**, but not the woman. It is unlikely that the church believed that only male offenders should be disciplined.[237] Even in the Mosaic law, the woman in this incestuous relationship would have been punished: Lev 20:11 – "If a man sleeps with his father's wife, he has dishonored his father. Both the man and the woman must be put to death; their blood will be on their own heads." If Paul does not refer to the woman, it is almost certainly due to her not being a Christian and thus not within the church's jurisdiction. They should leave her fate to God (1 Cor 5:12-13).

From the standpoint of the 21st century, we might prefer that Paul gave a clean bureaucratic procedure for expulsion. Instead, he speaks to them in words of the supernatural: **hand this man over to Satan.** "Hand over" (*paradidōmi*) is used here in its technical legal sense of handing someone over into custody; it appears in the New Testament for the arrest of John the Baptist and of the Lord Jesus. The end of this action is, literally, "for the destruction of the flesh" (KJV), see further along for the meaning of this clause. But beyond destruction there lies a positive goal: that his spirit be "saved on the day of the Lord." The church's expulsion is constructive and corrective rather than an act of revenge.[238] Our sole parallel to this verse is in 1 Tim 1:20: "Among them are Hymenaeus and Alexander, whom I have handed over to Satan to be taught not to blaspheme." Again, the aim is not to destroy the two false teachers, but to cause them to "learn" and presumably, change their behavior.

The verse alludes to a procedure that was already familiar to the Corinthians (and to

---

[235] Thus Chrysostom, *i ad Corinthios* 15.3: "For this is the meaning of being 'present in spirit:' as Elisha was present with Gehazi, and said, 'Went not my heart with thee?' (2 Kings 5:26). Wonderful! How great is the power of the gift, in that it makes all to be together and as one; and qualifies them to know the things which are far off." Origen also refers to this passage in 2 Kings and states that Paul as prophet was able to do the same thing.
[236] Conzelmann, *1 Corinthians*, 97, mentions six options.
[237] So Kümmel in Lietzmann and Kümmel, *An die Korinther*, 173.
[238] Thiselton, *First Corinthians*, 397, would like to say that not only the man's spirit but also the spirit of the church will be saved; while this is theologically interesting, it is more than the text says. See too Ambrosiaster (Bray, 46, emphasis added) – "If the man were not thrown out, *the spirit of the church* would not be saved on the day of judgment, because the source of the contamination was infecting them all."

Timothy in 1 Timothy) but which is not here described in detail. There have been a number of explanations for "hand over to Satan." (1) It may be to turn the man over to the civil authorities for punishment.[239] Strange as that may seem in light of what Paul will say in the next chapter, the difference may be due to the level of the crime. Here the man has broken Roman law; in 1 Cor 6 it is a question of a disagreement between two Christian individuals. (2) It may be a "dynamistic ceremony" that involves the naming of Satan. (3) More likely, it may be expulsion from the sphere of God's people, a casting out from the "holy temple" (1 Cor 3:16-17), an act that leaves the man at the mercy of the enemy.[240] Thus, Satan punishes the man because he wishes to harm people, but in so doing he also acts as God's agent. Two rough parallels would be Job 1:12; 2:6, where Job falls into the hands of Satan as a test, not to discipline him for sin; perhaps too Paul's "thorn in the flesh" (2 Cor 12:7). For want of more data, this third explanation must suffice. As said Theodoret of Cyrus (Bray, 46): "We are taught by this that the devil invades those who are separated from the body of the church because he finds them deprived of grace." If the language seems foreign to us, it may be because we think of the church not as a sanctuary from the devil but as a voluntary organization. As we shall see in 1 Cor 8-10, the ancients were keenly aware that outside of the protection of God's people they were vulnerable to demonic attack.

What does it mean that "the flesh" will be destroyed? The possibilities are: (1) he will receive corporal punishment inflicted by the civil authority or by the church itself. The use of corporal punishment for heresy was not uncommon in the synagogue and came to be a tool in the hands of the Inquisition, but it is out of place in this context; (2) physical illness, suffering or death, inflicted by Satan.[241] Parallels might exist in 1 Cor 11:30: "that is why many among you are weak and sick, and a number of you have fallen asleep"; see the CEV – "his body will be destroyed"; (3) the likely reading is that this is not the destruction not of the physical self (as in 6:16, 15:50), but of the flesh-as-carnality (as in 1:26, 29).[242] This is the view of the NIV with its **so that the sinful nature may be destroyed**, or even better, "for the destruction of what is merely human." **And his spirit saved on the day of the Lord** must be eschatological, and refer to the final judgment (see 1 Cor 1:8, 3:13, 4:5). Paul hopes that this man will repent in this life and be acquitted in the judgment.

It is likely that this offender is the same man who was punished by the congregation in 2 Cor 2:5-9. The data can be made to fit,[243] although Paul could be referring to an entirely different case and to an epistle other than 1 Corinthians. If he is not the same man, still he came to the same end that Paul desired in the case at hand in 1 Cor 5: a man

---

[239] So J. D. M. Derrett, "'Handing over to Satan': an explanation of 1 Cor. 5:1-7," en *Revue Internacionale des Droits de l'Antiquité* 26 (1979): 11-30; analyzed in Thiselton, *First Corinthians*, 397.

[240] Theodoret of Cyrus; Theodore of Mopsuestia; Severianus (all on Bray, 46-47); also Calvin, *First Corinthians*, 1:185.

[241] So Godet; Barrett.

[242] Origen says [my own translation]: "...not for the destruction of the soul, nor the destruction of the spirit, but of the destruction of the flesh – that is, 'the will of the flesh' [from Rom 8:7]." J. T. South, *Disciplinary practices in pauline texts* (New York: Mellon, 1992); also Grosheide, who resists calling this "excommunication," apparently because of his distaste for the ecclesiastical practice of his day; Fee, *First Corinthians*, 209-13, points out that the destruction of the flesh cannot be death, because then how could Paul imply that it might be remedial? Robertson and Plummer, *First Corinthians*, 99, think both excommunication and death are intended.

[243] Origen thinks they are the same man; Fee, *First Corinthians*, disagrees. See the full discussion in Godet, *First Corinthians*, 259-60.

was judged by the "majority," punished, was caused to grieve, repented, and now (says Paul in 2 Cor 2:7-8) should be re-embraced by the church.

Application: Discipline and the church 5:5

There is renewed interest today in the responsibility of the church to discipline its sinning members. It is a theme of great delicacy and must be handled in wisdom and love informed by the Scriptures.

What kind of church disciplines its members?

Some believe that the church of Christ is designed for the **consumer**. That is, an individual attends or does not attend as he wishes. He comes late and leaves early. She shares in the Lord's Supper if she happens to be there on the correct date, but if she misses there is no problem. If he does not like a certain preacher he stays away. He may not know the people around him on Sunday, and if he does it is just as likely that he knows them from work or the neighborhood. Care for the members tends to be in large groups or limited to the worship service. The individual contribution of each member is thought of in financial terms. The Christian consumer pays (contributes financially) in order to receive a product (teaching, spiritual uplift, worship music).

The biblical model by contrast is that the Christian is a **member of the body**. If one member is missing or ineffective, then it affects the whole church. The individual's contribution to the church includes financial support. Nevertheless the member is expected to contribute his or her very self, to be a growing Christian who is part of the church's light to the world.

In the consumer model of the church, discipline is rare. It will be limited to extreme cases and will probably take the form of pressuring certain people to leave the church to go find another. If there is any reproach for sin, it is done indirectly or through a general warning in a sermon. In this model a rich man who is a faithful tither may possibly find the standards of behavior less strict than does the man with few resources.

In the biblical model of the church, if members are in sin, its seriousness is gauged by how much they are offending God, and how much harm they are doing to themselves, the church and the witness of the gospel.

Church discipline is not easy within a megachurch, nor does it cease to be awkward within a small church. But each congregation needs to ensure that every member has pastoral care that is attentive enough that someone knows when a person has fallen into sin. There is no mathematical formula, but it's useful to recall that in Corinth every 25 or so people had at least one elder looking after their souls.

Church discipline is not some add-on to the life of the church. Rather it is an integral part of the ministry of the word, which is to be used "for teaching, rebuking, correcting and training in righteousness" (2 Tim 3:16). How ridiculous when a Christian receives his first visit from his pastor only in discipline! A leader rather earns the right to exercise discipline by being a constant friend and guide.

What sort of discipline?

It is loving. When a church disciplines a member, it must do so out of love. The fact that a church conducts discipline at all – an extremely difficult and draining task – is because it believes that it is doing the loving thing. When a church ignores destructive sin in its membership, it is not loving; rather it has become spiritual lazy.

It is measured and appropriate. The Bible's dictum "an eye for an eye and a tooth for a tooth" may sound strict to us. Nevertheless it makes an important point: discipline should correspond to the seriousness of the sin. Expulsion – which was what Paul ordered in this case – is the most extreme measure. But there are many other steps that a church may take to discourage its members from sin: not being able to teach for six months; sending them to counseling; telling them to make amends for their wrongs.

It is concerned more for reality than for image. Some churches refuse to exercise discipline because it looks and feels unpleasant. They choose rather to try to preserve the false image of the church as one big happy family, free from problems. But in grasping for the image of love they end up acting in hate: to allow a member to destroy himself with sin when loving intervention could have saved him is a rejection of the command to love.

It is applied evenly to all members. It does not exclude the wealthy, the influential members, the friends and relatives of the pastors. Nor does it excuse the poor. Uneven discipline may produce worse results than ignoring discipline altogether. This is especially important for a prominent leader. The church doubts how it can discipline someone whom the Spirit is obviously blessing (that is, the church is growing and the money keeps coming in). Yet it must be so. After all, a doctor who is famous for his skills but butchers just a few patients will still come under the swift action of his or her medical board.

It is for the resistant sinner, not for the repentant sinner. In Matt 18:15-17 and here in 1 Corinthians, it is the person who does not repent who receives discipline. That is, discipline is used to encourage people to repent, not to punish. Of course, a church needs to show great discernment to determine whether a person is really showing fruit of repentance, or is merely trying to fake it in order to avoid a disagreeable outcome.

It is corrective and hopeful. When the church disciplines a member it must be in hope that the discipline will help the person come back to Christ. A church without hope will merely toss the person away. Paul speaks of the salvation that he hopes this incestuous Christian will receive on the last day (5:5).

5:6

Paul speaks not to the offender, but to the church: **Your boasting is not good**.[244] Again, whether they are boasting about their tolerant spirit (see 5:2) or, as is likely, it is general background noise, it is not fitting for God's holy people.

Paul will now move to the metaphor of leavened bread, one that he used more than

---

[244] Ambrosiaster omits the negative particle "no," making it ironic: "How nice is your boasting!" See also Héring. Robertson and Plummer, *First Corinthians*, 97, have a similar opinion, without removing the negative particle.

once.[245] **A little yeast works through the whole batch of dough**: the metaphor works on levels that are difficult to follow for those without baking experience or without a background in the Jewish Passover rite. The purpose of leavening is to make bread rise to make it lighter. In the Passover week however all bread was to be unleavened, made into flat wafers (Exod 12:15-20; 13:7; 34:25). This was to symbolize the haste with which Israel left Egypt. In other instances, burnt sacrifices could not be leavened (Lev 2:4, 11; 6:17; 10:12), but offerings that were consumed by eating could be (Lev 23:17; Amos 4:5).

In antiquity people did not use powdered yeast as we do today. Where people baked bread with "leaven," it was by reserving a small uncooked lump from the previous batch of dough. This would be mixed into the new flour and water and left standing to allow the chemical permeation of the whole, exactly as described in Matt 13:33 – "yeast that a woman took and mixed into a large amount of flour until it worked all through the dough." Paul's point is that even a morsel of leavening cannot be contained when it sits in the bowl with good dough. Only by removing the sinner can the corruption of the church be checked.

5:7

With **get rid of the old yeast**, Paul goes a step further with the metaphor, and urges the congregation to be like the Passover bread **without yeast**, fit for an offering to God. Paul's point (with a parallel in 1:2, 3:16-17) is that the Corinthians must live as a holy people, because as his saints that is what in fact they **really are**.

Paul draws one more point from the Passover: we should be untainted by sin because **Christ, our Passover lamb, has been sacrificed**. Some have deduced that all this talk of Passover (see also 1 Cor 10:1ff.) is because Paul was writing in the spring, the Passover being celebrated in March or April of the year. He planned to stay in Ephesus until Pentecost (16:8), which always fell 50 days after the start of Passover. This theory is attractive but must remain speculative.[246] What is clear is that the death of Christ as the Passover lamb (1 Cor 11:23-26, see John 1:29) marks the Christian as God's redeemed people. As the redeemed they were "you were bought at a price" (1 Cor 6:20).

5:8

Let us keep the Festival, that is, Passover: Paul now summarizes his point, applying the old leaven to **malice and wickedness** (general terms for evil) and calling the church to live the unleavened life of **sincerity** (or with pure motive, as in 2 Cor 2:17) and **truth**.

---

[245] The Lord Jesus used leaven as metaphor in two instances: first in the parable of the kingdom, Matt 13:33 = Luke 13:21. There, leaven might be an agent of evil, but is more likely only to be a symbol of permeation. The true parallel to 1 Cor 5 is his teaching to "be on your guard against the yeast of the Pharisees and Sadducees" in Matt 16:6, 11, 12 = Mark 8:15 = Luke 12:1. In Gal 5:9, it refers to Judaizing, which is not only a contamination of the true gospel but also tends to infiltrate everything. Ignatius uses the same metaphor for Judaizing in his *Magnesians* 10.2 – "Throw out, therefore, the bad leaven, which has become stale and sour, and reach for the new leaven, which is Jesus Christ."

[246] See Origen (Kovacs, 86) – "He did not say this because Passover was at hand, or the feast of Pentecost, but to show that all time is a festal time for Christians, because of the abundance of blessings bestowed on them"; also the comments by Fee, *First Corinthians*, 217 n. 15.

b. Generally, Christians should expel worldly elements from the church 5:9-13

Paul will now broaden the theme to the responsibility of the church to police its own membership rolls.

5:9
Paul had already communicated **in my letter** about the need for separation from the ungodly. Some critics believe that this missing letter was later edited into 2 Cor 6:14-7:1, the part that begins with "Do not be yoked together with unbelievers." But there is no manuscript evidence to suggest that the 2 Corinthians passage is an interpolation; plus Paul does not say anything quite like 5:9 in 2 Cor 6:14-7:1. It is better to interpret Paul to be speaking of an earlier, now missing, letter.[247] The Corinthians had gotten Paul's teaching it precisely backwards, tolerating evil in its midst while frowning on the sins of outsiders. We suspect that Paul was for some motive or another being deliberately misunderstood in Corinth.[248] At any rate, what he had told them was **not to associate with sexually immoral people** (*pornoi*, the adjectival form of *porneia*, 5:1).[249] The verb for "associate with" (*sunanamignumi*) means to mix together with, in this case socially (see 15:33, "Bad company corrupts good character"). He picks a verb that fits well with the aforementioned leaven metaphor: the church is not to allow the sinner to mix together with the congregation.

Application: Separation from believers 5:9

It is fashionable to teach that *The church draws lines and separates people, but Jesus himself rejected nobody*. A corollary is that *The church teaches hell and condemnation, but Jesus always spoke of forgiveness: "Do not judge, or you too will be judged."* While this sounds plausible on the surface, it does not do justice to the canonical gospels. While Jesus indeed received sinners and ate with them, to the dismay of the Pharisees (Luke 15:2); yet no-one in the entire Bible spoke more of God's judgment on sinners than did he did. People too often draw conclusions about Jesus, based on their own partial and faulty memory. The only reasonable solution is to read carefully through all four gospels.

Jesus himself laid the basis for church discipline in Matt 18:17 – "treat him as you would a pagan or a tax collector." In context he is talking about a disciple who has been warned time and again about his sinful behavior, and who refuses to change his ways. The final step Jesus offers is to cease to fellowship with him.[250] In 1 Cor 5 Paul speaks

---

[247] Ambrosiaster; Godet; Walter; Thiselton; Schrage. Theodoret of Cyrus takes this as an epistolary aorist, that is, that Paul is referring to something he has just written in 1 Cor 5:6, see *Commentary*, 1:177; see also Calvin, *First Corinthians*, 1:190. Origen describes both viewpoints and does not offer a final opinion.

[248] So Nicoll; Barrett; Fee; Schrage; Thiselton.

[249] The Spanish Versión Popular is misleading with its "those who go to prostitutes [quienes se entregan a la prostitución]," which looks forward to 6:15 but the word itself will not bear that specific meaning in 5:9.

[250] I am well aware that some New Testament critics do not believe that Jesus ever spoke Matt 18:15-17. This is based on the critical method known as *Formgeschichte* or form criticism. That methodology has as one of its premises that if a saying of Jesus seems to reflect the later practice of the church, then it is unlikely to have come from Jesus himself. This is an unproven assumption, that Jesus could not have predicted the formation of the church or even known that he was going to die on the cross.

of the same step, breaking off normal contact. This is the way that Paul teaches here, and also in 2 Thess 3:14-15 and Titus 3:10.

It is human nature to want to rescue a person from isolation and suffering. Thus when we run into a person from whom we are supposed to remain separate, we may feel like giving them a hug and comforting them in their sorrow. But we must remember that the grief they are experiencing is a healthy one, and one that may lead them back to Christ (2 Cor 2:10). Would you embrace a non-Christian and tell them that, it's alright if they reject God, they will always have you? What a poor substitute our human affection is for the love of Christ.

The difficulty in our culture is that the ties of blood or friendship may prove stronger than the ties of the church. It may help us to remember that Jesus and Paul taught within Jewish and Greco-Roman cultures respectively; in both environments, as now, devotion to friends was fundamental. Jesus and Paul both pushed back against culture.

It is impossible that there be no accidental contact with someone under church discipline. Discipline does not mean that one cannot say hello to someone in the market or at work. Nor does it mean that the person should be ostracized from Christian family members. Rather, Paul tells us to not have contact that will encourage the person to stay as he is; nor that will give him the idea that we are sympathetic with him against the church. This can be fatal to the process of drawing the person back to Christ. It is after a person repents that we should welcome them back warmly (2 Cor 2:7).

5:10-11

Paul clarifies that of course Christians will live in the world and have regular dealings with unbelievers. In this way the gospel encourages a Christian presence in the world, a witness that far exceeded that of the synagogue, with its stricter social barriers. He will deal again with boundaries between church and world in his teaching about lawsuits and about prostitution (1 Cor 6), marriage to an unbeliever (1 Cor 7), and meat sacrificed to idols (1 Cor 8-10).

Paul gives three, successively larger, lists of sinful people:

5:10	5:11	6:9-10 (wicked)
(sexually) immoral	sexually immoral	sexually immoral
greedy	greedy	idolaters
swindlers	idolater	adulterers
idolaters	slanderer	*male prostitutes (see below)*
	drunkard	*homosexual offenders*[251]
	swindler	thieves
		greedy

---

[251] So the rendering of these two key words in the NIV 1984, a version that is usually highly accurate. Nevertheless, "male prostitutes" is a wholly unacceptable translation, and "homosexual offenders" is also problematic; see our comments on 6:9. In fact it is difficult to render the two Greek words with one or two words in English. An accurate sense for the first word would be "men or boys who submit themselves sexually to another man;" and for the second, "men who sexually use men or boys as they would a woman." Paul does not speak of motivation or sexual orientation, but only of sexual behaviors.

Commentary 5:1-6:20

> drunkards[252]
> slanderers
> swindlers

The nouns are similar in form, except that he uses the singular in 5:11 and the plural in the other two. The list in Gal 5:19-21 refers to fleshly *deeds* (for example "idolatry") not types of person ("idolaters").

The form the apostle uses has parallels to the literary device known as a "vice-list." The genre originated in Greek philosophy and was used in later Judaism.[253] The Stoics in particular wrote out long lists of vices and virtues. It has been suggested that Paul simply adopted traditional lists from earlier Greek or Jewish sources, but that theory has many flaws. Despite the similarities with lists written by philosophers, Paul's statements are relatively short. Even within this one epistle, no two lists are alike. They are specifically tailored to the problems at Corinth, "intricately connected to the epistolary situation of the letter."[254] A "sexually immoral" person has already appeared in 5:1, but there are other points of contact with Corinth. The basis for the suit in 6:1 is that some Christian has supposedly defrauded (6:7) another, or been "swindler" or perhaps a "thief" or "greedy." The "idolaters" may be linked to Christians who are too freely partaking in idols' banquets (10:14-22). And the list of 6:9-10 explicitly reflects what "some of you were" (6:11). In 5:11 he expands on the first list by adding **slanderer** and **drunkard**. The sin of slander was probably never far from the Corinthian church, rife with party divisions.

Paul's teaching on separation has to do with fellowship **with anyone who calls himself a brother but is sexually immoral, etc.** Such "brothers" are acting as the world does and are without inheritance in the eschatological kingdom (6:9-10). **With such a man do not even eat**, because partaking of a meal implies *acceptance*, especially in the ancient world.[255] The advice given in 2 Thess 3:14-15 is "take special note of him. Do not associate with him, in order that he may feel ashamed. Yet do not regard him as an enemy, but warn him as a brother." This tone is less strict than in 1 Cor 5, due probably,

---

[252] "Drunkards" is the correct translation; "alcoholics" has another meaning, see under 6:9.

[253] In German they are called *Lasterkatalogen*. See the Excursus in Conzelmann, *1 Corinthians*, 100-01. An example of a long list of vices is found in the writings of the Hellenistic Jew Philo, *Sacrifices of Abel and Cain* 32: "a bold, cunning, audacious, unsociable, uncourteous, inhuman, lawless, savage, illtempered, unrestrainable, worthless man; deaf to advice, foolish, full of evil acts, unteachable, unjust, unfair, one who has no participation with others, one who cannot be trusted in his agreements, one with whom there is no peace, covetous, most lawless, unfriendly, homeless, cityless, seditious, faithless, disorderly, impious, unholy, unsettled, unstable, etc." An example from the Dead Sea Scrolls is found in the *Manual of Discipline* (1QS col iv.9-10) – "to the spirit of deceit belong greed, sluggishness in the service of justice, wickedness, falsehood, pride, haughtiness of heart, dishonesty, trickery, cruelty, much insincerity, impatience, much foolishness, impudent enthusiasm for appalling acts performed in a lustful passion, filthy paths in the service of impurity, etc." Vice lists are also found in the testamentary literature, the apocalypses, the rabbinic writings and also in Christian writings of the 2nd century, for example, *Didache* 2.1-5.2, for example – "You shall not be greedy or avaricious, or a hypocrite or malicious or arrogant. You shall not hatch evil plots against your neighbor, etc." (*Didache* 2.6).

[254] P. 629 in Peter S. Zaas, "Catalogues and context: 1 Corinthians 5 and 6," *NTS* 34 (1988): 622-29; Thiselton, *First Corinthians*, 412, so too Fee. Contra Conzelmann, *1 Corinthians*, 101.

[255] See Gal 2:11-13. The transgression of Cephas ["Peter" in the NIV] in Antioch was that when he who "used to eat with the Gentiles" later "began to draw back and separate himself" from them. His action signaled that he did not regard them as fully Christian.

as Chrysostom notes, to the fact that the sin of work in Thessalonica is not of the degree of sins mentioned in 1 Corinthians.[256]

5:12

Although Paul publically preaches against sin, it is not his pastoral duty to regulate the behavior of non-Christians.[257] **Those outside** is traditional Jewish terminology for those outside the people of God.

5:13

God is the judge of the world, as he is of the Christian (4:4). The responsibility of the church is not to set up court to dispense God's eschatological judgment. It does have the obligation to **"expel the evil man from among you."** This is a quotation (with a simple change from singular to plural) of Deut 17:7 – "You must purge the evil from among you." In that context, an Israelite who is idolatrous should be stoned on the strength of two or three witnesses. The world is filled with idolaters, and God's people have no warrant to destroy them all. Here it is abominable and worthy of execution that such a thing "has been done in Israel" (Deut 17:4).

2. Lawsuits – 6:1-11

Paul changes abruptly to a new outrage. One member of the church had sued another, presumably to recover his losses from being defrauded (6:7). This action was objectionable on several levels: 1. It harmed the unity of the church; 2. The civic leaders of Corinth would see Christians together only when they were suing each other; 3. It widened the gulf between rich and poor in the church. In modern times, the oppressed have sometimes been able to use the court system to press its claims. In Corinth, only the wealthy could bring suit (see Application – The Christian and Lawsuits, below).

Some have suggested that the lawsuit in 6:1 had to do with the incest of chapter 5, but this is unlikely.[258] It is better to see the pair of problems as two of a kind: sins that are morally wrong, that display the church to the world's ridicule, and that uncovers the congregation's inaction in the face of internal wrongdoing. As always, it is Paul who is controlling the agenda of the epistle and who orders the various topics for his own reasons.

a. Situation – Christians are suing each other in court 6:1

6:1

Without transition Paul asks, how dare some Christian bring a lawsuit before the civil

---

[256] Chrysostom, *i ad Corinthios* 16.2 – "For [in 2 Thess 3] he is reproving indolence; but here fornication and other most grievous sins."

[257] So especially Barrett. Also Herman Ridderbos, *Paul: an outline of his theology* (Grand Rapids, MI: Eerdmans, 1975), 304-05.

[258] See for example p. 296 in Will Deming, "The unity of 1 Corinthians 5-6," *JBL* 115.2 (1996): 289-312. He argues that some Corinthians had taken the incestuous man to court, but that the judge had not punished him for his sin. Deming's hypothesis is weakened by the fact that he has to assume two points which are absent from the text, that a lawsuit had already been brought, and that it was unsuccessful.

system. The NIV, as the ESV, changes the original word order, making it less abrupt than it sounds in the Greek; the NKJV captures the emphasis: "Dare any of you, having a matter against another, go to law...?" The offense is not just that a Christian pursues a **dispute** (the technical legal term, *pragma echein pros*, literally "to have a matter against") against a fellow Christian, but that he would take the matter before the **ungodly** rather than before **saints**. Paul intends the reader to see several layers of meaning with "ungodly" (or "unrighteous," *adikoi*) *versus* "saints": (1) the judges of Roman Corinth are not part of God's holy people; (2) they are unjust judges and cannot be counted on to give justice; (3) the "ungodly" (rendered as "wicked" in the NIV in 6:9) will not inherit the kingdom of God, but the saints will. With **instead of** (literally, "and *not*") he uses the strong negative *oichi* to show how incredible is their behavior. Paul is not negating what he would say about obeying the civil authority in Rom 13:1-7; rather, he objects to a Christian causing a public imbroglio, when the church should have handled the matter.

b. Solution – the church should handle matters between Christians; failing that, it is better to drop the matter 6:2-8

6:2-3

Rather than offer a step-by-step plan of action, Paul uses eschatology to demonstrate a principle. He uses the repeated diatribe formula **Do you not know...?** (see 4:7 for a definition of "diatribe"). Not only will the saints be vindicated in the final judgment, but they **judge the world** and (6:3) even the **angels**.[259] The New Testament teaches in a few key passages that Christians will rule in the age to come (see especially 2 Tim 2:12; Rev 2:26-28), as well as judge the nations (Matt 19:28).[260] Conzelmann declares that the idea is foreign to the strict monotheism of Judaism, where God alone judges (and see 1 Cor 4:5).[261] Some even have suggested the far-fetched idea that Paul himself did not believe that they would be judges, but that he was ironically appealing to their spirit of triumphalism (1 Cor 4:8). At any rate, contra Conzelmann, there is now evidence from Qumran that in some sectors of Judaism it was thought that the saints would share in judgment and in ruling over the age to come: "God is not to destroy his nation at the hand of the peoples, but in the hand of his chosen ones God will place the judgment over all the peoples" (1Qp-Hab v.3b-4). In addition, the most plausible interpretation of Daniel's vision is that God's people will rule over the future kingdom – "the time came when [the saints] possessed the kingdom" (Dan 7:22).

Paul twice uses the logical argument "from the lesser to the greater": if you will judge angels in the future, then you should be able to **judge trivial cases** and **the things of this life**[262] during this age. He is not necessarily in favor of an ecclesiastical court as it later evolved, but for the church to take initiative in solving what amount to "small

---

[259] See also 2 Pet 2:4, where the angels are said "to be held for judgment."
[260] As notes Fee, *First Corinthians*, 233. See Héring or Thiselton, *First Corinthians*, 426-27, for the history of this doctrine, which was rejected by Theodoret of Cyrus, Chrysostom, *i ad Corinthios* 16.5 and others. Ambrosiaster said that the saints "judge the world" only in the sense of giving an example of faith before them during this age (Bray, 50).
[261] Conzelmann, *1 Corinthians*, 105.
[262] Similarly KJV, CEV, ESV, GNB, NET, NIV, NJB, NKJV, NLT, NRSV. Conzelmann, *1 Corinthians*, 104-05, renders it "pettiest cases." The alternative translation is "smallest law courts" (NASB), as also Thiselton, *First Corinthians*, 428.

claims."

6:4
This verse is hard to punctuate and interpret. There are three ways to understanding Paul's point about setting up judges (*kathizō*, to appoint or install) to hear these **disputes**:[263]

1. The Corinthians have from one angle already set up (*kathizō* in a weakened sense) for themselves judges in the world, that is, they have yielded authority to gentile judges whose character is despised by the church.[264]
2. The Corinthians have already appointed some of their members to handle such cases, but they are of such low reputation or skill that they cannot possibly handle the job. In this viewpoint, the sentence could be taken as a question (NIV) or as an exclamation: "You have as judges those who count for nothing in the church!"
3. The Corinthians might as well set up the poorest example of a Christian to be judge; anything within the church would be better than the gentile judges![265] The KJV has "set them to judge who are least esteemed in the church." Paul is being ironic, and does not literally wish them to pick the poorest candidates; yet even if they did so, it would still be an improvement.

In light of 6:5 ("nobody among you is wise enough?"), the reading #2 is best. The church had an existing, yet poorly-established system of arbitration. The original is stronger yet, more like "the despised of the church." The language is strong; perhaps it was the Corinthians themselves who used such arrogant words.

6:5
But no, Paul wants someone **wise enough** as judge, someone who could arrange a just solution between parties which voluntarily submitted to the church's system. Here he is being provocative, since some Corinthians boasted about being "wise" (and 1:5, Paul himself states that they are rich in "knowledge"), yet no capable person had stepped forward for this thankless task. The apostle speaks here (unlike his statement in 4:14, but cp. 15:34) **to shame you**. The judgment is to be not done by outsiders, but between **believers** (literally "brothers and sisters"). Again the point of chapter 5 is reiterated: the church is fit and responsible for arbitrating matters of Christian moral failure or of disputes between Christians, but it must not now handle the affairs of non-Christians.

6:6
This verse may be a question, a statement of fact, or an exclamation; the meaning changes but little. Again, Paul seems aware that brother Christians will have disagreements – else why concede to set up a church court? – but it is the crossing of the boundary to stand **in front of unbelievers** as judges that is offensive.

---

[263] See especially Garland, *1 Corinthians*, 204-07.
[264] So Thiselton, *First Corinthians*, 433; Hays, *First Corinthians*, 94.
[265] So Augustine, also Severianus (Bray, 51); Godet, *First Corinthians*, 290-91; Andrew D. Clarke, *Secular and Christian leadership in Corinth* (Leiden: Brill, 1993), 69-71.

6:7

Paul has settled the question of how to handle disputes, and now he turns to explore a more fundamental topic: an accusing attitude, which is not the best that a Christian should have. If there are **lawsuits** among Christians, **you have been completely defeated already** (or perhaps "you have failed completely," GNB). Isn't it more Christian to drop the matter entirely? Here Paul echoes the spirit of the teaching of the Lord Jesus, which the Corinthian congregation probably knew: "You have heard that it was said, 'Eye for eye, and tooth for tooth.' But I tell you, Do not resist an evil person, etc." (Matt 5:38-42).

The Greek philosophers used to say "better to suffer wrong than to do wrong," that is, suffering wrong does not detract from your virtue, but causing harm to another does. In the case of the church, the wrong done is not against the soul and reputation of the virtuous man, but against the name of Christ: *Better to suffer than that the name of Christ should suffer insult!* This is not at all to say that the church should remain indifferent. Toleration of injustice was one of the major sins of Israel, and Paul is not calling for a weakening of the church's revulsion against sins that can keep people from the kingdom of God. Paul promotes a better path, but he does not mandate suffering in silence. The Corinthian should have the right to justice in the church; but, he should also consider dropping the matter if that leads to the higher good. Paul will speak in greater detail about yielding one's rights in 1 Cor 9.

6:8

The fault does not lie with one party: **you yourselves cheat and do wrong**. And it is even worse when it is done between **brothers**. Here is a parallel with the radical ethic of Luke 12:13-15. The younger brother demands that Jesus force his older brother to pay what is his legal due. Although the younger brother has in fact been wronged, his reaction too is sin. Jesus replies, "Be on your guard against all kinds of greed." Better to have nothing to do with grasping for the world's goods! It is hardly coincidental that Paul three times includes "the greedy" and "swindlers" in the vice lists that he has crafted specifically for the Corinthian church (5:9, 11, 6:10), and twice he mentions "thieves."

Application: The Christian and lawsuits 6:1

A lawsuit is a claim brought before the legal system, usually to seek compensation from another for some loss. In Corinth, one member of the church had sued another, presumably to recover his losses from being defrauded (6:7). In Corinth, to a much greater extent than today, only the wealthy could afford to bring suit. One could almost never hope to win a case against someone of higher social scale, who could afford better lawyers and pay bigger incentives to the jurors. The man who brought suit in Corinth almost certainly was well off, and quite possibly was suing someone who could not properly defend himself.

On the other hand, the wronged have often been able to use the court system to press its claims. In some societies, even the poor successfully bring suit against a government, cooperation or private individual, especially if their cause attracts the attention of groups with a stake in supporting their own interest. In societies where the court system is corrupt or unreliable, people sue each other with less hope for a just outcome.[266] For example, Peruvian citizens in recent years tried to sue a mining company based in Colorado for allegedly dumping toxic mercury from the Yanacocha gold mine. The US company argued that they should be sued in Peru, but the Peruvians did not trust their own court system to give them justice (the case was eventually settled in the United States in 2009). In many such cases, the victims do not have the means to sue within their own national system.

We do Paul a disservice if we try to reduce his teaching here to the slogan "no lawsuits ever." In this world a lawsuit is sometimes the only legal recourse for those who have been wronged, especially if the offender is richer and more powerful. Yet what happens when today's poorer Christian tries to seek redress from the richer? Perhaps his church suddenly steps in and tells him that it is a sin to sue, that the wronged believer simply should submit and stop causing trouble. The same dynamic occurs concerning the sin of complaining. Let us imagine that a pastor of a church abuses his flock: he takes money from the offerings without accountability; when the church buys property and erects buildings, he registers himself or his relatives as the legal owner. Then a member of the flock speaks up and says that this ought not to be. What happens then? He might be rebuked with verses like 1 Cor 10:10 – "Don't you know how wicked it is to complain and murmur against your leaders?" And so a person who was wronged is magically transformed into the culprit. The leaders now feel that they can hold their heads high, because they have been "murmured against" just as Moses was. And in the process the victim is sinned against twice.

A church must love justice and right, no matter the status levels of the accused and the accuser. If it tells someone not to complain or not to bring suit, it must also follow the other half of Paul's instructions, providing the wronged Christian with a fair and efficient mechanism for obtaining justice. If a Christian might have gone before a non-Christian judge to ask for fair protection from theft, how can the church of Christ offer anything less? If a teenaged girl in the church denounces her Sunday School teacher for inappropriately touching her, how can the church demand that she stop embarrassing such an important man? No, the church should be in the forefront of standing for justice, fairness, protection of the weak and poor. It should be outraged that one of its members is harming another, no matter what amount of money and prestige the offender gives to the church.

Thus the church needs to ask what it is trying to accomplish when it discourages lawsuits among its members. Is its goal to maintain the existing power structure? Is it to silence the spread of uncomfortable information? Is it to keep people under control? Is it to maintain an image of unity and peace before other churches and before the world? Woe to the rich or powerful Christian who suppresses dissent merely to protect his own interests, and to do so invoking the name of Christ!

Let us explore another direction that offers promise today, which goes under the general title "Alternative Conflict Resolution." This is an attempt to resolve the parties' differences without direct court intervention. Another process is binding arbitration, where the participants yield their rights and promise to follow the decision of an arbitrator.

---

[266] On the theme of corruption in Latin America, an essential book is Arnoldo Wiens, *Los cristianos y la corrupción: desafíos de la corrupción a la fe cristiana en América Latina* (Barcelona: CLIE, 1998).

Commentary 5:1-6:20

Many Christians are looking to an alternative to lawsuits, especially when the conflict is not a simple case of sin by one party against the other. The advantage for Christians is that they may speak to each other about their grievances openly and positively, without being goaded by their lawyers toward a path of greatest possible financial gain. Christian mediators stress truth, love and forgiveness and use conflict to encourage all parties to grow in Christ.

The advantages of Alternative Conflict Resolution are several: the church may use such a system of mediation as a means to obey Matt 18:15-17 and 1 Cor 6:1-8. Within the church there are plenty of brothers and sisters who are lawyers and arbiters ought to be able to set up an appropriate system which glorifies Christ.

c. Rationale – Christians who sue are living like those who will be damned 6:9-11

6:9-10

The tone becomes more heated with two more diatribe formulas: **Do you not know that...?** followed up by **Do not be deceived** (as in 3:18; 15:33). **The wicked will not inherit the kingdom of God** (*basileia tou theou*). Here is the kingdom with its fully eschatological reference, the age to come which the resurrected saints will enter.[267] It is one of a handful of similar Pauline passages:

> 1 Cor 6:9 – The wicked will not inherit the kingdom of God (repeated almost *verbatim* in 6:10)

> 1 Cor 15:50 – flesh and blood cannot inherit the kingdom of God, nor does the perishable inherit the imperishable

> Gal 5:19-21 – The acts of the sinful nature are obvious: sexual immorality, impurity and debauchery; idolatry and witchcraft; hatred, discord, jealousy, fits of rage, selfish ambition, dissensions, factions and envy; drunkenness, orgies, and the like. I warn you, as I did before, that those who live like this will not inherit the kingdom of God.

> Eph 5:5 – No immoral, impure or greedy person – such a man is an idolater – has any inheritance in the kingdom of Christ and of God.[268]

---

[267] The eschatological kingdom is also found in John 3:3, 5; Acts 14:22; also 1 Thess 2:12; 2 Thess 1:5. According to Gustav Dalman the words associated with inheritance mean "to take possession of" and may imply a title or a right to inheritance that exists prior to taking possession. The idea of "inheritance" has its roots in the Old Testament process of receiving the land under the covenant. It came to be used in both the Old Testament and rabbinic literature for inheriting the blessings of salvation in the Eschaton. See Gustav Dalman, *The words of Jesus*, tr. D. M. McKay (Edinburgh: T. & T. Clark, 1902), 125-27. See Matt. 5:4 and James 2:5, for example, for predictions of the end-time reversal, when the poor will inherit the kingdom. An excellent study on the kingdom of God may be found in Rudolf Schnackenberg, *God's rule and kingdom*, Herder and Herder, New York, 1963.

[268] Eph 5:5 differs from the other inheritance sayings in several ways: (1) it refers to having no inheritance in the kingdom, using a present tense. Nevertheless, the present tense in this context carries the same futurist reference as the others, especially 1 Cor 15:50 (contra Markus Barth, *Ephesians 4-6* [AB 34A; New York:

See too the vivid expressions of eschatological exclusion in Revelation, again with vice lists that are appropriate to the underlying themes of that book:

> Rev 21:8 – But the cowardly, the unbelieving, the vile, the murderers, the sexually immoral, those who practice magic arts, the idolaters and all liars – their place will be in the fiery lake of burning sulfur. This is the second death.

> Rev 22:15 – Outside [the city] are the dogs, those who practice magic arts, the sexually immoral, the murderers, the idolaters and everyone who loves and practices falsehood.

It is conventional opinion in certain circles that *Jesus preached the kingdom of God, and Paul preached Christ*. In fact, Paul used kingdom language in Galatia, Achaia, Macedonia and Asia, that is, in all of the regions where he planted churches. He was comfortable using "kingdom of God" as a summary of his gospel work, thus, "fellow workers for the kingdom of God" (Col 4:11). Acts too remembers that Paul preached "the kingdom of God" (Acts 19:8, 20:25, 28:28, 31; also 14:22). The evidence suggests that Paul himself coined the phrase "will not inherit the kingdom of God." It was based on the Jesus tradition (Matt 5:3, 10; 25:34 and parallels; John 3:3, 5) and while related to certain concepts in Second Temple Judaism, has no exact parallels in Jewish literature. The nearest parallel to Paul is James 2:5 ("Has not God chosen those who are poor in the eyes of the world to be rich in faith and to inherit the kingdom he promised those who love him?") but beyond that, the closest parallels are found in patristic writings which show the influence of Paul.[269] The apostle blended the kingdom formula with vice lists to produce a package that was distinctively his.[270] "These wicked people will not inherit the kingdom of God" was a regular Pauline formula. In his epistles he reminded the Corinthians, the Ephesians and the Galatians of kingdom truths of which they should have been fully aware from his first teachings in their cities.

It is vitally important that the reader understand Paul's meaning. We may not paraphrase him to say that, for example, fornication is *inconsistent with the values of justice which we should follow*. Rather, he writes as one who believes in the final judgment and the coming of God's kingdom at some time in the future, at the return of Christ (especially 1 Cor 15:50; 2 Thess 1:5). His words about sinners in 6:9-10 have to do with real cases of people who in the end times will be excluded from God's new creation because of their wicked deeds. To be excluded from the kingdom is to be

---

Doubleday, 1974], 564-65); (2) it is the kingdom of Christ and of God (or perhaps, Christ who is God); see 1 Cor 15:24 and Col 1:13 for Pauline references to Christ's kingdom; also 2 Pet 1:11.

[269] *Clementine homilies* 10.25 – "by reason of your erroneous judgments, you have become subject to demons. However, by acknowledgment of God Himself, by good deeds you can again become masters, and command the demons as slaves, and as sons of God be constituted heirs of the eternal kingdom." Ignatius applies the formula to schismatics in *Ephesians* 16.1 – "those who adulterously corrupt households 'will not inherit the kingdom of God'"; also *Philadelphians* 3.3 – "if anyone follows a schismatic, he will not inherit the kingdom of God." There are quotations of 1 Cor 6:9-10 in Polycarp, *Philippians* 5.3; Irenaeus, *Against heresies* 4.26.4; 5.11.1; he quotes the Gal 5 version in 1.6.3. It is also found in the spurious *Ignatius to the Tarsians* 7.

[270] See Gary S. Shogren, *The Pauline proclamation of the Kingdom of God and the Kingdom of Christ within its New Testament context*, unpublished thesis, University of Aberdeen, 1986; also Shogren, "'The wicked will not inherit the Kingdom of God': a Pauline warning and the hermeneutics of Liberation Theology and of Brian McLaren," *TJ* 31.1 (2010): 95-113.

Commentary 5:1-6:20

damned. That is how the church father Irenaeus could quote 1 Cor 6:9-10 and say that it, like Matt 25:14, predicts that the disinherited will be sent to the "eternal fire."[271]

In 6:9-10, Paul is building on the shorter lists of 5:10 and 11. We will give brief definitions to most of the terms, and more attention to the difficult ones. He begins with sexual sins in 6:9 -

- sexually immoral (*pornoi*) – sexual sin of any kind in whatever sphere (also in Eph 5:5)
- idolaters – Jews and Christians taught that idol worship went hand-in-glove with sexual sin, see Rom 1:18-27; also Eph 5:5
- adulterers – sexual relations that betray the marriage covenant
- *malakoi* (see below)
- *arsenokoitai* (see below)

He then moves on to other sins that the Corinthians knew well:

- thieves – both common thieves and those who defraud others out of property
- greedy – greedy for gain, mentioned also in the list in Eph 5:5
- drunkards (see below for a more exact definition)
- slanderers – the verbally abusive, perhaps linked with "drunkards," as in 1 Tim 3:3; Titus 1:7
- swindlers

Three terms deserve our special interest, not because they are prominently featured in the letter, but because they require greater attention in our day. First is the word that the NIV 1984 mistranslates as **male prostitutes**. The second term, **homosexual offenders** is more acceptable but by no means the best rendering. It strikes me that the translators of English Bibles have difficulty with these terms, not because they are trying to be "politically correct," but because literal translations are too graphic.

It has been argued by some that Paul is not condemning homosexual behavior as such, here or in Rom 1:24, 26-27, but that he is rejecting certain forms of it which were practiced in the ancient world. Thanks to some recent lexical study it is clearer what these two terms meant:

malakoi – one of its meanings is "soft," such as fine clothing (Luke 7:25). The term could by extension refer to someone who loved luxury or who was weak in character.[272] Nevertheless, the term was conventionally used to denote a male with known or suspected homosexual tendencies. BDAG offers the definition "pertaining to being passive in a same-sex relationship, *effeminate* especially of *catamites,* of men and boys

---

[271] Irenaeus, *Against heresies* 4.26.4
[272] See "*malakos*," LSJ. Plato, *Republic* 556b-c speaks of "spoiled wantons averse to toil of body and mind, and too soft to stand up against pleasure and pain, and mere idlers." This is the view taken by John Wesley, *Notes on St. Paul's First Epistle to the Corinthians*, n. p. Online: http://wesley.nnu.edu/john_wesley/notes/1Corinthians.htm – "Nor the effeminate – Who live in an easy, indolent way; taking up no cross, enduring no hardship." Another approach is the interpretation that the term refers to men who masturbate, although this is difficult to prove from the usage of the term in antiquity.

who are sodomized by other males in such a relationship."[273] The best literal rendering, although discomforting to readers, is the NET: "passive homosexual partners."

The Greeks were traditionally more accepting of homosexual sex (hence the name "Greek love") than were the Romans, but all groups despised one who submitted himself to penetration by another man. Such men lost their dignity and the respect of the community. At times slaves or minors were used for sodomy, but consensual homosexual sex was also a common practice.

Why would a man or boy act in that way? One motivation was economic, that he was a prostitute. In ancient times as today, prostitutes are sometimes voluntary, while others are coerced. Corinth had both homosexual and heterosexual prostitutes; nevertheless, the word does not in itself denote a prostitute, nor does Paul restrict himself to them. "Homosexual prostitute" is therefore a mistaken translation (as is "male prostitutes" in NRSV, NTV; see also the NAB); besides importing the idea of an economic transaction, which the word does not denote, the NIV fails to communicate to the reader that Paul is speaking only of males. The "pervert" of the CEV is too general to be of any use at all.

Another common motivation would be to seek status: by having a sexual relationship with a powerful man, a homosexual concubine[274] would gain connections and opportunities. We might compare this person with the girls of our own era, who offer themselves sexually to musical or sports stars. Another possibility, of course, is that men acted as "women" because they enjoyed it.

In whatever case, Paul says nothing about their motivation, but focuses on action or conduct. For this and other reasons, the common rendering of *malakoi* as "effeminate" is problematic (KJV; NASB), since in English the word is typically applied to boys who speak or walk in a certain way, or use gestures which are commonly associated with women, but who do not necessarily practice homosexual sex. The definition that Paul has in mind is "males who submit themselves sexually to another man, and who perhaps also dress or act in such a way for purpose of attracting other men." That is why, in his commentary on this verse, Origen warns his young male students about submitting to such *consensual* sex, "to keep your youth pure and not to be defiled with such a womanish defilement."[275]

---

[273] For example, Dio Chrysostom, *Oration* 66.25 complains that people will always criticize you, no matter what you do: "if you give thought to learning you will be called simple-minded and effeminate." Later in the paragraph he speaks of "soft clothing," using *malakos* with its meaning of soft texture. The implication is that the first use of *malakos* is meant to be a sexual slur, not a remark about "soft" clothing.

[274] That is the sense of the Latin *catamitus*, a word derived from the name of the boy Ganymede, Zeus' cupbearer whom he also kept for homosexual sex.

[275] Kovacs, 97. See especially Fitzmyer, *First Corinthians*, 255-56, who gives a list of references where *malakos* implies sexually submitting to another man. For example Dionysius of Halicarnassus, around 7 B. C., wrote in his *Roman antiquities* 7.2.4 that people wondered why a certain king had the unflattering nickname "Malakos"; one theory was that "because, when a boy, he was effeminate and allowed himself to be treated as a woman" (note that this was supposed to have been voluntary submission, not coerced). Philo, *Special laws* 3.7 §37-38 condemns those who are not ashamed to voluntarily submit to other men – "Moreover, another evil, much greater than that which we have already mentioned, has made its way among and been let loose upon cities, namely, the love of boys, which formerly was accounted a great infamy even to be spoken of, but which sin is a subject of boasting not only to those who practise it, but even to those who suffer it, and who, being accustomed to bearing the affliction of being treated like women, waste away as to both their souls and bodies, not bearing about them a single spark of a manly character to be kindled into a flame, but having even the hair of their heads conspicuously curled and adorned, and having their faces smeared with vermilion, and paint, and things of that kind, and having their eyes pencilled beneath,

Commentary 5:1-6:20

arsenokoitai appears in the New Testament only here and in 1 Tim 1:10. It is inaccurately translated as "sexual perverts" in the RSV. "Homosexual offenders" (NIV 1984) and "homosexual perverts" (GNB) are misleading, leaving open the question, *So then, is homosexual sex permissible, so long as it is not offensive or perverted?* Nor is "homosexuals" an acceptable rendering (GW), as we shall see below. "Behave like a homosexual" (CEV), coupled with its rendering of *malakoi* as "pervert" is possibly the least felicitous English translation now in general use. The ESV is somewhat better with "men who practice homosexuality" (similarly KJV; NET; NAB; NIV 2011; NLT; see also NJB; NKJV; NRSV).[276]

The translation offered by the BDAG lexicon might be confusing: "a male who engages in sexual activity with a person of his own sex, *pederast*," since BDAG later adds that it cannot be limited to pederasty. For a working definition of this rare word, one must look to its two components: it is a compound made of *arsēn* ("male") and *koitē* ("bed").[277] The Hebrew equivalent, *mishkav zakur*, was the regular rabbinic term generally to describe homosexual sex between males.[278] It is highly likely that Paul was thinking of Lev 18:22, "Do not lie with a man as one lies with a woman; that is detestable." In the Septuagint the verb and preposition *koimaomai meta* ("sleep with") is a metaphor for sexual intercourse.[279] Again in Lev 20:13 it states – "If a man lies with a man as one lies with a woman, both of them have done what is detestable. They must be put to death; their blood will be on their own heads." This verse is found in the context of other sexual sins, such as incest and bestiality. There is nothing in the context of Leviticus to support the hypothesis that Moses was specifically condemning "sacred prostitution," that is, consorting with another male as part of the worship of some idol (a practice that appears in Deut 23:18). It is a logical fallacy to argue: *Moses condemns sex*

---

and having their skins anointed with fragrant perfumes (for in such persons as these a sweet smell is a most seductive quality), and being well appointed in everything that tends to beauty or elegance, are not ashamed to devote their constant study and endeavours to the task of changing their manly character into an effeminate one. And it is natural for those who obey the law to consider such persons worthy of death, since the law commands that the man-woman who adulterates the precious coinage of his nature shall die without redemption, not allowing him to live a single day, or even a single hour, as he is a disgrace to himself, and to his family, and to his country, and to the whole race of mankind."

[276] The KJV (originally 1611) does not use the word "homosexual"; in fact, the term was invented only in 1869, by a German-Hungarian physician. The KJV's "abusers of themselves with men," while a bit abstract, is a better translation than "homosexuals."

[277] Dale B. Martin argues that it is fallacious to define the meaning of a word by analyzing its etymology, thus he doubts that *arsenokoitēs* means "sex between men." While his point is valid in part, he fails to mention that word meanings in fact may often be found in their etymology, especially in the case of rarely used or newly coined compound words. In the case of *arsenokoitēs*, it is possible that Paul himself has invented the term with an eye to meta *arsenos* ou koimētēsē *koitēn* gunaikos in Lev 18:22. The fact that the Greek form is the mirror image of the Hebrew *mishkav zakur* is a strong indication that in this case, the etymology is indeed reflected in the Greek phrase's significance. Martin tries to define the word by looking at its use in a vice list, in *Sybilline oracles* 2:70-77; since the word occurs near other sins of oppression, therefore *arsenokoitēs* could mean "oppressive sex between men." In fact, a vice list is a poor context for defining a word: sometimes similar vices are grouped together, sometimes they are not. Martin concludes that while *arsenokoitēs* might mean some sort of oppressive sex, no-one today really knows what it means. See pages 119-20 in Dale B. Martin, "*Arsenokoites* and *malakos*: meanings and consequences," in *Biblical ethics and homosexuality: listening to Scripture*, ed. Robert L. Brawley (Louisville, KY: Westminster John Knox, 1996), pp. 117-36.

[278] Robin Scroggs, *The New Testament and homosexuality* (Philadelphia: Fortress, 1983), 107-08.

[279] The verb is passive in the LXX, which is the common Greek idiom. See the parallel in Gen 19:32, where the daughters of Lot plan, "Let's get our father to drink wine and then lie with him."

between men; there existed pagan cultic prostitutes in that day; therefore, when Moses condemns homosexual sex, he was limiting himself to cultic homosexual prostitutes.

It is important to note that Leviticus played a role earlier in this epistle. From Lev 18:8 – "Do not have sexual relations with your father's wife" – comes the very sin that Paul condemns in 1 Cor 5:1. Just as the incestuous man should be cast outside the community, so the *arsenokoitai* will be excluded from the eschatological realm. That is to say, the apostle who says that we are "not under the law" can also go on and define sexual sin by using that same Mosaic code. This is the reason why he can simply say that "fornication" (*porneia*) is a sin, in this epistle and in 1 Thess 4:3, using that term as an umbrella for all sexual sins. In the gentile world that required him to have taught his new converts what precisely he meant by "fornication."

With *arsenokoitai* therefore, Paul is speaking of "men who lie down with other men for sex." This was the interpretation given to Leviticus by the rabbis, presumably including the rabbi Saul before his conversion. It appears that Paul the apostle is teaching the same doctrine. The term is used in our literature only for males who participate in same-sex acts.[280] *arsenokoitai* is probably a broader term than *malakos*, which refers to the submissive participant. Some have suggested *arsenokoitēs* refers to the active (or "male") partner, as BDAG "of one who assumes the dominant role in same-sex activity;" nevertheless, this nuance is not certain.

Which English Bible best captures Paul's use of *malakoi*? For those with a high threshold for forthright talk, the NET Bible wins the award for its pinpoint accuracy: "passive homosexual partners, practicing homosexuals." The NIV 2011 chooses to take these two words, which to some extent are synonymous and overlap, and to combine both into the one English expression "men who have sex with other men." The ESV and HCSB likewise combine the terms into one with its "men who practice homosexuality" and "anyone practicing homosexuality," a translation which is not as precise as the NIV 2011 (the new NIV is, inexplicably, less accurate when it translates *arsenokoitai* as "those practicing homosexuality" in 1 Tim 1:10).

What is lacking from these terms is any suggestion that Paul was limiting himself to (or indeed, even thinking of) prostitution, or to the sexual coercion of minors or slaves.[281] In fact, it is doubtful whether Paul would go out of his way to exclude from the kingdom the *malakoi* if they had been forced to perform sexual acts. A condemnation of the coerced would be mooted, since in Paul's theology, as all in Christian teaching, where there is no freedom to act there is no moral culpability. How then, can theologians argue that Paul is damning those who are extreme examples of the oppressed: minors or slaves who are forcibly used for sex? Paul, along with Philo and Origen, condemns only those

---

[280] So Fitzmyer, *First Corinthians*, 255-58; Garland; Schrage, Thiselton, Fee.
[281] As believes Irene Foulkes, *Problemas pastorales en Corinto* (San José: DEI-SBL, 1996), 166 (my translation): "Judged by the love and justice of the kingdom, the practice of pederasty is condemned because it constitutes an unjust relationship in which a man satisfies his own desire, taking advantage of the youth (and also of the economic necessity) of a young man." While these thoughts on pederasty are in themselves true, Foulkes offers no proof that pederasty is the issue in *this* passage. Nor does she pay careful attention to the text: if we were to follow her line of thought, then Paul is not condemning "pederasty" but "victims of pederasty." She cannot explain why Paul would condemn the "young man" from eternal salvation. Along this line see also Scroggs, *The New Testament and homosexuality*, 126-27, who argues that this has only to do with pederasty and not with consensual adult relations. Martin, "*Arsenokoites* and *malakos*," 122, makes it speak of sexual violation, although the historical references that he cites do not prove his case. He adds that in the end our ethic should include the Bible, but does not necessarily have to take the Bible's teaching as authoritative.

who sin of their own volition.

There are those who argue that if one finds a condemnation of homosexual activity in 1 Cor 6:9, then that person must have approached the text with an anti-homosexual bias. An analogy is then drawn with the institution of slavery: just as many Christians once employed the Bible to justify slavery, so today people use it to condemn homosexual behavior. The observation is based on a truth, that no reader approaches the biblical text free of assumptions. Nevertheless, the slavery analogy – which is too often assumed to be a parallel, not proven – breaks down almost immediately. Those same exegetes often take *malakoi* to mean men and boys who are forcibly used for sex. So then, what if we swap out the two categories of 1 Cor 6:9 and replace them with "slave" and "slave-owner"? If Paul, in our hypothetical construct, wanted to condemn slavery, he would of course never say that both slaves and slave-owners will be excluded from the kingdom as "unjust people" (*adikaioi*). Likewise, if Paul wanted to condemn the practice of predatory sex, forced upon the unwilling, by no means would he say that *victims* of sodomy will be damned along with their oppressors. The slavery analogy simply does not hold up.

In Corinth and around the world, there existed every sort of sexual activity. Paul traveled widely and knew his environment well; he was no innocent. He knew that there were relationships that were violent, and others that were consensual. There were people in heterosexual, homosexual and bisexual relationships. For example, young men might take a lover of the same sex while he was single, and later marry a woman. Indeed, as Thiselton notes, in this verse the apostle seems to be painting in broad strokes: not only adulterers, but fornicators of any type! Not only so-called normal heterosexual relations outside of marriage, but homosexual! Not only the aggressor, but also the (willingly) receptive! All these sins result in exclusion from the kingdom. Paul will not allow people who commit "normal" illicit sex acts to look down on other sinners who are marginalized by society – all are subject to God's condemnation.[282]

We moderns tend to think of homosexuality in terms of sexual orientation rather than in terms of practice. Paul would certainly have been aware that some of his day practiced sexual acts on account of their own preferences. This is the case in the other key passage, Rom 1:26-27 –

> Because of this, God gave them over to shameful lusts. Even their women exchanged natural relations for unnatural ones. In the same way the men also abandoned natural relations with women and were inflamed with lust for one another. Men committed indecent acts with other men, and received in themselves the due penalty for their perversion.

Nevertheless, while men are said to be "inflamed with lust for one another," what is not said is if they have a strictly homosexual orientation as such, or if they are bisexual. In fact, neither in Romans, 1 Corinthians or elsewhere does Paul address whether people are born with homosexual tendencies or whether they are acquired; neither does his source, Leviticus.[283] He does not mention bisexuality, although probably such were the

---

[282] Cf. the excellent essay in Thiselton, *First Corinthians*, 447-53. In contra, John Boswell concludes that "The New Testament takes no demonstrable position on homosexuality." See *Christianity, social tolerance, and homosexuality* (Chicago: University Press, 1980), 103-17.

[283] Fitzmyer, *First Corinthians*, 250.

majority of men who engaged in homosexual acts in 1st-century Corinth. For Paul this does not make any difference in the matter of exclusion of the unjust from the kingdom. (See below, Application: Homosexuality and the gospel).

6:10

Another word that strikes discord in modern ears is **drunkards** (as *methusoi* is translated in most English versions, which is a better rendering than "drinkers"). We wonder how and whether this can be related to modern scientific studies of alcoholism, and once again Paul is thought by some to be out of touch with what we now know. Here, as in the case of homosexual sex, it must be kept in mind that Paul is using a term to describe *behavior*, not its underlying cause or results. It is a mistake to render this "alcoholics" in order to make Paul sound more modern; the two words are not the same at all. A "drunkard" is one who regularly drinks to intoxication. Whether he is an alcoholic, an occasional binger, or a weekend overdrinker does not interest Paul here. What is noteworthy is that "drunkard" makes the vice list, because it too is relevant for the church at Corinth (see 11:21).

While the New Testament nowhere forbids the use of wine, Paul does speak out against its abuse (Eph 5:18; 1 Thess 5:7-8; 1 Tim 3:8; Titus 2:3).[284] He follows the Scriptural injunctions against the foolishness of drunkenness, for example, Prov 23:20-21 –

> Do not join those who drink too much wine
>   or gorge themselves on meat,
> for drunkards and gluttons become poor,
>   and drowsiness clothes them in rags.

All the elements of this vice list focus not on the odd sin, but on "life-dominating" behaviors. Paul is not speaking of the man who one time slips into, say, drunkenness, but one who has becomes identified with that sin. These behaviors become public knowledge, and tend to color the whole person's life and personality. Thus, a man does not simply drink often and much, he has become, he is, a "drunkard," whose behavior may go on to include verbal abuse, physical violence, fornication, as well as greed or hatred or other fast-breeding vices.

We now come to the question of intent: why does Paul mention this kingdom teaching here? Why does he seem to assume that the kingdom of God self-evidently affects how Christians will manage lawsuits and fraud? The answer is a double-edged sword. First, the anticipated future kingdom reinforces Paul's teaching in 6:1 and 6:6 (and perhaps v. 4): these gentile sinners from 6:9-10 are the kinds of people you will find sitting at the local tribunal. God will not allow such into the kingdom. You will judge them in the end, so why not handle small claims without their interference?

The second point is more subtle and more pressing: Paul has seen in the Corinthian

---

[284] There is a long train of those who wish to prove that wine in the New Testament era did not contain alcohol, that it was only grape juice. Such exegesis is an example of the fallacy known as "special pleading" or "*ad hoc* reasoning." After all, how is it possible that wine (*oinos*) contain no alcohol if it is a product of fermentation (Mark 2:22) and, if used in excess, causes drunkenness (Eph 5:18), while at the same time *oinos* contains no alcohol? In fact, Paul's practical advice that Timothy "use a little wine (*oinos*)" (1 Tim 5:23) makes no sense unless that wine contains alcohol: Timothy's stomach ailments were due to drinking water that had contaminants, which the alcohol in wine would kill.

church behaviors which they already know characterize the damned. The fact that the vice list is directly oriented toward Corinth shows that it is a warning about their behavior and only secondarily a polemic against "outsiders." When a Corinthian brother defrauds, or fornicates, or steals, or slanders, it raises the question of whether he is only a "so-called brother." Those who do such things should not only be concerned for appearances, or for maintaining the unity of the church; they should take care to their own eternal destiny.[285]

Application: Homosexuality and the gospel 6:9

The word "homosexual" is of relatively modern origin: it seems to have been coined in 1886 in the German reference book *Psychopathia sexualis* by Richard von Krafft-Ebing; he argued that the inclination to homosexuality was produced during gestation in the womb. He treated homosexuality alongside other "neuroses" such as pedophilia and other "perversions" (his terms). Nevertheless, the idea that some were homosexually-oriented was not his invention; throughout the 19th century there was a growing trend to distinguish homosexuals from other people.

The current debate over homosexuality and gay rights has obscured what Paul actually says in 1 Cor 6:9. Paul shows none of our modern interest in "sexual orientation," its origin and its nature. Nor would he approach the topic using Krafft-Ebing's definition of homosexuality as a disease. Rather he speaks in this verse of *behaviors*, acts of sexual intimacy between males, whether a man is the aggressor or passive partner. He would include men who coerce others to have sex, but as we argued above, he is not here speaking of those who were compelled to perform homosexual acts. It is misleading, then, to translate 1 Cor 6:9 using the modern term "homosexuals" (as GW, NASB), a word that is freighted with implications which Paul did not intend. For Paul does not deal with what it means to be a homosexual by modern definition or, for that matter, bisexual or heterosexual. This stands in marked contrast to the conventional language of psychologists and of gay and lesbian groups and many traditionalists, who regard homosexuality as something one is rather than what one does.

To summarize, Paul's message in these two verses is that people who are bound to sin will be excluded from salvation. These include males who of their own will engage in same-sex intimacy.

Our culture responds to homosexuality, to use the modern term, in many ways. On the one hand, there exists a hatred of men who act effeminate or who are known as practicing homosexuals. Our large cities have running histories of gangs beating or murdering gay men. Perversely, it is not unknown for gangs to sodomize a homosexual in order to dominate and shame him. This is machismo at its lowest, and coincidentally it also comes close to the mentality of the Greco-Roman world: *you're not "gay" as long as you're the one taking charge and playing the aggressor-male*. That philosophy is nowhere more evident today than in the prison system of many nations, where sexual

---

[285] There is a striking exposition of this and other verses from 1 Corinthians in Irenaeus, *Against heresies* 4.27.4, to demonstrate against the Gnostics that the God of the Old Testament and the God of Christ are the same, and that the Old Testament was written for Christian instruction. Quoting 6:9-10 he reminds his readers, "And as it was not to those who are without that he said these things, but to us, lest we should be cast forth from the kingdom of God, by doing any such thing..."

predation is one way to establish the power hierarchy. In all these cases, Paul's words apply equally to ancient Greeks or modern Colombians or Mexicans or North Americans: it is the behavior that condemns you, not whether you feel "turned on" while you're doing it.[286]

In this commentary we will take the following approach:

1. A homosexual inclination is not, as was once the fashion in psychology, a disease to be cured.

2. A homosexual tendency is influenced by genetics and *in vitro* experience but not genetically determined. This is the general trend of the research up to this point, and it is consistent with the biblical teaching.

3. A homosexual tendency does seem to have a correlation with a poor or nonexistent relationship with the same-sex parent. While that is not the universal "root cause," still, many male homosexuals report that they were physically, emotionally or sexually abused by their fathers. They felt rejected by that parent and came to identify more with the mother, which at times lead to even more rejection by the father. We need to provide young boys with a positive male role model, whether uncle or grandfather or a man from the church.

4. Homosexuality is not eliminated by forcing boys to be more macho, or girls more feminine. In fact, it may make the situation worse if the father rejects the boy who likes music or poetry or is indifferent to football. All boys – and all girls – should feel comfortable with who they are and be accepted even if their tastes are outside of traditional masculine or feminine interests.

5. Homosexual practice is not a breed apart from other behaviors which bar one from the kingdom. Many Christians act as if it was the worst sin possible. Nevertheless, consensual homosexual sex is surely far removed from the wickedness of forced incest or child abuse (for example, by clergy who prey upon underaged boys or girls).

6. Homosexual temptation is not "cured" by finding the right girl or man. There are too many tragic cases of people who try to change themselves by a marriage which later falls apart.

7. Homosexual temptations do not have to be acted upon.[287] We might add that nursing any illicit sexual thoughts apart from marriage is against the gospel, no matter what form it takes (see Matt 5:28).

---

[286] The men of Sodom who wanted to rape Lot's guests used homosexual rape for a show of power. Gen 19:4-11 nowhere states that the men of Sodom were gay, nor that their sin was their sexual orientation. Rather, they wished to assert dominance over Lot and his visitors through the use of sexual force. Lot for his part offered his daughters for them to use sexually (19:7b-8) – that is to say, he followed the traditional Middle Eastern code of hospitality by sacrificing his family for the safety of guests who had come under his roof. In this way Lot "submitted" to the men, who for their part rejected the offer of substitute victims (because they were not attracted to women? The text is silent on this) and threatened to violate Lot instead (19:9). The close parallel in Judges 19:22-25 is useful: a Levite is staying in a home in Gilead. The men of the city pound on the door to make his host release the man to him; the host offers his own wife and the Levite's concubine, but the men refuse. Nevertheless, the Levite throws his concubine to them, and they gang-rape her until she dies: the men of Gilead were apparently lusted after "dominance" rather than homosexual sex as such.

[287] See the document by Cardinal Ratzinger (later Pope Benedict XVI), "Letter to the bishops of the Catholic Church on the pastoral care of homosexual persons," Rome, October 1986 (online http://www.vatican.va/roman_curia/congregations/cfaith/documents/rc_con_cfaith_doc_19861001_homosexual-persons_en.html).

8. Homosexual temptations may be extremely difficult to withstand. This behavior is deeply rooted in the lifestyle of the individual. It involves his social life and his inner life and also the way he presents himself to others.

We hear Christians raising the topic of homosexuality only to shake their heads over the advances of "gay rights." Evangelicals and Catholics typically stand together against the legalization of gay marriage. But can that be the focus of the Christian message regarding the homosexual? How should Christians approach this issue both within and without the church?

1. Be forthright about what the Bible calls sin. This is actually positive news, since the gospel is designed to save sinners. Of course, there is huge pressure today to eliminate homosexual behavior from the category of sin. Some try to prove from the Bible that we have misunderstood what it says about homosexuality. I have found their arguments ultimately unconvincing. Yet we must ever base our message squarely on the Word, not on some sense that "homosexuality just feels wrong."
2. Preach "Christ crucified" as the one answer for all questions. Although many Christians could also use professional help (particularly "drunkards"), still it is the cross that is the basis for all change and reconciliation.
3. Stand squarely against hatred, violence and discrimination. The Catholic church and the evangelical both speak out against homosexual behavior, but the message is misinterpreted by friend and foe alike. Christians are widely blamed by gay rights groups for fomenting violence and discrimination towarded homosexuals in society (under the law, in the workplace). The church must love and embrace gay and lesbian people as it does any other person, no more or no less than with the love of Jesus.
4. Accept that evangelical churches have members with homosexual issues. Yes, this means your church as well, not just the other congregations or denominations. Remember this the next time you are tempted to make fun of the gays, by mocking their way of speaking or acting. This is a knife in the heart of people who may be at this moment seeking Christ's love and power with all their might.
5. Do not commit the error of taking gay rights groups as the spokesman for all homosexual people; neither should you ignore them, since much is to be learned from organized groups.
6. Be a place of refuge for people with AIDS. "Unprotected sex between men is the main mode of HIV transmission" in North America, Latin America and the Caribbean.[288] Nevertheless, we do not have the authority biblically to proclaim AIDS as a plague sent by God to punish sinners. Nor are we wise to discourage protection against sexually-transmitted diseases. But we do have a fine opportunity to demonstrate that we are willing to stand by those who suffer, even when the sufferers are opposed to the gospel. Many evangelical churches have had an excellent ministry with AIDS patients and used it as an opportunity for evangelism and for proclaiming its love to the homosexual community.

---

[288] From the Joint United Nations Programme on HIV/AIDS, at the World Health Organisation. See online http://www.unaids.org/en/

6:11

Paul concludes this implicit warning with a positive note: **And that is what some of you were**. He contrasts the past with the present as he often does (see especially Eph 2:1-22). And he brings up the dynamic that is so typically Pauline: on the one hand, the Corinthians are saints and have already been delivered from these sins; on the other hand, they have to live out what they are, God's chosen people.

As in 1:30 ("righteousness, holiness and redemption"), there is a triad of salvation words: **But you were washed, you were sanctified, you were justified. Washed** is a common term for the cleansing of the inner person. Some have seen in this an allusion to water baptism.[289] Nevertheless, the point here is not the rite itself, but the deeper reality, the inner change that comes through the Spirit. Paul will speak to the Corinthians of the New Covenant in 1 Cor 11:25 and 2 Cor 3:6, the latter verse in particular showing how he viewed his ministry as a fulfillment of the prophetic word. "Washing with water" had been a part of the New Covenant language since the days of Ezekiel:

> Ezek 36:25-27 – I will sprinkle clean water on you, and you will be clean; I will cleanse you from all your impurities and from all your idols. I will give you a new heart and put a new spirit in you; I will remove from you your heart of stone and give you a heart of flesh. And I will put my Spirit in you and move you to follow my decrees and be careful to keep my laws.

It is likely that 6:11 (and John 3:5, "born of water") has its roots in that passage. Because the Corinthians are "spiritual" (people of the Spirit) and have been "washed," this means that they have been turned around from their old way of life. Even though Ezekiel had been speaking of Israel in his prophecy, now the gentile Christians too have been converted into new people. Along a similar vein, in other passages Paul will speak of believers as having put on the "new man" (Col 3:10).

Sanctified harkens back to the "sanctified" or "holy," God's chosen people (1:2), and the holy temple that is the church (3:17). He uses an aorist verb; as in 1:2, he is pointing to a past event, part of their conversion experience. Yet the past must influence the present; as Gordon Fee says of this section: "Theology for Paul is not an abstraction, but the application of the gospel to life in the real world."[290] The apostle is no friend to the notion that believers may be "positionally" sanctified and then go on living in sin: after all, "that is what some of you *were*," in the past. The called and justified will most certainly manifest a life of holiness. The obverse is also true: those who are not holy should beware of what excludes people from the kingdom of God. Be greedy, sue other Christians, commit sexual sin, and you are acting like the damned.

Justified (from *dikaioō*) is a key Pauline concept, but the verb appears only twice in this epistle. It is useful to compare 6:11 with the other reference, 4:4 – "For I know of nothing against myself, yet I am not justified by this; but He who judges me is the Lord" (NKJV). "Justify" (or "acquit," see ESV, NASB, NET) has to do with the decisions taken by a judge: if a judge finds the defendant to be righteous, then he has justified him. The opposite term is "condemn": God as judge condemns the wicked.

---

[289] Barrett; Conzelmann. Fee, *First Corinthians*, is less sure. See also Acts 22:16; 1 Pet 3:21.
[290] Fee, *First Corinthians*, 248.

"Justification" is primarily eschatological, that is, having to do with the final judgment, when the righteous will inherit the kingdom of God. Nevertheless, those who believe in Christ have the assurance that they are already acquitted by God, in anticipation of the end. "Those he called, he also justified" (Rom 8:30), and both of these are past events.

It is likely that **in the name of the Lord Jesus Christ and by the Spirit of our God** should be attached to all three facets of salvation in 6:11, not simply "justified." "Our God" is the Father who washes, sanctifies and justifies – the passive verbs are what is commonly known as the "divine passives" and have the Father as their unnamed doer. Barrett points out the "unconscious Trinitarianism" in 6:11, as God, the Lord Jesus Christ and the Holy Spirit all work in the believer (see likewise the even clearer statement in 2 Cor 13:14). Unconscious or not, the language has its roots in what Paul has said in chapter 2 – that there is one wisdom of God, and that that is revealed in the Holy Spirit and in the cross gospel of Christ.

3. Libertinism 6:12-20

Paul abruptly moves to a new sin, again with no transitional words. This section is complicated by the strong possibility that Paul is quoting or paraphrasing the words of someone in Corinth, "slogans" which he then refutes or reorients. But which are slogans and which are Paul's own sentiments? The Greek lacks quotation marks or other semantic signals, and so the reader must hunt for contextual clues.

6:12

The NIV uses quotation marks to denote what its editors believe to be Corinthian ideas, which Paul quotes. It is almost certainly correct when it designates **"Everything is permissible for me"** (*panta moi exestin*) as a Corinthian slogan. That conclusion is reinforced by the fact that Paul twice uses the phrase, only to refute it, and that he does the same thing twice more, in 10:23.[291] "Everything is permissible for me" is very like the attitude that Paul lampoons in 4:8 – *We are kings! We are rich! We can do anything we like!*

What could a Corinthian have meant by such a phrase? One explanation is that they have misinterpreted Paul's doctrine of grace, giving it an antinomian meaning: if God is all-forgiving, then the mature Christian can act as he likes without negative consequences. Paul certainly faced that sort of distortion of his teaching elsewhere, according to Rom 3:8 – "Why not say – as we are being slanderously reported as saying

---

[291] Modern commentators are almost unanimous in attributing "all things are permissible for me" to the Corinthians: Fee, *First Corinthians*, 251, says it is "almost certainly a Corinthian theological slogan." See the chart in Hurd, *Origin*, 68. Thiselton, *First Corinthians*, 460, says there is no question but that it is a quotation. Calvin, *First Corinthians*, 1:214, says that Paul invented the phrase, but did so to express what the Corinthians were in fact thinking. The underlying Greek is *exestin*, which is sometimes used for what is lawful or conforms to the Torah (e. g., Mark 3:4; Matt 12:2, 14:4). The ESV and others use a form of "lawful," which is suitable if it is not taken too strictly of legal freedom. Conzelmann, *1 Corinthians*, 108, likes "I am free to do anything," which combines the two typical meanings of *exestin*; similarly the GNB: "I am allowed to do anything." Ambrosiaster, Theodoret of Cyrus, Chrysostom and Clement of Alexandria (Bray, 55-56) imply that the phrase is Pauline, and so interpret it to be a positive reference to Christian liberty.

and as some claim that we say – 'Let us do evil that good may result'?" (see also 2 Pet 3:14-17). Another interpretation is that some Corinthians have rejected the call to sexual morality because they are "enthusiasts" or have an "over-realized eschatology" that renders fornication a matter of indifference for the spiritual person.[292] As with this model in general, the text gives no indication that people visit prostitutes or commit incest based on a faulty eschatology.

A better explanation is that the Corinthians derived their slogan from a superficial use of popular philosophy, especially Stoicism. For example, the Stoic Epictetus often used *exestin* in the sense of "what lies within the power of" a person:

> What then should a man have in readiness in such circumstances? What else than this? What is mine, and what is not mine; and what is permitted (*exestin*) to me, and what is not permitted (*exestin*) to me.[293]

He taught that true freedom was the freedom for independent action within the boundaries of "the possible." The Stoic hypothesis is further bolstered by a computer search of all ancient Greek literature: the slogan "everything is permissible for me" has as its closest parallel a Stoic phrase – "For why should one get angry at the deity, for whom all things are lawful (*hō panta exestin*)?"[294] In that case, a Corinthian influenced by Stoicism might seek to live free from unnecessary restrictions. If a Christian is wise enough to understand what he may or may not do, then he can make his own choices without some apostle's rules and regulations.[295]

Paul retorts **but not everything is beneficial**; his rejoinder to the slogan is framed in typical Stoic language to denote what is "suitable action."[296] He seeks to out-do the Corinthians by showing that no real Stoic, let alone a Christian, can simply act as he wishes.

The second pair of sentences is very similar: Paul repeats their slogan and replies, **but I will not be mastered by anything**.[297] The Stoics had a horror of being coerced, whether from their environment or from their inner passions. Enslavement for them was a state of mind, and was the destiny of the unenlightened. Paul replies that, freedom is fine, but the Corinthians are forgetting how life-dominating sin can be (see especially Rom 6:12-14; also 2 Pet 2:19-20).

Therefore we have:

> Corinthian: I'm a wise man, I can do as I please!
> Paul: Yes, but even the "wise of the world" know not to misuse their freedom to

---

[292] So Fee, *First Corinthians*, 251; Lietzmann and Kümmel; H. Schlier, "*eleutheros*," *TDNT* 2:493-96. Martin, *The Corinthian body*, 70-76, tries to understand this tension from a sociological perspective. Charles Talbert, *Reading Corinthians: a literary and theological commentary on 1 and 2 Corinthians*, Crossroads, New York, 1987), 29-30, points to an "over-realized eschatology" as the source.
[293] Epictetus, *Dissertations* I.1.21. See W. Foerster, "*exestin*," *TDNT* 2:560.
[294] See Cassius Dio, *Historiae Romanae* 71.24, my rendering from the Greek. Cassius Dio (early 3rd century AD), is quoting or inventing a speech by the 2nd-century emperor and Stoic philosopher, Marcus Aurelius.
[295] Thiselton, *First Corinthians*, 463, is pleasing in this regard, as he notes the Corinthians were not libertines in the normal sense. Rather they were "spiritual people" who were confused about where the body fits into the gospel.
[296] So K. Weiss, "*sumpherō, sumphoros*," *TDNT* 9:72-73.
[297] "Mastered" (*exousiazō*) and *exestin* both have *exeimi* as their root. There could be a play on words here, but it is unlikely that the Corinthians would have caught it or that Paul intended it.

their own harm

Corinthian: I'm a wise man, I can do as I please!
Paul: Yes, but even the "wise of the world" won't let themselves be trapped

6:13
Scholarly opinion is strong that this verse too is a Corinthian slogan.[298] Nevertheless it is difficult to determine how much is Corinthian thinking and where precisely Paul's voice comes in. Most take at least the first phrase as coming from Corinth: "Food for the stomach and the stomach for food!" Some stop there, making Paul begin with "but...." (so NIV 1984; HCSB; ESV; GNB; NRSV; the NLT is particularly insensitive to the context of the epistle, making Paul say, "This is true, though someday God will do away with both of them").

The other possibility makes better sense, and the NIV 2011 is an improvement on the 1984 version: "You say, 'Food for the stomach and the stomach for food, and God will destroy them both.'" Some Corinthians were saying that they could sin with the body, since God was going to destroy the body anyway. In that case, Paul himself begins with "The body, however, is not meant for sexual immorality, etc..." (NIV 2011).[299] The main evidence is that Paul's argument in 6:13-14 is an appeal to the future resurrection of the saints. Why then would he state that God would "destroy" the body, when his whole belief system informs him that the body matters? First, the Christian's body is the temple of the Spirit (6:19); second, God will resurrect the body (1 Cor 15); and third, those who deny the resurrection are the same ones who say things like "if the dead are not raised, 'let us eat and drink, for tomorrow we die'" (1 Cor 15:32). In fact, this latter slogan is the closest parallel to "God will destroy" the body in 6:12; the two should be seen as expressions of the same false premise.

In that case the exchange goes like this:

Corinthian: Food is for the body and the body for food! What does it matter, as God will do away with food and with the physical body? Eat and drink, for tomorrow we die!
Paul: (6:13) But our body isn't for fornication, but to serve the Lord. And in fact, the Lord *is* interested in the body (6:14) as shown by the fact that he raised Jesus' body and will resurrect our bodies too

Some commentaries detect in "food" or "stomach" a coded reference to sex.[300] This is improbable, although their attitude about food was the same about sex: it's a natural appetite, so satisfy it! In the second part of the phrase, they proclaim that God would destroy the body by abolishing that corporeal plane of existence. With this slogan about food, and with their actions with prostitutes in 6:15-18, they reveal that they saw little meaning for the physical body in salvation. Unlike Paul, they saw salvation as for the "soul" and not for the physical self.

---

[298] Contra Garland, *1 Corinthians*, 229-31.
[299] Thiselton; Jerome Murphy-O'Connor, *1 Corinthians* (Doubleday Bible Commentary; New York: Doubleday, 1998), 51; Hays; Fee; Héring; Fitzmyer.
[300] "Stomach" (*koilia*) is made a false god in Rom 16:18 and Phil 3:19. It could mean the stomach or the whole digestive system, but not the sexual organs. Alternatively it could mean "the womb" (e. g., see Luke 1:44).

It is possible that the Corinthians knew the Lord's teaching from Mark 7:19: "'For it doesn't go into his heart but into his stomach, and then out of his body.' (In saying this, Jesus declared all foods 'clean')." Some might have misapplied that saying to mean that one's bodily actions could not touch the inner person, the "real Christian." If that was the case, they did not know or did not take into account that Jesus was speaking of ritual hand washing (Mark 7:3-4), not sins of gluttony or fornication (which he goes on to condemn in Mark 7:20-21).

6:14

By his power God raised the Lord from the dead, and he will raise us also: thus Paul foreshadows his detailed argument in 1 Cor 15 – that if Christ was raised bodily, and we are in Christ, then it is obviously God's pleasure to redeem our physical bodies.[301] The doctrine of the resurrection is a good balance to an inward-oriented piety or an otherworldly Christianity which has no affect on the life in the world. The resurrection affirms that God is the creator of the cosmos, and that he will not abandon it to evil forever (see Rom 8:18-23, which deals with the resurrection of the body in tandem with the "liberation" of creation).

6:15

Paul comes around to the point that he started in 6:13, namely, that fornication cannot co-exist with life in Christ. With the language of diatribe (addressing an audience that is not present, as if it were) he reminds them that **your bodies are members of Christ himself**. He uses *sōma* ("body," 6:13, 15, 16, 18, 19, 20; see especially 7:34; also 1 Thess 5:23) and also *sarx* in the neutral sense of "body" (6:16), to underscore that the gospel has to do with the physical self. Christianity is not simply lived in the heart, but in a body that dwells in the world.

Paul asks rhetorically whether it is fitting to take bodies that belongs to Christ and **unite them with a prostitute? Never!** is his sharp reply, and will show why that is in 6:16.

It is not exactly clear what it was that the Corinthians thought they could get away with. The *porneia* of 6:13 could be used for all sorts of sexual sin (including incest, 5:1; the verb form refers to "orgies" in 10:8). Even though Paul is the one who mentions prostitutes in this verse, that is only one manifestation of "fornication" or "sexual immortality."

Visiting a prostitute may strike us as appalling behavior for a Christian, but we must keep in mind the sexual culture of the day. Corinth was a port town and boasted of many prostitutes to service the sailors and travelers. But even within the settled population, prostitution was a cultural norm. Young single men were especially prone to squander time and money with prostitutes. Even within marriage, a wife was not to be employed for sexual satisfaction, but to bear legitimate heirs. Slaves were used for sex, since whatever children they bore were no threat to the lines of inheritance. Beyond this, liaisons with prostitutes were considered a man's natural right. A few philosophers

---

[301] Ernst Käsemann makes an excellent observation concerning this verse – "…for Paul it is all-important that the Christian life is not limited to interior piety and cultic acts…In the bodily obedience of the Christian…the lordship of Christ finds visible expression, and only when this visible expression takes personal shape in us does the whole thing become credible as Gospel message." P. 135, "Primitive Christian apocalyptic," in *New Testament questions of today* (Philadelphia: Fortress, 1969), 108-37.

looked down on prostitution, but generally it was an acceptable part of society, so long as one did not go broke paying for sex or otherwise make a public fool of himself.[302]

Within this context, a Christian man might invent all sorts of rationalization for using a prostitute: he was sparing his wife bother and unwanted pregnancies; he was protecting his children's inheritance; he was helping the local economy; he was communing with the girl (or boy) only with his body – his wife still had his legal commitment, and of course Jesus had his soul.

6:16

Not so, says Paul, introducing another diatribe formula: **Do you not know that he who unites himself with a prostitute is one with her in body?** He caps off his point by quoting the foundational verse Gen 2:24 – **"The two will become one flesh."**[303] In context, Genesis refers to the first marriage between Adam and Eve, which the author holds out as the model for all unions. But for the apostle, the Genesis mandate does not cover only legitimate marriage (as in Eph 5:31). In God's eyes, the person is united into one with every single sexual partner, no matter how casual the encounter. In other words, it is impossible to categorize intercourse as something merely physical, or beneath God's notice or interest.

According to 1 Cor 7, it seems that other Corinthians took that same principal and went to the other extreme: that marriage to a non-believer was a link with evil and thus an abomination and should be dissolved (see 1 Cor 7:12-16).

6:17

Paul completes this circle by reminding them that the believer **unites himself with the Lord**. The NIV introduces verse 17 with "but," but a better rendering of the Greek word *de* in this context is "and":

> The one who unites himself to a prostitute
> is one with her in body, and
> the one who unites himself with the Lord
> is one with him in the Spirit.

This completes the thought of v. 15 – if a Christian is joined in union with a prostitute and also joined in union with Christ, then Christ through him is in some sense has trafficked with a prostitute. The sinning Christian is mixing two worlds together into an abomination (see 2 Cor 6:14-7:1).[304] The NIV speaks of being united to Christ by the "spirit," but as we have seen in 1 Cor 2, *pneuma* in Paul's language more often refers to the Spirit of God, not the human spirit. Thus he anticipates the truth that the Christian is united to Christ because he or she is the temple of the Holy Spirit (6:19).

---

[302]This sort of denunciation of prostitution on pragmatic grounds is reflected in the Hellenistic Jewish book Eclesiasticus 19:2-3 NRSV – "Wine and women lead intelligent men astray, and the man who consorts with prostitutes is reckless. Decay and worms will take possession of him, and the reckless person will be snatched away."

[303] Paul adds "two" (*duo*) to the Hebrew, but so too the Syriac version, the Targum of Jonathan, the Septuagint, Philo, Matt 19:5-6, Mark 10:8, Eph 5:31. The Septuagint uses *proskollaō* ("join with"), a cognate of Paul's verb *kollaō* in Corinthians.

[304] See too 2 Cor 6:14-7:1. See the detailed analysis in Martin, *The Corinthian body*, 174-79.

6:18

Now comes the command: **Flee from sexual immorality** (*porneia*) consciously echoes the account of Joseph's flight from Potiphar's wife in Gen 39:12, which in the Septuagint uses the same verb for "flee" (*pheugō*). Paul will repeat his warning in terms of the Exodus in 1 Cor 10:8 – "We should not commit sexual immorality" (the cognate verb *porneuō*). The all pervasive nature of sex and the daily encounters with temptation mean that the believer must make clear decisions and take strong action in order to avoid falling into sin and dishonoring Christ.

All other sins a man commits are outside his body has its difficulties in translation; the NIV is preferred.[305] What is questionable is whether fornication is the only sin that is committed **against his own body**. What about suicide? Substance abuse? Gluttony? Don't they harm the body too?

The possibilities boil down to two. First, perhaps Paul means that fornication is a qualitatively worse sin than others, since other sins don't invade and harm the person to the same degree. Along that line, NLT has "No other sin so clearly affects the body as this one does." Or, as is more likely, he is speaking in exaggerated terms, since he is thinking specifically of the Corinthians being united with Christ's body and being united with prostitutes. Nothing else is as grossly discordant as that sin, insulting as it is to Christ and to the Spirit.

Application: Prostitution 6:17-18

Fornication of all types, adultery, use of prostitutes and homosexual sex are the behaviors that Paul condemns in this letter. This is natural, since the Greco-Roman stereotype is that young unmarried men went to prostitutes to find relief, and Greeks often formed homosexual liaisons to last them until they were married. Adultery was widespread, as was the keeping of lovers, concubines or slaves for sex.

The Bible consistently condemns the prostitution of either sex. Normally, however, it speaks from a male perspective and tells men not to consort with female prostitutes (as in Prov 7:6-27; 23:27; 29:3). The Law forbad priests from marrying a prostitute (Lev 21:7-8) and condemned cultic prostitution (Exod 34:16; Deut 23:18 mentions male and female cultic prostitutes), the very problem alluded to later in this epistle (1 Cor 10:7-8). On the other hand it did not punish the prostitute herself, unless she brought special disgrace to her father (Lev 21:9; Deut. 22:21).

In the New Testament, prostitutes came in for special notice in the ministry of Christ, since by following Christ they and other known sinners would enjoy salvation ahead of the self-righteous (Matt 21:32). Despite what some versions do with 1 Cor 6:9 (especially those which have "male prostitutes"), the Bible does not prohibit prostitutes as such from the kingdom of God. This can hardly be taken as a lax attitude toward fornication (again, 1 Cor 6:9!). Rather, the gospel doles out punishment for the men who consort with prostitutes rather than for the (female) prostitutes themselves. This probably reflects the gospel being applied in a culture in which some prostitutes were under

---

[305] So the NJB has "done outside the body" (also NKJV); the GNB has "does not affect his body." Some have suggested, with less justice this time, that Paul is citing another slogan. Hypothetically the Corinthians' idea would have been that it's not sin unless it touches the *inner* person, and if it's merely a *physical* act it isn't sin. See Thiselton, *First Corinthians*, 470-74 for the various views; Fee, *First Corinthians*, 261-63, is especially good here, and concludes that the whole statement is Paul's.

compulsion. They therefore do not carry the same culpability as those who fornicate of their own volition.

Prostitution is not a victimless crime. Minors, boys and girls, are sold into virtual slavery. Their bondage is reinforced by violence and poverty and is also driven by drug addiction. Where I live, wealthy foreigners arrive on package vacations of "sex tourism," often involving underage prostitutes. But let us not imagine that this is the only abuse. Women and men of legal age are also exploited, partly by their own choices but also because of circumstances, such as addiction, into which they were led.

For this reason, liberation theologians such as Leonardo Boff in Brazil have helped prostitutes to organize themselves into labor unions in order to protect their rights and to regain some level of dignity. In this case, the sinful side of prostitution is thought to lie primarily in the societal structures that produce the oppression and dehumanization of sex workers. While we evangelicals may find this (partly) misdirected, there is insight there as well. If our response to prostitution is to arrest and jail the prostitute, are we not adding to their oppression rather than alleviating it?

Paul does not offer a structural remedy for prostitution, but focuses on the "demand" side of the equation. Specifically, men are taught not to unite themselves with prostitutes; to honor marriage; to affirm that their bodies belong to God and, if they are married, also to their wives. More broadly they are taught that Christ came to save those on the lower rungs of society. Thus, the cross teaches us to accept grace and to offer it to others who are yet trapped in and by sin.

Beyond that the church must take other, more active, steps. One is to minister to the prostitute himself or herself, to bring Christ to people who are often the most oppressed of our society. The other is to work to change structures, especially those in which wealth and power are used to imprison the weak for sexual exploitation.

6:19a

Here is a parallel to 3:16-17 (see comments on 3:16), but this time applied to the individual member of the church: **your body**[306] **is a temple of the Holy Spirit**. We have received the Spirit **from God**. The gift of the Spirit is a running motif in this epistle, beginning with 1:8. Here Paul applies that truth to everyday morality: if God has placed his Spirit in our body, then the body matters to God, and the temple of God cannot be mixed with wicked practices. In 2 Cor 6:16 he will make the same point, only in much stronger terms, and using "temple" in the sense of the whole people of God: "What agreement is there between the temple of God and idols?"

The presence of the Spirit does not obliterate the individual's personality, nor does it lead the Christian to some otherworldly existence, in which daily behavior does not matter. "The Spirit does not lead us away from the body, but defines existence in the body as existence before God."[307] One sometimes hears people saying that they eat well and exercise and avoid smoking and drugs because "my body is a temple." What they are saying is that their body is the vessel for their mind or soul, and that they believe they should properly care for it. This is the philosophy that the Romans had: *Mens sana in corpore sano* ("a sound mind in a healthy body"). While this is a positive approach to

---

[306] Some later manuscripts, Ambrosiaster and Methodius have the plural, "bodies," probably by influence of the plural in 6:15.
[307] Conzelmann, *1 Corinthians*, 112.

physical health, the Roman slogan is not at all what Paul is driving at. Rather, the Christian's body is the temple of another person, from without, the Spirit of God. He indwells Christians and makes them a temple, and conversely, those who do not have the Spirit are not temples in that same sense.[308]

6:19b-20

Paul moves to a second, though related, metaphor: **you were bought at a price**. He develops the theme to which he briefly alluded in 1:30 – Christ is "our righteousness, holiness and redemption."[309] Although redemption is usually described as freedom from bondage, here it is taken in a different direction: that Christians were redeemed by being bought by another master, God. Redemption implies a new owner, not autonomy, and certainly not "everything is permissible for me" (6:12, 10:23). The Stoics strove for the liberty that comes through wisdom and self-control. To the contrary, Paul says, **you are not your own**.

The **price** is not named here, but the clear reference is the death of Christ.[310] The same wording is used in the next chapter, 7:22b-23a – "he who was a free man when he was called is Christ's slave. You were bought at a price."

The body of the slave was not only his own control, but was the property of another. The ancient slave-owner could buy and sell the person, or more cruelly, beat, rape or kill him or her if he so chose. The slave did not even have the legal right to commit suicide or to harm his own health, since that would be stealing something that did not belong to him. The meaning for the Christian is that we have a new Lord, who is God: **Therefore honor God with your body**.[311] He directly confronts the idea of the Corinthians, that the notion of honoring God with one's body was philosophically moot. They believed that it was in the mind or soul or spirit that God was honored, not in the physical shell. But no; according to Paul, the body can sin; or the body can honor God; but above all, the body matters. According to the Platonists of Paul's time, the self dwelled in a body – weak, sick, tempted, mortal – and that upon death the real person would escape from that prison. Tertullian is superb when he shows how the gospel teaches differently: "Where the platonic doctrine sees the body as a prison, on the other hand the apostolic doctrine sees the temple of God, when it is in Christ."[312]

"Honor God with your body": what a fitting conclusion to the first half of the epistle:

---

[308] See Charles Hodge, *The first epistle to the Corinthians* (New York: Robert Carter, 1857), 59 – "This indwelling of the Spirit constitutes each believer, every separate church, and the Church collectively the temple of God"; Héring.

[309] Redemption is also a key doctrine in Romans, Galatians and Ephesians. See Gary S. Shogren, "Redemption," *ABD* 5:324-34. In his landmark study of manumission, Deissmann, *Light from the Ancient East*, 322-34, concluded that Paul based his concept of redemption, not on the Old Testament, but on the practice of the fictitious redemption of slaves by gods in a pagan ceremony. His theory has since been invalidated. In contra, see Garland, *1 Corinthians*, 239; also Thiselton, *First Corinthians*, 476-79, for a full analysis of Deissmann's viewpoint.

[310] As it is the sense of "redemption" in Rom 3:24; Gal 3:13; Eph 1:7; Titus 2:14.

[311] Some later manuscripts, including the Majority Text, add "and in your spirit, which are God's." As Fee, *First Corinthians*, 265-66, notes, this sentiment about the human spirit is true, but the addition waters down the point about the body. Irenaeus, *Against heresies* 5.6 has a lovely section to show that salvation is for the whole person. See also 5.13.3: "what is mortal shall be swallowed up of life, when the flesh is dead no longer, but remains living and incorruptible, hymning the praises of God, who has perfected us for this very thing. In order, therefore, that we may be perfected for this, aptly does he say to the Corinthians, 'Glorify God in your body'."

[312] Tertullian, *On the soul* 53.5 (Bray, 58).

Application: "Honor God with your body" 6:20

Chrysostom believed that there was a connection between the Corinthians' carnality and their denial of the resurrection: "Do not then disbelieve the resurrection; for this is a doctrine of the Devil. This is what the Devil is earnest for, not only that the resurrection may be disbelieved, but good works also may be done away with."[313] Some Corinthians may have come to believe that the body would be destroyed, erasing all evidence of its misuse (so our comments on 6:13). Paul corrects their error in 1 Cor 15 and anticipates the practical application of the resurrection doctrine in 6:14: "By his power God raised the Lord from the dead, and he will raise us also."

Although we may have no intention of eliminating the resurrection from our roster of doctrines, we may unconsciously reject some of its implications. Thus: *What does it matter if we damage our brains or our health, so long as everything will be fixed with Jesus returns? What does God care about having sex outside of marriage – a mere bodily function! – if my sexuality will be done away with in the kingdom of God?* That error turns up in other places as well: *Why should I be concerned with the environment, since Christ will come and take us away from all this pollution?*

Some Christians follow the lure of false mysticism, by which the inner life of prayer and meditation becomes an escape. True mysticism seeks an encounter with God, not to retreat from the world but to be Christ's light to others. False mysticism may take the form of bodily self-denial. Life in the body is strangled in order to build up the true, inner life. True mysticism focuses on the grace of Christ that cannot be encountered through mere self-denial or starvation, but which is a gift from the crucified savior. There may have been false mysticism in the way the Corinthians employed the charismatic gifts, using them to retreat from the world through speaking in tongues or other experiences. Paul points out that here, too, the gifts are to build up the body of believers. That is, they are *social*, they help us to minister from person to person in a group of Christians. We will develop this point further in 1 Cor 12-14.

If, as Paul has taught, God has redeemed our self, including our physical self, then it follows that what we do in the body matters to him. We must serve God with the feelings and the mind and the heart and with the body, which too is "for the Lord" (6:13).

Paul uses the metaphor of the temple to show why Christians should not consort with prostitutes. We evangelicals often use it to forbid certain vices, that is, the abuse of tobacco or drugs or alcohol. These are indeed legitimate applications but they are far too narrow if we stop there. For God is not interested in us merely avoiding certain harmful substances. As his slaves we are his in every single detail: eating and drinking; sleeping and working; relaxing and laboring; sex; relationships with others, especially with the other redeemed servants of God; speaking, thinking, feeling; what we allow ourselves to see and hear. All these will come under the scrutiny of Christ at his judgment seat "that each one may receive what is due him for the things done while in the body, whether good or bad." (2 Cor 5:10).

---

[313] Chrysostom, *i ad Corinthios* 17.3.

C. Issues that the Corinthians have raised in their letter – 1 Cor 7-15

1. Concerning marriage: "Isn't marriage just the institutionalization of carnal desire?" 7:1-39

The Corinthians had written Paul a letter, now lost to us. Paul has waited until now to begin to answer their questions (see Introduction), not necessarily in the order in which they were written, but in the order that Paul has chosen. 1 Cor 7 is a case study of how the apostle applies God's commands in a specific situation, based on what we might label "gospel pragmatism." With the exception of 1 Cor 8-10, it is Paul's longest treatment on any one social issue.

What makes 1 Cor 7 so difficult to interpret is the fact that we are not sure what the Corinthians had asked and with what motivation, nor how we should read Paul's response based on their "conversation." This commentary will follow the approach that some Corinthians were against sexual intimacy and therefore looked down on marriage, following "Viewpoint 2," see below. Nevertheless there is another, entirely different, way to exegete the chapter:[314]

Viewpoint 1. Paul permits marriage as a concession, because otherwise some Christians are going to live in fornication (7:2).[315] In this view, Paul believes that marriage is an impediment to holiness. His ideal, which he himself lives out, is that it is better to abstain from all sexual relations (7:1). In the 2nd century, the Christian fixation with celibacy reached its extreme. According to the fiction *Acts of Paul and Thecla*, Paul's gospel was a message of "self-control and the resurrection."[316] This idea was later mitigated by the church, partly in reaction to the Gnostics, some of whom rejected marriage altogether. Even then, the church from the 3rd century onward used 1 Cor 7 to promote celibacy as the higher spiritual standard. In Carthage, Cyprian wrote that "Virgins are advancing in both the higher and better part to the Lord."[317] Later, in the East, Theodoret of Cyrus

---

[314] See especially the review of literature by Thiselton, *First Corinthians*, 487-97.

[315] For example, Allo, *Corinthiens*, 154. José María González Ruíz, *El evangelio de Pablo* (Madrid: Marova, 1977), 66, my own translation, claims that "Paul starts out by affirming, in the new religious situation, the superior nature of sacred virginity over marriage." See especially Rudolf Bultmann, *The theology of the New Testament*, tr. K. Grobel (New York: Charles Scribner's Sons, 1951, 1955), 106-08: in 1 Cor 7 Paul combined apocalyptic Judaism with the ascetic values of Gnostic dualism.

[316] According to *Paul and Thecla*, Paul taught: "Blessed are the pure in heart, for they shall see God: blessed are they that have kept the flesh chaste, for they shall become a temple of God: blessed are they that control themselves, for God shall speak with them: blessed are they that have kept aloof from this world, for they shall be called upright: blessed are they that have wives as not having them, for they shall receive God for their portion: blessed are they that have the fear of God, for they shall become angels of God: blessed are they that have kept the baptism, for they shall rest beside the Father and the Son: blessed are the merciful, for they shall obtain mercy, and shall not see the bitter day of judgment: blessed are the bodies of the virgins, for they shall be well pleasing to God, and shall not lose the reward of their chastity; for the word of the Father shall become to them a work of salvation against the day of His Son, and they shall have rest for ever and ever."

[317] Cyprian, *On the dress of virgins* 24. Matt 19:10-12 and 22:30 were the other key passages in the early church: in the age to come there is no marriage; thus in this age the Christian ought to live as a eunuch, that is, asexually.

summed up 1 Cor 7: "The Corinthians were asking Paul whether it was right for lawfully married Christians, once they were baptized, to enjoy sexual relations with each other. Paul answered by praising chastity, condemning fornication and allowing conjugal relations."[318] Of course, Paul believed that the person who marries has not "sinned" (7:28). For Augustine, celibacy was preferable, but not universally mandatory; he called it the pearl of great price.[319] There still exists the long-standing Roman tradition that priests and bishops (in the Eastern church, bishops only) must remain unmarried.[320]

Viewpoint 2. Paul affirms both marriage and celibacy as two gifts of God, and that the choice of one or the other depends on the individual's gifts and situation.[321] Still, if a person does have the gift of celibacy and is unmarried, it is better to stay celibate. Before God we are not defined by married or single, Jew or gentile, slave or free. God's will is to use each person in the state he is in, and so the Corinthians should stay where they are unless circumstances push them one way or another – the slaves are freed, or a married woman loses her husband by death or by abandonment. This is the view we will affirm in this commentary.

In the case of #1, the Corinthians would have written in order to ask Paul, *Is it alright for a Christian to marry? I'm engaged, should I go ahead with the plans? I'm married, should I leave my spouse?* Or, as Theodoret states, *I'm married, am I under obligation to have relations with my spouse?* Paul's answer in that context would be that married people should not divorce, but that if you're engaged you are better to break it off, unless of course you cannot control your sexual drives.

In the case of #2 the Corinthians may have posed a leading question, luring Paul into rejecting marriage and discouraging sexual relations for those already married: *Isn't it better, Paul, for a Christian to live as a celibate? Doesn't this make him a better believer, more detached from the world and freer from lower activities such as intercourse? In fact, shouldn't a married Christian live as a celibate or leave his/her spouse? Shouldn't a man break it off with his fiancée? Musn't a widow remain unmarried?* In that case, 7:17 is key: "each one should retain the place in life that the Lord assigned to him and to which God has called him."

---

[318] Bray, 59.

[319] Augustine, *Confessions* 6.11, 8.1.

[320] For the Roman teaching on celibate clergy, see *Catechism of the Catholic Church* §915, 1579-80; in §1599 – "In the Latin Church the sacrament of Holy Orders for the presbyterate is normally conferred only on candidates who are ready to embrace celibacy freely and who publicly manifest their intention of staying celibate for the love of God's kingdom and the service of men."

[321] So Fee; Thiselton; Robertson and Plummer; Héring; "Sex: marriage and divorce" in Victor Paul Furnish, *The moral teaching of Paul: selected issues* (3rd ed.; Nashville: Abingdon, 2009), 28-54. See too the modern view of Rome in the *Catechism of the Catholic Church*, §2349 – "'People should cultivate [chastity] in the way that is suited to their state of life. Some profess virginity or consecrated celibacy which enables them to give themselves to God alone with an undivided heart in a remarkable manner. Others live in the way prescribed for all by the moral law, whether they are married or single.' Married people are called to live conjugal chastity; others practice chastity in continence. 'There are three forms of the virtue of chastity: the first is that of spouses, the second that of widows, and the third that of virgins. We do not praise any one of them to the exclusion of the others…This is what makes for the richness of the discipline of the Church' [St. Ambrose]."

Here once again, Paul might be quoting the Corinthians' belief back to them, only in order to qualify or refute it (see comments on 6:12-13, 10:23). Once the phrase "touch a woman" is interpreted correctly (see commentary on 7:1), it *cannot* be regarded as Paul's own belief, and it is likely that he is quoting them or at least summarizing their attitude.[322] The ESV is quite correct to put 7:1b in quotations marks. We may paraphrase: *Now, concerning the things you wrote about; first, this idea that it is better that a man not have sexual relations with a woman. Very well, nevertheless, because of fornication, men and women should be married, etc.* Paul has already shown himself in agreement with the institution of marriage, quoting Gen 2:24 (in 1 Cor 6:16), which in Genesis is the response to "It is not good for the man to be alone" (Gen 2:18). We do not even need to mention a passage such as Eph 5:22-33, with its pronouncement that marriage is a model of our union with Christ. Second Temple Judaism was almost unanimously in favor of marriage, and also of sex within marriage.[323] Paul too affirms that marriage is a gift of God (7:7; obliquely in 1 Tim 4:3), and that regular sexual relations are a must (7:3).

Before studying 1 Cor 7, it is necessary to pause in order to define *asceticism* and *celibacy*. People commonly confuse one with the other, and a review of commentaries and technical study of this epistle show that even scholars fail to properly define their terms, making *non sequitur* statements along the lines of "we know that Paul was an ascetic, because he chose not to marry." This lack of precision can only skew one's interpretation of Paul's teaching.

Celibacy ("abstinence" is a close synonym in this context, as is "chastity") – the decision to abstain from marriage and from all sexual relationships, usually for religious reasons. The person is not necessarily a virgin, and may be formerly married. But he or she has decided to live without sex forever or simply for the time being.

Asceticism – a strictly disciplined lifestyle, typically for the purpose of achieving a higher spiritual level. Asceticism may include abstaining from sex, certain foods, alcohol, bodily comforts, or activities that are thought to dull the believer through worldly comfort. The only positive model of asceticism in the New Testament is that of John the Baptist, whose rough clothing and food and abstinence from alcohol reflected the Nazirite tradition of the Old Testament (Luke 1:15). The Jews criticized him for being an ascetic; they also rebuked Jesus for *not* being an ascetic (Matt 11:18-19).

Based on these definitions, an unmarried person can (and according to Paul, must be) celibate, but that chaste lifestyle has nothing necessarily to do with asceticism. For their

---

[322] So many modern commentators, for example Barrett, *First Corinthians*, 154; see Hurd, *Origin*, 65; especially Garland, *1 Corinthians*, 247-54.

[323] The Essenes may have been celibate, an uncharacteristic lifestyle within Second Temple Judaism; see Josephus, *Wars* 2.8.2 §120-21; *Antiquities* 18.1.5 §21; Philo, *Hypothetica* 11.14-15 – the Essenes "repudiate marriage; and at the same time they practise continence in an eminent degree; for no one of the Essenes ever marries a wife, because woman is a selfish creature and one addicted to jealousy in an immoderate degree, and terribly calculated to agitate and overturn the natural inclinations of a man, and to mislead him by her continual tricks; for as she is always studying deceitful speeches and all other kinds of hypocrisy, like an actress on the stage, when she is alluring the eyes and ears of her husband, she proceeds to cajole his predominant mind after the servants have been deceived." There is debate over whether all or some of the Essenes and the Qumran members practiced celibacy.

part, the Corinthians' interest in celibacy may have arisen from a commitment to asceticism or from a desire to live free from family concerns.[324]

Paul was celibate, even though he may have formerly been married. He urges other unmarried Christians toward permanent celibacy if they have the gift. As we see below, this is for pragmatic reasons, not for ascetic belief that it makes one spiritually superior. Paul in fact condemns ascetic heretics in Col 2:8-23. The "Colossian Error" included abstention from foods, contact with certain substances, and "false humility" supposedly to make its devotees more holy. Paul views this not only as wasted effort, but positively distracting from the centrality of Christ. Again, in 1 Tim 4:3 Paul warns about a certain ascetical heresy in which "they forbid people to marry and order them to abstain from certain foods, which God created to be received with thanksgiving by those who believe and who know the truth."

Paul himself did not live as an ascetic, but perhaps his celibacy prompted the Corinthians to ask if his lifestyle allowed one to reach some higher plane. Paul affirms the value of celibacy and is glad to live that way, but his reasons are practical rather than inherently spiritual: for some Christians, it is useful to stay unencumbered with a spouse and family. He could have taken a wife if he liked (9:5), but it was better for him not to (7:7, 8, 40). Without a wife, Paul finds it easier to concern himself with the Lord's affairs (7:32-35). If some Corinthians want to stay unmarried, and they are gifted by God to do so, then Paul is very much in favor, because the church is in a crisis (7:26). He never suggests that celibacy helps anyone along the path to sanctification or salvation.

Paul gives specific instructions and suggestions to various groups. This is a style that he has used throughout the letter, for example, he deals with local issues while leaving other sins unremarked upon (see 1 Cor 6:9-10). Because of that, the reader must accept that 1 Cor 7 is no general rule book on singleness, marriage, divorce or widowhood. Paul's word to Corinth was grounded in their concrete reality. His comments on divorce, for example, must be understood within a context of Roman law and custom, and application to our culture must include the additional step of translating his words into a very different context. At other times, the alert student must be content to say "on this issue, we have no clear word."

Both Jews and Greeks maintained that a woman be always under the oversight of some man, be it husband, father or other male relative. Therefore, underlying Paul's teaching is an assumption that would have appeared radical to his contemporaries: he was careful to address both men and women directly. He affirmed a woman's rights within marriage and the right for her to remain single if she so chooses. He insisted that men, like women, "belonged to" their spouses, and that they must be faithful to them and not divorce them. Not only in terms of morality, but also in terms of its treatment of women, the gospel ran contrary to the mores of Roman Corinth.

a. General principle: People may be gifted for marriage or for celibacy; in general, Christians should marry, and married Christians must not abstain from sexual relations 7:1-7

---

[324] Contra Will Deming, *Paul on marriage and celibacy: the Hellenistic background of 1 Corinthians 7* (2nd ed.; Grand Rapids, MI: Eerdmans, 2004), who argues that Stoic desire to remain unattached were the basis for the Corinthians' objection to marriage. Deming also gives strong proof that asceticism as such was not Paul's goal in this chapter.

7:1

The Corinthians wanted Paul to confirm their view that "It is good for a man not to have sexual relations with a woman" (so the NIV 2011, which is superior to the 1984 rendering). The original is literally "not to touch (from *haptō*) a woman" (as KJV, NASB), a well-known euphemism for sexual contact (as NLT, NET, HCSB, ESV).[325] It is imperative that we do not read into the phrase the meaning "marry" (as the NIV 1984 paraphrases, also CEV, GNB), which is not a meaning of *haptō*. In Corinth, some are wondering if for a man all sexual contact is wrong – or at least, not the best option – whether in or out of marriage.[326] For them a sex-free life was a moral good.[327]

It is a puzzle, how a church that winked at incest and visits to prostitutes could have come up with such a notion. It may be that they were being sarcastic with Paul in order to buy themselves more sexual freedom: *You say we must not fornicate? So, if we took your viewpoint, then all sex must be dirty, correct? All couples should divorce, all fiancés break up, right?* It is more probable that some subgroup, seeing the messiness that sex was creating in the church, went to the other extreme and suggested that all Christians had better be celibate. Or they may have used the Stoic reverence for self-control to formulate an ideal that was contrary to the Scriptures on the one hand, and unlivable on the other.

7:2

Paul now begins to qualify their viewpoint, with **but**. The Corinthian viewpoint had mixed a little truth with much distortion, and Paul takes great pains to show what the Christian way is. "Immorality" is more literally "fornications" (*porneia*) in the plural: in the light of the multiple cases of immorality, **since there is so much** sexual **immorality**. Paul is not inventing a hypothetical situation when he points out that out that universal celibacy will obviously fail in Corinth (5:1 and 6:15-18, also the three vice lists in 1 Cor 5-6). In 7:2b-4, he gives three statements in favor of marriage, and of sex within marriage. Note that men and women are carefully represented with equality, unlike the slogan in 7:1 –

> **Each man should have his own wife,**
> **and each woman her own husband.**
> **The husband should fulfill his marital duty to his wife,**
> **and likewise the wife to her husband.**
> **The wife's body does not belong to her alone**
> **but also to her husband.**
> **In the same way, the husband's body does not belong to him alone**

---

[325] Especially Fee; also Thiselton; Witherington, *Conflict and community*, 175. See the Jewish usage in Gen 20:6; Prov 6:29. Josephus, *Antiquities* 1.8.1 §163 is a commentary on the same Genesis passage and uses *haptō*. His *Antiquities* 2.4.5 §58 has similar idea (touching another man's wife), but with a synonym for "touch," *psauō* instead of *haptō*.

[326] Contra Winter, *After Paul left Corinth*, 225-26, who leans toward the view that it means "not have intercourse with one's wife." See too Norbert Baumert, *Woman and man in Paul: overcoming a misunderstanding* (Collegeville, MN: Liturgical, 1996), 30, who renders this "good for a (married) man (on occasion) not to approach his wife (not to touch her)." Although they are technically correct, that *gunē* ("woman") could also mean "wife", the slogan seems rather to be a general dismissal of all sex, thus laying the foundation for Paul to address the unmarried, widow, and virgin.

[327] So Hurd, *Origin*, 158-61.

but also to his wife.

"Have one's own wife/husband" simply means "married"; it doesn't necessarily mean to become married or to take a spouse or to practice intercourse within marriage. In these early verses Paul is speaking generally of the goodness of marriage and sex within marriage.

7:3

Celibacy might be a useful lifestyle, but it is wrong to try to live as a celibate when one is already married. The Jews spoke favorably about the value of sex between husband and wife.[328] Paul would have had this positive attitude toward marital sex as a rabbi and as an apostle. Therefore, if there was a movement in favor of celibacy at Corinth, that influence must have come from the Greek world. For some Greeks, sex and marriage and children were thought to be distractions from a life of philosophical growth and wisdom.

The Greeks and Romans believed that the husband had certain responsibilities to the wife, primary among them the right of financial support. Beyond this, it was assumed that the husband would take lovers so long as he was discreet and did not embarrass his family. Paul will have nothing to do with this double standard; a Christian husband has a duty to his wife, not only to refrain from infidelity but also to have sexual relations with her. In Christ, the man is for the wife, and the wife for the man, and both have a **marital duty**, the responsibility to have sexual relations with one's spouse. If the concept of duty seems offensive to us moderns, we might remember that sex is not just an obligation but a gift from God (7:7b).

7:4

Of course, Greek and Roman men wanted their wives to be faithful, even if the men were not. Their traditional paradigm was:

> We have courtesans for our pleasures,
>   prostitutes for daily physical use,
>   wives to bring up legitimate children
>   and to be faithful stewards in household matters...[329]

But Paul plows directly against prevailing opinion, making both husband and wife obligated to each other. In **does not belong to** (better "does not have authority over" his or her own body, see ESV), he uses the same word, *exousiazō*, that he used in 6:12 with the sense of "I will not be mastered by anything." Here it is not of domination that Paul speaks, but conjugal rights. He starts with the part with which the cultural conservatives in his audience would agree, that **the wife's body does not belong to her alone but also to her husband**. But wait, there's more! Paul adds **in the same way** and applies identical rules to the husband: neither is the man a free agent, but his body belongs to his wife.

---

[328] For anyone who thinks that the Jews looked down on marital relations, a look at the Mishnah will suffice. See *m. Ketubah* 5.6, which recommends daily relations for those who are not called away from the home by their work.

[329] This formula is from *In Neaeram* 59.122, a text falsely attributed to the 4th century B. C. Athenian, Demosthenes.

That is a revolutionary statement for pagans, but also for Jews. It denotes that the man is free to have sexual relations only with his wife, and she possesses the right, not just the privilege, to his faithfulness and his company.

If someone in Corinth was the sort of super-spiritual person who wanted to pray rather than behave as a husband should toward his spouse, he should think on this: first, his body does not belong to himself, but to the Lord (6:19). But second, his body also belongs to his spouse (7:4). This means that even the spiritual person has no right to reject his spouse, supposedly in favor of the Lord.

Application: Sex and the Christian marriage 7:2-4

Traditional European culture has deep roots in the classical model that characterized Roman Corinth. The husband is thought to possess his wife's body, but the right is not always thought to be mutual. A man might engage in sex outside of marriage – with a mistress, with a prostitute, with a servant, with a casual acquaintance. He does this because he is a man and men have certain drives which must be satisfied. Men are thought obligated to support the babies they create, but often they abandon their wives and girlfriends with their children. Women are expected to have a lower sexual drive and to think of sex in terms of conceiving children. Women who otherwise show an interest in sex may be suspected of promiscuity.

Of course, with the urbanization and globalization of the world, with women taking university education and working outside the home, we have partaken of other values: that a woman has as much right as a man to be sexually active, to choose her partners and to verbalize her sexual needs. Delaying childbirth is valued, with the added incentive to finish one's education before starting a family. Then too, for our Westernized young men and women, sexual desire is often detached completely from love or marriage. It may come to be simply one more physical need which needs satisfaction in some fashion or another, often through casual and joyless "hookups." Or people may try to mimic what was God's plan by establishing a long-term relationship with someone to whom they expect to remain sexually faithful, but apart from marriage. But any of these alternatives will be destructive in the end. Even couples who live together to give monogamy a trial test are statistically much more likely to later be unfaithful in marriage and to land in divorce.

Paul's teaching confronts the classical and the modern Western cultures. What are some implications of his teaching for today?

1. Within marriage, sexual intercourse is a mutual responsibility and right

What of intercourse as a "marital duty"? It helps to think in these terms – in the Christian life there are many duties: church attendance, reading the Scriptures, prayer, doing good to the poor, etc. These are true whether we feel in the mood or not. On the other hand, we must not regard them as "*mere* duties" to be grudgingly carried out. We are not simply to give, but "God loves a cheerful giver." We are to pray regularly; but we may not do so reluctantly nor stop praying and wait until our feelings change. The right course is to turn our reluctance or resentment over to God as the first act of worship and go on to do our duty cheerfully. It is the same way with sex: we have a duty to be faithful to our spouses, and also to regard it as a positive, joyful responsibility.

Paul was not trapped in the sexism and patriarchal mores of his time. He stood alone in Corinth with his doctrine that marital sexual duty is to be shared equally by both husband and wife. This severely narrowed the Christian man's options, living in a city where prostitution was widely tolerated. To be told that "in the same way, the husband's body does not belong to him alone but also to his wife" was shockingly strict for a converted pagan. Such mutual ownership would strike philosophers as intolerable for an educated man: *His wife the owner/mistress of the husband's body? Then what good is the freedom that the wise man is trying to cultivate?*

In Paul's model of "mutual ownership," marital sex is freely given and received. This eliminates all sexual manipulation as a tool for control. Traditionally this has been a behavior associated with the wife, but men have used it as well, for example, by threatening to take his needs elsewhere if the wife will not bend to his will. Likewise, if a wife withholds sex in order to control her husband, she is in effect stealing what is not hers to withhold.

What of Paul's prescription of marital intercourse as the antidote to lusting, an idea that many of us might find offensive? Let us remember that he is not defining sexual intercourse as *merely* or even *primarily* a solution to lust; rather he says that regular marital intercourse *would in fact* help solve the very real problem of Christians going to prostitutes. He speaks concretely and pragmatically in a difficult situation. Sex is for married couples, so why not marry and enjoy a relationship with your wife?

We moderns are heavily influenced by the romanticism of the 19th century and through to today. Wives especially want to believe that their husbands will feel no sexual temptations if they "really love them." But this is an unrealistic and unearthly idea, as Paul knows and affirms. The apostle is no starry-eyed optimist. His teaching reflects the fact that for a married man or woman, sexual temptation rises in direct proportion to the lack of regular sex at home. If they feel deprived, not only are their sexual needs unfulfilled, but they may easily interpret the spouse's withdrawal as emotional rejection and to then use it to justify their own sexual affairs with others.

Paul takes sexual desire seriously and respects its strength. Conversely, in our culture lust has become a joke. Consider how many television comedy shows poke fun at the wife hiding her lover in the closet; or the confusion about who is a child's real father; or the antics of the man who is trying to keep his two lovers separate. We giggle at lust until the moment when it rises up to ruin our own lives.

2. Sexual intercourse is not just for procreation

Sexual intercourse was part of the original creation. God created Adam and Eve with genitalia and with the desire to sexually be with the other and only with the other. This was one of the things he pronounced "very good." The Fall was not caused, as some theologians would have it, by sexual desire. Nevertheless, the Fall did harm the marital relationship, made childbirth painful, and greatly complicated the sexual side of human existence.

Greco-Roman society, promiscuous though it could be, often held surprisingly negative ideas about sex. Marital sex was for the creation of legitimate heirs, not for pleasure between a husband and wife. For some, the ejaculation of semen was thought to weaken a man, an idea that has survived among athletes to this day. In later Gnostic thinking, a spiritual man would abstain from such animal activities and cultivate the spirit instead. In Judaism, by contrast, the attitude toward marital intercourse and procreation was a valued part of a godly man's life. But Paul goes beyond even this positive approach:

> For Paul, what legitimated marriage was not the biblical mandate to "be fruitful and multiply," and certainly not the [Roman] imperial call for larger families, it was the need of two people for each other, provided they are willing to commit themselves to each other in a mutually faithful and caring relationship.[330]

As is well-known, there is a long-standing difference of interpretation between Protestant and Catholic interpreters on the purpose of sexual intercourse. Most modern Catholic theologians have shaken off the ancient philosophical assumptions that make marital sex carnal or marriage a second-rate existence. Today their main difference with evangelicals lies in the role of procreation: they assert that the purpose of sex is inextricably tied with conceiving children. Let us explore this.

Gen 2:18 lays the foundation for a marital sexual relationship in Adam's need for companionship. The fact that Eve came from Adam leads to a sexual relationship in 2:24-25, with no reference to procreation. It is telling that in 1 Corinthians, Paul can speak of intercourse with practically no reference to childbirth or child rearing (apart from the side reference in 1 Cor 7:14). Paul's words are not limited to those of child-bearing age; nor those where the wife was not already pregnant; nor to those who did not experience infertility. No, all husbands and wives are to have a sexual relationship with their spouse.

This touches on the question of contraception. We will speak here of contraception used to prevent pregnancy within marriage, not to prevent pregnancy or disease outside of marriage. When a century ago artificial birth-control methods came into use, Protestant Christians tended to disallow them. But during the 20th century most denominations came to allow contraceptive barriers (condom, sponge, spermicide) and pills that regulate ovulation, while rejecting abortifacients such as the IUD or the RU-480 pill, which might abort fertilized ova, or fertilization methods which involve the destruction of such ova.

In Paul's day, the men wanted to cut down expenses and limit the number of their heirs, and the women were anxious to survive their child-bearing years. Due to poorer medical care and nutrition and ineffective birth-control, death and childbirth were closely linked. For those who wanted to regulate births, there were all kinds of herbal and folk contraceptives, most of them ineffective. Women often had one baby after another until they reached menopause, or until they died in childbirth, or until they decided to expel their husbands from their bed. Even then the human population did not grow by much. Many years it shrank, and it was considered a success when the population could simply replace itself in the next generation. Caesar Augustus created a system of incentives to punish divorce and childlessness, in part because of the low birthrate.

In Caesar's day, the world population may have been no more than 250 million. It first reached the 1 billion mark only around 1800. In our time, with better prenatal care, nutrition and medical attention, an average woman could in theory produce many more healthy children than her foremothers did and most of these children would survive. This is particularly relevant when the population of the planet has grown in my lifetime from

---

[330] Furnish, *The moral teaching of Paul*, 50.

under 3 billion to over 7 billion inhabitants, with no end in sight.

Of course, we should not try to deduce God's will simply by reading population figures. Nor should we take our cue from the clamor of the West against Rome's stand against artificial contraception, particularly as represented in 1968 with Paul VI's *Humanae vitae*.[331] However, our context does encourage us to look again at the biblical verses to try to discern whether we have understood God's will all along. The key verse "Be fruitful and multiply" in Gen 1:28 should be reexamined. Adam and Eve were told to do this and thereby "fill the earth and subdue it." The same command was given to Noah and his family in Gen 8:17, 9:7. The point seems clear: the command was given twice, both times when the human race was limited to a few acres in one corner of the globe. Adam and Eve were told to multiply and fill the earth; after the destruction of the race, Noah was told to fill it again.

There is no stated numerical limit on God's command. Does it contain an implied fulfillment? When might one consider the planet sufficiently "filled" that the human race need not double itself in every generation? Each theologians and expert in population growth will have his own opinion, but many reasonable people believe that 7 billion people (as of 2011) may reasonably be thought to make the earth full.

Nevertheless, the Catholic church has taken its famous stand against contraception by artificial means. It allows birth control so long as it conforms to nature, although "natural contraception" is a slippery concept to begin with. One of the reasons that our ancestresses breast-fed their children to such a late age (sometimes to 3 years old, probably the background of Gen 21:8) was that it delayed the return of ovulation and thus spaced out the babies. For its part, the modern Roman church allows the so-called rhythm method and encourages husbands to abstain from sex during ovulation if they wish not to conceive a child. It is well-known that this is unreliable for many couples.

Rome's rejection of artificial contraception is presented as a matter of self-control:

> For if with the aid of reason and of free will they are to control their natural drives, there can be no doubt at all of the need for self-denial. Only then will the expression of love, essential to married life, conform to right order. This is especially clear in the practice of periodic continence. Self-discipline of this kind is a shining witness to the chastity of husband and wife and, far from being a hindrance to their love of one another, transforms it by giving it a more truly human character.[332]

This sounds lofty, but isn't this the same sort of rationalism that worries Paul in 1 Corinthians 7? For the issue there was that some Christians will try to practice self-control and only land in fornication. Paul, with his deep respect for sexual temptation, gives more realistic advice when he warns married couples away from abstinence, except in the rare case of a short "sexual fast" for prayer. For him, self-denial with one's spouse is no virtue.

Let us look at the question from the perspective of marriage: does not modern birth control allow Christian couples to enjoy marital sex more and reduce the temptation to turn to another partner, without the constant fear of too many pregnancies? Does not the

---

[331] "*Humanae vitae*," Online http://www.vatican.va/holy_father/paul_vi/encyclicals/documents/hf_p-vi_enc_25071968_humanae-vitae_en.html
[332] *Humanae Vitae* §21.

40-year-old Christian woman with contraception have a greater chance to have a faithful husband than does a wife who excludes her husband from her bed for the sake of her health? I have always felt that, within our environment of high fertility and long life-spans, artificial contraception is a godsend for the Christian couple that values fidelity. It is much better than the classical tradition, still around today, in which middle-aged men keep a mistress, at times in order not to bother their wives.

3. Implications for the physical aspects of Christian marriage

Christian discipleship must encompass the sexual life. If anyone thinks that the Bible is shy about discussing intimate issues, they should look at the rules in Lev 18 or the frank descriptions of the sexual sins among Israel or Paul's teachings here or in 1 Thess 4. The church's young disciples must be clear on what is the biblical teaching and must be able to count on the support of other Christians. Teaching about marital intimacy should be likewise clear. Catholic writers have long and consistently spoken frankly of the nature of marital love; their books and sermons are often much more direct and biblical and positive than their evangelical counterparts. Evangelicals often seem to direct all their fire against fornication, but little time to building up and affirming what is healthy marital sex. When it does do so, the results are by turn comical and, well, smirking: some Christian books on the topic resemble nothing so much as a sex manual with some Bible references added in. I have heard sermons where the pastor says that whatever two Christians do in their bedroom is fine with God: I'm sure these preachers are not low-minded, but they are unconscionably naive about what goes on behind some doors.

The Lord is watching us even in the bedroom, and our sexual relationships should follow in the footsteps of Christ's love for us. Christ is loving, nurturing, edifying, patient, kind, generous, giving and forgiving: the fruit of the Spirit is the way of life for the intimate relations of a Christian husband and wife. Although the Bible does not go into details about specific activities, it does give the strong impression that marital sex should center on the unifying act of intercourse and not just the giving of stimulation as an end in itself. There should be no hint of coercion; forced intercourse; humiliation; violence; giving of pain, even if it is designed to produce sexual stimulation; transvestitism; sinful fantasizing. The Christian should not use pornography in any form for sexual arousal or satisfaction, which must have wholly to do with the marriage partner and not images of other people.

The Bible says a little about quantity of sex: a Christian couple should follow the model that Paul teaches and have regular intercourse where that is practically possible. The rabbis of Paul's day, who left no human activity to chance, held various views on how often a couple should have sex. One opinion seems to imply that if the man is working near his home – that is, is not "on the road" for his job – he should have sex every day (see comments on 7:3). No two people desire sex with the same frequency, so it is normal that one person will wish it more often than another. The spirit of Paul's words here are that a couple will have intercourse often enough that the more eager partner will not feel a regular strain of going unfulfilled. To put it in Paul's terms, you are not having intercourse frequently enough if you "burn with passion" (7:9). This will require a spirit of patience when there are two people with unequal sex drives – but should that be a problem for people of the Holy Spirit? Let not the spouse complain of his partner's lack of spirituality if he or she wants to have intercourse as a friend to, not the enemy of, a strong devotional life! Both men and women should accept that their partners are not carnal or sinful if they are at the same time sexual beings.

In modern times, and especially with the entrance of women into the workplace, many couples find it hard to make time for sex. With electric lights for reading, internet, cable television and other things to distract us around bedtime, both spouses may come to bed craving nothing but sleep or at least feeling distracted and tired. At times men and women work different shifts, or are ready for bed at different times. The couple must take active steps to avoid things which distract away from time together for intercourse – or just simply to be together. If a husband is too tired for intercourse at night, but the next day he finds himself transfixed by the secretaries at work, he must get his priorities straight, and quickly. And wives – and yes, husbands too! – do themselves a great favor and invests in their marriage if they are available and pleasant to be with. A healthy marital relationship is a joyful gift of God as well as excellent hedge against outside temptations.

Let us train ourselves to proclaim even these truths without fear. The Scripture is practical, not otherworldly, in its teaching on purity. Thus does the gospel of Christ, the mystery of God, take into account, affirm, and uphold even our sexual lives.

7:5

If there is any doubt that Paul was talking about the physical act of sex in 7:2-4, here is a third command: **Do not deprive each other** (with one strictly limited exception, dealt with below). He uses the term (*apostereō*) that arose in 6:7-8 to refer to defrauding someone of what is rightfully his or hers. Under these circumstances, to deny intercourse is robbery.

Most readers, ancient or modern, might assume that Paul means that the woman should not push the man away.[333] In antiquity, many women died or damaged their health in childbirth, lowering the average life expectancy for married women to something like 20's or 30's. Every woman knew that intercourse entailed a respectable amount of physical risk, or at least, one more child to care for. But Paul, surprisingly, goes on to mention the other side of the coin: neither may the husband steal from his wife of what is rightfully hers, including sexual intimacy with him. Some men believed, or claimed to believe, that a courteous husband didn't bother his busy wife with his sexual needs. But it may also be because he found someone younger or prettier – a slave who could not refuse him or someone whose children could not receive an inheritance. Other men preferred boys.

It is doubtful that Paul would have affirmed the importance of marital obligations, unless that was a problem for the Corinthian church.[334] The fact that Paul knows about such intimate details; that he can quote their slogan in 7:1; and that he refers to their

---

[333] Nonetheless, the Greeks and Romans also thought that women were filled with sexual lust. See Martin, *The Corinthian body*, 219-28. Only male sexual desires were justifiable; wives who showed interest in sex other than as being passively receptive to her husband, were thought to be wanton. That "the good wife doesn't move" during intercourse was an accepted truism, see Peterman, "Marriage and sexual fidelity in the papyri, Plutarch and Paul," 168.

[334] Fee, *First Corinthians*, 321, makes a case that 7:5a means, "Stop depriving each other!" He bases this reading on Paul's use of the Greek negative present imperative. It was once thought that type of imperative must mean *Stop doing what you're doing!* Although this "rule" has been discredited, still it seems to be its meaning in this context, as Fee notes.

desire for **prayer** in 7:5b, all indicate that some had stopped having sex with their spouses in order to seek a higher spiritual level. The deprived husband or wife who complained about this enforced celibacy would be branded as "unspiritual," since they were placing their own lower passions over the higher things of the Lord. But what happened? In their rush to achieve an illusory higher spiritual state, the overachievers opened the door to conflict and even fornication (7:2).[335]

It has lately been argued that the primary problem in Corinth was a group of women who were seeking a deeper spirituality. Perhaps it was the women who coined the slogan, "it is good for a man not to touch a woman" (7:1).[336] A. C. Wire defends these hypothetical women, complaining that Paul valued the sexual needs of the husband above the spiritual aspirations of the wife. In fact, Paul does not say who was doing the depriving, and there are two possible scenarios: (1) wives deprived their men; the men, angry and frustrated, justified their visits to prostitutes; (2) men announced to their wives that they would refrain from sex in order to pray more; later they decided they couldn't hold out, and secretly went to prostitutes in order that their wives not see their prayer experiment as a failure. The fact that Paul ends the chapter with a word to married women ("a woman is bound to her husband," see 7:39-40) *might possibly* tip the balance in favor of the women wishing to abstain from marital relations or seeking a divorce, but concerning this we cannot be dogmatic.

Paul allows one exception to regular marital intercourse: **so that you may devote yourselves to prayer**. Even then he hedges it carefully: it must be **by mutual consent** (not one person's leap of faith; not the husband as "head" of the wife telling her it must be so); it must be only **for a time**. This period of time must not last so long that it leads to sexual frustration, which would have the effect of making an undisturbed period for prayer a complete waste of effort. Then they must **come together again**. That is, they must not fall into a habit that will surely be harmful in the long term. Although Paul does not give any numbers, we might assume that he is thinking of the sort of sexual practice mentioned by the rabbis of the 1st century B. C., which would last a maximum of 1-2 weeks.[337]

The fact that men and women have sexual desires is not wrong or carnal. Sexual desire is part of God's creation of humankind, and thus it is good. However, sex is one of the areas where people frequently fall into sin. Thus when Paul warns Christians **so that Satan will not tempt you because of your lack of self-control**, he is doing what a good pastor does, steering his people away from unnecessary trouble. There is no merit in courting temptation in order to prove how strong one is.

---

[335] In his commentary, Origen states that "there was dissension in the households of the brethren: in some the men and in others the women were seeking to be continent, and they were at odds with each other" (Kovacs). Chrysostom, *i ad Corinthios* 19.3, thinks of a celibate wife: "Thus, suppose a wife and husband, and let the wife be continent, without consent of her husband; well then, if hereupon he commit fornication, or though abstaining from fornication fret and grow restless and be heated and quarrel and give all kind of trouble to his wife; where is all the gain of the fasting and the continence, a breach being made in love?"
[336] Antoinette Clark Wire, *The Corinthian women prophets: a reconstruction through Paul's rhetoric* (Minneapolis, MN: Fortress, 1990), 94.
[337] See the Mishnah, in *m. Ketubot* 5.6 – "He who takes a vow not to have sexual relations with his wife – the House of Shammai say, '[He may allow this situation to continue] for two weeks.' And the House of Hillel say, 'For one week.'" Also *T. Naphtali* 8.8 – "There is a time for having intercourse with one's wife, and a time to abstain for the purpose of prayer."

7:6

Depending on one's interpretation of the chapter, the **concession** may be read in two ways: (1) that Paul concedes being married and having married sex, but it's second-best; as such it could refer to 7:2-4 or to "come together again"; (2) that Paul concedes only what he has just described (7:5b) as the one exception to regular marital sex: *I give in to you having strictly controlled times of prayer and abstinence, but no more; I'm allowing it, but not commanding or recommending it.*[338] It is this second view which best fits the context.

7:7

Paul uses the word **wish** (or "prefer," *thelō*) here. Remaining unmarried is no command, but Paul himself values that option and would prefer to see people follow it. The basis for his pastoral counsel is the call of God, and his next statement is filled with implications: **But each man** [better "each person"] **see has his own gift** (Greek, *charisma*) **from God; one has this gift, another has that**. Paul uses the word that he uses to mean the spiritual gifts in 1 Cor 12; that is, both states are gifts of God:[339] if staying unmarried and celibate is a spiritual gift, so is the married state with a minimal allowance for temporary abstinence (7:2-6). If both are spiritual gifts, then both are good, and as he will state in 12:4, "There are different kinds of gifts (*charismata*), but the same Spirit." It is not a question of choosing the good *versus* the bad: for Paul it is a question of choosing what is suitable to the person's gift and "the place in life that the Lord assigned to him and to which God has called him" or her (7:17). A sexually-active life with a spouse can therefore be just as "charismatic" as living as a celibate, since it is a gift of God. Paul will develop this truth in 7:17-24. If the Stoics thought that self-control was the sign of a wise man, Paul saw celibacy as a spiritual gift that Christians received from above. He may or may not have been thinking of the Jesus tradition that "others have become eunuchs because of the kingdom of heaven" (Matt 19:12), that is, as a divine grace which enabled people to serve the kingdom better. As Schrage states:

> For Paul, Christian celibacy is a charisma (1 Cor. 7:7). This has two implications. First, it is not required of all Christians, but is a free gift of God's grace. Second, however, as a charisma, it gives special opportunity for special service to others – a capacity for *diakonia* ["service, ministry"]. There is nothing [in 1 Cor 7] about ascetic celibacy for the sake of cultivating one's own spiritual personality, based on disdain for the body, or celibacy based on egoism, contempt for the opposite sex, or the like.[340]

---

[338] So Fee; Schrage, *An die Korinther*, 2:71-72; Barrett; Hays. Contra Augustine, *Letter 262 to Eudicia* (Bray, 61), who chides such a wife for not going along with her husband's desire to be celibate: *If only she weren't so weak, they might have consented together to accomplish a greater good!* The same attitude is taken by Origen, *Commentary on Matthew* 14.2 – "if the one wished to be pure, but the other did not desire it, and on this account he who willed and was able to fulfil the better part, condescended to the one who had not the power or the will."

[339] As affirms especially Fee; Robertson and Plummer; Conzelmann. Origen (Kovacs, 109) – "And if marriage is a special gift, it is wrong to forbid the special gift of marriage. If 'one of one kind and one of another' is 'from God,' it is clear that it is one God who has given both purity and marriage..."

[340] Wolfgang Schrage, *The ethics of the New Testament* (Minneapolis, MN: Fortress, 1990), 229. Also Conzelmann, *1 Corinthians*, 118: "[Paul] differs both from the Gnostics and also from the legalists in holding not that everyone's gifts are the same, but that each has his own, peculiar gift..." On p. 120 Conzelmann shows that what is a *charisma*, a spiritual gift, should not be held as a virtue. On the other hand,

Application: Celibacy today 7:7

All Christians are required to live chastely outside of marriage; permanent celibacy is a special commitment to continue single and pure. Today celibacy sounds either horribly old-fashioned or "too Catholic." Who would freely choose to live like a monk or a nun, people who we all assume live frustrated lives because of their unnatural lifestyle? Surely "holy singleness" is reserved for the unhealthy, the weird, or the physically unattractive! But no: despite the pressure in our society to have a special person and to provide our parents with grandchildren, one's service of the gospel is ranked higher than family expectations, and singleness may improve the quality of what we do in Christ's name.

Who should be married and who single?

There are two issues that the person must ask about him or herself:

1. The issue of sin: Do I have the gift to be celibate or the gift to be married? It is of no value to stay single if one will break God's commandments.

2. The issue of service: Do my circumstances mean that I can serve the Lord better single or married? Paul implies that he has decided to abstain from marriage and thus all sexual relationships. He implies that (1) God has given him the gift of living without sexual intercourse and conventional family life, and (2) has shown him that he can better work as he is. He is not an ascetic, but a pragmatist: we cannot imagine that Paul would push for singleness if that state were not a genuine help for the gospel work. On the other hand, Aquila and Priscilla are a model of two people who serve the Lord within their marriage. Paul is clearly in favor of the celibate lifestyle for those who have the gift to live it. But he does not live alone in order to be more holy, but set apart (the sense of *hagios*, "devoted," in 7:34) in order to be more useful.

How should the church handle chasteness?

In the West, the age of marriage has risen, partly because young adults are pursuing education or career and partly because people are engaging in intercourse with less danger of pregnancy, thus with less incentive to marry while young.

Pastors sometimes have a blind spot when it comes to university students in their flock. They may imagine that such motivated and intelligent young people have no problem controlling their sexual desires. The pastor does not bring up the topic until there is an unwanted pregnancy. Yet it has been proven in the United States that there is a higher abortion rate among Christian students than among non-Christians: Christians stumble into sex unprepared, and then have secret abortions because a pregnancy would damage their spiritual reputation. So much ruin, and much of it stemming from a lack of appreciation for the strength of sexual desire – the very sort of respect that Paul shows in this epistle.

Reuss (quoted in Godet, *First Corinthians*, 328) has it precisely wrong when he states that, "If abstention, life in celibacy, is a particular gift of God's grace, it is evident that something is wanting to the man who does not possess it."

Another issue that the church fails to address is that university students face a prolonged adolescence. In some cultures a boy matures sexually at 14 and marries at 18, or a girl even younger. It is quite another thing in our culture for men and women to be sexually mature for 10 or 15 years or more while they finish their college degrees then try to establish themselves in a career, and only then marry and begin to think of children. Youth is no friend to chastity, and this delay of marriage may ruin the spiritual health or the career path of many of our youths. Well-meaning Christians urge that young men engage in rigorous exercise in order to control themselves, although it is now known that exercise elevates the level of the male hormone and thus the sex drive. Many couples do all sorts of things to satisfy their sexual drives, rationalizing that it is not "sex" unless there is actual vaginal penetration. But this is not holiness as God defines it. What will your church do to help those who do not have the gift of celibacy to live as celibates for what seems an excruciatingly long time?

How should the church minister to singles?

Another difficulty that many single people face is that they would like to marry and raise a family, but they cannot find a Christian partner. In some countries this has even led to the formation of Christian internet matchmaking services. These days it can be very difficult for young Christians to meet each other socially, and I have known many wonderful Christian people who have had a hard time finding a mate. Let us not mistake imposed singleness with a desire to serve God as a celibate single. For many Christian singles, there should be no question of lifelong celibacy; they should marry if they can.

What then should the church do? It should remember that single people have the same needs that married people have, for example, family relationships. Ideally the church is the perfect venue for genuine family life. Yet we may spend so much time emphasizing family values and marriage that we forget that Christ wants the church itself to serve as his new covenant family. Heaven help the church that makes singles feel defective or like outsiders! When it comes to ministry, friendships and socializing, "like seeks like": married people tend to spend their time with other married people. Single and divorced people frequently feel cut off from those who live in nuclear families. The church needs to be more active in creating an environment where singles are given the opportunity to interact, fellowship and minister together. It should also think through whether its "singles ministries" alleviate the isolation that people experience or make them feel even more like outsiders.

Should the church match up single people? This depends a great deal on the culture of your country, and some singles find it embarrassing to know that others are trying to arrange their romantic lives. There are ways to introduce people without being obvious or manipulative.

In some mission fields it is better to work single; in some, it is better to be married. The same is true for being a pastor, or writer, or church-planter or musician: sometimes one state is better, sometimes the other. Paul's point is: what does it matter if we do not have a "special someone" in our lives, so long as we are serving the gospel?

b. Specific directions to the "unmarried" and the widows 7:8-9

After his general statements affirming marriage, Paul moves to specific subgroups within the church. It must be repeated that Paul does not cover every contingency for every Christian, but addresses the needs of the Corinthian church at that time.

Paul first addresses the **unmarried** and the **widows** of the church. The first term (from the adjective *agamos*) is difficult to translate. The evidence from the literature and the inscriptions and papyri (see LSJ, MM) is inconclusive; it appears that *agamos* can refer to a person who was never married (for example, "Alas for my children, some *unmarried*, others married and without offspring," 4 Macc 16:9 NRSV) or one who is formerly married. The specific meaning depends on the context. "Never been married" (as the CEV) simply does not capture the meaning of *agamos* in the context of 1 Cor 7. Paul speaks of the "unmarried" as a group apart from "virgins" (young, chaste unmarried girls) in 7:25-28, 36-38. The woman who leaves her husband ought to remain *agamos* (7:11); thus *agamos* must at least sometimes mean "previously married." Thus *agamos* in this passage is not strictly "never married" but rather "not now married." This group includes the "formerly married," widows/widowers or the divorced.[341]

7:8

For them **it is good** that they remain like Paul. The fact that Paul identifies with this group has led some to conclude that he had at one time been married. In fact, it would have been strange if Paul as a rabbi had been single; some have conjectured that his wife died or abandoned him, but there isn't evidence to prove any of these hypotheses. That they stay like him is Paul's preference, not a command. **But if they cannot control themselves**, they should marry. Once again Paul points to the real problem of sexual failure. The same verb for "control oneself" (*engkrateuomai*) appears again in 9:25: an athlete "disciplines himself in everything." Paul does not discount the power of sexual urges or simply tell his people simply to pull themselves together; as a pastor, he seeks godly ways for them to resist temptation.

7:9

Why might people marry? Because, literally "it is better to marry than to burn" (so KJV; NASB). One ancient interpretation is that "burn" is a reference to hell or to the fire of God's judgment (as in 3:13).[342] Fornicators won't inherit the kingdom (6:9), so it is better to marry than to go to the fires of hell. This interpretation would fit with the Lord's teaching in Matt 5:28-29:

> But I say to you that everyone who looks at a woman with lust has already committed adultery with her in his heart. If your right eye causes you to sin, tear it out and throw it away; it is better for you to lose one of your members than for your whole body to be thrown into hell.

---

[341] So Thiselton, *First Corinthians*, 515; Schrage, *An die Korinther*, 2:93-94; Deming, *Paul on marriage and celibacy* 130. Fee, *First Corinthians*, 287-88, states that *agamoi* here are the male widowers, to balance with the female widows, but this view is hard to sustain.

[342] Cyprian, Epistle 61.3 – "it is better that [virgins tempted to fornication] should marry, than that by their crimes they should fall into the fire."

The other interpretation is more plausible in this context, **burn with passion** (so the NIV, similarly most English versions).[343] Paul has already brought in the problem of unsated sexual desire in 7:2-6. Plus it would mean that Paul speaks in parallel form, linking lack of control with burning with passion:

> A But if they cannot control themselves,
> > B they should marry,
> > B for it is better to marry
> A then to burn with passion.

We will later examine of the question of whether divorced Christians may remarry in our comments on 7:15. At any rate, the widowed may remarry according to 7:8-9 and 7:39-40.[344] A widow in ancient times was in a much more desperate state than her modern counterpart. She was typically left with no means of economic support. Even some wealthy husbands were generous with their children in their wills, but thoughtless of their widows. This led to the church's concern for widows (Acts 6:1-6, 1 Tim 5:3-16, James 1:27), a concern that had its roots in the synagogue and of course the Old Testament (Exod 22:22; Deut 10:18; Isa 1:17, and many more). Beyond poverty, the widow or widower might experience loneliness and sexual frustration. If we think of widows as mature women who must be beyond this sort of passion (and that in itself is a cultural assumption), we should remember that a widow in antiquity could be quite young, even an adolescent. Paul deals with that particular problem in 1 Tim 5:11-16. In v. 11 he gives a surprisingly harsh reproof that nevertheless accorded with the conventional wisdom of the day – "when their sensual desires overcome their dedication to Christ, they want to marry." As in 1 Cor 7:5, the tempter appears again in 1 Tim 5:15 ("Some have in fact already turned away to follow Satan"). To give these young widows a social and spiritual anchor, they should remarry, and not only that but bear children (1 Tim 5:14).

---

[343] So Fee, Garland. See also Hosea 7:4; Ecclesiasticus 23:16 NRSV – "Hot passion that blazes like a fire will not be quenched until it burns itself out; one who commits fornication with his near of kin will never cease until the fire burns him up."

[344] In the 2nd-century church there was to be a major argument about widows and remarriage. On the orthodox side, it was sometimes argued that if Paul *recommended* that a widow remain single, then she *should* remain single, despite his allowances for remarriage. Tertullian went further: along with the Montanists he taught that widows must not remarry; in fact, the death of a husband was a gift of God, perhaps the best opportunity a woman would ever have (see *On monogamy*; *To his wife* 1.7). Why did Paul allow remarriage? Because (again, according to Montanist doctrine) when Paul was writing 1 Corinthians, the Paraclete had not yet come, and Paul did not know that decades later the Spirit would give new revelation about widows and remarriage. After all, Paul himself claimed that "we know in part and prophesy in part" in the time before "the perfect comes," that is, the fuller revelation given to the Montanists. Tertullian, *Adversus Marcionem* 1.29 – "Now, if any limitation is set to marrying – such as the spiritual rule, which prescribes but one marriage under the Christian obedience, maintained by the authority of the Paraclete, – it will be His prerogative to fix the limit Who had once been diffuse in His permission." That is: if God once allowed widows to remarry, it was his right later to tighten that rule.

Application: Choosing a mate – "Where's MY special someone?" 7:9, 36, 39

The New Testament gives no formula for choosing a husband or wife. Yes, in 1 Cor 7, Paul speaks a widow who wishes to marry "she is free to marry anyone she wishes," but, literally, "only in the Lord" – that is, only if the new husband is a Christian. Apart from that, Paul does not offer a full set of rules. In short, the apostle is concerned that we marry a Christian and that we live righteously within marriage; he says nothing about how to figure out which Christian to marry. In the 1st century and in many cultures, it is not the young people who decide on a mate, but rather parents or other members of the family or tribe.

People today, including many Christians, have adopted a view of marriage that owes more to 19th century Romanticism and Hollywood movies than to the New Testament: that there is a special someone for everybody, that you have to find just the right person, that being true to your marriage vows is not as important as following your heart.

Despite the singular experience of Rebecca in Gen 24:10-21, God never promises in his Word to give us a special revelation to show whom we should marry. Nor does he say that there is one, and only one, person for each man or woman. What he says is that we should marry a believer and live without our spouse in a godly way. Anything beyond this instruction is of our own making, not the word of the Lord. And people who claim that "God showed me to marry this person" often land in disaster, when they realized that it was not God's will but the tug of emotions or bodily chemistry.

So, how do you choose a marriage partner? Pray and ask yourself these three crucial questions, in this order.

QUESTION I. Does God want me to remain single?

Although it is often avoided, it is the first question to consider – don't put it off until you're madly in love with someone. Meditate on 1 Cor. 7:32-35, which shows that some people are called to special service as a single Christian.

QUESTION II. Whom should I marry?

The Bible does not encourage us to seek our perfect mate or the one person we are meant for; rather it teaches:

FIRST: God's revealed will for you is that Christians should marry only another believer (1 Cor. 7:39).Therefore: any marriage of an unbeliever and a believer is outside of God's will, no matter what hopes the believer has of converting the unbeliever, no matter what feelings they might have that this is really God's will and an exception to the rule. Young women in particular might decide that, *I'll marry him, and he'll come to the faith because of how I live it in front of him!* This is a risky business indeed, and all of us know exes who realized too late that God cannot be out-thought.

SECOND: think and pray through the meaning of marriage, particularly 1 Cor 7 and Eph 5:21-33. In particular, Paul tells believers who are married to non-believers that they should stay right where they are in the marriage.

THIRD: get advice from someone godly, honest, and impartial. Interestingly, some Western Christians have moved away from total freedom and have placed more emphasis on finding a mate through other, older Christians, whether in the church or in the family. It is a foolish thing to throw away the advice of wiser Christian friends and relatives because of what our heart tells us!

FOURTH: don't throw away good Christian sense! In the movies, romance is thought to be the ultimate experience. They emphasize "meeting cute," love at first sight, casual marriages, and a general lack of godly sense. Why not give the marriage a firmer footing by finding someone you at least suspect you can tolerate for decades to come?

QUESTION III. When should I marry?

Some people avoid this question, imagining that if they've found the "right" person they ought to marry right away. Again, seek God's wisdom and the Word of God to guide you. Hasty marriages always are riskier marriages. On the other hand, modern people have an extraordinarily prolonged adolescence. They mature when in middle school and then spend years studying and getting themselves settled, meanwhile living under sexual pressure. A wise Christian should consider how valuable it really is to delay marriage in favor of economic stability.

c. Specific directions to men or women who are married to believers 7:10-11

Now Paul addresses himself to the (already) **married**. Although he is not explicit, the context shows that he is thinking of Christians married to Christians. For them he offers no opinion or suggestion, but a **command** directly from **the Lord**. Paul has to look no further than the teaching of the Lord Jesus while he was walking the earth. A direct quote or allusion to the gospel tradition is rare for Paul.[345] The fact that Paul alludes to this tradition gives the impression that Paul taught his converts at least some sayings of Jesus.

Although Paul does not quote any saying directly, the Lord made a pronouncement against divorce and against remarriage (see Mark 10:2-12 and its parallels). The debate had been initiated by some Pharisees, who asked Jesus, "Is it lawful for a man to divorce his wife?" They were probably trying to trap him into taking sides in an ongoing controversy. Among Jews only the husband had the right to initiate a divorce. The Mosaic Law obliged him to write out a formal certificate, in order to allow the woman to remarry (Deut 24:1-2). The school of Shammai allowed divorce if the woman were sexually unfaithful; that exception is absent from Mark 10, but present in Jesus' teaching in Matt 19:9 – "except for marital unfaithfulness." According to gospel tradition, Jesus did not permit remarriage.

In this epistle, divorce must also be understood within its Greco-Roman setting. Both men and women could secure a divorce. It was a matter of private choice and not normally a matter for the courts. It could be accomplished by mutual consent, or by leaving or sending away the spouse. The marriage ended when the husband dismissed the wife with the Latin formula *tuas res tibi habeto* ("take your things [and go]!"). In modern times we differentiate between separation and divorce, but that distinction did

---

[345] In his letters there are references to Jesus' teaching here in 1 Cor 7:10-11, 9:14, 11:23-25; see the list of other possible allusions in Fitzmyer, *First Corinthians*, 56. Note the quotations in 1 Tim 5:18; Acts 20:35; and possible allusions in Rom 12:14-21, 13:8-10.

not apply in Roman Corinth. What we would call a divorce in those times was when a couple simply split up and did not return to the marriage. In some contexts the woman was obliged to log the fact of the separation with the local government. Paul assumes that Christians who left their marriage would be following local custom and not necessarily the law of Deut 24. For that reason the NIV might be confusing, which uses "divorce" (7:11, 12, 13, 27) as if were distinct from "separate from" (7:10) or "leave" (7:15). These two English verbs provide a literal translation, one that is faithful to the cultural context.

In 7:11a (which is best read as a parenthesis) Paul gives the separated wife two options: she must remain *agamos* ("unmarried") or else **be reconciled to her husband**. The Deuteronomic law examines the possibility that a woman is divorced by one man, marries a second, is divorced or widowed by *him*, and then the first husband wants to remarry her. This is strictly forbidden as a defilement (Deut 24:4). One of the reasons for the certificate of divorce was to force the husband to make a public rejection of his wife, not to move in and out with her as he pleased. In the Old Testament and in rabbinic teaching, a divorced woman may marry another. But Paul adheres to a stricter standard, telling the woman to stay unmarried or to hold out the possibility of remarrying her original husband. This is a hope that, according to Deut 24:4, would be ruined if she married a second man.

Paul begins by speaking to the woman, that she must not separate from her husband. He speaks to the men perhaps for the sake of balance at the end of 7:11, that the man should not leave his wife. Since the message to the women is longer, it may be another hint that it is the women who wished for celibacy.[346] Paul's brevity is not to be thought of giving husbands more latitude; it is simply that Paul has already put himself on record as strictly evenhanded in applying the same rules to men or women.

d. Specific directions to "the rest," that is, those married to unbelievers 7:12-16

7:12-13
Paul speaks now to **the rest**; in context, they must be Christians who are married to unbelievers.[347] These people receive the more detailed instruction, and the reason is easy to guess. The Corinthians needed help in applying Paul's teaching "not to associate with sexually immoral people" (5:9), along with his later point, "Do not be yoked together with unbelievers" (2 Cor 6:14)? It would be very easy for those who were in a difficult marriage to rationalize that God could not possibly want them to stay bound to a pagan; how could they possibly serve God?

When he says, literally, "I say, not the Lord," we might imagine that this isn't divine revelation, that it is Paul's personal preference as in 7:7, or his "in my judgment" in 7:40. But no, it simply means: *I as your authoritative apostle will give you a word, given that the Lord Jesus did not address the issue of mixed marriage.* This is because it was after the gospel went into the Hellenistic world that the possibility arose for one spouse to

---

[346] Severianus (Bray, 63) indulges in special pleading when he says: "Paul did not intend this to apply to those who abandon their spouses for the service of Christ." In fact, Paul recognizes no such exception.
[347] So Conzelmann, *1 Corinthians*, 121.

become a Christian and the other remain a pagan. The apostle's command is that Christians must not separate from their spouse.

Not all households came to Christ in a bloc; not every household was like that of Stephanus (1:16). The situation – especially for a Christian wife – could be made extremely difficult by an unsympathetic pagan spouse. Traditionally, the male head of the family chose the house religion, showing special devotion to this or that divinity. The other members were not free to choose their own faith, but were expected to pay respects at the temple or household shrine which the man had chosen. To refuse to do so in favor of a unique loyalty to Jesus Christ would be a grave insult to the husband, the extended family, and to the community. A slave would invite a beating, the wife a divorce or worse. Paul does not speak hypothetically: his assistant Timothy came from such a family situation (see Acts 16:1-3). Timothy's father was a (pagan) Greek who did not permit his son to be circumcised. It is not clear why he had married a Jewish woman. Timothy's mother and grandmother were Jewish and raised the boy with an awareness of the Scriptures; later Timothy came to Christ, and implicit in 2 Tim 1:5, Eunice and Lois did as well. The fact that Timothy was likely in his twenties when he was circumcised by Paul indicates that his father's opinion still held sway in that household. Thus the family was divided by Judaism and later by Christianity, and Timothy and the women twice broke with the husband's paganism.

And so Paul was aware of potential hardship when he told the believer to stay in the mixed marriage. If there is any leaving to be done (*aphiēmi* is used for both sexes), let the pagan initiate it, not the Christian! Paul seems to believe that a pagan spouse might be **willing to live with** him or her. It is the same in 1 Pet 3:1, where Christian women might have husbands who "do not believe the Word," but the marriage continues on.

7:14

What does it mean that the unbelieving partner **has been sanctified** (from the verb *hagiazō*) by the believer, or that their children are **holy** (the cognate adjective *hagios*) rather than **unclean** (the word used in 2 Cor 6:17, Eph 5:5) by virtue of having one Christian parent? This cannot mean the baptism of infants, as some have imagined, since Paul is speaking of an effect over the spouse as well.[348] The key seems to be the godly influence that the believer brings to the home that might persuade others to accept the gospel (as is the direction of 1 Pet 3:1-7). In a limited way all the members of the household are shielded from the power of Satan (1 Cor 5:5).

7:15

And if the unbelieving spouse **leaves**? In that case the believer may let him or her do so, the Christian is **not bound** or "obligated." The translation of the Spanish version the TLA is helpful; we translate it: "In such cases, the Christian wife or husband is not obligated to maintain that marriage." In a culture where divorce occurred simply when one party walked out, God does not expect the Christian to bar the door or automatically assume guilt for the divorce. **God has called us to live in peace;** the Christian may accept and enjoy the relief that accompanies the end of a turbulent mismatch.

One persistent interpretation of this passage is that it establishes the so-called Pauline Privilege: that while Paul generally forbids divorced people from remarrying, he allows

---

[348] Héring, *First Corinthians*, 52-53 is useful here. Godet, *First Corinthians*, 346-48, declares that this passage cannot be understood *without* assuming infant baptism.

it in cases where the Christian had been abandoned by an unbeliever.[349] Some denominations recognize two exceptions, marital unfaithfulness (based on Matt 19:9) or abandonment by an unbeliever, to be legitimate grounds for remarriage after a divorce.

In his case, Jesus was rejecting the liberal policy of the school of Hillel: Jesus ruled out divorce altogether unless there had been adultery; he does not allow remarriage. For his part, Paul is not focusing on remarriage, but addressing the question of whether Christians could separate from a marriage for reasons of religious incompatibility. Is marriage binding for the Christian? Yes, except in the case where the unbeliever decides to leave – then you can breathe easily, you're not bound to make him or her to stay.

The Pauline Privilege interpretation hinges on the meaning of **is not bound**. Some take it to mean *free from the marriage, just as if the spouse had died, and thus (like the widow) free to remarry* (1 Cor 7:39). We are helped in the interpretation of "is not bound" in 7:15 by looking at the use of a synonym for "bound" later in the chapter: to be literally "bound to a wife" (from *deō*; 7:27) means to be "married," as it is translated in the NIV; see also Rom 7:2 which uses, literally "bound" (also from *deō*) to refer to a woman who is married. Becoming "free" in 1 Cor 7:15, then, simply means to be free from the marriage, un-married.

It appears that Paul simply does not address the issue of remarriage, even for those who were abandoned by unbelieving spouses. Thiselton argues that, given the situational nature of the chapter, Paul was content to leave that question as a "loose end."[350] As far as we can draw a conclusion from 1 Cor 7, the one married to a Christian is that he or she may only remarry the same person; the person married to an unbeliever is to remain unmarried, free from marriage.

7:16

Perhaps the unbelieving husband or wife will be saved through the influence of their spouse. Christians are naturally shy of using the verb "save" (*sōzō*) of human evangelistic activity; of course, salvation is of God alone. Nevertheless, it is not uncommon for the New Testament to use "save" for the work evangelism or for rescuing a straying Christian (here; 9:22; James 5:20; Jude 23).

While there is always hope that the unbeliever will become a Christian, there is no guarantee, and thus no need to desperately try to preserve the marriage if the unbeliever walks out: as the NIV translates it, *How do you know whether you will save your spouse?* The NRSV translation is possible but less plausible, "For all you know, you might sane your spouse." In that case, Paul would be telling them to stay with their spouse, because there is a possibility that they will turn to Christ; but that does not seem to follow the flow of Paul's thought.

---

[349] Against the Privilege interpretation: Fee, *First Corinthians*, 302-03. For the Privilege interpretation: Conzelmann, *1 Corinthians*, 123; Héring, *First Corinthians*, 53. David Instone-Brewer, "1 Corinthians 7 in the light of the Graeco-Roman marriage and divorce papyri," *TynBul* 52.1 (2001): 101-16, argues that remarriage was always assumed in the culture, and that since Paul does not contradict it he must have allowed remarriage. While this interpretation is conceivable, it is an argument based on silence. Since Paul seems aware of the Jesus tradition regarding divorce, and implies that the Corinthians also knew it, the better logic is to understand that Paul assumes that remarriage is prohibited.

[350] Thiselton, *First Corinthians*, 536-37.

e. General exhortation: right now, stay where you are; but don't use your circumstances as an excuse for laxity 7:17-24

7:17
He gives a new set of instruction here in 7:17-24, and provides his reasons in 7:29-35. The Corinthian Christians were tempted to change their situation, for example, by seeking a divorce or by trying to force their spouse to remain when he or she was determined to leave. Paul taught the very opposite: in fact, his word for every Christian in every situation – **the rule I lay down in all the churches** – was: *Don't seek for change! Be content with your circumstances and accept them so far as it is possible. If change comes, don't be the one who has taken the initiative. Don't seek a wife; don't seek a divorce. Don't change anything about your circumstances.* Paul's teaching strikes Western Christians with special force, since the modern ethos has everything to do with taking personal initiative, pursuing self-improvement and freely choosing among many possible options. It is useful for today's reader to remember that Roman Corinthians too worshiped change and mobility.[351] This means that Paul was no reactionary, clinging to society's *status quo*; rather, he was revolting against the contemporary culture.

One result of the craze for change was that divorce was rampant, and men and women frequently alternated spouses. At times people married for love, but usually they pursued social or monetary advantage. Marriage was about status, and it was the lazy aspirant indeed who did not discard a spouse if divorce was an opportunity for advancement. For his part, Paul stresses – with Jesus – that marriage is for life. He does not seem concerned over whether the marriages were arranged by the parents, contracted under social pressure, or based on romance. Christian husbands and wives should love one another, no matter how they entered into the marriage contract (see Eph 5:25, Titus 2:4).

Paul's teaching on marriage and social status is centered in God, not on social mores or personal choice. With other Jews and Christians he knew that one's circumstances come from the hand of God. Contrary to the opinion of most pagans, there is no Fate to which one must bend. Rather, **each one should retain the place in life that the Lord assigned to him and to which God has called him** (cf. 1:2). He uses the verb "call" (*kaleō*) seven times in this paragraph; likewise, three times "assign" (*merizō*), which invokes the idea of assigning one's inheritance or portion (2 Cor 10:13; Rom 12:3; the same word is used in 1 Cor 1:13 and 7:34, but with entirely different meanings). Paul reiterates that **each one should remain in the situation which he was in when God called him** (7:20), and yet a third time: **Brothers, each man, as responsible to God, should remain in the situation God called him to** (7:24). Here is a verse where a gender-neutral translation more literally captures the original: the NIV 2011 is much improved with "each person should live as a believer in whatever situation the Lord has assigned to them". This verse reveals a great deal about the universe in which the Christian dwells. He is assured that God is free to change circumstances as he wills, and that God rules even over small details, whether the person has a lower or higher status according to society's values.

---

[351] See the example of a certain Cnaeus Julius Agricola "allied himself with Domitia Decidiana, a lady of illustrious birth. The marriage was one which gave a man ambitious of advancement distinction and support." Tacitus, *Agricola* 6.1. Fortunately, that couple "lived in singular harmony, through their mutual affection and preference of each other to self."

7:18-19

Paul has already dealt with married and unmarried; he goes on to other pairings: **circumcised** and **uncircumcised**, **slave** and **free**. With regard to the first pair, the apostle makes a statement that may not seem impressive to us, yet it was a phenomenal declaration in his context: **Circumcision is nothing and uncircumcision is nothing. Keeping God's commands is what counts.** There is a close parallel in Gal 6:15: "Neither circumcision nor uncircumcision means anything; what counts is a new creation." For a Pharisee and a rabbi this would have been an utter contradiction in terms, since receiving circumcision was considered the gateway to obeying God's commandments. Thus the Judaizers wanted to eliminate the very possibility of "gentile Christian"; gentiles must become converts to Judaism: "The Gentiles must be circumcised and required to obey the law of Moses" (Acts 15:5). For his part, Paul seems to be laying aside the ancient sign of the covenant that God gave to Abraham (Gen 17:10-14). 1 Cor 7 and Gal 6 would sound as jarring as the following would be to us: *Commit murder, or adultery, or steal or do whatever you like, so long as you obey God's commandments!*

What he is saying is that the gospel creates a people in which there is no special value of being in one race or another (cf. especially Gal 3:28, 1 Cor 12:13). Paul does not develop the implications of 7:19 as he does in other letters: in Corinth the temptation was not to fall into Judaizing, but in another direction, toward Greek wisdom.

Paul does not just say that "circumcision is nothing" but also its opposite, "uncircumcision is nothing." For years Jews in the Hellenistic world had been tempted to "hide" their circumcision.[352] Sometimes this was entirely literal; some Jewish men even had surgery so that people wouldn't laugh at them in the gymnasium. More broadly, many Jews who wished to assimilate and advance in the Greek culture surrendered to the mocking of the Greeks.[353] This was why it was so serious when some Jews levied a false charge against Paul: he supposedly taught Jews "not to circumcise their children or live according to our customs" (Acts 21:21). Their accusation of apostasy was by no means accurate: Paul expected that the Jewish Christian would live in a Jewish way.

7:21

The other pair is **slave** or **free**. Some Corinthian slaves may have imagined that they could not fully experience the Christian life if they were owned by another person. To them Paul says, **Were you a slave when you were called? Don't let it trouble you.**

Perhaps one third of the residents of Corinth were slaves.[354] Although we might imagine that all slaves were trying to free themselves and all free people were trying to avoid slavery, this was not always the case. The boundary line between a poor freedman and a slave was relatively fluid. People could sell themselves into slavery for a limited time to pay off debts. Many slaves found their loss of freedom and personhood a small

---

[352] For example, Josephus, *Antiquities* 12.5.1 §241; 1 Macc 1:14-15 NRSV – "So they built a gymnasium in Jerusalem, according to Gentile custom, and removed the marks of circumcision [literally, "they made themselves uncircumcised], and abandoned the holy covenant. They joined with the Gentiles and sold themselves to do evil."

[353] For example, Philo, *Special laws* 1.1-7, especially – "we will begin with that which is turned into ridicule by people in general. The ordinance of circumcision of the parts of generation is ridiculed, though it is an act which is practised to no slight degree among other nations also, and most especially by the Egyptians, who appear to me to be the most populous of all nations, and the most abounding in all kinds of wisdom."

[354] So Witherington, *Conflict and community*, 183.

price to pay for having regular meals and adequate clothing and housing. Some slaves were able to save small amounts of money over time and buy their own freedom. Others became like a part of the family, and stayed on as part of the household to work for wages once freed. This is not to minimize the wrong of one person owning another, it is merely to show that for some, slavery had its attractions.

Paul himself says to slaves, **although if you can gain your freedom, do so**. At some point in its history, the church began to receive petitions that the church funds be used to liberate Christian slaves. Ignatius mentions the practice in AD 117, but he believes that it will only lead to abuse: "They should not have a strong desire to be set free at the church's expense, lest they be found to be slaves of lust" (Ignatius, *Polycarp* 4.3).

7:22

Again, the apostle shows that the yearning for change is based on a serious theological misunderstanding. His rejoinder is, *Don't wait until your circumstances change to begin enjoying your freedom in Christ! Don't wait to begin to be Christ's slave, since you were "bought" and are owned by him (7:23a, parallel with 6:20)!*[355] In Christ, categories such as **slave** and **free** do not define what it means to be a Christian. The slave may represent Christ too, in the position where God has put him (Eph 6:5-8; Col 3:22-25; 1 Tim 6:1-2; Titus 2:9-10). 1 Pet 2:18-21 gives encouragement to slaves based on the fact of Christ's own servitude and sufferings.

7:23

When Paul says **you were bought at a price; do not become slaves of men**, he does not mean to say – as some Christian slaves surely must have reasoned – that it is a betrayal of the gospel to remain enslaved by a human being. It may be read in two ways. Perhaps he is talking about literal slavery: *Don't put yourselves into slavery for the sake of advancement: you belong to Christ, not to yourselves.*[356] More likely he speaks figuratively: *Don't become enslaved to anything that is not Christ, whether sin or whatever.*

7:24

But Paul's theme in this chapter here is marriage, not slavery or circumcision. He has used these categories merely to broaden his point about God's providence and to show that his advice regarding marriage is akin to what he tells people in other awkward or disadvantageous situations: *stay where you are!* **Brothers, each man, as responsible to God, should remain in the situation God called him to.** As in 7:17, this refers to "brothers and sisters," not just the male believers.

---

[355] Ignatius, *Polycarp* 4 – "Do not treat slaves, whether male or female, contemptuously, but neither let them become conceited; instead, let them serve all the more faithfully to the glory of God, that they may obtain from God a better freedom." See also Hermas, *Mandate* 8.10 – "Next hear the things that follow these: serving widows, looking after orphans and those in need, delivering God's servants from distress..."

[356] Clement of Rome mentions as an example of love that many Christians "have had themselves imprisoned, that they might ransom others. Many have sold themselves into slavery, and with the price received for themselves have fed others" (*1 Clem* 55.2). Clement apparently does not see this as a transgression of 1 Cor 7:23; neither does Paul his practice of "I make myself a slave to everyone, to win as many as possible" in 9:19.

Application: Status changes and the kingdom of God 7:24

Paul was not a Stoic: he does not tell the Corinthians to resign themselves to Fate, that "que será, será." In Paul's gospel, there exists a sovereign God, one who can make and free slaves, or make and end marriages, or promote and demote as he wills. "The Lord sends poverty and wealth; he humbles and he exalts" (1 Sam 2:7). The Christian lives in the world, but also possesses a higher citizenship with its own values. The teaching in this chapter has a parallel 1 Thess 4:13 – do not "grieve like the rest of men, who have no hope." This is not to say that a Christian cannot mourn their losses; it means that a Christian, knowing what he knows about this world and the resurrection, should not grieve as a pagan does. Gain or loss takes place in the greater context of God's sovereignty.

Nevertheless, God's children dream of changing their social status. We mistakenly assume that "if only" things were different, it would make us much happier persons and better Christians:

Get a divorce; find a new mate: In Paul's day, divorce was rampant, and men and women frequently changed spouses, typically to "move up" socially. What of today? The United States, Cuba, Panama, and Puerto Rico rank in the top 10 of countries with a high divorce rate. Most of the time, these people are seeking something better, whether for emotional or economic reasons. They believe that there must be a perfect mate for them out there in the world; or perhaps they have concluded that being single must be better than what they have. The church is right to emphasize God's ideals in marriage, the devastation of divorce, and the harm to the partners and the children. But Paul's point in this letter has more broadly to do with change of status, whether through marriage, divorce or celibacy. He tells married and single people that it's better in that case to stay right where they are. Underlying all this is the assumption that God makes full use of both married and single people. How ridiculous, then, to hear a single person claim that he or she could really serve God "if only" they were married, while at the same time those with families are fantasizing about how well they could serve God "if only" they weren't tied down with so much responsibility! How sad to see single Christian young women promise to start serving God as soon as they can locate a pastor to marry.

Social climbing: Today, as in Corinth, the young person with drive and energy is urged to go out and make contacts with the rich and influential. This can happen within the church as well – I could be a better Christian "if only" I were the favorite of the pastor! If only I had contacts in important ministries!

Self-improvement: As a North American, I was raised on the gospel of self-improvement, and in many ways I'm still sympathetic with it: *If you're poor, work harder! If you're ignorant, seek an education! If you fall down, try again!* The problem comes when we imagine that this exactly parallels the values of the kingdom of God. It appalls some Christians to hear this, but to God it matters nothing what our income is or whether we are a professional instead of a manual laborer. Christ's teaching on possessions is, "Do not store up for yourselves treasures on earth, where moth and rust destroy, and where thieves break in and steal. But store up for yourselves treasures in heaven, where moth and rust do not destroy, and where thieves do not break in and steal.

For where your treasure is, there your heart will be also" (Matt 6:19-21). Of course this teaching has been used in twisted ways. How gross to excuse our own indifference toward the suffering of others by telling ourselves that these poor people should be content where they are. More wicked still is to use it as a means of those we directly oppress by underpaying them or by playing the status game, telling them that it is Christian of them to put up with it in silence.

Social demotion: This practice is the opposite of the previous point, but it is based on the same misunderstanding. That is, some Christians seek spiritual power and status by lowering themselves socially. They sell their houses and set up self-sufficient farms in remote places. They live in communes because everyone "knows" that that leads to spiritual growth. This utopian vision may be the right choice for some, but it has no inherent connection to our relationship with God.

Move to the country; or move to the city: Again, believers make changes in their lives, imagining that God is present more in one place or the other. *How can we serve God here?* they cry. *If only we were somewhere else!*

Leave "secular" work: Many evangelicals have a warped theology of work, one that partakes more of the traditional clergy/laity model than it does of the Bible. And so, when God begins to move in their lives, they automatically assume that they should leave their "secular" job and go into "Christian work." They disparage their job: *I only do it to pay the bills; I put in my hours and then I use the rest of the time to serve God; at least it gives me something to tithe, but I resent losing the time that I could be spending in church!* But this goes exactly against God's attitude toward our individual calling or, to use the theological term, vocation. In his kingdom, there is no "secular" work, but all is done is his name (Eph 6:5-8; Col 3:23-24). In my own efforts to pay for my university education, I worked in a number of factories. One job was on an assembly line, where we made small pumps that would circulate water in home heating systems. I was able to assemble over 1000 pumps during each shift. I worked over an oven and it was dirty and hot work, often 40 degrees C. But much worse was the mental part of the job: it was repetitive and it bored me terribly. I was glad that I wouldn't be doing it forever. But still, God saw my job not just as a way to earn an education, in order to serve him at some later poing. It was a way to bring him glory in that moment. I assembled pumps in Jesus' name and tried to make them of a high quality that would bring him honor.

Seek a different religious flavor: Paul tells Jewish believers to be Jewish believers, and gentile believers to be gentile believers. It makes no real difference if you worship God circumcised or not. Now, every evangelical would probably accept that, it makes no difference to your *salvation*. But underneath lies the suspicion that these things do make a difference in the quality of one's Christian experience. But can we not see that that is precisely what Paul rejects here? If it doesn't matter, then it doesn't matter, period. We are no more or less saved if we are Jewish or gentile. What is more, we are no better or worse for liking Jewish-style Davidic dancing over traditional hymn-singing; we are no more or less peacemakers if we bless people with "God bless you" or "Shalom." We are no more or less in contact with God by hanging banners in our church or hanging a cross, or by being liturgical or singing choruses.

In conclusion: Be content with your status and accept it under God. In Christ, even a slave can remain a slave and be completely pleasing in the eyes of God.

---

f. Specific directions to virgins 7:25-28

7:25

The reappearance of *peri de* here (as in 7:1) may signal that the Corinthians had asked a specific question about the "virgins."[357] In the New Testament story, Mary was a virgin (Matt 1:23, Luke 1:27). Philip had four chaste daughters (Acts 21:9), although according to tradition they later married. The translation of *parthenos* as "singles" would be incorrect: "single" and "virgin" are not equivalent terms. Paul distinguishes the virgins from the unmarried and widowed (1 Cor 7:8-9). Here Paul speaks of the young chaste who were never married. Although the term "virgin" will be used specifically of women in 7:36-38, technically the word could refer to either sex.[358] In 7:26 he develops the teaching about virgins and shows that he includes chaste men or women. The theme of this section, then, is "people who are chaste and unmarried."

We do not know much about the state these chaste persons were in: were they pledged to remain celibate? Engaged, but uncertain whether to marry?[359] In a "spiritual marriage" but facing temptation (see below, under 7:36)?[360] Several commentators argue that these people, whatever their own desires, were being pressured by voices in the church to embrace perpetual celibacy.[361]

Here Paul has no oral tradition from the Lord Jesus, but that does not stop him from giving them directions: **I give a judgment as one who by the Lord's mercy is trustworthy**. As seen in the next verse, Paul's advice here is closely linked to the current circumstances in Corinth, not necessarily a rule for all people at all times.

7:26

It is this apostolic application of known truths to a new situation that leads to language like: **Because of the present crisis, I think that...** Unfortunately, we do not know what the "present crisis (*ananke*)" was, as that might give us further light on how to apply Paul's instructions. The Stoics used this same term *ananke* with the same meaning of "present circumstances imposed by Fate" (Chrysippus of Soli). Or it may mean a time of unusual distress (3 Macc 1:16 NRSV – "Then the priests in all their vestments prostrated themselves and entreated the supreme God to aid in the present situation"), or even the end-time tribulation (Luke 21:23). "Actual" (the participle *enestōsan*) could mean either "now present" or "impending."[362] One way of reading this passage is that Paul uses the term in its apocalyptic sense: they are in the time of tribulation; "the time is short" (7:29); "this world in its present form is passing away" (7:31). In that case, Paul

---

[357] Conzelmann, *1 Corinthians*, 131, says they did ask Paul a question.
[358] So Thiselton, *First Corinthians*, 571. Contra Robertson and Plummer, *First Corinthians*, 151; or Héring, *First Corinthians*, 57.
[359] Fee.
[360] So especially Hurd, *Origin*, 177-80; Lietzmann and Kümmel; Héring, *First Corinthians*, 63.
[361] Notably Fee; Schrage; Thiselton.
[362] Fee, *First Corinthians*, 328-29, argues that it must mean "present," rather than "impending." It definitely refers to present time in 1 Cor 3:22, Gal 1:4; nevertheless, contra Fee, other Christian texts that use the word (here, 2 Thess 2:2, 2 Tim 3:1 and *Barnabas* 17.2) are capable of either sense.

thought the end was upon them, that the Corinthians were about to be made "like the angels," or perhaps he meant that it was too late in time for Christians to be thinking of marriage.

The alternate interpretation fits better, that Paul was thinking "we are now going through hard times" (CEV), some set of circumstances that affected Corinth in the 50's.[363] The crisis, whatever it may have been, reminded the Christian that this world is transient. Therefore, marriage, which looms so large, especially for young girls, is one more institution that will eventually be done away with. There have been recent studies of Corinth which show that there was a bad famine in the late 40's and again 51, which continued to affect the poor for a longer time.[364] Perhaps the scarcity of food created a situation in which "some remain hungry" (1 Cor 11:21). In that case, why marry, when that will strain your ability to obtain enough to eat? Why divorce if that means that women and children will suffer privation?

7:27

Paul is not penning a manual to answer every question about marriage: "he addresses specific difficulties that have developed in Corinth and is not presenting a marriage manual or his systematic thoughts on marriage."[365] He addresses various situations: **Are you married? Do not seek a divorce.** Of course, Paul has already ruled out divorce, but here is an additional pragmatic reason: the times make remarriage an awkward choice. **Are you unmarried?** which is literally, "Are you free from having a wife?" The phrase is less than clear, and must be defined by the context: he speaks of a man who is either widowed or never-married. He cannot be speaking of divorced men, since in the next verse he says "But if you do marry, you have not sinned"; were he speaking of divorce and remarriage, he would be contradicting his prohibition of remarriage in 7:11. To the widowed and never-married men he gives, not a command, but a counsel: **Do not look for a wife.**

7:28

For some Corinthians, celibacy was the higher good before God: they claimed that it was a lesser state, to have sexual contact with a woman (7:1). This is not God's will at all, answers the apostle: for a widowed or never-married man or for a chaste young woman, **if you do marry, you have not sinned**, since marriage, like celibacy, is in fact a gift of God (7:7). Paul also argues from the standpoint of practicality: he himself is celibate and he recommends it to others, not because the Lord commanded it, but: (1) **those who marry will face many troubles in this life, and I want to spare you**. He explains just what **troubles** he is speaking about later on; (2) because there is a real lack of self-control in Corinth (7:2, 5, 9, 36). Taking on celibacy without the spiritual gift to do so is to risk fornication – to court a grave sin in order to adopt a lifestyle for which God never asked. Thus Paul advises the single state, but only for those who can manage it.

---

[363] See Fee; R. Morganthaler, "*Anangkē*," *NIDNTT* 2:147-48.
[364] Winter, *After Paul left Corinth*, 216-25.
[365] Garland, *1 Corinthians*, 242.

g. General exhortation, continued: why you should stay where you are 7:29-35

Here Paul develops in greater detail his world-view: the Christian must adjust his sights beyond the world's institutions and focus on the greater reality, the age to come. It is a rebuke, not to marriage, but to putting one's emphasis on social status.

7:29-31

Paul speaks in an exalted poetic style here, showing the implications of **the time is short** and **this world in its present form is passing away**. How should a Christian live in this age after the cross, **from now on**?

> **those who have wives**
> **should live as if they had none;**
> **those who mourn,**
> **as if they did not;**
> **those who are happy,**
> **as if they were not;**
> **those who buy something,**
> **as if it were not theirs to keep;**
> **those who use the things of the world,**
> **as if not engrossed in them.**

This is typical language of "eschatological reversal." The Christian, while commanded to serve God in and through the world's structures, lives in another dimension. This is not panic at the end of the world, nor the rejection of the world: rather it is "the relativizing of worldly things."[366]

Paul's main concern is marriage. Unfortunately, his statement that **those who have wives should live as if they had none** was for many centuries a proof text for the doctrine of celibacy as the higher spiritual plane: *if you are married already, live apart from your wife or put her away altogether.* But that this statement cannot be a call to divorce or sexless marriage is shown conclusively in the earlier verses of this chapter, where Paul calls for spouses to stay married and to have regular sexual relations within marriage.

7:32-34

Paul goes on to speak first to the unmarried men, then to the unmarried women (the *agamos*, as in 7:8, 11) and to the never-married virgin girls. He affirms what the Corinthian ascetics must have also seen, that it is easier practically to serve the Lord as a single. Of course, this will vary from place to place and time to time, but in Paul's case it made good sense. The Corinthians too, if they are so endowed, might remain **free from concern** in the world, so that they might be **concerned about the Lord's affairs - how he can please him**; otherwise their **interests are divided**. Paul implicitly is luring the Corinthians away from the temptation toward worldly status, in which arranging a

---

[366] V. L. Wimbush, *Paul the worldly ascetic: response to the world and self-understanding according to 1 Cor. 7* (Macon: Mercer, 1987), 33.

beneficial marriage is a critical step for improving one's social position. But what is that in comparison to serving the Lord with greater attention?

The virgin's **aim is to be devoted to the Lord in both body and spirit**. That statement could play into the hands of the ascetics, if it weren't for the fact that Paul was not commending celibacy, let alone asceticism. Purification in body and spirit is the goal for every Christian, married or not: "let us purify ourselves from everything that contaminates body and spirit, perfecting holiness out of reverence for God" (2 Cor 7:1). Yet in practical terms of time and energy, the virgin can dedicate herself to God's work. In those same terms, she is free from the goal of **how she can please her husband**, and also the bearing and raising of children. Paul is not speaking of **the affairs of this world** as if it is "worldly" and sinful to be married. Nevertheless, there are so many tasks to be done to maintain a family.

7:35

In practical terms, isn't it better choice to use that energy in devotion to the Lord – in direct ministry of service and evangelism? But again, Paul is recommending a better way, not giving a list of commands and **not to restrict you** but that they **live in a right way in undivided devotion to the Lord**. "In a right way" (from *euschēmōn*) may mean "decent"; nevertheless it also has the sense of noble or of good reputation, as were the esteemed Joseph of Arimathea (Mark 15:43) and the women of high social status in Antioch of Pisidia (Acts 13:50; see LSJ). That is, men and women who choose not to marry should not worry about their loss of social status: before the Lord they are noble.

h. Specific directions to those engaged to virgins 7:36-38

Paul now returns to a very specific case, speaking to men ("his" is masculine) about how they are treating, literally, a **virgin**. Paul refers to female virgins, and as the NIV paraphrases, she is "engaged."[367] There is hesitation about whether the girl should go ahead and get married. Perhaps someone in the church is teaching that celibacy is the higher choice, and the girl or her *fiancé* or someone in the family is having doubts. Paul gives the same instruction as he has in 7:25-28 – the marriage may take place or not, but there is no compulsion; the reasons for not marrying are the pragmatic ones he has already mentioned.

This being relatively clear, there is a major difference of opinion concerning to whom Paul is speaking. Almost every modern version chooses a side and gives the other view as an alternate reading. The three main positions are:

#1. Paul is addressing a father about his daughter. There view with the long history is that Paul is speaking to the father or guardian of a virgin girl (GW, NASB);[368]

---

[367] Some have argued that this could not mean an "engagement," since betrothal was a Jewish, not Greek, practice. Nevertheless, Conzelmann, *1 Corinthians*, 135, n. 44, shows that the Greeks too contracted marriages in advance, and "*fiancée*" properly describes the girl to be married.

[368] So Theodore Mopsuestia, Chrysostom, Theodoret of Cyrus, Augustine; Robertson and Plummer, *First Corinthians*, 158, who state that the Corinthians had asked Paul a question specifically about such fathers; Allo; Leon Morris, *The first epistle of Paul to the Corinthians* (TNTC, Grand Rapids, MI: Eerdmans, 1958); Grosheide; Hodge; Goudge; Godet; Nicoll; W. Günther, "Marriage," *NIDNTT* 2:581.

less likely, to the owner or guardian of a female slave. The man has the right to give her away in marriage, but perhaps he has decided that the girl should remain pure, dedicated to the service of Christ. There are serious problems with this interpretation. First, one must supply the additional word "daughter," which does not appear in the Greek. Second, one would have to translate "thinks he is acting unbecomingly toward" her (NASB), an awkward handling of the infinitive verb "to behave dishonorably" (*aschēmonein*). Third, there is a clear problem with the translation "he does not sin; let *her* marry" (NASB, similarly GW), that is, that the man should give the girl in marriage. But in the original the verb is plural and so it would have to mean "let them [the virgin and her *fiancé*] get married."[369] That plural verb is evidence in favor of the second interpretation, below. Then too we know that in non-Jewish families the role of the father as guardian of his daughter and thus the arbiter of marriage had been greatly relaxed in imperial times. While the parents would be involved in the decision, the girl also had some say in the matter. That fact makes viewpoint #1 very difficult, since it would imply that the decision would be the father's alone

#2. Paul is addressing an unmarried man about his *fiancée* (most English versions). In modern times this viewpoint has become the most popular one.[370] Later Paul addresses a man who decides to marry, literally, "his own virgin" (7:38), which implies "his *fiancée*" (NIV). "Let them marry" (7:36, NIV) means that the young man may decide to marry, with the implication that the girl has consented, as Paul affirms in 7:28a. This is the view of the NIV: "if anyone thinks he is acting improperly toward the virgin he is engaged to" (7:36), probably that he is making improper sexual advances toward her.[371] This has the virtue of simplicity, in view of the context of the letter and of the historical context: if Paul had had the father in mind here, it would be the first time anyone's father has appeared in this chapter, and the Greek is too vague to support the introduction of this third party. Rather, Paul's main concern is that people be free to decide that they themselves should marry or remain celibate. Thus in 7:37, the man decides that he himself should remain celibate. But if he takes the decision to marry, it is that man himself whom Paul assures that "he is not sinning."

#3. Paul is addressing the "husband" in a so-called spiritual marriage.[372] This view looks toward a marginal Christian known from the following two centuries, wherein a couple would contract a "spiritual marriage": they would live together permanently or at intervals but without ever consummating the union. The technical term for these spiritual wives is *virgines subintroductae*. Tertullian, for example, promoted spiritual marriage for widowers who could not live without domestic help. He makes a widower say:

"In my present (widowed) state, too, a consort in domestic works is necessary."

---

[369] A very few manuscripts (including the uncorrected D) have the singular, which would mean "let *her* marry." This is a case of the scribe emending the text to suit what he perceives is the meaning.

[370] For example, Ambrosiaster; Fee; Lietzmann and Kümmel; Schrage; Barrett; Garland.

[371] Winter, *After Paul left Corinth*, 243-46, demonstrates that the phrase "acting improperly toward" (*aschēmoneō*) has clear sexual overtones in some Greek literature. See too the strong argument of Martin, *The Corinthian body*, 219-28.

[372] This is the view of Héring; Weiss, *Korintherbrief*, 206-09; cf. Hurd, *Origin*. See contra Fee, *First Corinthians*, 326-27; Garland, *1 Corinthians*, 338-39. See the evaluation of the view by Conzelmann, *1 Corinthians*, 135-36.

(Then) take some spiritual wife. Take to yourself from among the widows one fair in faith, dowered with poverty, sealed with age. You will (thus) make a good marriage.[373]

Although this idea is intriguing, it has serious difficulties: first, there is no evidence in the 1st century for the practice of spiritual marriage; second, the couple would in effect already be married, making "let them marry" redundant or forcing a translation such as "let them consummate their marriage."

It is best to take the terms in their most natural sense, (#2) that Paul is speaking of an engaged couple, and that the young man has doubts about the sanctity of marriage. This allows the paragraph to flow most easily from the reference to the virgins in 7:25-26, and without introducing new characters or hypothetical versions of marriage.

Let us explore another detail, rendered by NIV as **and she is getting along in years** (*huperakmos*). First it may mean that the girl has sexually matured but is not too old to marry. It was not at all unusual for a girl to arrange marriage well in advance of puberty. In this case, she has now matured and in theory is ready to marry (see CEV, GW, NASB). The second view has better evidence, that she "is past the bloom of youth" (NET, also NIV 1984, KJV, NKJV, HCSB, Vulgate): she is getting rather old for a girl with an arranged marriage; she is *superadultus* (Latin Vulgate) and there is social pressure for the marriage to take place (see BDAG). In the ancient context "virgins" were usually between 12-16 years old; "old" may allow that she is still an adolescent. The third option is that *huperakmos* does not refer to the girl at all, but to the man; in that case it would be translated "if his passions are strong" (ESV, also GNB, NIV 2011, NJB). Any of the three options could fit the context, although a reference to the girl is best; Paul has already mentioned the questionable behavior of the young man in the first clause, and bringing it up again seems redundant. We therefore understand this paragraph to mean that:

- a Christian man and girl have been engaged for some time
- the girl is 15 or 16 or more and it seems as if her betrothed is delaying marriage
- something has made the man unsure about the propriety of marriage, yet he feels sexual pressure and may even be making inappropriate advances toward the girl

Verse 37 stresses that if he chooses to end the engagement, he is free to do so, implicitly under the same conditions Paul has already mentioned. He had better be sure he has the gift of celibacy; his actions to this point suggest that he does not – already "he is acting improperly toward the virgin he is engaged to" (see 7:2, 9, 36). But if he does decide to remain celibate, then he literally "decides to maintain his own virgin."

---

[373] Tertullian, *De exhortatione castitatis* 12. Cyprian deals with this issue in detail in his *Letter* 61 – "virgins who, after having once determined to continue in their condition, and firmly to maintain their continency, have afterwards been found to have remained in the same bed side by side with men…We must interfere at once with such as these, that they may be separated while yet they can be separated in innocence; because by and by they will not be able to be separated by our interference, after they have become joined together by a very guilty conscience. Moreover, what a number of serious mischiefs we see to have arisen hence; and what a multitude of virgins we behold corrupted by unlawful and dangerous conjunctions of this kind, to our great grief of mind!" See also Eusebius, *History of the church* 7.30.12.

7:38

Paul's conclusion runs true to form: **So then, he who marries the virgin does right, but he who does not marry her does even better**. The verb "marries" is *gamizō*. In other contexts it means "give in marriage" (as in Matt 24:38) rather than "marry," that is, it could refer to the action of the parents of the bride. However it also can mean "marry," depending on the context; in this context "marries" is a parallel to "they should get married" in 7:36.[374]

The context gives a clear sense of what Paul means by **right** and **better**. Remaining celibate is better on the pragmatic grounds that he has mentioned; it is not morally better.

i. Recapitulation, with a word to widowed women 7:39-40

Paul ends this long chapter with a summary and a final appeal to widowed women. Leaving aside all contingencies and extended application, Paul summarizes very briefly the teaching of 7:10-11 – a wife must not separate from her husband; her marriage to her husband lasts until he is dead. If and when he dies, she may marry whomsoever she wishes; the woman has the right of consent. The only stipulation is that he, literally, be "in the Lord," that the new husband be a Christian; hence the NIV's expansion, **he must belong to the Lord**. Paul wants to avoid in future the problem of mixed marriages (7:12-16). Thus, her freedom to contract a second marriage or to pass on it is the same freedom that a never-married virgin possesses. And Paul cannot resist once more saying in 7:40 that she'd be happier **if she stays as she is**, that is, unmarried.

Paul's reiterates his epistemology: **in my judgment…I think that I too have the Spirit of God.** His opinion is his own, but it is a spiritual one and therefore to be taken very seriously indeed.

To summarize our conclusions:

Corinthian situation: In Corinth, the Christian faced pressures from inside and outside the church. Divorcing and marrying upward was a constant in that culture, since a good marriage gave a boost to one's social and economic prospects. Beyond that, some Christians (perhaps wives? we do not know) concluded that sex was wrong, or at least an inferior state. This notion may have developed under the influence of some philosophical idea that celibacy was more godly, or led to a deeper, more thoughtful Christian experience. Some might have drawn the conclusion that singles and widows had better stay celibate; that married couples should abstain from intercourse; that engaged couples had better break it off; that Christians married to pagans had better walk out on the marriage.

The Corinthian letter sounded something like: *Paul, don't you think that it's better that a man not have any relations with a woman? Don't you think virgins should remain as they are? Why are you celibate, Paul, if you do not believe that it is not the holiest way to live?*

Paul perceives that some Corinthians are trying to change their circumstances in

---

[374] See Thiselton, *First Corinthians*, 602; Fee; Schrage; Lietzmann and Kümmel; Walter. Paul does not mean to say that a husband and wife in a "spiritual marriage" should physically consummate their marriage.

order to achieve a higher plane. He sees this as a misplaced goal. Paul also believes that the Corinthians have severely underestimated the power of sexual temptation. He does not want them to start out with a high ideal, which would later become the path to fornication. In fact, Paul can point to specific instances in the church of fornicating with prostitutes.

Paul in 1 Corinthians speaks about marriage as a development of the gospel of the cross and its implications. Explicitly to a widow considering remarriage (7:39), but implicitly to all, a Christian should marry "in the Lord," that is, marry another believer. Primarily he urges people to stay in the state in which they were when called, since God has a purpose for them within their particular set of circumstances. Paul bases his preference for celibacy mainly on pragmatic grounds. He bypasses theological or philosophical proofs and goes to circumstances and personal capacity and preference, signaling that where something is not sin, a Christian has liberty to choose. On those grounds he encourages Corinthians who have a gift of celibacy to follow his example. Paul has a healthier respect for sexual temptation than the Corinthians do.[375] Behind all of his words to virgins, engaged, married, widowed, and divorced lurks the fleshly and Satanic dangers of fornication:

1. To currently married men and women (2-6) – It is mandatory that you have regular sexual relations. We must assume this command when Paul gets on to addressing subgroups of married people:

1a. To men or women currently married to believers (10-11) – Avoid fornication; have regular intercourse with your spouse (2-6). The sole exception is a "sexual fast" for a short limited season of special prayer, after which they must go back to regular intercourse. You must stay married, it's a command of Jesus.

1b. To "the rest," that is, those currently married to unbelievers (12-16) – Avoid fornication; have regular intercourse with your spouse (2-6). The Lord Jesus didn't teach about mixed marriages, but Paul will: Stay married if the unbeliever consents to it, and be a Christian influence on the spouse and children. If there is a divorce, let the unbeliever initiate it; whatever happens, don't feel guilty one way or the other.

2. To the unmarried (*agamos*) and the widows (8, 11, 39-40) – Avoid fornication; if you are unmarried because of divorce, remain unmarried or remarry your former spouse; if you are widowed you're free to remarry a Christian, or to remain celibate (which state Paul prefers, but does not mandate).

3. Concerning never-married men and women (virgins) generally (25-28) – Avoid fornication; Paul prefers that you stay celibate because of the present crisis, and because it leaves one free to serve the Lord more directly.

3 a. Concerning young men already engaged to virgins (36-38) – Avoid fornication; marry if you like, stay celibate if you can (Paul thinks this is better); but make up your own mind, considering whether God has given you the gift of celibacy and also your circumstances.

---

[375] Walter, *First Corinthians*, is useful here.

To marry or not is up to the individual, regardless of outside pressures. Making a decision about the next question that Paul addresses – meat sacrificed to idols – will involve not only individual conscience, but the conscience of other Christians and the consideration of the sensibilities of pagan Corinthians.

Application: When a Christian is married to a non-Christian 7:39

Is it permissible for a Christian to be married to a non-Christian? That seems to have been what the Corinthians were wondering about, whether a Christian wife or husband had the right, or perhaps the obligation, to leave a non-Christian. This may have been part of their misunderstanding that Paul mentions in 5:9-13. In general Paul says that, yes, mixed marriages should be allowed to continue:

1. Paul does not want Christian spouses to terminate their mixed marriages

Paul's very brevity in this chapter might give us the false impression that being married to an unbeliever is simply a matter of remaining married. He uses the phrase "is willing to live with" him or with her (7:13), as if the unbeliever has simply to indicate his or her willingness and then everything is fine. In fact, Paul does not attempt to explore every possible ramification of staying married. Especially in the case of the wife being Christian, there are plenty of cases from antiquity up to the present, where the husband will use coercion, violence or even murder to prevent the wife from practicing her faith.

Paul does not here address marriages where there is threat of violence; his comments are for those where "all things being equal" and the unsaved partner wants to continue. The Christian partner should not initiate divorce in order to end an uneven partnership.

2. Paul wants new marriages to be contracted only with believers

Paul then deals with people who are unmarried and looking for a spouse. In the one clear statement, he states that a widow, literally, "is free to marry anyone she wishes, in the Lord" (7:39). This statement cannot be pressed to mean "I may marry an unbeliever if the Lord shows me that it is alright." Rather "in the Lord" is shorthand for "a believer, a person in Christ" (as in 1 Cor 7:22; also, Rom 16:11, Eph 5:8). Paul does not mention in the other relevant verses (7:9, 7:28, 7:36, 7:38) that Christian should marry Christian, but if it is true for widows in 7:39 there can be no reason not to apply it to all cases.

Most interpreters regard 2 Cor 6:14 ("Do not be yoked together with unbelievers") as a prohibition against marrying an unbeliever. Although Paul is not speaking specifically of marriage there, it is a valid application. Yet we must also insist that Paul allows – even encourages – mismatched couples to continue together in 1 Cor 7.

Depending on the time and place, some marriages are arranged by authority figures in the family or tribe, meaning that some mixed marriages were never the choice of either party. But the greater tragedy is with people with full or partial freedom to choose, yet botch the opportunity and choose poorly. I have known too many Christians who have married unbelievers, against the strong advice of their pastor, parents and Christian friends. The young woman especially – although not exclusively – takes it into her mind to combine evangelism with romance: *If I marry this boy, then I will be able to bring him around to Christ! He will see the love of Christian in me as his wife, and I will win him for the gospel!* She may even claim that God has told her to do so. Can such wondrous conversions happen? Certainly they do, as Paul says in 7:16, but he hastens to add that God offers no guarantee. I have seen one or two happy examples where the unbelieving spouse eventual came to Christ. But in almost all the examples I have known, the end is divorce, or else a long lifetime of struggle against a spouse who resents being a mission field. There are many young people who could have poured their energies into evangelism or missions or Christian work, or even a marriage to a Christian, but instead spend all their powers simply coping with a difficult union.

How can this waste be prevented? It is next to impossible to halt a wedding once the process begins. Yet, if you tell a young couple that the odds are against them, in their romantic haze they will take this up as a challenge to prove the world wrong. No, if young people are to be told why they should not marry an unbeliever, it must be years ahead of time. We have to practice preventive medicine, not wait to reason with people who are in the bloom of romance. We need to tell teenagers not only what they should do, but why. Parents may want to point out mixed marriages and stress the damage they cause. In this and in other areas, we must teach that it is never wise to commit a wrong – "evangelistic romance" – in order to accomplish a greater good.

Paul allows as a principle that a Christian may marry a Christian. This is their right and their obligation. We must not infer from that, however, that it is wise to marry just anyone, provided only that they are believers. We can imagine Paul encouraging some couples not to use their freedom to marry each other, because on some level such a marriage would be unwise.

2. Concerning food offered to idols: "Shouldn't a well-informed Christian have the right to eat meat that has been sacrificed to idols?" 8:1-11:1

1 Cor 8-10 form a continuous, though winding, development of thought concerning food that had been offered to idols. The abrupt changes of material in 9:1, 10:1 and 10:14 have sparked theories that 1 Corinthians is really a collection of disparate Pauline teachings, sewn together into what looks like a single letter.[376] But even apart from the methodological dubiousness of these source theories, no two of which are yield the same conclusions, a closer reading of the three chapters reveals an underlying unity. The keys are the concepts that we know from earlier chapters: knowledge (*gnōsis*), rights and freedom (often with the noun *exousia*), the need to know one's rights, the close participation of every single believer in the fellowship of Christ and the virtue of setting aside one's rights for the sake of love and for the gospel. In 1 Cor 9, Paul seems to go off on a tangent about an apostle's rights – but even then he is using himself as a model of Christian behavior, showing which of his rights he has laid aside as an example for the Corinthians: *Here's how I live, now how should you live?*

The very length of Paul's treatment might give the reader the impression that it was an entirely new issue, or that the primitive church had not yet developed a firm view of it. This could not be farther from the truth. Acts 15, which we take to be an accurate reflection of events, indicates that the central issue had been settled before Paul

---

[376] So Héring, *First Corinthians*, 100; contra Hurd, *Origin*, 131-42, who argues for the unity of the section.

evangelized Corinth, at the Jerusalem Council. Some Jewish Christians (Acts 15:1, 5) had rejected the very concept of "gentile Christian": they believed that gentiles who came to faith in Jesus would need to receive circumcision and take on themselves the yoke of the Torah; that is, they would need to convert to Judaism. The council rejected that idea and affirmed that gentiles and Jews are saved by the grace of Christ (Acts 15:11). They also wrote to gentile Christians to tell them of their decision, and also to instruct them to avoid certain practices that Jews thought of as stereotypical gentile offenses (Acts 15:20, 29; 21:25):[377]

> Prohibition against food sacrificed to idols (the adjective *eidōlothutos*, as in 1 Cor)
> Prohibition against "blood" (probably in the sense of eating animal blood)
> Prohibition against eating strangled animals
> Prohibition against fornication (*porneia*, as in 1 Cor 5:1, 6:13, 6:18, 7:2)

These practices were derived from the rules given to Noah in Gen 9:1-7.[378] The book of Revelation strongly denounces fornication and the eating of meat sacrificed to idols in the letters to Pergamum and to Thyatira (Rev 2:14, 20).[379] This moral lapse is the "teaching of Balaam," a reference to the apostasy of Israel in Moab (Num 22-25; see 2 Pet 2:15-16). Balaam had ensnared the Israelites to rebellion against Jehovah through the lure of the Moabite women and the idolatrous banquet of Baal (Num 25:1-2; 31:16). Roughly contemporary with Revelation is the tradition behind *Didache* 6.3 – "Now concerning food, bear what you are able, but in any case keep strictly away from meat sacrificed to idols, for it involves the worship of dead gods."[380] *Didache* does not refer

---

[377] The work *Joseph and Aseneth* shows the Jewish abhorrence of meat sacrificed to idols, although the text as we now have it may be been later influenced by Christian teaching about the sacraments: "It is not fitting for a [Jewish] man who worships God, who will bless with his mouth the living God and eat blessed bread of life and drink a blessed cup of immortality and anoint himself with blessed ointment of incorruptibility to kiss a strange woman who will bless with her mouth dead and dumb idols and eat from their table bread of strangulation and drink from their libation a cup of insidiousness and anoint herself with ointment of destruction." (*Joseph and Aseneth* 8.5). Later on, when she repented from her idolatry, "And Aseneth took her royal dinner and the fatlings and the fish and the flesh of the heifer and all the sacrifices of her gods and the vessels of their wine of libation and threw everything through the window looking north, and gave everything to the strange dogs" (10.14). The book does not use the technical term *eidōlothutos*.

[378] There is some doubt about the original text of Acts 15; see the NA[28] edition and the standard commentaries on Acts. The Textus Receptus preserves the authentic text as do the English versions. Beyond that there is also some disagreement about the exact meaning of some of these terms.

[379] The early fathers reported that the Nicolaitans (see Rev 2:6, 15) ate meat sacrificed to idols. See Irenaeus, *Against heresies* 1.26.3 – they teach "that it is a matter of indifference to practise adultery, and to eat things sacrificed to idols"; Hippolytus, *Refutation of all heresies* 7.24 – "[Nicolaus] departed from correct doctrine, and was in the habit of inculcating indifference of both life and food. And when the disciples (of Nicolaus) continued to offer insult to the Holy Spirit, John reproved them in Revelation as fornicators and eaters of things offered unto idols." The 3rd-century Victorinus of Pettau's commentary on Rev. 2:6 says that the Nicolaitans taught "that what had been offered to idols might be exorcised and eaten, and that whoever should have committed fornication might receive peace on the eighth day."

[380] For other patristic discussions of this theme see Clement of Alexandria, *Stromata* 4.15; *Instructor* 2.1 – "We must therefore abstain from these viands not for fear (because there is no power in them); but on account of our conscience, which is holy, and out of detestation of the demons to which they are dedicated, are we to loathe them; and further, on account of the instability of those who regard many things in a way that makes them prone to fall, 'whose conscience, being weak, is defiled: for meat commendeth us not to God.'" Tertullian, *De spectaculis* 13 – "we do not offer sacrifices to the gods, and we make no funeral oblations to the departed; nay, we do not partake of what is offered either in the one case or the other, for we cannot partake of God's feast and the feast of devils." Novatian, *On the Jewish meats* 7 – "as far as

to Acts 15 or 1 Cor 8-10; it appears to be an independent tradition.

Why does Paul make no reference to the Jerusalem decree in this epistle? If Acts 15-16 is grounded in history, it would be astonishing if Paul had not promulgated the decree in Macedonia and Achaia as he did in Antioch (Acts 15:30-31) and Galatia (Acts 16:4). Some argue that the Jerusalem decree did not exist as such, or that if it did, Paul did not know of it.[381] Some have imagined that Paul did not accept the decree's authority. Both hypotheses are entirely unnecessary. In 1 Cor 8-10 Paul comes to the same conclusion as the council had, rejecting any sharing in sacramental meals with idols. But rather than simply banning the practice, Paul spends three long chapters showing why he is compelled to do so. The other issue is that Paul is dealing with circumstances which lie beyond the scope of the apostolic decree, which we may frame as: *What if a Christian accidentally eats such meat: is that a sin too? Or what if a Christian has come to the mature understanding that idols are a fiction: does the rule still apply?*

What was this pagan ritual that caused so many questions? The practice in Paul's day was the ritual offering of grains and sacrificed animals – whether of livestock, fowl, or even fish – to a pagan deity. Some translations use the phrase "meat sacrificed to idols." Although that is not strictly literal translation, it is clear that the issue at Corinth was indeed meat, as Paul shows in 8:13 – "I will never eat meat [*kreas*] again, so that I will not cause him to fall." Typically, a third of the animal was burned on the altar; a third was left in the presence of the idol; a third was returned to the worshipers or sold on the market. As with a parallel custom in the Jewish Temple (see 1 Cor 10:18), eating that food signified the cultic participation with the deity and thus an act of worship. Paul uses here a pejorative Jewish term, *eidōlothutos*, "that which is sacrificed to idols."[382]

---

pertains to God's creation, every creature is clean. But when it has been offered to demons, it is polluted so long as it is offered to the idols; and as soon as this is done, it belongs no longer to God, but to the idol. And when this creature is taken for food, it nourishes the person who so takes it for the demon, not for God, by making him a fellow-guest with the idol, not with Christ." Origen, *Contra Celsum* 8, has a long section to refute Celsus, who had written in the 170's to make fun of Christians for refraining from sacrificed meat; Origen concludes "for that which is offered to idols is sacrificed to demons, and a man of God must not join the table of demons" (8.30). *Apostolic constitutions* 7.21 is based squarely on 1 Cor 8-10 – "But do ye abstain from things offered to idols; for they offer them in honour of demons, that is, to the dishonour of the one God, that ye may not become partners with demons." Theodoret, *History of the church* 3.11 (NPNF² 3.101), records how the 2ⁿᵈ-century apostate emperor Julian contaminated the wells and all the food in the marketplace in order to harm the Christians' conscience – "He began by polluting with foul sacrifices the wells in the city and in Daphne, that every man who used the fountain might be partaker of abomination. Then he thoroughly polluted the things exposed in the Forum, for bread and meat and fruit and vegetables and every kind of food were aspersed. When those who were called by the Saviour's name saw what was done, they groaned and bewailed and expressed their abomination; nevertheless they partook, for they remembered the apostolic law, 'Everything that is sold in the shambles eat, asking no question for conscience sake [1 Cor 10:25].'"

[381] Conzelmann, *1 Corinthians*, 139, uses 1 Corinthians to overturn the reliability of Acts 15: "There is no trace of a rejection or circumvention of the apostolic decree on Paul's part. [This is because] neither he himself nor the community in Corinth has any knowledge of it." See also Fitzmyer, *First Corinthians*, 50-51, 334-35, who says that James' comment in Acts 21:25 proves that Paul had not been present in Jerusalem when the apostles wrote to the gentiles. If that were so, then Acts 15:30-31 and 16:4 are revisionist history. See Godet, *First Corinthians*, 403-04, who argues that the Decree was limited to Syria and Cilicia, and that Corinth raised complex questions that the Decree did not answer.

[382] The earliest certain appearance of the word *eidōlothutos* is here in 1 Cor 8:1. The earliest extant Jewish reference is 4 Macc 5.2 – "[Antiochus] ordered the guards to seize each and every Hebrew and to compel them to eat pork and *food sacrificed to idols*." The book is from the 1ˢᵗ century AD, although it may be later than 1 Corinthians, and perhaps influenced by Christian vocabulary; likewise *Sibylline oracles* 2.96. Still, it

Of course, pagans would not use this term, since they did not regard their gods as mere "idols." They themselves used *hierothutos* ("sacrificed to a divinity"). In the New Testament the latter word appears only in 1 Cor 10:28 to report what a pagan friend might say; Paul intentionally makes the pagan speak the word that was used in his own culture.[383]

Where might a Corinthian Christian have encountered such meat?

1. It might be on sale in one of the city marketplaces (*agora*) at a discounted price, since it had gone through a certain amount of handling; it would have been appropriately labeled (cf. 10:25). The average Christian lived on a grain diet and probably consumed meat infrequently, because it was expensive. Nevertheless, the fact that Paul could renounce eating meat (8:13) shows that it was not beyond the reach even of a poor apostle.[384]

2. It might be served with a prayer at special gatherings of trade associations, fraternal groups, guilds, or civic events. The importance of maintaining business and social contacts in a city such as Corinth cannot be underestimated. One's superiors might pressure their employees to attend such banquets for business.[385] At Corinth especially, sports events such as the Isthmian games would include the worship of the gods and sacred banquets.[386]

---

is likely that 1 Corinthians reflects earlier Jewish usage. See Witherington, *Conflict and community*, 189; also pags. 238-39 of his article, "Not so idle thoughts about *eidolothuton*," *TynBul* 44.2 [1993]: 237-54).

[383] Origen points out that he and Celsus used two different words, *Contra Celsum* 8.21 (also 8.31) – "idol offerings, or, still better, offerings to demons, although, in his ignorance of what true sanctity is, and what sacrifices are well-pleasing to God, he call them 'holy sacrifices.'" Severianus's commentary uses *hierothuta* and *eidōlothuta* interchangeably. See too Witherington, *Conflict and community*, 227.

[384] Fresh research has shown that common people might have eaten more meat than was once thought possible, see Fitzmyer, *First Corinthians*, 334.

[385] This was still an issue three centuries later, see Augustine, *Sermon on Matt 8:8 and 1 Cor 8:10*: "But thou wilt say, I am afraid lest I offend those above me. By all means be afraid of offending them, and so thou wilt not offend God. For thou who art afraid lest I offend those above thee, see whether there be not One above him whom thou art afraid of offending." Tertullian, *On idolatry* 16, had tried to nuance the applications of 1 Cor 10: "Touching the ceremonies, however, of private and social solemnities – as those of the white toga, of espousals, of nuptials, of name-givings – I should think no danger need be guarded against from the breath of the idolatry which is mixed up with them. For the causes are to be considered to which the ceremony is due...Let me be invited, and let not the title of the ceremony be 'assistance at a sacrifice,' and the discharge of my good offices is at the service of my friends. Would that it were 'at their service' indeed, and that we could escape seeing what is unlawful for us to do. But since the evil one has so surrounded the world with idolatry, it will be lawful for us to be present at some ceremonies which see us doing service to a man, not to an idol. Clearly, if invited unto priestly function and sacrifice, I will not go, for that is service peculiar to an idol; but neither will I furnish advice, or expense, or any other good office in a matter of that kind. If it is on account of the sacrifice that I be invited, and stand by, I shall be partaker of idolatry; if any other cause conjoins me to the sacrificer, I shall be merely a spectator of the sacrifice."

[386] Winter, *After Paul left Corinth*, 269-86, has suggested that the issue took on new meaning shortly after Paul left Corinth. The Isthmian games had become highly popular, and therefore sacred banquets were more common; the games were held in AD 55. See also Elizabeth R. Gebhard, "The Isthmian games and the sanctuary of Poseidon in the early empire," in *The Corinthia in the Roman Period*, ed. Timothy E. Gregory, *Journal of Roman Archaeology* Sup Series 8 (Ann Arbor, MI, 1993), pp. 78-94. She notes the discovery of a garbage pit near the site of the games which contains bones from roasted cattle. The games featured special banquets for the Romans living in Corinth, and Winter suggests that the guest list included some Christians from Corinth who were given the special "right" to attend (*exousia*, the word used in 1 Cor 8:9). They would have involved the worship of the emperor as well as rituals supervised by the sports complex's Temple of Poseidon. The male-only banquets would have possibly included drunkenness and visits from local prostitutes. The more-famous Olympic Games were dedicated to Zeus and held in front of his sanctuary.

3. It might be served at a special gathering of family or friends. The amount of religious ritual at such gatherings could vary (10:27-28).[387]

With regard to #2 and #3, the meal could take place in a private home or in a "temple dining hall." The archaeologists have done a great service by uncovering in Corinth a temple of Asclepius, which had three dining halls attached. The rooms held 11 each;[388] other facilities could hold as many as 22.[389] These rooms could be used by the temple for its own functions, as we might use a church hall. But they were also rented out as "catering halls." The seating arrangement was in the Roman style of *triclinium* – three tables in the shape of three sides of a square, around which the diners reclined on their left elbow and ate with their right. Some rooms were partially open to the street, not unlike *cafeterias* in Latin America. This meant that passersby could peek at a private gathering and spot a fellow Christian sitting at one of the tables and eating the food (the basis of 8:10).

4. It would be served to the worshipers in the temple precincts as part of the regular cult (8:10; 10:14-22).

The Corinthians wrote to Paul to ask whether it was acceptable for a Christian to be involved with such food. We do not know if one party or another had an opinion on the matter; Hurd doubts this, and is correct that the church did not split in half over this issue.[390] The letter suggests that some (certainly gentiles) in the church took the liberal line, and that other Christians, perhaps poor and uneducated ones, were offended by the practice.

It is likely that their question had to do with the practices described in #2 and #3 above, that is, gatherings of civic, business or family groups. Either they or Paul broke the issue down into two parts. First, *about the substance itself: is the Christian harmed or does he offend God by eating such meat, whether ignorantly or by choice?* Second, *what about the sacramental significance of eating a pagan sacred meal?*

As always, Paul takes the Corinthians' questions and reorients them according to the priorities of the gospel. While the Corinthians are concerned with liberty, knowledge and independent action, Paul emphasizes love, thoughtfulness, humility, and a concern with the repercussions of one's actions on other people and on God. He also pens one of the most important sections on evangelism in any of his letters. We will save until the end a comparison of 1 Cor 8-10 with Rom 14.

a. The basis for deciding the question 8:1-6

8:1

Now about introduces the next Corinthian question (see comments on *peri de* in 7:1). There is virtual unanimity that Paul is quoting a Corinthian slogan or paraphrasing their

---

[387] See for example Plutarch, *Quaestiones conviviales* 6.10.1 (696e): "Ariston's cook made a hit with the dinner guests not only because of his general skill, but because the cock that he set before the diners, though it had just been slaughtered as a sacrifice to Herakles, was as tender as if it had been a day old." *Septem saptientium convivium* 2 (146de): "Periander had arranged the entertainment, not in the city, but in the dining-hall in the vicinity of Lecaeum, close by the shrine of Aphrodite, in his honor the sacrifice was offered that day." Both quotations from Murphy-O'Connor, *St. Paul's Corinth*, 104.
[388] See Murphy-O'Connor, *St. Paul's Corinth*, 169-75.
[389] So estimates Witherington, *Conflict and community*, 195.
[390] Hurd, *Origin*, 123-25.

mentality: **we all possess knowledge** [*gnōsis*].³⁹¹ Paul concedes that their boast contains some truth; he cannot accept that knowledge by itself outfits the Christian for life: **Knowledge** [*gnōsis*] **puffs up, but love builds up.** "Puffs up" is not healthy growth, but swelling with pride (see also 4:6, 18, 19, 5:2, 13:8); it is antithetical to Christian love.

Yet Paul later undermines their basic assumption: in fact, not all Corinthians have this knowledge about God and the gods (see 8:7, 11); if they did there would be no conflict in the church. The arrogance of some Corinthians has led them to deride the legitimate anxieties of other Christians.

Paul uses the language of "knowledge" (such as *gnōsis*) and also a form of another verb of "knowing" (*oida*) in 8:4. In 1:5, 21, 2:12, 14, 16 Paul speaks of true knowledge, the divinely-revealed gospel. In fact, one of the spiritual gifts is the "word of knowledge" (12:8). There is also a partial knowledge which we experience in this age but which will be eclipsed when Christian returns (13:8-12). This last category suits the sense of 8:1 – the knowledgeable Corinthians possessed truth about the real nature of idols, but they misused that knowledge by not acting in love.³⁹²

The word *gnōsis* is a red flag for some exegetes. W. Schmithals argued that if Corinthians were using the term, then Gnostics must have already arrived in 1st-century Corinth.³⁹³ This is almost certainly mistaken, not least because there is no evidence that Gnosticism existed before the 2nd century AD. Rather, the Corinthians claimed to have a rationalistic knowledge of the cosmos and the nature of pagan gods. We seem to be dealing once more with the elitists of the earlier chapters, people who ran their lives based on their supposed philosophical depth. Another clue abets this identification: the issue of what meat to eat was likely an issue for wealthier Corinthians, not the poorer. After all they could afford meat; they were the ones who got invitations to nice dinners.³⁹⁴ Thus, their knowledge was formed in part by their education, in part by the monotheism of the gospel.³⁹⁵ And as in chapter 2, this knowledge led them to being puffed up. Paul points out the superiority of the way of love here, as he will in 12:31b.³⁹⁶

8:2-3

Paul will correct their manner of reasoning before he says one word about idols (beginning in 8:4):

---

³⁹¹ The commentaries that Hurd analyzes are unanimous about 8:1; the majority also regard 8:4 as the Corinthians' own language. See Hurd, *Origin*, 68.

³⁹² See Chrysostom, *i ad Corinthios* 20.3; Theodoret of Cyrus; Clement of Alexandria, *Stromata* 1.54.4 (all in Bray, 74-75). The church fathers tended to regard the Corinthians' "knowledge" as false data or as mere opinion, but this does not follow from the text: they did have some legitimate knowledge, as Paul shows in 1 Cor 8:6-7. See Hays, *First Corinthians*, 137-39, who correctly observes that Paul agrees substantially with the Corinthians' facts, but not with their application.

³⁹³ Schmithals, *Gnosticism in Corinth*, 143.

³⁹⁴ This is the theory of Theissen, "The strong and the weak in Corinth: a sociological analysis of a theological quarrel," in *The social setting of Pauline Christianity*, 121-43.

³⁹⁵ Contra P. D. Gardner, *The gifts of God and the authentication of a Christian: an exegetical study of 1 Corinthians 8-11* (Lanham, MD: University Press of America, 1994), 25, who argues that they thought their knowledge was a charismatic gift. Also Fee, *First Corinthians*, 366 n. 34.

³⁹⁶ Augustine, *On 1 John* 2.8 compares this verse with the demons of Gadara in Matt 8:29, who knew Christ but wanted nothing to do with him. Augustine says: "If ye have a mind to confess and not love, ye begin to be like the demons. The demons confessed the Son of God, and said, 'What have we to do with Thee?' and were repulsed. [You on the contrary must] confess and embrace."

> **The man who thinks he knows something**
> **does not yet know as he ought to know.**
> **But the man who loves God[397]**
> **is known by God.**

Paul uses the verb form of *gnōsis* (i. e., *ginōskō*) to turn their vocabulary back against them. True Christianity is not found in rational knowledge (which leads to trampling other believers), but in loving God and being known by him. Even the limited truth that Christians possess in this age comes from above, from the all-knowing God, by revelation to one who is **known by God** (see 2:6-16). Paul will deal with the limitations of knowledge in this age in 1 Cor 13:8-12. Chrysostom points out the connection between these two texts: "Now if we possess as yet exact knowledge of nothing, how is it that some have rushed on to such a pitch of frenzy as to say that they know God with all exactness? Whereas, though we had an exact knowledge of all other things, not even so was it possible to possess this knowledge to such an extent."[398]

8:4

With **eating** Paul returns to the specific issue. It is likely that he reiterates two Corinthian phrases. In fact, he observes, the informed Corinthians are quite right: **an idol is nothing at all in the world** and **there is no God but one.** These are basic tenets of the monotheism found in the *Shema* of Deut 6:4 – "Hear O Israel, Yahweh your God, Yahweh is one." Paul may intend to say that false gods do not exist,[399] or that false gods mean nothing for the believer. The second understanding is best, as shown by the phrase "for us" in 8:6. The Corinthians claimed that a Christian may live as though false gods do not exist, because for Christians God's supposed rivals are nothing. Either reading shows that the elitists have been influenced by the philosophical discussion of the existence of gods and goddesses. They rejected the "poetic" theology of Homer and Virgil, with their all-too-human deities. Few educated pagans thought that the actual statue was a god; rather, it pointed to some cosmic truth beyond, or it served as a channel for divinity.

8:5-6

Paul agrees with the educated Corinthians: of course, the physical idol is not a god, it's just an inanimate object.[400] Nevertheless within the boundaries of Paul's monotheism there remains room for spiritual realities which lie behind a statue. The **so-called gods** *do* in fact exist, although they are not deities as the pagans imagined. This is what Chrysostom means when he preaches: "...they have no power; neither are they gods, but

---

[397] Verses 8:2-3 have several textual problems; the most important is the omission of "God" in v. 3, making it "if anyone loves." The NA[28] has good reasons for rejecting the shorter reading, and this is the text from which we will work.

[398] Chrysostom, *i ad Corinthios* 20.3.

[399] Cf. Héring; Thiselton, *First Corinthians*, 630.

[400] As argued so forcefully in Isa 44:9-20; 46:5-7; also Ecclesiasticus 30:19 NRSV – "Of what use to an idol is a sacrifice? For it can neither eat nor smell"; Wisdom of Solomon 13:10-15:17 NRSV – "But miserable, with their hopes set on dead things, are those who give the name 'gods' to the works of human hands, gold and silver fashioned with skill, and likenesses of animals, or a useless stone, the work of an ancient hand", etc.

stones *and demons*."⁴⁰¹ We cannot be sure how far the Corinthians agreed with Paul:

> **For even if there are so-called gods,**
> **whether in heaven or on earth**
> **(as indeed there are many "gods" and many "lords")**

He will go on in 10:20-21 to explain that behind the idols stand demons, the enemies of God who wish to usurp the worship due him. This was the usual Jewish viewpoint of the Second Temple period,⁴⁰² and it was taken up by the church. The **heaven** and **earth** could be a reference to astral and terrestrial deities, or it may be a reference to the gods in the heavens and their earthly representations in the idols on earth. Pagan gods were given the title "lord" [*kurios*], which of course is the term used in the Septuagint and the New Testament to translate the Hebrew *adonai*. See comments on 16:22 with respect to *kurios* in the primitive church.

Verse 6 was possibly taken an older creedal statement, and was certainly something the Corinthians already knew.⁴⁰³ The NIV has:

> **There is but one God, the Father,**
> **from whom all things came and**
> **for whom we live; and**
> **there is but one Lord, Jesus Christ,**
> **through whom all things came and**
> **through whom we live.**

But the NIV is an expansion of a more cryptic original:

> One God, the Father,
> from whom (*ex*) all and
> for whom (*eis*) we;
> One Lord, Jesus Christ,
> through whom (*dia*) all and
> through whom (*dia*) we.

It was typical of early Christian vocabulary to make sweeping theological declarations with a simple preposition such as "from" or "through" (see John 1:3, 10; Rom 11:36; Col 1:15-20; Heb 1:1-2). In the first strophe, God the Father is the source of all creation but also the goal toward which Christians move. The Lord Jesus Christ is the underlying reason for everything, including Christians.

This means that, whatever could be said about the existence of demonic false gods, the Christian lives in a universe created and ruled by the true God and which is moving toward its consummation in the kingdom. The fact that both creation and history belong

---

⁴⁰¹ Chrysostom, *i ad Corinthios* 20.4, emphasis added.
⁴⁰² See Thiselton, *First Corinthians*, 634.
⁴⁰³ Some later scribes added "and one Holy Spirit, in (*en*) whom are all things, and we in him" in order to make this a Trinitarian statement. 1 Cor 8:6 was quoted very frequently by the church fathers in the christological debates and other contexts.

b. Eating sacrificial meat harms other Christians 8:7-13

8:7

Paul turns the Corinthians' slogan back at them: all anyone has to do is look around his own house church to discover that not everyone has this insight; literally, as the HCSB, "not everyone has this knowledge" [*gnōsis*]. The claim that this truth is universally known, that even a fool should know it, in itself is a proud boast and led some to be dismissive of those who hadn't caught on to the facts. Although by definition every genuine Christian confesses the one God and the one Lord Jesus Christ, that datum had not automatically erased the underlying fears of the **weak**. Calvin says that the weak were "not sufficiently instructed."[404] A better explanation is that the weak might have been well-taught and could even have repeated back all the correct answers about God and the gods; nevertheless, their deep assumptions had not yet been transformed and some were still acting according to their old framework.[405] Godet paraphrases the scorn heaped on the weak by the well-informed: "Freedom to eat meats offered to idols follows logically from the monotheistic principle common to all; so much the worse for those who [lack] logic! We are not called to put ourselves about for a brother who reasons badly."[406] Paul pushes them toward being lovingly aware of their brothers.

Although a Jewish convert would be scandalized by meat offered to idols, the typical case in Corinth would be the converts from an unsophisticated form of paganism. It is because they have a personal history in idol worship that the connection with demons lingers in their minds. Before coming to Christ, they thought little about the meaning of the idol statues: they were **accustomed** to think of these statues were gods; but now they "know" that idols are demonically infested. Their conscience is weak, overwhelmed by the myriad ways in which they might offend their new Savior, or of invoking demonic involvement in their lives. Thus, the freedom of those who eat leads to **their conscience is…defiled**, using a verb *molunō* that is often used of moral impurity.[407]

8:8

But food does not bring us near to God; we are no worse if we do not eat, and no better if we do. The NLT is helpful: "we can't win God's approval by what we eat."[408] Some or all of this statement could be a slogan of the philosophically refined Christian in Corinth.[409] Nevertheless, there is nothing here that Paul himself could not have

---

[404] Calvin, *First Corinthians*, 1:279.
[405] So Walter.
[406] Godet, *First Corinthians*, 420-21.
[407] Origen, *On Matthew* 11.12 is useful here: "He then eats in faith who believes that that which is eaten has not been sacrificed in the temples of idols, and that it is not strangled nor blood; but he eats not of faith who is in doubt about any of these things. And the man who knowing that they have been sacrificed to demons nevertheless uses them, becomes a communicant with demons, while at the same time, his imagination is polluted with reference to demons participating in the sacrifice."
[408] The text that the NIV translates "does not bring us near to God" might also possibly be rendered "will not bring us before God's judgment."
[409] Calvin; Thiselton; Barrett; the NRSV puts it in quotation marks.

heartily affirmed. Rom 14:17 reflects the same basic meaning: "the kingdom of God is not a matter of eating and drinking." We cannot take either statement in a reductionist way, that after all food is just food, it affects the body but cannot have any significance for the spirit. Not at all: flaunting your consumption of meat sacrificed to idols has two ramifications: the damage it does to one's brother (1 Cor 8:9-13), and the offense it gives to God (1 Cor 10).

8:9

Paul tells the well-informed Corinthians, **be careful**. They cannot glide through life, enjoying their rights with no regard for others. Rather they are to be "their brothers' keepers." We are not sure what specific attitude these "wise" Corinthians took. Perhaps they were merely careless about what they ate. Or maybe they thought a Christian should visibly dare to eat such meat as a sign of his liberty. In any case, their unconcealed exercise of freedom led to a **stumbling block to the weak**. This is the second time in this epistle that Paul has spoken about a "stumbling block." First, the gospel of the cross is offense to unbelievers who despise the cross (1 Cor 1:23); here in 8:9 it is the creation of an unnecessary risk of damaging a fellow Christian.

As I am writing this, a Christian has just now written me. She is going on a trip to Mexico, and wants to know whether she should climb around the ruins of the Mayan temples. She is concerned with the possibility of a lingering demonic presence. I told her that I did not think any demon would harm her if she explored the ruins, and that if it were I, I would go without hesitation. I also told her that, *of course*, if her conscience troubles her she should avoid them: whatever is not done in faith is sin for her.

8:10

Paul imagines a case that involves an accidental onlooker. It is not the only reason for avoiding meat sacrificed to idols, yet it is a real danger given the layout of pagan banquet rooms. A person of weak conscience **sees you...eating in an idol's temple**. "Idol's temple" is how the English versions translate *eidōleion*; like its cognate *eidōlothuton* it is a pejorative term used by the Septuagint (but not other Jewish authors) and Christians.[410] It might also be understood, not just a temple proper, but more broadly as "a place dedicated to an idol." In fact, the word is similar to other Greek names for halls where banquets are given to worship pagan gods.[411] In Corinth, idols were located in many places, not just in the actual sanctuaries.

And so, a Christian happens to spot another Christian eating meat in such a place. The onlooker's conscience is **emboldened**; the "encouraged" of many other translations is too weak. Paul speaks ironically, employing the popular Christian verb "edify, build up" (*oikodomeō*[412]): *You have edified your brother, all right! You've edified him so well that he goes boldly ahead and ruins his conscience!*[413] If the informed brothers were

---

[410] F. Büchsel, "*eidōleion*," *TDNT* 2:379 states that *eidōleion* is found only in the Bible and in ecclesiastical writers; so too LSJ. MM states "No instance has been found as yet in profane Greek." But in fact, there is an instance of the word in Aesop's fable of "Apollo and the Snake," where *eidōleion* refers to a temple of Apollo.

[411] Moulton and Milligan, *Vocabulary of the Greek New Testament*, 183.

[412] For other, positive, uses of *oikodomeō* see 8:1, 10:23, 14:4, 14:17; also *epoikodomeō*, "build on" in 1 Cor 3:10, 12, 14.

[413] Thiselton, *First Corinthians*, 652. See the useful rendering of the NET Bible – "someone weak" is "'strengthened' to eat food offered to idols."

mounting an educational campaign to drive those silly low-class ideas out of their brothers, their plan worked all too well.

8:11

Paul has kept calm up to this point, but now the dam bursts. For the sake of your knowledge you are willing to destroy a brother **for whom Christ died**.[414] The actions of the "informed" Christians are not trivial, but are an attack on the very cross of Christ. There are many levels of meaning:

- Christ died to redeem the weak: "God chose the foolish things of the world to shame the wise; God chose the weak things of the world to shame the strong" (1 Cor 1:27) – thus in the end these unsophisticated brothers are of greater importance in God's plan than are you "wise" people
- Christ's death on the cross (as in 1 Cor 1-2) unites all of us in humility
- Christ paid an extremely high price for this brother, and you risk overturning his saving work (cf. also Rom 15:1-3)[415]
- What kind of Christian are you, who so blithely puts his fellow in eternal danger, and all for the sake of showing off how much you know?

8:12

What is more, this is not simply an insult done to another human being. It is harm **against your brothers**, and beyond that, **you sin against Christ**. Such boasters show that their wisdom is based on rationalism rather than on the cross of Christ. They sin by hurting one of Christ's own, but also by insulting his cross in favor of their own worldly cleverness.

8:13

It is always a temptation to minimize the effect that one's actions have on others. Paul on the other hand challenges the informed Corinthians to take with all seriousness how their actions cause others to sin. He switches to the first person to show what he would do: **I will never eat meat again**. He is not advocating vegetarianism. Rather, he is speaking in hyperbole: *If this meat or that causes someone's downfall, I won't eat any meat at all if that is what is necessary.* As he says in Rom 15:1, "We who are strong ought to bear with the failings of the weak and not to please ourselves." So-called wise and sophisticated people might sneer at the idea of accommodating those who should know better. What love requires in this case is not subtle argumentation, or witty barbs at the expense of the foolish, or clever rationalizations. Paul wants to see decisive self-sacrificing action in favor of other Christians – in other words, to build them up in love

---

[414] See Hodge, *I Corinthians*, 148-49 – he is forced to label the phrase about "for whom Christ died" as purely hypothetical, so that it does not controvert his doctrine of limited atonement. Calvin himself, *First Corinthians*, 1:284, focused more carefully on Paul's own point: "nothing were more unseemly than this, that while Christ did not hesitate to die, in order that the weak might not perish, we, on the other hand, reckon as nothing the salvation of those who have been redeemed with so great a price." The early fathers used this verse to refute the so-called "adoptionist" christology, which said that the Christ spirit descended on the human Jesus, and that the man Jesus died on the cross. No – it is also legitimate, according to Paul, to say that *Christ* died; see too Rom 5:8, "Christ died for us."

[415] So Chrysostom, *i ad Corinthios* 20.10 (Bray, 78) - "That whereas Christ died for him, you cannot even lift a finger to help him in the slightest."

(8:1). It is what Paul would do, and they should imitate his attitude (11:1).

Application: Controversial practices (adiaphora) and our fellow believers 8:13

Like Paul, we will deal with the issue of controversial practices on two levels: how it affects our fellow believers; how it affects God (see the application at 10:21-22).

Adiaphora among Christians today

The adiaphora ("matters of indifference," the plural form of "adiaphoron") are traditionally defined as issues (1) which are not directly addressed in the Bible; (2) which do not have an implicit solution based on biblical teaching about a similar theme; (3) concerning which sound Christians might have different opinions. This third point is bothersome to some, since it implies that there may be genuine gray issues when it comes to holy living. They instinctively believe that any reasonable Christian should have the same opinion that they do! Like the authors of the Talmud, they feel that God must have given a commandment about every one of life's details. They demand that their church leaders offer a ruling on one behavior after another. But the apostle allows that two Christians might disagree and both be right.

The church's attitude toward questionable practices will change from century to century and from country to country. We suggest a few modern examples, although my choices of what things are adiaphora and which are not are of course also open to debate:

Not adiaphora

Heroin abuse does not belong to the list of adiaphora, since it stands in close parallel to biblical teaching on the abuse of alcohol.

Internet pornography is a form of visual stimulus to sexual desire, banned in Matt 5:28; that is, not among the adiaphora.

Homosexual sex is not one of the adiaphora, it being banned (we have argued) in the Bible.

Adiaphora or legitimately controversial issues

Dancing, whether in church or socially, belongs in this list. Dancing was a part of most ancient cultures. It formed a part of Israel's worship as well as its social life. On the other hand, dancing, even so-called "Davidic Dancing," was not a practice of the primitive church. Christians disagree on its appropriateness of secular or sacred dancing today. In a variety of cultures, Christians debate what sort of music is appropriate for music.

Wine drinking was, despite what some scholars try to argue, a legitimate part of Israelite and Christian culture as defined by the Bible. Jesus did not turn water into grape juice but into the wine with which the Jews were familiar – containing alcohol, albeit with a lower content than modern wines (see commentary on 6:10). It is a true adiaphora, and affirmed as such in Rom 14:21.

When I asked people in my church in Costa Rica, the following were mentioned as adiaphora: observing Christmas traditions, for example, putting up Christmas trees;

playing billiards; playing cards; going to the football stadium; going to bull fights; whether Christians can eat in restaurants that serve liquor; makeup and jewelry, what type and how much; women wearing pants; women wearing nail polish when they receive communion; certain Catholic practices such as viewing religious processions or observing feasts to honor a saint.

My Christian friends in North America often mentioned beer and wine. They also spoke of: Watching movies and other entertainments. Tattoos. Martial arts. Role-playing games. Dating *versus* courting. Homeschooling *versus* public schools. Use of tobacco. What is appropriate behavior on Sundays. Whether Christians should take antidepressants or other psychotropic prescriptions.

In both cultures, a number of "gray areas" have to do particularly with women: their work, hair, clothing, make-up.

The issue in Corinth

In Corinth some "weak" Christians thought it was wrong to eat meat sacrificed to idols. Paul disagreed with their reasons, but he endorsed their right to be free from criticism by other Christians. Their "wise" opponents had a better set of arguments, with which Paul was largely in agreement; yet he rejected their attitudes and their actions, since they were not based on love.

The difference of opinion in Corinth was in part determined by social level and education. In Latin America, as in many regions, Christians are drawn from all sorts of socio-economic levels, a range greater than even that represented in the Corinthian church. We have people who are multilingual and who have an international level of education. On the other hand, there are Christians who have grown up in the jungle, illiterate and isolated and whose view of the cosmos is still colored by animism. If these two extremes had to face the same issue of meat sacrificed to idols, their conclusions would be wildly different; and yet both groups could offer Bible verses to back up their viewpoints.

Paul gives priority to the person who is at greater risk. On the one hand, the "knowledgeable" believers of Corinth are using their wisdom to increase their own reputation. They wanted to be known as the Christians who feared no metal idol, and their freedom was a sign of their high social level. For them to give way put them at risk only of reduced status. For the weak Christian, the risk was far graver: it was their conscience and their relationship with Christ. Paul uses terms like "cause to stumble," "lost," "harm." What wickedness, to be able to look upon the damaged and shrug and say, *Well, if they don't continue on in Christ, I guess they were never genuine to begin with.*

Dealing with adiaphora when they cause a rupture between Christians

In a sense, 1 Cor 8 is hypothetical: they probably knew already that the Jerusalem Council had forbidden meat sacrificed to idols. Therefore in 1 Cor 8 Paul begins by speaking "as if" they were approaching the issue from zero. By contrast, the parallel passage in Rom 14 deals with issues that were more purely adiaphora, unregulated by the Bible or apostolic decree: vegetarianism, abstention from wine and Sabbath observance (see below, Special Theme: 1 Corinthians 8-10 and "the Strong and the Weak" in Romans 14).

What does Paul tell them to do, or better, teach and model?

1. Teach the truth. That is, we should be frank about what we know from God's revelation. Paul did not downplay the fact that "an idol is nothing at all in the world and that there is no God but one" (8:4). The weak Christians needed to hear this. We too must be willing to tell weak Christians: "You're wrong! Yes, because of your conscience we will be careful not to harm you, but you need to understand doctrine better!" Weak ones should not be imagine that just because the church tolerates their scruples that theirs is the best Christian stance.

2. Teach no more than the truth. God has not revealed answers to every question we might have. We must be willing to state "on this issue, God has not spoken."

3. Realize that when we instruct people, our message does not seep down as deeply as we might imagine. Educationalists have shown that people know facts on different levels. We can know things on the level of deep trust, at a level that will affect our actions; or, we might know things at a shallower level of simple acknowledgement. Probably many of the weak Corinthians "knew" that "an idol is nothing at all in the world and that there is no God but one." But just because someone has been told the facts about an issue, he may still not truly know it at a deep level that affects his conscience.

4. Watch out for those at greater risk. The "weak" person is not the one that complains the loudest or threatens to cut off tithes to the church if he does not get his way. Rather, it is the person who is in spiritual danger.

5. Don't let anyone hijack the gospel with their personal agenda. Don't abide it when people shout that God is on their side, even though they cannot prove so by the Scriptures. Their logic is:

Because I am a Christian, I do this.

This is certainly their right, but they might take a logical misstep:

Therefore to be a good Christian, one must do this.

When it comes to the scruple in 1 Cor 8-10, as Fee observes, "Paul does not allow *any* Christian to make food a question of *Christian* concern."[416] That is, he will not allow them to make their own scruple a part of the Christian gospel. This comes even more to the fore in Rom 14:3b, where the weak Christians become judgmental. It is stronger still in Col 2:16, when the scrupulous judge the practices of others. Don't let anyone imply that you do not have the Spirit or know Christ if you are exercising your liberty in a godly way. Don't let anyone imply that your adiaphora are sinful in themselves, just because they are controversial or because in theory others might be harmed by it. By definition, adiaphora are not sinful, if done in faith and love.

6. Love is more important than any personal preference. This is Paul's main point here. Love does not mean being mousy. Rather, Christians with stated viewpoints and practices in the adiaphora decide in kindness and humility to set their practice aside so as not to hurt another.

7. Urge holiness and excellence. This point is lacking in much of the discussion of the adiaphora. There is a statement attributed to Susannah Wesley: "If you would judge

---

[416] Fee, *First Corinthians*, 485, emphasis in the original.

of the lawfulness or the unlawfulness of pleasure, then take this simple rule: Whatever weakens your reason, impairs the tenderness of your conscience, obscures your sense of God, takes off your relish for spiritual whatever increases the authority of the body over the mind, that thing is sin to you, however innocent it may seem in itself." This is excellent, provided we emphasize "that thing is sin *to you*," not "it is sin *per se*."

Perhaps this is a recent trend: more and more I run into Christians who go out of their way to show off their liberty before others. They are eager to inform you that they drink beer or go to R-rated movies. They imply they are spiritually more sophisticated and free than their stricter brethren. They fancy themselves "renegades." When they are criticized, they are inordinately pleased with their martyr status. They urge others to join them. Our formula should instead be: *If you reject a habit, do so joyfully and for a greater end, because you perceive that it will be better for your walk with God! If you accept a practice, do it because you do so joyfully and gratefully in his presence!*

PARENTHESIS – PAUL'S GENERALIZING PARANAESIS (*Engressio*): CHRISTIAN LOVE MEANS THAT WE SET ASIDE OUR OWN LIBERTY IF IT IS FOR THE GOOD OF THE OTHER 9:1-27

In 8:13 Paul has already set himself up as an example: "I will never eat meat again, so that I will not cause [another believer] to fall." He will conclude this section with 11:1 – "Follow my example, as I follow the example of Christ."
He is careful to establish two principles:

One, that Christian rights as such do exist. He does not make the error of refuting the Corinthians' *but we have the right to eat!* with *you have no rights!* Of course they had rights – even as Paul had the special rights of the apostle (to have a wife; to ask support from his churches) which he could exercise at any time should he so choose.

Two, that the Christian's highest aim is love, being thoughtful of others and willing to make personal sacrifices for their well-being. Christian love does not consist in the abolition of individual rights, but in the decision to voluntarily forego (not involuntarily be robbed of) one's rights for the good of others.

Paul's stewardship of his individual rights – like his celibacy, like his "fear and trembling," like his marching in the parade of captured prisoners – is a model for Corinth. In his teaching of them is not simply by letter or words, but by inviting them to live as he himself does.

9:1

Paul moves abruptly from food to apostleship: **Am I not free? Am I not an apostle? Have I not seen Jesus our Lord? Are you not the result of my work in the Lord?** If a Corinthian could loudly claim his rights, Paul more: *If we will speak of rights, let's speak of the rights that I was specially guaranteed by Christ.*

This section is not some fully-developed theory of apostleship. Nor is it necessarily a defense of Paul's calling,[417] although he would need to do so in 2 Corinthians. No, the point is, *Here I am, your apostle, leading the way in foregoing my rights for the sake of people such as you Corinthians.* As a rule the Corinthians, like the Stoics, defended their

---

[417] Contra Fee, *First Corinthians*, who labels this chapter "Paul's Apostolic Defense."

every right as a symbol of their freedom.[418] Naturally, they might expect that an apostle could – yea, must – display every symbol of higher authority. Or else, what good is it to be an apostle? His refusal to take money or to lord over them, commendable humility in the eyes of some, led to him being despised. If he acts humble, the logic ran, he must be hiding his inferiority.

9:2

The NLT has "Even if others think I am not an apostle" (similarly the CEV, GNB), but Paul is not speaking about recognition. The NIV is a better translation, **Even though I may not be an apostle to others** (also KJV, ESV, NRSV), which is the other side of the coin of **Are you not the result of my work in the Lord?** He means, *I am not the apostolic founder of other churches, but I am of yours*. Paul had "laid a foundation" at Corinth (3:10), an historical fact that was not affected by whether his teaching was in fashion at any given moment.[419] Corinth is living proof that Paul is an apostle, the **seal** of his authority and rights (the NLT has "You yourselves are proof that I am the Lord's apostle"; see especially 2 Cor 3:1-3).

9:3

This is my defense to those who sit in judgment on me is the heading for what follows. Most of the rest of chapter 9 is a series of rhetorical questions mixed with Paul's commentary. We do not know who might have been the accuser here, just as it is not clear who judges in 4:3, where he says "I care very little if I am judged by you or by any human court." It may be that there is no specific attacker in mind, and that Paul is merely using a rhetorical device. If the Corinthians had in fact judged Paul, it was probably for what they thought was his inconsistency:[420] eating meat in this place, but not that; acting Jewish on Saturday and Greco-Roman on Monday.

Application: Wanted – an apostle with style 9:3

Paul was being ironic when he said that "you even put up with anyone who enslaves you or exploits you or takes advantage of you or pushes himself forward or slaps you in the face" (2 Cor 11:20). But he was not exaggerating much; according to the Corinthians, a leader who acted harshly was especially anointed by God.

Paul had a precise idea of how to serve God. He worked day and night with his own hands; he risked his life and his health; he "served" the churches and did not exploit them. As a teacher and a writer of epistles, he acted with patience and consideration: when people wanted answers he gave them careful, detailed explanations. He communicated the gospel in a way that anyone could understand (1 Cor 9:20-22).

From what we can glean in 1 and 2 Corinthians, that church wanted a different breed of apostle:

---

[418] Thiselton, *First Corinthians*, 666.
[419] In the centuries to follow, it was a great boast to have an apostle as one's founder. Thus Rome laid claim to both Peter and Paul, giving that city one more reason to claim papal primacy (see Eusebius, *History of the church* 2.25). It is ironic to hear the boasting of later generations of Corinthian Christians, considering the grief that the earlier disciples in that city had given the apostle.
[420] So Hurd, *Origin*, 128.

Commentary 7-15

Church at Corinth, Achaia
Wanted: an apostle with style

The church in Corinth is seeking applicants for the position of apostle. We wish to avoid leaders who do not measure up to the highest standards of Christian ministry. Hence we insist that all candidates fulfill the following conditions:

Professional demeanor
- *We want a man who holds his head high, not one with a slavish attitude of "service." We want to show the appeal of the gospel for people with ambition.*
- *He should own a vehicle; travel by foot is inefficient and gives the impression that one is a loser.*
- *He should have a good family life; a single man gives the impression of instability.*
- *He should dress well; he should know about different types of cuisine; he should know which fork to use.*
- *He should take care to cultivate a good image in the community.*
- *He should be well-spoken. He should not use a simple word when a more exact philosophical term exists.*
- *He should enjoy good health and avoid arrest, prison time and persecution. Suffering is waste of time – days and weeks lost in the hospital, in jail, in fleeing from one city to another – and it gives people the impression that the gospel is not for the successful.*
- *He should be able to defend himself against his detractors. When he is slandered he should be able to mount a decisive verbal counter-attack.*

Ministry priorities
- *He should know his own mind. He should have concise black-and-white answers to difficult questions.*
- *He should put his agenda above individuals and severs relations with those who do not accept his vision. If he speaks sharply, especially to the ignorant masses, he should command their respect and obedience.*
- *He shouldn't be wasting his time with the so-called "Pray without Ceasing" movement.*
- *He should not be trapped by the fundamentalist tradition of "winning the lost." That is, he should focus on satisfying those who are already "won" and who want deeper instruction.*
- *He should get enough rest that he doesn't go around looking sleepless, hungry, or exhausted.*

Contractual details
We are looking for someone who will devote all his time to teaching. We have found it unworkable for an apostle to get sidetracked by secular employment, to the diminishment of the church's reputation and the loss of ministry time. He should not be ashamed to demand a good salary. He should expect to reward those who pay him with strong leadership and an impressive presentation of the Christian message.

Paul crumpled up the announcement and tossed it in the waste basket.

9:4

What rights do Paul and all the apostles possess?
- The right to food and drink
- The right to take a wife on a missionary journey
- Most relevant in this chapter, the right to draw their livelihood from the gospel ministry

The right to **food and drink** is, more broadly, the right to receive financial support by their churches, see below. More specifically Paul includes the right to eat "meat" (8:13).

9:5

Paul is under orders to travel for the gospel but he isn't under orders to do so as a celibate. He might take **a believing wife** on his journeys rather than live simply in the company of his male fellows, sleeping over a leather shop. In fact, others exercise this right with perfect liberty. By his own choice, Paul was an exception, and apparently Barnabas as well.

He refers to the apostles and Barnabas and the brothers of the Lord, which included the same James who ruled on sacrifices to idols in Acts 15:20.[421] Modern critics paint the early church as a disjointed series of communities, out of touch with each other, ignorant of anything but their own local traditions and leaders, uninterested in the Lord's earthly teaching or in his twelve apostles. They ignore the fact that the early church sprung up in one of the most highly-mobile societies to exist up to that point in history. The church was interconnected enough for Corinthians to know who the apostles and the Lord's brothers were; to know which were married; to know who Barnabas was, Paul's partner before the second journey, a man who probably never visited Corinth; to know that Barnabas, like Paul, worked to support himself;[422] to know who Cephas was, and apparently, to have met him; to engage in a running series of letters with their apostle while he was abroad; to have some of their leaders cross the Aegean Sea to make contact with Paul; for Phoebe of the Corinthian port Cenchrea to go to Rome in order to deliver an epistle. For a group spread over millions of square kilometers, the early church kept itself remarkably integrated.

Even **Cephas** has a wife; in fact, the gospels record the healing of Peter's mother-in-law as one of the early miracles of Jesus (Mark 1:30 and parallels). These apostolic wives and any children go nearly unmentioned in the New Testament, although that is not unusual in ancient documents. Of course, the church fathers read this through the lens of their own experience: yes, Peter had a wife, also Philip (he had daughters, Acts 21:9), but after they followed Christ they no longer had sexual relations with them, living together as brother and sister.[423] This might fit with the practice in the 2nd century, but it

---

[421] See the full study by Richard J. Bauckham, *Jude and the relatives of Jesus in the Early Church* (Edinburgh: T. & T. Clark, 2000).

[422] Thiselton, *First Corinthians,* 682-83, offers the tantalizing suggestion that "Paul and Barnabas may have offered a well-known model of missionary-pastors who paid their own way rather than drawing financial support from Antioch or from those to whom they ministered."

[423] Tertullian expresses two interpretations of this verse at two different times: he speaks of female assistants in *On monogamy* 8; of wives in *De exhortatione castitatis* 8. The "spiritual marriage" interpretation of 1 Cor 9 is held by Clement of Alexandria, *Stromata* 3.6, who regards the women as wealthy sponsors of the apostles and ministers to women; nevertheless he affirms that the apostles Peter and Philip had had children earlier; he is cited with approval in Eusebius, *History of the church* 3.30.1 – "Or will they reject even the

utterly contradicts 1 Cor. 7:2-6, where Paul forbids sexless marriage.

It did not take long for exegetes to offer various interpretations of "sister wife" or "sister woman" (as *adelphē gunē* literally means). Some stretched Paul's intention to be a female assistant, something like a nun who served as a member of a missionary team. This hardly fits the Greek; in that case, Paul could simply have said "sister;" "sister woman" would be redundant. Nor does this hypothesis explain what right Paul has sacrificed in not taking a "nun" around with him.[424] The right he and Barnabas suspended was the right to be married. This all goes to show that Paul was not equivocating in chapter 7 when he says that celibacy was a choice, not an obligation. Celibacy and marriage were two real options for him as an apostle. By the same token, he offers no criticism of the other apostles for their free choice.

9:6

The reader expects Paul to say that only he and Barnabas are unmarried, but instead he moves on to another topic: are these the only two who must **work for a living?** This theme will consume most of his attention in this chapter, and it is a topic that Paul brings up repeatedly (especially in 2 Corinthians, Philippians; 1-2 Thessalonians).

There has been a good deal of study on the role of money and patronage in the ancient world, as well as the approach that Paul took toward his apostolic right. There is a fine overview of the issues by Dr. Janet Everts, which we here summarize:[425] The philosophers always had the problem of appearing mercenary, yet would need to find financial support. Some lived by charging fees; some (especially the Cynics) begged; some worked; others sought the patronage of a wealthy admirer. The problem with the last was that often a philosopher had to trim or tone down his message in order to not offend the one who paid the bills. This sort of compromise was what Paul wanted to avoid; he preferred the unquestioned freedom to proclaim the gospel without compromise.

Paul worked with his own hands, to support himself, to avoid the appearance of greed, and also to give his converts an example of quiet industriousness (see 1 Cor 4:12; 9:6; 1 Thess 2:9; 4:11; especially 2 Thess 3:6-15). This approach fit well within Judaism. A rabbi some years after Paul would teach: "Fitting is learning in Torah along with a craft, for the labor put into the two of them makes one forget sin. And all learning of Torah which is not joined with labor is destined to be null and cause sin" (*m. Abot* 2.2). The problem was that manual labor gave a bad impression to the Greeks and Romans: how could a teacher be worth anything when he has to work simply to eat, and manual labor at that? Beyond that, the apostle's refusal to receive patronage could be taken as an insult to the rich, and make Paul seem arrogant or standoffish. Some have theorized that that was a problem especially in Corinth, which later on allowed itself to be "robbed"

---

apostles? For Peter and Philip had children, and Philip gave his daughters in marriage…" Augustine thought that the women in this verse are female assistants (Bray, 80-81). Modern Roman scholars who take the same view include Walter; yet Kuss, *Die Briefe an die Römer, Korinther und Galater*, is uncertain if it is a wife or a "female servant." The Latin Vulgate of 9:5 renders the Greek literally as "sister-wife" (*mulierem sororem*). The Roman Catholic Bible de Jérusalem has the same ambiguity with "une femme chrétienne," (a Christian wife or woman) while its English counterpart the New Jerusalem Bible is more specific – and accurate – with its "a Christian wife."

[424] See Allo, *Corinthiens*, 212-14; today there are few who follow this viewpoint. See the analysis by Thiselton, *First Corinthians*, 680-81.

[425] J. M. Everts, "Financial Support," in *Dictionary of Paul and his letters*, pp. 295-300.

and ruled by smooth false teachers (see especially 2 Cor 11:20-21a). Paul argues here and in greater detail in 2 Corinthians (11:7-12, 12:13-18) that he freely decided not to take his due support from Corinth. If an apostle has the right to support, an apostle also has the right to turn it down.

Paul, as Everts notes, did not always refuse support. The letter to the Philippians was in part a thank-you note for their gift of money and practical help by their representative Epaphroditus, and he remarks that they had helped him from the beginning (Phil 4:15-16). The letter, though warm and courteous, also reflects Paul's reticence about these matters (Phil 4:18). One should also reflect on the hospitality he received while in Philippi, which Paul accepted only after pressure from Lydia (Acts 16:15). The rule seems to be that Paul took nothing from a church while he was in their own city, but expected them to support the mission work after his departure, and also to contribute to his Jerusalem Fund (1 Cor 16:1; 2 Cor 8-9). In fact, it may have been a gift from Philippi that allowed Paul to devote himself more deeply to the work in Corinth, once his team arrived from the north (Acts 18:5; cf. the likely allusion to this in 2 Cor 11:8-9).

"No good deed goes unpunished," and we may pity Paul for how his good intentions led to complications. We hope that this is not the whole picture, and that Paul in fact reaped great evangelistic benefits for his sacrifice. In fact, we must assume that a pragmatist like Paul would not have pursued a self-defeating policy unnecessarily; after all, it was the gospel that mattered more than anything else.

9:7

Paul moves on to give an array of metaphors, the majority of which are agricultural (see also 1 Cor 3:6-9).[426]

> A soldier paying his own expenses
> A planter not sharing in the produce of the vineyard
> A goat herder who doesn't get a share in the milk
> An ox treading out grain, which is muzzled to keep him from eating
> A plower, thresher or reaper on a farm, prohibited by the owner from taking a share
> Temple personnel sharing in the sacrifices

The agricultural images remind the reader of Paul and Apollos as field hands in 3:6-9. The point of the soldier, the farm worker, even the ox, is that there are many instances where a worker deserves a share of the goods that technically another person owns. This is not charity nor is it an example of greed – it is simple justice that a participant in an enterprise deserves a share of the reward.

Who serves as a soldier at his own expense? The Roman empire was maintained partly by its standing army. "Expense" (*opsōnion*) is the technical term for the food and other provisions that a soldier was given.[427] Of course, history provides a few examples of soldiers paying their own way, but that is not Paul's point, namely that it is unreasonable to enlist a man in the army at his own expense.

---

[426] The metaphors from the footrace and from boxing in 9:24-27 are not connected with these illustrations, and are meant to demonstrate another point. He uses the three comparisons, soldier, athlete and farmer in 2 Tim 2:3-6.
[427] So Thiselton, *First Corinthians*, 683-84. The word is applied to soldiers in Luke 3:14. See also 2 Cor 11:8.

The next illustration concerns one who **plants a vineyard**. The hired worker sweats and works, yet the owner pushes him away from the vines when he tries to snack on the growing grapes. The same meaning applies to the hot, thirsty shepherd who **tends a flock**, but is forbidden to take a drink of the goats' milk. Paul's illustrations show the affront of denying a laborer a portion of his own produce to ease his burden.

9:8

How striking that Paul contrasts here – as he did in 1 Cor 2:14-16 – simple justice **from a human point of view** and the divine revelation. That revelation exists not only in the gospel but also in the Old Testament **Law**.

9:9-10

Paul cites as his proof Deut 25:4 – **"Do not muzzle an ox while it is treading out the grain."** A threshing floor was a circular area into which the farm workers threw whole stalks of grain. The ox would walk around a center pole and crush the grain underfoot in order to break the edible grain from the chaff. Paul refers to the practice of binding the ox's jaws so that he could not bend over and eat while he worked. The law applies to animals the idea found in other laws which forbid the Israelites from clutching on to the goods God has given: laws of gleaning, pledges for loans, etc. The lesson is that since God is good to Israel, so you too be open-handed with man and animal.

Paul has not turned Deut 25:4 into an allegory; if it were, "ox" would through some ingenious deciphering be made to really mean "apostle," "treading" something else, and "grain" something else. When Paul says **Is it about oxen that God is concerned? Surely he says this for us, doesn't he?** he is not dismissing the importance of the humane treatment of oxen. Rather his meaning is similar to the Lord's in Matt 6:26 – "Aren't you much more valuable than the birds of the air?" That is, if God makes a point of provide for the ox at the threshing mill, how much more should you watch out for your human apostle working on the church of God.[428] All human workers should labor with the confidence (better than the "hope" of the NIV, see BDAG) of taking a share. Again, this is not charity: they should be able to do so, it is a "right" (9:12)

9:11-12a

An apostle who sows the **spiritual seed** has the right to expect back something in the form of the **material**. This too is not charity, but what is his due; else Paul's argument doesn't work. The same figure underlies Gal 6:6 (cf. also 1 Tim 5:17). Paul argues from the lesser to the greater: other people deserve Corinthian support; how much more does an apostle have this **right**?

9:12b

Finally, the argument which was long in preparation begins to crystallize: *Are all in agreement, then, that I as an apostle have this as a right? Then, my point is that we (Paul and his team)* **do not use this right**. *A Christian may leave some right or another*

---

[428] So Nicoll, *First Corinthians*, 2:848. The NLT captures the meaning by adding "only" – "Was God thinking only about oxen when he said this?" Calvin, *First Corinthians*, 1:294, observes that Paul could have if he wished cited plenty of verses that spoke directly to human beings; thus, why did he cite this verse about oxen unless his aim was to argue *from the lesser to the greater*? See similarly Hodge. Fitzmyer, *First Corinthians*, 361-63 has a full discussion of Paul's hermeneutic here.

uninvoked if it's for a greater good.

And what is the greater good in Paul's case? To put no hindrance before the spread of the gospel. It is this higher good that will consume the rest of this chapter. Far from exercising his due, they **put up with anything** (from *stegō*; as too love "bears all things" in 1 Cor 13:7), that is, burdens which in themselves were not mandatory.

9:13

Paul is not done with his illustrations, but heightens the effect by moving from the farm to the sacred duty of the Temple. **Don't you know that...?** is for additional rhetorical effect, since he refers to a known fact. The Corinthians certainly knew about this practice from their local pagan temples, and this verse could be made to apply to either Jewish or pagan practice. Nevertheless, it seems much more likely that Paul uses the Jerusalem temple to make his point, as in 1 Cor 3:16-17, 6:19 and most especially 10:18; it would be paradoxical if he had used the right to eat meat sacrificed to pagan idols as a positive example at this juncture. Paul is not necessarily describing two classes of people, that is, Levites who **work in the temple** and priests who **serve at the altar**; more likely he is using Hebrew parallelism to describe all sorts of temple workers.[429]

9:14

Paul shows the parallel between Old and New covenants with **in the same manner** and a reference to the teaching of Jesus, as in 1 Cor 7:10 – "To the married I give this command (not I, but the Lord)." Here **the Lord [Jesus] has commanded that those who preach the gospel should receive their living from the gospel.** This is not a direct quotation, but the obvious reference is Luke 10:7: "Stay in that house, eating and drinking whatever they give you, for the worker deserves his wages." In 1 Tim 5:18, Paul cites directly Deut 25:4 and Luke 10:7, calling both "Scripture." There he demonstrates why the Ephesian church should financially support its leaders, the "elders." Paul believes that the Lord's command creates a privilege for the apostle, which that apostle may then put it to one side if he so decides.

9:15

We must qualify the statement **I have not used any of these rights**: Paul did receive gifts from the churches, but he did not ask for them as his due. In fact, he does not bring up the issue in this letter **in the hope that you will do such things for me**. In a typically Pauline tone, he would rather die than take money from them.

9:16-18

When Paul says he has reasons to **boast** (as the NIV rightly translates), we must place it side by side with 1:31, which is literally "Let him who boasts boast in the Lord." Paul is boasting in Christ's gospel, not in his own cleverness or power.

The logic here may be a little difficult to follow:

What do I boast about?
Not that I preach the gospel; I am compelled to do that by divine obligation,[430]

---

[429] See Lev 7:6-10 where, for example, every male in a priest's family may eat the meat of a guilt offering; and the abuse of that right in 1 Sam 2:12-17.

[430] "Obligation" (*anankē*) is the word that refers to sexual impulse in 7:37, in a very different context. Here

so what's the credit for me?

I do have some room for boasting:
When I do my evangelistic duty, I do it free of charge. Not only do I do my duty, but I delight in finding ways to speed it along, even at great personal sacrifice.

It is not entirely clear what he means by **Woe to me if I do not preach the gospel!** The reference is almost certainly the future judgment by Christ. Less probable is the psychological interpretation, that Paul will feel badly if he doesn't obey his commission.

Verse 17 expands the idea of obligation. Unlike the boasting and arrogance of the Corinthian "wise," Paul cannot boast about himself. He didn't find the truth by his own reason or cleverness; he doesn't proclaim it as a favor to the unenlightened, but as an obligation to God; his reward is not fame, but knowing that his voluntary sacrifices allowed the gospel to go forth that much more freely.

Verse 18 is meant to be ironic: his compensation comes in being able to preach without compensation (*misthos*[431]) and **not make use of my rights in preaching it**. If this seemed irrational in the status-conscious world of Corinth, it made perfect sense for a Christian whose present life was shaped by the coming of Christ.

9:19

Paul is **free**, and this freedom means he can choose to turn money down and to work with his hands. At first glance what follows looks like a contradiction to what he said earlier:[432]

Paul to the Corinthians in 7:23:	Do not become slaves of anyone
Paul about himself in 9:19:	I make myself a slave to everyone

What matters is one's motivation: the Corinthians are not free to enslave themselves for some social or monetary gain, in effect selling what does not belong to them, their own bodies. Yet Paul, like all Christians, is free to "enslave" himself to others if that will help the gospel. This is not the submission to a slave owner or to a wealthy patron. Rather, Paul enslaves himself to his audience **to win as many as possible**. Five times he uses the verb "win" (or "gain," *kerdainō*) in the sense of "bring many to Christ" (so the NLT); this is a parallel to "save" (*sōzō*) in 7:16.

9:20-22

What is this bondage to which Paul freely submits? He is speaking very specifically about adapting his person and his habits to his audience: "Paul was not pretending to be what he is not, but showing compassion."[433] He acts on behalf of the gospel, so that more

---

the implied subject is God, who puts Paul under obligation.

[431] *Misthos* is a common Christian word for recompense from God. It may refer to eschatological or present reward or punishment, depending on the context (e. g., Matt 5:12, 46, 6:1, 5, 16; 10:41-42 and parallels; Luke 10:7; John 4:36; Rom 4:4; 1 Cor 3:8, 14; Rev 11:18, 22:12). Rom 6:23 ("the wages of sin is death") uses the synonym *opsōnion*, the same word that appears in 1 Cor 9:7. Here in 9:17, 18, as in Matt 6:1 and others, the time and nature of the reward are left vague.

[432] 7:23 has "don't become slaves" (*me ginesthe douloi*), while 9:19 has "I enslaved myself" (*emauton edoulōsa*); the basic language is the same.

[433] Augustine, *Letter 82 to Jerome* 82.3.27 (Bray, 86).

people will accept Christ from any cross-section of his world; see his broad reach in Col 1:28 – "We proclaim him, admonishing and teaching everyone with all wisdom, so that we may present everyone perfect in Christ." His language is repetitious in order to underscore his goal: to win the lost, the Jews, the gentiles, the weak, everyone, to save all kinds of people by whatever means:

- To the Jews
- To "those under the Law." This is more or less coterminous with "Jews," although strictly this second designation might include gentile proselytes to Judaism[434]
- To those outside the law
- To the weak
- To all people

It is an odd twist of history that the first "accommodation" is to win a Jewish audience. We forget that Paul moved freely about the synagogues of the Diaspora, and dressed and spoke and ate and lived as a visiting rabbi would. There were definitely limits to what Paul considered as acceptable accommodation. At Antioch, for example, he roundly condemned Peter for refusing to eat with gentile Christians (Gal 2:11-14). Peter's compromise with Jewish sensibilities was not principally an aid to evangelism but a denial of the equality of gentiles in Christ (Gal 2:15-21). The truth of the gospel always came first, and then secondly cultural or religious accommodation to help its spread.[435]

The Jerusalem Decree placed a few restrictions on gentile believers because "Moses has been preached in every city from the earliest times and is read in the synagogues on every Sabbath" (Acts 15:21). That is, why should gentiles flaunt their liberty when that will prevent Jews from coming to Christ? For similar reasons, Paul circumcised the Jewish youth Timothy to avoid a gross offense to other Jews (Acts 16:1-3).[436] Likewise he had no hesitation about taking a Jewish vow at Cenchrea just as he was finishing his long sojourn in Corinth (Acts 18:18); nor about participating in a Jewish purification rite on his last trip to Jerusalem, not only sponsoring four others but taking part in it himself (Acts 21:23-26).[437] One of the patently false charges against Paul was that he was commanding Diaspora Jews to apostatize from the Torah (Acts 21:21).[438] Still, **I myself am not under the law**. The Law has become for him a thing of free choice, a liberty

---

[434] Severianus says "those under the Law" are proselytes only, that is not born "Jews"; also Theodore of Mopsuestia.

[435] One must here mention the fine study by Eckhard J. Schnabel, *Paul the missionary: realities, strategies and methods* (Downers Grove, IL: IVP, 2008), 135-37. With regard to this passage he states: "the basic rule of missionary existence requires the missionary to take the listener seriously (1 Cor 9:19). The behavior of the preacher is subordinated to the preaching of the gospel. Paul is prepared to relinquish his Christian freedom if he can win people for faith in Jesus Christ...[But] the normative center of the missionary's accommodating behavior is the gospel, not pragmatic effectiveness."

[436] Conzelmann, *1 Corinthians*, 161 n. 24, rejects the historicity of Acts 16:3 and denies that it would fit the criterion of 1 Cor 9, since Timothy was already a believer. The logic does not follow, since Paul the Christian is having Timothy the Christian accommodate himself to Jewish unbelievers.

[437] Some argue that Paul was in error when he participated in the temple vow. In this reading, the riot and arrest of Paul appear to be his just desserts for sinning, or perhaps God's way of preventing him from going through with the ritual. But Acts gives no hint that Paul was in error, and offers no apology or retraction.

[438] See however, Calvin, *First Corinthians*, 304-05, who thinks that that description of Paul was basically accurate.

that any faithful Jew would have regarded as abominable.

The gentile is **one not having the law**. For the Jews, the world is divided into those with Torah and those without it; Paul uses those traditional categories even while he reinterprets their significance. Depending on its context, "without the law" (*anomos*) may mean to "without the Law" or, more generally, "evildoer" (1 Tim 1:9, 2 Pet 2:8, more than 100 times in the Septuagint). For a Jew both meanings were inherent in the term: those without the Law are immoral. Here Paul uses the neutral sense "without the Law" rather than a comment on gentile behavior: after all, Paul did not act "lawlessly" or "immorally" in order to relate better to gentiles. But, he curbed his cultural Jewishness and accommodated himself to the environment in order to facilitate the gospel.

Paul appreciates the double meaning of "lawless" and so adds **though I am not free from God's law but am under Christ's law** (the adjective *ennomos*, "under the law," appears only here and in Acts 19:39 in a different context). What this refers to this is not immediately clear, and there are various explanations: is the Law of God and Christ the same as the Mosaic Law? Or the moral standards of that Law?[439] Is it the teaching of Jesus? Or the law of love (Lev 19:18, Matt 22:39; Gal 5:14)? Paul says elsewhere that a Christian fulfills the "law of Christ" when he bears the burden of another Christian (Gal 6:2). It may not be a coincidence that in Gal 6 and 1 Cor 9 Paul speaks of taking others into account with humility and love. And Gal 5:14 specifically links Lev 19:18 with serving others – "the entire law is summed up in a single command: 'Love your neighbor as yourself.'" We conclude that the specific idea here is "the law that Christ taught," affirming with Leviticus and Jesus that Christians must love their neighbor as themselves.

Paul provides a strong example of how a Christian Jew might preach the gospel in a gentile world. It helped that, along with his rabbinic training, he was also a son of Tarsus, which was a university town and a center of Greek learning. Plus he had had more than two decades of being the apostle to the gentiles and seems to have taken pains to be a valuable one. As an example of **to the Jews I became a Jew** we note the synagogue sermon in Acts 13:14-41. **I became like one not having the law** finds its expression in his references to Greek religion and his quotation of Aratus (*Phaenomena* 5, see 17:28) in his message to Athens (Acts 17:22-31), not to mention his easy use of Stoic terms in 1 Corinthians. He exhibits fluency in Greek in his preaching and letters, but his choice of Aramaic (or, less likely, Hebrew) in Jerusalem was a tactic to help calm his audience (Acts 22:2). This does not imply any softening of the gospel – he used Aramaic to announce the unwelcome fact that God had told him to evangelize gentiles (Acts 22:21-22); he quoted the philosophers in order to announce the resurrection to skeptical Greeks (Acts 17:31-32). Paul accommodated himself, but he did not omit or downplay the facts of the gospel.[440]

What is more, **to the weak I became weak, to win the weak**. This seems an odd statement, when "Jews" and "gentiles" would seem to cover his two main audiences. In fact he comes finally to the point, which is why a Christian should watch out for **the weak**. In his ministry to gentiles or gentile Christians, Paul was sympathetic to the

---

[439] See C. H. Dodd, "*Ennomos Christou*," in *Studia Paulina*, ed. J. N. Sevenster (Haarlem: Bohn, 1953), 103-08.

[440] Clement of Alexandria quotes 1 Cor 9:20-21 in his *Stromata* 1.1 to justify his heavy interaction with Greek philosophy.

downtrodden and powerless, the fearful and the confused.[441] The Corinthians had only to look at their own history to find the perfect example: Paul was weak for them, for which they should thank God (2:1, 3:1-2).

What is Paul's underlying message?

If I, a privileged apostle, can curb my rights
> for the weak and ignorant and powerless unbeliever
>> in order to win him for Christ...

...then how come you Corinthians, the very beneficiaries of my attitude, cannot adapt your rights
> to the needs of the weak and ignorant and powerless believer
>> in order to preserve him in Christ?

It is typical Pauline hyperbole, and a justifiable one, that he says that he tries to win people **by all means possible**. Love demands an extra effort in evangelism and in the church.

9:23

Paul serves the gospel and wants to **share in its blessings**. He refers to the ministry of evangelism and how he denies himself in order to reap a greater harvest of converts. This verse is the key to unlock what follows in 9:24-27, which uses the metaphor of athletic competition to develop further the reason for his self-denial.

Application: Surrender your rights for the progress of the gospel 9:23

Paul solves the internal friction of the church and then broadens the principal to how to carry out evangelism.

One of the memorable Greek myths had to do with Proteus, a god of the sea. In order to escape capture, he could turn himself into other forms, such as animals or trees or water, and slip out of danger. Was Paul "protean"? Did he change himself to suit his environment, leaving people to wonder who he really was? Not at all. He reminds the Corinthians that he makes himself socially acceptable to his hearers, so long as he does not transgress any of the values of the gospel. He could interact comfortably with Jew or gentile, with people of different classes, with people from the city or from the country. "I beat my body and make it my slave" (1 Cor 9:27), that is, I actively sharpen my skills because it helps me to spread the gospel. Paul was not like those who stick to their own cultural preferences and then blame their audience – or, heaven help us, the Holy Spirit – when they did not respond.

Part of modern missionary training involves this very point. For, years ago, when North American and European missionaries evangelized other continents, they sometimes blurred the lines between the gospel and their culture. They taught the new converts to conduct their services in foreign-looking buildings and to sing imported music. That phase didn't last: one of the visible fruits of Two-Thirds World

---

[441] Thiselton, *First Corinthians*, 705-06.

evangelicalism in the last decades is the acculturation of the gospel.

On the other hand, it is virtually inevitable that when these new converts go forth as missionaries they too will commit the error of cultural imperialism: Latin Christians "know" how a worship service should look and sound. *Why, it should have a salsa rhythm, and be led with a loud sound system, and there must be keyboards and trumpets and bongos!* And if the target audience is put off by their cultural trappings (dress, food, music, social interaction), the missionaries might be tempted to write home and complain about how spiritually dead the natives are.

Missionaries of all cultures will have to learn the same hard lesson, to distinguish the essential from the cultural. In so doing they will be put in the same tension in which Paul lived. The apostle acted very Jewish when he was around Jews, but he laid aside his tradition whenever it suited him. Gentiles who spent time with him would find out that Paul was discomforted by much of Greek culture but tried to "act natural" for a higher purpose. Yet some of his listeners would be stunned by "his apparently chameleon-like stance in matters of social relationships"[442]; perhaps both Jews and gentiles could charge him with being a compromiser. Even the Corinthians doubted him (9:3).

So too, Christians today who have to straddle two cultures for the sake of the gospel will attract criticism from both sides. This will be one of the sacrifices that they will make, not to mention their feeling of cultural dislocation. Our response must be that of Paul: that we are people of the gospel first and foremost, and that our greatest goal is to win people to Christ.

9:24

9:24-27 is often read apart from the previous context (9:3-23) and turned into some generalization about straining to achieve Christian holiness. This is not the case at all: Paul is using the trope of the strict training of Greek athletes as an illustration to further develop his missionary strategy; it is parallel to 10:33b – "I am not seeking my own good but the good of many, so that they may be saved."

Paul seems to have liked sports; or perhaps he *became a sports fan to win sports fans* (see 9:19-22). Greeks and Romans adored sports, while Jews thought that they were too closely tied with idolatry and the shame of public nudity. It is probably no coincidence that Stoics favored sports illustrations.[443] For example, Epictetus wrote about athletic training:

> You must conform to rules, submit to a diet, refrain from dainties; exercise your body, whether you choose it or not, at a stated hour, in heat and cold; you must drink no cold water, nor sometimes even wine. In a word, you must give yourself up to your [sports trainer], as to a physician (*Enchiridion* 29.2).

Do you not know...? fits very well in this epistle, since Roman Corinth had reacquired the ancient right to host the Isthmian Games. These games were second in importance only to the Olympic Games, and like them ran on a regular cycle. A reference to the

---

[442] Fee, *First Corinthians*, 423.
[443] So Thiselton, *First Corinthians*, 713.

games would have been as natural an illustration as a reference to football in a city with a popular team. The ruins of the site of the Isthmian Games have been excavated in the last century and lie about 15 km north of the city.

As Paul hints, the ancient sports were more traditionalist than the modern Olympics, focused on track and field events as well as wrestling, boxing and other combat sports. The ancient pentathlon comprised leaping, foot racing, wrestling, discus throwing, and casting the javelin. The participants were typically men, although boys' and women's events were not uncommon. Winners won a "crown" (*stephanos*, 9:25), more properly translated in the ESV as "wreath: it was not a crown as a king might wear, but a circlet woven out of laurel or another plant. At the Isthmian Games the crown was of pine. The games had been held in 49 and 51, meaning that Paul was probably in Corinth at the time. If he had, it is likely that he made tents to sell to the thousands who had come as spectators. What is more, they might have been held around the time of 1 Corinthians, in the spring of 55.

The apostle refers first to foot racing, a metaphor he uses in Phil 3:12-14, and perhaps in 2 Tim 4:8: **in a race all the runners run, but only one gets the prize**. Although Paul is using himself as the model Christian, he clearly wants all to do as he does: **Run** [you Corinthians] **in such a way as to get the prize.** What it means to be a winner or to gain the crown must be defined in the verses that follow. Paul is not urging certain elite Christians to be "winners"; in Corinth, the elite were known for their "knowledge" and their careless treatment of the weak. Rather, Christians must discipline themselves to be considerate of others.

9:25

A Greek athlete wants to win the prize of **a crown that will not last**, but of course, that perishable wreath represents all the praise of the crowd, the adulation of women, the approval of the imperial elite and financial sponsors.

Like a winning athlete, the Christian should practice rigorous discipline. The apostle's words here must not be lifted out of context, especially **strict training**, and in 9:27, "I beat my body and make it my slave." Paul is not saying that he is an ascetic.[444] He has previously affirmed the goodness of marriage, he is adamant about the importance of sex within marriage, and he has the right to eat and drink what he likes and to take a wife. If he had freely exercised these rights, they would not have been an

---

[444] Nicoll, *First Corinthians*, 2:855, labels this section "Paul's Asceticism," which reflects both a fundamental misunderstanding of this context and a misunderstanding of the meaning of "asceticism." Irenaeus viewed the prize as eternal life, *Against heresies* 4.36.7 – "This able wrestler, therefore, exhorts us to the struggle for immortality, that we may be crowned, and may deem the crown precious, namely, that which is acquired by our struggle, but which does not encircle us of its own accord." Also Chrysostom, *i ad Corinthios* 23.2 – "to me neither preaching nor teaching nor bringing over innumerable persons, is enough for salvation unless I exhibit my own conduct also unblameable…"; also Ambrosiaster. Tertullian uses this section in *Ad martyras* 3 to show Christians how suffering in prison can lead them to the crown of eternal life; so also the emphasis on martyrdom in Cyprian, *On the glory of martyrdom* 28 – "And to return to the praise of martyrdom, there is a word of the blessed Paul;" he then quotes 1 Cor 9:24. Those moderns who think that the text speaks of how Paul disciplines himself in order to receive salvation are Godet, *First Corinthians*, 473, who understands the passage to teach, "so the Christian's self-denial should bear, not only on guilty pleasures, but on every habit, on every enjoyment which, without being vicious, may involve a loss of time or a diminution of moral force." Also Horton, *I & II Corinthians*; Kuss; Marcus Dods, *The First Epistle to the Corinthians*, Expositor's Bible (London: Hodder & Stoughton, 1906), 213; Conzelmann, *1 Corinthians*, 161; Garland, *1 Corinthians*, 443-45.

impediment to his sanctification, and certainly not to salvation.[445]

Rather, he is making the same point that he had been making from 8:1 onward: in order to win a race, an athlete denies himself certain things that in other circumstances he would be perfectly free to enjoy, because he wants to be successful in his exertion. In order to win people to the gospel, Paul freely limits his liberty, not because he has no rights, but because he has a higher goal – to win Jews, gentiles, everyone. It is this wider achievement in evangelism which is the crown **that will last forever**.[446]

9:26

To conclude, he uses the images of a foot race and then of boxing. The race metaphor is not the same as that of Phil 3:12-14, which pictures Paul racing toward the resurrection. Rather, the race in this context has to do with the *goal of successful evangelism*. The boxer too serves to illustrate his point: **I do not fight like a man beating the air**. This phrase is a tricky one in the original, and probably uses sports terminology with which Greek scholars today are not familiar. It may refer to shadow boxing, or it may refer to punches that fail to land on the opponent.[447] Either image suits his point, which is: *Why box, unless I'm planning to hit something? Why carry out a difficult evangelistic mission unless I do it in the way that will bring in the most converts?*

9:27

Paul is still thinking of sports training when he claims **I beat my body and make it my slave**. This is not the life of an ascetic; as Walter points out, he is thinking of the rigors of the apostolic live. These include refraining from certain foods (8:13), working to support himself (9:6), deciding not to take a wife (7:32-35, 9:5) or even the hardships he has faced while traveling or ministering within the cities (2 Cor 11:23-33). These apostolic hardships go even beyond rigorous athletic training: beatings with rods; stonings; shipwrecks.

What is the exact nature of the danger after I have preached to others, I myself will not be disqualified for the prize? Some take his point to be *I preach the gospel to others, but I myself might not receive salvation*.[448] But this is clearly not the context. Paul has taught others to set aside, not sin (Heb 12:1), but personal freedom, "to win as many as possible" (9:19). How foolish it would to urge that value on the Corinthians and not take the trouble to live it himself; as a preacher of the gospel he would be "disqualified" or eliminated.

Paul provides a model for the disciples, and a preview of what will be made clearer in chapter 10: that the issue of eating meat sacrificed to idols is nothing compared with the importance of watching out for one's fellow Christian. And, those who live for other Christians do not simply think in terms of their enclosed group – love for Christians is of a kind with concern for the lost. In this way, one's attitude toward sacrificial meat reveals a great deal about whether one values the evangelizing of the world.

---

[445] As demonstrates Witherington, *First Corinthians*, 715-17.
[446] So Kistemaker, *1 Corinthians*, 312-15; also Baker, *1 Corinthians*, 136-37.
[447] One patristic approach (e. g., Origen, *Contra Celsum* 7.52) was to read this through the lens of Eph 2:2 and interpret it as boxing with the Satanic powers of the air; this hardly fits the context.
[448] Barrett, *First Corinthians*, 218; also Fee, *First Corinthians*, 440, although he sees it as hypothetical.

c. Israel's history shows us the danger of dabbling in idolatry 10:1-14

In 1 Cor 8-9, Paul shows that the "knowledgeable" might sin by harming a fellow Christian. Here he goes deeper: they might sin by contaminating themselves with idolatry. Unlike Judaism, "the emphasis in Paul's paraenesis, however, is not upon the maintenance of boundaries, but upon the solidarity of the Christian community: the responsibility of members for one another, especially of the strong for the weak, and the undiluted loyalty of all to the one God and one Lord."[449]

Why does Paul now speak of how all Israel lived under the cloud, passed through the sea, ate spiritual food and drank a spiritual drink? One interpretation is that the Corinthians had developed a sacramental theology that went well beyond Paul's earlier teaching.[450] In that case, the Corinthians would have been saying:

If you have been baptized into Christ,
    and share at his Supper,
then you are free from demons
    and free from falling into apostasy:
Therefore: you may eat meat sacrificed to idols without fear.

This case is weak for several reasons. One is that Paul never addresses their theology of the sacraments as such, not even when he is teaching about the Lord's Supper in chapter 11. Second, we have suggested that it was the "wise" elite of Corinth that are likely candidates for being the careless Christians of ch. 8-10. Their philosophical depth has led them to a freedom to eat sacrificial food. By contrast, the weak lack such intellectual sophistication. They see demons around every corner. They see sacrificial meat as tainted with hellish power, a view that Paul will later correct with an appeal to creation (10:26). It is unlikely that "wise" Christians would develop a magical view of the sacraments as amulets against evil. We suggest rather that those Christians would see themselves as too sophisticated to connect idol banquets with scary demons.

Paul does not correct any doctrinal aberration, but shows how God provides from the church just as he did for ancient Israel:

Whatever you have, you received from the God (see 4:7),
    but with all that we must constantly guard against idolatry.
        Israel too received many gifts from God (the crossing of the Red Sea, miraculous
            food, the cloud of glory to lead them)
    yet for all vast numbers of them perished because of idolatry.[451]

The divine gifts that Paul lists are "Christianized" by adding the word "baptized into." Israel was blessed, guided, and "baptized" as it were. They had the same food in common, yet most perished (see also Heb 3:7-18; Jude 5).

---

[449] See p. 75, Wayne A. Meeks, "'And rose up to play': midrash and paraenesis in 1 Corinthians 10:1-22," *JSNT* 16 (1982), 64-78.

[450] See James D. G. Dunn, *Baptism in the Holy Spirit* (London: SCM, 1970), 124-27, and others. This might then be connected with the "baptism for the dead" in the highly difficult 15:29.

[451] So Witherington, *Conflict and community*, 219.

10:1

For I do not want you to be ignorant of the fact is a rhetorical formula which means, "now I would like to share some relevant information or insight." The new datum is hardly the fact of the Exodus, or the water from a rock or crossing the Red Sea. Even the gentile Christians of Corinth had ample time to have learned these key facts from the Scriptures, and Paul glides through the history as if it is familiar. Israel's general moral failure (1 Cor 10:5-10) would also be well known. No, his point is stretched across several verses: *I want you to be aware of the alarming contemporary relevance of this fact, that, even though the Israelites all experienced such blessings, "God was not pleased with most of them" (10:5a).* There is a strong contrast between "all" who escaped Egypt and "most of them" whose "bodies were scattered over the desert."

The ancient people of God **were all under the cloud** and **they all passed through the sea.** The pillar of cloud first appears in Exod 13:21. The text does not speak of two pillars, one of cloud and one of fire, but rather one shining cloud of the Shekinah glory that shone more brightly when it was dark. The cloud stood between Israel and the Egyptian army (Exod 14:19-20) as the Israelites prepared to cross the Red Sea. The parting of the Red Sea, with the escape of Israel and the destruction of the Egyptians, is detailed in Exod 14:21-31. The Song of Moses in Exod 15:1-21 shows the deeper purpose of that miraculous parting: to elevate Jehovah above all gods (15:11) and to show the uniqueness of his sanctuary (15:17); both of these points will become relevant in 1 Cor 10.

Paul refers to Israel as **our forefathers**, a phrase that would have sounded natural in a synagogue. Nevertheless, he wants gentile Christians to know that those faraway Jews of long ago are their spiritual ancestors too, and the children will tend to be like the fathers. This is the sort of argument that Jesus used in Matt 23:29-36.

10:2

We should not take **were all baptized** beyond Paul's intended meaning. The crossing of the Red Sea was not some sacrament of baptism. However, passing through the Sea and following God's visible presence were the initial elements which defined Israel's identity. They were events of initiation that showed God's salvation for them specifically. The NIV paraphrases the original with its **baptized into Moses**, by analogy with "baptized into Christ Jesus" (see Rom 6:3, Gal 3:27). The key lesson from baptism in 1 Corinthians is unity: all Christians were baptized into the one Spirit (12:13), thus all should watch out for one another's welfare.

10:3-4a

The reference to **spiritual food** and **spiritual drink** is most naturally from what immediately follows in Exodus: the giving of manna (Exod 16) and of water from the rock (Exod 17:1-7). The use of "spiritual" here should not be weakened, but invested with its typical Pauline meaning of "having to do with the Holy Spirit"; in this case it means "food provided by the Spirit."[452] Fee (with many others) is insistent that these

---

[452] See especially Hodge. Some suggest that this may have been language already used in Communion. *Didache* preserves what is probably the oldest extant liturgy for the Lord's Supper. In alludes to 1 Cor. 10:3 in its prayer of Thanksgiving after communion: "You, almighty Master, created all things for your name's sake, and gave food and drink to men to enjoy, that they might give you thanks; but to us you have graciously given spiritual food and drink, and eternal life through your servant." The referent for "spiritual drink" is

refer to the Lord's Supper, since that is the frame of reference for rejecting idols' tables in 10:14ss.[453] But it is better to take Paul's lesson as the identity of Israel as God's chosen people, not to provide a one-to-one correspondence with each Christian rite. For example, the Spirit-water here is not the wine of the Lord's Supper but rather the Holy Spirit that Christians have all been given to drink (1 Cor 12:13b).[454]

10:4b

The modern reader might be surprised by **the spiritual rock...that accompanied them**, and then that **that rock was Christ**.[455] What are we to make of the first phrase? Some Jews reasoned that, if Moses struck a rock in Rephidim and water miraculously poured from it (Exod 17), then what did Israel drink after they had moved on? According to some rabbis, that same rock went with them. It was shaped like a beehive and could roll; when they stopped to camp, it rolled to a stop in the courtyard of the Tent of Meeting. When they were ready to move again, the Israelites cried out to it "Rise up, O well!" (Num 21:17-18, which in context actually refers to a well sunk in Beer). In that case, Paul is saying something like: *The rock from which water sprung followed them around, and that Rock was the very presence of Christ.*

The difficulty with this exegesis is its anachronism: the "rolling stone" tradition is not clearly attested as early as Paul.[456] The suggestion of Fee is much more to the point: Moses himself had already identified Jehovah as the Rock of Israel a number of times in Deut 32, for example, "I will proclaim the name of the Lord. Oh, praise the greatness of our God! He is the Rock, his works are perfect, and all his ways are just" (Deut 32:3-4). In fact, he also contrasts the Rock with the false gods of the pagan nations: "For their rock is not like our Rock, as even our enemies concede...[Yahweh] will say: 'Now where are their gods, the rock they took refuge in...?'" (Deut 32:31, 37). This is the very point that Paul wishes to underscore in 1 Cor 8:5. The new element in 1 Cor 10 is that Paul christologizes the references to the Rock.[457] Thus his meaning is: *They drank water from a Rock, provided by the Spirit; but the Rock truly is Jehovah, who was with them in the wilderness; and that same Rock is our Lord Jesus Christ.*

Paul not only finds the roots of the Corinthian church in the Israelites; he also finds Jesus Christ and the Holy Spirit in the ancient acts of God. We cannot (as the 2nd-century Marcion would do) divorce the church from ancient Israel, nor Christ from Jehovah. Christ was with Israel, as he is with us. The Holy Spirit provided them food and water just as he now nourishes the church. And if a people with that divine presence apostatized, how grave a warning does that give the Corinthians?

---

not made clear, although one would assume it is the wine. But this does not make "wine" Paul's referent in 1 Corinthians. Chrysostom (23.4) and many other Fathers take these as prefiguring the two sacraments.
[453] Fee, *First Corinthians*, 446-47.
[454] Contra Calvin, *First Corinthians*, 1:312-21.
[455] See the detailed discussion in Thiselton, *First Corinthians*, 727-30.
[456] Fitzmyer, *First Corinthians*, 383.
[457] That Christ is Jehovah is made evident from the way Paul quotes the Old Testament and consistently applies Jehovah-passages to Jesus. See especially how "Jehovah" becomes the Lord Jesus Christ in Rom 10:9-10, 13; Rom 11:26-27. So Fee, *Pauline christology*, 577-78; Fee, *First Corinthians*, 447-49; Fitzmyer, *First Corinthians*, 72-73.

10:5

Now comes the crisis: **Nevertheless, God was not pleased with most of them**.[458] The evidence comes not only from the text of the Pentateuch, but also from the vivid imagery that **their bodies were scattered over the desert** (see also Heb 3:17 – "Was it not with those who sinned, whose bodies fell in the desert?").

10:6

If the reference to "our forefathers" was not clear enough, Paul makes his point explicit that **these things occurred as examples** (see also 10:10-13). As always, earlier events in history serve to warn and encourage those of later times, in this case **to keep us from setting our hearts on evil things as they did.** Paul also uses the cognate verb *epithumeō*; the cognate noun *epithumētēs* is found only here in the New Testament, but appears in the Septuagint in Num 11:34 for those who had craved meat in the incident of the quails. That is the incident that Paul had in mind: *You who want idolatrous meat are like those who whined for flesh in the desert and were killed in the plague*. This is strong language: the Corinthians are not as clever and sophisticated as they would like to believe.

10:7

Israel's rejection by Jehovah was no mere whim, but the result of an unbroken chain of disobedience. Paul mentions some of their more egregious actions in 10:6-10, sins with the Old Testament account also emphasizes. He briefly alludes to texts whose details the Corinthians seem to have known:

7 – Golden Calf at Sinai: Idolatry, including sitting down to eat and rising up to "play" (that is, commit fornication)
8 – Apostasy in Moab: Eating sacrificial meat, bowing to idols, fornication
9 – Putting the Lord to the test by complaining against him
10 – Bitter complaining against God and Moses

In 10:7 Paul quotes the key verse Exod 32:6 – "So the next day the people rose early and sacrificed burnt offerings and presented fellowship offerings. Afterward they sat down to eat and drink and got up to indulge in revelry." This took place while Moses and Joshua were on Sinai to receive the Law, and the noise of reveling is what Joshua mistook for a sneak attack in 32:17. Paul is in agreement with traditional Jewish theology, which connected idolatry together with meat sacrificed to idols and orgiastic parties.

10:8

When he says **we should not commit sexual immorality**, Paul underscores how ancient Israel fell into the same sin that Corinth did. Specifically he refers to the great apostasy in Moab, instigated by Balaam (Num 25:1-3). Once again, the triad of idol-food-fornication comes to the fore. As the penalty of their apostasy, **in one day twenty-three thousand of them died**. There is a well-known discrepancy between Paul's number of

---

[458] Paul uses the verb form *eudokeō* in 10:5. A parallel is found in Luke 2:14, with its pronouncement of peace "to men on whom his favor rests (*en anthrōpois eudokias*)."

23 thousand against the number of 24 thousand in Num 25:9; the major commentaries offer a number of explanations. The exact number is not of consequence here in 1 Corinthians: what matters is the horrific loss of life that came about due to meat sacrificed to idols.

10:9

The apostle continues, **We should not test the Lord** [or the better reading, "Christ," as many other versions].[459] The Israelites put God to the test ten times according to Num 14:22; nevertheless it is the test in Num 21 that is the specific reference here, an incident that happened near the end of the 40 years and not long before the apostasy in Moab. Their sin consisted in complaining against the Lord, and especially the perceived lack of food and water. The penalty was the plague of poisonous snakes, which the Lord stopped through the medium of the bronze serpent. This type of sin is commented upon in Psalm 78:18-20 –

> They willfully put God to the test by demanding the food they craved.
> They spoke against God, saying, "Can God spread a table in the desert?
> When he struck the rock, water gushed out, and streams flowed abundantly.
>   But can he also give us food?
>   Can he supply meat for his people?"

At the core of testing God is a lack of trust. It is a willful, faithless demand that God show his power to suit our own desires. It is an evil imitation of the prayer of faith. Were the Corinthians putting the Lord to the test by their actions? In a sense they were daring God to strike them down but believing that he would not. Eating in idolatrous dining halls may have been the Corinthian equivalent to the devil's invitation that Christ throw himself from the pinnacle of the temple (see Matt 4:5-7; Luke 4:9-12). Their response should have been that of Jesus, who quoted Deut 6:16, "Do not test the LORD your God."

10:10

And do not grumble: Paul uses the biblical term for murmur (*gonguzō*) which, with its cognates, is used 17 times in the Exodus narrative. It also appears in the New Testament to describe this habitual Israelite sin.[460]

Murmuring against God is bitter complaining that arises from unbelief, disobedience, ingratitude and forgetfulness about God's past blessings. In the Exodus, it usually occurred when the people lacked water or food (or more desirable food). Often they were nostalgic for their former life in Egypt and exaggerated the hardships of the desert. In the key passage Num 13-14 the people complain (*gonguzō*, *diagonguzō*) because the ten spies had reported on the giants in the land. They complained directly against Jehovah, but typically against Jehovah's leaders as well (e. g., Exod 15:24, 16:2, 17:3; Num 14:2). The Corinthians certainly complained about Paul their apostle, but

---

[459] Several early manuscripts and fathers have *kurion* (the Lord), but the critical text finally settles on "Christ" as the original reading. Fee, *First Corinthians*, 457, regards "Christ" as "almost certain." The church fathers used this passage to refute the Gnostic idea that the God of the Old Testament was not the Christian God. See Irenaeus, *Against heresies* 4.26.3-4.

[460] See Luke 5:20; John 6:43; see cognates in Jude 16 and Phil 2:14.

Paul sees their rebellion as directed against God. They even grew dissatisfied because they had not received the better spiritual gifts.

10:11

All these things were "*tupikōs*," that is, are a type.[461] The whole Exodus narrative yields **examples**, and specifically **warnings** for the Christians in Corinth. Of course, God's people in the Old Covenant were also to heed the examples of previous generations. For example, Psalm 95:7b-11 is an exposition of the incident at Meribah in Num 11 where the people desired meat to eat. When the psalmist or Paul looked to the past for examples, they did not seek detailed allegorical meanings behind each feature of the stories, as did Theodore of Mopsuestia: "The sea is a figure of baptism with water; the cloud of the grace of baptism in the Spirit."[462] Rather, God's people may find in the pages of Scripture patterns of human behavior and acts of God which may guide them in all ages.

In addition, in the case of the Christian church there is a heightened sense of urgency, since on them **the fulfillment of the ages has come**. This does not mean that Christians are an end-time sect like the Qumran community. At Qumran near the Dead Sea they taught that, because it is the end of this age, and because the Essenes are the elect remnant of God's people, therefore the Old Testament speaks specifically about their commune. Their founder, the Teacher of Righteousness, had given them the key to properly interpret the Scriptures. In Qumran, for example, the key verse from Hab 2:4 ("the just shall live by faith") was taken as a prediction of the Teacher's hermeneutical method.[463]

In his hermeneutic, Paul does not assume that the world is ending and that the Christians are to flee to the desert to await the final judgment. Rather, God has finally in this age revealed his mystery, through Christ and the Spirit: "a wisdom that has been hidden and that God destined for our glory before time began...God has revealed it to us by his Spirit" (see 1 Cor. 2:6-10). This wisdom is not available through human reasoning, nor through a mysterious exegesis of the Scriptures; it was revealed by God in the cross.

10:12

The Scriptures prove it over and again: not only that God's people may **fall**; not only that the self-confident fall; but that the self-confident are the most likely to fall. Hasn't Paul already proven from Scripture that God makes a special point of tripping up the "wise" (1:19-20, quoting Isa 29:14; also 1:26-29)? Corinth had more than its fair share of people who believe they were **standing firm**. This is not confidence in the magical efficacy of the sacraments. Rather, it is the cocksureness that comes from "we all possess knowledge" (8:1b). And the church must understand that, "wise" and "rich" as some of its members may be, it still cannot disregard its Scriptural heritage and act carelessly.

10:13

This well-loved verse is often taken out of context. First, one must look to the Old

---

[461] The adverb "typically" (*tupikōs*) or "serve as an example" is found only here in the New Testament, and may be used in this general sense. It is related to the noun form for "types" (*tupoi*) in 10:6.
[462] Bray, 91.
[463] 1QPesher Habakkuk (1QpHab) col. viii.1-3 (edición Martínez, p. 251): "Its interpretation [Hab 2:4] concerns all observing the Law in the House of Judah, whom God will free from the House of judgment on account of their toil and of their loyalty to the Teacher of Righteousness."

Testament background of **No temptation has seized you except what is common to man.** In the Scriptures, God's people are seen facing all kinds of temptation to power, sex, idolatry, cruelty, pride and any other imaginable sin. The latter phrase means that any and all temptation is "of human, not superhuman, measure."[464] The city of Corinth has not invented any innovative temptation; according to the history told by God's Word, it does not exceed what Israel experienced in the wilderness. Neither are the Corinthians tempted beyond what their fellow Christians experience in Athens or in Ephesus.

Second, one must correctly interpret what Paul says about the level of temptation. The path to victory does exist, but it belongs only to those who seek it. God himself, who is **faithful**, will see to it that they will not **be tempted beyond what you can bear**. Within this word of comfort there lies a warning: if a Corinthian succumbs to temptation, it is his or her own fault, not the fault of God or of the circumstances which he has allowed. This truth applies especially to a Christian who pridefully seats himself at an idolatrous banquet and laughs at those who are offended. These arrogant people are walking outside the safe pasture, testing God to see whether he will keep them safe. "Disporting themselves at idolatrous feasts is akin to deliberately drinking poison and then praying for miraculous healing!"[465]

Third, one must understand what Paul is saying about escape: **he will also provide a way out so that you can stand up under it**. Once again, Paul refers to temptation which arrives without being sought. "The *way out* is for those who seek it, not for those who (like the Corinthians) are, where idolatry is concerned, looking for the way in."[466]

Application: Bible study as a cure to Terminal Uniqueness 10:13

If the Corinthians read the Bible and remember that it deals with fellow human beings and with the same God, then they could take seriously the examples of past failures and avoid foolish temptations. Obviously some Corinthians were not making this connection between the Bible and their everyday actions. Why?

Did they not know the Bible? Paul takes his readers to the books of Exodus and Numbers. He alludes freely to the stories as if they already knew their basic content. How many people in your congregation would be able to identify the quotation from Exod 32 in 1 Cor 10:7? Bible knowledge is crucial, but it does not cure all problems.

Did they imagine that God had changed? That is, was God less concerned with idolatry than he had been long ago? Some later Gnostics would argue that the God of the Old Testament was different from the Christian God, but we see nothing of that philosophy in Corinth.

Did they think that human nature had changed? In Christ we are new creatures (2 Cor 5:17). Does that mean that Christians have been altered so much in their basic nature that apostasy is no longer a factor? Again, if the Corinthians were Gnostics, this

---

[464] See J. Jeremias, "*anthropinos*," *TDNT* 1:366-67.
[465] Garland, *1 Corinthians*, 469. Calvin, *First Corinthians*, 1:331 – "Let others take their own way of interpreting this. For my part, I am of opinion that it was intended for their consolation, lest on hearing of such appalling instances of the wrath of God, as he had previously related, they should feel discouraged, being overpowered with alarm."
[466] Barrett, *First Corinthians*, 229.

might have been at issue, but there is no evidence for it.

Did they think that certain mature Christians were beyond this temptation? The best explanation is that the elitists of Corinth assumed that idolatry was a temptation only for the misinformed. They thought that the ignorant masses were afraid of the devils which lived in the idols, believing in powers which didn't exist. On the other hand, the well-informed would be sophisticated enough to discern temptations long before they blossomed into sin. They could live in the gray ethical area but be too clever to stray into actual sin.

Therefore, Paul's word in 10:13 was both warning and promise. First, the elitists experienced temptations like all human beings before them. Second, rather than boast of their strength, they should avoid temptation or quickly head toward the escape route which God has surely provided.

Early on in this commentary we talked about the sin of Terminal Uniqueness (see Application on 1 Cor 1:2). Here Paul gives one more remedy for this faulty way of thinking. One must read the Scriptures as real examples of believers struggling to serve God. We will then realize that our situations are not unique; that we are not the first believers to face temptations with idolatry, false religion, compromises and sex; that Christians, like the Israelites, need to face temptation with humility and trust in God, not arrogance in our own steadfastness.

10:14

The conclusion is introduced by **Therefore**; the Greek word (*dioper*) is used in the NT only here and in 8:13, both times in order to introduce a practical application. Here is the way of escape for a Corinthian tempted by idolatry: **flee from idolatry**. The same verb *pheugō* appears in a similar verse: "flee from sexual immorality" (1 Cor 6:18).[467] The solution is not to know the right facts or to rationalize the rightness of one's behavior nor to sit and mentally resist the temptation – it is to physically remove oneself from the place of idolatry. Run, don't walk, out of that idolatrous restaurant! How undignified, how childish this must have seemed to the Corinthian elite. Like foolish sheep they are told to use their feet instead of their powers of reasoning.

The Corinthian situation was a strange one, containing two elements not covered in the Jerusalem Decree. First, the apostles had forbidden eating meat sacrificed to idols, on the natural supposition that it was always an act of worship. Thus they ruled it out entirely, without writing down their reasons, as Paul does at great length. The Corinthians on the other hand, did not think of themselves as idolatrous, because the statues were not really gods. They "knew" that the idols were illusions; they "knew" when and where they were free to transgress the rules which were set up for other people. Therefore the assumed that their partaking exalted the power of the Christ, or of the rule of rational thinking; it was not a compromise with demons, as the superstitious rabble feared. And so, if their situation was not what the Jerusalem Council had in mind, did the rule then apply to them? And what of meat sold on the market that is suspected or known to have been sacrificed to an idol? Is such meat forbidden by the decree? Paul has shown in 10:1-14 that there are hidden dangers for these proud Corinthians which

---

[467] See also Paul's use of "flee" (*pheugō*) in 1 Tim 6:11, 2 Tim 2:22. The verb may mean to flee for safety (Matt 2:13) but also to flee from temptation. Conzelmann, *1 Corinthians*, 170, prefers "shun idolatry," which fails to capture Paul's urgency.

he will explain in 10:15-22.

d. Eating sacrificial meat is a sign of divided allegiance and thus offends God 10:15-22

If a Christian is participating in a sacred meal, Paul finally will show, then in fact the Jerusalem Decree had already outlawed what some "knowledgeable" Corinthians were doing. In 10:1-14, Paul is in accordance with the Decree, arguing first from biblical history that such meals are the gateway to idolatry. He develops a second ramification of their behavior in 10:15-22: from the divine standpoint, even if there is no further moral slippage, it creates an offense against God. This is because an idolatrous meal cannot be reduced simply to a person eating a plate of food. It has social and religious implications: social, in that it can harm another person through its symbolism; religious, in that it offends God because it is a sacrament of evil.[468]

10:15

Paul is at his most ironic here. His specific targets are the supposed **sensible people**, who want to judge what Paul says and evaluate it by their own supposedly deep knowledge. Paul helps the modern interpreter, signaling that he is speaking to the elitists of Corinth. This verse could point forward or backward. We understand it to point forward: you who love to "judge" others, **judge** if what follows is true.

10:16

Eating meat sacrificed to idols has sacramental implications – it symbolizes that the partaker worships the god and has joined in **participation** or "communion" with its pagan devotees.

For all their boasting about their knowledge, the Corinthians had committed a fundamental logical error, which is known as "reductionism." An example of reductionism is the claim that a human being is "simply" worth a few dollars of chemicals, implying that the value of the parts is equivalent to the value of the whole. Again, one could claim that atomic fission is "just" the rapid disintegration of a uranium atom; yet try telling that to a survivor of Hiroshima! The Corinthians wanted to reduce a sacramental meal to its simplest component: it is "merely" a person eating perfectly good meat. But there is so much more to it than that, says Paul. Just because it is symbolic does not make it any less real. Nor is baptism "merely" a bath.

And so Paul compares the idolatrous meals with the sacrament of the Lord's Supper.[469] He assumes a knowledge of the tradition that he will cite in 11:24-25: "This is my body, which is for you...This cup is in the new covenant in my blood..." It may be that **cup of thanksgiving** (or "of blessing") was liturgical language.[470] The reference

---

[468] Walter implies that it is impossible to understand this section apart from the Roman doctrine of transubstantiation. Conversely, a number of Protestants argue that it is impossible to make any sense of the passage with that viewpoint.

[469] Let not the reader by confused by the term "sacrament," which arises from this author's Reformed theology. For purposes of this commentary, the reader may substitute the term "ordinance" without any change in meaning.

[470] The tradition of giving thanks (*eucharisteō*) for the bread and the cup (11:24; see *Didache* 10.1 – "give

to the breaking of bread too has its origins in "he broke it" (11:24).

The key word here is **participation** (or "communion," KJV; or "sharing in," NET Bible) which renders the Greek *koinōnia*.[471] The whole Christian life may be called a participation in or communion with Christ. Paul has already taught that God "has called [the Corinthians] into fellowship with his Son Jesus Christ our Lord" (1:9). Paul does not define here what sort of fellowship this is, not in what way the Christian partakes in the body and blood of Christ. He describes this *koinōnia* mainly to show why its evil twin, fellowship with idols, is an abomination.

10:17

Paul's reference to being **one body** is not parenthetical, but underlies his point that Christians must take care one of one another (8:9-13, 10:24, 32). In partaking of **one loaf**, the church too has become one loaf. So much for the reductionism of the Corinthian "wise"! The church is not simply a collection of individual grains; rather, the grains have been ground and baked together to form a loaf, in which the individual grains are incorporated to serve the whole. It is not unusual for Paul to alternate between the "body of Christ" (the typical Greek word *sōma*) shown in the bread of the Lord's Supper (11:24, 27) and the body of Christ (again, *sōma*) which *is* the church (most notably 1 Cor 11:29; throughout 1 Cor 12; Rom 12:4-5; Colossians and Ephesians *in loc.*). Here as in 1 Cor 12 Paul is affirming that the true unity of the church is real, despite the individualism of Corinth and even its occasional disunity.

10:18

Again he invokes Israel's history, but this time (as in 9:13) its temple *cultus*. The translation of the NIV as **the people of Israel** is a bit weak, the original being "Israel afer the flesh" (KJV) or better "the natural people of Israel" (NJB). Although he may speak of gentiles as spiritual descendants of "our forefathers" in 10:1 he means historical Israel, not the church. The Second Temple would still stand in Jerusalem for another 15 years, and sacrifices happened during every daylight hour. He asks rhetorically, **Do not those who eat the sacrifices participate in the altar?** These participants are not priests and Levites, as they were in 1 Cor 9:13. Rather they are those who have brought the animal to the Temple for sacrifice, and then later eaten some of its roasted meat. This took place most notably in the Passover ritual. The answer he seeks is that of course, eating meat that had been offered to Jehovah is much more than a normal meal; it cannot be reduced to a person eating some meat, but it proclaims one's allegiance to Jehovah. The **altar** (the same word used in 9:13) refers to the main altar for burnt offerings that stood in the courtyard of the tabernacle and later in the temple. The worshipers did not personally approach or use the altar; rather, they surrendered their sacrificial animal to the temple workers, and a priest would sacrifice and burn it. Later on the worshiper would be given a portion of the meat to eat there or in his home. The eating in itself it is an act of worship.[472]

---

thanks as follows") would lead already in the 1st century to the naming of the Lord's Supper as the "Eucharist" (*Didache* 9.1, 5; Ignatius, *Philadelphians* 4; *Smyrnaeans* 8.1; perhaps *Ephesians* 13.1). 10:16 in the critical text has *eulogia* (blessing), but some witnesses read *eucharistia* (thanksgiving), probably influenced by liturgical usage or by influence of the cognate verb in 11:24.

[471] See for example Acts 2:42; 2 Cor 6:14; 13:13; Phil 2:1; 1 John 1:3, 6, 7.

[472] See for example 2 Kings 23:21-23, where kingdom Josiah destroyed the pagan idols and then invited the

10:19

Now Paul will come back to the original datum on which the Corinthians levered their argument: *But idols don't exist! They're mere statues!* (8:4-6). This is true on one level, Paul has said, and the "weak" are mistaken if they think that Hera or Apollo actually receive the sacrifices offered them in Corinth. But some Corinthians took a theological truth and misapplied it, saying that if the gods mean nothing, then surely **the sacrifices of pagans are offered to demons** are also null and void.

10:20

To their credit, the weak Christians do at least acknowledge an invisible spiritual reality that other Corinthians seem to have missed: behind the masks of the pagan gods stand the power of the **demons**.[473] There is a fascinating double meaning to this word. The Greek *daimōnion* has for Christians come to mean a demon, devil, fallen angel or evil spirit (Mark 1:34), that is, the spirit which possesses a demoniac (Mark 1:32). But the pagan Greeks at least as early as Homer usually used *daimōnion* in a looser sense, as we might use the word "spirit," to designate any sort of supernatural being or god. This is its sense in Acts 17:18, where the word is correctly rendered "gods." But here is where there is a switch in the content of the word: the pagans would refer to their deities as *daimōnia* and the Christians would be able to claim, *Aha, they consciously or unconsciously worship demons.* In fact, one of the complaints that modern pagans have against us is that we accuse them of knowingly worshiping Satan; for the vast majority of pagans or practitioners of Wicca this is not true. What Paul says here is that in worshiping their *daimōnia* they worship Satan's demons unknowingly.[474]

Grammatically, Paul's analysis of pagan sacrifice may be translated in one of two ways, since *theos* could refer to God or a god:

Either
    They offer sacrifices to demons, not to [the true] God (NIV and the other versions)
or
    They offer sacrifices to demons, not to a supposed "god" such as Apollo[475]

The former is certainly correct, since the contrast that Paul is setting up is between the table of demons and the table of the Lord's Supper (10:21). Besides which, this is probably an allusion to Deut 32:17 –

> They sacrificed to demons, which are not God – gods they had not known, gods that recently appeared, gods your fathers did not fear.

---

true believers in Jehovah to celebrate the feast as a sign of their loyalty: "The king gave this order to all the people: 'Celebrate the Passover to the LORD your God, as it is written in this Book of the Covenant.' Not since the days of the judges who led Israel, nor throughout the days of the kings of Israel and the kings of Judah, had any such Passover been observed. But in the eighteenth year of King Josiah, this Passover was celebrated to the LORD in Jerusalem."

[473] Justin Martyr, *First apology* 5, on the other hand, believes that behind each pagan god is a single masquerading demon. This is the idea too behind Milton's theology of the pagan gods in his *Paradise Lost*, and seems to be Paul's sense here.

[474] See Hodge.

[475] See Orr and Walther, *I Corinthians*, 250. Apparently also the NJB version.

10:21

When Paul says **you cannot** he means it in the sense of "you must not." He contrasts the **cup**, whose contents of wine were blessed in the name of the god, and the cup which was blessed in the name of the God of Christ. Again, he uses **table** to represent the Supper – table, since the Corinthians were eating off a low table, not directly off an altar, in the idolatrous dining hall. The word "altar" was not yet used to refer to the Lord's Supper, as it came to be later in church history.

Paul's point is that one cannot call the Christian sacrament the reality and the pagan one a mere illusion. Some Corinthians were publicly splitting their allegiance between Jehovah and a false god, just as the Baal worshipers did in the days of Elijah. As in 1 Kings 18:21 their sin was two-fold; not only did they honor a false god, but negatively they did not give undivided devotion to the true God. Hence Elijah proclaimed: "How long will you waver between two opinions? If the LORD is God, follow him; but if Baal is God, follow him." And like the prophet, Paul demands a clean decision. This call to decisive loyalty only functions for a person from a Judeo-Christian background. No heathen idol would issue a call through his prophet, demanding exclusive worship: that goes against the very soul of paganism, which allows people to be devoted to one god so long as they neglect none of the gods. In the Bible story, only Jehovah makes a statement like "You shall have no other gods before me" (Exod 20:3).

10:22

Here is the conclusion to this section: **Are we trying to arouse the Lord's jealousy?** Paul adduces once again Old Testament language. The sophisticated Corinthian may suppose that he is beyond the wrath and jealousy of the Old Testament God; after all, he has figured out that the rivals to Jehovah don't even exist. How could God be jealous of an illusion? Especially with the infection of Greek philosophy, some Corinthians might have had trouble even imagining the Supreme Being as capable of jealousy at all. But the God who banned all other gods did so because he demanded exclusive worship: "I, the LORD your God, am a jealous God" (Exod 20:5, see also Exod 34:14, Deut 4:24, etc., especially Ezekiel *in loc.*). Paul may well be thinking of Num 25:11, which refers to the apostasy of Israel at Moab (see 1 Cor. 10:8).

The second question offers an even stronger blow: **Are we stronger than he?** One must bear in mind how the Corinthian elite reasoned:

Elitist: *I am wise and well-informed enough that I have the right to eat of idolatrous food and the power to do so without offending my conscience.*

Paul (1 Cor 8-9): *a Christian must take the weak conscience of the brother into account and set aside his rights for the other.*

But that being said, Paul points the "wise one" heavenward:

Paul (1 Cor 10): *You claim to be strong enough to carry out this action without offense to your conscience; but if that is the case, then your conscience must be stronger than even God's, since he reports in his Word that he takes offense at your action.*

It is no coincidence that the Lord's Supper appears in this section about idolatry, and later in the section that follows concerning church meetings. On the surface he seems to make two separate points: in 1 Cor 10, that the Lord's Supper is a partaking in Christ and thus declares to heaven and earth one's allegiance to him. In 1 Cor 11 he mentions it because of specific abuses in the cultus: not only their general divisiveness, but its manifestation in the Lord's Supper.

But what appear to be two distinct teachings have a strong inner unity. Paul affirms in 1 Cor 10 that not only does the partaker of the meal show his allegiance to an idol or Christ, but also to the other worshipers. It is a sign of communion on a horizontal and vertical level. But the same comes through in 1 Cor 11 – when one insults a fellow Christian at the Lord's table, it is an insult to God and to Christ (11:22, 27b). They don't discern that these other disciples constitute the Body of Christ (11:29) and they insult that Body. In other language, they do not discern that Christians taken together comprise "one loaf" (10:17).

Thus, the very different applications of 1 Cor 10-11 arise from a single perspective: that the Christian is a member of a body and cannot act as an individual; that an abusive exercise of one's individual freedom (10:23) may offend both man and God; that it is the Christian's duty to not offend God but also to put his fellow's well-being ahead of his own liberty. In neither case does Paul teach a full theology of the Lord's Supper: *Is the Lord present in the bread? Does the bread turn into the body of Christ? Or is it metaphorical?*

Application: Religious practices and the Christian – 10:21-22

In 1 Corinthians 8 Paul speaks of the meat issue on one level only. He argues that if eating meat sacrificed to idols harms my fellow Christian, than "I will never eat meat again" (8:13) in order to protect him. In that case, the transgression has to do with our relationships with other Christians: "When you sin against your brothers in this way and wound their weak conscience, you sin against Christ."

In 1 Cor 10:1-22, conversely, Paul focuses on the vertical level. The key word is "communion," that is, a partaking in a religious ceremony or spiritual union. The Corinthians were in a real way taking communion within two different faiths, the Christian and the pagan.

There are practices and ceremonies in which we offend God or signal to others that our allegiance to the one Lord is diluted. Here are some contemporary issues that merit our attention:

Literal meat offered to idols. This is still a problem with Christians in Asia, Africa and Latin America.

The Roman mass. Participating in the mass is not "merely" the partaking of a wafer; it is an affirmation of the doctrine of transubstantiation and the receiving of grace through the sacrament.

Syncretistic rites. Latin America, Africa and Asia are rife with mixtures of Christianity with indigenous practices. This is not limited to Catholicism; evangelicals too mix up their faiths. Thus in the jungles of Peru the shamanistic formulas for health, protection and power may include Christian terms and biblical quotations.

Other systems. Christians mix their faith in Christ with other systems, implying that they are part of the same package: Christianity and capitalism; or socialism; or pacifism.

Not all of these are of the same kind, and some Christians might decide, for example, that participating in a Saint's Day does not offend God. Yet let us remember that what Paul teaches us here is that we must give our God not only allegiance, but unmixed allegiance. When offense to our Lord is truly at stake, we should spare no effort to do well by him.

e. Specific instructions for some marginal related issues 10:23-11:1

In this conclusion to a very long section Paul will deal with some peripheral details. He spells out several hypothetical but all-too-likely situations for a person who lived in Corinth. Two principles drive his teaching: the ultimate reality of our God, and love for Christians and non-Christians.

10:23
Can it be mere coincidence that Paul again quotes the slogan **"Everything is permissible"**? For in 6:12 too the issue was freedom of the wise man to eat what he wants, when he wants. There Paul argued that these supposed wise men were foolishly setting a trap for themselves. Here in 1 Cor 10 the focus is turned outward: *So, you are permitted to eat whatever you want?* Actually, the Corinthians must qualify that boast by looking to the needs of their fellows. Not everything they eat is **beneficial**, not everything is **constructive** for other people.

10:24
If it is not clear for whom idol meat is harmful, Paul will spell this out now: **Nobody should seek his own good, but the good of others.** It is similar to other Pauline statements about brotherly care, and is a *leitmotif* throughout Philippians (e.g. 2:3-4). His teaching derives from the law of Moses and of Jesus, "Love your neighbor as yourself." The context of that love in Lev 19:18 is not simply a feeling of affection toward the neighbor; rather, it results in watching out for his interests, in concrete terms, his property interests as denoted by boundary markers. No Corinthian can claim to be loving who then tramples over his brother's conscience. Pagan religion had both an individual and civic aspect, but it did not encourage loving community as such. Christianity, by contrast, was manifested primarily by communities who were called to love God and one another. "The question is not merely whether you are eating with a clear conscience. It is whether what you are doing is of benefit to your brother."[476]

---

[476] Oecumenius (Bray, 100).

10:25

From a sweeping statement about one's responsibility for others, Paul moves abruptly to the realities of the local agora. First, **Eat everything sold in the meat market.** For "meat market," Paul uses the Greek *makellos*, which is the direct equivalent of the Latin *macellum*, the term they used in Roman Corinth.[477]

Without raising questions of conscience constitutes a serious break from the practices of Judaism, in which everything was considered unclean unless it could be proven otherwise. In many cities, Jews went to their own butchers, who could be counted on to sell them meat that was kosher, properly and humanely butchered, unhandled by gentiles and free from idolatrous connections. If that were not possible, the Jews felt obligated to ask plenty of questions. The Christian on the other hand is told to assume that meat is all right unless told otherwise.

Thus in one swoop he banishes the fears of the "weak": meat which is dedicated to a pagan god is not inherently tainted; the consumer will not ingest unwanted demonic influence.[478]

10:26

To justify his claim in 10:25, Paul now cites Psalm 24:1, a verse well-known to Jew and Christian alike: **"The earth is the Lord's, and everything in it."** That is, the Christian should view the created order as a friendly place: the Lord made it for the benefit of his people. To be sure, demons are trying to usurp God's place by manipulating human beings to sacrifice animals to them. But in the end, those animals remain God's, by right of creation. To deny this would be to yield to the demons the very ground they have been trying to grasp.[479]

Of course, the Corinthian elite have probably taken a similar rationale, but taken it to an extreme: *If demons don't exist, and if God is our Maker, then I should be free to eat in a pagan restaurant!* The difference here is in the realm of sacrament: the material meat means nothing, says Paul. But when you share in a pagan meal, you are assenting before humanity and before the cosmos that you love and follow a demonic deity.

10:27-29a

The next hypothetical is **some unbeliever invites you to a meal and you want to go.** Already we are beyond the strictures of Judaism, within which such a dinner meeting

---

[477] See David W. J. Gill, "The meat market at Corinth (1 Corinthians 10:25)," *TynBul* 43.2 (1992): 389-93.
[478] So Theodoret of Cyrus; Clement of Alexandria, *Instructor* 2.1 has a long commentary on Paul's instructions in this section, and concludes: "We must therefore abstain from these viands not for fear (because there is no power in them); but on account of our conscience, which is holy, and out of detestation of the demons to which they are dedicated, are we to loathe them..." The spurious *Recognitions of Clement* 2.71 takes a different approach, that an unbeliever is polluted by demons: "he has become a guest of demons, and has been partaker with that demon of which he has formed the image in his mind, either through fear or love. And by these means he is not free from an unclean spirit, and therefore needs the purification of baptism, that the unclean spirit may go out of him."
[479] *1 Clem* 54.3-4 cites the verse, we assume under the influence of 1 Corinthians because it seems oddly out of place in its context. He urges schismatics in the Corinthian church to make peace with their elders. They can be at peace wherever they are in the world, "for 'the earth is the Lord's, and all that is in it.' These are the things that those who live as citizens of the commonwealth of God – something not to be regretted – have done and will continue to do." Apparently he means that every church in the world will accept a righteous Christian brother, and that there is nowhere a schismatic can go that lies outside of the Lord's creation.

would be impossible. But if a non-Christian invites a Christian to a meal, the believer is entirely free to accept if he likes.[480] This cannot mean an invitation to eat in a pagan temple: Paul has already shown that such a dinner violates the gospel and offends God. More than that, the Christian in this new situation does not know that the meat was sacrificed. He finds out only when someone tells him that **"This has been offered in sacrifice"** to an idol. This could not happen in a temple precinct, since the Christian would already know where the meat had been. Thus, we are dealing with a situation where a pagan invites a Christian to a private meal in his home or in some neutral location.[481] It is a secular meal, but someone mentions what sort of meat this is.[482] Perhaps it is a casual statement; perhaps the pagan wishes to show his piety and does not realize it would shock his Christian guest; perhaps it is a ploy to trap or embarrass the Christian. Or perhaps the pagan knows enough about the gospel to make the assumption that his friend cannot eat that meat: as a good host he informs him, just as we might tell someone that a dish contains ingredients to which some guest is known to be allergic.

The context does not favor any of these explanations in particular. Most likely Paul is not thinking beyond general terms: if someone tells you that the meat was sacrificed, then protect his conscience by refraining from the meat. Paul has his eye on an informant from a pagan background. First, his aim is evangelistic: he doesn't want to harm the conscience of a pagan, nor to prevent him from a positive appreciation of the gospel (see also 1 Cor 9:19-27; 10:32-33). Second, the information is given from the viewpoint of a pagan, not a Christian or a Jew. Paul uses a pagan term *hierothutos*, that is, meat sacrificed to a deity. The speaker does not use the pejorative term "idol," because he is a pagan, and would not use the Jewish and Christian *eidōlothutos* (see our comments on 8:1). Once again, Paul makes clear that the conscience of the Christian is not, and should not, be offended: the meat in this context signifies nothing. It is the conscience of the outsider that is at risk.

There is in this passage a careful attempt to steer the church between two extremes. On the one hand is idolatry. But on the other hand is the danger that the church will withdraw from the world (see 5:9-13), will refuse to eat with sinners, will insist on elaborate rules of purity, will in effect move away from the example of Jesus and toward the model of the Pharisees. Jesus' ministry was notable (and for many objectionable) because of his habit of eating and communing with sinners, notably prostitutes and publicans. Of course, these were Jewish sinners, who despite their many defects were not idolatrous. But the issue continues on in the church: how to imitate the extended embrace of Jesus without offending God?[483]

The Textus Receptus adds to the end of 10:28 a repetition of Psalm 24:1 (the text Paul quoted in 10:26); the quotation is found in the KJV and NKJV. It seems to have been added to the Greek text by scribal error.

10:29b-30
For why should my freedom be judged by another's conscience? is difficult. Unless

---

[480] Although it goes against the tone of the verse, Calvin, *First Corinthians*, 1:345, takes 10:28 as a concession: "When he says – *and you are willing to go*, he intimates indirectly, that he does not altogether approve of it, and that it would be better if they declined, but as it is a thing indifferent, he does not choose to forbid it absolutely."
[481] So Fee.
[482] See Thiselton, *First Corinthians*, 786.
[483] See the extended development of this same tension by Tertullian, *On idolatry* 14.

Paul is being ironic (and what follows in 10:30 will not allow that), then it is uncertain whose conscience is judging the liberty of whom. Perhaps it refers back to the exchange with the informant at the dinner. Thus, Paul would be asking, *Why should this person's scruples or misunderstanding impinge on my liberty to eat what I like?*[484] In that case, "my" is Paul as a representative Christian.

Alternatively, Paul puts the words in the mouth of the "knowledgeable" Christian, who immediately objects to Paul's concession to someone else's conscience.[485] The difficulty with that view is that Paul leaves the question unchallenged until the end of the discussion.

The best interpretation is that "my" refers to Paul himself, who had been challenged about his own principals:[486] that he is free to eat any meat; that he stays clear of idolatrous banquets or eating places; that he looks to a higher good than simply satisfying his hunger or exercising his liberty; that those goals include attracting the pagan to the gospel and building up the other Christian. Thus some would have found Paul too loose; some too restricted; some too concerned with others' feelings; some too unconcerned about God's will. It is possible that this is one more reason that some Corinthians found to deprecate their apostle. *Why have I been judged?* he wants to know (see especially 1 Cor 4:3-5).

Paul invokes **God** to show that he is not offending heaven by his eating. Whatever food he eats has come from the Lord's creation (10:26), and he with a clear conscience thanks the one true God for it, even if somewhere along the line someone had dedicated it to an idol.

10:31

The **so** finishes the thought of three chapters, and has been a long time in coming. We may compare 10:31-33 with the summary in 7:39-40, where Paul once again addresses Christian wives who may wish to become "unmarried." Here as there, he summarizes what he perceives to be the heart of the matter. Yes, there is freedom; yes, there are scruples. But in the end what matters is **do it all for the glory of God**.[487] Of course, both the weak and the well-informed, before hearing this epistle, would have argued that their actions were already to the glory of God: *I refrain from eating meat sold in the market, to the glory of the one true God!* Or *I exercise my freedom to eat in a temple cafeteria, to the glory of the one true God!* What Paul has shown is that there is a second dimension: God is glorified by not putting an obstacle between anyone and God (10:32), and by seeking the other's good in love (10:33).

10:32-33

Paul has rejected putting an obstacle before another Christian, but here he is thinking more broadly: **anyone...whether Jews, Greeks or the church of God**. The Jews divided humanity into two distinct groups: the circumcised and the uncircumcised (a paradigm that Paul rejects in 7:19). The Greeks might divide the world into Greeks and "barbarians" (see Rom 1:15, 16). For his part, Paul knows that if there are two groups in

---

[484] See the review of options in Thiselton, *First Corinthians*, 788-93.
[485] Lietzmann and Kümmel, *An die Korinther*, 52. Cf. Thiselton, *First Corinthians*, 788-89.
[486] Fee.
[487] Ignatius, *Polycarp* 5.2 cites this directive in order to prove that every marriage should be approved by the bishop.

the world, it is those in Christ and those not; if there are three groups, they are the **Jews**, the **Greeks** (or gentiles) and **the church of God** (which phrase occurs in 1 Cor 1:2, 10:32, 11:22 and 15:9 and in 2 Cor 1:1; outside of the Corinthian correspondence only in Gal 2:18 and Acts 20:28).

We know already that a Christian might stumble over something, causing him to transgress his conscience and to damage his walk with God (8:9). By extension, Paul also avoids creating an obstacle that will keep a Jew or a pagan Greek from Christ. Here he harks back to 9:19-27, and finally succeeds in tying 1 Cor 8-10 together. Of what value is my liberty if by eating some meal I ruin the chances of winning some convert or another? How is God glorified by that? And so Paul's concern extends even to the conscience of the pagan bystander in 10:27-29a.

Positively, **I try to please everybody in every way**. This stands in apparent tension with Gal 1:10, where "trying to please men" (using the same verb, *areskō*) is a sin and the opposite of seeking to please God. But of course, the apostle has already defined what he means in the present context: a lifestyle that shapes itself in a limited way to its audience's cultural mores. When it comes to obeying God, then of course the Christian must not compromise; this is the issue of Galatians, where someone had apparently charged Paul with tailoring his message to the taste of others. But here, where it is a matter of personal liberty, Paul would rather suit someone else than please himself. He takes the conceptual framework of one's care for other Christians (Phil 2:3-4, 2:19-21), and applies it to evangelism: **I am not seeking my own good but the good of many, so that they may be saved**. Of course one need look no further than the example of Christ himself, who looked to the interests of the ignorant, the powerless and the poor when he went to the cross (1 Cor 1-2; Phil 2:5-11).

11:1

Here lies one of the most unfortunate chapter divisions in our Bibles, making of 11:1 the beginning of a new chapter. Paul did not divide his letters into chapters. Only in the 14th century did an editor place a division here, thinking that this verse went with chapter 11, or at least that it stood apart from chapter 10. Most modern editions correct that error and make 11:1 the conclusion of chapters 8-10, and specifically a summary of 10:31-33 – **Follow my example** (that is, as Paul just spelled it out in 10:33) in the matter of eating and, more broadly, living.[488] This verse, taken in isolation, may seem to reek of self-confidence, as if he is saying that following Paul is the same as following Christ.[489] Rather, the verse refers specifically to Paul's practices about eating. *In the matter of meat sacrificed to idols, do what I do; because I am doing what Christ himself would do.*

Modern readers often miss out on the key role of imitation in the New Testament, and especially in Paul's epistles. His converts did not simply take his abstract principles and then try to follow them; they also learned by following Paul's pattern, whether it is with regard to freedom and love, manual labor (1 Cor 9:6, 1 Thess 2:9) or style of teaching (1 Thess 2:5-6).

---

[488] So too thought Chrysostom, who included this verse in his sermon on 1 Cor 10:25-11:1.

[489] Ambrosiaster (Bray, 103) – "For just as God the Father sent Christ as the teacher and author of life, so Christ sent the apostles to be our teachers, so that we should imitate them, for we are unable to imitate [Christ] directly."

Special Theme: 1 Corinthians 8-10 and "the Strong and the Weak" in Romans 14

In Rom 14 Paul speaks of Christians who make choices about certain practices. We have argued in another place that Paul is dealing with a very different issue in that epistle.[490] The historical background is that Claudius had expelled all Jews from Rome (Acts 18:2). This left the church in that city for a time a purely gentile movement. After the death of Claudius in 54, Jews were able to return. Christian Jews (such as those we find mentioned in Rom 16) returned to find a fully functioning church, but one that was attuned to gentiles rather than Jews. Paul's letter to the Romans contains a warning to gentiles that they not be triumphalistic or be arrogant toward Israel (Rom 9-11). Rather, God's goal is that Jew and gentile worship together in one church of God (Rom 15:7-13). It is in that specific context that Paul deals with Christians who observe the Sabbath and who refrain from eating meat and drinking wine (14:5-6). In Rome the issue was not meat sacrificed to idols. Rather, some Jews were practicing vegetarianism as a way of keeping aloof from the paganism of the imperial capital. They followed the example of Daniel and others, who kept themselves from the king's meat and wine.

Thus Paul's instructions in Romans and in 1 Corinthians, while similar in language, deal with different circumstances. Yet in Romans as well, Paul affirms that food as such is a matter of indifference to God (Rom 14:17). Again, the key is to care for one's fellow Christians. As in Corinth, he demands that no Christian cause another to stumble (14:13b) or to ruin someone for whom Christ died (14:15b).

What are the differences? In 1 Corinthians he is more sympathetic toward the weak. In Romans he addresses the weak directly, and tells them not to despise those who have more freedom (Rom 14:13a), a thing he does not do in 1 Corinthians. In Romans he speaks about "strong" Christians without criticizing their practices; in 1 Corinthians he does not use the term "strong" as such, although he does criticize the well-informed with "Are we stronger than [God]?" (1 Cor 10:22). In Romans, eating meat or not is a matter of complete indifference; in Corinth it ceases to be a matter of indifference if taken in a cultic meal. The principle that underlies both is that "We who are strong ought to bear with the failings of the weak and not to please ourselves" (Rom 15:1).

To summarize 1 Cor 8-10:

Corinthian situation: In Corinth, there were two opposing viewpoints. Each was tightly held by groups that believed that their opinion was the natural outcome of the gospel and the correct application of the Apostolic Decree. In Corinth idolatry extended to the meat one consumed. The point of contention was the "gray" area of whether a Christian could sit down at a meal which was specifically dedicated to a pagan god. This probably took place outside the normal temple cult: at a restaurant attached to a temple, or at a private gathering where the god was to be honored. Other issues, such as going to a temple to worship, or buying meat in the market were only of secondary concern for the Corinthians.

---

[490] Gary S. Shogren, "Is the Kingdom of God about eating and drinking or isn't it? (Romans 14:17)," *NovT* 42.3 (2000): 238-56.

Many Christians, informed by the gospel, by philosophy and by reason, knew that the pagan gods did not as such exist. Therefore, any prayer or ritual to a deity was moot for the Christian, empty words addressed to no-one: thus, it was reasoned, such rituals did not offend God, and the Christian had the right (perhaps even the duty) to participate in such a meal. They had freedom; all things were lawful!

The rest of the believers certainly did not label themselves as "weak," but were so categorized by Paul and, as is likely, by their more sophisticated brethren in Corinth. They did not know that the gods were nothing; they had lived too long and seen too much to accept that! Their weakness lay in not seeing that Christ's lordship delivered them from the fear of other spirit beings.[491] The weak may have been reactionary and perhaps condemned the more liberal Christians, but if so, Paul doesn't mention it. The real culprits were the knowledgeable ones, who took it on themselves to educate the weak in their basic Christian freedom, even at the risk of trampling their consciences and risking their souls.

There is no indication in 1 Corinthians that the "knowledgeable" and the "weak" correlated in any particular way to the Paul, Apollos, Cephas or Christ groups.

The Corinthian letter to Paul seems to have come from the "knowledgeable," since it them whom Paul addresses. They may have believed: *Paul, doesn't every Christian know that the gods are nothing? Isn't the whole point of the gospel that there is one God and one Lord? Isn't it true that food does not bring us near to God; we are no worse if we do not eat, and no better if we do? Doesn't the Apostolic Decree ban only active participation in temple worship? Don't you yourself eat meat from the marketplace without asking questions? Don't we therefore have the freedom to eat in a temple cafeteria or go to a party dedicated to a god, since it is really the same meat? Doesn't our church debate simply boil down question of knowledge* versus *ignorance?*

Paul perceives that this is not purely a question of knowledge *versus* ignorance, but of knowledge operating apart from love *versus* knowledge with love. The knowledgeable are using their freedom, not to honor God, but to flatter themselves on their own intellectual depth. They have raised liberty to a higher value than helping another Christian or expediting the evangelistic mission. They have not seen that in the gospel one is given certain rights, but that these rights are to be used to serve God and others, or set aside if that is best. The apostle also perceives that some Corinthians are violating the spirit of the Apostolic Decree: whether in a temple or in a restaurant, the knowledgeable are taking part in pagan ritual. That practice at least must be removed from the realm of personal freedom, since God is offended.

Paul in 1 Corinthians addresses the "knowledgeable," not the weak. Typical of Paul in this letter, he transcends the original question of who is right and who is wrong with a higher ethic: how may we best glorify God? If Paul does not mention the Apostolic Decree, it is because the Decree as such was not under dispute, only its application.

1. The main issue: eating meat sacrificed to idols outside of the temple cult but still within a broader context of pagan worship and sacrifice. Paul says: *Don't partake in such a meal.* His reasons are:

---

[491] Clinton Arnold argues that behind Ephesians lay a similar fear of the cosmos. See his *Ephesians: power and magic: the concept of power in Ephesians in light of its historical setting* (Grand Rapids, MI: Baker, 1992).

1 a. It harms your brother, who may be tempted to follow your "well-informed" practice

1 b. What is worse, it offends God: the practice cannot be viewed through a reductionist lens; it is idolatry.

1 c. Further, you're entangling yourselves with the demons who are impersonating pagan gods and goddesses.

1 d. You are walking a path more dangerous than you imagine. The Bible is packed full of people who dabbled in idolatrous practices, and such people inevitably went apostate. Your arrogance makes you prime targets of such backsliding.

2. The subsidiary issue: eating such meat in a non-cultic context. Paul says:

2 a. Go ahead, buy and consume meat sold in the market; not only are you not required to investigate its origins, it is better that you don't raise questions at all.

2 b. Don't eat such meat if someone has communicated to you that he thinks it has cultic entanglements – it would only harm that person.

3. The real, higher issue: Paul says that pleasing God is the most important principle. He shows:

3 a. The best ways to please God:
- publically show your loyalty to God alone
- watch out for the welfare of your brother
- live in a way that shows you understand the importance of the cross, for example by treating your fellow Christians as part of the same "loaf of bread"
- live in a way that makes evangelism a higher priority than your freedom

3 b. The fastest ways to displease God:
- publically send mixed messages about your religious loyalties
- destroy a fellow Christian
- trample over the sensibilities of an unbeliever, be he pagan or Jew
- (harking back to 1 Cor 1-3) deprecate the centrality of the cross in human history by destroying your brother whom Christ bought through the cross

In 1 Cor 11 Paul will deal with two other community issues. The Corinthians had perhaps written about head coverings for women. In addition, and more critically, Paul had heard from someone that their meetings were fragmented along social and economic lines. He will speak of the Lord's Supper once again, applying its meaning in a fresh direction.

3. Concerning meetings (they perhaps had written): "How serious were you, when you said that women had to wear veils in the meeting?" 11:2-16

From 11:2 through 14:40 speaks about Christian meetings. 11:2-16 is the most difficult passage in 1 Corinthians. It is probable that Paul is responding to a written question, but it is not certain what that question might have been, and from what perspective they raised it. What is worse, it is not immediately evident what Paul means to say. On top of everything, it is difficult to apply his teaching in a modern context that is far removed culturally from the original.

Today's reader must remember that Paul was alluding to previous oral instruction, as well as the Corinthians' comments. Thus, he and his readers knew already whether the terms in 11:3 were meant to be understood as man/woman or husband/wife; whether the custom applied to the worship service or elsewhere; what was the sense(s) of *kephalē* (head); what were the local customs of dress and hairstyle; what was meant by "sign of authority" in 11:10; what was meant by "the angels" of 11:10; whether Paul understood long hair in itself to be a sort of veil, or whether it merely suggested a reason for a veil. This has led some scholars into a deep pessimism over whether we can really get to the bottom of this section. But fortunately, recent advances in historical-cultural investigation have served to give better focus to Paul's intent.

Paul does not mark the Corinthians' question with *peri de* as he does in other cases. Rather he begins with an affirmation – a sincere one, we believe – of the Corinthians' general obedience and adherence to his teaching. He uses the rhetorical form known as *epideictic*, wherein an authority figure writes to evaluate the behavior of his reader(s), using language like "I praise you"/"I have no praise for you" (see 11:2, 17, 22). Thus he affirms and reinforces desirable behavior and criticizes them when they have strayed from the true path. In this case, Paul praises them for their general obedience; he clarifies a point of contention from their letter (11:3-16); but he shames them for behavior at the Lord's Supper, of which he has learned by oral report (11:17-34; note "I hear that" in 11:18).

Some have speculated that the Corinthians' question had to do with women only, and that Paul's reference to male hair and dress was merely to round off the context. Others suggest that either men or women or both were rejecting Christian custom; and in fact, it is to the men that Paul speaks first in 11:4. It is most likely that they were raising doubts about the head covering of women rather than men, hence our hypothetical wording of their question as "How serious were you, when you said that women had to wear veils in the meeting?"[492] Paul speaks to men, but he speaks to the women in greater detail, by our count in seven and a half verses, to the men's one and a half. Therefore the dynamic in chapter 11 mirrors what takes place in chapter 7: that the Corinthians' question specifically had to do with the Corinthian women; but that Paul responded by broadening the issue to reinforce his previous teaching for men and women both.[493] Given his positive comment in 11:2 and the dispassionate tone in this chapter (as in chapter 7), we infer that here too the church had signaled their willingness to obey Paul even as they raised questions about his earlier teaching.

In this commentary we will argue that the most natural interpretation is:

Paul taught all his churches that in a worship service both men and women are free to pray aloud and to speak prophetically to the congregation. Men should pray and prophesy with their heads bared; women, who arrive already wearing a

---

[492] Hurd, *Origin*, 228-29, believes that Paul had taught them about veils in his Previous Letter.
[493] The fact that most commentators put labels such as "Head Coverings for Women" over this passage, which indeed speaks to both men and women, has been taken as proof of how male readers have tended to read it with a bias. Note the clearer labeling by Fee; Thiselton, who point out that the passage deals with women and men.

veil – like a shawl on their head, as dictated the local culture – should continue to wear it throughout the meeting. This rule was given for several reasons: it reflected the created order as described in Genesis; because it was "natural"; because to do otherwise would bring cultural shame. But later on, some Corinthian women wanted to shed the veil. Paul perceives that, while the veil in itself is not a fundamental issue of the gospel, the motivations for rejecting the veil were questionable: to declare independence from men/husbands; to reject the relevance of cultural mores for a Christian; to act as if gender differences did not exist; to once again act independently, as if the Corinthian church was not united "with all those everywhere who call on the name of our Lord Jesus Christ – their Lord and ours" (1 Cor 1:2). For these reasons he reaffirms that women and men must maintain the *status quo* that he has established for Christian meetings.

Thus, the issue of head coverings became an important issue mainly because some Corinthians had expressed a desire to reject it.[494]

11:2
Remembering me in everything and for holding to the teachings, just as I passed them on to you. Paul uses a pair of words here (*paradidōmi*, "transmit, pass on"; its cognate *paradosis*, "tradition") that would grow to become key terms to describe the oral transmission of the apostolic tradition (see 11:23 and 15:1, 3, in which Paul uses another technical term, *paralambanō*, "to receive a tradition"). Some have argued that Paul is being sarcastic here – *Oh, how nicely you are obeying my tradition!* – before showing how once again they had let him down. This is highly unlikely, given the nature of epideictic language. Besides, if Paul were being ironic here, his sarcasm would be bitter and unloving and not worthy of a pastor. His praise is genuine, although qualified.[495] This section also indicates that Paul was not being sarcastic in the exordium of 1:4-9. The Corinthians, disappointing as they could be, were doing well in many ways.

We do not know whether Paul was responding to some self-doubt that the Corinthians had raised, such as: *Are we really as disappointing as your tone leads us to suspect?* It is more likely that Paul himself chose the epideictic form.[496]

11:3
Paul now uses a favorite "disclosure formula," **I want you to realize**. He does not give them a new teaching. Rather he is offering fresh arguments in favor of the custom of how one should dress for a worship service.[497]

His first argument in favor of the *status quo* is the order of the cosmos as revealed

---

[494] So Hays; Fee, *First Corinthians*, 498: "Paul feels strongly enough about the issue to speak to it, even if his argument lacks its customary vigor…it is probably the larger theological issue that leads him to this answer at all."

[495] So believes Athanasius, *Festal letter* 2.6 – "Paul justly praises the Corinthians, because their opinions were in accordance with his traditions."

[496] As Conzelmann, *1 Corinthians*, 182 n. 13.

[497] Conzelmann, *1 Corinthians*, 183, is surely mistaken when he claims that in this passage, "It is plain that [Paul] has to break with an existing custom" in Corinth. Hence he translates *de* as "I would have you know, however…" A better explanation is that the Corinthian women had all worn veils, but that now there was some doubt about the practice.

in the creation account and later augmented by the gospel. He makes three statements using the much-analyzed word "head" (*kephalē*).

The head of every man is Christ, and
   the head of the woman is man, and
   the head of Christ is God.

In many quarters it is claimed that the true meaning of *kephalē* is "source."[498] Thus a statement like "x is the *kephalē* of y" is taken to mean that "x is the source from which y came into being or has its existence." While in some contexts (for example, in 11:8) *kephalē* may *refer* to something which is also a "source," that is not the *meaning* of *kephalē* in itself. Thus the woman is on one level the point of origin of the man (11:8), his source as it were; yet she is not called his *kephalē* .

The scholarly world has seen many years of debate over *kephalē*, helped now on our ability to search Greek texts through the magisterial software *Thesaurus Linguae Graecae*. The results: *kephalē* usually refers to the physical head, as opposed to the body. When it is used metaphorically, it indeed does often refer to a position of authority. It is difficult in the extreme to provide convincing evidence that it basically means "source" or that it does not mean "authority over" when used as a metaphor.[499] The most natural meaning of *kephalē* is this context is "foremost" or "authority over," although of course that must be carefully understood within the context of Paul's teaching. Paul does not develop *kephalē* in the context of human relations or marriage in 1 Cor 11; his point is that the order of God-Christ-man-woman has a fundamental role to play in how men and women dress when they meet with the church of Christ.

Contrary to popular myth, New Testament Greek is not a scientifically-precise language. Here, **the head of every man is Christ** presents another translation problem, since *anēr* may be translated as "man" or as "husband," depending on the context (it is not generic and may not be rendered as "person"). The same dynamic holds for *gunē*, which may be "wife" or "woman." This lack of distinction in Greek has already raised a question in the translation of 1 Cor 7:1. In 11:3 the commentaries are divided between man/woman and husband/wife.[500] "Man" and "woman" are the better option, as the NIV and most English versions. First, there is no reference to marriage in this section. Second, Paul is not speaking as if "Christ is the head of every husband" but rather "of every man" or, better, "of every Christian man."

The head of the woman is man (better than "a husband has authority over his wife," GNB) bears some resemblance to the instruction to husbands and wives in Eph 5:23. In that context the husband's role as head is to love the wife as his own body; the wife is to

---

[498] Barrett, *First Corinthians*, 248, says that *kephalē* means "origin." Fee, *First Corinthians*, 503, says that "Paul's understanding of the metaphor, therefore, and almost certainly the only one which the Corinthians would have grasped, is 'head' as 'source', especially 'source of life'." See too C. C. Kroeger, "Head," *DPL*: 375-77.

[499] See Joseph A. Fitzmyer, "The meaning of *kephalē* in 1 Corinthians 11:3," in *According to Paul: studies in the theology of the apostle* (Mahwah, NJ: Paulist, 1992), 80-88, who demonstrates that "authority over" is one of the metaphorical uses of the word; also *First Corinthians*, 410-11. *Kephalē* was taken in the sense of "an authority" by Tertullian, *Adversus Marcionem* 5.8 – "The head he has here put for *authority*;" likewise *Apostolic constitutions* 3.1 §6, see below.

[500] For man/woman generally, apart from the question of marriage roles: Tertullian, *On prayer* 21-22; *Veiling of virgins* 7; Conzelmann, *1 Corinthians*, 183-85. For husband/wife, see Philipp Bachmann, *Der erste Brief des Paulus an die Korinther* (KNT 7; 2nd ed.; Leiden: Deichert, 1910), 350.

submit herself to and revere her husband.[501] This metaphor grows out of the relationship of Christ to the church in Eph 1:22, 4:15. Christ as head has authority over the church, but his main role in Eph 5 is to save and nurture it. The language in Colossians is similar: there, Christ is the head of the church in Col 1:18, 2:10, 2:19, which is his body. In 1 Corinthians Paul is thinking of the creation, anticipating what he will say in 11:8-9, that woman is the glory of man, and that woman (Eve) came from man (Adam). What then is Paul's point? Does he mean that Christ is the head of male Christians, but that female Christians have male Christians as their head? No, all members of the body of Christ, no matter the gender, race, social position, have equal access to the Father through Christ and through the Spirit (see especially Gal 3:26-28; Eph 2:18).That every man has the right to order around every woman, he being on a higher level of creation than she? Not at all, and Paul does not draw that conclusion. Rather "the head of the woman is man" is addressed to women and shapes their behavior before the church. Those women who wish to pray without a veil need to realize that they are obligated to glorify God in part by honoring "the men," that is their brothers in Christ. Neither man nor woman in Christ is an individual unit; each must come to Christ through serving the other. Thus on the other hand, Paul reminds the men: *if you are tempted to lord it over women, remember that you came from a woman* (11:8) *and that you too have to answer to a head, that is Christ, and to make very sure that you are reflecting glory to another, not to yourself.*

The head of Christ is God. Paul will later refer to the inner life of the Trinity in 15:27-28, where Christ rules as the Father's regent until all enemies are defeated; then "the Son himself will be made subject to him who put everything under him, so that God may be all in all." According to some commentators, this double reference of the Son's submission to the Father is no coincidence: supposedly the Corinthians had in their charismatic ecstasy exalted the Son to the robbing of glory from the Father. Thus Paul muffles them while being careful not to dampen their fervor (likewise, supposedly, in Phil 2:11).[502] This interpretation is wholly improbable. One must consider how Paul could expend so much energy on head coverings, then merely take a very light poke at what for him would had to have been a fundamental blow against monotheism.

Those ancient heretics the Arians, like their heirs the Jehovah's Witnesses, used 11:3 to teach that Christ was a lesser, created god, not co-equal with the eternal Father. The church fathers replied that headship does not imply that Christ is not God eternal; rather, his submission to the Father is either temporary and part of his incarnation (the so-called Augustinian view)[503] or eternal, but implying no inferiority (the Tertullian view).

Paul has so far said nothing here about the relationship between gender and authority in the church. How striking then that this is exactly what the Fathers inferred from 11:3. In the 2nd century, Clement of Alexandria (*Stromata* 4.8) uses the verse as proof that "as there is difference as respects the peculiar construction of the body, she is destined for child-bearing and housekeeping." *Apostolic constitutions* 1.3 §8 (4th century, but containing material from the 2nd) apply this text to wives: "Let the wife be obedient to her own proper husband, because 'the husband is the head of the wife.'" Later on 3.1 §6 gives our text as its reason for "We do not permit our women to teach in the Church, but

---

[501] Clement of Rome assumes that the Corinthian church of the late 1st century taught wives to obey their husbands (*1 Clem* 1.3) – "you charged the women to perform all their duties with a blameless, reverent, and pure conscience, cherishing their own husbands, as is right."

[502] See a description of this position by Thiselton, *First Corinthians*, 1237.

[503] So Fee, *First Corinthians*, 505.

only to pray and hear those that teach"; neither may women perform baptisms (§9). According to the 4th-century father Epiphanius, the Montanists ignored this verse when they ordained women as bishops and presbyters.[504] For our part, we must read what Paul says here and not import into this context teaching which Paul does not mention, that is, the role of women in leading the church.

11:4

Paul's conclusion that **every man who prays or prophesies with his head covered dishonors his head** was apparently meant to be a self-evident implication of 11:3; however, we must take into account that this was not the first time the Corinthians had heard something of this theme.

There are commentators who take this as a fictional case: that Paul speaks of men covering their heads only to balance off the real issue, that is, the women uncovering their heads. But this is no casual parallel that Paul tosses off here, but a point that he will go on to prove in 11:7a. Did men in fact ever cover their heads to pray in the ancient world? The parallel that most evangelicals think of is that Jewish men and boys wear a small cap called a *yarmulke* when they enter the synagogue, or draw the *tallith* prayer shawl to cover their head. Thus, Paul would be reversing the synagogue custom, making it part of the New Covenant that men approach God bare-headed.[505] This interpretation is undermined by the lack of evidence that Jewish men covered their heads to pray as early as the 1st century.[506]

The actual context for Paul's teaching is pagan practice, not Jewish: it was a Roman custom for men to wear a special head covering while praying or sacrificing.[507] There is even local evidence that this was the custom in Roman Corinth.[508] When he tells men to pray with head uncovered, his point is, "Don't dress like a pagan when you pray."

Prays or prophesies, that is, aloud in a worship service; prayer is addressed to God, whereas prophecy is a supernatural revelation, typically a message from God for the church.[509] The entire context from 1 Cor 10:1-14:40 has to do with the meeting of Christians, whether for prayer, prophesying, edifying or observing the Lord's Supper. Paul does not address private prayer as such, although one assumes that Christian man should not cover their heads then either. See our comments on 14:33 for whether women prophesied in the meeting.

Men should not pray or prophesy **with his head covered**, which is literally "down from the head," indicating something which is covering and hanging off of the head; a full veil rather than a minimal *yarmulke*. Since Paul contrasts it with "uncovered" in

---

[504] Epiphanius, *Panarion* 49.3 (Bray 107-08).
[505] See Morris.
[506] See Fee, *First Corinthians*, 507-08.
[507] Pp. 68-69, Richard E. Oster, "Use, misuse and neglect of archaeological evidence in some modern works on 1 Corinthians," *ZNW* 83 (1992): 52-73. See too Cynthia L. Thompson, "Hairstyles, head-coverings, and St. Paul: portraits from Roman Corinth," *BA* 51 (1988): 99-115; D. W. J. Gill, "The importance of Roman portraiture for head-coverings in 1 Corinthians 11:2-16," *TynBul* 41 (1990): 245-60; Witherington, *Conflict and community*, 232-35. In 238-40 he argues that both women and men were sinning by rejecting the Christian tradition.
[508] So Thompson, "Hairstyles." Hence Horton, *I & II Corinthians*, 100, is mistaken when he says that Paul forbad veils for men in Corinth because local custom made that shameful; in fact, local custom made that an accepted pagan practice.
[509] Contra Thiselton, *First Corinthians*, 826, who wants to make this prophetic *preaching* as well as inspired speech.

11:5, most versions opt for a translation of "covered" in 11:4. Some have also taken the covering not as a piece of clothing but rather a long head of hair, anticipating Paul's comment about long hair on men in 11:14. But, Paul seems rather to be making two sets of points: that women's long hair suggests the appropriateness of a veil; that men's short hair suggests that his head should not be covered with a cloth.

There is a word play in 11:4 and 5, between the physical human head and the Head who is Christ. This makes it difficult to know exactly what is dishonored when a man with a covered head, literally, "dishonors his head." One reading is that the man is bringing shame on his own head, that is, on his person. The better reading is that he who is the head of the man (Christ, see 11:3) is dishonored, something like "dishonors his Head." This shame is directed toward Christ, in the same category as "arousing the Lord's jealousy" in 10:22. For a man to wear a veil detracts from Christ's glory and offends Christ, because it is a pagan symbol.[510] As Cyprian stated in the mid-2nd century, men who stood firm during persecution refused to offer sacrifices to idols: "Your head has remained free from the impious and wicked veil with which the captive heads of those who sacrificed were there veiled; your brow, pure with the sign of God, could not bear the crown of the devil, but reserved itself for the Lord's crown."[511]

11:5

Up to the last phrase, this verse closely parallels grammatically 11:4. Woman is the glory of man (11:7). Yet if she is in the worship service, praying aloud or prophesying, and chooses to remove her head covering, she shames "her head." Since the verse is parallel to 11:4, the Spanish counterpart the NVI is right to translate "dishonors him who is her head" (deshonra al que es su cabeza). If the "head" of the woman is the man, than this refers to the men who are assembled with the church.[512]

Some suggest that this should be translated "she shames her own head," that is, herself. But Paul's whole point here is, again, that every Christian is duty-bound to lift up others. If women were shamed by uncovering their heads, would they not have been the first to feel shame? The point rather is that, you are shaming the men, whether you realize it or whether you even care.

We are dealing here with something deeper than fashion choice. Clothing, especially in ancient societies, conveyed strong signals about social position, self-consciousness and gender. Customs vary depending on place and time, but this did not mean that the signals are without meaning. For example, not many generations ago, when a girl reached a certain age and started wearing her hear bound "up," she was signaling that she was available for marriage. For younger boys, the purchase of their first pair of long pants was a visible step toward manhood.

In Roman society, a married woman or widow went out in public with her hair worn up and covered with a veil or shawl as a sign that she was faithful to her husband and not sexually available to men she encountered.[513] This was not the extreme form of the

---

[510] Witherington, *Conflict and community*, 233, 236.
[511] Cyprian, Treatise 3, "On the lapsed."
[512] So Hays, *First Corinthians*, 184-85.
[513] On the Jewish tradition, *m. Ketubot* 7.6 allows a man to divorce his wife without returning her dowry, "if she goes out [in public] with her hair flowing loose." If her hair is loose, the text implies, neither is she veiled. 3 Macc 4:6-7 NRSV shows how respectable newlywed women were shamed when they were forcibly dragged out in public unveiled – "and young women who had just entered the bridal chamber to share married life exchanged joy for wailing, their myrrh-perfumed hair sprinkled with ashes, and were carried

Muslim *purdah*, which might cover most of the face and head. Rather was a cloth or full scarf pulled up over the top of the head, falling to the back, past the neck. According to apostolic custom, a meeting of the church, though in a private home, was considered a public meeting to which people walked. A woman would arrive with her head covered; she should stay that way.[514] To remove her veil would embarrass all the men, and her husband, if she were married.

A century and a half later, Clement of Alexandria described how people should walk to church; his culture was similar to that of Roman Corinth:

> Woman and man are to go to church decently attired, with natural step, embracing silence, possessing unfeigned love, pure in body, pure in heart, fit to pray to God. Let the woman observe this, further. Let her be entirely covered, unless she happen to be at home. For that style of dress is grave, and protects from being gazed at. And she will never fall, who puts before her eyes modesty, and her shawl; nor will she invite another to fall into sin by uncovering her face. For this is the wish of the Word, since it is becoming for her to pray veiled.[515]

We understand more about how a woman might enter church in a Roman city from the church father Hippolytus:

> All the women should cover their heads with a pallium [that is, a covering like a cloak or shawl], and not simply with a [small] piece of linen, which is not a proper veil.[516]

Why would a Corinthian woman, in a meeting where women traditionally wore veils, want to take hers off? The explanation by Clement is unlikely in this passage: that she did so to sexually attract the men in the church.[517] Another, also unlikely, is that some Corinthian women were working themselves into a charismatic frenzy, literally letting

---

away unveiled, all together raising a lament instead of a wedding song, as they were torn by the harsh treatment of the heathen. In bonds and in public view they were violently dragged along as far as the place of embarkation." Plutarch, *Quaest Rom* 267a (translated by Conzelmann, *1 Corinthians*, 185 n. 40) says that according to Roman custom "it is more usual for women to go forth in public with their heads covered and men with their heads uncovered." His *Apophthegmata Laconica* 232c, shows that veils had to do with sexual or courtship ritual: "And concerning the question of why on the one hand maidens are taken out in public uncovered, but wives covered; 'Because,' he said, 'the maidens on the one hand need to seek a husband, but the wives need to guard what they have.'" [my translation]. There are plenty of portraits of women from Roman Corinth that show wives with their heads *un*covered (Witherington, *Conflict and community*, 234-35), but this is because the portraits did not portray women as they dressed to go out in public. Bruce W. Winter, *Roman wives, Roman widows: the appearance of new women and the Pauline communities* (Grand Rapids, MI: Eerdmans, 2003), proves that the portraits of the royal family were meant as exemplars, to show how a Roman wife should wear her hair. This disproves the theory that Paul was seeking to introduce an Eastern custom into the West; in fact, the head veil was common Western, Roman practice.

[514] Barrett is certainly correct when he says: "it is not a necessary implication of Paul's words that provided she does not speak she need not be veiled." See Barrett, *First Corinthians*, 251.
[515] Clement of Alexandria, *Instructor* 3.11.
[516] Hippolytus, *Apostolic tradition* 18.5, paraphrased by author.
[517] As states Pelagius (Bray, 106) explains that in Corinth the women "were flaunting their locks in church. Not only was this dishonoring to them, but it was also an incitement to fornication." Keener, "Man and woman," in *DPL*: 585, takes the same direction. Also Craig Keener, *Paul, women & wives: marriage and women's ministry in the letters of Paul* (Peabody: Hendrickson, 1992), 19-69.

their hair down, letting their veil fall, whipping their hair around as they prophesied.[518] This is how a pagan prophetess might behave, but it is hard to imagine Paul not censuring that sort of frenzy directly. Now does this hypothesis explain why Paul insists that men leave their heads uncovered. The best solution is one which fits very nicely with 1 Cor 7 and perhaps with 1 Cor 14: that some women in the church, fully enjoying their new equality in Christ and their right to pray and prophesy, wanted to do away with social custom. Just as some women in 1 Cor 7 wanted to refrain from sex or to abandon their husbands in an attempt to improve their spiritual lives, so some women – the same women? – wanted to disassociate themselves from their husbands in the worship service. A modern equivalent might be a woman who removes her wedding ring, because supposedly the commitment to one's husband takes away from a full devotion to Christ.[519]

Thus, women without veils and men with veils bring shame to their "head," but in different ways: women who reject their interdependence on men, or men who detract from the unique glory that belongs to the one Lord Jesus.

Paul makes another cryptic statement, that without a veil, **it is just as though her head were shaved**. He presumes the custom of women wearing their hair long in order to signal their femaleness. Sometimes a woman was shaved as a punishment for prostitution, a "Scarlet Letter" to tell the community what she was. If the Corinthian women were promiscuous, Paul would be saying: "Since you're acting like 'that sort of woman,' you should be put to shame like her!" But we have argued that it was not sensuality that was the problem, but an unchristian spirit of autonomy from other believers. Thus Paul is thinking of a shaved woman as unsexed: *If you really don't think it's appropriate for you to have a female commitment to a husband or general respect toward all the men, then why not cast away all womanly trappings?*

The idea that even in the church women should be women and men should be men may offend some modern people. But let us look positively on what Paul is saying: in the church, women and men remain women and men; husbands and wives remain such. Being in Christ, though guaranteeing equality among believers, does not mean the end of gender nor of marriage, both of which were part of God's creation before the Fall. There is therefore no need for women to assume that being independent or more mannish will in some way make them more Christian. Paul's word is: a Christian woman, dressed appropriately, can pray and prophesy aloud, shoulder-to-shoulder with any male in the congregation.

---

[518] Godet, *First Corinthians*, 541, wants to have "pray" mean *pray in tongues*, since that is the thrust of chapter 14; this is hardly necessary. Hays, *First Corinthians*, 182-83, interestingly, says that the problem was two-fold: women removed their veils, and also let down their hair; Paul rejected both. But if that were the case, then why does Paul seem to affirm that long hair was an appropriate natural covering? Hays asserts without giving any proof (185) that Greek and Roman women were not normally veiled. Morris, *First Corinthians*, 156, states that veils were a local custom, because Corinth was particularly licentious; but this is precisely the opposite of what Paul says.

[519] Conzelmann, *1 Corinthians*, 182, lends credence to this view when he says that female charismatics/enthusiasts removed the veil as a consequence of the doctrine that all are equal in Christ. Hurd's explanation is better, see *Origin*, 183-84: that although we do not know why women wanted to shed the veil there are plausible reasons – perhaps because they were meeting in private homes; perhaps because the veil seemed to promote inequality between the sexes.

11:6

He is being ironic: if it is Christian that a woman has a feminine hairstyle, then it is Christian for a woman to veil herself in the worship service. Paul's argument rests on the assumption that **it is a disgrace for a woman to have her hair cut or shaved off**. In some cultures today, women wear their hair as short as a man's, although typically in what is considered by the culture as a woman's style.

11:7

Back to the men in the worship service: **A man ought not to cover his head**. The man is **the image and glory of God** (not, as one would expect, *of Christ*; Paul is now echoing Gen 1:27). For him to worship with head covered is to rob God of his glory, by publicly appearing before the Creator as one would approach Zeus or Apollo. Paul first alludes to the creation of man and woman in Gen 1:26-27. Both male and female are in God's image, and both have authority over creation. Gen 2:18-23 provides the point of departure for the statement **since he is the image and glory of God; but the woman is the glory of man.** This is a point he will take up in 11:8-9. Taking Paul and Genesis together, it can be said at one and same time that the woman is the glory of the man, yet man and woman together are the image and glory of God. Both men and women, therefore, must take heed for God and for other human beings.

11:8-9

For man did not come from woman, but woman from man summarizes Gen 2:21-23, where Eve was made from Adam. In the text of Holy Scripture the woman came from the man (Gen 2:18, 20) to solve his isolation. Thus, Paul shows, the origin of woman is the cause for her living as the glory of the man, and not to shame the man. Gender differences are shaped by culture but also rooted in the creation, that is, they are ordained by God.

11:10

For this reason...the woman ought to have a sign of authority on her head. The NRSV and most versions make the "reason" the next clause, "because of the angels," but this is not the best interpretation of the connective *kai* – the NIV (similarly the NLT and CEV) is preferred, "For this reason, *and* because the angels are watching, a woman should wear a covering on her head to show she is under authority"; that is, there are two reasons for the veil. It is unclear is what Paul meant when he said that a veil is a "symbol of authority."[520] Whose authority is signaled by a veil? A traditional viewpoint, adopted by the Greek fathers, is that it signals to the world that she recognizes her husband's authority over her and her submission to him. This flows from the use of *kephalē* in 11:3, which apart from this verse is not developed in terms of authority-submission as it is in Eph 5.

The main alternative recognizes that the text says nothing about the authority of a husband; thus, the veil symbolizes the veiled woman's own authority. If the losing of the veil signaled moral laxity, then wearing it is a sign that she has sexual self-control.[521]

---

[520] In place of *exousia* in the critical text, some manuscripts substitute the easier reading *kalumma* ("veil"). *Exousia* is not only the *lectio dificilior*, and thus the favored reading, but also has strong manuscript evidence; it should be accepted as original.

[521] See the full discussion by Thiselton, *First Corinthians*, 823-26; also Fitzmyer, *First Corinthians*, 416-

We have argued against this approach to the text. Or it may mean that it is a sign that, woman though she be, also has the right to prophesy in a Christian meeting: it is a sign of her own right, not that of a husband.[522]

The way to unlock this difficult passage is to remember that effect must flow from cause: that is, that a woman must wear a sign of *exousia* because Genesis teaches that she was made from man, and for the man. The man is her *kephalē*, and her headwear should reflect that. This makes 11:10 more closely parallel to 11:3 but also to 11:5-6: her veil/long hair both signal the relationship of the female to the male. What is more – although Paul does not draw that point out – a man prays bareheaded as a sign of God/Christ's authority over him – not as a sign of the man's own rights.

Why else should a woman wear a veil? **Because of the angels** (from the Greek *angelos*). This too is a hard saying, and some scholars have tried to escape it by making the reference a later interpolation. Both the Greek *angelos* and the Hebrew *malak* can refer to either a messenger in general, or an angelic messenger of God. This is the same issue that affects one's interpretation of the "angels" (guardian angels? messengers waiting to deliver the epistles? pastors?) of the seven churches in Rev 2-3. If the Corinthian "angels" are human messengers or pastors, then Paul is saying: *every church practices this; if you don't, what will people from other churches think when they see Corinthian women with bare heads (cf. 11:16)?*[523]

The fact that the English versions prefer "angels" and not "messengers" is a reflection of how difficult it is to find human messengers in 11:10. But if Paul refers to angels, which angels could he mean, and why would angels pay attention to what the women are wearing on their heads?

One ancient interpretation looks to Gen 6 –

When men began to increase in number on the earth and daughters were born to them, the sons of God saw that the daughters of men were beautiful, and they married any of them they chose. [vv. 1-2]

In that case, perhaps Paul is thinking of evil angels who might be tempted to fornicate with women.[524] Thus, Christian women should wear a veil to ward off sexual attention, whether it be from men or angels.

Another reading is more likely, given that "angels" typically refers to holy angels rather than demons or fallen angels. The church is God's glory, not only on earth but also to the heavens. Thus, the angels of God are watching how Christians behave.[525]

17.

[522] Morna Hooker, "Authority on her head: an examination of 1 Cor 11:10," *NTS* 10 (1964): 410-16; also Fee, *First Corinthians*, 518-21.

[523] See Ambrosiaster (Bray, 108): "the angels are bishops."

[524] 2 Pet 2:4; Judas 6; several Jewish sources, including *1 Enoch* 15.2-3 – "And tell the Watchers of heaven on whose behalf you have been sent to intercede: 'It is meet (for you) that you intercede on behalf of man, and not man on your behalf. For what reason have you abandoned the high, holy, and eternal heaven; and slept with women and defiled yourselves with the daughters of the people, taking wives, acting like the children of the earth, and begetting giant sons?'" Likewise Tertullian, *On prayer* 22.5 (Bray, 108) – "because the angels revolted from God on account of the daughters of men." Tertullian, *Veiling of virgins* 7.2, uses this to argue that if married women need to wear a veil because of the demons, how much more should a lovely young virgin.

[525] The idea has its roots in the Old Testament, for example Psalm 137:1 LXX (138:1) – "I will acknowledge you, O Lord, with my whole heart, because you heard the words of my mouth, and before angels I will make

Why that might be a particular concern of Paul or the Corinthians is now impossible to determine.

11:11-12

The difference between 11:11-12 and 11:8 is striking enough that Conzelmann speaks of a "contradiction," and labels 11:11-12 "a note of retreat."[526] This is unnecessary, as Paul continues to affirm what has already been said. With **however** he signals that he is amplifying the part of the truth already stated. If anyone imagines that according to Genesis women are dependent on men, but men are free, Paul will now decisively close that door.

Does **in the Lord** mean to say that in the creation order, women are subordinate and derivative, but in Christ women move up to equality? Or is it epistemological, that "in the Lord" it is revealed to us that interdependence between the sexes is mutual? The latter appears to be the case here, since the arguments Paul will now adduce are the earlier one from Genesis (Eve being formed from Adam) and from nature (childbirth) rather than from the gospel as such. Yet, we know these things "in the Lord," not through natural reasoning or philosophy. Genesis, after all, is part of the revelation of God too.

The Greek text has no verbs, but only prepositions (see our comments on 1 Cor 8:5-6). We bracket the verbs that the NIV editors have added:

> **Woman is not independent of man,**
>   **nor is man independent of woman**
> **For as the woman [came] from man,**
>   **so also man [is born] of woman**
> **But everything [comes] from God.**

Once again, the referents are men and women, not necessarily husbands and wives. Eve was formed from Adam, and this demonstrates the interdependence of woman with man. Nevertheless, every man comes from a mother. The lesson for both men and women is that neither can declare independence from the other; both exist in and for each other. If any man or woman wishes to reject that order, he or she needs look no further than last clause: **but everything comes from God**. Paul thus affirms here a point that comes up with extraordinary frequency in Corinthians: the Christian does not live by himself or for himself; he or she lives for God, but also for the other. This principle shows the way when an "informed" Christian wants to eat idolatrous meat in front of a weak Christian; when a super-spiritual spouse wants to break off marital relations in order to pursue greater holiness; when a charismatic wants to display his gift of tongues to distraction in the worship service; when a Christian wife flings off her veil to prove to all her equality in Christ. No: we live to God, and God in turn tells us to live for the Other.

11:13

Judge for yourselves: is it proper for a woman to pray to God with her head unveiled? Some commentators believe that Paul is faltering, as if he knows that his case is weak, and so he must ask his readers, *Look at the facts: doesn't it seem as if my conclusion is the correct one?* In fact, Paul assumes that the Corinthians would believe

---

music to you." See too Walter; Robertson and Plummer, *First Corinthians*, 233.
[526] So Conzelmann, *1 Corinthians*, 190.

by instinct – be it cultural or genetic or by the Spirit – that of course it feels wrong to see a woman praying with bared head. He invites the Corinthians to review the facts and draw the proper conclusion.

11:14-15

Schrage demonstrates **the very nature of things** (*phusis*) could refer simply to what seems natural, given a set of cultural assumptions.[527] And so, rather than "nature demands long hair for women, short for men" a better wording would be "it does feel natural to you, doesn't it?" This is a helpful insight. For while there is a tendency among the world's cultures to follow the pattern of hairstyles, in some cultures men wear long hair, and women wear theirs relatively short, perhaps shorter than the men's. We cannot appeal to 1 Cor 11:13 to prove that these people are rebelling against nature by doing so. On the other hand, in Roman times, some men and boys wore their hair long, at times to signal that they were homosexual, at other times creating unwanted suspicions about their orientation. Some lesbians wore their hair very short for the same reason.[528] Thus for the men, wearing **long hair** means to send mixed sexual signals. The same was true of clothing, and thus it was forbidden to wear clothes of the other sex in Deut 22:5.

At the end of his argument Paul makes a statement over which modern commentators stumble and lose the thread. **For long hair is given to her as a covering** is usually taken to mean that long hair is nature's covering and thus wearing a veil is also natural for a Christian woman. Alternately, some take "for" (or "as") in its sense of "in place of a covering" (so GW), which might imply that a woman with long hair need not wear a veil. But if that were the case, why doesn't Paul tell the Corinthians to wear their hair loose, rather than the normal style of wearing hear pinned up? This interpretation only serves to confuse what has been said before, that women with long hair must also wear a veil in the worship service, with the implication that they wear their hair bound up under the veil – and this is precisely how women in the 1st century went in public.[529]

11:16

Paul, having appealed to the Bible, common sense, culture, nature now appeals to Christian custom: the Corinthian church should not create its new rules and reject the tradition that every other church follows. Perhaps the issue of veils was not so important to him. Nevertheless, it did matter **if anyone wants to be contentious** about the matter. Besides which, **we have no other practice – nor do the churches of God**, that is, no other custom with regard to men and women in the worship service.

We do well to follow Fee: "The distinction between the sexes is to be maintained; the covering is to go back on; but for Paul it does not seem to be a life-or-death matter."[530] In this epistle, other issues – notably the abuse of the Lord's Supper – are

---

[527] Also, Thiselton, *First Corinthians*, 844-46, who points out that the Stoics used the term to refer to "the order of how things are." Fitzmyer, *First Corinthians*, 420.

[528] There are striking parallels from the late 1st and early 2nd centuries: *Apophthegmata Laconica* 232.C.16-17, attributed to Plutarch but perhaps spurious: "'Why do [maidens and women] grow their hair long?' He answered, 'This is the way of adorning themselves that is natural (*phusikos*) and without cost.'" Pseudo-Phocylides, *Sententiae* 212, says that a man should not wear his long hair and braid it or style like in a delicately feminine way, as that is not fitting.

[529] As interprets Ben Witherington III, *Women in the earliest churches* (SNTS 58; Cambridge: University Press, 1988), 78-90.

[530] Fee, *First Corinthians*, 530.

much weightier for Paul. However, Paul does not (contra Fee) simply appeal to human logic and custom here; the bulk of his argument arises from his understanding of the creation as described in Gen 1-2. We must therefore conclude that for Paul the principle of headship in 11:3 is unchanging and must be reflected in the church. In his particular historical-cultural context, headwear was one way to signal that.

Let us stop and paraphrase this difficult section so as to highlight our own conclusions (we follow in part the lead of the New Living Translation):

But there is one thing I want you to know:
    Men are responsible to Christ,
    and **women** are responsible to **men**,
    and Christ is responsible to God.

Therefore, a **man** dishonors Christ if he wears something to cover his head
    while praying or prophesying in a meeting of the church.
But a **woman** dishonors men if she prays or prophesies in the church
      without a covering on her head;
    if she wants to rid yourself of gender signals,
      why does she not go ahead and shave her head?
    Yes, if she refuses to wear a womanly head covering,
      she should cut off all her womanly hair.
    And since it is shameful for a woman to have her hair cut or her head shaved,
      then she should wear a womanly covering.

A **man** should not wear something to cover his head when worshiping,
    for **man** is God's glory, made in God's own image,
    but **woman** is the glory of man.

How do we know all this? Because according to Genesis
    the first Man didn't come from Woman,
      but the first Woman came from Man.
    And Man was not made for woman's benefit,
      but Woman was made for man.
    So a **woman** should wear a covering on her head
      as a sign of her responsibility to men [or to her husband],
      and also because the angels are watching.
But with the Lord's new revelation to guide us, we know that the interdependence is mutual:
    women are not independent of **men**,
      and **men** are not independent of **women**.
    For although the first Woman came from Man,
      all **men** have been born from **women** ever since,
    but it's from God that everything comes!

Does it seem to you right for a **woman** to pray to God in worship without covering her head?
    Doesn't it feel obvious that it's disgraceful for a **man** to have long hair?

And doesn't feel obvious that long hair is a **woman's** pride and joy?
For it has been given to **her** as a covering.

But if anyone wants to argue about head wear in the meeting, all I can say is that
> we have no other custom than this,
> and all the churches of God practice the same custom.

Application: Christianity doesn't abolish social signals 11:16

Paul's point is that to represent Christ well in the world, Christians should take note of the signals they are sending out. In this case, the Corinthian men should have short hair and the women long hair and a veil.

Every human society has social signals, mute messages that help its members to communicate things about themselves. These change radically from culture to culture and over time and place. They can be very useful: they save billions of hours in unnecessary explanation:

- It used to be normal for widows to wear black. Likewise, men would wear black armbands. By this they showed their respect for the dead. It also signaled to others, *I am mourning a loss; don't joke around with me as if things were normal.*

- In some cultures, a wedding ring is a signal to others that we are romantically unavailable. In North America, beginning in the 20th century, men as well as women might wear them. People who remove their rings in order to hide their married state are considered deceitful.

- As a North American, I had to relearn certain signals when I moved to Costa Rica. For example, I had to be told that it was rude in Latin America to make eye contact with young women on the street. My own birth culture had taught me the opposite, that it is cold not to smile at and greet everyone I see.

- There are myriad signals that we communicate via tattoos; earrings, and on which ear; hairstyle; T-shirts; our manner of speaking.

Even though we are citizens of heaven, we still live in the world and we must pay attention to our social signals. Our Lord himself was famous for breaking some conventional rules, and sometimes we should as well (see Mark 7:2, 5; Luke 15:2; John 4:27; even John 2:10). But he always did so for a purpose: to serve the Father better, not to prove that he was "free" and that society could not rein him in. Like him, let us send a clear message to those around us, whether it is by word, action or mute signal.

4. Paul – And by the way, about your meetings: don't you know that the Lord's Supper should show the church at its most unified in love? 11:17-34

Christians read the words of institution of the Lord's Supper in the worship service. This is legitimate; nevertheless we must read the entire context of this section in order to understand why Paul inserted the tradition into the context. He did not write to the Corinthians to teach them why we have communion or with what words to introduce it. Rather, he was showing that the gospel of the cross, represented in the bread and wine, unites rich and poor.[531]

The Problem (as reported orally to Paul):
- When you come together as a church, there are divisions among you
- Some of you go ahead and eat without waiting for the rest. One overeats, another gets drunk
- Many among you are weak and sick, and a number of you have "fallen asleep"

Paul's Analysis:
- Those with plenty to eat and drink are shaming the have-nots and insulting the church, ignoring the implications of the Lord's death[532]
- When the meeting deprecates the have-nots, it is not celebrating the Lord's Supper as handed down by tradition
- These unusual illnesses and deaths in the Corinthian church are the result of abusing the Lord's Supper
- The divine judgment would stop if this sin were ended

Paul's Solution:
- When you come together to eat, wait for each other
- If anyone [rich] is hungry, he should eat at home

Not everyone perceived that there was a problem with the Lord's Supper, nor did the church write asking about it. Paul has heard about what is going on; his wording is from the perspective of the poor of the church and how it appears to them. Whether he heard this from "Chloe's people" or from others we do not know. Probably he refrains from giving his source because, after all, the poor have informed on their "betters," and that behind their backs. It is Paul who makes the theological connection between the disparity between classes in the church and the meaning behind the Lord's Supper. He might just as well have used baptism as his point of reference, if the link given by eating and drinking were not so near to hand.

---

[531] Similarly in Phil 2:6-11 Paul borrows or composes a Christian poem about the incarnation. He does so, not specifically to teach christology, but to teach the Philippians to be as humble and obedient, as Christ was.

[532] We are going to use terms like "rich" and "poor" to describe these two divisions. In fact the relatively wealthy of Corinth would be no more than middle-class by today's standards: those with adequate food and shelter, with enough to give a fancy dinner for a handful of close friends. The "poor" might include slaves or the working poor.

Fortunately the excavation of Corinth has shed fresh light on our text.[533] It was Roman custom for the relatively rich to give fancy banquets for their friends, often for the purpose of establishing their social status. The dining room (*triclinium*) of a private home was small, and by modern standards the space was not efficiently used: perhaps nine could be invited for a meal. The diners – typically all adult males – reclined on their left elbows on cushions or divans around a low table.

Let us speculate on what was happening in Christian Corinth: a congregation meets at sundown in the home of one of its wealthier members. But on Sunday afternoon prior to the meeting, the host also invites his rich friends over for a large meal. This favored circle eats and drinks, even to excess. Toward the end, the other Christian brothers and sisters would trickle into the home and wait outside the dining room, perhaps in the open-air atrium. They may have been laborers who have just come in from the field, or slaves who have come by permission of their masters. There was no time for these to get a meal, and perhaps they could not even afford one. But, they stand, sweating, tired and hungry, waiting on their social superiors to wrap up their party. Later at the meeting, they share the bread and wine of communion. For some this is their first food in hours; for others, it lies heavily on top of a huge meal and many cups of wine. The rich feel no disparity; the poor, meanwhile either feel insulted, or conclude that equality in Christ is merely a hollow slogan.[534]

Paul's tone changes drastically from the relaxed one of 11:2-16. It is at this point in the epistle that he reaches his high point of holy fury.[535]

11:17

Paul continues the epideictic style (see 11:2) with the negative: **I have no praise for you**, that is, in the matter that follows.[536] His next statement is news for all but a few poor Corinthians. Despite all their wisdom, spiritual giftedness and apparent prosperity, **your meetings do more harm than good**. Paul uses the verb "to meet" (*sunerchomai*) here in 11:18, 20, 33, 34; 14:23, 26 in references to their church meetings.

11:18

Paul speaks of the problem of divisiveness as **in the first place**. It is difficult to tell whether he ever gives an "in the second place," although 11:20 might be considered a second issue. The report that he has been told is that there are **divisions** in the church. Do these divisions follow the lines drawn in 1:11-12? Apparently not: the split here is along the lines of rich and poor. The leader of House Church A might war with those of House Church B over status in 1 Cor 1; but the leader of A is in 1 Cor 11 also abusing

---

[533] See Murphy-O'Connor, "House churches and the eucharist," in *St. Paul's Corinth*; Witherington, *Conflict and community*, 241-52.

[534] People at the same banquet could also face radical disparity, with the favorites receiving the better food and wine, see Martial, *Epigrams* 3.60: "Since I am asked to dinner, no longer, as before, a purchased guest, why is not the same dinner served to me as to you? You take oysters fattened in the Lucrine lake, I suck a mussel through a hole in the shell; you get mushrooms, I take hog funguses; you tackle turbot, but I brill. Golden with fat, a turtle-dove gorges you with its bloated rump; there is set before me a magpie that has died in its cage. Why do I dine without you although, Ponticus, I am dining with you? ...[rather] let us eat the same fare."

[535] In a striking parallel, James argues that giving the poor the lower places in the assembly is a blasphemy against the name of Jesus (James 2:1-7).

[536] Schrage, *An die Korinther*, 3:18.

those in his own church who have no status.

To some extent I believe it means that he is giving them some benefit of the doubt, since he had heard only one side of the story. Yet, he found the report entirely plausible, given what he knew about the church's striving for status.

11:19

No doubt there have to be differences among you to show which of you have God's approval: this verse is a puzzle, capable of two reasonable explanations. The first is that Paul sees in their situation an allusion to Matt 24:9-13. Jesus predicted that in this age, especially toward its close, the wheat would be separated from the chaff and the true saints would be made manifest.[537] This view has several problems: first, that there is hardly any eschatological reference in this paragraph. Second, it is hard to see how Paul would have applied that teaching to the Corinthian situation: after all, they were dividing among selfish rich and unfortunate poor. A twist on this view is that the Corinthians themselves were justifying their divisions by an appeal to the Olivet Discourse. Nevertheless, this sort of exegesis seems too sophisticated for the Corinthian Christians.

The other explanation suits better, although it involves the delicate procedure of attributing a slogan to the Corinthians (as in 6:12, 7:1, etc.). That is, Paul is quoting the Corinthian rich or else ironically putting words in their mouths: "After all, if there were no differences between us, how could we tell who really has God's approval?"[538] Thus, the rich were justifying their cliquishness by pointing to their own philosophical depth or even to their own wealth as a sign of God's evident favor. In that case, the divisions are social rather than theological. As in 1:10ff., Paul allows no rationalization for these divisions.

11:20

Paul uses an adjective which is translated **the Lord's**; *kuriakos* appears only here and in Rev 1:10 ("the Lord's Day") in the New Testament but throughout all of the Greek fathers.[539] It is related to the Greek term for Lord (*kurios*) and means "belonging to the Lord."

Two senses are possible for **it is not the Lord's Supper you eat**, although the final meaning is about the same. One is, *You don't come anticipating the Lord's Supper, but rather your own feast*. The other is more likely, that it means *It is not in reality an eating of the Lord's Supper since you are abusing its meaning so badly*. As the NET Bible puts it, "you are not really eating the Lord's Supper."

---

[537] So Hodge; Fee; Kümmel against Lietzmann, in *An die Korinther*, 185; Schrage; Witherington. Grosheide, *First Corinthians*, 266, says this means that the church should allow discussions and not force uniformity, but that is hardly Paul's point here. That Paul was allowing theological division was the nearly universal view among the fathers, who applied it to the sectarians of their own age. Tertullian in several passages, such as *Against heresies* 5; Clement of Alexandria, *Stromata* 7.15; Cyprian, *Unity of the Catholic Church* 10; Chrysostom, Ambrosiaster, Augustine, Vincent of Lérins and others (see Bray, 110). See Justin Martyr, *Dialogue* 35, who may, however, be quoting an unknown saying of Jesus rather than 1 Corinthians: "[For Jesus said] 'There shall be schisms and heresies.'"

[538] Thus Thiselton, *First Corinthians*, 840, renders it: "For 'dissensions are unavoidable,' it is claimed among you..."

[539] The actual phrase *kuriakon deipnon* is not at all common in the fathers, apart from quotations of 1 Cor 11:20.

11:21

As you eat, each of you goes ahead with your own supper, that is, everyone who is fortunate enough to have supper comes to eat a meal. It is not certain when this eating took place. Over the last century it was fashionable to view the occasion of this eating as the so-called *agapē* meal before communion.[540] But in Corinth, what was supposed to be a light meal of fellowship was turning into a feast, to which the rich brought meals and poor little or nothing.[541] Other scholars follow the very convincing view of Gerd Theissen, that the special guests came earlier, to have a banquet prior to the church meeting.[542] The poor workers and the slaves and perhaps also the women and children would arrive only to find that the "party" had started without them.

Some commentators, especially those of the early church, saw the Corinthian problem as one of gluttony and drunkenness.[543] While these faults were an additional offense, it is not this behavior but rather the dividing of the church that so grossly offends the apostle.[544] Nevertheless, we need not picture a wild orgy with **another gets drunk**. Wine would be served, and the problem was not the alcohol content – substantially lower than in today's wines – but the quantity that people would have drunk over several hours. At a formal meal people would slip so slowly into inebriation that they would not realize what was happening; meanwhile, a newcomer would size up the situation at a glance.

11:22

Paul is speaking to the wealthy of the church, since the luxury of having one's own house to eat and drink in was hardly common in Corinth. These few overeat and overdrink at their host's house. If they would instead eat and drink in their own homes, consecrating the meeting's time and place for holier use, the offense would be lessened.

Paul now draws a theological conclusion: *You rich may have never thought of it like this, but when you eat your fill in a boisterous exclusive dinner as a prelude to a worship service, you show contempt for* or **despise the church of God.** The language of epideictic rhetoric (see 11:2) turns passionate: **Shall I praise you? Certainly not!**

Application: How we show contempt the poor 11:21-22

One of the gross manifestations of the Corinthian elitism was that it made the poor feel

---

[540] Refuted by Thiselton, *First Corinthians*, 851-52.

[541] Clement of Alexandria, *Instructor* 2.2 wrote a detailed condemnation of the evils of too much wine. In the meetings of the church "always must we conduct ourselves as in the Lord's presence, lest He say to us, as the apostle in indignation said to the Corinthians, 'When ye come together, this is not to eat the Lord's supper.'"

[542] Theissen, "Social integration and sacramental activity," 145-74; so too Fee.

[543] See Clement of Alexandria, *Instructor* 2.1 – "some, speaking with unbridled tongue, dare to apply the name *agape*, to pitiful suppers, redolent of savour and sauces. Dishonouring the good and saving work of the Word, the consecrated *agape*, with pots and pouring of sauce; and by drink and delicacies and smoke desecrating that name, they are deceived in their idea, having expected that the promise of God might be bought with suppers. Gatherings for the sake of mirth, and such entertainments as are called by ourselves, we name rightly suppers, dinners, and banquets, after the example of the Lord. But such entertainments the Lord has not called *agapē*." Also many modern commentaries.

[544] So Schrage, *An die Korinther*, 3:57. He argues that the Corinthians held to an individualistic sacramentalism which focused on the individual's spiritual benefit. For his part, Paul shows that the Lord's Supper has implications for community and church.

like second-rate members of the body of Christ. Humanly speaking, it requires no effort at all to look down on the poor: unless active steps are taken, it will happen naturally and unconsciously. Such neglect may be manifested in all sorts of ways:

- the poor are blamed for being poor; they are told they must not have faith or that they are sinful
- people separate themselves from the poor because of their "bad vibrations" – their lack of faith might be infectious
- people are given special places in the church depending on their status
- the children of the poor are not invited to play with other children

What follows is a direct testimony from a Christian sister in Latin America, whom I asked to speak freely about her expectations of what it would be like to become a Christian, and then her actual status in the church and in its meetings:

In society being poor is not a pleasant thing, since to be poor is something like having leprosy, like someone who is not welcome in any place.

You don't have a good job. You don't have a career.

You don't have a good last name and you are not the daughter of somebody and you don't have a husband or anything that can back you, and you feel without hope, nobody knows you. Since you are not important for anybody you feel hopeless and you're almost at the point of giving up.

But one day you realize that there is a good God with much love for you and he can change your life and give you new hope where there was none and from then on you give Him your life and your frustrations!

But there is a big problem. You ought to congregate with others and attend a church and you believe that you will have a family and friends and everything seems very good. At the beginning they tell us that things are different inside the congregation. But the reality is far from the claims. Because you realize that it is not the truth, since they remind you right away, no, you cannot get ahead, you're different, you're not equal to the others. Very quickly they remind you that you are limited, and the saddest part of that is that it is very difficult to overcome. It is sad because some people told us that the Christians are different, they love you not for what you have but because you are the child of God and He makes no difference between people, we are all equal. But we poor do not have much to give, so we are not important for anyone. They receive socially children from good families, not the poor ones. They collect money for the poor in far-off places, but do not help us within their own church.

At the end of it all you remain with no desire for anything and totally without hope and you have two courses of action: you back off from everything, or you realize that you cannot be alone and you decide to stay but you are full of bitterness and pain for the rest of your life. At times it is hard to listen to them, because in my heart I am saying that their words are a lie.

It is the same way with my single friends. Some of them are very successful and they do much for the church, but they never belong because they have no husband or wife or children.

The congregation is divided into at least 4 or 5 groups:

1. The rich
2. The famous
3. The popular
4. The poor (where I am)
5. The miserable

During the meetings or fellowship times, everyone goes to the correct group. You need to know your position, where you are in relation to the others. If you do not know, people have little ways of reminding you. They say that you act like a rustic (a "hick"). And of course, no-one mixes, each one is where he ought to be.

If Paul were here, he would declare that this class tension is the enemy of the cross.

11:23a
The words of institution in 11:23-25 (and possibly 11:26) were not new information for the Corinthians. Indeed, his argument would carry little weight if they were not already fully familiar with the Lord's Supper. In fact Paul uses the language of oral tradition: *I received, I handed on* (*paralambanō/paradidōmi*, See 11:2) to introduce it. In keeping with the language of oral tradition, we need not understand **I received from the Lord** to mean that Paul heard it directly from Jesus by revelation. Rather it means that Paul received the tradition that had its start in the Lord Jesus.

11:23b-24
What follows is "a form of words which was regarded as authoritative in the church generally and was not Paul's own composition."[545] The apostle lifts his converts above the local squabbles and jealousies of Corinth and shows them how they fit into the redemptive history in which the whole church participates. The formula transports the church back to the night when **the Lord Jesus** was **betrayed** by Judas ("betrayed" is also from *paradidōmi*, but with a different sense than "pass on tradition, as in 11:23a; the word appears in Jesus' warning of the betrayal in Luke 22:21, among other texts).

The tradition of the institution of the Lord's Supper appears in two forms in the New Testament: the so-called Markan form (found also Matthew) is the shorter; the Lukan form is followed for the most part in 1 Cor 11.[546] Paul and Luke 22:19 include the three

---

[545] I. Howard Marshall, *Last Supper and Lord's Supper* (Grand Rapids, MI: Eerdmans, 1981), 111.
[546] Paul does not mention the first cup, nor that the blood is "poured out for you." Luke 22:19 however has only a single reference to "do this in remembrance of me," a phrase we twice encounter here in 11:24-25. Paul does not mention that Jesus "gave" them the bread.

actions of taking bread, giving thanks for it (*eucharisteō*), and breaking it.

The tradition itself says little about a doctrine of the atonement (see 1 Cor 1:30, 6:11), which is assumed rather than explained by the words of institution.[547] There is a textual variant here, all the more memorable since it is an oft-repeated verse. Some testimonies have "*broken* for you" (see KJV; the verb *klaō* is used in the gospel tradition only to say that Jesus "broke" the bread). The better manuscripts, which underlie the critical text, read simply **This is my body, which is for you**.

Do this in remembrance of me shows that the Lord's Supper, like the Passover meal, is a memorial of God's redemptive works.[548] This in itself does not prove that the rite has no other sacramental meaning, only that a memorial is a part of that custom. The Corinthians too needed to remember: that their Lord, Christ crucified, is the one who overturns the superficial wisdom of this age and breaks down the barriers between people.

11:25

After supper probably suggests that in the original Last Supper there was an interval after the breaking of bread. Churches have for two millennia celebrated the two parts of the Supper one after the other, and that may have been what the Corinthian church was doing already in the 1st century.

The phrase **whenever you drink it** (the cup) is vague in the Greek. It does not provide a guide to the frequency of observing communion, although ancient testimony agrees that the primitive church observed it every week.

The reference to **the new covenant** is likewise from the longer version of the eucharistic tradition. Luke 22:20 augments it further with "which is poured out for you," making an even clearer connection to the sacrificial death on the cross, with an allusion to the work of the Servant of Jehovah in Isa 52:13-53:12. Nevertheless, it is not from the synoptic tradition alone that Paul draws. In 1 Thess 4:1-12, for example, he shows a clear dependence on the New Covenant predictions of the Prophets, in particular Isa 30:20b-21; Jer 31:31-34, 33:14-26; Ezek 36:26-27.[549] Paul had been raised to believe that at the end of the age, God would break through into the history of Israel and endow his people with the Spirit, forever breaking their tendency to apostasy. What the rabbis could not have foreseen was that the Covenant would come about through the crucifixion of the Messiah nor that gentile Christians would receive its blessings. That meant that when Paul speaks of being "spiritual" in 1 Corinthians, he means that Jewish and gentile Christians are people "of the Spirit," benefactors of the New Covenant. They can live in the love which God commands, not simply because they have received good teaching, but because they have been changed from the inside out and "have been taught by God to love each other" (1 Thess 4:9, an allusion to Isa 30:20b-21 – "your teachers will be hidden no more; with your own eyes you will see them. Whether you turn to the right or to the left, your ears will hear a voice behind you, saying, 'This is the way; walk in it'"). In the New Testament, the New Covenant receives its fullest exposition in 2 Cor 3 and

---

[547] The eucharistic section of *Didache* 9-10 do not give the words of institution. Rather its intention is to give prayers for before and after the ritual.

[548] The reader is directed to seek out commentaries on the gospels and monographs on the subject for the debate over whether the Last Supper was a Passover meal, on which night it was celebrated, and which of the several Passover cups of wine was used for the words about Christ's blood.

[549] See T. F. Deidun, *New Covenant morality in Paul* (AnBib 89; Rome: Pontifical, 1981), a wonderful and underappreciated book.

Heb 9-10.

11:26

It is possible, given the eschatological focus and the non-Pauline vocabulary, that 11:26 was also part of an earlier oral tradition.[550] Every single commemoration of the Lord's Supper is to be focused **the Lord's death**. Given the theory of Corinthian over-realized eschatology, some take **until he comes** to be a correction, to remind the Corinthians that their theology must be oriented to the return of Christ.[551] But this is hardly necessary; both the Markan and Lukan eucharistic traditions already contained an eschatological reference (Mark 14:25 and Luke 22:16, 18). The early liturgical tradition in the *Didache* 11.6 makes the *Maranatha* ("Our Lord, come!" as in 1 Cor 16:22; cf. Rev 22:20) a part of the closing of the Eucharist. If it was Paul who himself introduced the eschatological reference, it was not to correct their theology but to remind that Corinthians that they will need to appear before Christ with this sin on their hands (as in 11:32, "we are being disciplined so that we will not be condemned with the world").

Application: How to celebrate communion 11:23-26

Communion has several functions. One of them is a memorial of Christ's death. That is, it is an excellent way to make each worship service centered on the cross of Christ for our sins (1 Cor 2:2) and not on the preacher's eloquence or on the beauty of the worship. Although we can preach about the cross, it is also excellent to see it acted out in the bread and wine. Another purpose is that it forces each believer to a spiritual crisis week by week: *I must now confess my sins if I'm going to participate.* But there are other functions: here in this epistle, it reminds us of the union of each member in the body of Christ (10:17; 11:33). Do your fellow Christians realize what a weighty sin it is to harm the unity of the church or to look down on the weaker members while they take communion? Do they know how grave it is to skip communion?[552]

In the Catholic church, the celebration of mass is the culmination of the week's services, and the worship service is often simply called "the Mass." Some Protestant worship services, too, focus on the sacrament, notably in Anglican churches. Yet most evangelical and Pentecostal churches are centered on music, worship or the sermon. In reacting against Rome we have badly drifted to an unbiblical extreme. Communion is normally not celebrated weekly; some have it monthly, some quarterly, some annually, some not at all. In the churches of the Two Thirds World, where the worship service may be two or three or four times longer than its northern counterpart, the time for communion does not expand proportionally.

Surely a healthy portion of a worship service can be carved out to celebrate the Lord's Supper every week. It can include a special time of confession, or a time of fellowship, or a time of silent prayer. What if it were announced, based on 1 Corinthians:

---

[550] Fee and Schrage say it was not part of the tradition.

[551] Schrage, *An die Korinther*, 3:47.

[552] Again, Calvin, *Institutes* 4.17.44, 1422-23, refers to the 4th-century *Apostolic constitutions* and shows that not partaking in communion could be grounds for excommunication in the early church. Anyone today who helps to serve communion is aware that many people do not participate, even though they are professing Christians. When someone skips it week after week, this should become a matter for pastoral counseling.

Look around, each one of you, at the people in this room. If you have any doubts about your relationship with your fellow Christians, then would you walk over to that person during this time and take whatever time you need to be reconciled. Or you could have people pray in groups or two and three and then take communion together. What if you had everyone spend time in praying the old prayer, "thy kingdom come," based on the eschatological aspect of communion, "until he comes"?

After all the investment of time and energy in preparing the worship and the message, do the leaders of the church heave a sigh of relief that at least communion is uncomplicated and can run automatically? So much may be done to restore the importance of the Lord's Supper, but only for those who are devoted to doing so.

11:27

Paul is now going to move his readers from the known tradition to his own prophetic interpretation of the Corinthian situation. His language becomes repetitive and builds up slowly. He speaks generally of partaking **in an unworthy manner**. Without pointing the finger, he draws his readers into agreeing with the general principle: those who desecrate the Lord's Supper are defaming the Lord and his sacrifice. **Guilty of sinning against the body and blood of the Lord** need imply nothing about the supposed real presence of Christ in the sacraments; after all, their sin was not in desecrating the physical elements, but in claiming to honor Christ's cross while shaming Christ's people.

11:28-29

Examine (*dokimazō*) is a term of judgment, the verb that was used in 3:13 for the end-time judgment of God. This verse partakes of the same tension as 4:1-5 – *yes, we should know ourselves, but God is the true judge and his judgment will not be revealed before the end*. Nevertheless God also gives an opportunity for self-examination in this age (11:32).

Examine himself is often taken from its context. We read it before the Lord's Supper, urging the communicants to search their own consciences before partaking. This is of course an excellent practice,[553] but in this context, the self-examination has to do specifically with sins against the spirit of the gospel: shaming the poor; excluding the powerless; making the commemoration of Jesus' death a chance to feast and to exalt oneself before others.[554] The Corinthians should step back and re-evaluate their whole attitude toward the cross, the gospel, communion and their brothers. This cannot be managed in a few seconds just before the plate is passed.

---

[553] For example Calvin, *First Corinthians*, 1:385, is surely correct however when he says, "Some restrict [the call to self-examination] to the Corinthians, and the abuse that had crept in among them, but I am of opinion that Paul here, according to his usual manner, passed on from the particular case to a general statement, or from one instance to an entire class."

[554] Clement of Alexandria, *Stromata* 1.1, is exactly in tune with Paul when he quotes our text to say: "But the imitation of those who have already been proved, and who have led correct lives, is most excellent for the understanding and practice of the commandments. 'So that whosoever shall eat the bread and drink the cup of the Lord unworthily, shall be guilty of the body and blood of the Lord. But let a man examine himself, and so let him eat of the bread and drink of the cup.' It therefore follows, that every one of those who undertake to promote the good of their neighbours, ought to consider whether he has betaken himself to teaching rashly and out of rivalry to any; if his communication of the word is out of vainglory; if the only reward he reaps is the salvation of those who hear, and if he speaks not in order to win favour: if so, he who speaks by writings escapes the reproach of mercenary motives."

Paul shows what sin in particular brings **judgment** to the Corinthians. It is that a person **eat and drink without recognizing the body**. This passage is often cited to prove the doctrine of transubstantiation, as if Paul were saying *they do not recognize that the elements have supernaturally become the real presence of Christ*.[555] But this is not the sense here: rather, it is the body of Christ that is the *church* that is not respected, the people that Christ's body and blood constituted. The Corinthians forget that the cross has made the poor and powerless one with the rich and powerful. As is typically Pauline, he takes what seems to be merely a social issue and demonstrates that it has deep theological implications: to exclude the poor brother is to deny what must be believed about the body of Christ.[556]

11:30

Paul and the Corinthians had both observed that **many among you are weak and sick, and a number of you have fallen asleep** in death. "Many" must be taken as "*relatively* many," or "a number of you." What that means relative to the membership of this collection of small house-churches is hard to calculate; it was nothing like the death of the 23,000 Israelites (10:8). Still, the Corinthians had begun to notice a disturbing pattern of illness and fatalities.

Not all illness is caused by sin, that is, it does not always come as a direct result of a sinful action by the individual. The Supper which symbolized life and health had become a poison for the offenders in Corinth. Yet it was not some magical effect; if this were true, it would have already slain so many Corinthians as to make Paul's warning come too late.

11:31-32

Again, Paul urges the Corinthians to scrutinize themselves to determine whether they have shamed their brothers. This is not simply an examination of their feelings, but of facts that perhaps have completely escaped their notice. Soards greatly weakens the force of this passage when he says: "[Paul] is explaining that he perceives God to be at work disciplining the members of the Corinthian church. Whether or not he is right in his conclusions," etc.[557] There is nothing of the sort in this text. Rather, Paul as apostle is telling them the truth, and he does not need to caution them "in my opinion." As one informed by the Spirit, he asserts that the illnesses and deaths would cease if the Corinthians would do this.

11:33

By offering a solution, Paul helps us to understand what the problem was. The verb **wait for** implies that those who arrive early should wait for others to come in before they eat; or alternatively that they take their meal in their home and suspend the banquet altogether. Paul's command that they wait for each other may seem like only good

---

[555] A Protestant too might argue that this has to do with respecting what the elements represent; see for example the Swiss "free evangelical" Godet, *First Corinthians*, 592-93.

[556] The view of Schmithals, *Gnosticism in Corinth*, 246, is that the Gnostics in that church rejected any kind of sacrament, since it represented higher, spiritual values through "base matter." This hardly comports with Paul actually says in this chapter, that their disrespect for Christ's body is social (against the community) rather than theological-sacramental (against the use of actual bread and wine).

[557] Soards, *1 Corinthians*, 248.

manners to us. However, it slashed directly against the social system of Roman Corinth, where the poor were at the disposal of the powerful, and the rich waited for no-one. Paul is telling the rich to leave behind their right to do what they please when they please, and to act as if the poor worker or slave were their equal in Christ.

11:34
He says, ironically, that those who are hungry can **eat at home**, speaking to those who have homes and who have food there to eat.

After the appalling list of sins with which he has already dealt in this letter, we wonder what could possibly have remained for Paul to correct. But apparently the epistle handles only the most urgent issues: "About the other things I will give directions when I come" (ESV).

5. Concerning the spiritual gifts: "Is it true that speaking in tongues is the surest sign of spiritual status?" 12:1-14:40

Now Paul returns to the Corinthians' written questions. In chapters 12-14 he will answer their request for guidance regarding the spiritual gifts. Chapter 14 implies that the gift of tongues was their main concern; the church as a whole wrote that Paul might refute a charismatic minority who were claiming too much for tongues.[558] We will use the term "ultracharismatic" to describe this group.

Speaking in tongues (or glossolalia) had become an end in itself rather than a means of serving the church. Paul affirms that, indeed, the gift is genuine and desirable. He is critical only when Christians use it for personal edification; who speak aloud in meetings without the church knowing what is being said; and who are disorderly in the worship service, striving with each other for attention and creating an atmosphere of confusion. If there is one adjective to describe these Corinthians, it is "childish" (see 13:11-12; 14:20). In their pursuit of personal spiritual fulfillment they were cutting in on each other and being unruly. It may be that women especially were at fault (14:33b-35).

As we have seen in the Introduction, some try to trace the various Corinthian problems to an enthusiastic or charismatic triumphalism that included an over-realized view of the eschaton.[559] In this viewpoint, those who disrupted the meetings with tongues were the same who gloried in their wisdom, boasted of being kings and thought themselves above the normal sexual conventions.

A stronger case may be made that this is exactly opposite what happened in Corinth, and that the abuse of tongues was a reaction *against* the elitism of other Christians. After

---

[558] Contra most commentators, who think the Corinthians wrote to request some test between true and false manifestations of the Spirit. In that case 12:1-3 would be the heart of Paul's reply. Hence Chrysostom, *i ad Corinthios* 29.3, uses 12:3 as a tool for discerning between pagan soothsayers and Christian prophets – "'When thou seest,' saith he, 'any one not uttering His name, or anathematizing Him, he is a soothsayer. Again, when thou seest another speaking all things with His Name, understand that he is spiritual.'" Schrage, *An die Korinther*, 3:126, says that the point of 12.1-3 is to prove that not all spiritual phenomena as such are of Spirit. Hurd, *Origin*, 192, is better when he says, "The three chapters form one long attack upon the notion that speaking in tongues was the single or the best manifestation of the Spirit at work in the Church."

[559] See Fee; Schrage. This view is taken by D. A. Carson, *Showing the Spirit: a theological exposition of 1 Corinthians 12-14* (Grand Rapids, MI: Baker, 1987), 16-17.

all, Paul has already urged the well-informed to reject earthly wisdom in favor of the Spirit's revelation. The poor had no such choice to make, since worldly wisdom was forever out of their reach. If those who ate fancy meals in Corinth were the upwardly-mobile of the church, then those who went without were those likely to be drawn into ultracharismatic experience. These were not partisans of any of the spokesman of 1:12; they were too marginalized to be involved in that competition. In that case, 1:10-4:21 had primarily to do with the upwardly-mobile; 11:17-34 was a rebuke against the same group in favor of those who went hungry; and 1 Cor 8-10 were directed to sophisticated Christians in favor of protecting the simple. But we will argue that at last in these chapters, Paul focuses on "the foolish things of the world…the weak things" (1 Cor 1:27-28). For they too are trying to compete with other Christians, albeit under the banner of charismatic excess.[560]

In a given community it is the Christian who has little to lose who will adopt an emotionalistic faith: the poor, the uneducated, the powerless, those who could rebel against the social competition of the elite by brandishing tongues in the worship service. Do the elitists compete by hiring philosophers, by making reference to important people or deep books, by trying to outdo each other in the meals they provide, in effect trading in the Spirit for an earthly philosophical wisdom? Then what better way to assert oneself against them by being people of the Spirit, Christians who are so close to the God that they are carried away in ecstasy. Part of the charismatic competition involved boasting or implying that one's own gift released the individual from dependence on other believers and from the duty of building up the church. Some may have even claimed that those who did not speak in tongues did not have the Holy Spirit or should not be regarded as real parts of the body of Christ.[561]

Paul's tone is notably kinder in these chapters than when he is rebuking the elitists. His strongest words to the ultracharismatics are: "Stop thinking like children" (1 Cor 14:20). Compare this admonition with the irony of 4:8, or the rebukes of 3:17, 4:21, or 11:22. Paul does not squash the simpler brothers, but gives them a gentle scolding, and directs them toward a better way. His point is that even the weakest member of the church can be empowered by the Holy Spirit; but this empowerment must and can be used to the blessing of the whole body.

Thus he launches into his fullest discussion of the work of the Spirit both in the meeting and in the broader life of the church. Paul's argument, while directed primarily against the ultracharismatics, would also have been applicable to every Corinthian Christian, rich or poor, speaking in tongues or gifted in administration. He argues first of all that every Christian has the Holy Spirit; that every Christian has a part in the church of Christ and deserves the support of every other Christian; that gifts are wonderful, but that all must be used in love, the highest good; that prophecy is preferable to tongues, being more directly useful to the church.

---

[560] See in particular, Finney, *Honour and conflict*, 192-95, and his discussion on the relationship between tongues and the conferring of honor on their practioners.
[561] Thus, we must disagree in part with Thiselton, *First Corinthians*, 799, when he says that "the 'gifted' seem hardly to care if less 'gifted' believers somehow feel estranged or second-class." Rather, the charismatically "gifted" overused their gift because they themselves had already felt estranged or second-class.

a. The key truth is the unity of the body as fostered by the one Spirit 12:1-31

12:1

Paul once again uses **Now about** (*peri de*) to introduce the next question, which concerns matters of the Spirit. The translation of the NIV, "spiritual gifts," is not the best. The Greek is literally *tōn pneumatikōn*, a form of the adjective he uses 15 times in this epistle and only 9 times elsewhere. In 12:1 the form could be either a masculine or neuter gender. If it were masculine it would mean "now about pneumatics/people of the Spirit" (as in 1 Cor 2:15; 14:37; Gal 6:1). But the key is the parallel in 14:1, where Paul uses *pneumatika*, which could only be neuter. It is best to render 12:1 "concerning matters of the Spirit."[562] The apostle's main interest here indeed is in the spiritual gifts (the plural form is *charismata*, 12:4[563]), but this phrase in 12:1 is more general. The spiritual gifts are not some magical power but rather the works of the person of the Holy Spirit (cf. 12:7, "manifestation of the Spirit"). Paul will impart information to them, as he signals with the disclosure formula: **I do not want you to be ignorant.**

12:2

The verb may be an imperative ("Know this, then!"), but as this remark is not new information, we agree with the NIV in rendering it as an indicative: already **you know**. Paul speaks to the church as mainly converts from paganism (as is implied in 8:7). The phrase **you were influenced and led astray** is difficult to render; the NIV offers the most likely interpretation. The statues that they worshiped were not simply symbols; even though they were speechless and impotent (see Isa 46:7), they had the power to deceive. Paul is thinking of the malignant powers that stand behind idol worship (1 Cor 10:20). This is not an extraneous observation but leads to Paul's next point: if any Corinthian has escaped from that deception, it was only through the powerful intervention of the Spirit.

12:3

Now at last comes the information that Paul anticipated in 12:1. He gives a two-sided message:

> No one who is speaking by the Spirit of God
> says, "Jesus be cursed,"
> and
> no one can say, "Jesus is Lord,"
> except by the Holy Spirit.

---

[562] So Nicoll; Godet. The Greek father Severianus takes *pneumatika* as neuter, saying that they are *tas tou hagiou pneumatos energeias* – "He now speaks of the *manifestations of the Holy Spirit*, which he distributes to each person according to his worth, to one evangelizing, to another prophesying, to another some other thing" [my own translation]. The NIV 2011 is an improvement on the 1984 version with its "the gifts of the Spirit."

[563] Ralph P. Martin, *The Spirit and the congregation* (Grand Rapids: Eerdmans, 1984), 8, and others define the *pneumatika* to the gifts having to do with worship, or the "charismatic gifts" by today's definition. Some argue that the term is the Corinthians', not Paul's. This could be true, but it cannot be proved from these chapters that *pneumatika* was a Corinthian term.

First Corinthians

He includes the two utterances *Anathema Iēsous* ("may Jesus be accursed"; in 16:22 and elsewhere *anathema* refers to God's damnation) and the ancient Christian creed *Kurios Iēsous* ("Jesus is Lord"; see Rom 10:9, Phil 2:11).

This reference to cursing Jesus was destined to mystify Bible students for the next two millennia, spawning, according to Thiselton, no fewer than twelve interpretations. Some scholars have imagined that Paul is referring to an actual ritual: there is a reference in Origen that indicates that the Gnostic sect the Ophites required their new initiates to curse Jesus.[564] Gnostics rejected the belief that Christ became incarnate; so they either rejected the real humanity of Jesus; or they pictured the spirit of Christ resting on a human man Jesus. Some scholars imagine that Corinthian Christians were cursing the human Jesus as a way to affirm his heavenly origin.[565] Alternately, it is theorized that while in mystical ecstasy, some Corinthians were uttering dark things of which they were unaware.[566] These theories lack credibility: not only is the evidence from Gnosticism late and also questionable, but these theories assume that Paul could spend three chapters regulating the practice of glossolalia, but only indirectly frown on a ritual or ecstatic cursing of the Lord Jesus.[567]

Rather, Paul's purpose is to make an absolute distinction between Christian and non-Christian, in the same way he does in Rom 8:9b – "And if anyone does not have the Spirit of Christ, he does not belong to Christ." Conzelmann is probably correct in saying that Paul here gives the formula *Anathema Iēsous* as something the unbeliever might say. It was designed to be the mirror image, the evil twin, of "Jesus is Lord." Nor was the idea created out of thin air: Paul says that he himself was a former blasphemer (1 Tim 1:13) and tried to get Christians to blaspheme against Jesus (Acts 26:11).[568] Only

---

[564] See Origen *Contra Celsum* 6.28; also from his commentary on 1 Corinthians (Kovacs, 198) – "there is a certain sect [the Ophites] that will not accept as a member anyone who will not curse Jesus."

[565] So Godet, *First Corinthians*, 611-15.

[566] So Héring; Barrett; Thrall, *I and II Corinthians*, 87, who think of a Christian resisting the Spirit of Jesus as it comes to take ecstatic control of him; as also states Allo. Contra this opinion Garland, *1 Corinthians*, 564-67.

[567] We agree with Hurd, *Origin*, 193: the Corinthians would presumably not need fresh guidance to know that cursing Jesus was wrong!

[568] See also *Martyrdom of Polycarp* 9.3, where Christians in Smyrna were invited to curse Christ in order to be delivered from martyrdom; to Polycarp the governor said – "But when the magistrate persisted and said, 'Swear the oath, and I will release you; revile Christ,' Polycarp replied, 'For eighty-six years I have been his servant, and he has done me no wrong. How can I blaspheme my King who saved me?'" From the early 2nd century, the *Letter of Pliny the Younger to the Emperor Trajan* 10 [http://www.earlychristianwritings.com/text/pliny.html] shows that in Northern Asia Minor those who were accused of being Christians were released if they would publically reject Christ: "Meanwhile, in the case of those who were denounced to me as Christians, I have observed the following procedure: I interrogated these as to whether they were Christians; those who confessed I interrogated a second and a third time, threatening them with punishment; those who persisted I ordered executed. For I had no doubt that, whatever the nature of their creed, stubbornness and inflexible obstinacy surely deserve to be punished. There were others possessed of the same folly; but because they were Roman citizens, I signed an order for them to be transferred to Rome. Soon accusations spread, as usually happens, because of the proceedings going on, and several incidents occurred. An anonymous document was published containing the names of many persons. Those who denied that they were or had been Christians, when they invoked the gods in words dictated by me, offered prayer with incense and wine to your image, which I had ordered to be brought for this purpose together with statues of the gods, and moreover cursed Christ – none of which those who are really Christians, it is said, can be forced to do –these I thought should be discharged. Others named by the informer declared that they were Christians, but then denied it, asserting that they had been but had ceased to be, some three years before, others many years, some as much as twenty-five years. They all worshipped your image and the statues of the gods, and cursed Christ. They asserted, however, that the sum and

an unbeliever can curse Jesus, or slander his gospel, or speak against the truth in this manner. It is a sin that parallels the "unpardonable sin" of blaspheming against the Spirit (Matt 12:31-32), the utter rejection and denunciation of the Spirit's work.

Paul was not saying that it is physically impossible for non-Christians to mouth the phrase *Kurios Iēsous*, or for Christians to say *Anathema Iēsous* aloud (after all, if the Corinthians were receiving this message from Paul, it is because some Christian in their church was reading 12:3 aloud to the congregation). He uses the phrases to distinguish between Christian and non-Christian, as he does in 12:13 – every Christian, no matter what his or her spiritual gifts, has the Spirit and is thus part of the body; no-one may claim to possess of the Spirit exclusively by experiencing glossolalia. Thus 12:1-3 is the foundation for what will follow in 12:4-30:[569]

I want you to think about what this means: that there are two and only two groups of people in the world:
1. Those without the Spirit, who reject Christ, the unbelievers
2. Those with the Spirit, who confess Christ, the believers

It is only by the Holy Spirit that anyone moves from cursing Christ to confessing him as Lord. Therefore, if your fellow church member has rejected dumb idols and turned to confess Jesus as Lord, then he has the Spirit and is one with you in the body of Christ. That implies that, whatever gift of the Spirit you or your brother possesses, it is given by the one Spirit. This is Paul's warning that the ultracharismatics in Corinth had better stop thinking that the others do not really have a part in Christ and the Spirit.[570]

12:4-6

He will now deal with the question: Do people who *don't* conspicuously speak in tongues have the Spirit, and are they necessary within the Body of Christ? Paul's style becomes highly repetitive, as if he were speaking to children (see 13:11). He will lay a theological foundation for understanding all the gifts before he focuses on tongues and prophecy in chapter 14. His formula, **different kinds of gifts** (*charismata*), **but the same Spirit**, will provide the theme throughout 12:30, after which point he intimates a new direction in 12:31.

Charismata (the plural form of *charisma*) in the technical sense of gifts of the Spirit

---

substance of their fault or error had been that they were accustomed to meet on a fixed day before dawn and sing responsively a hymn to Christ as to a god, and to bind themselves by oath, not to some crime, but not to commit fraud, theft, or adultery, not falsify their trust, nor to refuse to return a trust when called upon to do so. When this was over, it was their custom to depart and to assemble again to partake of food – but ordinary and innocent food. Even this, they affirmed, they had ceased to do after my edict by which, in accordance with your instructions, I had forbidden political associations. Accordingly, I judged it all the more necessary to find out what the truth was by torturing two female slaves who were called deaconesses. But I discovered nothing else but depraved, excessive superstition."

[569] This is also the view of Hays. Carson, *Showing the Spirit*, 30-31, wisely says of the theories about cursing Christ: "...most of them depend heavily on the presupposition that Paul is attempting a quick if rough criterion to enable his hearers to distinguish between 'true' and 'false' spiritual gifts. If we free ourselves from that and perceive that Paul's purpose lies rather in establishing who truly has the Holy Spirit, then the pressure to identify a precise and believable background is reduced...Paul's point is to draw a sharp contrast" between what Christians and non-Christians say about Jesus.

[570] With good reason the 6th-century Second Council of Orange (see Schrage, *An die Korinther*, 3:128) used this text, along with John 6:44 and Matt 16:17, as proof texts for an Augustinian soteriology: one believes in Christ through direct divine intervention which leads to free choice, and not through a natural freedom of the will.

is used in 1:7, 12:4, 9, 28, 30, 31; Rom 12:6; 1 Tim 4:14; 2 Tim 1:6; 1 Pet 4:10. Paul has also spoken of the *charisma* of celibacy and marriage in 1 Cor 7:7. The root of the noun *charisma* is *charis*, "grace."

There is clearly a Trinitarian reference underlying these three verses:

Different kinds of gifts (*charismata*)	but the same Spirit
Different kinds of service (*diakonia*)	but the same Lord [Son]
Different kinds of working (*energēmata*)	but the same God [Father]

Paul is not suggesting three levels of spiritual gift, as if some came from the Father and others from the Son. Rather, he is using the formula *Spirit, Lord and God* in order to drive home the (often-obscured) oneness of the church. This anticipates the same language of "Spirit, Lord, God" in Eph 4:4-6, where Paul demonstrates again the unity of the church of Christ. It is also reflected in the Trinitarian benediction that closes the other letter to the Corinthians: "May the grace of the Lord Jesus Christ, and the love of God, and the fellowship of the Holy Spirit be with you all" (2 Cor 13:14).

Different kinds of service (*diakonia*) reminds the Corinthians that their gifts are not given for their own enjoyment, but to serve others. In the third part, there is a play on words: the "workings" (*energēmata*) exist because, literally "God is active" in them. "'It is not as if you could complain that he was shown favor by the Spirit but you were favored merely by an angel. The Spirit showed favor to both you and him.' That is why Paul adds, 'but the same Spirit.'"[571]

The gifts are special capacities given by the Holy Spirit, so that each member might be equipped to build up the body of Christ. Through the spiritual gifts the individual is a channel for what God himself wishes to provide to the church: teaching, information, direction, discernment, healing, or other means of encouragement.

12:7

Each gift within these three categories may be labeled **the manifestation of the Spirit** [*pneuma*], bringing us back to the theme of this whole section in 12:1: *pneumatika*, "spiritual things," or better "things of the Spirit." **Is given** (the verb *didōmi*) reminds the Corinthians that they are the recipients, not the inventors, of whatever gifts they have.[572] These are all given **for the common good**; the word Paul here uses is the same he uses to speak of benefiting other Christians in 6:12 and 10:23 ("not everything is beneficial"; see also 2 Cor 8:10, 12:1 for the other two uses).

Grammatically, it is not clear whether **to each one** means that every believer has at least one spiritual gift; implicitly that is Paul's assumption. Notwithstanding his specific point here is that every single gifted Christian must acknowledge his dependence on the Spirit and his duty to the church.

12:8-10

Paul dictates no less than three lists of spiritual gifts in this chapter, not to mention the

---

[571] Chrysostom, *i ad Corinthios* 29.4 (Kovacs, 202). The 4th-century Macedonian heretic taught (like the Jehovah's Witnesses and other sects today) that the Spirit is not a person but a force. Gregory of Nyssa, *Against Macedonius*, argues from this verse that the Spirit, since he is one who makes decisions, is a person and not merely an impersonal power.

[572] See similar usage of *didōmi* in 1:4, 3:5, 3:10, 7:25; the same idea in 4:7.

lists in Rom 12 and Eph 4. The fact that one gift or another is present or missing from a list is an indication that Paul is tailoring these lists to his audience and not trying to give an exhaustive inventory.[573] For example, the gifts in 12:8-10 are almost all "supernatural" manifestations, unlike the emphasis in Eph 4:11.

12:8-10
message of wisdom message of knowledge
faith
gifts of healing
miraculous powers
prophecy
distinguishing spirits
different kinds of tongues
interpretation of tongues

12:28
apostles
prophets
teachers
workers of miracles
gifts of healing
help others
administration
different kinds of tongues

12:29-30
apostles
prophets
teachers
work miracles
gifts of healing
speak in tongues
interpret

It should come as no surprise that the spiritual gifts that keep appearing in this epistle are prophecy and speaking in tongues; "work miracles" also shows up three times. This reflects the local concerns of the church, and also paves the way for Paul's comparison of prophecy and tongues throughout 1 Cor 14.

Some of the gifts are fairly well-defined, but others are left as mere names. Two of the undefined gifts are **message** [lit. "word"] **of wisdom** and **of knowledge**. First, they appear to be distinct from each other and from prophecy, tongues and interpretation; second, we have no idea from the context what were their function; third, we are not told whether and to what extent they involve supernatural revelation; fourth, it is unlikely

---

[573] Martin, *Spirit and congregation*, 13, rightly adds that "we must allow...the sovereign Spirit to fashion new gifts for fresh occasions and special needs as they will arise in the life and service of the church..."

that the second gift is what Paul refers to later, that knowledge will "come to an end" in 13:8 (see our comments there). Many Christians have offered their own definitions which are not necessarily what Paul had in mind, but they are not strictly derived from the Scriptures.

Faith – every Christian by definition has faith, so this is an unusual expression of it, one would imagine, the ability to exercise trust in God in such a manner that, by definition, benefits the congregation.

Gifts of healing and **miraculous powers** are better-known to us from other passages of the New Testament (for example, Acts 5:12-16). Healing the sick is miraculous too, so it seems right to understand these as "miraculous healings of the sick" and "other miraculous deeds that are not primarily healing." Paul performed healings (Acts 14:8-10, 19:11-12; 28:7-9; probably in 20:10), and did other non-healing miracles: the blinding of Bar-Jesus (Acts 13:11); exorcisms (Acts 16:18; 19:12); being spared from a snakebite (Acts 28:3-6). Paul's team did "signs and wonders" (Acts 14:3; 15:12; Gal 3:5; Rom 15:19; probably also 1 Thess 1:5).

How do these gifts manifest themselves in the church? Does having the gift of "healing," for example, mean that the person may heal at any time, or only occasionally? Does the gift mean that any Christian may at any moment receive the power to heal someone, but does not necessarily have a lasting gift to be used at other times? This first list tells us very little, but the later context helps us along. First, Paul asks rhetorically whether in 12:29-30 whether all Christians have some particular gift. The implication is that some Christians do not possess and will never possess, for example, the gift of healing. Second, although Paul writes out a list of gifts, he will speak in 12:28 and Eph 4:11-12 of *gifted people*: a Christian has the gift of prophecy; he is therefore a *prophet*. This would indicate that the gifts become attached to specific people. Thus a quick glance around the room might reveal that the member with the gift of interpreting tongues does not happen to be present at a worship service (as Paul implies in 14:28). Third, having a certain gift does not mean that it is in use every moment. There are prophets who presumably come to the worship service without any message for that week; this does not make them any less a prophet (14:26; cf. 14:30).

Prophecy (see below, *Special Theme: Speaking in Tongues and Prophesying – what are they?*). The gift of prophecy is the supernatural ability to receive and communicate messages that are directly from God; it is not the same as preaching or teaching.

Distinguishing spirits. The New Testament sheds a little light on this gift:

> 1 Cor 14:29 – Two or three prophets should speak, and the others should weigh carefully what is said.

> 1 Thess 5:19-22 – Do not put out the Spirit's fire; do not treat prophecies with contempt. Test (*dokimazō*) everything. Hold on to the good. Avoid every kind of evil.

> 1 John 4:1 – Dear friends, do not believe every spirit, but test (*dokimazō*) the spirits to see whether they are from God, because many false prophets have gone out into the world.

In the case of 1 John 4:1 the discernment is a test of the teacher's doctrine: if someone pretends to give a revelation that denies the incarnation of Christ (1 John 4:2-3), then it is not of God but the spirit of antichrist. In 1 Cor 14:29 and 1 Thess 5 we are not told whether the testing is by supernatural discernment, or by a doctrinal litmus test or by some other means. The gift of discernment of spirits in 1 Cor 12:10 is likely a supernatural power of discernment.

Two early Christian works provide additional parallels. *Didache* 11.8-10, 12 probably contains tradition from the 1st Christian century:

> However, not everyone who speaks in the spirit is a prophet, but only if he exhibits the Lord's ways. By his conduct, therefore, will the false prophet and the prophet be recognized. Furthermore, any prophet who orders a meal in the spirit shall not partake of it; if he does, he is a false prophet. If any prophet teaches the truth, yet does not practice what he teaches, he is a false prophet... But if anyone should say in the spirit, "Give me money," or anything else, do not listen to him.

Thus, a true prophet practices as he preaches, and is not greedy for gain: he does not go into a trance and demand that money or food be given to himself. The same problem is treated in the *Shepherd of Hermas*, from the first half of the 2nd century (Hermas, *Mandate* 11). The test has to do with the prophet's character: the true prophet is humble, tranquil and not grasping; he takes nothing for his message. Meanwhile, the false prophet is proud and greedy. Thus both the *Pastor* and the *Didache* address the problem of people who act as charlatans for gain; what needs to be discerned is personal character. The fact that three canonical epistles and various fathers of the early 2nd century speak of the need for discernment is an indication that false prophecy was a regular occurrence.

Different kinds of tongues (See essay on *Special Theme: Speaking in Tongues and Prophesying – what are they?*). The noun *glōssa* is very similar to our English *tongue*; it may refer to the literal physical organ (Luke 16:24) or to a human language (Acts 2:6; Rev 5:9).

Interpretation of tongues. The gift of supernaturally translating or interpreting tongues is found only in 1 Cor 12, 14. On Pentecost, the disciples spoke in languages which expatriates who were visiting in Jerusalem understood as known dialects. In 1 Cor 12, 14 the interpreter has the divine gift of translating tongues into the vernacular, so that the rest of the church can then participate in the prayer or worship directed to God.

12:11

The key here is the constant alternation between **one and the same Spirit** and the diverse gifts. There is a rich variety in the possibilities, but only one Spirit. The spiritual gifts reflect the variety that God put into the original creation (Gen 1:11, 12; 21-22, 24-25; 1 Cor 15:38-41).

The new information that the apostle gives here is that it is the Spirit makes the decisions concerning the spiritual gifts, **just as he** [lit. "the Spirit"] **determines**. This principle must be placed side-by-side with other statements:

   12:31   "eagerly desire the greater gifts"

   14:1   "eagerly desire spiritual gifts, especially the gift of prophecy"

   14:13   "anyone who speaks in a tongue should pray that he may interpret what he says"

   14:39   "be eager to prophecy"

Taken together these references give us a full picture: the Holy Spirit decides according to his own counsel who will receive what spiritual gift; nevertheless a believer may desire and pray for one spiritual gift or another, not because they are more glamorous but because they could be of help to the church. Although the reader of 12:4-11 might infer a static situation, in which each believer has his gift and that's that, Paul goes on to imply that the Spirit might, if asked, bestow other gifts on a person.

12:12

In 12:12-26 Paul will go into great detail with the central metaphor of this section: One Body, Many Parts. The human body provides a parallel to **so it is with Christ**, that is, with what takes place in Christ's work in the church. He launches it with a chiasm:

   A   The body is a unit,
   B   though it is made up of many parts,
   B   and though all its parts are many
   A   they form one body.

Paul uses **body** (*sōma*) 18 times in these 15 verses. He has also used body language in 10:16-17 to underscore the unity of the church, and this may be the point of 11:29 as well.[574] In Rom 12:4-8 he gives much the same point, albeit in abbreviated form: that even with the variety of gifts, there is one body.

Colossians and Ephesians contain a further development of the body-metaphor:

   Eph 1:22b-23b   God appointed Christ to be head over everything for the church, which is his body
   Eph 2:16   this one body
   Eph 4:4   there is one body and one Spirit

---

[574] *1 Clem* 37.4-5 uses the body imagery (and also the metaphor of an army) to urge Christians to stay in their assigned place: "There is a certain blending in everything, and therein lies the advantage. Let us take our body as an example. The head without the feet is nothing; likewise, the feet without the head are nothing. Even the smallest parts of our body are necessary and useful to the whole body, yet all the members work together and unite in mutual subjection, that the whole body may be saved." Here as in 1 Cor 12 the head is but one more body part. *1 Clem* 46.7 alludes to 12:27 – "Why do we tear and rip apart the members of Christ, and rebel against our own body, and reach such a level of insanity that we forget that we are members of one another?"

Eph 4:12	so that the body of Christ may be built up
Eph 4:16	"from him the whole body, joined and held together by every supporting ligament, grows and builds itself up in love, as each part does its work"
Col 1:18	Christ is the head of the body, the church
Col 1:24	Christ's body, which is the church
Col 2:19	"from [the Head] the whole body, supported and held together by its ligaments and sinews, grows as God causes it to grow"
Col 3:15	Christians are members of one body

Now not only is the church the body, but the body has a head, who is Christ. Also the husband (Eph 5:23, not in the parallel teaching in Col 3) is the head of the wife, in a way that is further developed than what Paul teaches in 1 Cor 11:3. There is nothing in Colossians and Ephesians that Paul hasn't said in kernel form in 1 Cor 11:3; yet in 1 Corinthians, Christ is "the head of every man," not of the body which is the church. In fact, 12:21 makes clear that in this chapter, the head, along with the hand, the ear, and the foot, is but one more member of the church, not its Lord. The head as such is not even mentioned in Rom 12:4-5.

Paul's use of **parts** (*melē*) here and in Rom 12:4 is traditionally rendered as "members," which accidentally yields a play on words that is absent from the original. In English we use "members" to speak of parts of the body (arms, legs), but also for individuals who belong to a congregation. Paul does not intend that second definition, which would have been foreign to a Greek speaker. He refers to any distinguishable part of the body (ear, eye, head, foot, hand, nose, the "less honorable" [genitalia?]; see also Matt 5:29; Rom 6:13, 19; 7:5, 23; 1 Cor 6:15; James 3:5; 4:1). Eph 5:30 (cf. 3:6) uses "members" (*melē*) in a similar way as 12:12.

12:13

Paul now reasons backward from the present state of the church to its beginnings. The original goal of the Holy Spirit is not simply to baptize individuals with power, but to form a body: **we were all baptized by one Spirit into one body**.[575]

This verse is one of the key texts for the "baptism of the Holy Spirit." The few verses that mention it are not easy to harmonize.[576] This is made even more difficult by various statements in Paul's letters that could be interpreted as water baptism, Spirit baptism, or both (Rom 6:3-4, Gal 3:27, Col 2:12). Here are the principal references:

Matt 3:11 = Mark 1:8 = Luke 3:16 contains a saying of the John the Baptist that will become key in the synoptic gospels and Acts. Mark 1:8 – "I have baptized

---

[575] The NIV renders the Greek preposition *en* as "by"; it could also be translated as "in." Although much is made of the "baptism in" *versus* "by" the Spirit, there is no theological difference between them.
[576] J. D. G. Dunn, *Jesus and the Spirit: a study of the religious and charismatic experience of Jesus and the first Christians as reflected in the New Testament* (Grand Rapids, MI: Eerdmans, 1997), is still one of the best analyses of the theme. For a different view, see John W. Wyckoff, "The baptism in the Holy Spirit," ch. 13 in *Systematic theology*, ed. Stanley M. Horton (rev. ed.; Springfield, MO: Gospel Publishing House, 1994); also Michael Green, *I believe in the Holy Spirit* (rev. ed.; Grand Rapids, MI: Eerdmans, 2004), ch. 8.

you with water...but he will baptize you with the Holy Spirit." Matthew and Luke adds "and with fire." The meaning of "fire" is the judgment of Christ, not the tongues of flame that appeared over the disciples in Acts 2:3.

Acts 1:5 – Christ again contrasts John's baptism with the baptism of the Spirit: "John baptized with water, but in a few days you will be baptized with the Holy Spirit." The Pentecost account in Acts 2 does not mention the phrase "baptism in the Spirit," but rather "they were filled with the Spirit" (Acts 2:4). Nevertheless, since this is presented as the fulfillment of Acts 1:5 it is implicitly a recounting of their baptism in the Spirit. The disciples speak in tongues in Acts 2.

Acts 8:15-16 – "When they arrived, they prayed for them that they might receive the Holy Spirit, because the Holy Spirit had not yet come upon any of them; they had simply been baptized into the name of the Lord Jesus." The Samaritan converts believed and were baptized with water. However, the Holy Spirit did not come until the apostles came to lay hands on them. The experience that they were missing was "receiving" (*lambanō*) the Spirit, who "came upon" them (*epipiptō*). There is no reference to speaking in tongues, but that is the most natural cause for Simon's reaction in 8:17-19.

Acts 10:44, 45-47 – "While Peter was still speaking these words, the Holy Spirit came on all who heard the message. The circumcised believers who had come with Peter were astonished that the gift of the Holy Spirit had been poured out even on the Gentiles. For they heard them speaking in tongues and praising God. Then Peter said, 'Can anyone keep these people from being baptized with water? They have received the Holy Spirit just as we have.'"

Acts 11:15-16 – "As I began to speak, the Holy Spirit came on them as he had come on us at the beginning. Then I remembered what the Lord had said: 'John baptized with water, but you will be baptized with the Holy Spirit.'" Once again the Spirit fell upon (*epipiptō*) the first gentile Christians even as they were listening to the gospel message; they received the Spirit (*lambanō*) and began to speak in tongues; Peter cites the Acts 1:5 promise about the baptism of the Spirit.

Acts 19:4-5 – "Paul said, 'John's baptism was a baptism of repentance. He told the people to believe in the one coming after him, that is, in Jesus.' On hearing this, they were baptized into the name of the Lord Jesus." There is one final contrast between the disciples of John the Baptist and the Christians. These had not received (*lambanō*) the Spirit; when they were baptized in water as Christians the Spirit came upon them (*erchomai*), and they spoke in tongues.

Is it possible to harmonize these verses?

- "Receive" the Spirit/the gift of the Spirit (Acts 2:38, 8:20, 10:47, 11:17),[577]

---

[577] "Gift" here is *dōrea* rather than *charisma* in these four verses; the idea is "the gift *which is* the Holy Spirit."

likewise the Spirit "came on" someone; being baptized in the Spirit. All of these refer to one and the same experience. It occurs once and for all in any individual's experience.

- "Filled with the Spirit." There exists a contrast between Acts 2:4 and Eph 5:18. The Ephesians passage implies that a Christian should seek to live filled by the Spirit, that is, that it is a state rather than a one-time event. It may be the Acts 2:4 (and 9:17) is using "filled" as a one-time event, synonymous with "baptized"; or it is possibly using "filled" as a repeatable experience (as it clearly is in Acts 4:8, 4:31, 7:55, 13:9, 13:52) that nonetheless also accurately describes but is not limited to an initial experience of the Spirit.

- In Acts, the baptism of the Spirit is a reception of his power, and is frequently evidenced by speaking in tongues; in 1 Corinthians it is the initiation of a person into the invisible body of Christ. Some wish to argue for two distinct Spirit baptisms, but the texts indicate the one baptism of the Spirit has various results.

- The baptism of the Spirit is sometimes associated with water baptism, but is not identical to it. The Holy Spirit fell on disciples with no connection to water baptism in Acts 2:4; he baptizes gentile converts immediately before their baptism in water, in Acts 10-11; shortly after water baptism in Acts 19; some time (at least several days) after baptism in Acts 8; in an unspecified connection in Acts 2:38. Catholic scholars and some Protestants[578] wish to make 1 Cor 12:13 and the other Pauline verses references to the sacrament of water baptism, that is "through water baptism you received the Holy Spirit." This is nowhere specified in the Pauline texts, and it is contradicted by the Acts texts.

Paul goes on to use a phrase that is unique in the Scriptures: **and we were all given the one Spirit to drink.** It is not coincidental that Acts 2:13, 15 and Eph 5:18 draw a contrast between being drunk on wine and being filled with the Spirit.

Paul does not command any Christian to be baptized in the Spirit; this implies that all of his addressees had already been baptized in the Spirit. There is little room here for splitting hairs, to say, for example that every Christian *has* the Spirit (as states Rom 8:9), but is not *baptized* in the Spirit; or, worse, to speak of baptism *in* the Spirit and baptism *by* or *with* the Spirit.[579] Although these phrases look distinct in some versions, in fact they all represent similar Greek constructions. As in 1 Cor 12:3, the point of 12:13 is: *either a person has the Spirit, and is fully in the body of Christ, or does not have the Spirit and is therefore not a Christian.* His point in this verse makes sense first if all Corinthians had been baptized in the Spirit, and second if not all have the spiritual gift of tongues (12:30) nor any spiritual gift in common.

The apostle's design here is to stress the unity of God's work:

Don't misinterpret the obvious diversity in the divine empowerment;
the Holy Spirit has come to baptize us into one body,

---

[578] Barrett, *First Corinthians*, 289.
[579] As believes Horton, *I & II Corinthians*, 119; contra Dunn, *Baptism*, 150-51; Carson, *Showing the Spirit*, 46-47.

and though often not visible to the eye, that unity is the underlying essence of the church.

He now gives a typically Pauline list of disparate human beings, **Jews or Greeks, slave or free**, to demonstrate the unity of the body (see Rom 1:15-16, 10:12; 1 Cor 7:18-19; Gal 3:28, 6:15; Col 3:11). Discrimination against gentiles Christians is not at issue in Corinth, as it is in Galatians.

12:14-21

We will handle these verses as a group. The proposition, echoing 12:12, is contained in 12:14: **the body is not made up of one part but of many**. The church of Christ is like a body, and a body by definition is a combination of very different parts. Paul launches a series of rhetorical conditional questions along the lines of, *if this were true, what would happen?* These questions arise from the insinuation that "every member of the church should be like me, with the same gift."

That the ear is an ear and the foot a foot **it would not for that reason cease to be part of the body**. Quite the contrary! To be a real vital part of the body, the foot must do what feet do, and the ear likewise. The body and the church both need a variety of functions (12:17). Was it the case that some Corinthians devalued their own gifts?[580] Did the poor who craved the gift of tongues foolishly discount the spiritual gifts that they already possessed? Or are the jealous foot and ear representative of those who don't speak in tongues, and who are therefore rejected by those who do? We do not know, and the fact that Paul leaves us in doubt is perhaps for the best: on some occasion any Christian may doubt the worth of his or her spiritual gift; any Christian might wish to be transferred to another function in the body.

12:19 repeats the idea of 12:17, and 12:20 the main point of 12:12, 14.

12:21 explores further the thought of 12:15-16 – it is wrong for a member to depreciate his own gift, but now also wrong for one member to diminish the other: **The eye cannot say to the hand, "I don't need you."** This may be the closest Paul comes to revealing the attitude of the ultracharismatics, implying that they believed: *Because you do not speak in tongues, you are not a valuable member of the church.*

Here again, Paul introduces one side of the issue, which he will balance off in chapter 14, where he will argue that in fact some gifts better edify the church: "One who prophesies is greater than one who speaks in tongues" (14:5). The boastful members in 12:21 are in fact those who possess gifts that build themselves up personally. Therefore, not only can that member not reject another member, but that member must think in terms of respect for the body. It is a matter of indifference to be a hand or a foot; it is not a matter of indifference when a member rejects the concept of the body.

12:22

The point of this next paragraph is clear, even if we are not sure to what body parts Paul is referring. He is apparently going from the more to the less presentable as he moves from **weaker** to **less honorable** to **unpresentable** in 12:23-24. Common experience tells us that Paul is quite right about the importance of minor body parts. Those who have lost even one toe can testify what a difference that makes to walking; losing the tiny gall

---

[580] Martin, *Spirit and the congregation*, 20-21, thinks that both superiority and inferiority complexes were operating in the Corinthian church.

bladder likewise reminds the person what an important role a small member might play even when unnoticed – or even when a person is unaware of its very existence.[581]

12:23-24

There are weak members, but also members **less honorable**. He uses the adjective *atimos*, the very one he used of the dishonored apostles in 1 Cor 4:10. Paul generalizes about body parts which he would rather not name, but they still function as parts of the organism. **Unpresentable** is a euphemism, probably for the genitalia. Since they are not presentable we make sure that they're covered up (as in Gen 3:7, 10-11). In fact, it is God himself who arranges the church so that **the parts that we think are less honorable we treat with special honor**. Roman society did not watch out for its weak members, but exalted the strong and powerful. Giving special consideration to the weak – as we would, for example, by making a wheelchair ramp into a building – went against the Roman ideal. Even the emperor Claudius was for a long time excluded from public service because of his limp and his speech impediment. Christians on the other hand must watch out for weaker members of the church, since that is the very thing God himself does.

12:25

Thinking in terms of God's work in 12:24b, Paul shows the divine purpose: **so that there should be no division in the body, but that its parts should have equal concern for each other**. With a jolt, the reader leaves the biology lecture and finds himself transported back to the very real frictions within the Corinthian church. Mutual care is not some unreachable ideal; rather, Paul expects each member to avoid divisions and to live for the other. It is for the good of your brother, for the good of the whole, for your *own* good as a member of the body, and in accordance with God's pleasure. It is a statement like this that led us to conclude that Paul was being ironic in 11:19.

12:26

If selfless love does not motivate the Corinthians, perhaps this will: if another Christian suffers, then you as a member of the body also suffer. If he is honored (as opposed to humiliated), then you (as a member of the body) will rejoice along with him ("rejoice with," *sunchairō*, as also in 13:6).

12:27-28

Paul is now firmly back to the church, making sure his hearers will now draw the correct lessons about the spiritual gifts: **you are the body of Christ…God has appointed** the following. We now move from ears and feet to spiritual gifts that are familiar to the Corinthian church.

First of all apostles, second prophets, third teachers, then etc. It is debated whether Paul means "of greatest importance, apostles, of second greatest, prophets" and so forth, or whether he is just numbering off spiritual gifts without regard to their

---

[581] Augustine, *The usefulness of fasting* 6 (Bray, 127) is worth quoting at length here: "Aren't the hairs of your head certainly of less value than your other members? What is cheaper, more despicable, more lowly in your body than the hairs of your head? Yet if the barber trims your hair unskillfully, you become angry with him because he does not cut your hair evenly. Yet you do not maintain that same concern for unity of the members in the church."

importance. In fact, both are true: Paul can affirm the equality of the gifts, and also arrange them in order. Here the list is in descending order, according to their usefulness to the congregation. The apostles are invaluable, even though he has said that "God has put us apostles on display at the end of the procession, like men condemned to die in the arena" (4:9). By contrast, it seems significant that he mentions speaking in tongues last in the list; as he will go on to demonstrate, this highly-craved gift was the least useful for building up other people.

Let us compare this list with the one in Eph 4:11 –

1 Cor 12:28
apostles
prophets
teachers
workers of miracles
gifts of healing
help others
administration
different kinds of tongues

Eph 4:11
apostles
prophets
evangelists
pastors and teachers

The list in Eph 4:11 is shorter, but adds "evangelists" and "pastors and teachers"; the latter should be taken as one gift, the "pastor-teacher."[582] The fact that both places list apostle and prophet first – and that Eph 2:20 make those two gifts foundational to the church – suggest that their placement first is intentional.[583]

Apostles – An apostle is one of a limited group of people especially commissioned to represent Christ to the world and to the church. They are not identical to evangelists, pastors or teachers, although an apostle at times performs any of those functions. Many seem to have been pioneer missionaries (Rom 15:16-21).[584] We need to distinguish

---

[582] In Eph 4:11 the sense of "pastors and teachers" (*tous poimenas kai didaskalous*) has been debated. The word "pastor" has the definite article, "teacher" does not, and they are joined by the word "and" (*kai*). This, some argue, means that the Granville Sharp Rule of Greek grammar applies (as in Eph 5:5, 2 Pet 1:1 and Titus 2:13), and that there is a single gift, a "pastor-teacher." Others argue that, no, the Granville Sharp Rule is guaranteed to work only with singular nouns; these are plural, thus it must be two persons: *pastors* on the one hand, *teachers* on the other. In fact the Granville Sharp Rule *may* work with plural nouns, but it is only *guaranteed* to work with singular nouns. In the case of Eph 4:11 the Rule apparently applies to two plural nouns; otherwise there is no reason for Paul to have omitted the definite article with "teachers" (*didaskalous*). In short: Paul refers to persons who are "pastor-teachers" or "pastors who are also teachers."
[583] Yet how strange the remark by H. L. Goudge, *The first epistle to the Corinthians* (WC; London: Methuen & Co., 1915), 115, emphasis added – "The order in the enumeration is the order of importance...*It is characteristic of St. Paul to prefer what is orderly and rational to what is ecstatic and merely emotional*."
[584] In his commentary here, Ambrosiaster (Bray, 129) equates "apostle" with the office of bishop; that is not what Paul intended in this epistle. By definition, a bishop stays in a fixed location, whereas an apostle is

between the Twelve and other apostles. The Twelve was a specific set of men, and excepting the replacement of Judas before Pentecost, the posts were not filled when the apostles died. Acts 1:21 gives as the criteria for membership in the Twelve: "choose one of the men [from *anēr*, that is a man and not a woman] who have been with us the whole time the Lord Jesus went in and out among us, beginning from John's baptism to the time when Jesus was taken up from us. For one of these must become a witness with us of his resurrection." As for other apostles, Paul saw the risen Christ (1 Cor 9:1, Gal 1:16), but only after his ascension, and he did not accompany Jesus at all during his earthly ministry. Others were also called apostles too (Acts 14:4, perhaps 1 Cor 15:7; Rom 16:7) but were not enlisted with the Twelve. The apostles were especially endowed with the Spirit's power (2 Cor 12:12), but were also called to suffer in unusual ways for the gospel (1 Cor 4:9-13; 2 Cor 11:16-33). Apostles had the authority to teach and direct the churches.

The **prophets** are listed second after apostles. If it were not for 1 Cor 14 we would be hard pressed to explain what would elevate prophets so highly here and in Eph 2:20 and 4:11. Even in churches today that practice the gift of prophecy would likely place its value under that of pastor, teacher, missionary, evangelist or even administrator.

Teachers teach the Christian message, but do not necessarily hold an office in a church. **Help others** is not further defined. With the elitism of some in Corinth, it is likely that this gift would be ranked well below the others – a *charisma* suited to a slave or a woman, but not to a leader among men! **Administration** has to do with a person who holds a position of responsibility and management. Again are mentioned **work miracles**, **gifts of healings** and **different kinds of tongues**.

It is instructive that Paul classifies administration, helps, healings and tongues together as spiritual gifts. We do a grave disservice by labeling the miraculous gifts "charismatic" and then throwing the others into the category of "talents" or, worse, "mere human talents." There is a movement abroad today that claims that an "apostle" should have unlimited power, and that mere board members or administrators should have little. This strange idea, which claims to revive the Spirit's gift, in fact constitutes a rejection of those very gifts and a rejection of certain gifts of the Holy Spirit.

Application: Are there apostles today? 12:28

We live in a time, according to some, when God is restoring the office of apostle. For some this takes the name of New Apostolic Reformation, a movement associated with C. Peter Wagner. The drift of this commentary so far has already hinted that I reject the existence of modern apostles. But first, let us mention some fallacies regarding the gift of apostleship:

1. Some argue that all spiritual gifts must be operative in every generation. Of course this is the discussion that also has taken place over the last hundred years regarding all the so-called "charismatic gifts." But whereas in the case of tongues or prophecy there is no clear indication in the Scriptures that they would cease, it is different with apostleship. The only time anyone spells out criteria for being an apostle is in Acts 1:21 – they were to serve not just as proclaimers but also as eye-witnesses of Christ's resurrection. Paul affirms the same in 1 Cor 9:1 – he, an apostle, by definition had seen

---

peripatetic.

Christ. This event on the Damascus road was more than a simple vision of Jesus, which many Christians have had. His experience was a resurrection appearance.

2. Some argue that if there are false apostles today (and there certainly are) then there must be true apostles: for how can there be a counterfeit if the real article does not exist? Yet this logic does not hold up. I just read of a man who foolishly tried to open a bank account with a million dollar bill. The bill was false and counterfeit, but those labels do not imply that real million dollar bills exist (in fact they never have). To use another parallel, Jesus predicted that there would be false messiahs in the end times (Matt 24:5, 23-26), but that does not demand the *simultaneous* presence of the true Messiah *on the earth*.

3. Others argue that people who do things of an apostolic nature – pioneer evangelism, discipling, church-planting, miracles and healings, unusually influential teaching – are thereby apostles. Thus, we speak of Patrick as the apostle of Ireland. But Patrick's nickname is a good one if we take "apostle" in its broader sense of a pioneer missionary; no-one would place him on a par with the Twelve or with Paul.

Let us think through the phenomenon of modern apostles and see if they measure up to the biblical standard. The facts are alarming:

1. There are a high number of new apostles. If we consider that there were only a dozen apostles in the early church – and most died with a few years – there would appear to be a grossly disproportionate number of apostles nowadays, and the number is growing rapidly. One of Paul's points in 1 Cor 9 or in 2 Cor 10-12 is that apostleship is by definition a very rare gift. Would it really be expected that every urban center have its own apostle or even plural apostles?

2. Apostleship is being defined in terms of authority and control, not servanthood. Our constant enemy raises its head once again: even within the body of Christ it is a natural human tendency to want to dominate others. Some modern apostles testify that for them, titles such as pastor or minister didn't carry enough weight for what they wanted to do. But let us remember that the apostle John was content with the unostentatious "elder" (see 2 John 1 or 3 John 1). The new-fangled doctrine of "apostolic covering" has little to do with God's blessing, and much to do with yielding power and money to an already powerful and rich man. It is no wonder that these "apostles" are quickly gaining the reputation of being womanizers and swindlers: no-one has the authority to reprove them.

3. Modern apostleship has no link with the biblical teaching of apostolic suffering. True apostles are liable to suffer. Today, modern apostles talk about the energy they have invested in the ministry, the time and the effort. They speak of the personal rejections and emotional pain they have experienced. I suppose that I believe them; but on the other hand, who in any ministry cannot report the same? And missionaries who are serving in Muslim lands or in dangerous urban ministries run a much greater risk of real suffering than today's "apostles," who use jets and limousines to whisk them from one speaking venue to another.

4. Modern apostles give their attention to their own "priesthood" and *de facto* deny that all believers are priests and kings.

5. Modern apostles give out new extrabiblical or antibiblical teaching. Individuals are inventing new doctrines or changing the Bible's doctrine, particularly about the nature of spiritual warfare or of Christ's second coming. In fact, the very idea of a New Apostolic Reformation is proclaimed as a new teaching. In addition, the movement carries on this new doctrine of "prosperity" or "*rhēma*," an approach to power that has nothing to do with prayer and faith as the Bible teaches.

If we want to determine the real precedent of the New Apostolic Reformation, we should look no further than the Roman Catholic system. One of the pope's titles is "apostle," and he and the bishops are the authoritative interpreters of the Bible (*Catechism* §2034). He claims to have the power to do so just as Peter or Paul would have were they alive today. The pope also has the authority to appoint bishops in every city and to grant them apostolic authority. The modern apostolic movement follows that pattern with precision.

Thus there exist serious reasons doubting this new enterprise. But even more, we must remember that we serve a Lord who told us "If anyone wants to be first, he must be the very last, and the servant of all" (Mark 9:35). People who are most like Christ disdain power, titles, money, goods and illicit sex, and serve in humble ways.

12:29-30

Paul has not listed out the spiritual gifts because they were unfamiliar to the Corinthian church, but to show how they follow his congregation-as-body metaphor. They now provide the basis for the rhetorical questions that follow. It is not readily obvious in English how repetitive are these verses is in the Greek. Each begins with **Are all?** (*mē pantes*) then the position, starting with **Are all apostles?** From the context it is obvious that the answer is "No," not everyone is an apostle; or a prophet; or an interpreter, etc. After all this is the whole point of 1 Cor 12:17. What is more, the Greek construction that Paul uses removes any doubt that this is his intention. The Greek has two main negative particles meaning "no"; they are *ou* and *mē*. If a writer uses *ou* in a question, he is expecting a positive answer of "yes." If he uses *mē* he is expecting a negative answer of "no." Paul's use of *mē* here is the equivalent of saying: "Not all are prophets, are they?" (NET Bible; see also GW). This is why the CEV paraphrases the statement as "Not everyone is an apostle," etc.

Paul's main point arrives at the end: **Do all speak in tongues?** that is, "Not all of you speak in tongues, do you?" This may seem to contradict this that Paul says: "I would like everyone of you to speak in tongues" (14:5). After all, why would he say this if it were not in the realm of possibility? Or is he saying, "Every Christian has a supernatural prayer language, but I wish you could all speak in tongues in the congregation"? Two points need mentioning: first, when Paul wishes that all spoke in tongues, it is far different than believing that all could speak in tongues if they would only seek it. Rather, his meaning in 14:5 is, *I wish you all could, but you all can't! And besides, I'd wish other, better gifts for you if I could (prophecy!).* The other point has to do with the hypothetical "prayer language." Paul is speaking of private prayer and worship in 14:2, 4, contrasting it with the public blessing that comes through prophecy. People who speak in tongues speak to God, speak mysteries in the Spirit, and build up themselves. Paul wishes (14:5) that all Christians could have that experience, that is, the experience of having a special "prayer language" for their private devotional life. But in fact they do not and most likely will not. It is the Spirit's decision, not the individual's. The fact that a few are apostles; that some prophesy; that some are gifted administrators; that some and only some speak in tongues – this fact is a sign of a healthy church, for without this variety there would be no functioning body.

12:31

Should this be translated as a command (But **eagerly desire the greater gifts**, as the NIV and most versions), or is it merely an observation ("You only want the better gifts," GW)? Grammatically either one is permissible,[585] and so we are thrown back on the vocabulary used and the context to determine Paul's sense. The options are:

1. "You eagerly desire the greater gifts." If the verb is taken as indicative, then this might express Paul's disappointment with the Corinthians: *Here I am talking about serving the body, and showing that not everyone can have every gift, but you are lusting after showier manifestations for your own glory!* There may be a parallel in 14:12 – "Since you are eager to have spiritual gifts, try to excel in gifts that build up the church."

2. "Eagerly desire the greater gifts" is the better interpretation, see the NIV, most versions and commentaries. The arguments in favor of this are the parallel in 14:1: "Follow the way of love and eagerly desire spiritual gifts, especially the gift of prophecy," a thought that is repeated throughout chapter 14. Chapter 13 interrupts the point that Paul is beginning to make in 12:31a. When Paul returns to his argument in 14:1, it is naturally the same thought found in 12:31a and repeated as the conclusion in 14:39, "Be eager to prophecy." The verb **eagerly desire** (*zēloō*) in 12:31a may in other contexts have a negative sense of "lust after" or "carnally hunger for." Nevertheless, it may also be used in a neutral sense of "desire earnestly." Paul uses *zēloō* in this neutral way in 14:1 and 39 and its cognate *zēlōtēs* in a negative (or perhaps ironic) way in 14:12. Therefore either sense is possible in 12:31. However, the obvious continuity between 12:31a and 14:1 is key, and demands the imperative reading #2.

Thus Paul's lesson is a positive one: *there are in fact greater and lesser gifts; go ahead and seek the greater ones!* The reader must wait until 14:1 to see where he wishes to take this idea.

And now I will show you the most excellent way. "Most excellent" is strong language (see the use of this noun *huperbolē* in 2 Cor 1:8, 4:7, 17, 12:7 and other passages). It denotes something superlatively better, the highest good. Striving after spiritual gifts can be a positive goal, but there is something much better.

Let us be clear: Paul is not going to say that spiritual gifts are worthless or harmful or a distraction from the real Christian life. He does not state – as I hear too often – that the fruit of the Spirit should concern them and not the Spirit's gifts. He does not tell them

---

[585] In the present tense in Greek, the second person plural indicative and imperative are normally the same form, and could thus be confusing to the reader. Usually the context indicates whether the verb is meant as an indicative (a statement or a question) or an imperative (command). At times both possibilities make good sense. The most famous New Testament example of this is John 14:1, and most modern versions have a footnote to show the various possibilities.

to pursue love instead of the spiritual gifts. Rather, he will raise the (entirely valid) discussion of spiritual gifts to a higher plane, reminding them that they must be used in love. For Paul it is not acceptable that the Corinthians separate the spiritual gifts from *agapē*. Love is not an abstract; in chapter 14 he will show in very concrete terms how to use prophecy or discernment or tongues or interpretation in a loving Christlike manner. But before he lays down rules and principles he will make certain that every Corinthian knows that the highest principle is *agapē*, love.

Special Theme: Speaking in Tongues and Prophesying – what are they?

Today's Christians have been trying to define the meaning of tongues and prophecy. Naturally enough, people want to read their experience and theological framework into the text of 1 Corinthians (and Acts). The result is, if we added up everyone's experience for the last hundred years we would end up with every single possible interpretation of the biblical text. For our part, we want to know is what 1 Corinthians meant in its original context, so that we may apply it more carefully to our own day.

For this quest we have several resources: first is the biblical text itself, given as an inspired commentary on what was happening but also on a human level the closest witness of the early church. Secondly, the history of the early church sheds a great deal of light on the experience of the 1st century: the early fathers of the 2nd century claimed that prophecy and tongues were being experienced in their own day and they perceived an unbroken continuity with the practice of the spiritual gifts in the apostolic age. Also, the rise of the Montanist or "New Prophecy" movement in the 160's drew forth reactions from many church fathers, who offered comments on the true charismatic gifts even as they condemned Montanism.

The following questions are key for understanding 1 Corinthians:

Tongues:
1. Are tongues human languages, angelic languages, or unintelligible noise?
2. What is the relationship between tongues in 1 Corinthians and tongues in Acts?
3. Was the speaker "ecstatic," that is, in a trance or out of control?
4. What was the content of tongues?

Prophecy:
1. What is the nature of New Testament prophecy?
2. Was the prophet "ecstatic"?
3. What was the content of prophecy?
4. Was prophecy infallible?

Tongues:
1. Are tongues human languages, angelic languages, or unintelligible noise?

Outside of 1 Corinthians the only certain references to speaking in tongues are in Acts (2:4ff., 10:46, 19:6).[586] On the day of Pentecost the apostles found themselves in an

---

[586] The so-called "Longer Ending of Mark" contains a reference to glossolalia: "they will speak in new

unusual situation, speaking in tongues publically, during a festival that had drawn in Jews from all over the known world. The crowd responded that "we hear them declaring the wonders of God in our own tongues!" (Acts 2:11, reflecting 2:6 and 2:8). Later, in Acts 10:46 and 19:8 the Christian onlookers knew that certain people had received the Spirit when they heard them speaking in tongues; that is probably the implication of Acts 8:17-19 as well, even though tongues are not explicitly mentioned.

The majority view today is that Pentecost did not involve a miracle of speech but the miracle of hearing, that is, that God enabled the crowd to hear their own languages even though the speakers were not speaking in those languages.[587] This is an improbable reading from an *a priori* perspective: one would expect that a divine spiritual gift is not given to unbelievers, but believers. They do the miracle, and the others are onlookers. In fact, the text is clear that the believers "began to speak in other tongues" in Acts 2:4, *prior to and apart from* the point at which Diaspora Jews drew near and heard their own languages. This is the case in 1 Corinthians as well: in a congregation a person might speak in tongues, even when there is no-one who happens to know that language.

In Acts 2, it was due to special circumstances that foreigners understood the tongues as their own languages, without the gift of interpretation. Some have interpreted 1 Corinthians in the same manner, that the Corinthians spoke foreign human languages that needed an interpretation. But others have argued that the gift in Corinth is a different sort of experience. What is the evidence?

First, in 1 Cor 13:1 there is a reference to speaking in "tongues of angels"; some have taken this as the Corinthians were speaking in heavenly tongues that no human could possibly understand.[588] However, it is better to interpret the phrase as hyperbole (which Paul uses throughout 1 Cor 13:1-3), that is, he adds "tongues of angels" in order to boost the illustration well beyond normal experience. Paul probably knew that some Jewish mystics claimed to have heard the angels worship in their own heavenly language.[589] This may even be what Paul is hinting at when he says he was caught up to paradise and "heard inexpressible things, things that man is not permitted to tell" (2 Cor 12:4); this does not prove that he thought glossolalia was speaking in angelic languages.[590]

Another interpretation is that the tongues in 1 Corinthians were not languages at all, but some sort of ecstatic experience.[591] The speaker went into a trance and from a deep psychological level uttered random syllables and sounds. They are "mysteries" in the sense that the sounds have no intrinsic meaning.

The best interpretation is that in Corinth as at Pentecost, "tongues" were unknown, foreign human languages:

---

tongues." Although Mark 16:17 is missing from early manuscripts and is probably not part of the original text, nonetheless it does reflect the belief of the early church. The meaning of "*new* tongues" is not that the language were newly-invented, but that they were "new" to the speaker, who previously had not been able to speak it.

[587] Dunn, *Jesus and the Spirit*, 151-52 states that the disciples spoke with ecstatic speech on Pentecost, and that some onlookers *thought* they heard other languages, but their testimony was not credible.

[588] Witherington, *Conflict and community*, 267; Fee; Hays.

[589] The best example is in the *Testament of Job* 48-50, where Job's three daughters miraculously begin to sing praises to God in three angelic languages. This apocalypse is roughly contemporary with Paul. See Fee, *God's Empowering Presence*, 83.

[590] Contra many commentators, including Schrage, *An die Korinther*, 3:284, who says that this term can be "scarcely ironic."

[591] Nicoll, *First Corinthians*, 2:889; Thrall and many others. Thiselton's opinion is a variation of this view.

a. It would be highly unlikely that the early church knew of two distinct gifts that were both called "speaking in tongues." Thus, we would give priority to an interpretation in which Acts and 1 Corinthians refer to the same kind of experience with the same terminology.

b. Paul compares tongues to foreign human languages in 1 Cor 14:21: they have meaning, but the meaning is not known because the language is unfamiliar.

c. As with human languages, the tongues utterance means one thing and not another; without an interpreter an onlooker could say that "he does not know what you are saying" (1 Cor 14:16). If the utterance is ecstatic and nonsensical sound, by definition it has no meaning and the speaker is not "saying" anything. Tongues are not *per se* unintelligible noise (1 Cor 14:7-12), but only unintelligible in the sense that the content is not understood by anyone present. An interpreter is enabled to say in Greek what the speaker said in another tongue (1 Cor 14:14).

Therefore, tongues are "unknown" in most circumstances, but not (as the NIV implies in 1 Cor 14:9) unintelligible in absolute terms. They are "intelligible" to someone who, as in Acts 2, knows the language. We therefore agree with the ancient interpretation of which Chrysostom is representative: "So very many tongues used to go into one man; and he would pray and speak in tongues in Persian and Latin and Indian and in many other languages, while the Spirit was speaking through him."[592] Likewise Theodoret of Cyrus, who picked out what would have been foreign, barbaric languages for his examples: he who spoke in tongues might be "speaking the language of the Scythians or Thracians."[593]

2. *What is the relationship between tongues in 1 Corinthians and tongues in Acts?*

The one experience of tongues functions differently in Acts than it does in 1 Corinthians. In Acts 2, 10 and 19 the tongues show that the Spirit has fallen on people for the first time. We are never told in Acts how tongues functioned in the Christian's devotional life or in the church. By contrast, 1 Corinthians deals exclusively with the latter and says nothing about any initial experience of tongues.

There is a special issue that surrounds "Do all speak in tongues?" in 1 Cor 12:30, which we have shown to mean, "Not all speak in tongues, do they." This rhetorical

---

[592] Chrysostom, *i ad Corinthios* 25.1 [my translation]. Chrysostom took the position that a person with the gift of tongues could miraculously speak in multiple unknown languages, according to *In principium Actorum apostolorum* 3.4 [my translation] – "And the one who was baptized immediately spoke both in our language (Greek), and in the Persian, and in the Indian and in the language of the Scythians, so that even the unbelievers could perceive that he was thought worthy of the Holy Spirit." Yet in *i ad Corinthios* 29.1 [my paraphrase] he seems to say that each person spoke in just one language – "one immediately spoke in the Persian, another in the Roman, another in the Indian, another in some other such tongue." With regard to Paul, since he said that "I speak in tongues more than all of you" (1 Cor 14:18), this means that he spoke in more languages than anyone in Corinth; Chrysostom, again in *In principium Actorum apostolorum* 3.4 [my own translation] – "Let us see therefore how the apostle also had this spiritual gift (of tongues), and all others. Concerning this he says, 'I speak in tongues more than all of you.' Did you see how he spoke in various kinds of languages, and not only that, but that he had exceedingly more than all the other believers? For he did not just say, 'I can speak in tongues,' but also 'I speak in tongues more than all of you.'" Hodge, *1 Corinthians*, 277-78, gives an essay on why tongues are real languages; see also Godet.
[593] Theodoret of Cyrus, *Commentary*, 1:212.

question runs counter to what some Christian groups teach: that while everyone must speak in tongues as evidence of Spirit baptism, not everyone will have the permanent spiritual gift of speaking in tongues. Horton, for example, states the Greek present tense in 12:30 might be a "continuous present," as if it were "Do all continue to speak in tongues after their initial experience?" This reflects a basic misunderstanding of Greek syntax, where the present tense may be "continuous" but usually is not. Horton also ignores that the rhetorical questions about the other two gifts in this verse use the Greek present tense; yet Horton does not advocate a translation of, "Do all continue to have a gift of healing after their conversion experience?"[594]

Another theory is that each Christian speaks in tongues as a prayer language for use in private, but that not every Christian has the gift of speaking in tongues for the purpose of giving a revelation to the whole church. But nowhere does Paul differentiate between any such species of tongues: one either does or does not speak in tongues, and many Christian do not, never will, and should not be concerned about it. In 1 Cor 14 he assumes that people who speak in tongues in church should pray in tongues at home: he speaks of two functions of the one gift, but nowhere speaks of two distinct gifts of tongues.

3. Was the speaker "ecstatic," that is, in a trance or out of control?

Some scholars have compared 1 Corinthians with certain supposed parallels in the Greco-Roman world. They then argue that the Corinthians had brought in a pagan practice and were going into a trance to prophesy or to speak in tongues. Their babblings were unintelligible but sounded to any bystanders as supernatural. In the 2nd century, the Montanists prophesied in an ecstatic trance, bringing down the condemnations that their practice did not accord with the apostolic pattern.[595]

On the contrary, Paul insists that tongues speakers (as also the prophets) control themselves, and that they consciously seek the best edification for the church. "They are able to count the number of speakers, discern if someone is present to interpret, and curb the impulse to speak" if it is necessary to be silent (1 Cor 14:27-28).[596] The most that we can say is that some Corinthians who were truly speaking in tongues, were doing so in a pagan fashion. They were *acting as if* they were so possessed by the Spirit that they could not help speaking uncontrollably and overlapping each other. Paul puts this behavior down to self-indulgence. God the Spirit gives the spiritual gifts, and "God is a God not of disorder but of peace" (1 Cor 14:33).

4. What was the content of tongues?

In every instance in the New Testament, when tongues are interpreted it turns out that the words were "God-directed": people pray in tongues (14:14-15; possibly Rom 8:26, although it is doubtful that Paul is speaking about tongues there); sing (14:15); offer praise and thanksgiving (14:16-18). This fits well with tongues at Pentecost, where the onlookers heard "the wonders of God," that is, praise about God (Acts 2:11). By contrast prophecy is usually (but not exclusively) a message from God to man.[597]

---

[594] So Horton, *I & II Corinthians*, 123.
[595] See Eusebius, *History of the church* 5.16-17, quoted below in the section concerning ecstasy and prophecy.
[596] Garland, *1 Corinthians*, 569.
[597] Fee, *God's empowering presence*, 218 – "Although it is quite common in Pentecostal groups to refer to

The gift of tongues, especially as manifested in Acts 2, was God's way of reversing the confusion of tongues at Babel (see Gen 11:1-9). God scattered the builders by diversifying their language, making them unable to work together for their own human glory. At Pentecost God once again makes people speak in other tongues, but this time to draw in and unify the various nations to hear of God's glory.

Some opponents of the Pentecostal movement raise a challenge: *If you have a gift of tongues, prove it by going on the foreign mission field and speaking the gospel to them in their own language. Why spend years learning a language,* they taunt, *if you can just trust in God and speak the language automatically?* [598] From the perspective of the Word this idea makes no sense: the gift of tongues was not designed for use in missions. If in Acts 2 they served to attract an audience, the gospel message itself was preached in Greek. Conceivably a foreign visitor to Corinth might have heard his own language, but this is an atypical event which Paul does not explore.

Rumors abound of people recognizing a tongue as a language that they know. Many of these stories are "urban legends," fictitious stories with no known origin which circulate and evolve over decades. Everyone tells the tale as something that happened to someone they met in college or a "friend of a friend," but no-one seems able to give verifiable details. Many of us have heard or passed along the story of the missionary who is captured by African tribesmen. He is taken to the chief, and knowing his end was near, he kneels and begins praying in tongues. The natives fall strangely silent, they confer, and they let him go. Later on the missionary is told that he had been heard praying in the native language. I first heard this story in the 1960's; yet who can produce the confirmed testimony of the tribesman or the missionary, or report the details of how it happened? Such stories are extremely difficult to trace to a source, let alone to prove.

'a message in tongues,' there seems to be no evidence in Paul for such terminology." Contra Horton, *I & II Corinthians*, 133, who states that interpreted tongues might function the same as a prophecy.

[598] Pentecostals also toyed with this use for tongues, notably in the early 20th century. See R. P. Spittler, "Interpretation of Tongues, Gift of," in *Dictionary of Pentecostal and Charismatic Movements*, ed. S. M. Burgess y G. B. McGee (Grand Rapids, MI: Zondervan, 1988), 469-70. There is no indication from the biblical text that the primary purpose of tongues was foreign evangelism, see Dods, *First Corinthians*, 314-15. On the other hand, Theodoret of Cyrus, *Commentary*, 1:209, said – "To the divine apostles, on the other hand, the grace of the Spirit had given the knowledge of tongues, since being appointed teachers of all the nations they had to know the languages of all so as to bring the evangelical message to each in their own language." Theodoret is the only father I know of to teach this idea; other church fathers thought that the gift was to *remind* the church to take the gospel to all nations, but not to *facilitate* the mission to people of other languages. Eusebius, *Demonstratio evangelica* 3.7 [online: http://http://www.tertullian.org/fathers/eusebius_de_05_book3.htm], comes tantalizing close to Theodoret's viewpoint, but then backs away from it: the disciples communicated the gospel in the power of Jesus' name, not through tongues: "Whereas He, who conceived nothing human or mortal, see how truly He speaks with the voice of God, saying in these very words to those disciples of His, the poorest of the poor: 'Go forth, and make disciples of all the nations' (Matt.xxviii. 19). 'But how,' the disciples might reasonably have answered the Master, 'can we do it? How, pray, can we preach to Romans? How can we argue with Egyptians? We are men bred up to use the Syrian tongue only, what language shall we speak to Greeks? How shall we persuade Persians, Armenians, Chaldeans, Scythians, Indians, and other barbarous nations to give up their ancestral gods, and worship the Creator of all? What sufficiency of speech have we to trust to in attempting such work as this? And what hope of success can we have if we dare to proclaim laws directly opposed to the laws about their own gods that have been established for ages among all nations? By what power shall we ever survive our daring attempt?' But while the disciples of Jesus were most likely either saying thus, or thinking thus, the Master solved their difficulties, by the addition of one phrase, saying they should triumph 'In MY NAME.' For He did not bid them simply and indefinitely make disciples of all nations, but with the necessary addition of In my Name."

In addition we should take into account the many recent scientific studies of tongues. (1) They have yet to find a discernible human language; (2) utterances which have been reported to have "sounded like" one language or another turn out not to be those languages, when analyzed by those who know them; (3) when people speak in tongues they use sounds which are familiar to their own language, that is, they do not use vowels or consonants outside of their linguistic comfort zone; (4) the utterances of people have been shown to be identical to those of people who have been asked by scientists to *pretend* to speak in tongues.[599]

There are roughly 7000 known languages in the world today, plus undiscovered languages and many more dialects on top of that. It is conceivable that people are speaking real human languages but that they haven't been discovered. Yet the hundreds of tests that have been done in laboratory conditions indicate that modern tongues-speakers neither are speaking human languages, nor that they are not following the patterns of *any* human language; that is, they tend to be repetitive and lack the sort of framework that all languages have. This weakens the claim that Christians are speaking in real if unknown tongues, which is how Acts and 1 Corinthians define the gift. While we cannot rule out the genuineness of a spiritual gift by laboratory tests, still, it should make us pause to ask what precisely people are doing when they speak in tongues in private or in a meeting. The most reasonable response is that many are speaking "ecstatically," using the sounds that they come from their own first language. Whether God is working through that experience is for him to say; it is not the experience of the Christians in Acts and 1 Corinthians and has no solid biblical base.

Prophecy:

1. What is the nature of New Testament prophecy?

Some in antiquity and also in recent times have suggested that prophecy was a charismatic interpretation of the Old Testament, that it was "inspired exegesis." This is not a credible explanation, given that there is no biblical example of "prophecy as Bible interpretation." Nor is prophecy the gift of preaching, even of preaching a specially prompted message.[600] Preaching or teaching is the gift of presenting God's Word to others in a faithful and spiritually powerful manner. Prophecy on the other hand involves the receiving and giving of information that accords with the Bible but that is not a written part of it.[601]

---

[599] See the detailed article by Vern S. Poythress, "Linguistic and sociological analyses of modern tongues-speaking: their contributions and limitations," *WTJ* 42.2 (1980): 367-388. These data have been glaringly overlooked by Pentecostal teachers, for example, Ron Phillips, *An essential guide to speaking in tongues* (Lake Mary, FL: Charisma House, 2011), chapter 9: "Speaking in tongues and science." In five pages brings up and then discredits a single study and uses that to dismiss all such studies, showing no real acquaintance with the published reports.

[600] Thiselton, *First Corinthians*, 1017-18 develops a variation of this viewpoint in detail. Also Calvin, *First Corinthians*, 1:415: "Let us, then, by Prophets in this passage understand, first of all, *eminent interpreters of Scripture*, and farther, persons who are endowed with no common wisdom and dexterity in taking a right view of the present necessity of the Church, that they may speak suitably to it, and in this way be, in a manner, ambassadors to communicate the divine will."

[601] There is no better text than Christopher Forbes, *Prophecy and inspired speech in Early Christianity and its Hellenistic environment* (Peabody, MA: Hendrickson, 1997). He expands and corrects the view taken by D. E. Aune in his seminal *Prophecy in early Christianity and the ancient Mediterranean world* (Grand

In the New Testament, people gifted by God might speak a supernatural message to his people or to outsiders. A useful definition is:

> It consisted in occasional inspiration and revelations, not merely or generally relating to the future, as in the case of Agabus, Acts 11:28, but either in some new communications relating to faith or duty, or simply an immediate impulse and aid from the Holy Spirit, in presenting truth already known, so that conviction and repentance were the effects aimed at and produced...[602]

Much confusion has arisen from our modern distinction between *foretelling* (prediction of future events) and *forthtelling* (communication about the present). This is a false and unnecessary distinction: if prophecy is supernatural revelation, then it may take the form of predicting the future or speaking to the present (see below). For example, Paul predicted that the ship he was on would be destroyed, but that everyone on board would be saved (Acts 27:22-23). The early church father Irenaeus said that prophets in the late 2nd-century church prophesied about the present and also "have foreknowledge of things to come."[603]

2. Was the prophet "ecstatic"?

Some have argued that prophets went into a trance. That was what pagan prophets did, but this was not the gift of prophecy as Paul knew it. As with speakers in tongues, prophets too remain in control of themselves (1 Cor 14:26-33a). A prophet receives a revelation (14:30), in this case, while in the worship service. We are not told what this experience is like, but most certainly the prophet does not lose control. When one prophet signals that he has a message, the prophet who is speaking can chose to pause and to allow the second one to speak. Prophets can speak one at a time (14:31). They do not suddenly begin to shout, then wake up and ask, "What did I say?"[604]

Later, the 2nd-century church had wide experience with true and false prophets. They rejected prophets who went into a trance, since they regarded that as a pagan practice, counter to what the apostles taught. With regard to the sectarian leader Montanus, a certain Apollonius wrote:

> [Montanus] was filled with spiritual excitement and suddenly fell into a trance and unnatural ecstasy. He raved, and began to chatter and talk nonsense, prophesying in a way that conflicted with the practice of the Church handed down generation by generation from the beginning. Of those who listened at that time to his sham utterances some were annoyed, regarding him as possessed, a demoniac in the grip of a spirit of error, a disturber of masses.[605]

Another said:

Rapids, MI: Eerdmans, 1983). See also Witherington, *Conflict and community*, 276-81.
[602] Hodge, *I Corinthians*, 247. See also Godet, *First Corinthians*, 695-96; M. E. Boring, "Prophecy (Early Christian Prophecy)," *ABD* 5:496.
[603] Irenaeus, *Against heresies* 2.32.4. See also the predictions of the future by Polycarp, *Martyrdom of Polycarp* 16.2.
[604] This is possibly what the false prophets did in *Didache* 11.9, 12.
[605] Quoted by Eusebius, *History of the church* 5.16.

> ... But the pseudo-prophet speaks in a state of unnatural ecstasy, after which all restraint is thrown to the winds. He begins with voluntary ignorance and ends in involuntary psychosis, as stated already. But they cannot point to a single one of the prophets under either the Old Covenant or the New who was moved by the Spirit in this way – not Agabus or Judas or Silas or Philip's daughters; not Ammia at Philadelphia or Quadratus; nor any others they may choose to boast about though they are not of [the Montanist group].[606]

Origen also wrote that Christian prophets are conscious, and understand what they are saying:

> Moreover, it is not the part of a divine spirit to drive the prophetess into such a state of ecstasy and madness that she loses control of herself. For he who is under the influence of the Divine Spirit ought to be the first to receive the beneficial effects...and, moreover, that should be the time of clearest perception, when a person is in close contact with the Deity.[607]

3. What was the content of prophecy?

Unlike tongues, prophecy is usually directed toward human beings from God: predicting the future (Acts 11:27-28; 21:10-11); directing people to take specific action (Acts 13:1-2; 1 Tim 1:18 along with 4:14); revealing God's knowledge of what is hidden in the human heart (1 Cor 14:24-25); giving people divine encouragement (Acts 15:32, 1 Cor 14:3, 31). Prophecy could less frequently be praise directed to God (Luke 1:67-79, 2:36-38).

The role of the prophet often differs from that of his Old Testament counterpart.[608] In the New Covenant it is typically the apostle rather than the prophet who proclaims new doctrine. The prophet usually gives directions from God or else applies God's truth to a specific situation. Severianus said as much in regard to Acts 5:3-4 –

> There is a difference between ancient and recent prophets, as follows. The ancients prophesied about the redemption of Israel, the calling of the Gentiles and the incarnation of Christ, whereas recent prophets prophesy about particular things or people, as Peter prophesied about Ananias, for example.[609]

Nevertheless, the New Testament also contains instances where the Spirit gives a message which we would consider "doctrinal." Paul quotes "a word of the Lord" about the resurrection of the Christian dead (1 Thess 4:15) and later a "mystery" (1 Cor 15:51), probably both prophetic words. He predicts future apostasy with "the Spirit clearly says"

---

[606] Quoted by Eusebius, *History of the church* 5.17.
[607] Origen, *Contra Celsum* 7.3. In *Contra Celsum* 7.4-9 he contrasts true prophecy with the pagan and argues that the Holy Spirit beings clarity, not ecstatic confusion. Celsus had claimed (in 7.10) that Christian prophets were like those pagans: "to these grand promises are added strange, fanatical, and quite unintelligible words, of which no rational person can find the meaning; for so dark are they as to have no meaning at all; but they give occasion to every fool or impostor to apply them so as to suit his own purposes."
[608] Wayne Grudem, *The gift of prophecy in the New Testament and today* (rev. ed.; Wheaton, IL: Crossway, 2000), ch. 2.
[609] Severianus (Bray, 106, commenting on 11:4).

(1 Tim 4:1). The prophets in Eph 2:20 worked with the apostles to provide a doctrinal foundation for the early church.

As an example of applying truth that is already known, the prophets in Acts 13:1-2 did not invent the Great Commission; rather, the Spirit speaking through them set aside Barnabas and Saul for the task that had already been commissioned by Jesus. In the worship service, the prophet does not define new sins; rather, he reveals what sins are hidden in the heart of someone present (1 Cor 14:24-25).

When people today argue that, if God were giving prophecy, then this would have to be written up and added to the Bible, they reveal a distorted understanding of the New Testament gift. The 27 books of the apostolic literature are God's revelation to the church of all time. The church is not to write down and circulate prophecies such as "Julius is secretly visiting a prostitute and must repent" or "a certain widow who lives above the grocery store is in great need and you should help her." This is God's direction of a local church, not his Word for all time. That is why in the 2nd-century, when Montanists claimed to be giving prophecies on the level of the New Testament and wrote them down for publication, the church as a whole rose up in horror against them.

4. Was prophecy infallible?

Although Paul warns that Christians must take prophecy very seriously, he also wants the churches to carefully analyze prophetic utterances (1 Cor 14:29; 1 Thess 5:21-22). This accords very well with the instructions in Deut 18:18-19. In the Old Testament the penalty for false prophecy was death (Deut 18:22). The implication is that a true prophet will receive a divine message and communicate it accurately.

Wayne Grudem famously argued in *The gift of prophecy in the New Testament and today* (originally published in 1988) that New Testament prophecies are of a different kind. He studies the prophecies of Agabus from Acts and the warnings about discernment in 1 Corinthians and 1 Thessalonians. From these he deduces that Christian prophecies might be garbled in their transmission. While they arise from a genuine impulse from God they are not infallible, but that does not mean a mistaken prophecy is "false."

This is unnecessarily complicated. When Paul tells the churches to discern prophecy, he means to determine whether the content is true, whether the prophet is of godly character and whether the message accords with the apostolic doctrine. This is what happens in the majority of cases in the 2nd century (see *Didache* 11; Hermas, *Mandate* 11). In the prophecy imagined above – *Julius is secretly visiting a prostitute and must repent* – this can be compared against the gospel: yes, in fact, Christians already know that it is a sin to consort with prostitutes, and Julius should repent immediately. But there is no way in which this can be dismantled word for word, labeling some parts true and some false (1 Thess 5:19-20). Throughout the Bible, prophets who were "often" or "usually" correct were called false prophets.

Summary:

Tongues in Acts or in 1 Corinthians is a spiritual gift of speaking in an unknown human language. It may function as a sign of the Spirit's presence and serve as a private prayer language or as a means of declaring God's praises in a meeting. The gifted person spoke not knowing what he was saying. Despite what some Christians from the pagan world thought, the speaker was to remain under his own control. Paul's only objection to uninterpreted tongues was that while they made the speaker feel close to God, they did not help Christians, which was the purpose of every spiritual gift.

Prophecy might be praise directed toward God but is usually a message from God to humans. It is directly inspired by God, and prophecy is either all true or it is false. In the New Testament, prophecy usually functions on a more personal and local level than in the Old. The prophet senses when something is revealed to him, and he does not lose control or consciousness. He can share the word when he wants.

PARENTHESIS – PAUL'S GENERALIZING PARANAESIS (*engressio*): THEIR ROOT PROBLEM IS A LACK OF *AGAPĒ*. WITH LOVE, ALL THESE PROBLEMS ABOUT CHARISMATIC GIFTS WOULD RESOLVE THEMSELVES 13:1-13

1 Cor 13 is a popular text for weddings; it was read aloud at the wedding of Prince Charles and Lady Diana in 1981. It was a shameful indication of Bible illiteracy that many wrote in to ask where they might get a copy of that lovely poem!

This chapter is as beautifully poetic as anything Paul has written, but it is not a mere literary adornment. It is *paranaesis*, that is, a parenthesis that broadens and generalizes the ethical instruction of the section in which it is found. It is just possible that Paul wrote something like this text for another occasion and quoted it here. Nevertheless, he very specifically adapted it to the Corinthians' situation and it cannot be exegeted out of its context.[610] Paul writes that "love is patient, love is kind. It does not envy, it does not boast, it is not proud, etc.," because the Corinthians were notably not patient or kind, and were envious, boastful and proud. The emphasis on love here is *horizontal*, that is, how one treats fellow Christians and other people. Paul speaks to the ultracharismatics in 13:8-11, but his general message applies to all Corinthians.

13:1

Paul begins with a series of conditional sentences: even if a Christian were to experience dazzling charismatic endowments or to make extreme sacrifices, these would still be nothing if I **do not have love**.[611] He uses the word he normally uses for love, that is, *agapē*. The noun appears 116 times in the NT, the verb *agapaō* 143 times, plus several other cognate words such as "beloved" (*agapētos*).[612] Contrary to popular belief, the

---

[610]Contra Conzelmann, *1 Corinthians*, 217-18. Héring, *First Corinthians*, 134, argues that chapter 13 is a later interpolation (of a genuine Pauline text) and that 14:1 is the editor's attempt to smooth the transition; see also Weiss, *Korintherbrief*, 309-16. In favor of reading it as an integral part of the context, see Calvin, Schrage, Fee, Grosheide, most commentaries.

[611] Schrage, *An die Korinther*, 3:283, is correct when he says that "I" is rhetorical rather than personal, just like the "we" in 9:12.

[612] Pagans used the term *agapaō* (see, for example, Homer); it is the content of the Christian message of love, not the word itself, that made it unique in the ancient world. A century and a half ago, Hodge, *I Corinthians*, 265, could still claim that there was no evidence that the Greeks had used the noun form, and conclude that "the Greek word *agapē* is not of pagan origin. The heathen had no concept of the grace that in the Scripture is expressed by this word." Such a view is untenable for two reasons: first, it is fallacious to confuse "word" with "concept," as if the word *agapē* could not exist without special revelation. If that were

word *agapē* was not a Christian innovation; nor was it invented by the Jewish translators of the Septuagint (as claims Thayer's *Lexicon*).[613] The word does not always refer to divine love or selfless love. It could be used of love for one's wife or neighbor; or love for God. The word group may also be used for low desires, such as love of human honor (Luke 11:43, John 12:43) or this world (2 Tim 4:10, 1 John 2:15) or darkness (John 3:19).[614] Here of course it is used to denote Christian love, which is made possible only in the gospel and through the Holy Spirit (as in Gal 5:22). Paul has already showed the importance of *agapē* over mere human reasoning (1 Cor 8:1); now he exalts love even above supernaturally revealed knowledge.

The interpretation of this section is complicated by several factors: first, the difficult statement **if I hand over my body so that I may boast** contains a textual variant; second, Paul is speaking poetically and it is not certain what is literal and what is hyperbole, that is, exaggeration for the sake of emphasis.

The question of hyperbole appears immediately: **If I speak in the tongues of mortals** [better "of humans"] **and of angels**. He uses the normal term for tongues[615] and is referring to the spiritual gift that is the theme of this section. We have argued above that Paul thinks of glossolalia as foreign *human* languages that are at least potentially knowable by some person. His point in this verse is exaggerated and hypothetical, as it is in all three verses: *If I speak supernaturally in all kinds of human tongues, or even if I spoke in angel languages, it would mean nothing without love!*[616]

Paul's hyperbole extends to "have not love." Surely even the most pitiful Corinthian occasionally manifested some love. But Paul is not interested in quantifying how much love one should have: for the sake of argument, one is either loving or not.

What it meant by **a resounding gong or a clanging cymbal**? The first is a gong. The second term is the Greek *kumbalon*, from which we derive the word "cymbal." However these are not cymbals in our modern sense of two discs that are banged together, but rather a metal plate that is struck with a stick. Some have tied **cymbal** to a specific religious context: the mystery religions often used gongs as part of their rituals. Thus Paul might be saying that a Christian who speaks without love is tantamount to participating in pagan worship.[617] It is better to take a "gong" and a "cymbal," not for their religious connotations, but because they make a lot of jarring and unpleasant noise.

---

the case, how could the pagan Greeks possess words for "God," "savior" or "redemption" apart from the Bible? Yet possess them they did, but assigned them different meanings that those found in God's revelation. Second, we now possess proof that the noun *agapē* existed previous to the Septuagint and Greek New Testament and free from any influence from those texts. This evidence is still widely ignored.

[613] Thayer's continues in popular use, since it is keyed to the Strong's numbering system; nevertheless, it is badly outdated and should not be regarded as reliable.

[614] Popular belief also has it that the noun *philē* and the verb *phileō* must always denote mere human love or affection. This too is not the case: the disciple "beloved" by Jesus is so described with both the *agapē* and *philē* word group (as in John 21:20 and 20:2 respectively); as is the love of God for humanity (John 3:16 and 16:27 respectively). Thus the words are sometimes interchangeable, although it is also true that the *agapē* word group was the conventional one for the early Christians.

[615] [*tais*] *glōssais...laleō*; as in Acts 2:4, 2:11, 10:46; 1 Cor 12:30 and nine times in 1 Cor 14; plus there are three more references in this epistle simply to "tongues."

[616] Kistemaker, *1 Corinthians*, 452, points to the conditional syntax in 13:1 to argue that Paul never spoke in tongues in an assembly. This is clearly incorrect; the statement says nothing for or against it. Martin, *Spirit and the congregation*, 43, makes this phrase refer to both human eloquence and to charismatic speech. That would, he points out, make the verse include both the elitist and charismatic in its scope. Martin too has overstepped the context here, which principally has to do with glossolalia.

[617] So Héring, *First Corinthians*, 136.

"Clanging" nicely captures the original; it is a harsh, grating racket.

13:2
The original is "If I have prophecy," but the NIV rendering captures the sense, **the gift of prophecy**, the significance that *prophēteia* also has in Rom 12:6, 1 Cor 12:10, 13:8. In chapter 2 Paul castigated the elitists for their love of rational philosophy, when as Christians they might instead enjoy supernatural revelation, both in the gospel message and in the life of the church. And later on in chapter 14 prophecy is ranked higher than speaking in tongues, to the extent that it yields the greater blessing to the rest of the church. Yet here, contrary to what we might expect, he ranks prophecy lower than God's call to love. He broadens out from prophecy with **and can fathom all mysteries and all knowledge**.[618] It is a blessing to all to reveal some astonishing divine mystery (as in 1 Cor 2:1, 2:7, 15:51). Yet, if the person who is passing along that information does not have love, he is nothing.

And if I have a faith that can move mountains goes back to the teaching of Jesus (Matt 17:20, also 21:21), which gives Paul's words added weight:[619]

> He replied, "Because you have so little faith. I tell you the truth, if you have faith as small as a mustard seed, you can say to this mountain, 'Move from here to there' and it will move. Nothing will be impossible for you."

Paul's point here is striking: even if you Corinthians could do what according to the Lord Jesus was the most striking demonstration of faith, you are nothing without love.

13:3
Up to this point, a Corinthian pseudo-philosopher might feel smug: *That's right, tongues and prophecy are nothing; therefore these ultracharismatic upstarts deserve a rebuke.* But Paul now digs even deeper and compares love with what are universally recognized Christian virtues: faith and self-sacrifice. **If I give all I possess to the poor and surrender my body** is charity in extreme terms: first, to give away, better, to "dole out" all one's goods to the poor (see the same verb in Rom 12:20, where Paul is quoting Prov 25:21 LXX). It connotes an almost reckless generosity toward the needy. Normally, of course, Christians think of helping the poor as being one of the highest expressions of *agapē*. In fact, James castigates those who say kind words and yet offer no material help to the poor (James 2:15-16). But as Schrage states, it possible to go through the motions of excellent Christian deeds and still be unloving, that is, to be proud, boastful, impatient, divisive and antagonistic: the Corinthians have "Liebeswerke" without "Liebe" ("works of love without love").[620]

The second phrase of this verse is difficult. The NIV's **surrender my body to the flames**, with most versions, follows the text of the majority of manuscripts, which have some form of the verb *kaiō*, "to burn or to burn up." In that case the idea is probably being burned at the stake. The historical difficulty is that burning at the stake was not how 1st-century Romans executed their enemies. The critical text NA[28] is preferred; it

---

[618] Contrast this with the partial knowledge we possess during this age, in 13:9-10.
[619] The version in Luke 17:6 says that, "If you have faith as small as a mustard seed, you can say to this mulberry tree, 'Be uprooted and planted in the sea,' and it will obey you."
[620] Schrage, *An die Korinther*, 3:290.

chooses the more difficult reading "to boast" (*kauchēsomai*), which is very similar in sound to the various words for "burning" and probably led to a scribal error. This reading produces something like "if I give my body in order to boast" (HCSB; similarly NET, NLT, NRSV, NIV 2011). In that case, the two phrases might be parallel:

> if I give the poor all that I possess,
> if I can even boast of giving over my whole person.

Paul has already spoken of this type of self-sacrifice: "To this very hour we go hungry and thirsty, we are in rags, we are brutally treated, we are homeless. We work hard with our own hands" (1 Cor 4:11-12a). But even a person who undergoes apostolic rigors is nothing if he has not love! How much more will this be true of a Corinthian whose boasts consist of a spiritual gift which he did nothing to earn.

13:4

Paul uses the literary device of "personification," that is, speaking as if love were a person. He does not give a dictionary definition of love, nor an exhaustive list of characteristic; Paul focuses on attitudes and behaviors that were lacking in Corinth.[621] One might even paraphrase 13:4-7 as: *Love does not act as you Corinthians act!*

First, **love is patient, love is kind. It does not envy, it does not boast, it is not proud.** How relevant are these manifestations of love, in a church where the elite cannot wait with patience (*makrothumeō*, note the cognate noun in Gal 5:22) for the poor (1 Cor 11:21, 33-34). Love is **kind** (see again Gal 5:22 for the cognate noun). This does not mean that the loving person ignores evil: after all Paul, who loves the Corinthians and did not wish to cause them pain, spoke sharply to them when it was necessary (2 Cor 2:4). The Christian must not confuse goodness with indifference.

What is more, love **does not envy**. *Zēloō* may have a neutral sense of "desire," as it does in 12:31. Here it means an active striving envy rather than a quiet resentment. **Boast** is a characteristic of Corinth. **Proud** is a weak translation of the verb "is not puffed up" (*phusioō*); Paul repeats the term he used in 8:1, "This 'knowledge' puffs up, but love builds up" (see also 4:6, 18-19, 5:2).

13:5

It is not rude, it is not self-seeking, it is not easily angered, it keeps no record of wrongs. Again, these are the exact traits of the fractious church of Corinth. The game of the elite was not only to build oneself up, but also to demean those who were not a part of their circle. **Rude** is the same verb used of mistreatment of the "virgin" a man is engaged to, in 7:36. **Self-seeking** is a sin that Paul rejects in Phil 1-2 in favor of humble sacrifice.[622] **Is not easily angered** means that the person is not irritable or easily aroused, as a divisive person is bound to be. **Keeps no record of wrongs** is a nod in the direction

---

[621] Clement of Rome makes much of this chapter in his words to the Corinthian church of the AD 90s. For example, *1 Clem* 49.4-5 – "The height to which love exalts is unspeakable. Love unites us to God. Love covers a multitude of sins. Love beareth all things, is long-suffering in all things. There is nothing base, nothing arrogant in love. Love admits of no schisms: love gives rise to no seditions: love does all things in harmony."

[622] Phil 2:3 – "Do nothing out of selfish ambition or vain conceit, but in humility consider others better than yourselves." See also Rom 15:3a – "For even Christ did not please himself..."

of the person who brought the lawsuit in 6:1.

13:6
Love does not delight in evil but rejoices with the truth. In an interesting parallel, we might consider the parable of the Pharisee and the publican in Luke 18:9-14. On one level, the Pharisee is disgusted at the sins of the publican; but on another, he secretly harbors satisfaction, because those sins supposedly validate that he is righteous and his enemy is condemned. One of the common crimes of factionalism is delight at seeing someone from another group fall into sin, shame or stupidity. For its part, love rejoices when one's opponent avoids doing the wrong thing and finds the true and right path.

13:7
It always protects, always trusts, always hopes, always perseveres. The Christian need not be gullible or falsely optimistic; love does not mean we should fantasize that our fellows are better than they really are.[623] Paul himself challenges people when he thinks they are misleading him; otherwise, what kind of apostle would he be? He forgives sins, but he does so at the right time and in a way that upholds God's justice and the reconciliation of the sinner (2 Cor 2:5-11). Still, *agapē* makes the Christian forgiving, trusting, hopeful and patient.

13:8
Love never fails. Here in 13:8-12 Paul moves away from ethical considerations and invites his readers to think of love and the spiritual gifts within the God's plan for human history. Already in 1 Corinthians Paul has looked backward in time, to show how the revelation of the gospel overturned the wisdom of the ages past. Now he and the other apostles "do, however, speak a message of wisdom among the mature, but not the wisdom of this age" (2:6). But there is another side of this: the Christian must look forward to the age to come in order to properly evaluate the present. And so Paul appeals to what theologians call the tension of the *Now-Not Yet* to show the Corinthians why they should be humble about what they know and do in the now.[624] It is true that already the Spirit has revealed to us the mysteries of God in an unparalleled way. Yet at the return of Christ we shall learn that our knowledge, while true, has been incomplete. The gifts will serve their purpose and then come to the end of their utility; by contrast, love will never come to an end of its usefulness or validity.

If 13:8a is relatively clear, that which follows is more complex. A literal translation would be:

> If their are prophecies, they will come to an end;
> if their are tongues, they will cease;
> if there is knowledge, it will come to an end.

This triad is meant to show the transience of two (or possibly three?) spiritual gifts. They

---

[623] Here the reader will benefit by reading Dietrich Bonhoeffer's *Life together*.
[624] See too Gary S. Shogren, "How did they suppose the 'the perfect' would come? 1 Corinthians 13:8-12 in patristic exegesis," *Journal of Pentecostal Theology* (Sheffield) 15 (1999): 97-119. Utterly unconvincing is the view of R. Bultmann (also Weiss) that here Paul is contrasting love with Gnostic mysticism: R. Bultmann, "*gnōsis*," *TDNT* 1:709.

are gifts of God but not of eternal duration. We are familiar at this point in the letter with tongues and prophecy; the last term is more difficult, as "knowledge" (*gnōsis*) could have a variety of possible meanings in this context, including the gift the "word of knowledge" (*gnōsis*) in 12:8. A better interpretation is that Paul is not speaking of a spiritual gift,[625] but to all the supernatural insight in which the ultracharismatic boasted. This is the same as the knowledge of 13:2, "If I have the gift of prophecy and can fathom all mysteries and all knowledge."

The verbs follow an ABA pattern: the verb in the first and third lines is a form of *katargeō*, "to destroy." It is in the future tense and passive voice, and as such its meaning is reflexive: **cease** or "end." The NIV translates the same verb in two different ways: prophecies "will cease" and knowledge "will pass away." I see no justification for disrupting the parallel between the first and third lines.

The verb in the second line, which the NIV paraphrases as "they will be stilled," has been invested by some exegetes with more meaning than Paul ever intended. It is a so-called middle voice of the verb *pauō*. In the active voice it is a transitive verb, "to stop [something else]." In the middle voice it is intransitive, meaning "to cease." The myth persists that because this is in the middle voice, it must mean that it will stop because of its own built-in obsolescence; its batteries will run out without some outside force stopping it.[626] This is a over-exegesis of the verb. The simple meaning of the clause is that "tongues will cease."

Application: Love, Part I: What is love? 13:1-8

Jesus ranked love for God and love for others as the two great commandments (Mark 12:29-31). Love for ones neighbor flows from love for God, as Paul also implies in 8:3. It is this second love, human to human, that the apostle now explores in 1 Cor 13 (also Rom 12:9; Col 1:4; 1 Thess 4:9; see also 1 John). If they could only get love for their fellow Christians in order, then other issues would fall into place (see especially 8:1-3).

Every Christian is at least going to pay lip service to the importance of love. This in itself is worthless; our actions will show what our deep priorities really are. The church of Corinth had become distracted by peripherals (status; knowledge; spiritual gifts) instead of focusing on the best thing.

What are some false forms of Christian love? –

1. Mere feelings of love or good will. James 2:15-16 deals with a religion of mere talk or feeling: "Suppose a brother or sister is without clothes and daily food. If one of you says to him, 'Go, I wish you well; keep warm and well fed,' but does nothing about his physical needs, what good is it?" (see also James 1:27). There are plenty of people who feel badly when they see a hungry person. They may use that uncomfortable feeling to prove to themselves that they are sensitive to the needs of others. James rejects this completely. Love is not just feeling a certain way, it is acting lovingly.

---

[625] The Greek Church Fathers, who might have been expected to link the knowledge of 13:8 with the spiritual gift "word of knowledge" in 12:8, do not link them together.
[626] See a clear and accurate interpretation of *pausontai* in Carson, *Showing the Spirit*, 66-67. For the fallacious interpretation, see Robert L. Thomas, *Understanding spiritual gifts: a verse-by-verse study guide of 1 Corinthians 12-14* (rev. ed.; Grand Rapids, MI: Kregel, 1998), 78.s

2. Mere activism. On the other hand, while love will lead to action, we must not confuse action for love. For example, Paul mentions giving away all your possessions or your whole life for the faith. A loving person might do these things, but doing these things does not make one loving. Nor does being a missionary; nor singing or teaching or giving. The Ephesian church (Rev 2:2-4) was a major center of Christian ministry yet had already lost its "first love."

3. Correct doctrine. In some circles, it is assumed that love is the same as having sound teaching. What is more loving, after all, then to defend God's truth? As usual there is a legitimate insight, but in itself it is a weak substitute for what the Bible teaches. To return to the case of James 1:27 (see #1 above), it does no good to have a well-reasoned and biblical doctrine of poverty if in fact people are going hungry all around us.

4. Love and biology. Sometimes people experience a biological or emotional response to another person and imagine that this is Christian love. A young man sees a pretty girl struggling with some heavy boxes and he offers to carry them for her. He may convince himself that he is a kind and Christ-like person. But let us first see him carrying the boxes of angry old men or people he dislikes, and then we may draw more accurate conclusions.

5. Love and sociology. People hit it off with other individuals, often because they share the same interests, or background or sense of humor. This is normal, but this too is not Christian love:

> If you love those who love you, what reward will you get? Are not even the tax collectors doing that? And if you greet only your brothers, what are you doing more than others? Do not even pagans do that? (Matt 5:46-47)

What is the positive side of Christian love? A few points must suffice:

- Christians who love seek the good of others, even at the cost of their own inconvenience.
- Love involves our emotions, because God made us emotional creatures. But Christian love is a supernatural gift that flows through and beyond our human feelings.
- Love means seeing others as God sees them through the cross, not as we pretend them to be.
- Love shows itself in both attitudes and behaviors.
- Love takes action, even if it doesn't give us a warm feeling for helping someone or doing the right thing.
- Love does not simply react to situations, but actively seeks ways to express itself.
- Love is content to do things quietly and not seek glory.
- Love acts in both small ways and large.
- Love should show up not just in large loving gestures but in everyday issues – you speak to people politely; you show up when you say you'll show up; you make a point of paying people on time; you are carefully to give people the

information they need; you listen carefully to others.
- People who love do not try to play god with others or manipulate or control them to make them into my own image of what they should be.
- Love cannot be learned from a manual or a list of hundreds of rules. "God is love," and we learn love when we know God through the crucified Christ himself.

13:9

Paul now gives us help to understand why tongues, prophecy and knowledge will not last forever. The NASB gives a clearer sense of the original:

> For we know in part, and
> we prophesy in part;
> but when the perfect comes,
> the partial will be done away.

The phrase **in part** is *ek merous*. It shows up twice in 13:9, once in 13:10, and then later in 13:12. No prophet, no matter how blessed, gives more than a fragment of the divine truth; even the most spectacular gifts are "only able to lift a corner of the impenetrable veil that now hides the mystery of God."[627] Paul is including himself in this state of limited knowledge. The very existence of the spiritual gifts is proof that we are not in God's direct presence.

13:10

We now come to a sharper definition of when 13:8-9 will take place, when the imperfect will be **done away** (again, *katargeō*, as in 13:8). This will happen **when perfection comes**. "Perfection" or "the perfect" (*to teleion*) stands opposite "the imperfect" (*ek merous*). The adjective *teleios* may mean perfect or complete, depending on the context. But what is "perfection" that is still future to Paul? There are several explanations:

(1) Eschatological: The interpretation that has prevailed for 2000 years and is the overwhelming favorite today, is that Paul is referring to the Parousia. The church fathers (with the exception of Tertullian) taught that 1 Cor 13:8-11 could only refer to the final coming of Jesus.[628] Proof of this is readily to hand, since the coming of "the perfect" is laid side-by-side with seeing Christ "face to face" (13:12). Paul later on uses a cognate word, *to telos*, to refer to the eschatological "end" in 15:24. The church fathers typically cited 1 Cor 13:10, 12 alongside verses like 1 John 3:2 – "But we know that when he appears, we shall be like him, for we shall see him as he is."

(2) Additional revelation to come later in history: Some heretics claimed that this passage referred to some new revelation that would come along after Paul, but during this age. The most notable example of this was the New Prophecy movement founded by Montanus in the 2nd century:

---

[627] Kuss, *Die Briefe an die Römer, Korinther und Galater* [my translation].
[628] See Shogren, "How did they suppose the perfect would come?"

...[supposedly] Montanus possessed a fulness of knowledge such as was never claimed by Paul; for [Paul] was content to say, "We know in part, and we prophesy in part," and again, "Now we see through a glass darkly."[629]

As an example of new doctrine, the Montanists claimed that the Spirit had revealed to them that widows should not remarry. The rest of the church responded by quoting 1 Cor 7:39-40, where Paul says it is not a sin. The Montanists replied that Paul's theology was incomplete, as he himself admitted in 13:8-12, and that "the perfect" had only recently come through the Montanist prophets.

(3) The maturing of the church. This third alternative is first attested in Chrysostom: he held to view (1); nevertheless he added the miraculous gifts of revelation were designed to get the early church started and stabilized and for the gospel to spread widely. But at some point they ran their course and later ceased to function. "For if tongues and prophecy were brought in for the purpose of aiding the spread of the faith, when the gospel is every where sown abroad, the use of these gifts is made superfluous."[630]

(4) The completion of the New Testament canon. In Dispensationalist and some Reformed circles over the last century, "the perfect" has been taken to mean that once the canon of the New Testament was completed, there would no longer be any need for charismatic revelations.[631] Since "the perfect" is of the neuter gender in Greek, it could not refer to the coming of Christ – in that case Paul supposedly would have had to have used the masculine gender, "the perfect person." Therefore it must refer to a perfect *thing*, such as the canon. In this viewpoint, around the end of the first Christian century, tongues and prophecy ceased.[632]

There are a number of serious flaws with viewpoint (4): (a) it is based on a misunderstanding of Greek gender: in fact "the perfect" could refer to the end or to the return of Christ, as neuter adjectives do; not one of the Greek Fathers had any problem taking "the perfect" as the Second Coming; (b) nowhere does Paul give any hint that he is thinking of a New Testament canon; how could the Corinthians have known to read "completed New Testament canon" for "the perfect"? Some scholars refer to Psalm 19:7, "the law of the Lord is perfect," as proof that Paul is speaking of the canon of Scripture. This argument is self-defeating, given that the psalmist wrote when not even the Old Testament was complete; in addition, the Septuagint version uses *amōmos* ("blameless, perfect"), not the word *telos*; (c) not a single church father refers to the canon as a

---

[629] Jerome, Letter 41.4, *To Marcella*.
[630] Chrysostom *i ad Corinthios* 34.2, paraphrased. Godet, *First Corinthians*, 678, agrees with the eschatological interpretation, but adds that the gifts may be altered in the interim between the apostles and the end.
[631] Kistemaker, *1 Corinthians*, 464-65, states that prophecy as *revelation* has ceased, but prophecy as powerful *preaching* continues until the end of the age. For Dispensationalists, the cessationist view is implicit in the notes on 1 Corinthians 12-14 in the *New Scofield Reference Bible*.
[632] Thomas, *Understanding spiritual gifts*, 78-80, manages to combine three viewpoints: that the need for revelatory gifts ceased at the end of the 1st century, with the completion of the New Testament canon, *and* that the church had grown in maturity, *and* that we would see Christ at his coming. Thomas' treatment of 13:8b is generally disappointing, given that he does not prove his case from the text as such but instead asks the reader to speculate why these gifts, supposedly, ceased. He also insists that tongues were rare by the time Paul wrote 1 Corinthians, a statement that is hardly credible if one has read the epistle or the fathers of the 2nd century.

fulfillment of 1 Cor 13; (d) the church fathers, possessing a completed canon and with the gift of prophecy still being exercised, saw no incompatibility between the two. The early church knew that the prophetic gift did not exist to give new normative revelation, but rather to guide the congregations from year to year.[633]

All the linguistic evidence favors the interpretation that has convinced Christians for two millennia: that when Christ comes and we see him "face to face" (13:12), then these highly-regarded charismatic gifts will cease to be of use. After his return "to prophesy would be like switching on a torch [flashlight] in the full light of the noonday sun."[634] No matter how new and profound is the revelation we have in the gospel or through the spiritual gifts, they still add up to mere glimpses of God's full truth and person. One church father concluded:

> For all gifts are given for a time as use and need require, but when the dispensation is ended they will without doubt presently pass away: but love will never be destroyed.[635]

It is falsely believed that history records that the gift of prophecy died out around the year AD 100. In fact, most church fathers of the 2nd century affirmed that the prophetic gift was still practiced throughout the church. Both the *Didache* and the *Shepherd of Hermas* speak of ongoing prophecy. Polycarp of Smyrna was "in our own times been an apostolic and prophetic teacher, and bishop of the Catholic Church which is in Smyrna. For every word that went out of his mouth either has been or shall yet be accomplished."[636]

The great fathers Justin Martyr (AD 135) and Irenaeus (AD 180) were adamant:

> For the prophetical gifts remain with us, even to the present time.[637]

> In like manner we do also hear many brethren in the Church, who possess prophetic gifts, and who through the Spirit speak all kinds of languages, and bring to light for the general benefit the hidden things of men, and declare the mysteries of God.[638]

> [Some Christians today] have foreknowledge of things to come: they see visions, and utter prophetic expressions.[639]

Far from dying out with the apostles, gifts such as tongues, prophecy and healing thrived long into the next century. Only at the end of the 2nd century would Origen comment that the gifts were gradually less frequent:

> ...but since [the ascension of Jesus] these signs have diminished, although there

---

[633] See Shogren, "Christian prophecy and canon in the second century."
[634] Thiselton, *First Corinthians*, 1061.
[635] John Cassian, *First conference* 11.
[636] *Martyrdom of Polycarp* 16.2.
[637] Justin Martyr, *Dialogue* 82.
[638] Irenaeus, *Against heresies* 5.6.1
[639] Irenaeus, *Against heresies* 2.32.4. He goes on to say that Christians lay hands on the sick to heal them and even raise the dead.

are still traces of His presence in a few who have had their souls purified by the Gospel, and their actions regulated by its influence.[640]

Nevertheless, the gifts were by no means rare, according to Origen. He claims to have seen prophecy and miracles,

> traces of which to a considerable extent are still found among Christians, and some of them more remarkable than any that existed among the Jews; and these we ourselves have witnessed.[641]

Two centuries later, in the late 4th century, Chrysostom announced that tongues and prophecy no longer occurred in the church:

> See how now, at least, there is no prophecy nor gift of tongues.[642]

> [The teaching about the gifts in 1 Corinthians 12] is very obscure; but the obscurity is produced by our ignorance of the facts referred to and by their cessation, being such as then used to occur but now no longer take place.[643]

13:11

Paul now contrasts childhood and adulthood. This is not a prediction of the maturation of the church after AD 100 – and if it were, a very uneven maturity it would be! – nor to the maturing of the individual disciple. Rather all of 13:8-12 refers to the end of the age. In that moment, one's boasted charismatic knowledge will be revealed as the limited knowledge one gives a child.

> For now we know "in part," and as it were "through a glass," since that which is perfect has not yet come to us; namely, the kingdom of heaven and the resurrection, when "that which is in part shall be done away."[644]

Love, on the other hand, is a virtue for this age and the age to come.

13:12

The NIV has attempted to put in understandable terms a phrase that could be confusing: **Now we see but a poor reflection as in a** mirror. To understand the metaphor, we must lay aside our modern conception of mirrors, which are made of glass with silver backing and reflect a very accurate image. The mirrors of Paul's day were made of polished metal, giving only a clouded reflection. Paul is not talking about seeing our own reflection or knowledge of our own selves, that is, 1 Cor 13:11 is not a true parallel of James 1:23-24. Rather he is contrasting poor mirror image with seeing something **face to face**, seeing Christ in his return. **Then I shall know fully, even as I am fully known** means that our future resurrection will clear away the fog and give us accurate

---

[640] Origen, *Contra Celsum* 7.8.
[641] Origen, *Contra Celsum* 2.8.
[642] Chrysostom, *Contra anomeos* 1.9.
[643] Chrysostom *i ad Corinthios* 19.1, a message preached in the 390s.
[644] Methodius, *Symposium* 9.2.

knowledge of God.

In one paragraph Paul has dispensed with the claims the rationalists, who trust in the human mind; but more especially, the ultracharismatics, whose revelations do not after all take them directly to God's presence. Our little glimpses of God now, imperfect and fragmentary, will be swallowed up when we see Christ face to face. Paul's reference to the eschaton also reminds the believers that when we see Christ at last, he will be coming to test our works by the fire (1 Cor 3:13); works which are not done in love are going to burn.

Application: Love, Part II: Love the opposite of childishness 13:8-12

Where did we ever get the idea that love is a nice lesson for the new believer, and that being discerning, wise, or effective in our work are signs of maturity? In fact, this is the very opposite of what Paul teaches.

Even the most mature of Christians in this age is a mere infant in God's eternal plan. Paul hints at that in 13:11-12: "when I became a man," that is, when I see Christ at the resurrection, I will realize how silly I was during this life. Our arguments, our boastings, our priorities will all seem like so much playground noise.

Do you brag that you have some special, deep knowledge of God, his principles and his Word? Do you feel unique because you speak in tongues more than anyone else? Then in the end we will see that that was only baby-talk. Why not save ourselves future embarrassment by stopping our boasting now? We should seek what is the real adult virtue, the one that will last for eternity. According to Gregory Nazianzen:

> [Paul] is not undeveloped in knowledge, [yet even he] claims to see in a mirror, darkly...What is the lesson and instruction he would thus impress upon us? Not to be proud of earthly things, or puffed up by knowledge, or excite the flesh against the spirit.[645]

Jesus taught us to "love each other as I have loved you" (John 15:12). Let us not imagine that this is a simplistic faith. Let us never think that this is what we tell the little ones because they can't think more deeply, but that the really important issues lie somewhere else.

13:13

And now these three remain: faith, hope and love. It is not entirely clear what Paul means by "remain" or "abide." Is he speaking of the eschaton: "then these three will remain forever"? Or of the present: "now these three important qualities remain for this age"? Or perhaps the logical present: "these three remain 'on the table'"? The first is possible, but it runs counter to common sense, since one can speak about hope and faith as virtues that will not be necessary in the age to come. The third reading is a bit obscure. The strongest case may be made for the second: glossolalia may be popular, prophecy

---

[645] Gregory Nazianzen, *Orations* 2.55.

desirable, but the real jewels in the crown are these three virtues; what is more, love triumphs over faith alone (13:2) and, presumably, hope. For the Corinthian Christian in this age, **the greatest of these is love.**

b. From the perspective of love, it is obvious that prophecy is a better blessing to others than is the gift of tongues 14:1-40

We come to the heart of why Paul is addressing "matters of the Spirit" in 1 Cor 12-14. He will show how in a worship service, prophecy far surpasses tongues in usefulness and as a sign of the Spirit's true presence. Of course, tongues too are a spiritual gift. They are utterances directed toward God and at a minimum edify the gifted one. But prophecy is a better spiritual gift in that it brings a direct blessing to the church.

Some Corinthians were exalting glossolalia far beyond its purpose or usefulness. The entire church was "charismatic" in our modern sense of the word, but some "ultracharismatics" exalted certain spiritual gifts. What if we, like "some who do not understand" (14:23), entered a Corinthian house-church in the middle of a worship service? Some members would be speaking in tongues aloud, noisily, all at once. They would tend to overwhelm those who wanted to teach, or to lead in a song, or who had a revelation to share with the group. You might be standing next to someone shouting in tongues; others might respond with "Amen!" when he is done. But you don't know how to respond: *What did he say, and how do I know if it deserves an Amen?*

The pressure to speak in tongues was partly a fruit of social jealousy. The poor of the church were already badly alienated because of social and economic stratification. These craved some method of distinguishing themselves as God's own special people. It was only in the worship service that they could break out and be extraordinary: no-one could forbid them from being the center of attention, as this was the Spirit's work!

The assumption ran among some that the more raucous and contorted the person, the clearer it is that the Holy Spirit has taken possession of him. From the pagan environment came the idea that the sign of spiritual presence was wild frenzied behavior, indecipherable words and even glossolalia. Some simple converts may have transferred this assumption to their Christian experience and (probably unconsciously) emulated what they thought of as charismatic behavior.

Paul's analysis of the problem is:

1. The aim of any spiritual gift is to build up the church, not the gifted individual
2. Confusing and untranslated glossolalia in no way builds up the church, and in some ways harms it
3. Therefore, untranslated tongues have no place in the worship service
4. Godly "intelligible words" are more edifying than the incomprehensible
5. Therefore: pray for the gift of interpretation or of prophecy or word of knowledge. Find some charismatic way to be a blessing to the group!

It is because inward-turning spiritual experience is unloving that Paul wrote the Love Chapter. The poor are being asked to relinquish, for the sake of *agapē*, their last possibility for status. They are to throw away their mysterious appearance and have their glossolalia translated for all; or they are to prophesy – in Greek – and to submit their message to the discernment of the others. They are being asked to speak or serve in some way that doesn't make them immediately astonishing and notable. This can only be done by the Spirit's power: to gift them and most especially to fill them with love.[646]

14:1

Paul recapitulates 12:31, where he had said "eagerly desire [from *zēloō*] the greater gifts."

> **Follow the way of love and**
> **eagerly desire spiritual gifts,**
> **especially the gift of prophecy.**

Love is the superlatively better way; prophecy is also relatively better than speaking in tongues. Those who love should pursue the more useful gifts, even if they seem less glamorous (see our note on 12:11).

14:2-4

Paul chooses prophecy as the foil for glossolalia: it too is supernatural utterance, yet unlike tongues it is intelligible and edifying. Tongues in this chapter are not a message from God to the church: the person **does not speak to men**. Nobody understands the message (failing an interpretation), **since the person utters mysteries with his spirit**. The GNB, HCSB, NET, NLT and NIV 2011 take *pneuma* here to be the Holy Spirit. Nevertheless, it is better here to take this as the human spirit (NIV 84), since that is what is in view in 14:14-15 – "*my* spirit prays." "Mystery" is a favorite Pauline word to speak of the hidden mystery which the Spirit has now revealed apart from human rationalism (1 Cor 2:1, 7; 4:1; 13:2). Yet there is irony here: a divine mystery, shared only between the worshiper and God, becomes mere noise for those who cannot understand.

The prophet, on the other hand, does speak to other people. Paul uses some of his favorite terms to describe it: strengthening, encouragement and comfort (see the cognate words in Phil 2:1; 1 Thess 2:12, 5:14). A prophetic message, given in love, will build others up (cp. 8:1). Besides, prophecy is multi-faceted, extending help to the guilty, the sad, the weak and the discouraged.

The speaker in tongues **edifies himself**. Some have seen this as ironic, as if building oneself up in the Spirit is *per se* wrong or equal to being "puffed up" with pride. But no: Paul grants that it is better that an individual be edified than not edified; he also unapologetically enjoys speaking in tongues (14:18).

14:5

Paul values the gift of tongues and **I would like every one of you to speak in tongues**. He distinguishes between its use in private and its employment in a worship service, but this does not mean that they are two different gifts. There is only one gift of tongues in this epistle. Not all Christians speak in tongues (12:30), either in private or in public.

---

[646] So Calvin, *First Corinthians*, 1:434 – "Lest the Corinthians should object that they wronged God, if they despised his gifts, the Apostle anticipates this objection by declaring, that it was not his design to draw them away even from those gifts that they had abused – nay rather he commends the pursuit of them, and wishes them to have a place in the Church. And assuredly, as they had been conferred for the advantage of the Church, man's abuse of them ought not to give occasion for their being thrown away as useless or injurious..."

Many Corinthians crave this gift, and Paul would like them to have their wish. However in the end many Christians will never speak in tongues, nor should they feel less spiritual for that.[647] "Would like" is a wish, not a command. Likewise, he wishes that **I would rather have you prophesy**, although many never will.

Paul is not being drawn into the status game. His ranking of gifts is based, not on personal glory, but on service: *how useful a servant does this gift make you?* It is in this sense that **he who prophesies is greater than one who speaks in tongues**. There is one exception: the church might **be edified** if there is an interpretation, the rendering in the local language praise or prayer that someone has addressed to God in a miraculous tongue. Commentators often assume that the interpreter is a second individual, a natural assumption in light of 1 Cor 12:10 and 30 (see ESV – "unless someone interprets"; also GNB). But Thiselton points out, with the NIV (and KJV, HCSB, NASB), that the likelier translation is **unless he interprets**, that is, that the person himself translates what has been said. This assumes that at some point during or subsequent to the utterance, the person comes to know what he/she is saying.[648] That would make this verse fit nicely with 14:13 (the speaker in tongues should pray that he or she may interpret). The interpretation makes the utterance intelligible and the church built up, not by hearing a message from God, but by understanding and participating in praise directed toward him.

14:6

Paul creates a hypothetical case, one uncomfortably close to the situation that already existed in Corinth: **if I come to you and speak in tongues, what good will I be to you…?** Some Corinthians might have responded: *What good is it, Paul? Well, it helps my fellow Christians to see how remarkably our congregation is blessed with the Spirit's presence!* By using himself as an example, as Paul often does with difficult issues, he invites the Corinthians to view the situation as others see it. What if Paul broke off his current work; made the long sea voyage all the way from Ephesus to the port of Cenchrea; walked over to Corinth; waited until the Lord's Day; entered the worship service; stood before a congregation eager to hear him; and then contributed nothing more than hours of himself speaking in tongues. Would not the disappointed audience question his motivation? *What is Paul doing: showing off that he too has the Spirit?* But this is precisely how the ultracharismatics appear to others.

If someone really wants to channel the Spirit's help to a church, how much better to direct oneself outward with something to help the other Christians. The apostle mentions four kinds of intelligible speech that is just as charismatic as tongues. **Prophecy** and **instruction** we already know from the list in 12:28; **revelation** and **knowledge** (*gnōsis*) might cover "message of wisdom," "message of knowledge" in 12:8; or it may be that Paul is speaking in general terms of different types of speech. Instruction is as charismatic and spiritual as tongues and prophecy.

---

[647] As he does in 12:30, Horton, *I & II Corinthians*, 132, engages in a strained exegesis of the Greek present tense here, forcing it to mean "keep on speaking in tongues," meaning, apparently, after their initial manifestation of tongues when receiving the Spirit.

[648] So Schrage, who calls tongues without interpretation "Sinnlosigkeit und Vergeblichkeit" ("senselessness and vanity"), *An die Korinther*, 3:392.

14:7-8

As in 14:6, Paul in 14:7-11 uses a series of rhetorical questions and analogies to prove his point: that it is not the loud manifestation of the Spirit that blesses the church, but an intelligible manifestation. He speaks of the harp and the flute, probably for no other reason than that they were so common. The NIV captures the sense nicely with **how will anyone know what tune is being played unless there is a distinction in the notes?** It is the differences in sounds that produce useful communication. In the same way, language without a meaningful pattern of changes is no more useful than gibberish.

The reference to music brings us around again to 13:1. There Paul used loud, monotonous instruments to illustrate how tongues can sound to the other person. No message is coming through; it is loud and disruptive and giving people headaches. In the same way, tongues without love are not only fruitless, they're positively disagreeable.

The **trumpet** here is not for entertainment but to direct an army. But this bugler **does not sound a clear call**, is not sending any intelligible message. The illustration has been current right up until a few years ago, when hand-held radios began to take the place of trumpets. But in an earlier generation the bugler was the main means of communicating over distance and over the horrible din of battle. Each battalion would have its special signal, and each command – *Retreat! Advance! Disperse! Gather up!* – its own code. Understanding the code and obeying it would often be a matter of life or death. But what if a bugler sounded a random series of notes, or even chose to play a pretty tune? The army will lose the battle and perhaps even die while listening to it. The same is true of the church: *why make random noise when you might give your brother some information that is vital for his walk with God?*

14:9

Again, the key is **intelligible words**, that is, words not only from the Spirit but which form a coherent statement. Otherwise, speech is mere noise thrown into the air, not to your brother, who is standing by waiting for help. Like the shadow-boxing or aimless running in 9:26, it is fruitless, and therefore, not done on the basis of love.

14:10

There are all sorts of languages in the world. If the Corinthians had tried to guess how many, they would have badly underestimated the number.[649] Today there exist around 7000 identified languages, not counting the dialects, but we still do not have an accurate count of how many other unknown languages exist around the globe. The people who know the languages receive meaning through the combinations of sounds and tones and morphemes and gestures and everything else that goes into a language: **none of them is without meaning**.

---

[649] Jewish and early Christians inferred from the Bible that there existed 70 (or 72 or 73 or 75) languages in the world. Clement of Alexandria, *Stromata* 21 – "there appear to be seventy-two generic dialects, as our Scriptures hand down. The rest of the vulgar tongues [i. e., local variations] are formed by the blending of two, or three, or more dialects." Chrysostom, *i ad Corinthios* 35.4, comments on 14:10 that there are "countless nations" in the earth, but he names only seven. The mission of the seventy (some manuscripts, seventy-two) disciples in Luke 10:1 is probably a foreshadowing of the gentile mission, the number symbolizing all the nations of the earth. The multinational audience of Acts 2:5-11 represented perhaps 12 languages, plus a number of local dialects (this information is thanks to my graduate student, Robby Richard).

14:11

A person who hears foreign tongues will feel like **a foreigner**. Paul uses the term *barbaroi*, which is a milder word in Greek than is "barbarian" in English, but even in the Greek it implies an outsider. This is significant on two levels: first, the intellectual – without understanding there is no edification; the message fails. And secondly the problem is social – your fellow-Christian is being made to feel like the outsider. You are excluding him, whether that was your purpose or not. To the ultracharismatic Paul is saying: your upwardly-mobile brother may have insulted you over the pre-worship service feast, but you should not retaliate by making him an outsider in turn.

Application: The Sheep and the Goats on Sunday Morning – A Parable 14:11

When the Son of Man comes in his glory he will separate the people one from another as a shepherd separates the sheep from the goats. He will put the sheep on his right and the goats on his left.

Then the King will say to those on his right, "Come, you who are blessed by my Father; take your inheritance. For I was lonely and I felt like a foreigner but you made me feel welcome; I was confused and you cleared things up; I was beaten down by life and you lifted me up; I was anonymous and you called me by name."

Then the righteous will answer him, "Lord, when did we see you lonely and feeling like a foreigner and made you feel welcome; or confused and we made things clear for you; or beaten down by life and lifted you up; or anonymous and we called you by name?"

The King will reply, "One Sunday I visited your church in disguise. I sat by myself, shy and without a friend, and you came over and talked with me and asked me about myself. I came without a Bible, and you shared yours with me and pointed out where we were reading. Your leaders spoke clearly so I could understand and showed me the words to the songs with a projector. I cried during the prayer time, and you put your hand on my shoulder and asked me what you could do to help. You asked my name and you remembered it when you saw me after the service, and you introduced me to your friends. That was my experience, but besides that, whenever you did such things for the least-attractive person to wander in, you did it for me."

Then he will say to those on his left, "Depart from me. For I was lonely and I felt like a foreigner but you made me feel even more unwelcome; I was confused and you disdained to clear things up for me; I was beaten down and you didn't lift me up; I was anonymous and you left me without a name."

They also will answer, "Lord, when did we see you lonely and feeling like a foreigner and left you feeling unwelcome; or confused and disdained to clear things up; or beaten down by life and didn't lift you up; or anonymous and left you without a name?"

The King will reply, "One Sunday I visited your church in disguise. I sat by myself, shy and lonely, and you never turned your head to look at me, but went on talking and laughing with your friends. I came without a Bible and you frowned at my ignorance. Your leaders spoke so fast and with the volume turned up so loudly I could hardly make out what they were saying. When we sang, everyone but me seemed to know the words, but I couldn't identify them. I cried during prayer time, but you were jumping up and down and waving your arms and didn't notice. A bunch of people grabbed the microphone and made weird noises, and everyone yelled and applauded and praised God, but it only frightened me and left me more confused. People interrupted each other and I could not figure out what was going on. You finally asked my name, but it was to see whether I would pledge to give 10% of my income to the church; when I said I was unemployed you scolded me for my lack of faith."

"That was my experience, but besides that," concluded the King, "whenever you forgot to do good things for any person to wander in, you were forgetting me."

14:12

Paul addresses those who are **eager to have spiritual gifts** (using the cognate noun form of *zēloō*, see 12:31, 14:1). Probably they wanted to speak in tongues. But they should rather pour that zeal and energy and prayer into something that will build up the church, embracing the central Christian paradox, that excellence is found in a servant spirit.

14:13

The tongues-speaker, to exercise his gift most lovingly, needs to make himself intelligible: he should pray that he may **interpret** (the NIV adds "what he says"). This introduces to the reader a new datum, but it is one that must have been familiar to the Corinthians. The speaker in tongues did not know what he was saying; the language is foreign to him too. It will take another supernatural gift to render intelligible what has been said.

14:14

Paul develops the idea of unintelligibility a step further by exploring what the tongues-speaker experiences. He knows from his own experience that when he speaks in tongues **my spirit prayers, but my mind is unfruitful**. Although the speaker receives a spiritual blessing and is charismatically speaking to God, he himself receives no message that he can communicate to his neighbor or even understand for himself. *Is that so bad?* the ultracharismatics might ask. *Doesn't the sterile intellectualism of our elitist brothers prove that the mind is overrated?* Again, Paul has to prove that where there is no understanding, there is only limited edification for the speaker and none for the hearers. "It was not enough that the prayers and praises should be spiritual, they must be intelligible."[650] To think otherwise truly is childish (14:20), as other Christians well know.

14:15

Hence the best combination is to **pray with my spirit [or sin or praise], but I will also pray with my mind**. Paul is not contrasting praying by the Spirit with praying with the mind, as if these were mutually contradictory. Rather it is in the human spirit: I will pray in tongues; I will also pray in an intelligible way, so that both I and my neighbor will understand what I am praying.[651]

---

[650] So Hodge, *I Corinthians*, 277.

[651] Tertullian, *On prayer* 28 takes this in a different direction, equating praying in the Spirit with the worship "in spirit and in truth" of John 4:23-24. See also Gregory Nazianzus, *Orations* 31.12 – "Therefore to adore

14:16-17

The same could be said of praise and thanksgiving. A person gives thanks to God in tongues; God hears, but neither the person nor the church understand. It is impossible, even risky, for another person to say **Amen** to such an utterance. This word was originally from the Hebrew and has now, like the Hebrew "Hallelujah," gone all over the globe. The meaning of Amen is something like "so it is" or "may it be so." If I hear someone praying in a foreign language, who knows what he is saying or whether a Christian ought to affirm it? One might argue: *but, I'm speaking with God; he knows what I'm saying, and that's all that matters!* On one level that is true, but on another level, you are in a meeting and worshiping, not as an individual, but as part of a group.

Among those who do not understand is much better in the NIV 2011 – "who is now put in the position of an inquirer"; the last word translates *idiōtēs* (here and 14:23-24). The word is a distant cousin of our "idiot," but the meaning in the Greek is an amateur or an untrained person. These people are mentioned alongside the unbelievers in 14:23-24. It may refer in all these passages to "inquirers" or to those who have expressed interest but are not yet taught in the gospel.[652] It may simply refer to people who are untaught in the particular language. He is made into a "foreigner" by the lack of intelligibility.

14:18

The apostle holds himself up as a model: he has the gift of tongues; he recognizes that it comes from God and he uses it often. Yet, he implies, he would never do what some Corinthians are doing, speaking in tongues in a worship service without interpretation or in a disruptive or self-centered way.

It is possible that the ultracharismatics had questioned Paul's spirituality because they thought a true apostle ought to appear "possessed"; or they concluded from his concern to speak clearly in the worship service that he did not speak in tongues at all. And why listen to someone who has never experienced the exalted state of glossolalia? Not so, says Paul: not only do I have the gift of tongues, but I use it, often; I know too that it does not build up the other brother.

14:19

Paul is not making a mathematical statement that five clear words are better than 10,000 unknown ones, but is speaking in hyperbole. 10,000 words is the product of a couple of hours of uninterrupted speech.[653] Yet even a sentence of five words or less could convey a more powerful message: "Christ loves you!" or "Christ died for sinners!" or "I forgive you, beloved sister!" or even a prophetic "Your sick baby will recover." Whether it is supernatural speech or everyday words said in the power of the Spirit, it's all evidence of God's grace to his people.

---

or to pray to the Spirit seems to me to be simply Himself offering prayer or adoration to Himself."

[652] Along this vein, the Catholic version BJ of 14:16 is anachronistic with "the uninitiated person" (French original, "celui qui a rang de non-initié"). This refers to a distinct class of people, the catechumens, that did not exist in the 1st century. The NASB has to paraphrase in order to make this "the place of the ungifted," but that is not the point either: Paul refers not to the person who doesn't have the gift of tongues, but to the person who can't decipher the foreign tongue.

[653] It is worth noting the number of words within this epistle: in the original Greek text it contains roughly 7,300 words; in the NIV 1984 about 8000.

14:20

Stop thinking like children is a rebuke, albeit a gentle, fatherly one. The reader should compare this word with Paul's comment about adulthood in 13:11 – we are moving toward this goal, so let us strive to be mature in our lives now. Of course, a Christian should be *un*skilled in practicing **evil** or "malice," ill-will toward others (Eph 4:31, Col 3:8, Titus 3:3).

14:21

Paul now alludes to **the Law**, with "Law" broadly defined to include the Hebrew prophets, not just the five books of Moses. His quotation differs both from the Septuagint and the Hebrew of Isa 28:11-12. He may have had another version in mind, although the fact that he shortens the quotation and rearranges the order may mean that he is quoting freely. In the original context, the elite of Israel burlesque Isaiah message. They hold wild parties, filled with vomiting, and they think the prophet's message is childish. When they complain that God's Word sounds like baby-talk, Isaiah replies that indeed they will hear from God again: but this time in the foreign language of the Assyrians. They will invade Israel and their foreign gibberish will be God's rebuke to them.

14:22

It is Paul's application of this verse to Roman Corinth that leaves interpreters confused:

> **Tongues, then, are a sign,**
> **not for believers but for unbelievers;**
> **prophecy, however,**
> **is for believers, not for unbelievers.**

The apostle appears to contradict this conclusion in 14:23-24, where an unbeliever will think a tongues speaker is out of his mind, but if he hears prophecy he will repent. This has led to a number of proposed solutions: one, by the English translator J. B. Phillips, is to emend 14:22 on the assumption that some scribe mixed up "believers" and "unbelievers."[654] Since there is no manuscript evidence to support this proposed reconstruction, we should hold back from emending it and interpret the text as it stands in all the manuscripts.

Some Dispensationalists understand Paul to mean that, just as God spoke to unbelieving Israel through Isaiah and then through the Assyrians, so God will judge 1st-century Jews through the glossolalia of the gentile Christians. Israel is made to be "jealous" over the faith of the church (see Rom 11:11-16) and the "unbelievers" here are strictly Jewish ones. As in Isaiah's situation, tongues ceased to fulfill this purpose once Jerusalem was destroyed and the Jews taken into a new exile in AD 70.

The problems with this interpretation are manifold: first, there is no evidence that Paul was thinking specifically of *unbelieving Corinthian Jews*. He speaks simply of "unbelievers," and indeed, either Jew or gentile who heard uninterpreted tongues will say that **you are out of your mind** (14:23).

A better approach is that we are dealing with the motif of social alienation. When a

---

[654] Phillips' English translation: "That means that tongues are a sign of God's power, not for those who are unbelievers, but to those who already believe."

church member hears an ultracharismatic speaking away in tongues without an interpretation, he is excluded, and made to feel like an outsider. And indeed, Paul says, this is how "foreign tongues" worked in the Old Testament: they were a note of judgment and exclusion from God. Thus, an ultracharismatic will be proclaiming with every syllable that "you do not belong here." This is why Paul says that they are **a sign**, a label that people are unbelievers, not a "message" for them. The signal is a social one, symbolizing that some do not belong to the mystical inner circle and belong with the non-believers.

Thus we paraphrase Paul's sense here:

> Speaking in tongues is a sign
>> not to affirm that the other believers are believers
>> but to declare that they are like unbelievers, excluded from blessing.

With **prophecy, however, is for believers, not for unbelievers** he is not eliminating the possibility that an unbeliever will be convicted by a prophetic word (see 14:24). Rather, he means to say that it is prophecy through which God communicates with his own people. It affirms the Lord's interest in them when he directs a prophet to give a special message. In short, the apostle has declared in a roundabout way that prophecy, not tongues, is the appropriate speech for other believers to hear. If the ultracharismatics truly are filled with the Spirit, then they will possess the depths of *agapē* that will make them strive to bless and affirm the others.

14:23

Paul introduces a hypothetical situation: he says **if the whole church comes together and everyone speaks in tongues**, when he has already said in 12:30 that Christians *don't* all speak in tongues. Then **some who do not understand or some unbelievers come in**. A large house in Graeco-Roman times had less privacy than the homes of today; there might be a fair bit of traffic during the hour of the meeting – deliverymen, servants, friends or relatives, neighbors looking to chat. Their ultracharismatics, who regard uncontrolled speaking tongues as the highest manifestation of the Spirit's presence, will be taken by such bystanders as crazy. A loving Christian will want to communicate with the lost how they might be saved, not simply push them further away.[655]

14:24-25

This is still hyperbole, but one that is not far from possibility: what if the same person comes in, hypothetically, **while everybody is prophesying**. Here Paul shows what is only implicit up to this point: that a prophet's message might lend itself to evangelism.

---

[655] The 2nd-century apologists made use of the *charisma* of prophecy as a sign that the church was now the true people of God. Thus Justin Martyr, *Dialogue* 82, contrasted the church with Israel: "For the prophetical gifts remain with us [Christians], even to the present time. And hence you ought to understand that [the gifts] formerly among your nation [Israel] have been transferred to us." Irenaeus focused more on the role of the gifts within the church. In *Against heresies* 5.6.1: "...we do also hear many brethren in the Church, who possess prophetic gifts, and who through the Spirit speak all kinds of languages, and bring to light for the general benefit the hidden things of men." Also *Against heresies* 2.32.4: "Others have foreknowledge of things to come: they see visions, and utter prophetic expressions." See also *Contra Celsum* 2.8, quoted above.

Thus an unbeliever, like a believer, will hear a message of truth that is perhaps tailored specifically for him or her. For a prophet might speak of the facts of the cross-gospel in a clear manner, but also add something like: "and you, friend, although you have a believing wife, you have not yet repented. This is because you are reluctant to give up your cleverly-concealed liaison with a prostitute, and because you secretly resent the spiritual changes in your wife, even while professing to admire her new devotion to you and the children!"

Paul uses language of repentance, with the person falling prostrate: **So he will fall down and worship God, exclaiming, "God is really among you!"** This is not simply an admission that God is present, but a confession of saving faith. The apostle quotes Isa 45:14, in which gentiles bow down before the Israelites; in Paul's paraphrase they bow down and worship *God*.

Application: What is the worship service for? 14:25

A worship service should be to glorify God. This sounds so simple! But how easy it is to make worship service an end in itself. Like the disciples in the Jerusalem temple, we stand in awe of the pretty things we see around us (Mark 13:1) rather than focus on the Lord of the temple. But this can soon descend into the idolatry of sights, sounds and above all feelings, instead of the adoration of God.

14:26
As he has done with the themes of idolatrous meat or marriage, in 14:26-38 Paul will apply these larger principles to the specific context in Corinth. "Everyone has" of the NIV could be misleading, since it implies that everyone can speak in tongues, teach, prophesy, etc.; although it is a paraphrase, the GNB version "one person has a hymn, etc." captures the meaning. Paul gives the alternative of *all* prophesying or *all* speaking in tongues. Alright then, what if we act as we should act, and we all come with a different contribution, reflecting the body metaphor of 1 Cor 12? In that case, someone might have a **hymn**, or **word of instruction**, or a **revelation** (prophecy in this paragraph, but the same could be said of other types of revelatory word), or a **tongue** or an **interpretation**. The GNB's "message in strange tongues" reads far too much into the phrase, implying that tongues are a coded message from God to the church. The Greek is simply "each has a tongue."

Tongues are good, prophecy is good, variety is better, but, Paul will hammer home once again, **All of these must be done for the strengthening of the church**.

Application: Spiritual gifts and the megachurch 14:26

The verse is often taken as a sign of how spontaneous and democratic was the early church. But in fact Paul leaves unspoken whether people arrived prepared or (apart from the obvious 14:30) whether all was spontaneous; whether someone chaired the meeting or it moved along as individuals led. "Has a hymn," for example, is broad enough to include the person who comes prepared to lead music or the person who suddenly suggests the singing of a chorus. What the passage does tell us, however, is that the worship service is not left in the hands of any one individual or small group, no matter how gifted. And everyone should come expecting to participate.

There are forces today that work against the exercise of spiritual gifts in the worship service, so much so that many of us cannot even picture of 1 Cor 14:26 might look like in our church. Much of worship today is a spectator sport. Let us identify three important issues:

1. Professionalism. As a church grows in numbers and in finances, is may move away from people getting up and strumming the guitar or leading in choruses. People can listen to professionally-recorded Christian music at any time, and the music in the church suffers by comparison. And so the tendency will be to professionalize the music. Oh, the leaders are still Christians, exercising their gifts! But the ordinary Christian can never hope to "have a hymn." There arises a priesthood of the specially-trained: musicians, technicians, counselors, youth workers, etc. People without special training will become discouraged about serving in the church, or may feel that they exist merely to assist the "real" leaders.

2. Spiritual hierarchy. Once the church decides that some Christians are specially anointed and others are not; or that people with a certain gift are the real leaders, and others are not; then 1 Cor 14:26 inevitably falls by the wayside. Paul on the contrary wants all believers to participate. For a few to dominate the worship service, for whatever theological justification, is to quash New Testament worship.

3. Megachurch. I have been in very small churches and fairly big ones. For example, I have preached in a number of small assemblies of Brethren Christians. One of their emphases is taken from 1 Cor 14:26 – that every week, all members of the church should be able to exercise their gifts. Large churches have great advantages, especially in the range of specialized ministries they can offer, for example, to addicts, to the handicapped, to the divorced. Nevertheless there is loss. The model in this text can work well with a group of 20 people in Corinth. On the other hand, 1 Cor 14:26 has little hope of surviving in a worship service of, let us say, 2000 participants, in which a smaller percentage personally contribute to the worship service. Like Zacharias of old (Luke 1:8-10), you might wait a lifetime to get your one chance to minister in the temple! And so, the rest are invited to watch or participate: *let's all sing this song; it's time to give your offering; let's all listen to today's teacher! And only the small group of leaders will be given access to the loudspeaker system.*

Large churches inherently have special issues which will require some careful thinking and planning. One positive solution is to have cell groups, where 14:26 is fulfilled, and then large worship services where other ministry is done. This is not simply to satisfy a sociological or psychological need: it is what the Lord of the flock wants.

14:27

Since speaking in tongues is the main issue in this chapter, he will give a specific word about speaking aloud in the worship service. **Two – or at the most three** may do this, and only one at a time. Gone is the noisy clamor of one speaking over another, and all to give themselves a spiritual thrill. If the aim is to edify the church (14:26b), then each tongues-speaker must see to it that the church is blessed: one at a time, in order to allow someone to interpret what is being said. Two or three were a generous percentage of people in a church of only a few dozen.

14:28
As we have said earlier, the gift of interpretation seems to have been permanently given to individuals: if not, it could not be known in advance that someone was could give an interpretation.[656] Speakers must not overlap each other; they must not claim to be so controlled by the Spirit that they cannot restrain themselves; after each one, someone gives an interpretation: the rest of the body hears the praises of God in their own language, to which they can then say "Amen!"

If there is no interpreter, the speaker should keep quiet in the church and speak to himself and God. Horton argues that uninterpreted tongues do have a place in the worship service but that the Corinthians' mistake was to speak too long (14:23).[657] Nevertheless, Paul's law of silence is absolute; the person may speak in tongues later when alone (1 Cor 14:2-4), not aloud in the church.

Application: At what point have we violated 1 Cor 14:28?

Paul said of glossolalia: "If there is no interpreter, the speaker should keep quiet in the church." Christians today react in various ways to his teaching:

- Some act as if 1 Cor 14:28 did not exist.

- Some complain that other Christians are trying to put them into a box when they apply it to them.

- Some argue that it does not apply to them: for example, the verse only has to do with a single 1st-century congregation that abused the spiritual gifts, and not with today; or that it has to do only with a certain kind or usage glossolalia but not with the sort of thing that the church normally does. Of courses, our old acquaintance "terminal uniqueness" shows its face here, where people assume that in their situation the Spirit of God has been poured out so strongly that they cannot be limited by the "letter" of 1 Cor 14:28.

- On the other extreme, for those who theology does not allow for glossolalia, 14:28 does not apply any longer. They say: *If people were really speaking in tongues (which they aren't!), then we would have to insist on 14:28 being*

---

[656] We simply cannot agree with Thiselton, *First Corinthians*, 1139, that the gift of interpretation was only given at the moment, and that there were no regular "interpreters" as such in the congregation. This could imply that Paul was effectively ruling out tongues altogether by a logical tautology: *unless you know for certain that which cannot be known [i. e., that someone will be able to interpret], you cannot speak in tongues aloud.* This would be more than a little disingenuous on Paul's part. Why would he not simply say that tongues are for private use only, and may never be used in church?

[657] Horton, *I & II Corinthians*, 137-38.

applied; but in this day and age it is a moot issue.

- Thankfully, some Christians take very seriously what Paul says here. They believe that if the apostle taught this, then it is the will of God, given for our good and for God's glory. All that is left is to apply this faithfully to our own situation.

To put the question positively: what does it look like for a church to interpret speaking in tongues so that all may hear their meaning, and yet to not fall into a confusion of all speaking and the body going unedified? What does it mean to "keep quiet"?

Here is where cultural differences will play an important role. In North America, where Pentecostalism first manifested itself roughly a century ago, this takes place in a context quite different from the Latin American one. For in North America, it is not traditional for a whole group of people to pray aloud. Rather, they pray one by one.

In the contemporary Latin American church as in the Korean church and many others, the norm is that many people in a group may pray aloud and at once. What happens when this includes speaking in tongues? It means that an observer from the North might say, *You're violating 1 Cor 14:28! I can plainly hear more than one person speaking in tongues, all at once, and yet there is not a word of interpretation!* Meanwhile, the Latin Christian might respond that 14:28 is not the issue – after all, the intent is to seek God in prayer, and if someone prays in tongues loud enough to be overheard, that is no more problematic than if you overheard them praying in Spanish. After all, they "speak to themselves and God," just as Paul wanted! And they "keep quiet," but "quiet" of a Latin American type, not a traditional Northern type.

Let us hold the cultural issue in abeyance for a moment and think about what it was that Paul wanted to happen:

1. That the church might be edified by intelligible speech

2. That everyone have a chance to use whatever gift they have

3. That the worship service, while including elements of individual praise, might encompass the whole group

4. That no-one be made to feel like an outsider

5. That no-one think the church is irrational

6. That there be order

These are not negotiable cultural values, but principles that God wants in our worship services wherever we are. Based on them, we might ask ourselves these questions:

1. Is there any speech within the church that may reasonably be regarded as unintelligible by the average local person? Does anyone ever say "that made no sense" in my church? You might retort that, of course, things don't make sense to those without the Spirit, but that begs the question. Paul says that no person,

believer or unbeliever, should feel like a foreigner in a worship service.

2. Could anyone in my church justifiably observe that people with one kind of gift – whether glossolalia or preaching or any gift – consistently occupy the center of the worship service and those with other gifts are pushed aside?

3. Do people during the service withdraw into private worship, even though the meeting is to be a time of group worship? We may worship God in our home, privately, individually; but when we are with other Christians, we must take them into account and worship God as a group. Yet many Christians close their eyes, speak to God one on one, praise God as solitary units, and seek his blessing for themselves. This is the heart of Paul's objection to the Corinthian practice: they wanted to ask, *And what could possibly be wrong with worshiping God?* Nothing of course; but it is inappropriate to act as a solitary unit when God wants to be worshiped by a body of believers.

4. Does any believer ever look at the worship service as something that specific leaders do, an activity which he or she may only observe?

5. Do things happen haphazardly? Do people talk over each other? Do some people get shut out and not have the opportunity to participate because the louder elements are grabbing the attention of the group? Even when the order does not conform to some premade plan, would people leave saying that things happened in a recognizable pattern?

Paul does not specify a decibel level, but describes a situation in which tongues are audible to others. I would say that, speaking in tongues without interpretation in anything above an inaudible or barely audible whisper is a transgression of 14:28. It is the responsibility of church leaders that they expect all persons to follow all of the Spirit's leading in chapter 14.

14:29
For prophets the rules are similar, except that there is no need of a third party to interpret the prophetic message. With the warning that **two or three prophets should speak** Paul affirms what has already been said so many times: that every single gift of God is valuable, and therefore every Christian should present his contribution in a way that will be clearly received.

Prophetic messages are to be taken very seriously, so seriously that they should be examined for their content. This is the sense of 1 Thess 5:19-22: prophecies are never to be rejected out of hand; but they are to be examined first to make sure that they are indeed genuine.

Paul is not clear whether it is the rest of the congregation or the other prophets that are meant by **the others should weigh carefully what is said**. Also missing from the directive is on what criteria the "others" discern the prophetic message. Do they discuss the personal character of the prophet, as in *Didache* and the *Shepherd of Hermas*? Do they examine the doctrine of the message, as in 1 John 4:1-2?

Application: Discerning prophecy 14:29

Paul orders that prophecies be discerned, that is, that the church carefully examine them; once approved, the prophecy should be conscientiously obeyed. Yet there is an almost universal tendency today to ignore the call to discern prophecy.

For Dispensationalist Christians or others who believe that the gift has ceased, discernment is not an issue. For why would one bother to spend time discerning something which is thought to be false from the beginning?

In other circles where the gift of prophecy is welcomed, many Christians refuse to exercise any discernment: why, after all, question something that is so obviously from God? We would be doubting God and showing a lack of faith or obedience. The reader can find many illustrations of this on websites that are supposedly "apostolic": question the apostolic leader, and that means you are a rebel against God! But this goes directly contrary to the will of the Spirit himself, who told us to "Test everything. Hold on to the good. Avoid every kind of evil" (1 Thess 5:20-22).

False prophecy exists and it is dangerous. Prophecy is not true just because it is loud, or delivered in extreme emotion, or delivered with foaming and groaning. It is true if it is true, that is, if it is truly from God and not from Satan or from the human imagination.

Why are we not more discerning? In many cases, it is because the church is impatient or unwilling to discern a prophecy. It half-accepts it but risks nothing on its trustworthiness. This accounts for why many prophetic messages, overwhelming and striking when given, are forgotten within hours – people do not leave the worship service deeply convinced that God had spoken.

What are the signs of a *lack* of discernment?

1. Prophets announce "thus says the Lord." but that claim is not examined

2. When people want to compare the prophecy with the Bible or with other known truth, it is implied that they are being rebellious or serving the "letter," not the Spirit, in a misinterpretation of 2 Cor 3:6

3. When a prophecy does not come to pass, no-one remarks on it; the church has a short memory

4. No-one examines the moral character of the prophet

5. Words of prophecy that uphold the power structure of the church are welcomed, those that do not are ignored

6. There is no space given after the end of the prophecy before it is announced that this was indeed God's message

The clearest examples of prophecy in the New Testament are from Agabus and the apostle Paul himself. Agabus in Acts 11:27-28 predicted a world-wide famine. The author of Acts comments as an aside that indeed this famine later took place during the reign of Claudius (the Roman emperor from AD 41-54). One of the prophecies of Paul is found in Acts 27:21-26, which is full of specific details: the ship will be run aground on an island and be destroyed; yet all the passengers will survive; later, Paul will appear before Caesar in Rome.

Agabus and Paul gave prophecies that were:

> 1. Unequivocal. In no case did a prophecy fail to come true and the prophet then say, well, it's because I prayed and changed the direction of the event; or, this *could* have happened or *would* have happened if other events had taken place.

> 2. Capable of being disproved. In the case of Agabus, if a world-wide famine did not come within a reasonable time, his prophecy would have been shown up as false. In Acts 27:21-44, if but one of the 276 persons on board Paul's ship had drowned or otherwise died, the prophecy would have been disproved. In our day, there are "prophets" who misspeak time after time; perhaps they are right once in a while, which is not a difficult thing to do with a little practice; but the church continues to listen in awe and amazement as though the errors did not matter.

> 3. Detailed. These were not general messages but ones with numbers and other incidental references. In the case of 1 Cor 14:24-25, a non-Christian seems to hear his hidden sins listed in front of the congregation; he is so shocked by the accuracy of the word that he immediately turns to God.

Some modern prophecies fall far short of this criterion of precise fulfillment. For example, Benny Hinn in the 1990's prophesied that God would give the North American homosexual movement a death blow within a short time. When it did not happen, he offered no apology. People could begin to rationalize: *But what is a "short time," after all? And what does "destroy" mean? Or maybe God really destroyed it, it's just invisible to the human eye.*

The New Testament prophecies were not like elusive messages such as: "I am the Lord, I will shepherd my people" or "Fear not, I am with you always"; comforting words, but not revealing anything specific, timely and urgent from heaven. Are such prophecies false? Not necessarily, but they cannot be proven or disproved. Yes, prophecies are meant to be a comfort or a rebuke to the listeners, but they usually do so by providing some new or hidden data so that the hearer is made aware that it is God who is speaking. This is the weakness of the view that says "we will accept anything as true so long as it does not directly contradict the Bible." For if one speaks in Christian generalities, they will not contradict the Bible, but neither are they special immediate words from God.

What may the church do to return to the apostolic pattern?

First and foremost, we must accept that there is such a thing as false prophecy and that it is prevalent; that it may even come from people we know well; that it is to be carefully set aside. Second, we will expect true prophecy to supplement what we already know from regular Bible study, not be a substitute for it. There is too much excitement when an "apostle" claims to have new truths from God; it seems so much more interesting than the hundreds and thousands of hours that a believer should put into the study of the

Scriptures.

Third, we will expect true prophecy to come from the holy of the church, not necessarily from the powerful.

Fourth, the church must arrange for some way to discern prophecy and makes known to everyone what that plan is. Someone should announce, *We respect the gift of prophecy so much that, when a word is given to someone, this group over here will immediately take the message and pray and discern it and then report back to the church whether they think it is from God. This may take more than a few minutes, but it is so important that we get this right that we will take what time is needed.*

Fifth, if the church decides a prophecy is not genuine, it announces so clearly and forcefully. If it decides that it is from God, the leaders and church should begin to talk about how to follow it. The church will set aside what is not proven true, and hold on to and obey what is proven true. Thus, if your church received a prophecy last year, and it was discerned to be true, then the church ought to be following it this year, and everyone in the congregation ought to be able to recite the gist of it.

To reiterate, it is no disrespect to God to be discerning; rather, discernment is the sign that we will take this word with great seriousness. To the skeptical and to the gullible alike, the Bible says, "Discern"!

Application: False prophecy and taking Lord's name in vain 14:29, 37

The Ten Commandments stated emphatically, "You shall not misuse the name of the LORD your God, for the LORD will not hold anyone guiltless who misuses his name" (Exod 20:7). Thus when Israelites took oaths in court or to ratify treaties, they were to swear by Jehovah's name as a sign of their fidelity (Deut 6:13). It was a grave sin to swear deceitfully (Lev 19:11-12).

But there is another application of this commandment: some false prophets misuse Jehovah's name. We are not speaking here of the explicitly pagan prophets of Deut 13, people who might speak in the name of Baal, for example (as in the account of Elijah in 1 Kings 18). Rather, it is that other breed of false prophet: those who invoke the name of the Lord and deceptively claim that God has revealed a message to them. Both types of false prophet are mentioned in Deut 18: "But a prophet who presumes to speak in my name anything I have not commanded him to say, or a prophet who speaks in the name of other gods, must be put to death" (Deut 18:20). Also, "If what a prophet proclaims in the name of the LORD does not take place or comes true, that is a message the LORD has not spoken. That prophet has spoken presumptuously. Do not be afraid of him" (Deut 18:22). The test is whether the prophecy comes to pass or not. If it does not, the prophet is false, even though he used God's name and seemed to be encouraging people to follow Jehovah. The Mosaic penalty for both kinds of false prophets was the same: capital punishment.

Where does the content of false prophecies come from? From out of their own imagination; it is what the prophet would like to be so, but he has no sure idea of whether it is God's truth or not (Jer 23:16-22; Ezek 13:1-10; 1 Kings 22:5-6). Jeremiah has several examples of this, notably 14:14:

Commentary 7-15

> Then the LORD said to me, "The prophets are prophesying lies in my name. I have not sent them or appointed them or spoken to them. They are prophesying to you false visions, divinations, idolatries and the delusions of their own minds.

Imagine how this looks from God's perspective: here are men and women who claim God's own authority and announce a message; but God knows that he never authorized these persons. This constitutes a violation of the commandment not to misuse God's name.

False prophets are not limited to Old Testament days. It is probable that false prophets in 1 John 4:1-6 were claiming to speak in the name of God: that is, they took the Lord's name in vain when they stood up to announce, *Thus says the Lord – Christ the Spirit did not take on flesh; this was only an illusion to make it easier for simple people to accept his message.* The false prophets in Matt 24:24 lead people away from the true Christ, and also back up their words with signs and wonders. 2 Thess 2:2 may imply that the church had heard a false "word" of prophecy. Let no one imagine that God keeps false prophets from the church; rather, it is the church that must learn to please God by being discerning and filtering out false messages.

Let us focus on three fictional scenarios where people are taking the Lord's name in vain:

- A leader of a Christian organization is being pressured by others to change direction. They have had meetings to try to settle the dispute, and now it looks like the leader is going to lose. But suddenly he announces that "God has told me" that they must follow the plan that – surprise! – the leader was promoting all along. He now becomes stubborn, since who would disobey what God wants? Plus, those who oppose his plan are told that in reality they are opposing God. Did God really speak to him? Perhaps, but if not, the leader is pulling out God's name as if it were the trump card to win a game.

- A teacher is speaking on some issue on which the Bible does not clearly speak. For example, there is a political election, and in a message she proclaims, *It is God's will that we vote for so-and-so, and if we don't we are in sin!* She does not say, "Here is why this choice is more biblical, or seems to me more godly." Rather, she is announcing God's own opinion in God's name. But, we have no right to tell what God thinks if God has not revealed it!

- A man gets up in the congregation and announces that God has given him a message: *Within 30 days the economy of this country will collapse, says the Lord. Therefore, store food and water in your homes for the hard times that are coming!* Some people do this, but after 30 days, 45 days, three months, the economy continues as before.[658] What happens then? It is common that the church will simply have a case of amnesia: it is uncomfortable to mention the awkward prophecy, and so nothing at all is said. Alternatively, the prophet may get up to announce: *Here is what really happened: I prayed for the economy not*

---

[658] The reader might profit from the classic sociological study, *When prophecy fails: a social and psychological study of a modern group that predicted the destruction of the world*, by Leon Festinger, et al., 1956.

to collapse; the Lord has shown me that my prayers changed the situation. That is, he implies that despite appearances, his first prophecy was set aside, that his prayers changed things, and that God gave him a second revelation to confirm that fact to him. Now, I do not doubt that this can happen; the case of Jonah 3:10 (see also Exod 32:14) is a Bible example, but it is also a rare occurrence. This is why the Bible can put so much emphasis on true prophecies coming to pass and false prophecies not coming to pass – that is what happens in all but a tiny number of cases. If so many of today's prophecies seem to need updating and revising, it is likely that the "prophet" took the Lord's name in vain, that is, proclaimed a revelation that he had never been given.

These hypothetical people are all violating one of the Ten Commandments. How fearful we should be to use the words "Thus says the Lord" or "The Lord told me" or "This is the Lord's mind on this issue" if we are not absolutely convinced that it is a supernatural revelation from God, and if we are not willing to put it forward to be tested. To presume to speak otherwise is a wickedness that, had it taken place in the days of the Old Testament, should have led you to being stoned to death. And if being stoned is a fearful fate, how much worse is it to fall into the hands of the God who said of the false prophets: "I will make them eat bitter food and drink poisoned waters" (Jer 23:15b).

14:30-31

Paul affirms throughout that true prophecy leads to order, not to frenzy. He pictures the church as a meeting where people are seated to participate but then stand to prophesy, and presumably, to teach or to speak in tongues. Now he thinks of spontaneous revelation.[659] Someone is prophesying and suddenly another person is conscious of receiving a word from the Lord. The rule is curious, since Paul could have told the seated person to wait, but instead has the person with the floor pause to allow the second one to speak. There seems to be a level of urgency to this second revelation message that does not characterize the first: so the new message should be given, and then the other can be completed too. That way, both messages are communicated **so that everyone might be instructed and encouraged.**

14:32-33a

The gift of prophecy is the model for any other gift, especially tongues: **the spirits of prophets are subject to the control of prophets**. Here "spirit" carries the sense of 14:14-16, the human spirit as endowed with charismatic gift. The GNB reads this as an admonition rather than a statement: "The gift of proclaiming God's message *should be* under the speaker's control." While this also true, Paul's likely meaning is a *declaration*: no matter how ecstatic they might feel, people with a true gift of prophecy are *de facto* always able to control themselves. Christian prophecy is not like the prophecy of the raving pythoness (as in Acts 16:16-19), **for God is not a God of disorder but of peace**. The Corinthians must not blame the Spirit if his messages are not being heard! It is your rudeness, the opposite of love, that is blocking the transmission.

---

[659] So Schrage, *An die Korinther*, 3:452; contra Thiselton, *First Corinthians*, 1141-42.

14:33b

As in all the congregations of the saints is an appropriate word is for the Corinthians, who yearn to be unique. We agree with the majority of the versions (including the NIV 1984; but contra the KJV, NASB, NIV 2011), that the phrase belongs to what follows and refers to how women behave in all the churches.

14:34-35

Some scholars (most evidently Gordon Fee) have argued that these two verses were not part of the original text of 1 Corinthians and were a later interpolation, added by some scribe; therefore they should be eliminated from the biblical text.[660] This seems shocking; nevertheless, the scholars who wish to remove these two verses from the English versions do so because they are convinced that, at some time in the past, someone mistakenly added to God's Word and that that error should now be corrected. Thus the question here is, *What was the original text of his Word?*

In fact, every single Greek manuscript of 1 Cor 14 includes these two verses. However, beginning with the late 4th century commentary by Ambrosiaster some witnesses in the Western tradition put them in a different location, after 14:40. Since the verse numbers were not added until centuries later, the ancient reader might not have noticed a disruption. The end of the chapter would look like this:

> But everything should be done in a fitting and orderly way. Women should remain silent in the churches. They are not allowed to speak, but must be in submission, as the Law says. If they want to inquire about something, they should ask their own husbands at home; for it is disgraceful for a woman to speak in the church [and then on to 1 Cor 15:1].

Gordon Fee argues that the verses originated as a note that someone wrote in the margin of some manuscript; the next scribe to copy that manuscript assumed that the marginal gloss was (as it often could be) verses that the previous copyist had accidentally left out and wanted included.[661] Thus when he copied 1 Cor 14 he included them in their current location, while in other cases, scribes decided to put them at the end of the chapter. Thus Fee claims that the verses are not from the hand of Paul, but from some later person whose views on women in the church were more restrictive. Others have criticized the interpolation hypothesis, since in other New Testament books, whole verses occasionally do appear out of order, and this is not necessarily taken as a sign of their inauthenticity.[662]

Every single Greek manuscript does include the verses, and the evidence isn't even

---

[660] See especially Fee, *First Corinthians*, 698-705; Conzelmann; Weiss; Barrett, *First Corinthians*, 330, leans to this view. Murphy-O'Connor, *1 Corinthians*, 150-51, calls the section "An Attack on Women."

[661] This is almost certainly how 1 John 5:7 came to be included in our NT, although that happened centuries later in the copying process; the verse is not found in any Greek manuscripts prior to the late Middle Ages. In the case of the two principal textual difficulties of the New Testament (the ending of Mark 16:9-20 and the passage of the woman taken in adultery in John 7:53-8:11), we possess actual early Greek manuscripts that omit the passages. This cannot be said for 1 Cor 14:34-35.

[662] Fee, *First Corinthians*, 700 n. 9, accepts that authentic verses were accidentally transposed in some manuscripts of Matt 5:4-5 and Luke 4:5-10, but he decides that this parallel is not relevant. But see J. M. Ross, "Floating words: their significance for textual criticism," *NTS* 38 (1992): 153-56; Ross demonstrates that when there is a whole sentence or two that moves from place to place, they are usually authentic.

strong enough to produce serious doubt about the original order. The UBS[4] edition rates the reading as it stands with the letter B, that it is "almost certain" that Paul wrote these verses *and* that they originally appeared in this place in the epistle as opposed to at the end of the chapter. The verses appear here in all the English versions. We agree that Paul wrote these verses and he included them at this point in the chapter.[663] The language, while differing from Paul's in some ways, does follow neatly on what has been he has been saying (references to women in the worship service in ch. 11; the tension between speak/remain silent). In fact, the entire section of 14:14-35 has to do with who should be speaking in the church and who should be quiet so that others may be heard.

Another possibility is that Paul is quoting or paraphrasing some statement that came out of Corinth.[664] In that case, it was the Corinthians who said that "Women should remain silent in the churches, etc." Then, when Paul says in 14:36 "Did the Word of God originate from you?" he means, "Was it only to you Corinthians that God revealed this 'truth' about women keeping silent?" This viewpoint is highly unlikely, since if anything the Corinthians were more liberal in such matters than Paul – some even thought women could prophesy without a veil. And besides, if Paul were citing the Corinthian view only to dismiss it, he did so in an extremely vague fashion, and the Corinthians could have been forgiven for not understanding what he meant. We will approach the text, therefore, that Paul wrote 14:34-35, and that it is a positive expression of his teaching.

Women should remain silent in the churches. They are not allowed to speak seems to be at variance with 11:5, where the discussion of the veil reveals to the reader that women *were* allowed and expected to pray and prophesy aloud. This tension has not arisen only recently; the church fathers commented on it, ages before the modern feminist controversies. Paul also mentions corporate speech or singing (e. g., 14:26), in which we assume that women participated. How is it possible that they may speak, but at the same time must stay quiet? Some commentators have concluded that Paul was not seriously affirming female participation in 11:5,[665] but this is hardly likely. Why would he have spilled so much ink about how women were to pray and prophesy with a veil if in the end it were a moot issue?

There are two points at issue: (1) Was it expected that women would have the gift of prophecy? (2) Were they permitted to prophesy in the meeting?

With regard to (1), the evidence from the New Testament and from the early church fathers is unambiguous: some women as well as some men received the prophetic gift and conveyed messages directly from God. The prophet Joel had predicted that "Your sons and daughters will prophesy" (Joel 2:28, quoted by Peter in Acts 2:17). Neither men nor women were prophesying on the day of Pentecost, but apparently the women

---

[663] So Thiselton, *First Corinthians*, 1147-50.

[664] So Talbert, *Reading*, 91-95, who thinks that Paul disagrees vehemently with their anti-woman attitude. Also Fitzmyer, *First Corinthians*, 530-33.

[665] See Hodge; also Origen. Robertson and Plummer, *First Corinthians*, 230, will only concede that there existed "a bare possibility that that Spirit may compel [women] to speak." Similarly, Godet, *First Corinthians*, 545, says: "while rejecting, as a rule, the speaking of women in Churches, Paul yet meant to leave them a certain degree of liberty for the exceptional case in which, in consequence of a sudden revelation (prophesying), or under the influence of a strong inspiration of prayer and thanksgiving (speaking in tongues), the woman should feel herself constrained to give utterance to this extraordinary impulse of the Spirit…Moreover, Paul does not seem to think that such cases should be frequent." But this idea raises more questions than it solves: are women incapable of controlling themselves in the manner Paul mandates in 1 Cor 14:27-33a? Does the Spirit force women to break the rule of silence that he himself has inspired Paul to write?

present were speaking in tongues. Women implicitly have the gift of prophecy in 1 Cor 11:5. The four daughters of Philip have the gift (Acts 21:9) just as do men such as Agabus (Acts 21:10-11).

The fathers of the 2nd century were the immediate heirs of the apostolic age and wrote of practices that had their roots in the 1st century. This is how we know of the prophetess Ammia, who lived in the city of Philadelphia, the city addressed in Rev 3:7-13. Ammia may have been active at the time of Revelation, if not, then in the early years of the 2nd century.[666] Justin Martyr, speaking around the year AD 135, quoted Joel's prophecy and added, "Now, it is possible to see amongst us women and men who possess [charismatic] gifts of the Spirit of God."[667] Centuries later, Chrysostom says of 1 Cor 11:4 that "for then [at the time of 1 Corinthians] women also used to prophesy."[668]

On a few occasions, the church looked askance at prophetesses. Beginning in the 160s, Montanus started the "New Prophecy" movement. His two co-leaders were the supposed prophetesses Priscilla and Maximilla. The church as a whole rejected the two, not because they were female, but because their prophecies were false.[669] Around the year AD 180, Irenaeus criticized women who were disciples of a certain Marcus, not because they were female but because they imagined that Marcus could give them the prophetic gift.[670]

With regard to (2) Were women permitted to prophesy in the meeting? For example, Bachmann argues that 11:5 has to do with worship in the woman's home, where she might prophesy to a small group of friends.[671] Nevertheless, here again, the New Testament and the early fathers give implicit, unanimous approval to women and men prophesying in the meeting.

First, the social context of 1 Cor 11:5 is that women are not in their own homes, where they would not be wearing a veil. A woman would put on a veil only to go from her home to a meeting of men and women, and then leave the veil on throughout the meeting, including when she prayed or prophesied aloud. If men are not present when a woman prophesies, then it makes no sense to say that removing the veil would shame the men (see comments on 1 Cor 11:5). Neither this epistle or any other New Testament passage says nothing about women being allowed to prophesy only in their own home. In the same way, as late as AD 180, Irenaeus interpreted Paul to be saying that women

---

[666] Eusebius, *History of the church* 5.17.
[667] Justin Martyr, *Dialogues* 87.
[668] Chrysostom, *i ad Corinthios* 26.2 and 4. Again Chrysostom, *i ad Corinthios* 37.1: "For if to them that have the gifts it is not permitted to speak inconsiderately, nor when they will, and this, though they be moved by the Spirit; much less to those women who prate idly and to no purpose."
[669] See Shogren, "Christian prophecy and canon in the second century," 615-18.
[670] Irenaeus, *Against heresies* 1.13.4.
[671] Bachmann, *An die Korinther*, 352. Likewise, Calvin, *First Corinthians*, 1:467-68 – "[1 Cor 14:33-35], however, we must understand as referring to ordinary service, or where there is a Church in a regularly constituted state; for a necessity may occur of such a nature as to require that a woman should speak in public; but Paul has merely in view what is becoming in a duly regulated assembly." Contra the view expressed by Kuss, *Die Briefe an die Römer, Korinther und Galater* [my translation], that "the passages deal with two different types of meetings: in ch. 11, house meetings; here [in 14:34-36], full meetings of the whole church." Of course, contra Bachmann, Calvin and Kuss, Paul makes no mention of this sort of distinction. See the clear problems with this "private prophecy" view as pointed out by Grosheide, *First Corinthians*, 252-53.

prophesied in the meeting: "For, in his Epistle to the Corinthians, [Paul] speaks expressly of prophetical gifts, and recognises men and women prophesying *in the Church*."[672]

Second, the church generally banned people from prophesying "privately," that is outside of the meeting. According to Hermas, when Christians assemble together and pray, then God might decide to send a prophetic message. False prophets, on the other hand, are fortune-tellers who prophesy whenever people visit them and give them money for some message. Thus, Hermas' experience in the church at Rome was that all true prophecy takes place during the meeting.[673] The church became more conservative throughout the 2nd century. In the early 3rd century, Origen was the first to say that women may not prophesy within the Christian assembly, but that they may prophesy outside the church.[674]

Let us return to the text of 1 Cor 14. Paul tells women to be silent, but in a context that strongly indicates that the silence is not absolute but relative. He uses the same verb "remain silent" (*sigaō*) that appears in 14:28 and 30. In 14:28, tongues-speakers who perceive that there is no interpreter present in the worship service should "remain silent." Similarly a literal translation of 14:30 is, "if a revelation comes to someone who is sitting down, the first speaker should stop." This gives us some help, as does the use of the word elsewhere in the New Testament:

- Luke 9:36 – the disciples do not tell what they know about Jesus
- Luke 18:39 – Jesus silences the demons who were blurting out his true identity
- Luke 20:26 – Jesus' opponents are silent, they stop testing him with hard questions
- Acts 12:17, 15:12, 13 – *sigaō* means to cease talking so as to listen or to think in silence

That is, depending on the context, *sigaō* could mean to maintain silence, to pause from speaking or to cease from speaking. In 1 Cor 14:28 and 30 it means "refrain from speaking" and "stop speaking" respectively, but not maintain absolute silence.

In addition we are greatly helped by the context. Beginning at 14:29, Paul moves from speaking in tongues to prophets. For prophets the rules are:

---

[672] Irenaeus, *Against heresies* 3.11.9, emphasis added.

[673] Hermas, *Mandate* 11.8-9 – the genuine Christian prophet "gives no answer to anyone when consulted. Nor does he speak on his own (nor does the Holy Spirit speak when a man wants to speak), but he speaks when God wants him to speak. So, then, when the man who has the divine Spirit comes into an assembly of righteous men who have faith in a divine Spirit, and intercession is made to God by the assembly of those men, then the angel of the prophetic spirit which is assigned to him fills the man, and being filled with the Holy Spirit the man speaks to the multitude, just as the Lord wills." Note: in this section, when Hermas refers to a prophet as *anthrōpos*, he uses it with the generic meaning "person" and not necessarily "man." Hermas, *Mandate* 11.2 shows that the false prophet gives private consultations – "These double-minded ones come to him as to a fortune teller, and ask him what will happen to them. And that false prophet, not having the power of a divine spirit in himself, answers them in accordance with their questions and their wicked desires, and fills their souls just as they themselves wish."

[674] In his commentary, Origen mentions the daughters of Philip, Deborah, Miriam, Huldah and Anna and concludes (Kovacs, 239-40) – "…even if we should concede, on the basis of a prophetic sign, that a woman is a prophetess, still she is 'not permitted to speak' in church. When Miriam the prophetess spoke, it was to certain women whom she was leading. 'For it is shameful for a woman to speak in church' [1 Cor 14:35b]. And 'I permit no woman to teach or to have authority over men' [1 Tim 2:12]."

Commentary 7-15

> Two or three speak
> The others should weigh carefully what is said
> All prophesy in turn

Then he adds:

> Women remain silent in the church
> Women with questions should ask their husbands at home

Paul has said in 11:5 that women may prophesy, so long as their heads are covered. This indicates that "two or three prophets should speak" (14:29) could include bare-headed men or veiled women. He turns in 14:29b from discernment of the prophetic word: "and the others should weigh carefully what is said." Part of the reason for prophesying in turn is to allow everyone to hear every word, but also to allow for times of discernment. The church needs times of speaking but also times of quiet reflection on what has been said, here primarily to discern whether it is truly a message from God. It is in this context that women are to maintain silence (to stop talking and to reflect, which is one of the uses of *sigaō*).[675] In that case Paul is saying to the women: *Stop talking! Let the church have silent time to discern! Don't keep asking questions that will serve to distract!*[676] This means that the two clauses **they are not allowed to speak** and **it is disgraceful for a woman to speak in the church**, according to the context of Corinthians, must be qualified and not be taken absolutely.[677] The directive continues the theme of silence while prophecy is being discerned. As in 11:6, "disgraceful" (*aischros*) refers to behavior that erodes fitting gender roles.

Some have suggested that the rule is designed to prevent a wife from judging what her prophet husband has said, thus controverting his headship (11:3); the wife should ask her husband **at home** about the meaning of the prophecy. In fact, there is no compelling need to limit the verse to a wife and own prophet-husband. Paul speaks broadly of not allowing **women** to speak. This is probably an application of the truth "the head of the woman is man" (11:3): for women of the church to probe and test a man who has prophesied is bringing shame to men. They should listen and **be in submission**. Submissive to the husband?[678] To the men? To the church? We are not told.

One more difficult point is **as the Law says** (the word *nomos*) in 14:34b. Some have suggested that this is some sort of "canon law," that is, that there existed somewhere a list of rules that governed the churches, one of which deals with women speaking in

---

[675] So Thrall, *I and II Corinthians*, 102; the detailed discussion by Carson, *Showing the Spirit*, 121-31; James B. Hurley, *Man and woman in biblical perspective* (Grand Rapids: Zondervan 1981), 193 says that they should be silent and not judge prophecies; Witherington, *Women in the earliest churches*, 90-104, see p. 102 – "it only restricts her from judging prophecy in some manner so as to lord it over either her husband or men in general."

[676] Witherington, *Conflict and community*, 278-79, suggests that some women were treating the prophet like a pagan oracle, to whom the people would "put questions" about life, love and money. While this would in fact be a distraction and contrary to the Spirit, one wonders why they should ask their husbands such questions in the home. Why not simply warn the Corinthians that such questions are beside the point?

[677] So Thrall; Walter; Grudem, *Gift of prophecy*, chapter 11.

[678] This is the direction taken by Ambrosiaster: "For if it is the man who is the image of God and not the woman, and if she is subjected to the man by the law of nature, how much more ought the woman to be in subjection when she is in church, as a sign of respect for the man who is the ambassador of the One who is his head."

church. This is speculative, and presumes the existence of another, unknown document. Those who argue for an interpolation believe that the reference to this restriction cannot have come from the hand of Paul, champion of Christian liberty, since the author of these words is speaking positively about the law of Moses. Even taken superficially, this argument will not work: Paul has already adduced the Old Testament law as a guide to the Christian in 9:8-9, and even more strikingly in this same context in 14:21, where he introduces a quotation from Isaiah with, "In the Law it is written," as in 14:34 using the same word, *nomos*. That seems to make the best sense here as well: *As the Old Testament says, women should be in submission* (so the NIV). The best guess is that he is thinking again of Gen 2:18-23 as proof for the headship of men over women, just as he did in 1 Cor 11:7-9.[679]

Is this passage synonymous with "women should not teach men"?[680] Although that might be the conclusion one will take after comparing this passage with 1 Tim 2:11-15, it is not teaching that is in view here but a process of discerning prophetic words.

Reading these verses as an absolute prohibition of women speaking in church is not, as some claim, the obvious or "literal" interpretation of the passage. Our interpretation takes into account the most relevant exegetical data, that is, 1 Cor 11:5, the immediate context of 1 Cor 14:29-33, the flexible meaning of "remain silent" and the majority testimony of the early church.

We may paraphrase the passage thus:

Two or three prophets should speak, and the others should weigh carefully what is said...And as in all the congregations of the saints [during that time of weighing], women should remain silent in the churches. They are not allowed to speak [either for or against the prophet or prophetess], but must be in submission, as the Law of Moses says in Gen 2. If women with a Christian husband want to inquire about something, they should ask their own husbands at home; for it is disgraceful for a woman to speak in the church when prophecy is being tested.

This means that 14:30-33 flows naturally into 14:34-35, which is not a parenthesis which breaks up the flow of the passage.

In the end, one cannot get around there here is a rule specifically for women in **all the congregations of the saints**. Paul's reference to the other churches indicates that this is not specially designed to rein in the Corinthian women for being uniquely disruptive. Rather the Corinthian women must behave as do all Christian women everywhere.

14:36

We take 14:36-37 to be directed, not to the rationalist elitists of Corinth, but toward the same ultracharismatics to whom Paul addresses the bulk of 1 Cor 12-14. Whereas he earlier had to urge the elitist to begin to pay greater attention to the divine revelation, here he speaks to those who act as though they alone were its proprietors. And so, like

---

[679] So Kistemaker. Most others take it as a reference to Gen 3:16 – as early as Origen – but it is to Gen 2:18-19 that Paul had earlier appealed in 1 Cor 11:8-9, making that text the likely referent here.

[680] Robertson and Plummer, *First Corinthians*, 302: "So far from preaching, [women] ought not even to ask questions." Ambrosiaster says (Bray, 146): "If they dare to speak in church, it is a disgrace, because they are veiled in order to appear humble."

their rationalist brothers and sisters, the ultracharismatics too fell into the trap of believing themselves unique and beyond the rules that applied to other congregations.

14:37

Even the ultracharismatic, anyone who **thinks he is a prophet or spiritually gifted**, must submit to the word of the Lord as given through his apostle. So many of the strands of 1 Cor 12-14 are wound together here: *the Spirit makes some apostles and other prophets, but both are sent by God to bless the church. The prophets cannot claim that the Spirit is giving them a message different from that which the apostles gave them – because that would make the Spirit's word contradictory*. Paul speaks of the **prophet**, but also more generally of the **spiritually gifted**, which translates the adjective *pneumatikos*, used in 12:1 and 14:1. It is better rendered in all three verses as "that which as to do with the Holy Spirit," thus "a person of the Holy Spirit." A person truly in communication with the Spirit will affirm that another word of the Spirit is **the Lord's command**, that is, what Paul writes in this letter or, perhaps, what the Lord commanded in the Law (14:34).

14:38

Here is a warning to those who are proud of their spiritual gift: **If he ignores this, he himself will be ignored**; if you claim to be a prophet, yet will not accept the apostle's teaching, the apostle (or perhaps, the church of God) will in turn deny your authority. Or it may be a reference to the final judgment. Whatever the reference, Paul is giving a chance to the Corinthian to evaluate his attitude and to repent.

14:39

Paul has finally reached his conclusion, opening with the attention-getter **Therefore, my brothers**. The command **be eager to prophesy** repeats closely as his theme in 12:31, 14:1, using the same verb *zēloō*. Added now is a word about tongues, **do not forbid speaking in tongues**. If some leader of the church has been tempted to shut down all glossolalia, because it had become annoying and connected with status-seeking, he should stop right now. Paul allows tongues in the worship service since, under the conditions he has previously stipulated, it is the work of the Spirit.

14:40

Tongues, or whatever spiritual gift, must fit within the context that **everything should be done in a fitting and orderly way**. This reflects what Paul has already said in 14:33, that "God is not a God of disorder but of peace." The orderliness of the worship service is not designed to muffle the Spirit's work, but in love to allow full play to all the gifts that he has given for the benefit of all present.

6. Concerning the Christian's future: "Do we really need to accept that crass superstition of the resurrection of the body, or doesn't the idea of an eternal spiritual existence do complete justice to the Christian tradition?" 15:1-58

First Corinthians

We leave behind one long section only to land in another long, tightly-woven essay. There is no "Now about" (*peri de*) to introduce it. However, because it is sandwiched between two Corinthian questions (12:1, 16:1) we take this to have been a concern that they expressed in their letter to Paul.[681] His answer to them is that, when Christ returns, all dead believers will be resurrected and all living Christians will be transformed before they can enter the kingdom of God. To deny this, he says, is to badly misunderstand and misapply certain fundamental gospel truths.

Paul obliges us more than usual by giving some hints about their new ideas:

15:12 – some of you say that there is no resurrection of the dead

Later on he gives a real or potential objection to the Pauline doctrine:

15:35 – How are the dead raised? With what kind of body will they come?

There are several ways to interpret what the Corinthians were saying:

1. *The Christian will perish when he dies; there is no future existence.*[682] This might answer why Paul says in 15:19 – "If only for this life we have hope in Christ, we are to be pitied more than all men." The Epicureans taught the annihilation of the individual upon death. It is less certain what the Sadduceans believed about the afterlife. The 1st-century witnesses to their doctrine are found in the New Testament and in Josephus: Matt 22:23-33 and its parallels have the Sadduceans denying and mocking the resurrection, but not offering their alternative. Acts 23:8 is unclear on the very same point: "the Sadduceans say that there is no resurrection, nor angel, nor spirit" (ESV), which may mean they denied the resurrection, either in the form of angels or in the form of spirits. In that case, they taught annihilationism, which is the Sadducean teaching as related by Josephus (*Antiquities* 18.1.4 §16). If this was the Corinthian doctrine, it may be reflected in 6:13 (see our commentary on that verse), that God will destroy the human body.

2. *The Christian experiences only an inner spiritual awakening*, a view that anticipated the later Gnostics: "God raised us up with Christ" (Eph 2:6), and that is all the resurrection there is. It may have been the error described in 2 Tim 2:18, "the resurrection has already taken place," the details of which doctrine are not obvious.[683] In

---

[681] Contra Nicoll, *First Corinthians*, 2:917. Karl Barth, in his remarkable little volume *The resurrection of the dead*, tr. H. J. Stenning (New York: Fleming H. Revell, 1933), goes so far as to take 1 Cor 15 as the main point of the letter.

[682] Bultmann, *Theology of the New Testament*, 169, argued that Paul misunderstood the Corinthians, that he was refuting that which they did not really believe, that is, the denial of any future existence. Schmithals' view is a variation of this, see *Gnosticism in Corinth,* 261-62. Alternatively, Andrew Lincoln, *Paradise now and not yet: studies in the role of the heavenly dimension in Paul's thought with special reference to his eschatology* (SNTSMS 43; Cambridge: Cambridge University Press, 1981), 35, suggests that they viewed the future kingdom as a continuation of the type of pleasant life they now enjoyed.

[683] Tertullian connects the Corinthian error with Marcionite and Gnostic ideas in *Prescription* 33; with Marcion in *Adversus Marcionem* 1.24 – "those whom [Marcion's god] saves are found to possess but an imperfect salvation – that is, they are saved only so far as the soul is concerned, but lost in their body, which, according to him, does not rise again." The Gnostic document *Treatise on the resurrection* 4 (http://www.thepearl.org/Mystery_of_the_Resurrection.htm) teaches: "The body is a shell. It has been

this case, some Corinthians believed that at death the Christian would become a liberated spirit. In this camp are those who find in Corinth an over-realized eschatology (see Introduction, also comments on 4:8): some Corinthians felt themselves so filled with the Spirit that they cannot imagine any future improvement on what they already have:

> In their view, by their reception of the Spirit, and especially the gift of tongues, they had already entered into the true "spirituality" that is to be (4.8); already they had begun a form of angelical existence (13.1; cf. 4.9; 7.1-7) in which the body was unnecessary and unwanted, and would finally be destroyed.[684]

Through some over-realized view of the kingdom of God some believe themselves to have been speaking in angelic tongues and perhaps spiritually resurrected to the point where the eschaton lost its meaning. Once again, it must be insisted that no known group in the early church combined charismatic excess with over-realized eschatology; neither the Gnostics nor the Montanists of the 2nd century held to anything like this hypothetical construct – it exists only on paper.

3. The Christian will live forever with Christ, but as a disembodied spiritual being.[685] This is not the same as the second option, which stresses an inner resurrection of conversion. Rather at death or at the second coming the Christian's soul or spirit will go to be with Christ in heaven, leaving bodily life behind forever.

The third option is best. In 1 Cor 15, Paul is specifically proving the resurrection and nothing else. Nowhere in this chapter does Paul set up arguments in favor of the future eschatology any more than he tries to prove that Jesus died for our sins and rose from the dead. Rather he uses these hopes to prove a different point: that if Jesus reigns, he reigns over enemies; death is the ultimate enemy; therefore the kingdom of Christ must involve the defeat of death. Along another line, he shows that death comes through Adam; Christ died and rose again to save us from sin and from its effects; therefore, part of salvation will be from death, that is, bodily resurrection. Likewise the Corinthians needed to hear of the bodily (and secondarily, eschatological) transformation of the living Christians. In 2 Corinthians, Paul delves more deeply into the issue: heavenly

---

compared to a tent. It is not the body that is saved, for salvation is a spiritual gift, which is received by the spirit, but the body is renewed by the spirit, and carried with it into the Eternal worlds. What then is the reality of the resurrection? It is always the disclosure of those who have risen. We rise [in this life] when we fulfill the new life which we have entered through Christ Jesus." The reader might be aware of the Gnostic societies throughout the Americas; the modern Gnostic Society in California offered as one of its lectures in March 1999: The "Key to the Future: The Gnostic Resurrection. How to rise from Spiritual Death while we are still in the body" (see http://www.gnosis.org/gnostsoc/gnostsocpast.htm). The label "Corinthian Gnosticism" fails to explain the facts of history: for example, Pagels, *The Gnostic Paul*, 80-86, shows how handily the later Gnostics reinterpreted this chapter to buttress their own theology, turning the "resurrection" of 15:12 to spiritual awakening, and the "mystery" of 15:51 into a hidden, superior teaching for the pneumatic Gnostics. See also the treatment by Wire, *The Corinthian women prophets*, 159-76.

[684] Fee, *First Corinthians*, 715.

[685] Justin Martyr, *Dialogue* 80.4-5 speaks of "some who are called Christians...who say there is no resurrection of the dead, and that their souls, when they die, are taken to heaven...But I and others, who are right-minded Christians on all points, are assured that there will be a resurrection of the dead..." In the context of *2 Clement* 9.1 the author alludes to both Corinthian epistles when he says "And let no one of you say that this very flesh shall not be judged, nor rise again." Similarly *Polycarp to the Philippians* 7.1: "and whosoever perverts the oracles of the Lord to his own lusts, and says that there is neither a resurrection nor a judgment, he is the first-born of Satan."

First Corinthians

existence without a body is compared to "nakedness," and the Christian ultimately waits to be "clothed" with the resurrection body (2 Cor 5:2-4).

The various errors and tendencies are easily explained by social and philosophical influences rather than by the presence of a specific alternative eschatology. In the case of the resurrection, the elitists dabbled in Stoicism and other philosophies, all of which vehemently scorned the concept of bodily resurrection.[686] The denial of the final resurrection had as much to with social climbing as it did to theological allegiance. The same sort of social factor may be seen in the Sadduceans of Palestine: according to the traditional interpretation, their eschatology was a sign of trying to fit into Hellenistic society, but was also a reflection of their wealth and privilege in this world.

Paul begins his proofs of the Christian's resurrection with Jesus' own death and resurrection. We cannot believe that any Corinthian denied the resurrection of Jesus, since that would mean that they were not Christians at all. But "it was probably held that Christ's rising from the dead was a unique, symbolic occurrence, bringing about for believers in Him a redemption wholly spiritual, a literal and full deliverance from the flesh and the world of matter."[687] This is the contradiction that Paul underscores in 15:12: "But if it is preached that Christ has been raised from the dead, how can some of you say that there is no resurrection of the dead?" Paul was uniquely qualified to make this point: as a Pharisee, Paul had upheld the teaching of the bodily resurrection against the Sadduceans.[688] And as a Christian his whole experience centered around his encounter with the risen Jesus on the Damascus Road.

The apostle's style here is well-reasoned, but it has the patient tone that one might use with a child. He is repetitive, taking the reader carefully through each step (see especially 15:12-14). His argument is that:

- The rising of Christ from the dead is an essential fact of the gospel
- If Christ rose from the dead, then the idea of resurrection from the dead cannot be impossible; the dead can rise, so now it is only a question of *who* rises
- If Christ rose from the dead, and we are in Christ, then we will rise too
- If we believe in the fall of Adam and in the need for salvation, then we will see death as an aberration, and resurrection to be an integral part of God's redemption of the human race
- If we believe in a universe made by a sovereign creator, we will have no trouble believing that he can raise the dead, even if the idea strains our limited imaginations
- The resurrection doctrine is a strong motive for holiness, and its denial leads to immorality[689]

---

[686] Plutarch, *Romulus* 28.8 cites some burlesque examples of bodies disappearing from their caskets, and then favorably quotes the poet Pindar: "All human bodies yield to Death's decree, The soul survives to all eternity." Chrysostom, *i ad Corinthios* 1.2 and indeed many Fathers made this same point: "The doctrine of the Resurrection, too, was lame among [the Corinthians]: for some of them had no strong belief that there is any resurrection of bodies, having still on them the disease of Grecian foolishness."

[687] Nicoll, *First Corinthians*, 2:917-18.

[688] Dan 12:2 – "Multitudes who sleep in the dust of the earth will awake: some to everlasting life, others to shame and everlasting contempt." The resurrection is portrayed in *1 Enoch* 51.1 – "In those days, Sheol will return all the deposits which she had received and hell will give back all that which it owes. And he shall choose the righteous and the holy ones from among (the risen dead), for the day when they shall be selected and saved has arrived." Also *2 Baruch* 49-51.

[689] See also Clement of Rome in *1 Clem* 24-27, especially 27.1-3 – "With this hope, therefore, let our souls

But Paul does not simply form a logical argument for the resurrection; he surprises the reader by adding a divine revelation (15:51) to cap off his argument: "Listen, I tell you a mystery," that is, a word that God has revealed through the Spirit. This new datum, which no philosopher could have conjured up through logic, is that at the return of Christ all believers will receive an "imperishable" body (15:51-52). But Paul waits many verses before revealing God's direct answer to their question. As a good teacher he takes them through many steps in order to prepare them to accept the "mystery" when it comes.

a. The saving gospel is a gospel of the bodily resurrection of Jesus 15:1-11

15:1

Paul does not refer to a question of the church or to oral reports. Rather he uses a reminder formula **I want to remind you** to take them back to the first facts of the Christian message. Their denial of the resurrection is not a detail of eschatology; it is inextricably tied to what they believe already, that Christ was resurrected and seen by many eyewitnesses.

He introduces the gospel, using technical terms of oral transmission, as he did in 11:23:

15:1 – of the gospel I preached to you, which you *received*
15:3 – what I *received* I *passed on* to you

That is, *I am telling you Corinthians the basic assured facts of the gospel, as transmitted to me, as preached by every apostle, as testified by all believers*. Even the Corinthians, with all their problems, may be said to **have taken your stand**.

15:2

By this gospel you were saved, that is, this gospel and not another; it is not possible to dispense with the eschatological resurrection and leave the saving message intact. **If you hold firmly to the word I preached to you** means that they cannot attach themselves to some other message and still enjoy salvation. No-one may alter parts of it according to one's taste.

Otherwise you have believed in vain is not a parallel to the failure to win the prize in 1 Cor 9:27. For there Paul speaks of the prize of being a successful evangelist, not the prize of eternal life. The traditional reading is best, that unless the Corinthians follow through on their reception of the gospel, they have believed to no good end (see 2 Cor 6:1).

15:3

Paul did not invent what he taught them, but had faithfully passed on the gospel tradition

---

be bound to him who is faithful in his promises and righteous in his judgments. He who commanded us not to lie all the more will not lie himself, for nothing is impossible with God, except to lie. Therefore let our faith in him be rekindled within us, and let us understand that all things are near to him."

he and all Christians had received. He did so "first," which might be chronological, the first lesson, but is probably logical, the most important one (so the NIV, **as of first importance**). 15:3b-5 contains the content of his message. Its structure and language imply that Paul is quoting it in a traditional form, that this is a primitive outline of the gospel that all early Christians learned and could recite. At the least it looked like this:

> Christ died for our sins
> > according to the Scriptures,
> he was buried,
> he was raised on the third day
> > according to the Scriptures

Most scholars today believe that 15:5 was also part of the fixed tradition:

> He appeared to Cephas (in the NIV "Peter"),
> and then to the Twelve.

This outline bears a strong resemblance to the later Apostles Creed and possibly helped to form it:

> He was crucified, dead and buried.
> > The third day he arose again from the dead.

The tradition may or may not have included resurrection appearances in 15:6-7. We take at least 15:8ff. as Paul's fresh commentary to the Corinthians.

Christ died for our sins according to the Scriptures. The language of expiation is based on the Servant passage of Isa 52:11-53:12. Paul does not develop the concept, but invests his time correcting what his readers failed to grasp. If they had denied its atoning value, Paul would have gone into greater depth. As it is he has already implied, Christ was crucified for the Corinthians (1:13, 8:11) and it is the manifestation and the channel for God's saving power and wisdom (1:18, 25) and their redemption (1:30). The cross of Christ in fact may stand as symbol for the whole gospel message (2:2) and the death of Christ is what is represented in the Lord's Supper (11:23-26).

Paul is true to his apostolic roots in appealing to what the Old Testament said about Christ's work. This was of great prominence in an era when so much evangelism was being done among Jews or gentile God-fearers. The post-resurrection accounts of Luke-Acts stress that the Scripture was being fulfilled in Jesus' death, resurrection, ascension, the giving of the Spirit and the proclamation of the gospel (Luke 24:25-27, 44-49; Acts 3:18, etc.). The New Testament preachers and writers regularly make reference to Psalm 16:8-11, Psalm 110:1, Psalm 118, Joel 2:32, 2 Sam 7:13-14, Isa 8:14, and other texts as being key predictions of Jesus, a list that is amplified in writers such as Justin Martyr in the next century (see especially his *Dialogue with Trypho*). One theory is that there existed a document or oral tradition called the *Testimonia*, a list of Bible verses with their fulfillment in Jesus, from which early Christians drew. Although this theory as such appears less and less likely, the fact remains that it was a key concern to prove that the gospel was biblical, that is, based on the Jewish Scriptures.[690] This is especially true for Paul in his epistles to the Galatians and to the Romans.

15:4

That he was buried has its parallel in the Apostles' Creed. To us it may seem unnecessary to stress the burial of Jesus' body or that he physically "he suffered under Pontius Pilate." But in the Creed it was needful to refute the Docetic heresy, the idea that Jesus was a phantom that could not suffer or die. Paul's argument here is in a slightly different direction: Jesus' burial was proof that he had died; therefore, when he was raised it was a true resurrection and not just the revival of a coma victim. For the same reason the gospel contains the detail about the soldier spearing Jesus (John 19:33-35).

That he was raised on the third day is repeatedly testified in the New Testament, especially in the apostolic preaching in Acts. The difficulty with Paul's statement is the reference **according to the Scriptures**. Did the Bible predict the detail that he would rise *on the third day*? If so, then the most likely reference is the deliverance of the prophet Jonah from the belly of the whale on the third day (Jonah 1:17; especially Matt 12:38-40). Beyond this possibility it is very difficult to take a concordance and find a biblical prediction that the Messiah would be in the grave three days and nights.[691]

Far too much has been made of the fact that Paul does not mention the "empty tomb" of Jesus, as all four gospels do. Some argue that the original resurrection tradition included only visions of the risen Jesus; later on the "empty tomb" story made the Easter experience into more than a vision of Jesus but rather the resurrection of his dead body. This is a false dilemma: the entire theology of resurrection in 1 Cor 15 assumes the transformation of the physical body and its continuity with the resurrection body. Paul cannot conceive of a resurrection that is merely continued spiritual existence while the body continues in a tomb.

15:5-7

This list of witnesses to Jesus' resurrection does not match any one gospel account, and seems to follow an inner logic of its own. Lacking is any reference to Mary and to the other women. Rather, the emphasis is that Jesus appeared to the apostles as eyewitnesses, as in 9:1.

That he appeared to Peter (in the Greek, "Cephas") is not mentioned as such as the gospels; only with difficulty do we make this an allusion to the event of John 21:7. Peter's Aramaic name is used here. The Corinthians thus knew personally – in Cephas and Paul – at least two independent eyewitnesses of the resurrection. And strikingly, in light of 1:11-12, Paul and Cephas are held up not as competitors but as witnesses of the same truth.

Since Judas was already dead, should not **the Twelve** be "the Eleven," as in fact a few manuscripts read? And what about the appearance to only "the ten" the time Thomas was absent (John 20:19-23)? Some (e. g., Chrysostom) have argued that Matthias, who would later be called an apostle, was one of these Twelve mentioned here, but Paul is not being mathematically precise. It is rather that "the Twelve" very quickly became a

---

[690] See the further refinement of this view by C. H. Dodd in his *According to the Scriptures* (London: Nisbet, 1952).

[691] See Fitzmyer, *First Corinthians*, 548-49, who detects a reference to Hos 6:2 – "After two days he will revive us; on the third day he will restore us, that we may live in his presence."

title for the group, even if someone happened to be missing at any one time (see for example Acts 6:2; also Rev 21:14). As in the appearance to Cephas, this appearance is not clearly attached to any one of the gospel accounts.

15:6

Paul now makes an addition of his own: not only to the inner circle did Jesus appear, but in fact to all kinds of people. We do not know who were the **five hundred of the brothers**,[692] but the reference is an important datum to understand the early church. Paul had proclaimed this gospel to the Corinthians around the year AD 50, that is, about 20 years after the resurrection. He knows enough about this group of 500 to be able to report that the majority still live in 55, and also that some have died. How completely at odds are these historical data, written very close to the event, with the reconstructions of some modern critics! For them the resurrection appearances were, at best, the experiences of people coming to believe that Jesus was after all the victor over death. Supposedly these highly individualistic feelings evolved into the resurrection stories that we possess in the gospels. For Paul, on the other hand, speaking shortly after the event, the resurrection was no hallucination or mystical event for scattered individuals; it was a fact repeatedly demonstrated to many different people at different times and places. Yet, **some have fallen asleep**: even these 500 have not yet escaped death. They too are falling one by one, pointing ahead to the need for the resurrection.

15:7

Again, this appearance of Jesus to **James** is not mentioned in the gospels.[693] Matt 28:10 is a possible reference to Jesus' "brothers," although it probably is his name for the disciples. This James is almost certainly the brother of Jesus and son of Mary and Joseph. He rose quickly to leadership in the Jerusalem church (Acts 12:17, 21:18; Gal 1:19, 2:9, 2:12). Paul seems to have considered James an apostle (Gal 1:19). James announced the decision of the Jerusalem Council (Acts 15:13-29; 15:19). He is the mostly likely candidate for the authorship of James. Josephus and later Christian tradition portray him as a pious Jew and also that he was martyred in the year 62. The steady unbelief that James and his brothers expressed toward Jesus (Matt 12:46-50, Mark 3:31-34, Luke 8:19-21, especially John 7:1-9) changed radically after the resurrection. The tradition speaks similarly of the other brothers of Jesus, among whom may have been Judas, author of the epistle of the same name.

Then to all the apostles could again be one of several recorded appearances in the

---

[692] Some have speculated that Sosthenes (1:1) was one of the 500, although it is unclear how that same man could have later been synagogue leader in Corinth (Acts 18:17). The spurious *Acts of Pilate* 14 has Nicodemus paraphrase the ascension account of Mark 16, adding: "And both we and many others of the five hundred besides were looking on." We have no way of knowing if this is derivative of 1 Corinthians or an independent tradition. The reference to the 500 by Eusebius, *History of the church* 1.12 is clearly derived from 1 Cor 15 and does not provide an independent tradition.

[693] An appearance to James takes place in the apocryphal *Gospel of the Hebrews*, as reports the church father Jerome, but the document places that appearance before any of the others: "And when the Lord had given the linen cloth to the servant of the priest, he went to James and appeared to him. For James had sworn that he would not eat bread from that hour in which he had drunk the cup of the Lord until he should see him risen from among them that sleep. And shortly thereafter the Lord said: Bring a table and bread! And immediately it added: he took the bread, blessed it and brake it and gave it to James the Just and said to him: My brother, eat thy bread, for the Son of man is risen from among them that sleep." Cited by Jerome, *De viris illustribus* 2.

gospels. The unusual point here is the apparent distinction between the Twelve and "all the apostles." Either they are synonymous and the change is to avoid redundancy, or Paul refers to apostles, as he sometimes does, as a group broader than the Twelve.

Why list all these witnesses, if no Corinthian rejected Jesus' resurrection? Paul desires to proclaim the gospel to them in all its detail, point to the Scriptures, and list the witnesses to underscore for the Corinthians *the historical reality of at least one resurrection*. Every Christian must believe in Jesus' resurrection; therefore every Christian must believe in the *possibility* of resurrection.

15:8

Paul describes his experience in 15:8-11. This passage is not designed (as is Gal 1:11-24) to prove that Paul is an apostle. Rather he is making every attempt to show that everyone, Paul, Cephas, James, the 500, whomever one could name, all preach the same gospel of the risen Christ. The gospel that the Corinthians had heard is not Paul's individualistic theory about Jesus, but the same one that he received and faithfully passed along (1 Cor 15:1-3), and that they could have gotten from any of the hundreds of aforementioned people. This, and nothing less, is the Christian faith.

Because he saw the risen Lord after his ascension, Paul is **one abnormally born**. *Ektrōma* may mean a premature birth or an abortion/miscarriage. Paul became an apostle without the time of gestation that the others had had, beginning from the days of John the Baptist (Acts 1:22). Paul and not the Corinthian elitists have seen Christ alive; thus he is an apostle and can tell them what is God's truth, even about the Christian's eternal destiny.

15:9

Paul's experience of the resurrection was indeed unique, since he saw Jesus and was commissioned an apostle only after the ascension. Although Paul and others might have a vision of Jesus from heaven (Acts 7:55-56, 9:10-17; 10:13; 18:9-10 in Corinth), only the Damascus Road experience is presented in terms of a resurrection appearance.

15:10

Paul was forgiven for his sins, but he is still the persecutor of the church from a quarter-century earlier. 1 Tim 1:12-16 expounds the same theme: that Paul had been a blasphemer (against the Lord Jesus) and persecutor, but he is a living testimony to the power and grace of God's forgiveness. If he was a great sinner and one born out of time, what he is now is purely due to **the grace of God**.

15:11

This verse captures the point of this section. This is the basic Christian message that one could have received from any number of witnesses: **this is what we preach.** And Paul now shows where he is going with all of this basic gospel talk: **this is what you believed**. The Corinthians could have had nothing but *Amens* for Paul's words thus far, including their faith in Jesus' resurrection.

b. Denying the resurrection of the body means denying the resurrection of Jesus, and thus the saving gospel 15:12-19

15:12

Now comes a reproach, anchored firmly in the evangelical message: **But if it is preached that Christ has been raised from the dead, how can some of you say that there is no resurrection of the dead?** That is, how can a Christian on the one hand proclaim the risen Jesus but on the other hand deny the very possibility of any resurrection?

Paul uses logic in this chapter, notably that cornerstone of human reasoning, the Law of Non-Contradiction: *A and non-A cannot be true at the same time and in the same way.* In this case, one cannot affirm both of the following:

Christ rose from the dead.
No-one rises from the dead.

Paul will not allow the Corinthians to hold both ideas. He will now follow their error to its natural end: *if you reject the resurrection, you do not understand the gospel.*

Application: Is the resurrection of the believer a "practical" doctrine? 15:12

The Day of the Dead (Día de los Muertos, celebrated on Nov 1) in Mexico is a classic syncretistic mixture of pre-Columbian traditions with Catholicism. Like their Aztec ancestors, Mexicans celebrate the holiday in order to reconcile themselves to the inevitability of death and to lessen its sting. But the Bible tells us otherwise: death is not a nuisance who can be intimidated or shooed away by either mourning or partying. It is an enemy to the plan of our God, and must be destroyed.

Yet sadly there are even some in the evangelical tradition who do not fully grasp the resurrection of the body. Oh, they affirm the doctrine, but in effect give it no place in their world view. For example, at Christian funerals we comfort each other with the thought that our loved one is right now with the Lord in spirit (Phil 1:21-23). That is only part of the truth: Jesus died and rose again, not simply to deliver our spirits to heaven when we died, but to deliver us from sin and its terrible result, death.

But we modern Christians like our theology to be practical. Is the resurrection of the Christian only a fine point of doctrine, or does it make a real difference?

Paul implies that there to reject the resurrection of the Christian means (1) that we doubt the power of God; (2) that we have cut ourselves off from a central motive for holy living.

(1) Doubt the power of God. Jesus told the Sadduceans (Mark 12:24) that their rejection of the resurrection was not simply an intellectual choice, but that they fell short in their faith in the God who could raise the dead. Paul, perhaps thinking of this tradition, makes the same point in 1 Cor 15:35 – people rejected the doctrine because they reasoned: if I, being a wise man, cannot imagine the resurrection of the body, then the idea must be absurd; and everyone who believes in the doctrine is a simpleton and worthy of contempt.

(2) Loss of a motive for holy living. If we do not believe that God is powerful enough to figure out how to raise the dead, then how could he be powerful enough to ever cause me any trouble over my moral choices? Another way to reason would be, if my body will perish when I die, then in effect my bad moral choices will perish with it (as in 1 Cor 6:13, see our comments); everything physical passes away and I will enter eternity with a pure spirit or soul; therefore, I do not have to take care about moral choices.

I have met Christians who thought nothing of throwing trash on the ground and polluting the environment. They justified themselves by saying that the Lord was going to return and destroy the earth anyway, so why bother keeping in clean now? Some make that same error with respect to the physical self. Nevertheless, God will not do away with our body; he will raise us and judge us (1 Cor 6:13b-14). Because of that hope, Christians can remain steadfast despite all obstacles: "stand firm. Let nothing move you. Always give yourselves fully to the work of the Lord, because you know that your labor in the Lord is not in vain" (1 Cor 15:58; see also 15:30-34).

15:13
"If there is no resurrection/if the dead are not raised" is the key to 15:12-19. That is, if resurrection is an unacceptable concept, than it is invalid whether applied to millions of dead people or only to one man, Jesus.

15:14-16
The Corinthians do not deny that Christ was raised; yet they stumble over the concept as such, which should logically entail the denial of Jesus' resurrection. And if their philosophy were true, what then? Paul emphasizes two aspects: first of all, *that the gospel does not function if the resurrection of Jesus is removed*. Secondly, he lays a great deal of emphasis on being a true witness: *if Jesus is not raised, then I, Paul, also Cephas, James, the Twelve, all the apostles, the 500 are all liars.* It matters not at all whether one prefers Paul, Cephas or Apollos (1 Cor 1:12) – they all proclaim the same resurrection faith. If there is doubt about resurrection, there is doubt about Jesus' resurrection; if there is doubt about that, then all Christian leaders you could possibly name are **false witnesses** because all are "lying about God, because we said that he raised Christ from death" (GNB). In that case, **you faith**, sincere though it may be, is rooted squarely in a lie and is **useless** or worthless (*kenos* is used twice here, also in 15:10, 58).

15:17
Paul affirms as he does in 15:14-16 that there are severe ramifications for denying the resurrection: if Christ not raised your faith is **futile** (*mataios*, as in 3:20, a synonym for *kenos* "useless" in 15:14). Paul draws out another soteriological point here: if the gospel is discredited, **you are still in your sins** (cf. 15:3; also 6:9-11). Once again the centrality of the cross is displayed even in a chapter on resurrection: no philosophical speculation can buy what the (culturally offensive) cross has accomplished.

15:18
In 15:18-19 Paul draws some eschatological implications of the Corinthians' error. In that case, dead Christians are lost forever. He uses here a form of *apollumi* that is similar to "those who are perishing" in 1:18 and to perishing by serpent bite in 10:9. Is Paul saying that if there is no resurrection at all, then dead Christians are annihilated? Taken out of context the verse might say that (see 15:29-34). But in this context he is speaking

of the resurrection of Christ: "if Christ is not raised...Then those also who have fallen asleep in Christ are lost." Without his resurrection there can be no distinction between "those who are perishing" and "us who are being saved" (1:18): all are lost.

Whereas some versions (correctly) paraphrase "those who have died," Paul in fact says literally (NIV, ESV, HCSB, NET, NASB, NJB) **those who have fallen asleep**, from the verb *koimaō*. That idiom appears with regularity in the New Testament (John 11:11-12; 1 Thess 4:13, 14, 15; 1 Cor 7:39, 11:30, 15:6, 18, 20, 51). It was once thought that this metaphor was a Christian invention, that dying in Christ is like falling asleep, a rest from which the believer will one day awaken. Hence Christian burial places are called "cemeteries" (from a cognate of *koimaō*, literally, "bedrooms, dormitories"). But in fact, the pagan Greeks had for centuries spoken of the sleep of death, even when they spoke with no expectation of awakening. The metaphor, though especially fitting for the Christian's theology, was not a specifically Christian one. Since the Greeks used it to speak of the dead whose spirits were still conscious, Paul's use of the verb gives no support to the doctrine of "soul sleep" or conditional immortality.

15:19

Paul speaks ironically of a hope which is **only for this life**, as if that sort of thing were any hope at all. What good is salvation which ends in the grave, and invites persecution during this short existence? So much for those who fantasize that they are kings now and rich (4:8)!

c. The resurrection of Jesus must imply the resurrection of his people 15:20-28

15:20

Of course Paul has been speaking hypothetically, because every Christian knows that **Christ has indeed been raised from the dead**. One can almost sense the Corinthians letting out their breath at last, as Paul begins to explore the good news that is anchored in reality. The word *nuni* here may be chronological ("But now in history") or even better, logical (**indeed**, NIV).

In this section he shows what has been implied earlier: that our destiny is inextricably entwined with Jesus'. His death and resurrection for our sins means that our death will be resolved in resurrection at the return of Christ. That makes Christ a kind of **firstfruits** (from *aparchē*; here and 15:23, 1 Clem 24.1 – "Let us consider, dear friends, how the Master continually points out to us the coming resurrection of which he made the Lord Jesus Christ the *firstfruit* when he raised him from the dead"; the same concept appears in Acts 26:23 and Col 1:18).[694] The metaphor has its foundation in the Old Testament system of sacrifices. The Israelites were commanded: "When you enter the land I am going to give you and you reap its harvest, bring to the priest a sheaf of the first grain you harvest" (Lev 23:10; see also Exod 23:16, Num 15:19-21, Deut 26:1-11).

The firstfruit offering included bread made from the first wheat of the year. It was a means of giving thanks to God, but it was served as a hopeful precursor of the full harvest to come. Also known as the Feast of Weeks (its Greek name is "Pentecost," which means

---

[694] *aparchē* as "first convert of many" appears in 1 Cor 16:5; also Rom 16:5, 2 Thess 2:13, Rev 14:4.

"on the fiftieth day"), the feast typically fell in June and anticipated to the harvest festival of Tabernacles in September or early October. The fact that Paul was staying in Ephesus until Pentecost of that year (1 Cor 16:8) may have suggested this metaphor.

Firstfruits of those who have fallen asleep shows that there is an underlying unity between the first-fruit offering and the full harvest to come: they are of a piece with each other. Paul will develop this further with his Adam-Christ doctrine in 15:21-22, 45-49. Everyone in that agricultural economy knew that harvests did not come gradually, but suddenly exploded on the scene, calling for myriad helping hands hired on the spot to bring it in immediately.[695]

15:21

Paul begins with Adam and Christ, a pairing he will develop further in 1 Cor 15:45-49 and Rom 5:12-21. Paul departs from Judaism in two crucial points here. First, Judaism expected that the Messiah would be human, or perhaps a being like an angel. It never created a doctrine of God participating in humanity as in the Christian doctrine of incarnation. Only in the Christian gospel may one say that death and death's cure came **through a man**.

Digging deeper, we recall that Judaism never had a doctrine of the Fall that resembled the Pauline teaching. The closest it came to "we all fell in Adam" is a passage in *4 Ezra*, which probably was written in the years after Paul.[696] Judaism believed that each individual had the ability to choose righteousness or wickedness. Paul broke radically with this viewpoint: Adam did not simply create a bad example for the following generations. Rather, his fall corrupted his descendants also. If there is any doubt about the effect of his sin, one has only to look at the universality of death. God told Adam that "when you eat of it, you shall surely die," and die he eventually did. But none of his descendants have had the choice to choose righteousness and thus avoid death. In Christ and his resurrection it is possible to see that death was an unnecessary aberration due to sin: "the sting of death is sin" (15:56).

How does this help Paul's case? His point is to show that just as Christ died for our sins (15:3) he came more broadly to redeem his people from sin's effects. In Christ his people receive pardon, but they will eventually also receive liberation from death.

15:22

This key verse makes explicit what he has implied in 15:21, that he is speaking of two men, Adam and Christ. All humans are subject to death, even though a very few will not die (Enoch, Elijah, and those alive at the return of Christ, 15:51). Yet after the catastrophic fall of Adam into sin and death, a man brings about the resurrection by dying and rising again.

The second "all" demands scrutiny: what is meant by **all will be made alive**? Does he mean all humanity in a general resurrection? Or does he mean that all who are in Christ will be resurrected, the point that is his focus in this chapter? There has been some

---

[695] The harvest comes all at once, and woe to the farmer who allows it to stand in the field until it rains or rots! This provides the tension in the parable of the hired workers in the grape harvest in Matt 20:1-16; the urgency of evangelism in Matt 9:37-38. In the book of Ruth, Boaz works all day, and rather than go home he sleeps at the threshing floor; see also Prov 10:5.

[696] *4 Ezra* 7.118 – "O Adam, what have you done? For though it was you who sinned, the fall was not yours alone, but ours also who are your descendants."

debate over whether Paul taught a general resurrection of the dead in the sense of John 5:28-29. Some have detected this in 15:24, as we shall see. Others have argued, based on Paul's epistles, that he held only to a resurrection of the righteous and that the wicked suffer only fiery punishment (2 Thess 1:8-9).

The "all" is best taken to mean the whole human race. In this context Paul's interest is the resurrection of the Christian (see also Rom 5:17, 21).[697] The apostle also taught a general resurrection of all people. The account of Paul before Felix in Acts 24:15 has Paul say that "there will be a resurrection of both the righteous and the wicked," and there is no compelling reason to reject that report. Yet for Paul the resurrection of the unjust is not a "victory" (as in 15:57) but rather the portal into divine judgment and exclusion from the kingdom (6:9-10).

15:23

People will be resurrected place, **each in his own turn** (*tagma*). The word was used to speak of military divisions or parts of a parade, or it could refer as here to classes or groups more generally. In God's work it is so ordered that Christ comes first from the dead, alone. Only later will come those in Christ.

When does this second order pass by and experience the resurrection? **When he comes** (see "Maranatha," "Come, O Lord!" in 16:22). The noun *parousia* can be used of the return or presence of any person (as in 16:17; 2 Cor 7:6-7). Nevertheless the early Christians used it as a technical term for the return of Christ in glory (1 Thess 4:15). The parallel passage in 1 Thess 4:13-17 is directed to those Christians who have seen their fellows die, and who were grieved beyond what was proper for people who believed in resurrection. His emphasis in that epistle is the meeting with Jesus and the priority of dead Christians in being with him. There is no mention there of the mystery that living believers will also be transformed (15:51), a point that becomes relevant to Paul's argument with the Corinthians.

15:24

What follows is distinctively Christian teaching; nothing in the Jewish apocalypses prepares us for a Messiah who dies to rise again;[698] who defeats the powers by dying and rising and then reigning; who fulfills Psalm 110:1 or Psalm 8:6 in his person; whose ultimate enemy is death. The Corinthians know that Jesus died, was buried, rose and reigns from God's right hand. There was no doubt in Corinth that Christ would return. But have they truly thought through what it is the goal of the gospel? Is it merely to purchase forgiveness for individual Christians? Or does it have universal implications? Thus Paul invites the Corinthians to think of the resurrection in anthropological and in cosmic terms: what is God doing in Christ in and for the human race? In and for the cosmos? And how does the Christian's destiny fit into those plans?

Like "when he comes" (*parousia*), **the end** (*to telos*) had the technical meaning of "the end of this age" (e. g., 1 Cor 1:8; also Mark 13:7; 2 Cor 1:13; 1 Pet 4:7). It is possible

---

[697] When Paul speaks of "eternal life," he always means the life of the eschatological resurrection – "the wages of sin is death, but the gift of God is eternal life in Christ Jesus our Lord" (Rom 6:23). It is "life" in that the dead are made undead. In this point his vocabulary differs from John's, who speaks of eternal life as a present possession. See the study by Murray J. Harris, *Raised immortal: resurrection and immortality in the New Testament* (Grand Rapids: Eerdmans, 1983), 200-01.

[698] Not even *4 Ezra* 7.22 teaches this when it says that the Messiah will reign for 400 years and then die.

Paul distinguishes between Christ's "coming" and the "the end." Much depends on the use of the adverbs that link the stages together:

Christ, the firstfruits
(*epeita*), when he comes, those who belong to him
(*eita*) then the end will come

epeita and *eita* could have a logical sense ("thus"); or they might be chronological ("then, later"). The evidence points to the latter meaning: immediately before this section (15:5-8) he has used similar terms for the chronology of the resurrection appearances: "he appeared to Peter, and then (*eita*) to the Twelve. After that (*epeita*) he appeared to more than five hundred of the brothers at one time…Then (*epeita*) he appeared to James, then (*eita*) to all the apostles, and last of all (*eschaton*) he appeared to me also." If his meaning is "then, later, after," it is possible that he implies a future millennial kingdom, as in Rev 20:4-6 (see below).

Then comes **the end**.[699] *Telos* is a cognate of *teleion*, "the perfect," which Paul uses of the end of the age in 13:10. Paul leaves untouched the questions of whether Christ continues to subject the powers to himself between the *parousia* and the *telos*, and when he might resurrect the wicked. Rather, Paul's point is that all will rise from the grave (15:21) and that all powers will be subjected (15:24); the chronological point that interests him here is the period between Jesus' resurrection and the resurrection of the church. They are not two events, but two aspects of the same act.

Paul speaks in chiasm in 15:24-28 –

> when he hands over the kingdom to God the Father
>   after he has destroyed all dominion, authority and power.
>   For he must reign until he has put all his enemies under his feet.
>   The last enemy to be destroyed is death.
>   For he "has put everything under his feet"…
>   When he has done this,
> then the Son himself will be made subject to him who put everything under him, so that God may be all in all.

His logic is: we Christians know that Christ will exercise absolute rule over all his enemies. But, Christ cannot be said to rule over all if he doesn't rule over Death. And how does he destroy death? By undoing it: by resurrecting the dead, he defeats Death. Only then he will turn the sovereignty over to the Father as a completed job.

Some have asked whether Paul was assuming a so-called "interim kingdom" of Christ, as is pictured in the millennium passage of Rev 20:4-6. Some Jews believed that this age would blend into the age to come through a messianic kingdom of a specific length of time.

There are three main interpretations of Christ's rule:

---

[699] Lietzmann takes *to telos* as "the rest," that is, the rest of the human race, see Lietzmann and Kümmel, *An die Korinther*, 81. Against this view the majority through the centuries: see Conzelmann, *1 Corinthians*, 270-71; Thiselton, *First Corinthians*, 1230-31.

1. The kingdom of Christ is present and lasts from the resurrection/ascension of Christ until the Parousia.[700]
2. The kingdom of Christ is a future "millennium" which corresponds to Rev 20:4-6 and begins at the Parousia.[701]
3. The kingdom of Christ begins with the resurrection/ascension and ends sometime after the Parousia; it spans the two ages.[702] It is this third view that represents the biblical data best, especially the teaching that Christ began to put all enemies under his feet as soon as he ascended into heaven (for example, Eph 1:20-22, 1 Pet 3:22). If that is what Paul believed, it must always be kept in mind that Paul's emphasis is driven by the Corinthians' skepticism over the resurrection, not interest a messianic kingdom.[703]

15:25

Christ died and rose again according to the Old Testament predictions (15:3-4). Beyond that, the apostles preached that he fulfilled prophecy in his ascension: 15:25 and 27 are rooted in two such passages. 15:25 has the phrase **under his feet**. This is an allusion to Psalm 110:1, the most popular verse in the New Testament. The image comes from the ancient practice that conquered kings were made to grovel at the feet of the victor. It is a verse that Jesus applied to himself in the debate over David's Son in Mark 12:35-37 and parallels. The early church applied Psalm 110:1 to the ascension of Christ, not to the second coming. It could at the one hand affirm that Christ is Lord over all now, but also that some elements are still in rebellion. This is the tension dealt with in the commentary of Heb 2:8b on Psalm 8: "Yet at present we do not see everything subject to him." Paul's aim here is to show how the creed "Jesus is Lord" (12:3) will be played out through the rest of human history. Until that time **he must reign** and conquer.

15:26

Destroyed (*katargeō,* 15:24, 26) is a favorite Pauline term, and is at times used for eschatological destruction (so 2:6, 6:13, and possibly in 1:28; see too 2 Thess 2:8). The Corinthians must not think of God's enemies exclusively as Satan and his angels, but also death. Death is the **last enemy**; it is personified here and in Rom 6.

15:27-28

Paul now directly quotes Psalm 8:6 – "**has put everything under his feet.**" Because of that shared "feet" metaphor, these verses were linked together in the early church's proclamation. Psalm 8 is of a different nature than the royal Psalm 110. It is a description

---

[700] Ridderbos, *Paul*, 556-62.
[701] Scholars such as Stauffer, along with a number of millenarian and Dispensationalist theologians, would place the inception of this reign of Christ at the Parousia. Stauffer, *New Testament theology*, 218-19. See also Albert Schweitzer, *The mysticism of Paul the apostle*, tr. W. Montgomery (Baltimore: The Johns Hopkins University Press, 1998), 84-94.
[702] Ladd, *Theology*, 604; Oscar Cullmann, "The kingdom of Christ and the church in the New Testament," in *The early church*, ed. A. J. B. Higgins (London: SCM, 1956), 104-37.
[703] Hodge, *I Corinthians*, 329, states that a millennialist interpretation is nothing other than the re-adoption of Judaism and a denial of the spiritual nature of the gospel. Conzelmann, *1 Corinthians*, 270, states that "he takes over from the [traditional Jewish] schema the notion that death is not annihilated until the end of the messianic kingdom. But he transposes this kingdom into the present. For Christ is risen. His kingdom fills up the period between the resurrection and the consummation of the work of salvation after the parousia." Against his opinion, Horton, *I & II Corinthians*, 153, says that the millennial kingdom is "clearly" present in these verses.

of creation, rooted squarely in Gen 1:26-31, with humankind at its head. The psalmist comments that people seem so small in comparison with the cosmos, yet God has made them and put creation under their feet. The psalm looks before the fall of Adam, to the original ideal of God's creation. For Paul the verse fits neatly into his Adam-Christ schema: Christ recovers what Adam lost; all things will be put under his feet, and in this way the church will reap eternal benefit.

Some have seen in the second half of the verse an echo of a christological disagreement with the Corinthians. According to this viewpoint, Paul as a Jew was reticent about making Christ equal with God the Father. But when the gospel spread to the Hellenistic world, with its possibilities for multiple gods and lords (1 Cor 8:6-7) some gentile Christians went beyond the original gospel and began thinking of Jesus as Lord and God. The theory runs that Paul was offended by this, but that he could not bring himself to directly contradict their attitude. So, we are told, he went as far as he could in affirming their christology but then slipped in phrases like "every tongue confess that Jesus Christ is Lord, *to the glory of God the Father*" (Phil 2:11) to try to cool down their misdirected ardor for Christ. In this case, the Corinthians' theology – Hellenistic, ultracharismatic, non-eschatological – went too far and saw no difference between the reign of Christ and the kingdom of God. Hence Paul must remind them that Christ's kingdom too has an end, and that the final eternal goal is in the hands of God the Father.

This hypothetical reconstruction is unworkable for two reasons: first, Paul is not above damning those who preach a different gospel (Gal 1:8-9; cp. 2 Cor 11:4). *A priori* it is improbable that Paul would trifle over celibacy and head coverings in this epistle, but not make a fuss over a distortion of the main fundamental of the faith, monotheism.[704]

The other reason is found in the context: his point is that Christ's kingdom is *telic*, that is, it has a goal. His work is to destroy whatever sets itself against the Father, and then to turn the kingdom over to God only when his work is complete. History is driving toward that eschatological kingdom of God and it will only come with resurrection as an established deed. What God does is done through Jesus Christ; he **put everything under Christ**.

We can know little about **the Son himself will be made subject to him who put everything under him, so that God may be all in all**. Some early heretics, such as the Arians, took this to be a denial of the eternal deity of Christ, that his lordship is a temporary expedient until the coming of God's eternal kingdom.[705] But this is not what Paul says, which is that the kingdom of God is in Christ, and that Christ's rule is what in the end will constitute the kingdom of God.

God will be all in all. The Stoics were pantheists; that is, they believed that the universe was ontologically "in God." What happens is not only from God, it is part of God. Paul cites the words of the pantheist Aratus, although with his own sense, in Acts 17:28: "in him we live and move and have our being." What happens in the gospel is entirely different from the Stoic framework: although God is the creator of all and the Lord of all, the creation is alienated from him due to sin and death. That is, the creation will not return to its right state only in the resurrection of the human race.

---

[704] See Thiselton, *First Corinthians*, 1237.
[705] See Theodoret of Cyrus and others (Bray, 163-64).

d. The acceptance or denial of the resurrection of the body affects one's lifestyle in this age 15:29-34

Christians act as if certain things are true, even as they deny the doctrine with their lips. In these verses Paul demonstrates that the elitist Corinthians act as if there is a future hope, even while they smirk at the philosophical superficiality of that hope. He shows the foolishness of their behavior if there is no final resurrection.

15:29

We must imagine that when Paul refers to those who are **baptized for the dead**, he was confident that the Corinthians could understand the reference. His use of the third person "what will those do" may indicate that he is speaking of others, apart from the Corinthian church, but we have no way of knowing. The generations after Paul have had little idea what he meant by it, whether it was a Corinthian practice, and whether he approved of it.[706] The church fathers knew of a heretical baptism for the dead, that is, that a living person was baptized in proxy for a dead person.[707] There is no way of proving that this was a 1st-century practice and not a later misinterpretation of 15:29, as is the case in the modern Mormon rite.[708] Or the reference might have its roots in Mark 10:38, where baptism is used metaphorically of martyrdom. A better option is that Paul means to say, "why are people baptized if they're only going to wind up dead anyway?" That would lead in very naturally to the next few verses.

15:30

Paul refers to **we**, the apostles, as he does in 4:9-13, "like men condemned to die." The apostles model what is normative Christianity. If the apostles suffer it's because they are Christians, and if other Christians do not suffer it may be because their priorities are awry. Paul takes risks and faces dangerous situations, some life-threatening and others dangerous or bothersome. Why would Paul risk his life if there was not a resurrection life to come? Modern Christians may stumble at his logic, since they often reason as the Corinthians do: if Paul dies in the service of Christ, he as soul or spirit will go immediately to heaven "which is better by far" (Phil 1:23).[709] For his part, Paul expects to go to heaven when he dies; nonetheless he sets his sight beyond that to the final resurrection in the pattern of Christ's (Phil 3:10-11).

---

[706] See the full essay in Thiselton, *First Corinthians*, 1242-49; he concludes with the view that this means that people were baptized *for the sake of the dead*, that is, so that they would be reunited with their dead Christian relatives in the resurrection. See the full discussion by Gardner.

[707] Chrysostom, *i ad Corinthios* 40.1 mentions the Marcionites doing so. Cf. also Tertullian, *Adversus Marcionem* 5.10 – "Do not then suppose that the apostle here indicates some new god as the author and advocate of this baptism for the dead. His only aim in alluding to it was that he might all the more firmly insist upon the resurrection of the body, in proportion as they who were vainly baptized for the dead resorted to the practice from their belief of such a resurrection."

[708] The Latter-Day Saints take the baptism for the dead as a new revelation through Joseph Smith, but also point to 1 Cor 15:29 and Hermas, *Parables* 9.16 as a reference to an ancient Christian practice. Their rationale is that spirits of dead human beings heard the gospel proclaimed during the three days that Jesus was in the spirit realm (1 Pet 3:19). These dead people believe, but may receive eternal life only through baptism. Their descendants may stand in for them and be baptized in the name of the dead one.

[709] Note the imbalance for example in William Hendriksen, *The Bible on the life hereafter* (Grand Rapids, MI: Baker, 1987), who has much more on the intermediate state than he does on the resurrection.

15:31

I die every day is not some ascetic dying to self; rather, Paul is daily risking his physical life (so NIV 2011: "I face death every day"). This anticipates his later word to the Romans, that "we face death all day long" (Rom 8:36a, citing Psalm 44:22). This is something of which he boasts, since it is done for the God who raises the dead. The rest of the verse is not clear in the original, but the NIV captures its sense with **just as surely as I glory over you [i. e., am proud of you] in Christ Jesus our Lord**.

15:32

Paul poses the question of why **I fought wild beasts** (*thēriomacheō*) **in Ephesus** if there were no resurrection. The verb appears only here in the New Testament; in other contexts, it typically referred to facing lions or other beasts as punishment, not a chance encounter with an animal in the wild. The difficulty with taking this literally is that Paul as a Roman citizen normally would not be exposed to such a punishment; nor is this experience mentioned in Acts or even more significant in his fuller catalogue of sufferings in 2 Cor 11:23-33; nor do we know how he escaped what was in effect a capital punishment. Some therefore leave open the possibility that this is hypothetical: "if I had gone so far as to fight with wild beasts."[710] The more likely reading is that the wild animals are metaphorical, referring to savage opposition by other humans (as for example, in Acts 19:23-41). Here again, the Corinthians must have already been told what Paul was referring to.

If there is to be no resurrection, better to eat than to be eaten! **"Let us eat and drink, for tomorrow we die"** may be a quotation from Isa 22:13, or from the Lord's parable in Luke 12:19; then too Paul might have been simply quoting a popular expression. Of course it is as true for all that "tomorrow we die." But for the Christian there lies beyond the grave a resurrection and by implication a judgment (1 Cor 3:10-17; 2 Cor 5:10). The resurrection doctrine makes a serious impact on daily ethics.

It is likely that the denial of the resurrection in Corinth went hand in hand with immoral use of the body: they consorted with prostitutes and overate and drank (1 Cor 6:12-20), arguing that God would destroy the body anyway (see commentary on 6:13; also 11:21). Thus there was in Corinth a mixed situation: some denied the resurrection and their ethics followed suit; others denied the resurrection but still believed in the Christian ethic. It is to these people whom Paul appeals here.

15:33

Paul drives the point further: **"Bad company corrupts good character."** As he does in other texts, Paul demonstrates a Christian point by quoting a pagan poet, Menander (4th century B. C.). Some Corinthians were consorting with Greeks, not to win them, but because they spoke the same philosophical language as the Christian elite. The pagans denied the resurrection and also lived according to pagan morals. What surprise is there if Corinthian Christians, by lusting after pagan (pseudo)-intellectualism fell too into the sins of pagan Corinth? Such Christians should be wary of being beguiled, hence, **Do not be mislead**.

---

[710] So Héring, *First Corinthians*, 171-72.

15:34

The earlier chapters have revealed some stunning moral lapses in the Corinthian church. He tells these people **stop sinning**. The next sentence is mishandled by the NIV, implying as it does that some church members have no knowledge of God: "In effect, there are some of you who have no knowledge of God." The original does not contain "in effect" nor "of you" but is simply as the ESV words it, "for some have no knowledge of God," living their lives outside the revelation of God in Christ. Paul already spent a great deal of energy in 1 Cor 1-2, dealing with the Corinthians who found in Greek philosophy a higher knowledge. They must realize that their pagan heroes have no idea of the truth of God. That the Corinthians follow them should be to their **shame**.

e. The objections to the resurrection stem from a lack of faith and a poor understanding of God's power as creator 15:35-49

Paul is an example to other Christian teachers, since he is not dismissive of genuine doubts or questions. He takes the time not only to affirm what is true but also to handle the philosophical difficulties at Corinth.

15:35

Paul stresses, as he does in 2 Cor 1:9, that our God is more than powerful enough to resurrect the body. As was the style in classical rhetoric, Paul interacts with an imaginary opponent in a "diatribe" (see 1 Cor 4:7): **But someone may ask, "How are the dead raised? With what kind of body will they come?"** These questions did not arise from Paul's imagination, but were rather the very sort of question he dealt with as a Pharisee or as a Christian. Those who denied the resurrection relied on ridicule as one of their tools. The Greeks portrayed the resurrection as the mere reanimation of rotten corpses as zombies, something like the myriad zombie movies that are currently flowing out of Hollywood. Who, they would taunt, would wish for that instead of existing as pure spirit?

The Sadduceans used a similar argument with Jesus: *If a woman marries seven brothers in succession and is widowed by all, then to whom does she belong in the resurrection?* (Mark 12:18-27 and parallels). Paul's argument takes the same tack as Mark 12:24 – mere human reasoning cannot uncover what a powerful God wants to do (1 Cor 2:9). These mysteries can only be revealed by the Spirit (2:10, 15:51).

15:36-37

So those without God's revelation are speaking **foolish** words. Paul now makes a number of remarks, based squarely in the Genesis account of creation (as he did with the issue of meat sacrificed to idols in 8:6, and that of women and men in 1 Cor 11:7-12, 14:34). These are not simply illustrations from nature, but from nature that is interpreted by divine revelation.

First in 15:36-37 he uses the illustration, common enough in many cultures, of a seed that grows into a full plant. Paul underscores the fact that the seed must, as it were, die and be buried. But everyone knows that that "burial" is only a hint of something greater to come; death is the prerequisite for new life. His argument is not far off from the firstfruit/harvest metaphor of 15:23-24, but here he takes advantage of the plowing under of a seed to suggest the burial of the human body.

A seed may look nothing like the plant that is to come; yet there is continuity between the two. The seed is sown literally "naked," a metaphor that the NIV loses with "just" a seed, which misses out on the parallel with the nakedness that is death (see 2 Cor 5:1-5). He now makes a transition to his next thought in 15:38: that there exist many types of seed, **perhaps of wheat or of something**.

15:38
The Greek has a play on words that works only poorly in English: they could use "body" (*sōma*) to refer to a body of a plant, animal or person, while we typically would not use it of a plant. This allows Paul to speak of the plant's body and move neatly to human bodies or even celestial bodies. God gives each seed whatever body he chooses, and different kinds of seeds receive different kinds of bodies, according to the third day of creation in Gen 1:11-12. Paul will use this principle of seed/plant body in greater detail beginning in 15:42.

15:39
Paul now moves to the fifth and sixth days of creation, as recounted in Gen 1:20-31: man and woman were made on the sixth day, but previous to them there came forth terrestrial **animals**, **birds** and **fish**. God who made these things by his own plan gave each kind of animal or man its own kind of body. This is obvious to anyone with eyes, but scientists have for many years discovered more and more distinctions between the animals: for example, birds possess lighter, hollow bones to facilitate flight. It is God who decides and assigns to each the body he chooses and creates.

15:40
The fact that there are **heavenly bodies and there are earthly bodies** will lay the basis for Paul's Adam-Christ motif in 15:45-49. What does Paul mean by these two types? He is thinking not of angels, but rather the sun, moon and stars; in fact, the study of the heavens was a major occupation of the Stoics, and that may have provided Paul with the illustration.[711] The apostle did not follow the popular thinking that the heavenly bodies were gods who influenced human life – the cosmological basis for astrology. This is a transitional statement that leads us to 15:41 – not only on the earth (land, seas, sky) are their different beings. In fact there are celestial bodies too, objects placed in the sky that are also the handiwork of God. He distinguishes them by their **splendor**, their unique glory.

15:41
To show more distinctions between bodies Paul now goes ahead and returns to the fourth day of creation, the making of sun, moon and stars (Gen 1:14-19). There sun is the greater light, the moon the lesser (1:16-18), but God created their dissimilarity for a reason: the moon is appropriate to give light during the night, but the sun gives light for the day. Beyond stars, sun and moon, Paul notes that each star is different: **star differs from star in splendor**. He is speaking of what is scientifically known as "apparent visual magnitude" – not the absolute amount of light, but the brightness of a star from

---

[711] Inwood, *The Stoics*, 328-37.

the perspective of an observer on earth. The higher the magnitude, the dimmer the star, from Sirius in the 1st magnitude to the barely visible stars of the 6th. Paul sees each and every star as the handiwork of God (as in so many Psalms, e. g., Psalm 8:3, 19:1-4, 33:6, etc.). The apostle's point is this: *God can create a myriad of kinds of bodies, most of which are well beyond our comprehension. So what is the problem with this God resurrecting the dead to a new kind of body?*

15:42-43

We now come back to an application of natural creation: **So it will be with the resurrection of the dead**. He draws four parallels: perishable/imperishable; dishonor/glory; weakness/power; natural/espiritual. These contrasts will lead Paul even deeper to the Adam-Christ pairing in 15:45-49. For Paul, death is not some natural process, but a result of Adam's sin. Rudolf Bultmann labeled this as a myth, that is, a figurative story by which the primitives explained death to themselves.[712] Paul would have none of this: in his reflection of Genesis, he regards death as an aberration, the corruption of the Creator's original good work. God did not create Adam to be corrupt, shamed and weak, but rather to rule over nature as his regent (Psalm 8:5-6, see 1 Cor 15:27). The Gnostics would later proclaim that it was material bodily existence that was at the heart of humankind's problems, that an inferior creator deity had condemned the race to being an abomination of spirit chained to matter. Their gospel was that Gnostic humans were really sparks of spirit that would one day be unfettered. Paul, on the other hand, proclaims the cross of Christ as that which undoes the false turn of death and takes the human race back to God's original aim.

Much confusion has arisen because of the church's adoption of the Greek concept of the "immortal soul." For Paul the human being is mortal, that is, the body is subject to death and corruption. He does not speak of the immortal soul, but rather of the future immortality and incorruptibility of the body no longer subject to death.[713] "That is to say that the salvation of the soul is not enough to counter death. Man is indivisible, and indivisible is his salvation."[714]

15:44-45

Paul draws another contrast, literally "it is sown a body of the soul (*psuchikos*), it is raised a body of the spirit (*pneumatikos*)." This language is made difficult by our own misconceptions of the nature of soul and spirit, and because our minds do not move in the language of creation in Genesis. Let us examine the second term first. Some Christians have taken this to mean that Christians die, but they live forever as spirits without bodies.[715] But this is not the sense at all. In terms of Pauline theology, a disembodied spirit is still a dead being. Normally when Paul uses *pneuma* or *pneumatikos*, he is thinking of the Holy Spirit, who gives life (15:45). That works well here: the Christian will be raised, not as a spirit but in a body resurrected by the Spirit's power.[716] This same truth appears in 1 Pet 3:18-22 and 4:6: Christ is raised by the Spirit

---

[712] Bultmann, *Theology of the New Testament*, 187-203.
[713] See Harris, *Raised immortal*, 140-41.
[714] Walter.
[715] See the refutation of this view by Thiselton, *First Corinthians*, 1277-78.
[716] So also Thiselton, *First Corinthians*, 1275-81; Fitzmyer, *First Corinthians*, 593-600; Lincoln, *Paradise now and not yet*, 39-42.

(3:18), and in that resurrected state (in the Spirit) he proclaimed his victory to all the imprisoned angelic powers (3:19), as part of his ascension to God's right hand (3:22). Likewise, dead believers will be made alive in the Spirit (1 Pet 4:6), that is, resurrected. See also the power of the Spirit in the resurrection in Rom 8:11, 2 Cor 5:5 and Eph 1:13-14.

What then of the "body of the soul" (*psuchikos*)? Although some scholars wish to attribute the term to Gnosticism,[717] in reality we need look no further than the language of Gen 2:7, which Paul will quote in the next verse. God breathed his Spirit into the man made of dust, and Adam became a soul. Note that Adam does not receive or possess a soul, but that the animated body is a soul. Paul is contrasting mere people of the earth, the soulish, with people who have the Holy Spirit, just as he does in 1 Cor 2:14. The NIV tries to capture all of these implications with **a natural body**, but one might also paraphrase it "body of a mere earth-person." "Physical body" (NRSV; GNB; CEV) is far from the original language and is totally misleading. Paul never denies that the resurrection body is material and physical; he does deny that it is *merely* physical and earthly.

We will paraphrase this as:

the body is planted in the ground a merely earthly thing
it is raised a body fashioned by the powerful Spirit

If Adam is a soul, by contrast Christ is a spirit. Not only that: Adam was given life, but Christ is the lifegiver. Why is Christ called **a life-giving spirit**? (see too 2 Cor 3:17-18, where the Lord Jesus "is the Spirit"). It does not mean that there is no distinction between Christ and the Spirit. Christ, while human, is at the same time above and the limits of this world, and as the agent of creation is the Spirit who gives life.

15:46

How is Christ, the second Adam, the prototype for the Christian? Once again Paul appeals to the divine order in things: Christ must rise first, then his people (15:23). Again, the mortal Adamic race must appear first and only later the new people of God in Christ.

15:47

Paul switches back and forth from the proper name "Adam" and "man [human being]" (*anthrōpos*). This follows a play on words in the Hebrew, since "Adam" is used both as a generic term for "human being" and as the proper name of Adam, the first Human. Paul amplifies Gen 2:7 in 15:45 by adding the word **first**, in order to prepare us for a "later" or **second** Adam.

The two Adams had different points of origin: the first **of the dust of the earth**. The second Adam or Human is **from heaven**. Christ was raised by God and his body is one that is from heaven, not from earthly soil. And in the end, Christ will come from heaven as the life-giving Spirit, to raise his church in the same way.

---

[717] So Robert Jewett, *Paul's anthropological terms* (Leiden: Brill, 1971), 352-53.

15:48-49

There are two images or patterns for human beings. **Those who are of the earth** are the human race who live like Adam. **Those who are of heaven** are the people of Christ, and in the future resurrection **we shall bear the likeness of the man from heaven**. The Christian is in the position of being born in the one image, and looking forward to the second. Paul is not refuting here a "realized resurrection," as may be the problem in 2 Tim 2:18, making Paul say that "there is still something in the future, a resurrection." Rather his point is that "in the future what we can expect is resurrection, not some perpetual existence as pure spirit."

f. Besides, the resurrection of the body is revealed truth 15:50-58

There is a sense in which this is a new, second *confirmatio* or logical proof of what Paul has been saying: first, we believe in the resurrection of the believer, because that is the only doctrine that fits with the gospel we preach; secondly, here, we believe in the resurrection because God has shown us that doctrine by a divine revelation. In other words, it is true because God says so, even if his truth conflicts with philosophical reasoning (2:6-16).

15:50

Now he interjects **I declare to you** and in 15:51 communicates a divinely revealed "mystery;" the divine revelation is not to be debated, but humbly believed.

15:50 is one of a cluster of Pauline verses about not inheriting the kingdom of God (see our comments on 6:9-10). Typically Paul speaks of sins that keep people out of God's final kingdom. This saying is of a different nature: **flesh and blood cannot inherit the kingdom of God**. That is to say, no-one may enter into the kingdom in the mortal form of Adam's race.[718] "Flesh and blood" is synonymous with the "natural body" in 15:44-45 and gives rise to the NJB's "mere human nature."

In the resurrection accounts, Christ is tangible; he has scars in his body, feet, hands, flesh and bones, can eat, and has a body not like a ghost but like a man. He appears to his disciples to say, "Look at my hands and my feet. It is I myself! Touch me and see; a ghost does not have flesh and bones, as you see I have" (Luke 24:39). It is no good trying to argue that flesh and blood cannot enter the kingdom but that flesh and bones may; this is not the point at all. Rather Paul is pushing the Corinthians to the truth that he will make in 15:51 – that not even Christians who manage to live until the *Parousia* will enter the kingdom unchanged.

---

[718] See Calvin, *First Corinthians*, 2:56 – "Flesh and blood, however, we must understand, according to the condition in which they at present are, for our flesh will be a participant in the glory of God, but it will be – as renewed and quickened by the Spirit of Christ." This view over against Tertullian, *Adversus Marcionem* 5.14, who relates this to *sins* done in the body: "[1 Corinthians 15:50] was not with the view of condemning the substance (of the flesh), but the works thereof." Cf. too the important article by J. Jeremias, "'Flesh and blood cannot inherit the Kingdom of God' (1 Cor. xv. 50)," *NTS* 2 (1955-56): 151-59; he argues that the verse is not intended to prove the resurrection, but that the *living* must be transformed at Jesus' coming.

15:51

Here is the newly-revealed **mystery**. We are told nothing of how Paul has come by this revelation. It is implicit that the Corinthians had not heard it before, else why would he brandish it as new information? Interestingly, Paul gives a doctrine that is absent from the Olivet discourse and from the parallel in 1 Thess 4:13-17, written some five years earlier. For while all speak of the resurrection of the dead and the "gathering" of living and resurrected believers to Christ (Matt 24:31; 1 Thess 4:17), there is no reference to any change in the bodies of saints who are still alive. The new mystery element is that even living Christians must be **changed**. In the view of some Corinthians the only thing needed to enter the kingdom of heaven would be the eradication of the body: in that sense, a stab of a knife would provide the escape that the spirit craved. But according to the gospel, the dead will be raised and the living will be transformed.

15:52

The transformation will be instantaneous: **in a flash, in the twinkling of an eye**. The first phrase uses the Greek *atomos*, from which we get the word "atom." Just as the atom was once thought to be indivisible, Paul is thinking of the tiniest split-second, a time so brief it cannot be divided up. Some versions (CEV, GNB, HCSB, NET, NLT) render the second phrase as a "blink of an eye," although the original implies something faster than a mere blink. Paul is eliminating any idea of gradual growth or evolution toward a better existence. The event happens instantaneously at the return of Christ, so quickly and decisively does he overpower death.

The sounding of **the trumpet** was a feature of long standing in Jewish and Christian eschatology. Its roots are in the trumpet sounds at Sinai, which heralded the glorious appearing of Jehovah on the mountain (Exod 20:18). It also signaled the day of Jehovah's future coming (Isa 27:13; Zech 9:14). In Jewish tradition, the last trumpet is blown by God or by an angel. It appears in Matthew's version of the Olivet discourse in Matt 24:31 and again in 1 Thess 4:16. Some try to connect this with the last of the seven trumpets of the Revelation (Rev 11:15). At that trumpet blast **the dead will be raised imperishable, and we will be changed**.

There is no indication in this paragraph nor in the parallel in 1 Thessalonians that Paul means to distinguish between a secret rapture of the church and a later, visible, second coming of Christ. This is widely assumed by students of Scripture, but the assumption must be imported into 1 Corinthians from outside; it does not appear in the text.[719] Indeed, a careful comparison of 1-2 Thessalonians, 1 Corinthians and Matt 24:29-31 (which deals with Christ's coming *after* the tribulation) reveals a striking coincidence between the four texts, including shared details such as angels, the trumpet and the gathering of the saints. The natural interpretation of these data is that there is one single coming of Christ, at which he will gather the saints and then rule over the kingdom.

15:53

Paul likes to use language of **clothe itself**, a metaphor that one finds in *1 Enoch* 62:15 – "They shall wear the garments of glory." Yet the resurrection body is not *merely* a

---

[719] See the influential study by Pentecost, *Things to come*, 201-02, whose proof for a pretribulational rapture rests heavily on a theological belief, that Israel is distinct from the church.

garment, but a body with which Christians are clothed and enclosed. He makes a similar point between the nakedness of death and being clothed in 2 Cor 5:2-4. But here in 15:53 the crux is the use of the Greek verb *dei*, which is properly rendered as **must**. In God's program this must happen, just as it is necessary that (again, *dei*) Christ rules until death is destroyed (15:25). Only then in the resurrection will Christians receive immortality, that is, an existence that is free from death.

15:54

This forceful passage is a favorite at funerals, and for good reason. He quotes from two Old Testament verses, Isa 25:8 and in 15:55, Hosea 13:14. Paul has already quoted from this section of Isaiah in this chapter (see 15:32). His unspoken assumption is this: the Scriptures are God's revelation and must come true. Isaiah predicts a day when it will be true that **"Death has been swallowed up in victory"** (Isa 25:8). This must happen, but only at the day of resurrection. If death is not swallowed up, then Christ's kingdom has failed and so has God's Word.

15:55

Paul's view of death is nowhere at greater variance with the Greek views than at this junction. The philosophers typically thought of death as natural, or even as a welcomed release from the prison of the body. For Paul death is a catastrophe and a curse, something that must be put right if God's righteous kingdom is at last victorious.

The quotation from Hosea 13:14 is taken from a verse in which Paul would have perceived strong resurrection language:

> I will ransom them from the power of the grave;
> I will redeem them from death.
> Where, O death, are your plagues?
> Where, O grave, is your destruction?

In the original context, the verse is a threat to unrepentant Israel. God promises to abandon them to death, and calls for Death and Sheol to punish the wicked; not rescue or redeem them. But here in Paul the questions are turned to blessing: *God called for Death to come for the wicked; but wait, where is death? Why doesn't death have a sting for the Christian?* It's because death and Sheol are for the wicked, but Christians have been redeemed from sin by the cross of Christ. Christ, not Death, must have the final **victory**. Christ has removed the harsh sting from death by defeating it. This echoes what he said 1 Thess 4:13 – "Brothers, we do not want you to be ignorant about those who fall asleep, or to grieve like the rest of men [the pagans], who have no hope."

15:56

And finally, at the conclusion of his argument, Paul circles around once more to the gospel of Christ and shows how the end times, the cross and creation are not separate ideas but are inextricably linked in his gospel:[720]

---

[720] Irenaeus well describes this integration of the gospel in *Against heresies* 3.23.7 – "Therefore, when man has been liberated, 'what is written shall come to pass, Death is swallowed up in victory. O death where is your sting?' This could not be said with justice, if that man, over whom death did first obtain dominion, were not set free. For his salvation is death's destruction. When therefore the Lord vivifies man, that is,

Death is a result of sin (15:56)
But Christ died for our sins (15:3)
And rose from the dead (15:4)
And will defeat death (15:27)
By resurrecting the Christians (15:53-54)

It is **sin** that gives sin its sting, and it is **the law** that makes things even worse. There is some debate on what Paul means by "law" or "Law" in this verse. The language in this verse, brief though it be, reflects the condemnatory role of the Law of Moses as found in greater detail in Gal 3:10-14 or Rom 7:14-25. Even as the Old Testament provides Paul with his theological framework, especially the hope of the resurrection, the same Scriptures confirm that sinful people deserve death.

15:57

Paul ends his long discourse, not with a satisfied smile at his own logic, but with a heartfelt burst of praise, which captures in brief the truth of the gospel (see also Rom 7:25a, 11:33-36): **But thanks be to God! He gives us the victory through our Lord Jesus Christ**. He also underscores a point that is latent throughout the chapter: that Jesus will defeat death for "us," the people of God.

15:58

How then should the Corinthians live, based on the resurrection hope? Surely they should already know, but Paul will briefly underscore a key point:

> Stand firm. Let nothing move you.
> Always give yourselves fully to the work of the Lord,
> > because you know that your labor in the Lord is not in vain.

Paul is alluding to the problems posed by a lack of resurrection in 15:30-32. Christians without a resurrection hope should not expose themselves to danger or "wild beasts." Why risk the one life you have when your effort is not going to be rewarded? And why cultivate a holy lifestyle if, after all, God will simply throw away the body (6:13)?

The resurrection of the body provides a base for holy and faithful courage. In light of the coming resurrection, the Corinthian disciples can **stand firm**, no matter what pressure the world applies. Their death will be reversed and rewarded many-fold. *Keep working in the work of the Lord, because you are most definitely moving toward eternal resurrection life. Your work is not **in vain**, just as you have not believed in vain (15:2).*

7. Concerning the collection for the believers: "What should we do about this Jerusalem offering?" 16:1-4

Now about (*peri de*) marks what was perhaps the seventh issue concerning which the

---

Adam, death is at the same time destroyed."

Corinthians had written. Paul is done with the complicated theological issues and is now passing over to the more mundane details of charitable collections, travel arrangements and itineraries. But we would be mistaken if we labeled this paragraph as a mere detail with only shallow connections with the deeper "doctrinal" issues.

16:1

Paul is brief and to the point and assumes that the Corinthians already understand what he is talking about.[721] This is because **the collection for God's people** (literally "the saints") was no spontaneous plan, but one which had been on Paul's mind for his entire third journey.[722] It seems to have its roots in earlier interaction with Jerusalem: Saul and Barnabas arrived with food during a famine (Acts 11:27-30). The Jerusalem apostles charged Paul that he not neglect the Jewish Christian poor (Gal 2:10). That event is difficult to date; it likely happened during the famine visit. Now years later, the collection is to provide financial relief to poor Jewish Christians living in and around Jerusalem. It is mentioned in Acts, here and in 2 Corinthians, and may be alluded to in Romans and Galatians. The famous section about giving and generosity in 2 Cor 8-9 has to do with that same offering. The epistles and Acts hint at just how widespread the collection was – Christians across Achaia, Macedonia and Asia Minor were raising funds (here, 2 Cor 8:1, Rom 15:31). The plan was elaborate enough that each church was asked to appointed stewards, who would accompany Paul with their gift and be able to confirm that it arrived (1 Cor 16:3-4; 2 Cor 8:18-21; Acts 20:4).

The New Testament hints that Christians there suffered chronic financial hardship: in the 30's (Acts 2:44-45, 6:1), in the famine in the 40's (Acts 11:27-30), and still now in the 50's. The motives for the collection were varied: for the sake of simple Christian charity (2 Cor 8:19); because the gentiles should show gratitude to the church from which the gospel had gone forth (Rom 15:27); and perhaps to provoke unbelieving Jews to faith in Christ when they saw gentile Christians contributing to Jews (Rom 11:11-15).

The collection was yet another point of contention between Corinth and Paul. He later came to suspect that they were not going to follow through on their promises of only a year earlier, and so he gave a lengthy teaching about it (2 Cor 8-9). In 1 Cor 16, Paul seems to be answering a sincere question; only later did it turn out that it was an implicit complaint as to why Corinth should give money.[723] Paul, typically, reminds the Corinthians that they are not unique or to be singled out: **Do what I told the Galatian churches to do**.

16:2

What plan were the Galatians following? That **on the first day of every week, each one of you should set aside a sum of money**.[724] Paul's hope that **when I come no**

---

[721] See Hurd, *Origin*, 201; also Gary S. Shogren, "Una ofrenda para los pobres," *Apuntes Pastorales* 23.4 (2006): 18-24; and the fine article by S. McKnight, "Collection for the saints," *DPL*: 143-46.

[722] Still, McKnight, "Collection for the saints," goes too far when he claims that the collection was "Paul's *obsession* for nearly two decades."

[723] So reasons Hurd, *Origin*, 201-02.

[724] In the 4th-century church Chrysostom says in *i ad Corinthios* 43.7: "And let us make a little chest for the poor at home; and near the place at which you stand praying, there let it be put: and as often as you enter in to pray, first deposit your alms, and then send up your prayer; and as you would not wish to pray with unwashen hands, so neither do so without alms." Perhaps Chrysostom is thinking of Joash's collection box in 2 Chron 24:8-11.

collections will have to be made. His instruction is for "each one of you." In a world where the poor had little to spare, and where the rich were expected to make generous gestures, it would be difficult to find a parallel to this universal participation in a charitable fund. By the next century the church would direct its charity appeals principally to the rich.

They were setting aside money **the first day of every week**.[725] The seven-day week was introduced into the Roman Empire by the Jews and other eastern cultures some time before the 1st century AD. It was officially adopted by Rome in AD 321 after the conversion of Constantine. Why does Paul specifically point out the first day of the week (which the pagan Romans would come to call the day of the Sun)? Some, particularly Seventh-Day Adventists, argue that the church met on Saturday, and that this collection therefore took place on the day after the Sabbath. For this there is no evidence whatever. In the scant references to Sabbath observance, Paul says either that it is a matter of personal choice (Rom 14:5) or, negatively, a law that must not be imposed on gentile Christians (Col 2:16).[726] The references to the church's meeting are few, but there is clear evidence that from apostolic times meetings were on the first day of the week.[727] This setting aside of funds is part of the church's weekly observance, whether it took place in the home or in a collection in the meeting. Clement is probably alluding to this custom when he says to the Corinthians that "we have searched into the depths of the

---

[725] Calvin, *First Corinthians*, 2:68, badly misreads this as "on one of the Sabbaths," that is, "on some Sunday, which is the Christian Sabbath." The Greek idiom should be translated as "on the first day of the seven-day week."

[726] Justin Martyr, *Dialogue* 47 states that there are Christians who practice circumcision and the Sabbath, but that so long as they do not try to persuade gentiles to accept the Law of Moses, "then I hold that we ought to join ourselves to such, and associate with them in all things as kinsmen and brethren."

[727] Sunday worship was the custom of the late 1st and early 2nd century AD. Pliny wrote that the Christians met on a "fixed day" but did not name the day – "They asserted, however, that the sum and substance of their fault or error had been that they were accustomed to meet on a fixed day before dawn, etc."; *Letter of Pliny the Younger to the Emperor Trajan* 10 [http://www.earlychristianwritings.com/text/pliny.html]. *Didache* 14.1 spoke of weekly meetings on the "the Lord's Day." Around the year AD 117 Ignatius explicitly rejects the Sabbath in favor of the Lord's Day, the day of Jesus' resurrection: *Magnesians* 8.1 – "Do not be deceived by strange doctrines or antiquated myths, since they are worthless. For if we continue to live in accordance with Judaism, we admit that we have not received grace"; *Magnesians* 9.1 – "If, then, those who had lived in antiquated practices came to newness of hope, no longer keeping the Sabbath but living in accordance with the Lord's day, on which our life also arose through him and his death (which some deny)"; also *Barnabas* 15.9 – "This is why we spend the eighth day [Sunday] in celebration, the day on which Jesus both arose from the dead." Justin Martyr wrote in *First apology* 67 – "And on the day called Sunday, all [Christians] who live in cities or in the country gather together to one place" for the weekly meeting. Totally mythical is the claim that Constantine or the Roman church changed the day of worship from Saturday to Sunday, nor that he did so in order to honor the Sun god. As early as Justin the first day is called the day of the sun, but the sun reference is not objectionable. Justin by the same token argues with the Jewish Trypho that Christians do not observe the Sabbath (*Dialogue* 92). Irenaeus, *Against heresies* 4.16.2 points out that, like Abraham, Christians do not keep the law of circumcision or of the Sabbath – "that they were given as a sign to the people [of Israel], this fact shows, - that Abraham himself, without circumcision and without observance of Sabbaths, 'believed God, and it was imputed unto him for righteousness; and he was called the friend of God.'"; Tertullian, *Answer to the Jews* 4 said that neither Adam, nor Abel, nor Enoch, nor Noah, nor Abraham nor Melchizedek observed the sabbath: "Whence it is manifest that the force of such precepts was temporary, and respected the necessity of present circumstances; and that it was not with a view to its observance in perpetuity that God formerly gave them such a law." Only gradually did Sunday come to be the "Christian Sabbath." The Lord's Day was not a formal day of rest until after the conversion of Constantine in the 4th century. See the very useful study, D. A. Carson, editor, *From Sabbath to Lord's Day: a biblical, historical and theological investigation* (Grand Rapids: Zondervan, 1982).

divine knowledge, we ought to do, in order, everything that the Master has commanded us to perform at the appointed times. Now he commanded the offerings and services to be performed diligently, and not to be done carelessly or in disorder, but at designated times and seasons" (*1 Clem* 40.1-2).

Among the Jews, some levies were equally imposed on all (for example, the temple tax, Matt 17:24-27); the majority were like the Jerusalem offering, gifts which were proportionate to the wealth of the giver.[728] The NIV has **in keeping with his income** (similarly CEV, GNB, NLT, NRSV), but this translation is shaped by the modern middle-class conception of weekly "income" as the primary source of wealth. The original is closer to "as he may prosper" (NKJV; also ESV, HCSB, NASB, NET); it accords with "according to your means" (2 Cor 8:11-15).

16:3-4
It is possible that Paul will travel to Jerusalem with the trustees. As it turned out, Paul would go (Acts 20:3-5). In fact, the presence of the gentile steward Trophimus in that party led to a riot and Paul's arrest, some accusing that he had illegally sneaked a gentile into the temple precincts (Acts 21:27-29). At this point Paul did not know what his plans would be, but merely made provisions that **the men you approve** would carry the fund. As was typical in that century, Paul would write **letters of introduction** for them. Paul uses what might be generic pronoun, that is, the grammar of 16:3 does not require that the couriers be male; nevertheless, the names that are mentioned in Acts indicates that they were all men.

Such was Paul's plan: simple yet well thought out. As it turned out, the Corinthians were about to balk on their promise, but eventually they would fulfill it (as Rom 15:25-26 implies). And Paul's charitable trip to Jerusalem would land him in prison for four years.

Application: Stewardship 16:2-3

What does the New Testament teach about stewardship of our goods, and what role does 1 Corinthians play?

1. Tithing. The New Testament nowhere tells Christians to tithe; not even the lengthy 2 Cor 8-9 refers to any specific percentage, to be given to the church; nor does 1 Cor 16:1. History helps us too: Christians did not tithe as a rule before the 4th century AD; up to that time the fathers were not in agreement as to whether tithing was even acceptable as a Christian practice.[729] Nor does the New Testament state that the tithe is the *minimum*

---

[728] Garland, *1 Corinthians*, 754.
[729] Irenaeus, *Against heresies* 4.18.2, was specifically against tithing – "they (the Jews) had indeed the tithes of their goods consecrated to Him, but those who have received liberty [the Christians] set aside all their possessions for the Lord's purposes, bestowing joyfully and freely not the less valuable portions of their property, since they have the hope of better things [hereafter] ..." Also 4.13.3. The first positive reference to Christians tithing which I have been able to locate is from Augustine, *On the morals of the Catholic Church* 67 [NPNF[1] 4] from AD 388. He describes how monks give a tithe of their labor and live communally; in that passage he does not specify that tithing is a norm for all Christians, but only a voluntary offering made by the super-dedicated. Around the same time, Chrysostom commented on 1 Cor 16 and recommended that Christians give ten percent as a minimum, but did not say so as "laying down a law." See

that a Christian must give. If the doctrine of tithing is to be upheld for Christians, it would have to be proven that the Old Covenant law (reflected in Mal 3:10) is somehow binding on Christians today.

2. Support for local leaders. Paul taught his disciples to support their local church leaders ("teachers" in Gal 6:6; "elders" in 1 Tim 5:17-18). He does not stipulate any level of support in his epistles, although Paul in theory an apostle deserves full support (1 Cor 9:3-14; see a parallel in 3 John 5-8). Decades later, the *Didache* told the church to support its local prophets from the "first-fruits" of their farms (*Didache* 13.3). It also warned that false teachers would try to live as parasites in the church; these should be turned out after two or three days (*Didache* 12).

3. Management of funds. Nowhere does Paul teach that all Christian donations should be managed by the leadership of the church.

4. Charitable giving to others. In 16:1 and in 2 Cor 8-9 Paul is speaking about the Jerusalem fund. This was apart from their support of their leaders in #2. It was voluntary but strongly advised; once a church made a commitment to the fund, Paul expected it to fulfill it.

By what principles are Christians to give to charity? We provide an outline that is suitable for a series of sermons.

Principle I = Why should I give? We should give because God gives to us

God is the source of all of our goods according to 1 Cor 16:1; 2 Cor 8:7, 9; 9:8-11. Our model is Jesus Christ, who gave up everything for us in his incarnation (2 Cor 8:9).

This stands in contrast to what we hear today, which is "give so that you may receive." Rather the apostle tells us "give because already you have received."

Principle II = How do I give? We must give with the right attitude

The attitude we have in giving is more important than the amount we give (2 Cor 8:8, 11-12). Our highest priority is to give willingly, cheerfully and eagerly. We should also have clear heads when we give, not in a moment of high emotion during a worship service that we later regret, but in our quiet moments. Our gift is purely voluntary (2 Cor 8:7). A cheerful giver is not stingy, but generous: how could he pass out stale bread and unwearable clothes?

There is another aspect of attitude which is critically important today. That is, people who are working hard, perhaps with exhausting jobs, are naturally going to resent helping those without jobs or who do not work as hard as they do. This calls for a great deal of wisdom. Paul himself told the church of Thessalonica not to support people who would not work (2 Thess 3:6-15). But what of those who were physically or mentally unable to support themselves? What of mothers whose husbands had abandoned them with many children? What of able-bodied people who would work if they could but cannot find enough work or work that pays sufficiently to support themselves? What of a whole congregation – as Jerusalem – where famine combined with job discrimination

---

Chrysostom, *i ad Corinthios* 43.7.

prohibited the Christians from supporting themselves? In those cases, Paul indicates that it is proper for a Christian to give them help.

People who give to a fund for charitable giving today have every right to know that their money is being disbursed according to a clearly-enunciated policy. There should be no hint of favoritism, no case where people receive money when their problem is laziness. This is why Paul used "stewards" or "overseers" so carefully in his ministry. Any church that raises money for any reason is under the obligation of telling its members how the money is uses.

Principle III = What should I give? We should give according to what we have

1 Cor 16:1-2 and 2 Cor 8:7 show that the Corinthians themselves make the decision of how much to give. In their case, the decision may have been made well ahead of time (here in 1 Cor 16; also 2 Cor 8:6, 10, 9:2).

Paul wants people to give more if they have greater resources; yet he also commends the poor for giving generously, that is, more than would have been reasonably expected. The apostle does not teach people to give recklessly or to "give until it hurts." He expects giving to be proportional and that everyone will participate according to their means (2 Cor 8:13-15).

Principle IV = What happens when I give? We should give knowing that it will result in an increase in God's financial blessing

God promises to bless us in response to our giving (2 Cor 9:6-11). He blesses us in spiritual ways and in financial ways. This does not contradict what we have said in Principle I. A Christian gives because he has already been blessed. Giving is not a mechanism to make ourselves prosperous. We cannot appear before him claiming that he now owes us because of what we have given to his work. How twisted to use the term, as does one group, "The Magic Law of Tithing" or to go around teaching, "Do you want to be Rich? Then call this number to 'prove' this spiritual law!" 2 Cor 9:7 gives the right attitude, that "Each man should give what he has decided in his heart to give, not reluctantly or under compulsion, for God loves a cheerful giver."

IV. CONCLUSION (POSCRIPTO) 16:5-24

The form of the rest of the chapter uses the conventions of letter writing. For example, in a short note to his mother, a Roman soldier closes with greetings and a wish for health:

> Many salutations to my brothers and Apollinarius and his children, and Karalas and his children. I salute Ptolemaeus and Ptolemais and her children and Heraclous and her children. I salute all who love you, each by name. I pray for your health.[730]

Paul uses such conventional forms, but in his hands they sparkle with the truths of Christ.

A. Itinerary 16:5-12

16:5-7

Here is yet another innocent comment that would land Paul in a dispute: **After I go through Macedonia, I will come to you**. From what we read in 2 Cor 1:15-2:4 the Corinthians must have concluded that they were being cheated. Paul had, as he affirmed in 2 Cor 1:15, "I planned to visit you first so that you might benefit twice," when he returned to Corinth, his point of debarkation. Not only did he want to buy more time for the church to settle down, but he also decided that he should stay with them longer than he had originally planned. In addition, Paul seems to have made a quick visit, sailing across the Aegean to check in on the church, and had a "painful visit" (2 Cor 2:1); but of this we know almost nothing (see Introduction).

Here Paul hints that this is a change of plans, and says twice that he wants not to rob them of his presence but to spend **awhile** with them. He is likely also concerned with the effect that this delay might have on the arrogant (1 Cor 4:6-7). As with all ancient travelers, Paul planned his journeys around the seasons, trying to find a place where he wanted to lay over once sea travel was closed by Roman law for the **winter**. If he left Ephesus after Pentecost (16:8), that is, in May or June, he could sail to visit Macedonia, leaving him enough time to walk to Achaia and then winter there. Were he to travel to Corinth first, he would have to winter in the north. Paul makes the pastoral decision that Corinth should have its apostle later but for a longer stay. Acts 20:3 puts this stay in Achaia at three months. Perversely, the Corinthians would take change of plans as a sign of caprice on Paul's part.

As he often does, Paul concedes his plans to God: **if the Lord permits** shows his humility before the Lord, but also the fact that Paul does not now know what God's will is (see in Introduction, Application: God's Will and Paul's Missionary Plans, or, How did Paul know where he was supposed to go?). Acts corroborates the information found in this itinerary (see Acts 20:1-6).

16:8-9

This is the only reference in Paul's letters to **Pentecost**. This Jewish holiday is best

---

[730] Select Papyri I (1932) #111 (2nd century AD).

remembered now for the descent of the Spirit (Acts 2:1). Here we find out the other pressure on Paul's itinerary: he doesn't want to leave Ephesus when there is **a great door for effective work**. We are not told what it is, although the language and that of the parallel in Col 4:3 make the reader think of evangelistic opportunity. As sometimes happens in the face of success, the same time **there are many who oppose me**. Acts puts the near-fatal riot in Ephesus immediately before Paul's departure, making it yet in the future at the time he writes this epistle (see also 2 Cor 1:8-11, written after he left Ephesus).

16:10-11

16:10-12 is part of the Itinerary, although it might also be labeled along with 16:15-18 as "Commendations." Timothy will at some point arrive in Corinth, having departed before 1 Corinthians but apparently with other work to do (1 Cor 4:17; according to Acts 19:22, he and Erastus went first to Macedonia). Thus **if Timothy comes**, while a literal translation, could be misleading to the reader today. We might take this in the sense of "when Timothy comes."

Paul uses typical language of the 1st century to commend another and to ask that he receive hospitality (cf. Rom 16:2). Timothy should be made to feel at home, and again he asks that **No one, then, should refuse to accept him. Send him on his way in peace**. In antiquity it was the duty of all to show hospitality to a traveler; how much more to a person who is in Corinth for the sole purpose of ministering to the church. Paul perhaps guesses that the church will be disappointed at seeing Timothy when they had specifically requested a visit from Apollos.[731] He stresses that they not only need to receive him but also to willingly let him go so that he might rejoin Paul. For a church that was so hard on its apostles, Corinth seems reluctant to let them leave.

16:12

This sixth **Now about** (*peri de*) probably signals that the Corinthians had asked a question about Apollos.[732] This man, unlike Timothy, was not one of Paul's lieutenants. Thus, Paul sends Timothy, but **I strongly urged** Apollos as a colleague to travel to Corinth with some of Paul's people. Apollos had been in Corinth some three years earlier, just when Paul was arriving in Ephesus (Acts 19:1). Apparently he is back in Ephesus and in contact with Paul.[733] It may be that Apollos, like Paul, had other things to do, and was only waiting for when he had the opportunity. Yet the language seems too strong for this, and may indicate: *Don't imagine that I am sending my lieutenant Timothy in order to keep the Apollos faction at bay! Not at all! I begged Apollos to go, and Apollos* **was quite unwilling to go now**. Many commentators view his reluctance as Apollos denying his partisans a chance to pit him against Paul. Perhaps that too is why Paul wished to send him in company with members of the Pauline team, for a demonstration of unity.

---

[731] Thiselton, *First Corinthians*, 1332.
[732] So Hurd, *Origin*, 206.
[733] Didymus the Blind (Bray, 188) says that Apollos was the bishop of Corinth, but that he had fled to Paul when the schism broke out. There is no evidence for this.

Conclusion 16:5-24

B. Final exhortation 16:13-14

Again, many letters and most Christian epistles end with a list of terse final appeals to recapitulate the main point of the letter (cf. especially 1 Thess 5:14-22):

> **Be on your guard;**
> **stand firm in the faith;**
> **be men of courage;** [better "be courageous," as in NIV 2011]
> **be strong.**
> **Do everything in love.**

All this fits well with what has gone before in the epistle. Not only moral alertness, but a strong commitment to the faith – including faith in the resurrection – are necessary. Even more fitting is a final exhortation to do everything **in love**.

C. Commendations 16:15-18

Many Greek and Roman letters contained commendations for the bearers of the letter or for other persons whom the author wants to uphold. **Stephanas, Fortunatus and Achaicus** are commended because they had made the trip to see Paul; they had helped Paul while they were there; and now they were returning to an unruly church: the wording most likely implies that the three are returning to Corinth now with this letter. We do not know much of these three, except that Paul had baptized the household of **Stephanas** (see 1 Cor 1:16) and that in fact they were **the first converts in Achaia** (literally, "first-fruits;" see also Rom 16:5). These were not the very first believers, who were Christians in Athens (see Acts 17:34), but they were part of the first wave of the Corinthian Achaeans.[734] Besides these notable experiences, **they have devoted themselves to the service of the saints**. Perhaps the letter contains implicit rebukes or affirmations of these three men, but we cannot tell.

Nowhere in the Corinthian letters does Paul speak of paying the leaders a salary; the only collection he mentions is for Jerusalem, not for the local church. But here there is a general appeal that the church give such people **recognition**, which might have included financial support.

D. Secondary greetings 16:19-20

The Greek and Roman letter often ended with "secondary greetings," that is, greetings from local people other than the author. Paul here twice uses the conventional verb for "greet" (*aspazomai*). Those who wish to be reminded to the Corinthians are, strikingly, not simply the Christians around Paul but **the churches in the province of Asia**. How often did Corinth try to be its own isolated spiritual nexus, fighting out its little internal

---

[734] *1 Clem* 42.4 says that the apostles appointed the initial converts of each city as bishops and deacons – "So, preaching both in the country and in the towns, [the apostles] appointed their firstfruits, when they had tested them by the Spirit, to be bishops and deacons for the future believers."

battles and thinking itself above the rules that other churches had to follow? The greeting is a reminder to Corinth: you are part of a world-wide community, and the rest of the Christian world is watching you.

That ubiquitous Christian couple, **Aquila and Priscila**, is back in Ephesus. True to their generous natures, they are hosting a church, just as they had hosted the original mission in Corinth (Acts 18:2-3) and would later do in Rome (Rom 16:3-5a). There is an even later reference to them being back in Ephesus in 2 Tim 4:19.

Paul summarizes: **All the brothers salute you**. His call to **Greet one another with a holy kiss** is similar to Rom 16:16. All the churches of Christ send greetings." The "holy kiss" was have been a known custom to the Pauline churches in Corinth (see the parallel in 2 Cor 13:12) and Thessalonica (1 Thess 5:26), but also in the non-Pauline churches in Rome (Rom 16:16) and in northern Asia Minor (1 Petro 5:14). In the Old Testament a kiss in greeting or farewell was usually reserved for close relatives or intimate friends.[735] Such is the sense in Luke 7:45, 15:20, Acts 20:37, and in the deceptive greeting of Judas, mentioned in all three synoptic gospels. In the Christian house churches people kissed each other as they would kiss their closest family members, as indeed in Christ they were.

Some have argued that this was limited to same-sex kissing on the mouth or cheek, but the testimony of history points to the kissing of everyone, although in a pure and brotherly manner.[736] In the 2nd century, the holy kiss (or "kiss of peace") grew to be a part of the liturgy of the Eucharist: before partaking of the bread and wine the believers would kiss each other to show their oneness in Christ.[737] It fits the context better to think of Paul's reference as non-Eucharistic, celebrating this moment of contact between the family of Christ in Achaia and in Asia.

E. Autograph 16:21

I, Paul, write this greeting in my own hand. Paul's 1st-century contemporaries normally dictated letters (see Rom 16:22) and then added final greetings in their own

---

[735] For example, Joseph is made to say that "a man who worships God will kiss his mother and the sister (who is born) of his mother and the sister (who is born) of his clan and family and the wife who shares his bed, (all of) who(m) bless with their mouths the living God" (*Joseph and Asenath* 8.6).

[736] In the latter half of the 2nd century AD, Clement of Alexandria, *Instructor* 3.11.2 – "But love is not proved by a kiss, but by kindly feeling. But there are those, that do nothing but make the churches resound with a kiss, not having love itself within. For this very thing, the shameless use of a kiss, which ought to be mystic, occasions foul suspicions and evil reports. The apostle calls the kiss holy." If there were "suspicions," then men and women must have been kissing each other. Around the same time, Athenagoras of Athens, *Supp* 32, remarks that men and women kiss each other, but with caution: "On behalf of those, then, to whom we apply the names of brothers and sisters, and other designations of relationship, we exercise the greatest care that their bodies should remain undefiled and uncorrupted; for the Logos again says to us, 'If any one kiss a second time because it has given him pleasure, [he sins];' adding, 'Therefore the kiss, or rather the salutation, should be given with the greatest care, since, if there be mixed with it the least defilement of thought, it excludes us from eternal life.'" Around AD 200, Tertullian mentions the kiss, but does not say whether it was same-sex (*On prayer* 18). In the 4th-century *Apostolic constitutions* 2.57.17, men and women were not allowed to kiss each other – "Then let the men give the men, and the women give the women, the Lord's kiss."

[737] Justin Martyr, *First apology* 65.2 – "Having ended the prayers, we salute one another with a kiss" and then celebrate communion.

hand, in what is technically labeled the "autograph." Over the last century and a half, scholars have unearthed many ancient letters that have their final greetings written in different (more amateurish) handwriting. It should therefore be no surprise to see Paul signing his letter here: he took the pen (from Sosthenes?) to write 1 Cor 16:21-24. In the same way, the "large letters" of Gal 6:11 signal the point at which Paul took the pen and scratched out his closing remarks in his own handwriting (see also Col 4:18). In Philemon 19, Paul's signs a promise to repay what is owed Philemon. Paul's signature was also a sign of a letter's authenticity: from the first, he had to frustrate forgers (compare 2 Thess 2:2; 3:17).

F. Benediction (and malediction) and Final Greetings 16:22-24

16:22

Many letters, whether pagan or Christian, ended with some sort of prayer, blessing, benediction or well-wishing. But before Paul issues a benediction he offers the modern reader one last small puzzle. After the blessing he also offers a curse: **If anyone does not love the Lord – a curse be on him.** Unusually, Paul uses the verb *phileō* rather than the typical *agapaō* for "love" directed toward God – probably echoing the *philēma* ("kiss") of 16:20. As we have seen (comments on 13:1), some scholars define *phileō* as a weak form of love; nevertheless, Paul is hardly speaking of mere affection here. The apostle is demonstrating that there are only two kinds of human beings: those who love God, and those who do not. The curse here must be given its full value of "damnation," exclusion for eternity from God's presence, as it is with Gal 1:8-9 and Rom 9:3 (and compare with 1 Cor 6:9-10). Most strikingly, the other two references to the Maranatha prayer in early Christian literature (Rev 22:20; also *Didache* 10.6, see below) occur in strong warnings about the division of humankind into two groups when Christ returns.[738]

The next word, like the Hebrew *Amen* and *Alleluia*, has passed into Christian vocabulary around the globe: *Maranatha*. This is an Aramaic saying, meaning that it originated in the early church in or around Palestine. There has been some debate on what the original phrase was. The NIV with the other versions assumes that the Aramaic was *Marana ta* ("Come, O Lord!"). It is also possible that it should be divided *Maran ata* ("The Lord is present!"), in a sacramental sense: "the Lord is now really present [in the Lord's Supper]." The first, eschatological, view is correct, based on the Greek translation of the phrase in Rev 22:20 and also because it has a basis in Jewish eschatology in *1 Enoch* 1:9 – "Behold, he will arrive with ten million of the holy ones in order to execute judgment upon all" (cited in Jude 14).[739] The *Maranatha* prayer bears a strong resemblance to the clause in the Lord's Prayer "your kingdom come" (Matt 6:10).

This phrase played a role in the 20th century controversies surrounding early christology. There were those, like Wilhelm Bousset, who claimed that the church came to think of Jesus as "the Lord" (*ho kurios*) only in the later, Greek-speaking church, that

---

[738] See Thiselton, *First Corinthians*, 1350-51, following the view of Eriksson.
[739] So the analysis by Fee, *First Corinthians*, 838.

is, outside of Palestine.⁷⁴⁰ In paganism, each divine "lord" (see 1 Cor 8:5-6) had his own sacramental supper, and, says this theory, Christ was added to the list of divine lords by converts from paganism. Later Christians read the Greek Septuagint and found verses where Jehovah was referred to as *Kurios*. Thus, the theory ran, gentile Christians evolved into thinking that Jesus was God and departed completely from the original Jewish idea of Jesus as a human Messiah. Nevertheless, this one little Aramaic phrase proves that Aramaic-speaking Christians acclaimed Jesus as "Lord" beginning in Palestine, a fact that Acts resoundingly affirms (see especially Acts 2:34-36).⁷⁴¹ Beyond this, we are helped by the presence of Paul, who was thoroughly acquainted with both the Hebrew Scriptures and the Septuagint, and had no hesitation in applying Jehovah-passages to Jesus (see our comments on 1:8).

Rev 22:20 has this same cry, but translated into Greek: "Come, Lord Jesus!" *Didache* 10.6 uses similar language in the liturgy of the Lord's Supper, where the *Maranatha* cry warns of coming judgment: "If any one is holy, let him come; if any one is not so, let him repent. Maranatha. Amen." This is part of the closing of a prayer after the Lord's Supper. And in liturgy that has survived in some circles to the present day is proclaimed, "Let grace come and let this world pass away."

Application: Maranatha – preaching the Second Coming 16:22

There is hardly a topic that for 2000 years has been more electrifying than the end of this age and the return of Jesus Christ. The phenomenal success of the books by Tim LaHaye in the *Left Behind* series show a hunger for the topic. We have weekly interpretations of prophecy in the news by Jack van Impe as well as myriad prophecy conferences, books and tapes.

On the other hand, there are whole groups of Christians that seem to have left off entirely from thinking about the Lord's literal return. Some wonder if the age to come is a device of the oppressor class to keep the oppressed under control by making them think that they'll be rewarded in the age to come. Liberals typically underplay the second coming as an outdated myth. Many simply are so concerned with prospering in this age that they are not in tune with the age to come.

Let's analyze some false ways to proclaim this truth, and then some biblical ways.

False ways, beginning with the mildest error and move to the gravest:

1. Obsession with End-Time Details. What is the first thing you look at when you come to a prophetic passage? Are you fascinated by the trumpet? Or the voice of the archangel in 1 Thess 4:16? Or by the exact fulfillment of each one of the seals in Rev 6? Or whether instant cash machines were foreseen on the island of Patmos? Or are you keeping your gaze focused on the more important issues of judgment, resurrection, vindication? Revelation, for example, is not obsessed with each and every plague, but rather with the

---

⁷⁴⁰ Bultmann, *Theology of the New Testament*, 51 – "Since W. Bousset's book, *Kyrios Christos,* there has been debate whether this implies that the earliest Church had already entitled Jesus 'Lord' and invoked him as such in prayer. Bousset, who vigorously denied it, is probably right. In any case, the earliest Church did not cultically worship Jesus, even if it should have called him Lord; the Kyrios-cult originated on Hellenistic soil. Judaism, at any rate, never entitled the Messiah 'Lord'."

⁷⁴¹ See Oscar Cullmann, *Christology of the New Testament* (rev. ed.; Philadelphia: Westminster, 1963), 203-19; also W. Mundle, "Maranatha," *NIDNTT* 2:895-96.

victory of the Lamb of God and the deliverance of his people. 1 Cor 15 is meant to show how the resurrection of Jesus makes a massive difference in the future of God's people: it signals that God intends to redeem our bodies. Do you focus on the larger picture or only on the shiny details?

2. Setting a date. This is a further abuse of #1 but one that deserves its own paragraph. Those who have been Christians for only a short time will have no memory of the date-setters that have come before. But in fact, every 3-4 years someone announces that his or her calculation is the only true one, that all others have been mistaken, and that Christ must come back by a certain date. In fact, several such dates have come and gone while I was writing this commentary, including the famous prediction of May 21, 2011 by "Family Radio." Such false prophets will never tell you that they may themselves have set dates in the past and been proved false. Do their Bibles not contain Matt 24:36, which says "No one knows about that day or hour"? *Oh, they say, we don't know the day or hour...but we do know the month or the year!* Or, *No, Jesus didn't know the day or the hour back then, but we have a new prophecy today that reveals it to us!* Historically, whole sects – Jehovah's Witnesses, Mormons, and the Millerites to name some well-known ones – arose when someone set a date for the second coming. The Jehovah's Witnesses taught that they were the end-time people of God, raised up to testify to the truth before the return of Jesus in 1914. When Jesus did not return, they kept on presenting themselves as the remnant. They predicted the end of the world again in 1925 and in 1975. Much more deceptive is when someone you trust, who seems to have a solid grasp of the Bible, who has done many wonderful good works, starts to make the same sort of claim.

When Jesus told us no one knew the day or the hour, he was not joking. He gave it as a warning that we not play around with timetables but instead concentrate on how we should live in the light of his return. Even with such a stern warning, Christians have broken his commandment time and again.

3. Secret knowledge. The idea that some give is, *We all have the Bible; but I have in hand extra information that gives more light than the common Christian possesses.* It is scandalous to hear Bible-believing Christians turn away from their Bibles and place their faith in the writings of ancient Jewish rabbis; the supposed *Epistle of Barnabas*, which was not written by the biblical Barnabas at all, but dates from the 2nd century[742]; Nostradamus; occult sciences; ancient scrolls or tablets that have supposedly just come to light; mathematical calculations based on the Egyptian pyramids or the Temple mount in Jerusalem; Mayan calendars; rumors about Satanic super-computer called "The Beast" or about plans to implant computer chips into people's foreheads. I have just found a website by a man who claims to be the prophet Elijah. What foolishness, to turn away from the very Word of God to follow fables.

The Jews too have always had their fringe groups. The Essenes, for example, known from the Dead Sea Scrolls from the time of Jesus, thought that they were the end-time

---

[742] *Barnabas* 15.3-4 is often cited by prophecy students to "prove" that the history of the human race will last 6000 years – "And he himself bears me witness when he says, 'Behold, the day of the Lord will be as a thousand years.' Therefore, children, in six days – that is, in six thousand years – everything will be brought to an end" (also found in Irenaeus, *Against heresies* 5.28.3). This notion led some to set dates for Christ's return around the year 2000.

righteous remnant. They have been extinct for thousands of years, as is the fate of all such groups.

4. Ungodly behavior. Every once in a while a sect will arise that is so convinced that it is the end-time remnant that it will commit actual sins in the name of God. There are sects that are white supremacists or anti-Semitic. They justify their sin by claiming that in the end of times the conventional rules of morality do not apply. People kill their opponents, set off bombs, ask their members to commit group suicide – remember Jim Jones in Guyana – all with the absolute conviction that it is God's will. Then too, prophecy teachers may be trying to manipulate their hearers into the things that many preachers commonly want: for you to donate to their ministry, buy gold bars from them, or expensive survival kits.

Right ways: these appear in no particular order. Any godly, wise presentation of the Lord's return ought to be heavy in the following elements:

1. The second coming and personal holiness. This is the connection that is most evident in 1 Corinthians. Christians are to look at the second coming as a warning against sin and an encouragement to righteousness. If a denial of the resurrection might lead to moral corruption (15:30-34), the opposite is also true – that the Christian can take encouragement from the return of Christ to remain firm (15:58). For the worldly-wise Corinthians who disregard God's revelation (2:6-10) and split into status factions, there is the warning of fire that will destroy their accomplishments (3:13).

2. The second coming and justice. This is a theme more apparent in the gospels or in James than in Paul, mainly because of the specific problems that each author was dealing with. James warns those who are oppressing their agricultural day-workers that they had better not cheat the poor. Those who do so are hoarding riches in the last days (James 5:3b). The return of Christ will bring the great reversal of fortunes for rich and poor.

3. The second coming and persecution. This overlaps with #2, but we will consider it separately. In the New Testament, references to the second coming are more frequent in books that have to do with the persecution of God's people. The clearest example of this is Revelation, which describes how Christians must cling fast to the Lamb and refuse the mark of the beast and the false religion of Babylon, even though it may mean their death (see especially the key verse Rev 2:10b). The teachings of Jesus himself mix the two themes of persecution and the second coming (see for example in Matt 5:1-12; 10:5-42; 16:24-28; 24:4-22; see also Rom 8; 1-2 Thessalonians). It is often observed that people in persecution and distress have special insight into God's power to vindicate the righteous. This does not mean (see #2) that we should tell the poor, the disenfranchised, the downtrodden to fix their hope on the second coming as a substitute for pursuing justice in this age. Rather, it is the hope of the age to come that gives us a light to steer by; and it reminds all Christians that no matter what improvements they make in the current system, final liberation comes only from Jesus' personal return. Our thirst for justice must never lead to bitterness, slander or impatience (James 5:7-12), but rather quiet trust in God's coming redemption.

Conclusion 16:5-24

4. The second coming and evangelism. Paul's greatest treatment of evangelism and missions appears in Rom 9-11 and 15. For Paul, his evangelistic work is interrelated with the plan of God for the nations, Israel and the church. In Rom 15:16 he uses the concept of "an offering" in a way that has roots in the Old Testament prophecies of the nations bringing tribute to Zion. Our Lord himself taught that "this gospel of the kingdom will be preached in the whole world as a testimony to all nations, and then the end will come" (Matt 24:14). Revelation describes how an end-time persecution is compatible with a great harvest of souls (Rev 7:9-17), a theme that has some echoes in 1 Thess 1:4-10. Why is this important? The phenomenon of end-time fervor, as seen above, has historically had two contradictory effects. One is paralysis: *if we really are in the end times and in the days of evil, they we should concentrate on protecting ourselves rather than finding new converts.* The other effect is that Christians, focused on the Lord's coming, suddenly found new energy to go out and share the gospel.

5. The second coming, prosperity and healing. The return of Christ reminds us that full healing and prosperity come only in the resurrection. The resurrection heals us from the ultimate breakdown, death, and leaves us in a state where we will never again be sick, weak or dying. The future kingdom is the time of ultimate and eternal prosperity as well. Why is this important? One of the key features of the Christian message is the tension between what is "now" and what is "not yet." There are false teachings (Gnosticism, for example; the Prosperity Gospel) that arise directly from the neglect of that tension. The most useful method is to begin with the second coming, and to remember that it is there that we will find perfection:

- God's plan is that I will have perfect healing and perfect prosperity in the age to come
- God's plan is that I have some measure of healing and prosperity in this age
- Therefore: whatever healing and prosperity I experience now is partial and an anticipation of the full reality; it is not the perfection itself

This will help with the question: *If God is healing people around me, and he has healed me in the past, then why am I dying from cancer?* Part of the answer must be that God does not intend perfect healing for us in this age – if he did, then we would never die but go on living like we are forever.

16:23

The blessing, **the grace of the Lord Jesus be with you**, is typical of Paul with its mention of divine "grace" (*charis*), although fuller than most (see the end of all of his epistles; depending on the manuscript, Romans contains four benedictions in 15:13, 15:33, 16:20b, 16:25-27).

16:24

What a contentious and difficult letter this has been; yet Paul goes beyond the normal blessing of "grace to you" and adds a personal note: **My love to all of you in Christ**

Jesus.[743] This is no mere formality; this apostle speaks what is true, not what is merely pleasing to the ear (see comments on 1 Cor 1:4-9). Thiselton also wishes to underscore the use of "all of you," that is, not just the rich but the poor, not just the obedient but the boastful.[744] Not for Paul is a love that falters and turns away in disgust when it is let down; not for Paul is a theology that argues each small point of doctrine past the bounds of love. In Christ, Paul "always protects, always trusts, always hopes, always perseveres" (1 Cor 13:7).

Concluding thought

By the grace of Christ (1 Cor 16:23) the Corinthians have experienced God's love. Paul's love for them (16:24) is a reflection of that divine love. Their love for Christ (16:22), the churches' love for them (16:19-20a), the love the Corinthians can have for each other (16:20b) – all of these flow from God, who has reconciled them through the cross of Christ.

Where, then, is the need for boasting in such a universe? What need of status? What need of stepping on other Christians? What need of anything but God in Christ, even as the universe hurtles toward its conclusion? Let us love you, Lord, and through you love one another! Let grace come and let this world pass away! *Maranatha!*

---

[743] The closing "Amen" is missing from manuscript B and was possibly not part of the original text.
[744] Thiselton, *First Corinthians*, 1353.

About the Author

Gary Steven Shogren has a Ph. D. in New Testament exegesis from Kings College, University of Aberdeen, Scotland. He is the author of numerous articles, focusing mainly on Pauline theology. He is also the author of the volume on 1-2 Thessalonians in the Zondervan Exegetical Commentary on the New Testament.

After serving for some years as a pastor and profesor in the United States and part-time in Romania, Gary moved with his wife Karen and four children to Costa Rica, where they learned Spanish and have ever since served in the church of Latin America. Gary and his wife Karen both teach at Seminario ESEPA, San José, Costa Rica. They are missionaries with WorldVenture (www.shogrens.com).

Gary is a regular blogger, in English (www.openoureyeslord.com) and in Spanish (www.razondelaesperanza.com).

www.ingramcontent.com/pod-product-compliance
Lightning Source LLC
Chambersburg PA
CBHW081124170426
43197CB00017B/2747